ESEA IVB

THE CONCISE
ENCYCLOPEDIA OF
ANCIENT
CIVILIZATIONS

THE CONCISE ENCYCLOPEDIA OF ANCIENT CIVILIZATIONS

EDITED BY JANET SERLIN GARBER

Franklin Watts/New York/London/1978

874

Library of Congress Catalog Card Number: 77-71166

Library of Congress Cataloging in Publication Data
Main entry under title:

The Concise encyclopedia of ancient civilizations.

  Includes index.
  SUMMARY: Surveys ten great civilizations of the ancient
world.
  1. Civilization, Ancient—Dictionaries, Juvenile. [1. Civilization, Ancient]   I. Garber, Janet Serlin.
CB311.C74   930'.003   77-71166
ISBN 0-531-01330-8

CONTENTS

CONTENTS

INTRODUCTION

This book offers a concise survey of the great civilizations of the ancient world. The subject matter is presented in compact form so that the interested reader or researcher can have basic information about these cultures readily available in one reference source.

At a glance, the contents page reveals the breadth and scope of the material covered. The ten main divisions, one devoted to each of the civilizations represented, are subdivided into sections giving the background and a general overview of the main features of the particular civilization. A section titled "People, Places, and Terms," arranged alphabetically, presents the aspects of major significance in that civilization. Photographs and drawings are included throughout to illustrate concepts of visual interest.

The purpose of this sectionalized format, rather than a strictly alphabetical one, is to coordinate in one place the multi-faceted information about a particular culture or people and thereby eliminate the need to consult a number of widely scattered entries when investigating any one general topic. In some instances, a topic is discussed in one of the introductory sections about the culture as well as in a separate entry in the "People, Places, and Terms" section that follows. In these cases, the topics will have more than one reference listing in the index. For example, in the section about Greek civilization, the Acropolis is discussed under the general heading of architecture, and also in a separate subject entry in "People, Places, and Terms." In other cases, a subject is discussed in a general category such as art or literature in relation to other subjects of which is is an integral part, and does not have an additional separate listing. Also, because many cultures influenced each other and overlapped in time, a topic may be covered in only one of the cultures—usually the one in which it had its major development. In all cases, the index will clearly and easily guide the reader to the exact page or pages where the topic is presented.

This book includes as much reference material pertaining to the ten major ancient civilizations as is possible and practical within a single introductory volume. It is hoped that this overview will serve both as a basic reference source and as a thought-provoking guide to areas of knowledge that the reader will want to subsequently explore in greater depth.

THE CONCISE
ENCYCLOPEDIA OF
ANCIENT
CIVILIZATIONS

BYZANTINE CIVILIZATION

ARCHITECTURE

BYZANTINE [bĭz'ən-tēn, bĭ-zăn'tĭn] **ARCHITECTURE,** style of building that developed in the eastern Mediterranean area after 330 A.D., when Constantine established his new capital at Byzantium, renaming the city Constantinople. The Byzantine style had its roots in Italy and crystallized in Ravenna and Constantinople. It spread thence throughout Greece and the Balkans to Asia Minor, Armenia, parts of Syria, and finally to Russia, southern Italy, Sicily, and even more distant regions such as Egypt and the Perigord area in southwest France.

The style was the product of late Roman methods of construction and design, modified by new aesthetic concepts of enclosed space and utilizing new methods of adornment with strikingly colorful materials. These, though sometimes considered Oriental, are, in fact, the logical outgrowth of trends already observable in Roman imperial structures of the first three centuries of the Christian era. Although these changes were accomplished gradually, a new and distinctive style of building had emerged within two centuries after Constantine, and had developed to a point where obvious similarities to classical architecture had largely disappeared.

The earliest form of the Christian church, the basilica, had established a type of structure beautifully planned to meet the liturgical needs of the new religion. Its characteristic scheme and essential features, first embodied on a grand scale in the sumptuous churches founded by Constantine at Rome and in the Holy Land, soon became so popular that the basilica type has largely dominated the subsequent evolution of Christian architecture, not only during the Middle Ages but even down to modern times. Yet the Constantinian basilica had one serious flaw. Although its walls of brick and its columns of marble resisted fire, the wooden roofs of its long nave and aisles did not. Ignited by lightning or careless workmen, these roofs often roared into flame and ruined the rich interior, making necessary a costly restoration and at times a complete rebuilding. Hence, one of the primary aims of Byzantine architects was to create a fireproof church, a problem eventually solved by devising new forms of masonry vaults and domes to replace the flammable roofs of earlier churches.

Early Byzantine Architecture. In the reign of Justinian (527–65), Byzantine architecture attained its first defini-tive expression in a number of great buildings. Chief among these are the octagonal Church of San Vitale at Ravenna, whose dome is ingeniously constructed of clay pots suggesting modern work in hollow tile; the cross-shaped Church of the Holy Apostles at Constantinople, crowned with five domes of brick; and the world-renowned Hagia Sophia (532–37), designed by Anthemius of Tralles as the cathedral church of the imperial capital.

Interior of the 14-centuries-old Byzantine masterpiece Hagia Sophia. Its richly decorated interior is sheathed with colored marbles and flashing gold mosaics. First a cathedral and later a mosque, it has now been converted into a museum.

Alinari

1

BYZANTINE ARCHITECTURE

In Hagia Sophia, the acknowledged masterpiece of the first phase of the Byzantine style, a lofty central dome of brick—its form suggesting the massive concrete dome of the circular Roman Pantheon (124 A.D.)—was raised above a rectangular structure of basilican plan, a feat accomplished by the perfection of new architectural devices called pendentives. These spherical triangles of masonry made possible the support of the dome on a square framework of four huge equal arches, of which the two on the longer east-west axis of the church are extended and but-

Alinari

The Church of St. Mark's, Venice, Italy, rebuilt in the 11th century, is considered second only to Hagia Sophia as an achievement of Byzantine architecture. The mosaic (*above*) depicting the Ascension of Christ with the Virgin, Angels, and Apostles on a gold background lining the central dome exemplifies the décor. Much of the intricate exterior embellishment (*below*) was added in later centuries.

Jordanidis

The Church of the Holy Apostles in Salonika, Greece (*above*), is an example of late Byzantine architecture. It continued the tradition of Byzantine churches not only in plan but also in depending on its architectural form and patterned brickwork for exterior decoration.

tressed by great half-domes, themselves resting upon smaller half-domes and arches. All interior wall surfaces of Hagia Sophia are sheathed with slabs of colored marbles richly veined and polished, while the vaults, arches, half-domes, and dome are clothed in flashing gold mosaic. These features, plus the height of the lofty monolithic columns of purple porphyry and dark green marble that support the structure and the flood of light from a crown of windows high in the great dome, give an amazing sense of airiness, and all combine to produce an effect of space and light that has exerted a profound influence on later architecture.

Throughout their history the Byzantines, in true Roman fashion, formed their walls and vaults of thin square bricks laid with mortar joints as thick as the bricks themselves. A powerful carcass, or shell, was thus created, the interior of which was richly colored by materials incrusted as a decorative veneer. Ornamental carving of capitals, moldings, and balustrades was rendered in low, flat relief, its pattern achieved by incision rather than by the plastic modeling of ancient ornament. Its special character depended on the use of the drill rather than the chisel to produce the effect of a rich and colorful tapestry. Structurally, these buildings employ a distinctive system of thrusts, one acting against another and concentrated upon selected points in the edifice, much as in the great vaulted baths and basilicas of the pagan Roman period. Also, like the latter, their exteriors exhibit broad wall surfaces, rarely broken by moldings or detail, but diversified above by the boldly swelling shapes of vaults and domes roofed with sheets of lead.

Middle Byzantine Architecture. The second or middle phase of Byzantine architecture, in which Eastern influences first became unmistakable, is best represented by the Church of St. Mark's in Venice, rebuilt in the 11th century but greatly modified and embellished in succeeding centuries. St. Mark's is generally considered the greatest achievement of the Byzantine style except for Hagia Sophia. Modeled on Justinian's lost Church of the Holy Apostles—said to have been designed by Anthemius and known to have been destroyed to make way for a Turkish mosque—its plan is that of a Greek cross with a dome over the crossing. The structure has four smaller domes, one over each arm of the cross, all surmounted by elaborate exterior cupolas of fantastic bulbous form and later date. In contrast to the unadorned outside surfaces of the earlier period, St. Mark's is richly decorated both inside and out. Its exterior is sheathed with colored marbles and richly carved ornament; its interior is a treasure house of rare stones and magnificent figure mosaics showing Biblical scenes on a background of twinkling gold. Many of its treasures are doubtless spoils from Hagia Sophia, brought back to Italy in the 13th century by members of the Fourth Crusade, whose freebooters from Venice captured and sacked Constantinople.

Late Byzantine Architecture. In its final stylistic phase, realized in the 13th and subsequent centuries in Greece, Constantinople, south Italy, the Balkans, and Russia, Byzantine architecture assumed more ornate and exotic forms, while the churches themselves became progressively smaller. The preferred plan was that of a cross inscribed in a square, the crossing crowned by a dome. This dome rose on an elaborate cylindrical drum pierced by narrow arched windows; similar subordinate domes were grouped picturesquely about it at lower levels. To the present day this is the accepted style of the Greek Orthodox Church. Among a number of examples in Greece is the Little Metropolitan Cathedral in Athens (13th century) and the Church of the Holy Apostles at Salonika, the latter noted for its beautifully patterned brickwork on the east façade.

In Armenia at this time and earlier a distinctly local interpretation was developed, with cut stone instead of brick being used as the chief material. This was often carved with Biblical scenes in relief. And in Russia, also, Byzantine forms were reworked to a national style—for example, in the cathedrals of Moscow, Kiev, and Novgorod—in which the exterior false domes were multiplied and assumed a pointed bulbous form. The interior decoration, as in most late Byzantine churches, was realized largely in fresco.

Aside from churches, the surviving examples of Byzantine architecture are chiefly monasteries, such as the Meteora and those of Mount Athos in Greece; a few ruined castles and town sites, such as Monemvasia and Mistra in the Peloponnesus; baptisteries in Naples, Palermo, and Ravenna; and city walls and gates, as in Constantinople. Little is left to testify to minor structures.

ART

BYZANTINE ART, style of artistic expression that developed in the eastern Mediterranean area after 330 A.D., when the Emperor Constantine established his capital in the old city of Byzantium, changing its name to Constantinople. The style flourished from Italy eastward through Greece to Anatolia and the Near East. Although it has been said that the Turkish conquest of Constantinople and the fall of the Byzantine Empire in 1453 ended Byzantine art, it in fact lingered for several centuries, particularly in Greece, the Balkans, Armenia, and Russia. Its influence extended well into the period of the European Renaissance, and is reflected sporadically in the arts of modern times.

Arising from the styles of late antiquity and developing further their already obvious trend toward abstraction, deep colors, and rich patterns in design, Byzantine art combined in varying degrees elements from the art of Roman Italy with others from late Hellenistic and Oriental sources. From Alexandria and the Near East in general it drew important themes of iconography, that is, its system for representing Christian subjects by means of pictures or images. Although its origins were diverse, Byzantine art succeeded in fusing these elements into an original and distinctive style that remained vital for almost 12 centuries and produced some of the greatest masterpieces of the Christian Middle Ages—not only in architecture, decoration, and mosaic, but also in the minor arts of manuscript illumination, ivory carving, enamels, tapestries, and metalwork.

History of Byzantine Art

Scholars distinguish four successive phases in the stylistic evolution of Byzantine art: (1) the early or Proto-By-

Alinari

Detail of the mosaic depicting the Empress Theodora in the 6th-century Church of San Vitale in Ravenna, Italy. Mosaic was the principal form of Byzantine architectural decoration.

zantine period, (2) the Byzantine Renaissance, (3) the third or Middle Byzantine period, and (4) the final or late Byzantine period.

The Early or Proto-Byzantine Period. The first phase dates from the foundation of Constantinople in 330 A.D to 726, when Emperor Leo III instituted iconoclasm by forbidding the creation of religious works of a representational nature. These centuries comprise the formative phases of the style as well as its first golden age, in which were erected its greatest architectural monuments, such as Hagia Sophia and the Church of the Holy Apostles in Constantinople; the Churches of San Vitale and Sant' Apollinare Nuovo in Ravenna, Italy; and resplendent basilicas in Rome and in the Holy Land. In the late Roman tradition, all were sheathed internally with sumptuous colored marbles, their ceilings richly gilded or their vaults encrusted with gold mosaic. The earliest centers of this art were in Italy—in Rome, Milan, and Ravenna—and later in Constantinople, while Alexandria, Antioch, and Ephesus played subordinate roles.

The Byzantine Renaissance. The second phase evolved under a dynasty of Macedonian emperors (867–1057). It is called a renaissance because it was, in fact, a classical revival following more than a century of political, religious, and artistic decline occasioned by disorders attending the iconoclastic controversy, an ecclesiastical contest of the 8th and 9th centuries. Iconoclasm was instituted by Em-

peror Leo III (reigned 717–40), an adventurer from Isauria, an ancient district in present south-central Turkey. There, with puritanical Jews and Arabs, he had acquired a deep hatred of all images, particularly of icons, which were believed to be endowed with such mysterious powers that they could work miracles by invoking, in some occult way, the intervention of the saints. Although opposed by his people and his clergy, Leo joined the iconoclasts, and in 726 prohibited the creation of religious works. Under his leadership countless works of art were destroyed.

Under the Empress Irene at the Second Council of Nicaea in 787 the veneration of images was revived. But the bitter violence of iconoclasm had produced unexpected results, the most important of which was the secularization of art. Because the old monastic schools had been ruined by the iconoclasts, their artists now turned to secular themes under patronage of the nobility, producing works of an aristocratic type inspired by ancient classic models. Persecuted by the iconoclasts, many artists had fled to Italy and Provence where their descendants exerted a strong Byzantine influence on European art in the 8th and 9th centuries.

Another result of iconoclasm was the stimulus it gave to secular learning, which naturally fostered a revival of the older classical styles. Thus, a true renaissance occurred when peace was restored under the Macedonian Dynasty, fostered not only by the revival of the old faith, but also by political stability and a return of material prosperity. The art of this period is therefore distinguished by numerous elements from pagan classic sources, by the colorful, decorative, and formal qualities always seen in Byzantine art, and by the use, for didactic purposes, of the continuous narrative method of representation still employed in the modern comic strip.

The Third or Middle Byzantine Period. The third phase developed under the Comnenian Dynasty, which began with the reign of Isaac Comnenus in 1057, and ended with the Latin conquest of Constantinople in 1204. The city was sacked by French and Venetian troops of the Fourth Crusade, and held for more than half a century. Middle Byzantine art, justly esteemed as representing a second golden age, is distinguished by the final and perfect fusion of the Hellenistic, Roman, and Near Eastern elements in the full-blown Byzantine style, characterized by slight naturalism, an abstract intellectual quality, and a wonderfully decorative effect. St. Mark's in Venice, with its famous 11th-century mosaics, is the masterpiece of this period.

The Final or Late Byzantine Period. The final phase began in 1261 with the expulsion of the Latins by the Palaeologan Dynasty and ended in 1453 with the Turkish conquest of Constantinople. Although the arts still flourished, the empire was impoverished and already in decline. Hence, the churches undertaken during this era were smaller and less richly decorated, with more attention to exterior ornament in patterned brickwork, and with frescoes instead of mosaics on their inner walls. Although the art shows a superficial trend toward realism, the figures suggest puppets, jerky and uncontrolled in movement. This style nevertheless inspired the early Italian Renaissance painters Giotto and Cimabue. Later, in

The Byzantines excelled in making small objects like the ivory carvings and cloisonné enamels shown here. They give an idea of the decorative effects and formal quality that are characteristic of Byzantine art.

"St. Gregory the Theologian," cloisonné enamel on gold, of the 11th or 12th century.

Cloisonné enamel representation of the archangel Michael (10th–12th century). Byzantine artists used gold for the background and for the bent wire fillets (cloisons) that form the pattern and hold the enamel in place.

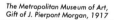

A 10th- or 11th-century carved ivory plaque representing Christ.

An ivory chest of the 10th century.

the 16th century, it formed the basis for the distinctive manner of El Greco.

Present-Day Survivals

Painting. Aside from frescoes in late churches, our knowledge of Byzantine painting derives largely from illuminated manuscripts, such as the sumptuous *Vienna Genesis, Joshua Rotulus,* and *Rossano Gospel.* The pages of the last are dyed purple and lettered in gold. These manuscripts show that this art was never dramatic or filled with the warmth of human joys and sorrows. Instead, it was formal, splendid, and hieratic, strictly controlled by the Church in expounding a dogmatic system of salvation. Although few frescoes have come down to us, the panel paintings (icons) have survived in considerable number, and from these and the manuscript paintings come the clearest indications of stylistic evolution.

Mosaics. Famous Byzantine mosaics survive in Rome and Ravenna, but most of those farther east have been lost. The fact that Muslim rule required such representations to be plastered over when a church was rededicated as a mosque has resulted, however, in some remarkable discoveries. Since 1930 an American expedition in Constantinople (Istanbul) has uncovered in Hagia Sophia and in the Kahrie-Djami several great series of mosaics that reveal the perfection of this art in the capital of the Byzantine Empire. The sonorous harmony and depth of color, the visual charm of complex ornament, and the conventional dignity of the figures form sumptuous decorations on the golden background of wall and vault.

Sculpture. Figure sculpture, because of its pagan associations, was generally neglected by the Byzantines and soon became of slight importance. The sculptor's art was therefore largely confined to architectural ornament, to church furniture, and to ivory panels for book covers, reliquaries, and episcopal thrones such as that of Archbishop Maximian at Ravenna.

EMPIRE

BYZANTINE EMPIRE, successor to the Roman Empire. In 330 A.D. Constantine the Great transferred the capital of the Roman Empire from Rome to Constantinople, a city that he had erected for that purpose on the site of the ancient Greek town of Byzantium. In the century and a half that followed, the Roman Empire lost virtually all its western provinces and in 476 the imperial office in Italy was abolished by the barbarian Odoacer. The Roman Empire was now reduced to the eastern provinces—Egypt, Syria and Palestine, Asia Minor, and the major part of the Balkan Peninsula—with Constantinople as its capital. This is the Empire that modern historians call "Byzantine" and sometimes "Greek": "Byzantine" because Constantinople occupied the site of Byzantium and was sometimes itself called Byzantium, "Greek" because of its Greek character, at least in language. Thus the Byzantine Empire was the Roman Empire restricted in its territorial extent but also, in the end, radically transformed in civilization and culture. Its capital, located at the crossroads of commerce and protected by impregnable fortifications, became the richest and most populous city in Europe.

Constantine. In the rise of the Empire, the reign (306–37) of Constantine the Great was of particular significance. Besides transferring the capital to Constantinople, Constantine laid the basis of the political and religious system of the Empire. Building upon the reforms of Diocletian, Constantine definitely established, with the help of Christian thinkers, the centralized, absolute monarchy that remained the fundamental feature of the political system of the Empire throughout its existence. Under Constantine the Empire became Christian. Not only did he confirm the legal status that Galerius had granted to Christianity but also became converted himself and granted privileges to the Church. But more important was his active participation in the affairs of the Church in order to help it define its doctrine and assure it unity. Thus Constantine took the initiative in convoking (325) the Council of Nicaea in order to settle the Arian controversy, provoked by Arius, a priest of Alexandria, who believed that Christ was a created being and therefore inferior to God. The Council of Nicaea rejected the belief of Arius and formulated a creed that declared Christ to be consubstantial and coeternal with God. This eventually came to be accepted as the true doctrine of the Church, but the significance of the Council of Nicaea lies also in its setting a precedent for the settlement of future disputes. Under Constantine, church and state related closely and thus they remained throughout the duration of the Empire. The attempt made by Constantine's nephew, Julian the Apostate (331–63), to re-establish paganism ended in failure.

Goths and Heretics. In 378 the Empire suffered a serious defeat near Adrianople. Goths routed the imperial forces and killed the Emperor, Valens. The situation was retrieved by the new Emperor, Theodosius the Great (346?–395), who pacified the Goths and settled them south of the Danube in Byzantine territory. Theodosius outlawed paganism and, with the help of the First Council of Constantinople, which he brought together in 381, liquidated the Arian heresy. The Gothic problem grew serious again under Arcadius, but the bulk of the Goths finally turned toward Italy, while those who remained in Constantinople were removed from all positions of influence. The Huns under Attila were the most dangerous enemies of the Empire during the reign (408–50) of Theodosius II, but diplomacy and subsidies kept them at bay. Theodosius II was a weak ruler, but his reign is noted for three important accomplishments: the foundation (425) of the University of Constantinople; the issuance (438) of the first official code of laws; and the erection of the massive fortifications of Constantinople. It was troubled, however, by the controversy over the nature of Christ. On the one hand, there were the Nestorians who separated the divine in Christ from the human; on the other, there were the Monophysites who posited only one nature in Christ, the divine. Although the Council of Ephesus (431), called by Theodosius, condemned the Nestorians, and the Council of Chalcedon (451), brought together by Marcianus (392–457), condemned the Monophysites, the controversy continued. Zeno tried to solve the problem by a compromise (*The Henotikon*, 482) that Anastasius (430?–518) also tried to enforce, but with no success. The controversy ended only after the conquest of Egypt and Syria, the two important Monophysitic provinces, by the Arabs in the 7th century. Anastasius gave to the Empire an efficient and

frugal administration and when he died he left a surplus of 320,000 pounds of gold which Justinian used to finance his enterprises.

Justinian. Justinian was one of the most brilliant Emperors of the Byzantine Empire. His wars against Vandals and Berbers in Africa (533–48), the Ostrogoths in Italy (535–54), and the Visigoths in Spain (554) enabled the Empire to recover North Africa, Italy, part of Spain, and the islands of the western Mediterranean and to make that sea once more a Roman lake. In accomplishing this, however, Justinian neglected the eastern and Balkan regions of the Empire, which were subjected to invasions by Persians, Bulgars, and Slavs. A most notable achievement was the codification of Roman law, which still remains the basis of the law of virtually all Europe. A great builder, Justinian was responsible for the erection of the magnificent church of Hagia Sophia, one of the most remarkable architectural monuments of all times. In an unsuccessful effort to conciliate the Monophysites, Justinian called the Second Council of Constantinople (553). Justinian had able collaborators, including his wife Theodora, a woman of remarkable ability, the great generals Belisarius and Narses, and the jurist Tribonian.

Arabs. The system built by Justinian collapsed after his death. The Lombards conquered the major part of Italy, while in the Balkan Peninsula and in the east, Avars, Slavs, and Persians roamed almost at will. Mauricius (539?–602), who checked the Persians in the east and pushed the Avars beyond the Danube, retrieved the situation somewhat, but his violent overthrow, which put the incompetent Phocas (reigned 602–10) on the throne, plunged the Empire into another crisis. Heraclius, who deposed Phocas, stopped the Avars (626) and crushed the Persians (622–28), but he had hardly finished his task when a new and more formidable enemy appeared. The Arabs, helped by the Monophysites of the eastern provinces who offered them no resistance, quickly conquered Palestine, Syria, and Egypt and penetrated deep into Asia Minor. In 674–78 they besieged Constantinople, but they were routed by Constantine IV, who made effective use of the famous Greek fire. They came back in 717 but were again repulsed by Leo III. Leo III, who founded a new dynasty, the Isaurian (717–802), also stopped the Arabs in Asia Minor, while his son and successor, Constantine V, crippled the Bulgar state that had been established south of the Danube in the reign of Constantine IV. In Italy, however, Constantine V lost Ravenna to the Lombards. The deposition of Irene, who had become sole ruler (797) by blinding her son and coruler, Constantine VI, brought to an end the Isaurian Dynasty. Irene is famous for her role in the restoration of the veneration of icons, which had been prohibited by Leo III. Iconoclasm, revived in 813, was definitely abandoned in 843.

Apogee. Early in the 9th century the Empire survived the devastating attacks of the Bulgars under Krum (d.814), who defeated and killed (811) the Emperor Nicephorus I, but the Arabs soon conquered Crete and invaded Sicily. In the meantime a new dynasty, the Amorian (820–67), came to power. During its sway, the Empire won some successes against the Arabs in the east, turned back the Russians, who in 860 attacked Constantinople, asserted the independence of the Greek Church against

Rome (the Photian Schism), and converted the Bulgars to Christianity, thereby laying the foundations for the propagation of Orthodoxy among the southeastern Slavs. At the same time the revival of the University of Constantinople opened the way for the development of learning.

In 867 Basil I, born of Armenian parentage in Macedonia, plotted the assassination of Michael III (reigned 842–67) and replaced him on the throne. The dynasty that Basil established (the Macedonian Dynasty, 867–1056) was responsible for the most brilliant period in the history of the Empire. Led by able soldier-emperors such as Nicephorus II Phocas (913?–969), John I Zimisces (925–76), and Basil II (958?–1025), the Empire humbled the Arabs, subjugated the Bulgars, cleared the Mediterranean of corsairs, and strengthened its position in southern Italy. It took Greek Christianity to the Russians (989) and definitely asserted the independence of the Greek Church (the Cerularian Schism, 1054). At the same time it saw a flowering of learning, literature, and art. At the time of the death of Basil II (1025), the Byzantine Empire was the greatest power in the Christian and Muslim worlds.

Decline. This was not to last. The successors of Basil II neglected the army and undermined the social structure of the Empire by ignoring the interests of the small peasant proprietors. In 1071 the forces of the Empire under Romanus IV (d.1071) suffered a crushing defeat at the hands of the Seljuk Turks at Manzikert. This defeat and the civil war that followed enabled the Seljuks to occupy Asia Minor. In the meantime, the Normans conquered southern Italy and nomadic tribes from the north repeatedly devastated the Balkan Peninsula. Alexius I Comnenus, an able soldier and diplomat, finally established

order, checked the Normans, turned back the nomads, and, with the help of the First Crusade (1096), in the instigation of which he played an important role, recovered the western part of Asia Minor. His son John II Comnenus (1088–1143) increased both the prestige and territory of the Empire but failed in his efforts to check the commercial penetration of his Domain by the Venetians, who had entrenched themselves as a result of the privileges granted to them by Alexius I. John's son, Manuel I Comnenus (1120?–80), sought to re-establish the universalism of the Empire but in the end failed, having suffered defeat in Italy and also in Asia Minor, where his army was crushed (1176) by the Seljuks in the battle of Myriocephalum. Nor was he able to check the commercial exploitation of the Empire by the Venetians. In 1185 the Angeli replaced the Comneni on the throne giving way in turn to the Latins of the Fourth Crusade (1204), who, instead of fighting the Muslims, plundered Constantinople and carried away its wealth.

The Latins made Constantinople the capital of a new Latin empire organized on the feudal basis of the West, but failed to crush completely the Greeks, who now formed three states: the empire of Nicaea under the Lascarids; the empire of Trebizond under a branch of the Comneni; and the despotate of Epirus under a branch of the Angeli. There followed a terrific struggle in which Greeks, of both Epirus and Nicaea, Latins, and Bulgars were involved; in the end the Greeks of Nicaea won. In 1261 Michael VIII Palaeologus, who usurped the throne of the Lascarids, recovered Constantinople and made it the capital of a restored Byzantine Empire. An able soldier and a skillful diplomat, Michael not only coped

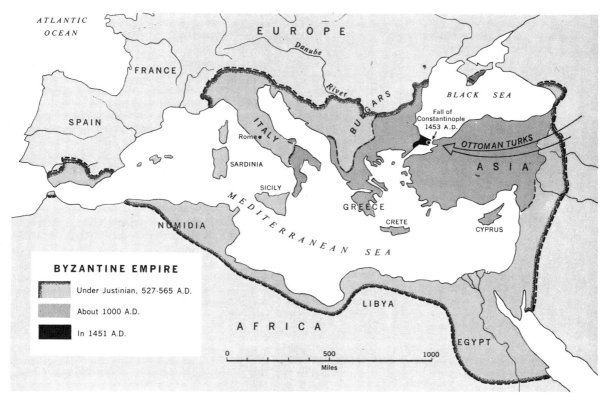

BYZANTINE EMPIRE

Under Justinian, 527-565 A.D.

About 1000 A.D.

In 1451 A.D.

successfully with the enemies of his state, the most formidable of whom was Charles I of Naples, but also increased its prestige and territory. Michael founded a new dynasty, the Palaeologi; his successors, however, were unable to equal him. Hampered by Venetians and Genoese who controlled the economic life of the Empire, and troubled by civil wars, they stood helpless in the face of the steady decline of their power and resources. In 1354 the Ottoman Turks, who had by now deprived the Empire of its possessions in Asia Minor, occupied Gallipoli and made it the base of their operations in Europe. By 1400 they were the masters of virtually the entire Balkan Peninsula. Their defeat (1402) by the Mongols in Asia Minor checked them only temporarily, for they soon resumed their march and finally, in 1453, under the leadership of Mohammed II, attacked Constantinople. The city fell on May 29. Although the Empire had been in full political decay for many years, its final struggle for survival was not unheroic. Constantine XI, the last Emperor, was killed fighting valiantly to stave off disaster. Today he is one of the heroes of the Greek national tradition.

LITERATURE

BYZANTINE LITERATURE, the natural continuation and development of classical and Hellenistic Greek literature from the reign of Constantine the Great (306–37) to the fall of Constantinople (1453). All types of literature were cultivated: theology, history, geography, philosophy, rhetoric, antiquarian studies, natural sciences, religious poetry, and secular poetry. The writers of these genres all used classical Greek, which was no longer spoken but was the basis of instruction in the schools. Some writers, however, began to employ colloquial Greek, which had developed from the classical. In this medium, from which modern Greek developed, were written popular histories, romances, animal fables, chronicles, and collections of proverbs.

Since the Greek authors of the classical epoch were regarded as models of literary perfection, as well as guides to the best material for education and character formation, the educational curriculum was based on the study and imitation of the classical writers. Under the influence of the Cappadocian Fathers of the 4th century, the Church recognized the value of the Greek classics, if taught within the framework of Christian education. The methods and terminology of classical Greek philosophy had an important effect on the development of Greek theology. As a result, education became primarily literary in character and even the natural sciences were taught from the philosophical and literary point of view. Literary accomplishment was essential for advancement in the legal profession and the civil service and many of the most distinguished authors were lawyers or civil servants.

Since the basis of the Byzantine society and state was essentially religious, theological writing played a large part in Byzantine literature. Many scholars, both clerical and lay, wrote on both ecclesiastical and secular subjects. It was due to the Church's interest in classical literature as a part of the national heritage that the classical authors were preserved, edited, and studied.

Literary Scholarship was diversified. Men of letters had to be able to write upon, and teach, a variety of subjects. Typical of such men was Theodorus Prodromus (12th century), whose literary activity was manifold. Tools of literary scholarship were available, such as the encyclopedic lexicon of Suidas and the learned collections and antiquarian treatises of the imperial scholar Constantine VII Porphyrogenitus (reigned 912–59), best known for his compilation of the rules for the ceremonies of the imperial court law. A typical ecclesiastical man of letters was Eustathius, Archbishop of Thessalonica (d.1194), who annotated Homer and other classical authors, and wrote religious and historical treatises. Manuel Philes (13th–14th century), one of the most productive Byzantine authors, wrote, always in verse, on a wide range of subjects, including natural sciences and works of art. John (or Johannes) Tzetzes was another typical scholar and commentator.

Historical Writing was one of the main achievements of Byzantine literature. For the most part history was written by imperial officials and diplomats who had played an active part in public affairs. Procopius, the last great Greek historian of antiquity, was a legal officer in the military service. His work was continued by Agathias (6th century), a lawyer and civil servant, who also wrote poetry. Theophylactus Simocattes (7th century) had a great influence on future historians. Zonaras (12th century), an imperial official, compiled a widely used historical handbook. Johannes Cinnamus (12th century) was another historian in the imperial service. Laonicus Chalcondyles and Georgius Phrantzes, imperial officials and diplomats in the 15th century, wrote histories of their own times. Emperor John VI Cantacuzene (reigned 1341–55) was a historian of considerable ability, and Princess Anna Comnena wrote a history of the reign of her father, Alexius I Comnenus. A popular historical genre was the chronicle, in which the material was arranged in strictly annalistic order. The leading exponent of this form was Theophanes the Confessor (8th century).

Byzantine Poetry continued the classical tradition in such works as *Hero and Leander* of Musaeus. Georgius Pisides (7th century), the best secular poet of the Byzantine period, wrote on a variety of subjects. Byzantine literature was especially distinguished by the work of the woman poet Casia (9th century), a writer of original gifts and deep religious feeling, who dealt with both secular and religious themes.

Religious poetry, however, followed new lines in the Byzantine period, as accentual verse replaced the quantitative meter of the classical period. A writer of the new style was Romanos (5th–6th century), the greatest Byzantine poet and a gifted religious writer. His work was continued by Andreas, Archbishop of Crete in the 7th century, and Cosmas of Jerusalem in the 8th century. The Emperor Justinian (reigned 527–65) composed a hymn which is still used in the Greek Church.

The examples of colloquial writing which have been preserved are fewer in number than those in the classical style, since books in the vernacular were not as carefully preserved as those in the cultivated language. One of the earliest and best-known compositions in colloquial Greek is the chronicle of Johannes Malalas, a Syrian monk of the 6th century. It sets forth an abbreviated history of the world beginning with Adam and continuing down to the author's day.

Role in Politics. Literature played a major role in keeping alive Byzantine patriotism and awareness of the link to classical antiquity, two of the bases of the strength of the Byzantine state. When Photius, the learned patriarch of Constantinople (9th century), wished to lead a political revival and encourage the Byzantine people to resist the ambitious plans of the West, a revival of the study of classical authors was one of the means he employed. The classical tradition in literature flourished down to the last days of Constantinople. The account of the capture of the city by the Turks, written by the Greek official Critobulus, was composed in imitation of the style of Thucydides.

In the 15th century, a period of political and territorial decline in the Byzantine Empire, there were a number of distinguished scholars and humanists such as Johannes Bessarion, Georgius Gemistus Plethon, and Manuel Chrysoloras. Their teaching of the Greek language and literature in Italy contributed to the development of the Renaissance by the transmission of classical Greek and Byzantine literature to Western Europe.

MUSIC

BYZANTINE MUSIC comprises the secular and sacred music of the Eastern Empire from the 6th century to the fall of Constantinople (1453 A.D.). Musical manuscripts are preserved from the 9th century onward. However, no specimen of secular music has survived, although the *Book of Ceremonies* by Constantine Porphyrogenitus (913–59 A.D.) gives a vivid picture of secular music at the court in Constantinople. There is, however, a 17th-century collection of folk songs in Byzantine neumes (see neumatic signs below) discovered in the binding of a codex on Mount Athos. The melodies are stylistically akin to the liturgical music of the 13th century.

Byzantine ecclesiastical music derived from that of the Syro-Palestinian church, which itself derived from the chant of the synagogue. The music is divided into two groups: the cantillation of the lessons, and the singing of the liturgical chants and hymns. Byzantine musical notation as well is divided into two types: ekphonetic signs, guiding the reader of the lessons, and neumatic signs, indicating the general flow of the melodies, rhythm, and

The Codex Sinaiticus, a 4th-century Byzantine manuscript, was discovered in a monastery on Mount Sinai and is now in the British Museum. Musical signs to guide the reader of the lesson can be seen above the words (in Greek) of John 1:28, which ended the Gospel reading for Easter Monday.

New York Public Library—Music Room

expression. From the 11th century onward, signs were added to indicate the approximate interval value. In the 12th century this notation was perfected; it now gives precise interval values. From the 13th century onward, additional red signs were introduced to facilitate the execution of groups of notes.

In the Epistle to the Ephesians (5:19) St. Paul admonishes the followers of Christ to speak to themselves "in psalms and hymns and spiritual songs." These three types of Jewish sacred music were taken over by the Byzantine Church. Psalmody, as in the West is, more or less, a recitative with fixed formulas at the half and full closes, or cadences. Hymns are composed in a syllabic style. In the beginning, at least, the Hirmoi, the model stanzas of the odes, have one note to a syllable; at a later stage one finds two or three notes to a syllable, and some important words even have a melisma (several notes to one syllable). The stichera are monostrophic, or single-versed, hymns and slightly more ornamented. All these genres were sung by the choir, which knew the melodies by heart. Except for the choirmaster, nobody had a book containing the music. The spiritual songs mentioned by St. Paul are the Alleluias and Doxologies, composed in a richly ornamented style. They were sung by a soloist. These melismatic chants are preserved in late manuscripts only, and so are the melodies of the kontakia, poems of homiletic character in 20 to 30 strophes.

The kontakion poem dates from the 6th century, and its most famous author is Romanos, the greatest poet of the Eastern Church. It has been established that countless Latin hymns in praise of the Blessed Virgin derive from the *Akathistos Kontakion*, written originally for the Feast of the Annunciation, but later turned into a Song of Victory when, by the intervention of the Virgin, Constantinople was saved from the enemy in the 7th century.

In the same century the kontakion was replaced by a new poetical form, the *kanon*, since the Council in Trullo (691) made preaching after the Gospel obligatory. The kontakion, the sung homily, therefore had to be dropped to avoid duplication. The *kanon* consists of nine odes. Each ode has its own meter and melody. The model stanzas, the hirmoi, of all of the odes of the *kanons* are collected in the Hirmologion. The most famous writers of *kanons* at the end of the 7th and the beginning of the 8th centuries were Andreas of Crete, John of Damascus, and his foster brother, Cosmas of Jerusalem. They adorned the main feasts of the year with *kanons*.

At that time (7th and 8th centuries) the Arab conquest destroyed monastic artistic endeavors in Asia Minor, and the monastery of Studios in Constantinople became, in the 9th century, the center of hymn writing. Although persecuted and tortured by the Iconoclasts, the monks adorned all the feasts with numerous *kanons* and shorter hymns. In the 11th century the church had to stop the introduction of new hymns. Now began the activity of the composers (*maïstores*), who extended the melismatic chant by coloraturas, but who also replaced expressive and beautiful melodies with insignificant ones. Finally, the Turkish influence changed the character of Byzantine music. Only on Mount Athos and in some other monasteries has the greatness of Byzantine chant been preserved. A complete edition of Byzantine music, *Monumenta Musicae Byzan-*

tinae, was started by Carsten Hoeg, Egon Wellesz, and H. J. W. Tillyard, and others in Copenhagen in 1935. It contains six volumes of facsimiles, four volumes of studies, and nine volumes of transcriptions.

PEOPLE, PLACES, AND TERMS

ARCADIUS (c.377–408), emperor of the Eastern Roman (Byzantine) Empire (395–408). Arcadius ascended the Eastern throne following the death of his father, Roman Emperor Theodosius I; Arcadius' brother Honorius inherited the Western throne. Weak, dull, and uninspiring, Arcadius was dominated by the strong personalities of his court: his wife, Eudoxia; the praetorian prefect of the east, Flavius Rufinus; the eunuch Eutropius; and other ministers. The most important problem of his reign was the rise of the Visigoths, whom his father had settled in the Balkan peninsula. Eventually, however, the Visigoths, under the leadership of Alaric, moved into Italy, while the Goths, who remained in the East and threatened to dominate imperial military and political life, were largely massacred in 400. Arcadius exiled (404) the patriarch St. John Chrysostom.

BASIL I (d.886), Byzantine Emperor (867–86). Born of Armenian parents in Macedonia, Basil, as an unknown youth seeking his fortune, went to Constantinople. His athletic prowess attracted the attention of a courtier who introduced him to the Emperor, Michael III. Michael, fond of Basil, made him head groom of his stables and then high chamberlain. Basil was instrumental in the assassination (866) of Bardas, Michael's uncle and the real ruler of the state. Made co-Emperor by Michael, Basil instigated Michael's murder in 867 and thus became sole Emperor. Basil founded the most brilliant of the Byzantine dynasties, the Macedonian, so named in honor of his birthplace. Under the reign of this dynasty, which endured more than 170 years, the empire reached the apogee of its power and its widest influence as a cultural source. Basil laid the foundations for this greatness. Although he ultimately failed against the Arabs in Italy, he made important territorial acquisitions in Asia Minor, and extended Byzantine authority among the Slavs in the Balkans. Internally, he revived the legal codes of Justinian, and protected the interests of the Byzantine Church against those of the papacy, although at the beginning of his reign he gave way in the controversy concerning the patriarch Photius. Basil's death was accidental.

BELISARIUS [bĕl-ə-sâr'ē-əs] (c.505–565), Byzantine general in the service of Justinian I. Perhaps of Germanic origins, Belisarius was born in Germania, in the Balkan Peninsula. He was a well-known general by 529, when he was appointed to an important military post in the eastern provinces of the empire. In 532 Belisarius saved Justinian by suppressing the popular rebellion in Constantinople known as the Nika revolt. Belisarius' greatest military successes occurred in his wars against the Vandals in North Africa (533–34) and the Ostrogoths in Italy (535–40; 544–48). Hampered by insufficient troops and lack of supplies, Belisarius did not finish the war in Italy. Recalled

from Italy in 548, he was put in command in the east but soon retired (551). In his late years he was temporarily in disfavor.

CONSTANS II (630–68), Byzantine Emperor (reigned 641–68). Constans II succeeded his father Constantine III as Emperor. The most important events of his reign were the advances of the Arabs, who, having already conquered Syria, Palestine, and Egypt, overran part of Asia Minor and Armenia and, taking to sea, attacked Cyprus and plundered Rhodes. A man of strong will and relentless energy, Constans made a serious effort to stop the Arabs at sea, but suffered a crushing defeat at their hands off the coast of Lycia in 655.

The civil war that soon broke out among the Arabs, however, enabled Constans to turn his attention to the Slavs in the Balkan Peninsula, whom he forced (658) to acknowledge his suzerainty. Never popular in Constantinople, Constans went (662) to Italy, hoping to establish his capital in Rome. He met with little success there and settled in Syracuse, where he was murdered. Constans is credited with having reorganized the administrative machinery of the Byzantine Empire as well as for having issued an edict forbidding the discussion of religious matters.

CONSTANTINE IV (652?–685), Byzantine Emperor (reigned 668–85). He succeeded his father, Constans II, who was murdered in Syracuse. The two important events associated with the reign of Constantine IV are the failure of the siege of Constantinople (674–78) by the Arabs and the establishment (679) of the Bulgar kingdom in the Balkan Peninsula. Both events affected the course of history. The Arab failure saved Christian tradition in eastern Europe, and the founding of the Bulgar kingdom conditioned the subsequent history of the Slavs as well as that of the Byzantine Empire.

CONSTANTINE V (718–75), Byzantine Emperor (reigned 741–75). Constantine V succeeded his father Leo III in 741 but for two years he had to fight his brother-in-law Artavasdus, who sought to replace him. War with the Arabs and the Bulgars and the vigorous pursuit of the iconoclastic policy of his father were the principal features of his reign. An able commander, Constantine was usually victorious in the field. His successes against the Arabs, however, brought no new territories to the Empire, and his victories over the Bulgars brought about no permanent settlement, though they did weaken the Bulgar state. Meanwhile, the Empire lost Ravenna in Italy to the Lombards. Constantine, strongly antimonastic, called the church council that met in Hieria in 754 and approved his iconoclastic policy. He died during a campaign against the Bulgars.

CONSTANTINE VI (c.770–97), Byzantine Emperor (reigned 780–97). Constantine succeeded his father, Leo IV. Since Constantine was a minor, he was put under the regency of his mother Irene, who was proclaimed Co-Emperor. In 790, discontented under the tutelage of his mother and supported by the iconoclastic elements in the army that had been alienated by Irene, Constantine removed her from power. He recalled her two years later, an act that estranged him from his friends. At the same time he aroused the indignation of Orthodox circles by divorcing his wife and marrying his mistress. Left without support, he was deposed and blinded (797) by his mother, who could then satisfy her ambition to rule alone.

CONSTANTINE XI (d. 1453), last Emperor of the Byzantine Empire (reigned 1449–53). Constantine XI was Despot (Governor) of Morea when he was called upon to succeed his brother John VIII, who died in 1449. Honest, generous, valorous, and energetic, but patriotic above all, Constantine made a last determined effort to save the Greek world from Turkish domination. The great event of his reign was the capture of Constantinople by the Turks in 1453. Because of his stalwart defense of the Byzantine capital, in the course of which he lost his life, he is a national hero to the Greeks.

CONSTANTINOPLE. See ISTANBUL.

HAGIA SOPHIA [hä′jə sō-fē′ə] (Gr., "Holy Wisdom"), also called Santa Sophia, originally the cathedral church of Constantinople, later a mosque, and now a museum. Considered the supreme masterpiece of Byzantine architecture and one of the world's greatest buildings, it was erected in 532–37 by the Emperor Justinian on designs of his architect Anthemius of Tralles who was assisted by Isidorus of Miletus. The spacious nave, 265 ft. long by 102 ft. wide, is covered by a lofty central dome 184 ft. high carried on four huge arches and pendentives. The latter, employed here for the first time in monumental construction, are the curved triangular pieces of masonry used to effect the transition from a rectangular structure to its circular dome. The nave, entered through two spacious vestibules, has a vaulted sanctuary at its east end and is flanked by side aisles with galleries above. Their massive vaults, supported by monolithic columns of green and white marble and gleaming purple porphyry, buttress the

great dome, which appears to float like a weightless golden shell high overhead. All interior surfaces are sheathed with sumptuous colored marbles and gold mosaic, which enframe glowing mosaics of figures and religious scenes. The last have been cleaned and restored by American archeologists.

HARUN AL-RASHID or **HAROUN AL-RASCHID** [hä-rōōn′ äl-rä-shēd′] (763?–809), the fifth Caliph of the Abbasid Dynasty. The dynasty reached the height of its power under Harun, who later achieved legendary fame in the *Arabian Nights*. Harun's career was decisively influenced by two developments which occurred in his youth. In 782, during a victorious campaign against the Byzantine Empire, Harun so impressed his father, the Caliph al-Mahdi, that the latter nominated him as the second in the line of succession, according him also the honorific title al-Rashid, meaning the "Straightforward." The second development was the appointment of Yahya ibn Khalid, a prominent member of the Iranian family of the Barmecides, as Harun's tutor. As a result of this association, the Barmecides controlled the affairs of state from the accession of Harun in 786 until his brutal liquidation of them in 803. The social and economic prosperity of Harun's reign was mainly achieved by the administrative talents of these Iranian viziers.

The general prosperity was also enhanced by the relative security of the empire both internally and externally. Harun's armies successfully coped with a number of rebellions, and the security of the empire was strengthened by new fortresses erected along the Byzantine frontier and by raids launched against Christian territory. The Caliph's military campaigns in 789–99 forced the Byzantine Empress Irene to pay tribute to the Muslim ruler. When Emperor Nicephorus rejected that treaty, Harun reimposed even more humiliating terms on the Byzantine Empire by means of victorious campaigns between 802 and 806.

Although the anti-Byzantine wars did not result in any

Istanbul's Hagia Sophia, originally a Byzantine church (begun, 532), is today a public monument. The building, an architectural masterpiece with an opulent interior, was used as a mosque after the Turkish conquest (15th century).

Pix, Inc.

permanent territorial gains, they contributed greatly to Harun's international prestige. His court was visited by foreign diplomats; according to Western sources even Charlemagne exchanged embassies with his great Muslim contemporary. Apart from economic, political, and military splendor, the reign of al-Rashid was famous for scientific and artistic activity in which the Caliph showed great interest.

With all its splendor, the reign of Harun al-Rashid had an adverse effect on the development of the Abbasid Caliphate. By allowing a Governor in Africa to establish a hereditary dynasty, Harun legalized a secessionist tendency among provincial governors, which led ultimately to the disintegration of the empire. The brutal suppression of the Barmecides alienated the Iranian aristocracy, the support of which had been so essential to the rise of the Abbasid Caliphate. His incompetent handling of an oppressive Governor in Khurasan (eastern Iran), and above all his division of the empire between his two sons, al-Amin and al-Mamun, cast further doubt on his abilities as a statesman. It was mainly because of Harun's political errors that, soon after his death, the Caliphate was plunged into bloody civil war.

HERACLIUS [hĕr-ə-klī′əs] (c.575–641), Byzantine Emperor (610–41). He was instrumental in the overthrow of the incompetent Emperor Phocas, whose place he took in 610. A brilliant general, Heraclius launched a series of campaigns against the Persians, who had threatened the empire with extinction. The war assumed the character of a crusade, for one of its objectives was the recovery of the true cross, which the Persians had carried away when they took Jerusalem in 614. In the absence of the Emperor, the Avars made a vain attempt to seize the city of Constantinople. Toward the close of his reign the Arabs conquered the eastern provinces that he had taken from the Persians.

ICON [ī′kŏn], painted or sculpted image with extraordinary mystical or religious power attributed to it. The supernatural quality associated with an icon differentiates it from an ordinary religious image. Although veneration of icons is inimical to the Roman Catholic Church, they are an integral part of the worship of the Greek and Russian Orthodox churches. The architecture of Greek and Russian churches includes the iconostasis, designed to hold the icons, as an integral part of the building.

Most icons were painted on wooden panels by anonymous monks. They reached their first great importance in the 8th-century Byzantine Empire. The "iconoclastic" period, lasting a little over 100 years, prohibited production of icons in the Byzantine world. By the 10th century they were produced again and assumed an even greater importance throughout the Greek and Russian east. The Russian, Andrei Rubliev (1370–1430) stands out as one of the greatest icon painters of all times. The "Virgin of Vladimir" and Rubliev's "The Saviour," in Moscow are among the most famous and venerated of icons.

ICONOCLASTIC [ī-kŏn-ə-klăs′tĭk] **CONTROVERSY**, 8th- and 9th-century controversy concerning the use of icons in the Byzantine Church. In 726 Emperor Leo III of Byzantium ordered the destruction of all images on grounds of idolatry. Pope Gregory II objected, as did St. John of Damascus, the most eminent contemporary Greek theologian. Nevertheless, a synod of Eastern bishops in 754 pronounced the use of images heretical. Later, Empress Irene took the lead in convoking the 7th ecumenical council at Nicaea in 787, where the Greek bishops reversed themselves and authorized the veneration of images.

In 813 Emperor Leo V renewed the earlier prohibitions. Patriarch Nicephorus of Constantinople opposed him but was deposed. St. Theodore, abbot of the monastery of Studios in the capital, suffered exile for denouncing the Emperor's caesaro-papism. The Greek monks in general opposed iconoclasm, but the army and court circles upheld it. Finally, under Empress Theodora another Greek synod, in 843, again permitted images. With that, the controversy ended.

IRENE [ī-rēn′] (752–803), Byzantine Empress (797–802). A woman of great force and ambition, Irene married the Emperor Leo IV in 769. When her husband died (780), she ruled as regent during the minority of her son, Constantine VI. In 790 rebel soldiers removed her from power, but she schemed her way back (792), ordered her son's eyes stabbed out (797), and became the sole ruler of Byzantium. Irene was the first woman to govern the Empire in her own right, but so strong was the prejudice against the rule of a woman that she signed herself Emperor, not Empress. The restoration of the worship of icons (Council of Nicaea, 787) and the revival of the imperial title in the west (coronation of Charlemagne, 800) were the two leading events of her reign. Overthrown in 802, she died shortly after.

ISTANBUL [ĭs-tăn-bōōl′], the largest city in the Republic of Turkey, formerly the capital of the Ottoman Empire, and earlier, under the name Constantinople, the capital of the Byzantine Empire (q.v.). It is strategically located on the European shore at the southern end of the narrow straits of the Bosporus that connect the Black Sea with the Sea of Marmara, thus separating the Asiatic and European mainlands. The site must have known settlement since remotest antiquity, though legend attributes the first city founded (c.667 B.C.) here to a Megarian captain, Byzas, from whom it received the name Byzantium (q.v.). The original city occupied the triangular promontory lying between the Sea of Marmara on the south and a Bosporus inlet, the Golden Horn (Haliç), on the north and was defended on the west by a wall stretching between these two bodies of water. This in principle remained its plan until the Ottoman period. With the security then brought to the region by Turkish military power, the city was able to overflow its natural defenses and to incorporate the cities of Pera (now Beyoğlu) on the opposite side of the Golden Horn and of Üsküdar (formerly Scutari) on the Asiatic shore of the Bosporus. The modern city exhibits the common features of metropolitan sprawl, with suburb after suburb stretching along its several littorals; and now Greater İstanbul consists of 16 boroughs, including the nine Princes' Islands in the Sea of Marmara, administered by an elected mayor and an urban council. The city with its environs is also a province (vilayet) of the Turkish re-

Ewing Galloway

The imperial mosque of Sultan Ahmed I in İstanbul was built from 1608 to 1614 as a burial place for the Sultan and his family.

public, under a governor responsible to the minister of the interior and a provincial council elected by popular vote.

History. The history of Istanbul properly begins in the year 324 A.D., when the Roman Emperor Constantine I, having seized the city and destroyed its walls in punishment for the support it gave to his rival Licinius, decided to found it anew and to transfer here from Rome the capital of his empire. The economic, religious, and above all, the military center of gravity of the Roman Empire had since the time of Emperor Diocletian (reigned 284–305) been steadily shifting eastward. Rome had squandered the material resources and the man power of Italy in attempting to maintain its empire, and it was now bankrupt. Its pagan associations and its history of persecution made it an unsuitable center for an empire that, whatever may have been the faith of Constantine himself, was henceforth to be Christian. Rome was remote from the areas where its military forces were needed to combat its most menacing enemies, the barbarian tribes of the Danube and the Persians. New Rome, or as it was soon to be known, Constantinople, protected by a new wall that increased fivefold its former area and lavishly adorned with the most precious objects of art to be found in the whole Mediterranean world, was formally dedicated on May 11, 330. For over 1,100 years it was to remain the bastion of Christianity against the pressure of the non-Christian East.

Like Rome, the city was founded on seven hills (actually prominences in a gradual elevation from east to west, only four of which were included within the wall constructed by Constantine); and also on the model of Rome, it was divided into 14 administrative districts. Each of the hills became the site of a monumental edifice. Proceeding

westward from the tip of the promontory along the Golden Horn side were: (1) the Acropolis and, later, the Church of Hagia Sophia (q.v.); (2) the Forum of Constantine with its column (Çemberlitaş); (3) the cistern of Nymphaeum Maximum and the Forum of Theodosius (subsequently the university and the Mosque of Bayezid); (4) the Church of the Holy Apostles (the Mosque of Mohammed II); (5) the open cistern of Aspar (the Mosque of Sultan Selim I); (6) the Monastery of Chora and the Charisius Gate (the Mihrimah Mosque and Edirne Kapısı); and (7) the Forum of Arcadius with its column (Avret Taşı). Only the last hill lies on the Marmara side of the city, and originally the valley running between it and the other hills was the principal thoroughfare (the Mese), which at the third hill branched northward toward the Charisius Gate and southward toward the Golden Gate beyond the seventh hill.

The ambivalent religious attitude of the Constantine emperors (324–63) was definitely changed under Theodosius the Great (reigned 379–95), who destroyed all the pagan temples and made Christianity not merely the state religion but a virtual state monopoly. It was in his reign, also, that the empire was divided into two; but while Rome, the capital of the West, continued to decline under anarchy, Constantinople thrived and grew. So great had the population become that in the reign of Theodosius II (408–50) the land walls had to be moved westward, and those newly constructed were of such impregnable strength as to defy all thought of assault. The sea walls of the Marmara were strengthened; and with access to the Golden Horn cut off in times of danger by an enormous chain stretching across its entrance, the city assured its in-

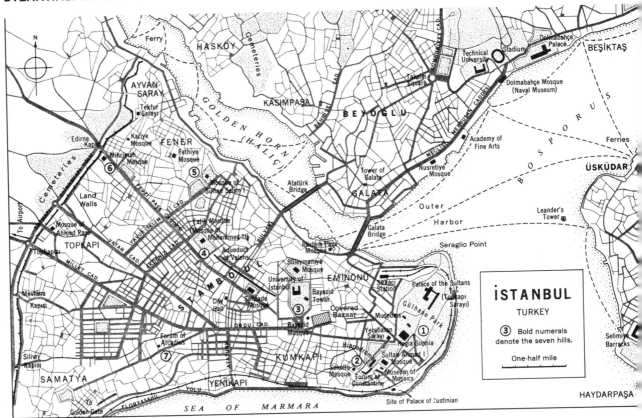

Warehouses line the water front of Galata, a commercial district on the northern shore of the Golden Horn. Nusretiye Mosque, with the minarets, is one of over 400 in Istanbul.

Ewing Galloway

vulnerability from the sea. But probably even more important than its military security was the economic advantage given the city by its location. Here was the inevitable nexus of the trade routes of the ancient world, and the revenues of commerce allowed Constantinople the luxury that is still the first connotation of the term Byzantine.

Culture. Constantinople tried to mimic Rome in more than mere externals: its laws and its administration were both Roman, and Latin remained the language of the court and of the bureaucracy down to the end of the 6th century. But environed as it was by a Hellenistic culture, which since the time of Alexander the Great (4th century B.C.) had become highly orientalized, and with its attention never allowed to waver from its enemies to the north (the Slavs) and to the east (the Persians and later the Arabs), it was unavoidable that Constantinople should succumb to their influence. Out of this medley of cultures developed the synthetic, characteristic Byzantinism that is attested to most vividly in its art and in its architecture. In religion, too, Constantinople had to assert her individuality. Although the formal break with the Latin Church of the West did not come until 867, for centuries previously contention and dissent provided the pattern of ecclesiastic history. Whatever the issues, dogmatic or confessional, the underlying cause was always a divergence in mentality that prevented understanding and made communication all but impossible. The Greek Orthodox Church, with its elaborate ceremonial and sumptuous adornments, was ultimately born of the same spiritual and aesthetic values that produced the churches and palaces with walls and ceilings decorated by mosaics and frescoes. Constantinople was not only the capital of the Byzantine Empire but also its purpose and its meaning; and even in its latter centuries when the whole of the empire's territories hardly exceeded the confines of its walls, the world still regarded the city with wonder and admiration as something unique and superior. When it was captured by the Turks in 1453, even Western Christendom felt that it had lost one of its polar points.

Bastion. It seemed incredible that a city that had resisted so many sieges and assaults could fall. In 616 and in 626 it had repulsed the Persians and the Avars; in 675 and again in 717–18 it had withstood Arab attacks from land and sea, destroying their fleets with the terrifying incendiary weapon called Greek fire. The Bulgarians failed to take it in 813, and on four occasions between 864 and 1043 Russian fleets were destroyed in the attempt. The participants in the so-called Fourth Crusade, which was really a Venetian enterprise designed to win exclusive control of the trade that passed through the city, succeeded in capturing Constantinople in 1204 and in three days of massacre and pillage destroyed the greater part of the artistic legacy of the previous eight centuries. But the tenure of the Latins was brief; and in 1261 Michael VIII Palaeologus recaptured the city, though it was now but a shambles compared with its former splendor. In the 14th century the Ottoman Turks crossed from Asia Minor and launched their campaigns of plunder in the hitherto unexploited regions of Greece and the Balkans. The ease of their victories encouraged them to remain and to incorporate the lands conquered into an empire of their own, an empire that was, in reality, to be a Muslim continuation of Byzantium. But so long as Constantinople remained in the heart of their territories as a spiritual and moral enclave, their ambitions could not be realized; and on at least four occasions siege was laid to the city before its final capture by Sultan Mohammed II on May 29, 1453.

The Sultan had prepared for his assault on the city by constructing in 1452 a fortress (Rumili Hisar) to its north on the shores of the Bosporus, directly across from an existing fortress (Anadolu Hisar) on the Asiatic shore, thereby cutting off access to the Black Sea. Enormous cannon were cast for breaching the walls; and an immense army, over 20 times as many as the 50,000 or so Greeks who were to defend the city, was mustered. The most spectacular coup of the siege was the transportation overland in a single night of the Turkish fleet of 70 ships from the harbor in Beşiktaş into the Golden Horn, under the protection of which a bridge was constructed above present-day Ayvansaray. The main assault was directed against the Romanus Gate (Topkapı), which was subjected to a continuous bombardment from the mighty cannon; but the first entry was made at the Charisius Gate (Edirne Kapısı). From dawn to noon of May 29 the city was delivered over to massacre and pillage.

One of the first acts of Sultan Mohammed after his conquest was to order that the great Church of Hagia Sophia be converted to a mosque, and this became the precedent for many more such conversions. In taking Constantinople (henceforth to be known as İstanbul) the Turks achieved the ultimate in all Islamic military aspiration and were well aware of the prestige value of their trophy. In contrast, therefore, to the witless vandalism of the Crusaders two centuries previously, they made every effort to preserve what remained of the once glorious city and to embellish it further with their own building. If in the course of time many of the Byzantine churches became mosques, this can be attributed to the relative proportions of the Christians and Muslims in the changing population of the city. Even in converting these churches, the Muslims retained all that was not offensive to Islam. Rather than destroy the frescoes and mosaics, they whitewashed them; or they effaced specifically human features, such as the eyes (Muslims regard as sacrilegious the representation of

The Galata Bridge, which spans the mouth of the Golden Horn, connects the Beyoğlu section of İstanbul with the original city site.

Ewing Galloway

the human form). Minarets were added without destruction to the original fabric of the walls, and internal proportions were maintained.

Archeology. In a city subject to fire and earthquake, a great number of these Byzantine buildings have completely vanished or survive merely as ruins. Hagia Sofia is now a museum, as is also the Church of St. Saviour in Chora (the Kariye Mosque), a 14th-century construction, the mosaics and frescoes of which, with their fluidity of design and composition and their still vibrant colors, are unique among the productions of this highly immobile and formalistic art. The Church of St. Mary Pammacaristos (the Fethiye Mosque), charmingly situated on a hill overlooking the Golden Horn, has probably the most pleasing exterior of all the Byzantine remains; and the mosaic dome of one of its chapels is hardly inferior to those of the Kariye. Of the other 20 or so edifices wholly or partially extant, few present anything of immediately perceptible beauty; and they remain more the concern of the archeologist and of the art historian than of the artist.

The great residential buildings of the Byzantine emperors survive, when at all, only as unprepossessing ruins. Near the Edirne Gate, the palace (Tekfur Sarayı), attributed to Constantine Porphyrogenitus, the walls of which are still standing, alone retains some of its original charm. Only a mosaic pavement has so far been unearthed on the site of the great palace in the Hippodrome, while the so-called Palace of Justinian, on the shores of the Marmara, exhibits nothing but the ugliness of decay. Many of the old cisterns are still to be seen, the most interesting of which is the underground construction known as Yerebatan Sarayı, with its 336 columns ranged in 12 rows. It supplied the old imperial palace. Also connected with the water supply of the city are the numerous aqueducts in its northern suburbs and the great one, dating from the time of the Emperor Valens (reigned 364–78) running between the third and fourth hills of the city itself. These aqueducts were maintained in use and augmented by others in the Ottoman period, and they have been so frequently restored and repaired that it is almost impossible to establish the original sections.

JUSTINIAN [jŭs-tĭn′ē-ən] **I** (483–565), Byzantine Emperor (527–65). He was born in Macedonia, the nephew of the Emperor Justin. His original name was Petrus Sabbatius, but he changed it to Justinian after his uncle brought him to Constantinople. He was well educated and already influential during Justin s reign, and when his uncle died in 527 he succeeded to the throne.

Justinian was perhaps the greatest of the Byzantine Emperors. He recovered much of the lost Roman territory in the west by successful campaigns against the Vandals and Berbers in North Africa, the Ostrogoths in Italy, and the Visigoths in Spain. But while fighting these wars he neglected the eastern provinces, and they were repeatedly devastated by Persians, Bulgars, and Slavs.

More permanent than his conquests was Justinian's codification of the Roman law: the *Code*, consisting of imperial edicts; the *Digest* of the decisions of the great Roman jurists; the *Institutes*, a textbook for law students, and the *Novels*, edicts issued by Emperor Justinian himself. Together they constituted the body of the Roman law—*Corpus Juris Civilis*—which still forms the basis of the law of virtually all Europe.

Among the buildings erected by Justinian, the most notable is the Church of Hagia Sophia in İstanbul (former Constantinople), one of the outstanding architectural monuments of all time. An autocratic Emperor, he intervened actively in the affairs of the Church and did not hesitate to interfere in matters of doctrine. His notable collaborators included his wife Theodora, a woman of lowly origin but remarkable ability; Belisarius and Narses, great generals who led his armies; and Tribonian, who supervised the codification of Roman law.

LEO III (c.680–741), Byzantine Emperor (717–41). Born in Syria, he began his military and political career in 705 when he helped Justinian II regain his throne. He was sent on a difficult mission to the Caucasus and distinguished himself both as a diplomat and a military commander. Anastasius II appointed him governor of the Anatolic theme, then the largest province in Asia Minor; but when Anastasius was overthrown, Leo rebelled against his successor and seized the throne. His family, known as the Syrian (or Isaurian) Dynasty, occupied the imperial office till 802.

War with the Arabs, prohibition of icon worship, and the promulgation of a new legal code were the principal features of Leo's reign. The law code, the *Ecloga*, was published in 739 and consisted of sections drawn from the codes of Justinian I revised to conform to the social conditions of the period. The veneration of icons, denounced by Leo in 726, was formally prohibited by an edict issued in 730. This was the beginning of the iconoclastic controversy, which was to trouble the Byzantine Empire for over a century. Leo won two important victories over the Arabs, the first from 717 to 718 when they had besieged Constantinople, and the second at Acroinon in Asia Minor in 740. The immediate Arab threat to the empire was thereby removed.

MANUEL [măn′ū-əl] **I** (c.1120–1180), Byzantine Emperor (1143–80) of the Comnenian Dynasty. The youngest son of John II, Manuel's skill in battle won him his father's designation as successor to the throne. He believed the Byzantine Empire to be a later development of the Roman Empire and his greatest ambition was the re-establishment of its world supremacy. To this end he negotiated with the Papacy and repeatedly intervened in Italian politics, but suffered military defeat and was forced to withdraw from most of Italy. He was more successful in Syria and Palestine, where the Latin princes acknowledged his suzerainty, and to some extent in the Balkan Peninsula, where Serbs, Croats, and Hungarians were brought under his influence. Manuel allowed the Second Crusade (1147–49) to pass through Byzantine territory, which the Crusaders devastated. His most serious defeat came at the hands of the Turks in the battle of Myriocephalum (1176); it undermined both the position of the Empire in Asia Minor and that of the Comnenian Dynasty. A brilliant Emperor in many ways, Manuel nevertheless brought financial strain to the Empire by his frequent military involvements, and his introduction of Western ideas and customs in his court antagonized his subjects.

MICHAEL VIII (1234–82), Byzantine Emperor (1261–82). The scion of a noble Byzantine family, he forced himself on John IV Lascaris, then a boy of seven, and became regent in 1258. Early in 1259 he was proclaimed co-Emperor, but not content with this, he soon deposed and blinded young John, and so became sole Emperor. Michael founded a new dynasty, that of the Paleologi, which ruled the Byzantine Empire until its end in 1453. An able military commander and a clever diplomat, he nearly succeeded in restoring his Empire to its former greatness. In 1261 he realized the dream of every Greek when he reconquered Constantinople from the Latin Empire and restored it as the capital of the state. Thereafter he successfully defended his Empire against the Seljuk Turks and Charles of Anjou.

MOSAIC [mō-zā′ĭk], pictures or designs made by setting small pieces of colored stone, marble, glass, and related materials in wet mortar. Since the colors are permanent, mosaic is peculiarly fitted for decorating floors and walls. Its name comes from the Greek *mouseios,* "belonging to the Muses," because mosaic was used to adorn artificial grottoes dedicated to these mythological patrons of the arts.

The earliest mosaics, laid in simple patterns with natural pebbles of uniform size, appear in the 5th century B.C. as small panels in pavements of Greek temples. Pebble mosaics with formal designs were found in private houses of the next century at Olynthus. At Delos a century later the finer homes had floors picturing mythological subjects, their compositions rendered with tesserae, small cubes of colored marbles prepared expressly for this purpose. Roman floor mosaics, first based upon Greek examples, became very popular after 100 B.C. not only in Rome itself but also throughout Italy and every land where Roman rule extended. These floor mosaics vary from simple geometrical designs to large pictorial

Below, "Presentation of the Child in the Temple," a 5th-century mosaic in the Church of Santa Maria Maggiore in Rome.

Alinari—Art Reference Bureau

Alinari—Art Reference Bureau

Above, "Christ Pantocrator," a monumental figure against a golden background, is a Byzantine mosaic (12th century) decorating the apse of the Cathedral of Monreale, Sicily.

subjects, some obviously copies of famous ancient paintings. The most renowned is a remarkable pavement from Pompeii, showing a spirited combat scene of Alexander the Great at the battle of Issus, now in the National Museum, Naples. Roman wall and ceiling mosaics were generally restricted to small niches for household shrines or fountains. In these, brilliant glass tesserae eventually supplanted the less colorful marble.

Mosaic achieved its artistic peak on the inner walls and vaults of medieval churches, even though it was here used primarily for religious instruction rather than for adornment. The earliest medieval masterpieces, dating from the 4th to 6th century, are in Rome, notably in the churches of Santa Maria Maggiore, Santa Prudenziana, and Saints Cosmas and Damian.

The most distinctive feature of Byzantine mosaic, its sumptuous golden background, developed gradually in Italy. Lavishly used in 6th-century churches at Ravenna, gold mosaic thereafter became universal in Byzantine churches. Its most dazzling display is in Hagia Sophia in Constantinople, where an estimated four acres of vault and wall surface are clothed in the glittering fabric. To prepare this type of mosaic, a delicate layer of beaten gold was spread on a glass slab and fixed in place by a thin protective coating of molten glass. The cooled slab was then broken into tiny quarter-inch cubes, each one of which was set by hand in the moist plaster until broad areas of wall were gradually covered. The irregularities of the numberless hand-set tesserae cause light to be reflected at different angles, thus producing an effect of shimmering vibration unobtainable by any other means.

Skilled Greek artists were driven from their Byzantine homelands by the iconoclastic controversy, and in some cases found refuge in Italy. Their influence brought about a great revival of the mosaic art from the 11th to the 13th century Outstanding masterpieces of this phase—distinguished by tall, quiet figures, simple compositions, and rich symbolic ornament against the golden ground—

are found in St. Mark's in Venice and in famous churches at Palermo, Monreale, and Cefalù in Sicily. During this same period, mosaic decoration was extended to church furniture such as pulpits, episcopal thrones, marble candlesticks, and the twisted columns of cloisters. Known as Cosmati work, from a guild of decorators (*cosmati*) who employed it, the effect is that of a colorful inlay producing rich geometric patterns.

THEODORA [thē-ə-dôr'ə] (508?–548), Byzantine Empress, wife of Justinian. The daughter of a bearkeeper at the Hippodrome in Constantinople, she went on the stage at an early age. In those days an actress was almost synonymous with a prostitute, and it was as a prostitute that Theodora became notorious. Abandoned by a provincial official whom she had followed to Libya, she went to Alexandria and then returned to Constantinople. This experience is said to have reformed her, and when Justinian discovered her she was allegedly making a scanty living by spinning wool. Justinian took her as his mistress, and she later became his wife and Empress. A woman of beauty and irresistible charm, she also possessed a strong will. Until her death she was a tower of strength to Justinian. He actually owed his retention of the throne to her, for she gave him the necessary courage to suppress the dangerous Nika revolt in 532.

THEODOSIUS II (401–50), Eastern Roman Emperor (reigned 408–50). The son of Emperor Arcadius, Theodosius was a child when he ascended the throne. Not a very strong personality, he was successively dominated by the able prefect Anthemius, by his sister, his wife, and his chamberlain. His strong-willed sister Pulcheria, called the Augusta, picked Eudocia, a cultivated Athenian girl for his wife in 421. After 440, Theodosius was dominated by the corrupt grand chamberlain Chrysaphius. His reign is notable for three reasons. New walls were constructed, which rendered Constantinople almost impregnable. The school of higher learning in Greek and Latin grammar and rhetoric was re-established. Most important was the Theodosian Code, a compendium of the still valid imperial edicts issued since the time of Constantine the Great. This code was the forerunner of the more extensive Code of Justinian. The reign of Theodosius II was marked by successful wars against Persia and unsuccessful attempts to block the advance of the Huns under Attila into the Balkans. Diplomacy and massive bribery were used to induce the Huns to move westward.

ZOË [zō'ē] (d.1050), Byzantine Empress (1028–50). She was the eldest daughter of Emperor Constantine VIII (1025–28). Just before the death of her father, when she was almost 50 years of age, she was married to the Byzantine nobleman Romanus Argyrus who, as a result, became Emperor when Constantine VIII died. Romanus was the first of four Byzantine Emperors who ascended the throne through Zoë, three as her husbands (Romanus III, 1028–34; Michael IV, 1034–41; and Constantine IX, 1042–55) and one as her adopted son (Michael V, 1041–42). Michael V drove her away from the palace and forced her to enter a convent, but a popular uprising brought her back and put her on the throne along with her sister Theodora. She ruled the state as Empress in 1042, but when she married Constantine IX that year, she relinquished its direction to him. Zoë was a notorious debauchee, and had no conception of public affairs.

CELTIC CIVILIZATION

CELTS

CELTS [*sĕlts, kĕlts*], Indo-European people whose prehistoric roots go back into the Bronze Age to at least 1000 B.C. Their main center of earliest cultural development was southern Germany and the eastern Alps, where the Celts represented the western branch of the early Iron-Age Hallstatt culture. Archeological evidence confirms that the dominant physical type of the early Celts was Nordic in character. Numerous traits of the east European horse nomads, such as a feudal social organization and the use of the war chariot, were assimilated. Additional Greek and Etruscan elements are noticeable in their technology, the final product of which is seen in the advanced Iron-Age La Tène culture appearing in the 5th century B.C. Linguistically the Celts show closest relationship to Italic and Germanic tribes.

Expansion. In the 8th century B.C. the Celts began to occupy a large area between the Meuse, Weser, and Danube, and between the Alps and the North Sea. Major expansion into the remotest parts of Europe came in several waves, the first of which occurred in the 7th century B.C. when they occupied large parts of Gaul and

CELTIC METALWORK
The earliest known Celtic art was created in a late Iron-Age culture known as La Tene. The basic material of the culture was bronze, with silver and gold used occasionally.

Hurault—Illustration Research Service
Celtic bronze helmet from France, dating from early La Tène period.

British Museum—Illustration Research Service
Bronze torque, feminine adornment for the neck, 1st century B.C.

British Museum—Illustration Research Service
A bronze shield from the Thames at Battersea, London, 1st century B.C.–1st century A.D.

British Museum—Illustration Research Service
Bronze mirror from Desborough, Northamptonshire, exemplifies the refinement of La Tène art.

Britain, and one group burst into Spain. These oldest tribes indicate distinct Hallstatt affinities and anthropologically represent an introduction of Nordic types into western Europe. A second, attenuated wave brought carriers of the La Tène culture into other regions of Gaul, Scotland, Ireland, Bohemia, and Silesia during the last half of the 5th century B.C. About 400 B.C. other Celtic tribes under Brennus invaded Italy, defeated the Romans on the Allia, and sacked Rome in 390. About 335 B.C. Celts moved into the middle Danube-Sava area, where they intermingled with Italic and Illyrian tribes. A third wave broke into the Aegean area, 280 B.C., where the fierce barbarians moved through Thrace and Macedonia, sacking the temple of Delphi in 279 and crossing the Dardanelles to Asia Minor in 278. Here, known as the Galatians, they devastated the countryside until defeated by Pergamum c.230 B.C., after which they were forced to settle in central Anatolia. This represented the furthest extension of the Celtic peoples, who by now had absorbed the older ethnic groups of the British Isles, France, Germany, and the areas lying south and east of the Alps.

Culture. In the conquered lands the Celtic social order consisted of a ruling caste of nobles and priests, or druids, more or less distinct from the largely indigenous common people. These were peasants and warriors, the latter often appearing as mercenaries in the Mediterranean world. Hierarchical in constitution, the priestly caste was responsible for sacrificial rituals, legal decisions, and education. Unfortunately, the oral tradition of the druids is lost so that Celtic religious concepts are only poorly known from outside sources. The Gallic pantheon recorded by Caesar included the gods Taranis (Jupiter), Tentates (Mars), Esus (Mercury), and Grannus or Belenus (Apollo). Archeological finds have added Epona, goddess of horses, Cernunnos, a god with stag antlers, several mother goddesses, and a mounted giant-killer. Numerous animals were worshiped and graphically symbolized on war standards or in the form of masks, among them the Gallic cock, of Iranian origin. The Irish gods included a mother goddess, a war god (Nunado), a lord of the heavens (Ehu, "father of all"), along with a variety of local demigods, elves, and dwarfs. Celtic music is best preserved in its original form among the Gaelic peoples of the British Isles and is dominantly pentatonic in character.

Pottery, textile, metal, and art production were important and of good quality. The Celts introduced the millstone and the potter's wheel to central and northern Europe, and were excellent craftsmen and smiths. Whereas the Celtiberi (q.v.) of Spain and Galatians of Asia Minor had few cities and lived in villages or as seminomadic pastoralists, the other tribes had well-organized towns, protected by massive walls of quarried but unmortared stone, reinforced by wooden palisades. The Celts produced valuable achievements with the creation of the Celtic La Tène culture in the 5th century B.C. Another interesting form resulted from contacts with Iranian Scyths and Greeks in the middle Danube area, attaining a climax about 150 B.C. The third peak of Celtic culture, according to Arnold Toynbee, was the Far Western civilization of Christian Ireland during the early Middle Ages (5th–10th centuries A.D.). Excepting Ireland, almost all written knowledge of

the Celts is derived from the classic authors Diodorus Siculus, Appianus, Strabo, Livy, and above all, Caesar.

Decline. The decline of Celtic hegemony over western and central Europe was due to expansion of the Roman Empire and the aggression of migrant Germanic tribes. Diffusing from northern Germany, they replaced the Celts between the Weser, Danube, and Rhine by 100 B.C., and in part penetrated into what are now Belgium and Alsace, where they were checked by Caesar, 58–57 B.C. The Celts of Gaul and Spain were conquered by Rome before the close of the 1st century B.C., and those of England before the close of the 1st century A.D. The last Celtic tribes in the Danube area had disappeared before the time of Augustus. Only in Ireland, Scotland, and Wales did the Celts remain independent, although those of England retained their national identity. The Gauls, Belgae, and Celtiberi were gradually Romanized and had lost their language before 400 A.D. But the Celtic tongue in France was revived in Brittany during the 6th century A.D., when large numbers of Britons (Bretons) emigrated from southwestern England during the Anglo-Saxon invasion.

CHURCH

CELTIC [sĕl′tĭk, kĕl′tĭk] **CHURCH,** Christian churches of the Celtic and Pictish peoples of Britain and Ireland, and their missionary offshoots. Between the 5th and 12th centuries, in relative independence of Continental and English Christianity, they developed a distinctive culture, marked by their monastic organization, intense asceticism, missionary zeal, and devotion to learning, with notable artistic achievements in sculpture and manuscript illumination.

LANGUAGES

CELTIC LANGUAGES, a number of related languages which form a subgroup of the Indo-European language family. The earliest stage of a distinctively Celtic language is known as Common Celtic. This made its first appearance as a dialect of Indo-European, and is closely related to Common Italic, from which Latin and the modern Romance languages are descended. From Common Celtic developed P-Celtic and Q-Celtic. The former is the ancestor of the Gallo-Brythonic languages, in which the Indo-European sound qu became p; the latter is the ancestor of the Goidelic, or Gaelic, languages, in which the Indo-European sound was preserved. P-Celtic dialects were at one time widely spread over Europe and part of Asia, from Galatia, in what is now Turkey, to France, northern Italy, Spain, and Portugal. Speakers of P-Celtic invaded Britain in the latter part of the 1st millennium B.C.; their language developed into what is known as Brythonic. On the continent, P-Celtic developed into Gaulish, which died out during the first centuries of the Christian era. Brythonic survived, and subdivided into Cymric in the south of Scotland (extinct after the 12th century); Welsh, in Wales; Cornish, in Cornwall (extinct since the 18th century); and Breton, the language of the British settlers in what is now Brittany.

There is some evidence that there was a Continental form of Q-Celtic; however, the term Goidelic refers only to the Q-Celtic languages of the British Isles. Of these, the most important is Irish, which developed in Ireland. From the early modern stage of Irish, Scottish Gaelic developed in Scotland and Manx developed on the Isle of Man.

PEOPLE, PLACES, AND TERMS

AIDAN [ā'dən], **ST.** (d.651), Irish monk from Iona, and first bishop of Lindisfarne. He was important in the struggle between Celtic and Latin Christianity in England. His friendship with Oswald, King of Northumbria, enabled him to establish Celtic churches and monasteries in Northumberland, and to resist during his lifetime the Romanizing influences of St. Augustine.

ALLOBROGES [ə-lŏb'rə-jēz], ancient Celtic tribe living between the Rhone and Isère rivers and Lake Geneva. They aided Hannibal in crossing the Alps in 218 B.C., and were subjugated by Rome in 121. Revolting unsuccessfully in 61, they subsequently appealed to Caesar for help when attacked by the Helvetii in 58 B.C., thus sparking the Gallic Wars. Their principal towns were Vienne (now in France), Geneva (now in Switzerland), and Gratianopolis (now Grenoble, France).

BARD, singer and poet of the Celtic peoples, especially in Ireland and Wales, in ancient and medieval times. The bards wielded political influence and, their positions being hereditary, they constituted the intellectual class of their nations. Their poems were heroic ballads. Little is known of their music except they accompanied themselves on a kind of bowed harp, the *crwth, cruit,* or *crowd.* They met at singing contests called, in Wales, "Eisteddfods," which were revived about 1820.

BELGAE [bĕl'jē], warlike tribes of mixed Celtic and Germanic ancestry which inhabited northern Gaul between the Seine and Rhine. They were first reported to the Romans by Caesar, who later came in contact with recently arrived Belgic tribes in southern England. The Ambiani, Atrebates, Bellovaci, Remi, Suessiones and Viromandui were mainly of Celtic origin, while those tribes living east of the Scheldt and Meuse, the Atuatuci, Eburones, and Nervii, were largely of Germanic descent. Attacked by Caesar in 57 B.C., they strengthened their confederacy, which was finally defeated and subjugated in 46 B.C.

BRIGANTES [brĭ-găn'tēz], Celtic tribes which occupied northern England between the Trent and the Cheviot Hills, as well as Wexfordshire in Ireland. Their capital was Eboracum (York). The most powerful tribe in Britain, they were finally subjugated by Agricola in 79–80 A.D.

CARNUTES [kär-nū'tēz], Celtic tribe located in Gaul between the Seine and Loire rivers. They initiated the Gallic revolt of 52 B.C. by attacking the Roman garrison at Cena-

bum, but were subjugated by Caesar in the same year. Their principal towns were Autricum (Chartres) and Cenabum (Orléans).

CELTIBERI [sĕl-tĭ-bēr-ī], important warlike tribes of the Iberian Peninsula centered in Castile, Galicia, and on the lower Guadiana. Their origins went back to the amalgamation of a wave of early Celtic immigrants (c.600 B.C.) with Iberian groups. After 230 B.C. they were in conflict with Carthage and from 215 B.C. with the Romans, who conquered several strongholds (Clunia, Segovia) in 179 B.C. and made the tribes nominally dependent on Rome. The Vaccaei of the upper Douro persistently defeated the Romans until Scipio Africanus the Younger took the Celtiberian capital, Numantia, after an extended siege in 133 B.C. Guerrilla warfare and bitter revolts continued into the time of Augustus.

DRUID [drōō'ĭd], member of the Celtic priestly class which together with the military composed the aristocracy of Gaul and the British Isles. The classical writers Caesar and Strabo are the earliest extant sources for modern knowledge of the Druids. Strabo describes a threefold class of Druids, bards, and prophets, which corresponds to the Druids, bards, and *filid* of ancient Ireland. If, as Caesar suggests, Druidism originated in Britain, it was perhaps pre-Celtic, but nothing certain is known.

The Druids are associated with religious beliefs which included the transmigration and immortality of souls and with ceremonies involving human sacrifice. Doctrine was preserved and transmitted in oral verse to candidates for the Druidhood. In addition to the religious role, Druids had great political, educational, and judicial influence. A chief Druid presided over an annual judicial gathering.

The Gaulish Druids were proscribed by the Roman Emperors Claudius and Tiberius for their rebellion against Roman rule in the province, but in the 4th century A.D. the Roman poet Ausonius records a family still claiming descent from the Druids. Anglesey, perhaps the Druids' British center, was sacked in 60 A.D., but the existence of British and Irish Druids was recorded as late as the 6th century. No connection has been established between Druidism and Stonehenge, or with the Welsh Eisteddfod.

EARLY BRITAIN. There are traces, from the stone age, of Paleolithic man in England. But he was superseded (c.2500–2000 B.C.) by Neolithic man, who introduced a rudimentary agriculture, mined flints for tools, built fortifications, and established well-worn lines of communication. Next to arrive were the Beaker People (so called from their distinctive pottery), who instituted the working of copper and bronze. The use of iron spread from Europe as early as the 5th century B.C. with the arrival of the Celts, whose culture soon dominated England. Little is known of contemporary tribal organization, however. "Kings" like Cunobelinus (Cymbeline), who flourished on the eve of the Roman conquest, are shadowy, legendary figures, and powerful institutions, such as the religious sect of the Druids, are little better known.

The Roman occupation left remarkably few permanent traces. Raids by German seafaring tribes of Angles, Sax-

THE ANGLO-SAXON KINGDOMS
IN THE
EARLY 7th CENTURY

0   50   100
Miles

N

of English civilization and, in association with Ireland, had a profound influence upon contemporary European culture.

FRANCE. France, because of its location, has over the centuries been accessible by sea and land to a variety of migrating peoples and has experienced a remarkable mingling of different ethnic elements. Marseille, the oldest city of France, was founded by the Greeks about 600 B.C., but they were soon succeeded by the Celts from Central Europe. The Celts invaded Gaul and gradually pushed the native Ligurians and Iberians down to the Mediterranean and across the Pyrenees to Spain.

The important ethnic contribution of the Celts was later profoundly modified, first by the Roman conquest and then by the Germanic invasions. Whereas the Roman conquest was of cultural rather than ethnic importance—there was no true implantation of Italian colonies —the Germanic hordes, chief among them the Franks, drove the Celts completely from certain regions of France. In the 9th century the Norsemen from Scandinavia, later known as Normans, established themselves in northern France. After the 10th century France experienced a long period without migrations. This ethnic stability made possible the unification of the country under a single authority, and also facilitated the growth of a single language.

GAUL [gôl] (Lat. **GALLIA**), ancient Roman name designating two areas: Cisalpine Gaul, the area in northern Italy between the Apennines and the Alps; and Transalpine Gaul, the area between the Alps, Pyrenees, Atlantic, and Rhine, corresponding roughly to modern France.

Cisalpine Gaul was inhabited by Ligurians, Veneti, and others in prehistoric times, but in the 5th century B.C. Celts crossed the Alps, seized the fertile Po Valley, and inflicted severe defeats even upon Rome. Rome, however, began conquering these Celts before 222 B.C. and by 191 B.C. had subjugated them. Acquiring many south Italian settlers, Cisalpine Gaul became very populous, productive, and prosperous. In 42 B.C. it was incorporated into Italy.

GAULISH or GALLIC, member of the Celtic subgroup of the Indo-European family of languages. It was spoken during Roman times in what is now France, Belgium, the Rhineland, and northern Italy; these areas formed a part of the vast portion of Europe once overrun by the Celtic tribes. Gaulish was closely similar to Brythonic, the Celtic language of Britain whose surviving descendant is Welsh. Since only a small number of inscriptions have been preserved, our knowledge of the structure of Gaulish is scant. It has been supplemented through careful study of names of places and of persons, like Vercingetorix, whom Caesar and other ancient authors mention.

GERMANY. Like other European peoples, the Germans are a mixture of several ethnic strains. Their land, lacking clearly defined geographical boundaries, has been subjected to repeated invasions over the centuries, and each group of conquerors has contributed to the national stock. But if Germany is a melting pot no less than the United States, the diverse elements are more difficult to identify.

ons, and Jutes had begun in the 3d century, A.D., and with the retirement of the Roman legions in 410, Britain lapsed into a chaos of dissociated tribes, led by legendary figures like Vortigern, Germanus (Saint Germanus of Auxerre), and Arthur. The Saxon settlement began in the late 5th century, but not until the 7th century is it possible to distinguish the tribal kingdoms of Sussex, Wessex, Kent, and Essex in the south; of Mercia and East Anglia in the Midlands; and of Northumbria in the north.

Kent was converted to Christianity in 597 by the Roman missionary Augustine, first Archbishop of Canterbury. Northumbria was converted a generation later by Aidan and other missionaries from Iona, the center of Celtic Christianity, and the differences between the two communions were reconciled at the Synod of Whitby in 663. For two centuries Northumbria remained the center

The west is generally Celtic and Latin in character, reflecting the centuries of close association with the Roman Empire. The population of the central region is largely Celtic and Teutonic, while in the east Teutonic and Slavic influences are particularly strong. Yet these generalizations are at best only half-truths. They do not account for the Syrians and North Africans who settled along the Rhine and Danube in the days when Rome ruled the ancient world.

HELVETII [hĕl-vē'shē-ī], ancient Celtic tribe originating in southwestern Germany. Helvetians moved into western Switzerland under pressure from Germanic tribes about 200 B.C. Some had joined the Cimbri by 102 B.C. Caesar forestalled their migration into Gaul at Bibracte in 58 B.C., after which they returned to their former boundaries as Roman allies. They preserved their integrity until the Alamanni conquered them after 450 A.D.

IONA [ī-ō'nə], **MONASTERY OF,** monastery founded by St. Columba and a group of Irish monks in 563 on the island of Ioua (later misspelled Iona) in the Hebrides. From here monks went forth to spread Christianity among the Picts and the Saxons. Iona soon became a great center of Celtic learning. The Book of Kells is supposed to have been written there. In the 9th century the incursions of the Danes forced the monks to move to Kells, in Ireland, and those who remained on Iona were put to death. In 1203 a Benedictine monastery was erected on the island, which remained until the Reformation in Scotland (16th century). Many of the early Scottish Kings and nobility were buried at the old Columban monastery, and Iona was long regarded as the holiest place in Scotland.

IRELAND. The earliest inhabitants arrived during the Mesolithic Period (c.6000–2500 B.C.). They hunted and fished along the northeast coast, where there was a plentiful supply of flint for making implements. Later (c.2500–2000 B.C.), Neolithic man introduced farming to Ireland and built tombs of stone (megaliths) to commemorate the dead. One of the most spectacular of these tombs is at Newgrange in County Meath. In the Bronze Age (c.2000–500 B.C.) the inhabitants began to make use of Ireland's mineral resources and traded their gold, copper, and other metal products on the Continent. It was during the Iron Age (c.500 B.C.–100 A.D.) that Celtic culture, language, and social organization became established. Because Ireland never experienced a Roman occupation, the Iron Age continued until the early Christian period, when the Pope sent St. Palladius to the island to proselytize. After St. Palladius' death in 431, St. Patrick carried on the work of converting the Irish to Christianity. Monasteries were established throughout the country, and their patronage encouraged the production of the splendid treasures of Ireland's golden age on parchment, metal, and stone. Beginning with the early 9th century Norsemen from Scandinavia began to raid the country and first disrupted and finally destroyed the monastic culture.

Norman and English Domination. The Normans, already firmly entrenched in England, invaded Ireland in the late 12th century. They developed a manorial economy, with expanded and intensified agricultural activities concentrated mainly in the open lowlands of the east and south. In addition, they built many trading towns within reach of navigable waters, selected Dublin as their capital city, and introduced an elaborate system of local government based on county divisions. The number of new settlers remained small, and they created a labor force to work the land by reducing the Gaelic people to serfdom. In the north and west, however, the local Celtic rulers fought more successfully against attempts by Henry II of England to grant their areas to Norman subjects and were able to hold their society intact somewhat longer.

SENONES [sĕn'ō-nēz], Celtic tribe which occupied territory on the Seine and Yonne rivers. Some Senones invaded Italy and sacked Rome in 386 B.C., settling in the Marches. These Italian Senones, allied with the Italici and Etruscans against Rome, were defeated at Sentinum and subjugated in 283 B.C. The Gallic group was conquered by Caesar in 52 B.C. Their chief city was Agedincum (modern Sens).

SILURES [sĭl'yə-rēz], ancient Celtic tribe of southeastern Wales and Monmouthshire. Their chief town was Venta Silurum (modern Caerwent, near Chepstow). They offered fierce resistance to Roman aggression (c.48 A.D.) and only after a legionary fortress had been set up at Isca (modern Caerleon) were they subdued (78 A.D.) and later incompletely Romanized.

TALIESIN [tä-lē-ĕ'sĭn] (fl.6th century), one of the *Cynfeirdd*, the earliest Welsh poets. His poems were composed between 570 and 600 A.D. and are preserved in the *Book of Taliesin* (c.1275). He is first mentioned in the 8th century by Nennius. Legends became attached to his name.

TRINOBANTES [trī-nō-băn'tēz] or **TRINOVANTES** [trī-nō-văn'tēz], ancient Celtic tribe of Suffolk and Essex, England, allied with Caesar's expedition in 54 B.C. Subdued during the Roman invasion of England in 43 A.D., they unsuccessfully rebelled with the Iceni in 61. Their chief town was Camulodunum (Colchester).

WALES. The delimitation of a physical territory which can be looked upon as Welsh occurred in the 8th century when Offa (757–96 A.D.), King of Mercia in midland England, built a bounding dike which defined the border between Mercia and the Welsh. Isolated in separate regions in Cornwall, Cumbria, Scotland, and Wales, the Celtic peoples began calling themselves compatriots, or "Cymry," while the Saxons called them foreign, or "Wælisc" (hence, "Welsh"). To the west of "Offa's Dyke" the Welsh did not form one political group, but were divided into a number of small kingdoms. These became the basis for later territorial units, the Norman lordships, and the present counties. Prior to 1066 and the Norman occupation there were repeated attempts to unite the diverse kingdoms. The two most important efforts were made by Rhodri Mawr, or Roderick the Great (reigned 844–78), and by Hywel Dda, or Howel the Good (reigned 910–50), of Dyfed in southwest Wales. Hywel Dda ruled over most of Wales and codified Welsh law. Such unity as was attained was short-lived, however, and the continued division made conquest easier for the Normans.

WELSH LITERATURE. In the mid-6th century Welsh was the language of Wales, northern England, and southern Scotland. In those areas the native bardic tradition had long been in contact with Christianity and Latin literature. The poetry of the *Cynfeirdd*, or early poets (c.550–c.1100), is thus metrically and rhetorically sophisticated. The 6th-century bards Taliesin and Aneirin exploited an elaborate technique of rhyme, syllabic meter, alliteration, and vocalic correspondence. This eulogistic and elegiac poetry originated in the south of modern Scotland. The later poetry associated with the name of Llywarch Hen, a 6th-century leader, was probably composed during the 9th century in Welsh Powys, and perhaps served as the framework for prose narrative, which, because it was improvised orally, has since been completely lost. Oral narrative poetry probably ultimately underlies the collection of Celtic tales written between the 11th and 13th centuries, usually referred to as the *Mabinogion*, which preserves much early, even pre-Christian, material. The mnemonic *Triads* indicate the extent to which other early Welsh saga literature has been lost.

Celtic Renaissance in Wales. In the early 20th century the rise of cultural nationalism in Wales gave new impetus to the study of the Welsh language and literature. An extensive body of modern literature in Welsh has been produced by writers of short stories, novels, poetry, and drama.

CHINESE CIVILIZATION

ARCHITECTURE

Throughout its history, Chinese architecture has been primarily based on the use of wood. The most important parts of the typical building, both structurally and visually, are its wooden pillars and the brackets, beams, and rafters that frame the roof. Almost all the important changes in proportioning and design that have marked the evolution of architectural style have involved these members. In particular, bracketing—the system of interlocking arms built up from the level of the column tops to support the wide, projecting eaves—has been more consistently developed than any other part of the architectural vocabulary. It is possible to date an old Chinese building fairly accurately by study of the bracketing design alone.

For protection and decoration all these wooden parts are painted, typically the pillars in a deep red, and the other parts in colorful abstract patterns.

The important secondary materials in a traditional Chinese building are tile and masonry. Tiles have been used to cover and ornament roofs from very early times. For roughly 1,000 years their manufacture has been continuously improved by the high technical standards of the ceramic arts in general. Buildings of first importance, like those of the old imperial palaces in Peking (Peiping), erected during the Ming (1368–1644) and Ch'ing (1644–1912) dynasties, are covered by lustrous glazed tiles of green, deep blue, or imperial yellow, which add greatly to the colorful beauty of the whole. Roof ridges have usually been emphasized by sculptured tile ornaments, particularly by monster forms with high raised tails at the ends of the main ridge. In some examples in South China this sort of tile roof sculpture reached fantastic extremes. The well-known Chinese curving roof is also seen at its greatest development in the South, curvature having always been much more restrained in the North. In the Peking palaces the eaves run horizontally through most of their length and tilt up only at the corners.

Chinese walls in the old tradition are mere screens that support nothing. In the temperate South they too may be made of wood. In the North they are usually of brick, and may be several feet thick. They never rise beyond the level of the column tops, however, so that the wood construction above may show. Brick or stone platforms raise the buildings well above the ground. Where materials are

used most extravagantly, as in Peking, these terraces with their carved balustrades and stairs are of a dazzling white marble. When special richness is desired, the front portico of columns may occasionally be of carved stone or the walls may be faced with colorful glazed tiles.

Types of Buildings. Important groups of buildings are designed symmetrically around courtyards. A main hall faces south toward the entrance of the yard. The principal hall—no matter whether it belongs to a palace, temple, imperial tomb, government office, or city mansion —is almost always a simple rectangle in ground plan. It features a high, spacious central room, usually enclosed by free-standing columns, surrounded by one or two continuous, lower aisles. The left and right sides of the building are symmetrical, and often the front and rear also. The entrance is at the middle of the long side, the hall extending across the plan axis, not along it, as in Greek and Roman temples and Christian churches. A building of this sort is normally only one story high, though a separate aisle roof at a lower level may suggest two stories. There are no clerestory windows of the sort familiar in European aisled churches, so the upper part of the interior is relatively dark.

The Chinese at an early date learned how to construct multistoried buildings used for pleasure, and developed the type enthusiastically for many centuries. These often reached heights of well over 100 ft. The typical high pleasure pavilion had an open top floor for maximum visibility and coolness. A special variation designed for use with Buddhist temples was the pagoda, a tapering, many-roofed tower raised on a relatively small square or polygonal base. The pagoda type has normally no usable interior, and serves chiefly as an architectural symbol, this function being emphasized by some sort of conspicuous finial at the top. Its materials, too, are often unusual—stone, brick, tile, or even metal, instead of wood.

In recent centuries, when traditional Chinese culture has been in decline, this emphasis on great height and bold construction has all but disappeared. In the relatively modern city of Peking, except for the great roofs of the largest palace halls and the pavilions over the entrances of the high fortification walls, the skyline is low and horizontal.

Historical Survivals. Emphasis on construction in wood has given Chinese architecture a normally short life. The earliest structures preserved in quantity are tomb chambers of brick or stone, dating from the 1st to 3d centuries A.D. These are usually roofed by tunnel vaults, a technique probably borrowed from the West, and are almost exclusively underground. A group of masonry pagodas from the 6th to 8th centuries shows variations on the pagoda theme, the earliest being Indian in style.

Extant wooden buildings of the Orient appear first in Japan, at the 7th-century monastery Horyuji, and in the old capital, Nara. The former probably shows the Chinese style as it filtered into Japan through Korea. The Nara buildings are very close to the designs of the Chinese T'ang Dynasty (618–906). In Northwest China at the great Buddhist pilgrimage center of Wutai Shan two temple halls from the 8th and 9th centuries have been saved. From the 11th century on, remains become increasingly numerous, widely distributed, and varied in type.

Most old buildings belong to temples. Remaining palace architecture is concentrated in the North, in Peking and the Manchurian city of Mukden. In Peking, also, can be seen the traditional great Chinese city, with its checkerboard of broad avenues and surrounding high fortification walls and towering gates. In the countryside are the remains of the splendid tombs of the Ming and Ch'ing emperors, templelike groups of buildings leading back to an artificial hill.

A kind of classic perfection was reached by the T'ang Dynasty architects. Their forms were sturdy, large-scaled, and clearly interrelated. Their bracketing rose in boldly expanding, widely spaced groups, from the pillar tops only. Under the Sung Dynasty (960–1279) design became more ingenious and complicated. The bracketing was then multiplied to become a kind of rich, nearly continuous frieze. From the 14th century on a stereotyped formula was repeated, in which the details became merely ornamental and the old noble beauty survived only in general outlines.

ART

The oldest extant art of China is the pottery and other artifacts made by the late Neolithic peoples from the 3d into the 2d millennium B.C. The principal centers of manufacture were in Kansu Province in the northwest and in the area of the Yellow River, which remained the focus of Chinese civilization throughout the early period. A painted pottery, similar to that found in the Near East and parts of Europe, appears to be the earliest ware; later it was replaced by a burnished black pottery, the manufacture of which continued into the Bronze Age.

Shang, Chou, and Han Dynasties

To the Bronze Age belongs the Shang Dynasty (c.1523–c.1028 B.C.), the first period both historically documented and known from archeological finds. Early Shang sites have recently been excavated at Chengchow and Huihsien, north of the Yellow River, but the major site is Anyang in Honan Province, the Shang capital from around 1300 B.C. The chief artistic productions of the Shang are vessels and other objects cast in bronze; they show an amazingly high artistic and technical level. The symbolic designs on their surfaces—highly formalized animal motifs and abstract patterns—relate to their use in ancestral sacrifices. The Shang artisans also produced jade carvings, some marble sculpture, and various objects in perishable materials that have not survived.

During the early part of the succeeding Chou Dynasty (c.1027–256 B.C.), Shang artistic traditions were retained, but the special blend of barbaric fervor and refinement was soon lost as the art of the bronze caster declined. In the latter part of the dynasty, known as the Warring States period because of the political fragmentation of China at that time, fine bronzes were again produced, but their makers seem to have aimed more at decorative beauty than at religious significance. Inlays of gold and silver and incrustations of semiprecious stones gave a new lavishness to the surfaces, and the décor, although still made up of semiabstract animal motifs, became more fanciful and graceful. Along with a revival of jade carving and a flourishing manufacture of lacquerware, the true beginnings of representational painting in China are in the late Chou period. Two fragments of painting on silk from around the 3d century B.C., executed in fine line and color with a brush, have been discovered at Changsha in Hunan Province.

Another important innovation of the same period is a high-fired and glazed ceramic, which was perfected under the Han Dynasty (202 B.C.–220 A.D.). Glaze colors of Han wares range through brown and green tones; the shapes are sturdy and practical. Painting also flourished under the Han. Portraits, mythological scenes, and anecdotes from history were the favorite subjects. The great wall paintings of the palaces survive only in literary descriptions, but a few paintings on tomb walls or clay tiles have been preserved, as well as translations of paintings into other media, such as low-relief engravings in stone and stamped clay bricks. It is fundamentally an art of line and silhouette, although primitive attempts at foreshortening and spatial rendering may be observed.

"Six Dynasties" Period

After the collapse of the Han empire in the early 3d century A.D., China was divided into small and short-lived states for several centuries. The period 317–589, known as the "Six Dynasties" period, produced the greatest of Chinese calligraphers, Wang Hsi-chih (321–79), and a number of major painters, of whom only one, Ku K'ai-chih (c.344–406), is represented in surviving copies. The best-known and earliest is the handscroll titled "Admonitions to the Court Ladies," now in the British Museum, London. It was during the Six Dynasties period that Buddhism took hold in China, and much Buddhist art, chiefly stone and bronze sculpture, dates from these centuries. Cave-temple complexes at Yunkang, Lungmen, and other sites contain many thousands of Buddhist images, and stone steles and gilt bronze figures have also been preserved in quantities. The earliest are based fairly closely on Indian or Central Asian prototypes, but a characteristically Chinese style evolved, reaching its peak in the austere, formal figures of the Northern Wei Dynasty in the early 6th century.

Sui and T'ang Dynasties

With the Sui (590–618) and T'ang (618–906) dynasties, a combination of new influences from the west and a native Chinese development produced a more plastic, full-bodied sculpture, with greater naturalism in posture and expression and some sense of movement. The same qualities appear in painting, both Buddhist and secular. Extant pre-T'ang and T'ang Buddhist paintings, aside from a few isolated pieces in Japan, have been preserved almost entirely at the oasis city of Tunhuang, in the far northwest of China. Scroll paintings on silk and paper from Tunhuang have nearly all been removed to New Delhi, Paris (Musée Guimet), and London (British Museum), but the compositions executed on the cave walls are still at the site.

The greatest secular artists of the T'ang Dynasty worked for the imperial court. To Yen Li-pen (d.673) is attributed the "Portraits of the Emperors" scroll in the Museum of Fine Arts, Boston. Masters active in the 8th century include the horse painter Han Kan; Chang Hsüan and Chou Fang, whose palace scenes are transmitted in various copies; and the greatest of T'ang painters, Wu Tao-tzu, whose masterworks, mostly wall paintings, have disappeared entirely.

In the minor arts, the T'ang period is distinguished by the highest technical refinement and a luxuriance of expression that blended the native taste of the T'ang aristocracy, opulent and assured, with influences from the Near East and India. Foreign styles and techniques were introduced through a thriving trade and through the importation of craftsmen, especially smiths who worked in gold and silver. Typical of T'ang ceramics are the three-color wares, so called after the deep blue, apple green, and yellow-brown colors of the glazes. A white ware, precursor of the later porcelains, also appeared in this period. Besides

vessels for practical use, thousands of ceramic tomb figures, representing humans, horses, camels, and similar subjects, were manufactured for burial with the dead.

Sung Dynasty

In painting from the late T'ang period onward, the human figure was gradually supplanted by landscape as the dominant theme, and a decorative style in bright colors began to give way to the technique of ink monochrome, in which only black ink and washes in tones of gray were employed. Such 10th-century masters as Ching Hao, Tung Yüan, and Li Ch'eng founded schools of landscape that set the course for the great Sung Dynasty (960–1279) developments in this genre. It is doubtful that any of them is represented by extant work. The earliest Chinese landscape that can be safely ascribed to a particular painter is the "Traveling Among Streams and Mountains" (Palace Museum Collection, Taiwan) of Fan K'uan, who was active in the early 11th century. It is a supreme example of the monumental compositions of the early Sung, with their solid construction in mass and their increased sense of space and atmosphere. Later in the century Kuo Hsi, whose landscape "Early Spring" (Palace Museum Collection, Taiwan) is dated 1072, made further advances in the rendition of space through an accomplished use of atmospheric perspective and deep recessions into distance.

Under the patronage of Emperor Hui-tsung (reigned 1101–26), the Imperial Academy of Painting drew the best artists from all parts of the empire. Hui-tsung himself was a gifted painter of bird-and-flower subjects. The leading artist in his academy was Li T'ang, who was

The contrasting shapes and textures of natural objects are explored in this brush and ink study "Cypress and Rock," painted in 1550 by the Ming Dynasty poet and painter Wen Cheng-ming.

Nelson Gallery and Atkins Museum, Nelson Fund

Freer Gallery of Art

Shang Dynasty (c.1523–c.1028 B.C.) bronze vessel, decorated with abstract patterns and animal motifs, was used for ritual purposes.

largely responsible for the course taken by landscape away from the awesome and austere toward a more lyrical and intimate mode. This development, which has been termed "romantic," culminated in the late 12th and early 13th centuries, in the Ma-Hsia school, named after the most prominent landscapists then in the academy, Ma Yüan and Hsia Kuei. By the middle of the 13th century the academy was in decline, and the only significant achievements in painting of the last decades of Sung are the work of Ch'an (Jap. Zen) Buddhist monk-artists, the most famous of whom was Mu-ch'i. They painted in a spontaneous, expressive manner, using ink monochrome and loose, free brushwork.

Buddhist sculpture under the Sung Dynasty, while technically superb and often of great decorative beauty, is overly ornate and conveys little sense of religious conviction. The Sung Dynasty is now generally recognized as the peak period of Chinese ceramics. In celadons (gray-green or gray-blue in color) and other monochrome wares, the color and texture of glazes reached an unparalleled refinement, as did the shapes of the vessels. The typical pottery of Sung is a high-fired stoneware with feldspathic glaze; it is usually decorated, if at all, only with incised or molded designs.

HISTORY

From Antiquity to the Classical Age. The Chinese not only enjoy the oldest of the contemporary civilizations, they also have the longest, continuous recorded history, which dates from, at least, the Chou Dynasty (c.1027–256 B.C.). According to legend the Chinese culture was first developed in the 3d millennium B.C. under the successive reigns of the Five Emperors—(The Yellow Emperor, Chuan-hsü, Ti-k'u, Yao, and Shun). Tradition has it that Emperor Shun was followed by the Hsia Dynasty (c.1994–c.1523 B.C.), whose founder, Great Yü, controlled the floods and opened up the waterways.

According to archeological findings, the ancient Chinese people lived in pits in the Yellow River region in North China during the Neolithic period around 3000 B.C. They used stone implements and stone wheels, made and painted pottery, had silk, hunted, fished, and farmed, but possessed neither metal nor writing.

During the Shang Dynasty (c.1523–c.1028 B.C.), which followed the Hsia, China was no longer a tribal society but a kingdom, with a ruling family, nobles, commoners, and slaves. Bronze tools had replaced stone implements and society had become mainly agricultural. People were organized into clans, each with a family name; they lived in houses, did weaving, had writing, used jade, and employed horse-drawn chariots. They worshiped their ancestors and *Shang-ti* ("Lord on High"), and allowed spiritual beings to exercise strong influence on them. They also waged war with their well-organized armies against surrounding tribes.

If in a real sense the Shang represented the period of formation of the Chinese civilization, the succeeding Chou Dynasty (c.1027–256 B.C.) was its period of development. During the dynasty's 800-year period of dominion, when the early Chou rulers established their capital near the great bend of the Yellow River, Chinese society and culture evolved rapidly. In time the Chou empire covered most of the North China Plain and extended southward to the Yangtze Valley. Politically, the *feng-chien* system of the Chou was somewhat similar to the feudalism of medieval Europe, with political power vested in the ruler. Feudal vassals were installed in the Chinese states comprising the "Middle Kingdom" in the region of present Shensi, Shansi, and Honan provinces, whence Chinese culture spread to the surrounding areas. Socially, the clan structure was further strengthened by a definite family lineage primogeniture. On the economic side, great public works were undertaken, especially water tanks and reservoirs, flood control, irrigation, and canal building. Agricultural production was developed to a high degree of efficiency, and some form of communal farming was in practice. Trade began to flourish and, along with it, urban centers.

While a great many of the surrounding barbarian tribes, particularly those of the Yangtze region and the eastern seaboard, were assimilated, those of the northern deserts and western steppes resisted Chinese influence. They became such a threat to the security of the Middle Kingdom that in 770 B.C. the Chou court moved its capital eastward to the present site of Loyang in Honan Province. This marks the transition from the Western Chou to the Eastern Chou.

In the earlier part of the Eastern Chou—known as the period of Spring and Autumn (722–481 B.C.) from a historical chronicle of the same name—as the power of the Chou court declined, the feudal barons gradually asserted their independence and began to war among themselves. Although during this period the number of vassal states was reduced through hegemony from over 800 to 124, there was still some general recognition of the titular authority of the Chou court. As time went on, the remaining feudal barons formed alliances and engaged in constant fighting, so much so that later historians named this period (403–222 B.C.) the time of the Warring

Pagoda in the Western Hills near Peking. A former royal capital, Peking is noted for its many elaborate palaces and pagodas.

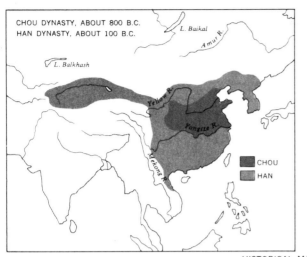

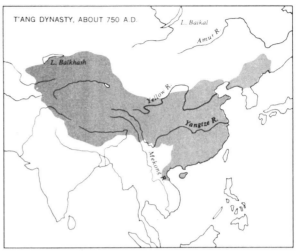

HISTORICAL MAPS OF CHINA

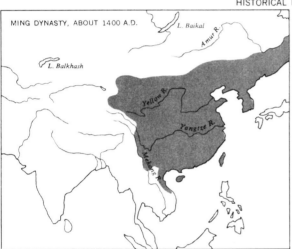

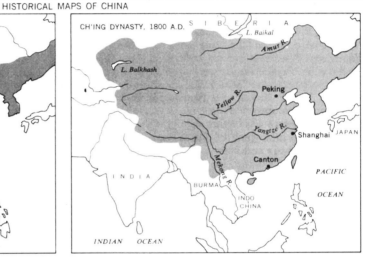

States. Finally the multitude of rival states was reduced to seven major contenders, one of which, Ch'in, was able to conquer the rest and establish a unified empire and centralized authority.

The four centuries of civil strife were accompanied by fundamental economic and social changes. The introduction of iron not only made possible the making of deadlier weapons, but also the production of more efficient agricultural and industrial implements. As the feudalistic hierarchy set up at the beginning of the Chou Dynasty began to decay and crumble, class distinction began to lose its significance. Forced by circumstances to earn a living, the displaced noblemen became scribes and teachers, and some traveled from state to state offering their services. The greatest of this newly constituted middle class was Confucius (551–479 B.C.), who advocated, by virtuous examples, benevolent rule based on moral principles. His chief emphasis was on humanity or love as the root of all virtues and filial piety as the foundation of family life. Recognized as a sage in his own time, his theories developed in time into a code of ethics which dominated Chinese thought and life for the next 20 centuries.

The First Empires. The Ch'in Dynasty (221–207 B.C.)

ruled the first really united empire in Chinese history. Under the leadership of the Legalists, it abolished the feudal system and divided the country into 42 prefectures with governors appointed by the central authority—a pattern of political organization retained by succeeding dynasties. It centralized the command of armed forces; unified measurements, laws, and currencies; and standardized script writing. To unify thought, all books, except those on medicine, agriculture, and divination and those in the imperial archive, were ordered burned, and some 460 scholars and magicians who incurred the wrath of the Emperor by refusing to conform were put to death. The bureaucracy was made nonhereditary, and nobility was no longer based on birth, but on merit. Many roads, canals, and palaces were built. Invading nomads in the north were expelled, and the existing defense walls were connected and extended to form the Great Wall, some 1,500 mi. in length. In the southwest, the Ch'in penetrated the northern part of present Vietnam, and in the east, the first contact was made with Japan.

However, the Ch'in's totalitarian rule—excessive regimentation, inhuman punishments, and oppressive taxes —were too severe and ruthless to endure. Within 14 years, following the death of Shih-huang-ti, the Ch'in Dynasty came to an abrupt end and was succeeded by the Han.

The Han Dynasty (202 B.C.–220 A.D.) was founded by Liu Pang, who eliminated the rival rebels against the Ch'in and established his capital at Changan (now Sian), in the Wei River Valley. He consolidated his government by a combination of feudal vassal states and prefectures directly under his control. Court procedures were regulated, but most of the Ch'in political machinery was retained. Externally, however, for a few decades, China was constantly harassed by the Hsiung-nu tribes in the north. They were not checked until the time of Wu-ti (reigned 140–87 B.C.). Thereafter, Chinese power began to expand rapidly into Central Asia. Korea in the northeast and northern Vietnam in the southwest were penetrated, and southwestern China was pacified. Internally, Wu-ti established Confucianism as the state cult. He dismissed non-Confucian scholars from the Board of Doctors in 141 B.C., and set up a new Board of Doctors of the Five Confucian Classics five years later. From then on Confucianism remained dominant in Chinese thought for some 2,000 years.

This was also a period of economic and cultural growth. Trade with the Middle East flourished, bringing in ivory, horses, wool, grapes, and similar commodities in exchange, mainly, for silk. Paper was invented, porcelain was produced, and astronomy and iron casting were greatly advanced. The development of sculpture, painting, and poetry reached great heights, and the writing of history set a standard unsurpassed for centuries. Around 2 B.C. Buddhism was introduced from India. Later, in 142 A.D., the Taoist religion was founded.

But Wu-ti's military operations and public works programs put undue strain on the economy. To stabilize prices, an "ever-normal" granary was established to store up grains when there was surplus and sell them in times of deficiency. To raise revenues, the state sold titles and granted monopolies for the distribution of salt, iron, and wine.

In 9 A.D. a scholar-official Wang Mang usurped the power of the Han Emperor and set up a Hsin (New) Dynasty (9–23). To curb the power of the aristocracy he nationalized all land, taxed owners of slaves so heavily that they were forced to free most of them, imposed an income tax, and instituted loans to farmers at low interest rates. But popular uprisings soon ended the Hsin Dynasty. When the Han Dynasty was restored under Kuang-wu-ti (reigned 25–57), the capital was again moved eastward to Loyang. Kuang-wu-ti and his successors quickly re-established central power, and within a few decades South China and northern Vietnam were incorporated into the empire, and Chinese power once more extended to Central Asia. Himself a Confucian scholar, Kuang-wu-ti encouraged learning and proceeded to establish his capital as a cultural center. For three generations thereafter China experienced peace and prosperity. However, from 88 A.D. on, the throne was occupied by a succession of child-Emperors, allowing political power to fall into the hands of eunuchs and relatives of empresses. Influential families retained their hold on the government and ex-

empted themselves from taxes. The peasants were forced into banditry and, before long, the Empire disintegrated.

The collapse of the Han precipitated 350 years of civil war and general disorder. The country was first divided into three kingdoms—the Wei (220–265) in the north, the Shu (221–264) in the west, and the Wu (222–280) in the southeast. The reign of the Chin (Tsin) Dynasty (265–420) that followed was able to achieve a semblance of political unity. But pressure from the Toba tribes in the north forced the Chin to move its capital in 317 to the south to Nanking. Only after the Chinese victory in the historic battle of the Fei River (383) which prevented a barbarian conquest of South China, was China able to enjoy relative peace in the south. There the Chin was succeeded by the four native dynasties, known as the Southern Dynasties (420–589), which managed to preserve a continuous Chinese culture. Meanwhile North China was ruled by five different dynasties of nomadic tribes, known as the Northern Dynasties (386–581). For some years thereafter, the northern, alien kingdoms constantly subjected the south to military pressure. However, they were gradually assimilated by the Chinese. They adopted Chinese names, language, and family organization. Their rulers employed Confucian scholars and used Chinese ceremonial systems. They encouraged intermarriage with the Chinese and, in some instances, went as far as prohibiting the use of their own language and dress.

In spite of civil strife and disunion, the migration of Chinese aristocrats and scholars to the south stimulated renewed cultural developments. During this period, the quality of landscape painting, calligraphy, and literature reached unprecedented heights. The cave sculptures of the Northern Wei (386–535) are particularly famous. Spiritually, the age was alive: Buddhism began to spread to South China and Korea, a new Taoist philosophy emerged, and the Taoist religion became widespread. Astronomy, medicine, and other branches of learning flourished. Coal was used for the first time. Tea, fruits, flowers, folk tales, games, trousers, large hats, and new architectural and sculptural styles were introduced.

The Golden Age. After 264 years of disunion, China was finally reunited under the Sui Dynasty (581–618). During this short-lived dynasty China reasserted control over northern Vietnam, invaded southern Vietnam, conquered northern Tibet, and again spread its influence to Central Asia. Long canals were built, facilitating commerce between North and Central China. But the tremendous drain of manpower and resources required by these foreign military campaigns and large-scale construction works at home caused hardship and resentment among the people. Within a matter of two decades popular uprising ended the Sui rule.

The reign of the T'ang Dynasty (618–906), which followed the Sui, was a period of such military renown that to this day Chinese living overseas still proudly refer to themselves as "Men of T'ang." Through the military prowess of its early rulers, notably T'ai-tsung (reigned 627–49), the second ruler, T'ang was able to build an empire larger than that of the Han Dynasty. They subdued the Turks in the west and established a protectorate over Turkestan, penetrated Mongolia, destroyed the land and sea forces of Japan and Korea, and a Chinese military expeditionary force even went into India. At the zenith of its power, the influence of the T'ang extended over the entire Asian continent. Tibet, Korea, and Manchuria acknowledged Chinese suzerainty. Tribute came from Japanese rulers in the east, Indian princes in the west, and chieftains in the South Sea Islands.

Internally, the country was divided into large provinces. The central government, with three secretariats and six departments, became the model for later ages. Land was redistributed by breaking up the large estates. Trade flourished and tax and labor conscription were both reduced. Farmers served in the army when needed, thus making the army both economical and huge. An elaborate postal system was established over the country. The population of the capital, Changan, which covered an area of 5 by 6 mi., grew to almost 2,000,000.

In the absence of external harassment and serious internal strife and because of the active encouragement of the imperial court—Emperor T'ai-tsung promoted learning, art, and religion; Emperor Hsüan-tsung (reigned 713–55) encouraged education and art—the T'ang period grew to become the golden age of Chinese civilization. It was the age of the great poets, Li Po (699–762) and Tu Fu (712–70). Great painters, such as Wu Tao-tzu (d.792), and some of the greatest writers and Buddhist theologians flourished. Schools were opened in villages as well as in towns. The Hanlin Academy, the highest institution of literature, was formed. The civil service examinations through which officials were selected, already begun under the Sui, were now refined and extended. Block printing, gunpowder, the compass, and some astronomical instruments were invented. Astronomy, geography, mathematics, porcelain, stone carving, and textiles were all greatly advanced.

Land and sea routes extending as far as Persia and the Red Sea were opened. Merchants, missionaries, entertainers, and students came from many lands and in great numbers. Zoroastrianism, Nestorian Christianity, Islam, Manichaeism, and Judaism made their inroads into China. At the same time, Chinese culture was adopted wholesale by the Japanese.

By the 8th century, however, the T'ang power began to ebb, partly because of the continuous usurpation of political power by empresses. The rule of Empress Wu (reigned 684–705) was a disaster. In 755 a rebellion led by An Lu-shan, favorite of Emperor Hsüan-tsung's consort, Yang Kuei-fei—the most famous beauty in Chinese history—broke out. Although within eight years the rebellion was quelled, the country never recovered from its devastation. From then on regional commanders assumed more power, while at court scholars and eunuchs engaged in bitter struggle for control. The revolt under Huang Ch'ao in 874 also hastened the downfall of the once mighty T'ang Dynasty, which was finally toppled in 906. The fall of T'ang was followed by the short-lived Five Dynasties (907–960) in North China, while South China was divided among 10 minor states.

Although the Sung Dynasty (960–1279) was able to reunite the Chinese Empire, the reunification was never complete. The founding Emperor of the Sung, T'ai-tsu, tried to consolidate his empire through the concentration

An artisan adjusts the strings of a zither (tseng). The Communist regime encourages the revival of old forms of Chinese music.

of political, military, financial, and judicial power. But his troops were old and weak, and there was little wealth in the country for local constructive enterprises. Parts of north and southwest China were never recovered and, in the end, his domains were smaller than those of the Han and the T'ang. Most significant was the fact that these lost territories included the horse-raising regions, without which it was impossible for the Sung to build an efficient land army. Furthermore, although throughout the dynasty literary men were in power, thus freeing the court from the intrigues of eunuchs and empresses, the scholars were bitterly divided in their theories of government. As a result, the dynasty, though remaining in power over three centuries, was politically and militarily weak throughout.

In 936 the Khitan, a seminomadic people who had been harassing China since the T'ang, occupied part of North China and in 947 declared an empire, called the Liao (907–1125). Through concessions and humiliating terms, China maintained an uneasy peace with it. In the northwest the Tangut state of Hsi-hsia (990–1227) also had to be accommodated by compromising peace terms. As both the Hsi-hsia and the Liao declined, the Chin (1115–1234), a Tungusic people (also known as Kin or Jurchen) of the Amur River Valley, in the extreme northeast of China, replaced the Liao rule in North China, and came into constant conflict with the Sung. In 1127 the Sung Emperor was forced to move the capital from Kaifeng in North China to Hangchow in the south. Thus, for 300 years part of China, and for about 150 years half of it, was occupied by alien tribes. Culturally, however, the Hsi-hsia, Liao, and Chin were gradually assimilated by the Chinese.

In spite of its military weakness, both before and after the retreat to the south, the Sung was a period of political experiment and brilliant cultural accomplishments. With the support of the Emperor, the court reformer

CHRONOLOGICAL TABLE OF CHINESE DYNASTIES

T'ang Kingdom	3d millennium B.C.
Yü Kingdom	3d millennium B.C.
Hsia Dynasty................	c.1994 B.C. – c.1523
Shang (Yin) Dynasty..........	c.1523 B.C. – c.1028
Chou Dynasty................	c.1027 B.C. – 256
Western Chou	c.1027 B.C. – 770
Eastern Chou	770 B.C. – 256
Spring and Autumn	722 B.C. – 481
Warring States	403 B.C.– 222
Ch'in Dynasty	221 B.C. – 207
Han Dynasty	202 B.C. – 220 A.D.
Western (Earlier) Han	202 B.C. – 9 A.D.
Hsin	9 A.D. – 23 A.D.
Eastern (Later) Han	25 – 220
Three Kingdoms	220 – 265
Shu	221 – 264
Wei	220 – 265
Wu	222 – 280
Chin (Tsin) Dynasty..........	265 – 420
Western Chin..........	265 – 317
Eastern Chin..........	317 – 420
Southern Dynasties...........	420 – 589
Liu Sung..............	420 – 479
Ch'i.................	479 – 502
Liang................	502 – 557
Ch'en................	557 – 589
Northern Dynasties	386 – 581
Later Wei..............	386 – 535
Eastern Wei	534 – 550
Western Wei............	535 – 556
Northern Ch'i...........	550 – 577
Northern Chou...........	557 – 581
Sui Dynasty	581 – 618
T'ang Dynasty...............	618 – 906
Five Dynasties	907 – 960
Later Liang.............	907 – 923
Later T'ang.............	923 – 936
Later Chin.............	936 – 947
Later Han.............	947 – 950
Later Chou.............	951 – 960
Sung Dynasty...............	960 – 1279
Liao.................	907 – 1125
Northern Sung...........	960 – 1126
Hsi-hsia...............	990 – 1227
Chin (Kin).............	1115 – 1234
Southern Sung...........	1127 – 1279
Yüan Dynasty...............	1260 – 1368
Ming Dynasty...............	1368 – 1644
Ch'ing Dynasty.............	1644 – 1912
Republic..................	1912 –

Wang An-shih (1021–86) inaugurated a national budget, an unemployment tax, and a graduated income tax; instituted loans for farmers at low interest; established price regulation and commodity control; enforced compulsory military service; and introduced collective guarantee and joint responsibility among families. Bitterly opposed by scholars, these measures ultimately failed. But the vigor it represented found expression elsewhere.

Many cities were built. Movable type was invented, and gunpowder was used for warfare. The compass was applied to navigation. Naval architecture, history, poetry, fiction, painting, architecture, porcelain, and landscape gardening all reached a high degree of excellence. The great number of academies of learning, libraries, huge encyclopedias, and works on natural science and political economy testify to the intellectual progress. Under the influence of Buddhism and Taoism, Confucianism was reborn in the form of Neo-Confucianism, which was destined to dominate Chinese intellectual life for the succeeding 800 years. Paper money was invented. Cotton, medicine, pearls, and precious stones came in from the outside and left their impact on Chinese textiles and art. After the Sung court's flight to the south, the Chinese began to travel by sedan chairs instead of by horseback.

Already weakened by the harassments of the Tangut, the Khitai, and the Jurchens, the Sung now faced a new threat from the Mongols. Under Genghis Khan (reigned 1206–27) the Mongols had gained control of the region north of the Yellow River by 1214. By 1259 they had overrun Central Asia, northwestern India, northeastern Europe, Russia, and Korea. Under Genghis Khan's grandson Kublai Khan (1215–94), they pushed south against the Sung. In 1271 Kublai Khan declared himself Emperor after establishing the Yüan Dynasty (1260–1368) with its capital in Yenching (Peking). By 1282 the Mongols had conquered all China, becoming the first alien power ever to achieve so vast an undertaking.

During their century of rule, the Mongols adopted the Chinese governmental system, language, and dress. They employed Chinese in the government and directed most of their own attention to watching them. They declared their own religion, Lamaism, the state religion, but made no attempt to impose it on the Chinese. A great number of scholars in self-imposed exile from the court turned to art and literature as a pastime, thus making the Yüan period famous for the number and quality of its dramas, novels, and paintings. But the inability of the Mongols to pacify the upsurge of national consciousness among the Chinese peoples finally resulted in the downfall of the Yüan.

LANGUAGE

CHINESE [chī-nēz'], the most widely spoken language in the world. There are more than 500,000,000 speakers in China, with millions more in various other countries of Southeast Asia. It is one of the five official languages of the United Nations. Chinese belongs to the Sino-Tibetan family of languages. There are many Chinese dialects, some of them mutually unintelligible. Mandarin, the modern standard dialect, is based on the pronunciation of Peking and is understood with very little difficulty throughout the northern, central, and southwestern provinces by over two-thirds of the population. The more divergent dialects, such as Cantonese, Amoy, and Hakka, are found in the coastal provinces of the southeast and are also spoken by Chinese immigrants in Southeast Asia and Taiwan (Formosa).

History. The Chinese language has a long history. The

earliest remains are inscriptions on bones, shells, and bronze vessels dating from the middle of the 2d millennium B.C. These inscriptions are usually short, and although progress has been made in deciphering and interpreting them, many difficulties remain. During the last six or seven centuries B.C., the great Chinese classics were written in a language that Sinologists call Archaic Chinese. The system of sounds of this period has been reconstructed to a considerable extent. Our knowledge of the language of the 6th century A.D. (called Ancient Chinese) is better documented; for this later period we have rhyme books (dictionaries arranged according to rhymes) and a system of spelling (known as *fan-ch'ieh*). The period of Modern Chinese begins with the 13th century; from this time on the standard language that was used in the north began more and more to resemble modern Mandarin.

Very early there arose a literary language (*wen-yen*), which is still in use. Because of the unity of vocabulary and grammar maintained by a large body of literature and by a system of writing common to all dialects, it became the common language in which practically all government documents, histories, essays, and letters were written. It was only in the beginning of the 20th century that colloquial Mandarin gradually began to replace this literary language; it has not yet completely done so.

Structure. Though the system of writing Chinese is generally called ideographic, the written characters are symbols which stand for words rather than for ideas. A Chinese word may be monosyllabic or polysyllabic, but in a great majority of cases the meaningful unit consists of one monosyllable. It is for this reason that Chinese is often labeled a monosyllabic language. Chinese is called a tone language, because pitch distinguishes between words which would otherwise be homonyms. Thus the syllable *pa* may have any one of the four stressed tones in Standard Mandarin, or a neutral tone, usually unstressed. It forms, therefore, five different words, namely, *pā* (high level tone), "eight," *pá* (high rising tone), "to pull out," *pǎ* (low rising tone), "a handful," *pà* (falling tone), "to cease," and *pa* (neutral tone), a final particle.

There are thousands of characters which an educated person has to know. A number of characters were originally pictures: 日 "sun"; 月 "moon"; 馬 "horse." Others indicate concepts: 一 "one"; 二 "two"; 上 "up"; 下 "down." However, the majority of characters are compounds composed of two parts: a signific, which indicates the meaning of a word, and a phonetic, which indicates the sound of the word. For example, the word "pillar," 柱 , pronounced *chu*, consists of the signific 木 , meaning "wood," and the phonetic 主 (meaning

EVOLUTION OF CHINESE WRITING

	servant	to fish	turtle	chicken	horse
Shell and Bone Characters B.C. 1700-1400					
Ta-chün (Great seal script) B.C. 776-A.D. 250					
Hsiao-chün (Small seal script) B.C. 250-A.D. 25					
Li-shu (Scribe script) A.D. 25-220	僕	漁	龜	雞	馬
Kai-shu (Regular script) A.D. 380-present day	僕	漁	龜	鷄	馬
Current Simplified Forms	仆	渔	龟	鸡	马

"master" when it appears alone), which is also pronounced *chu*. The creation of most phonetic compounds was completed in very ancient times; changes of pronunciation through the ages have sometimes rendered it difficult to see what phonetic similarity underlies the phonetic compounds. The writing system was systematized and codified in the 3d century B.C., and in spite of minor modifications it has maintained its identity since that time. After World War II the Communist regime attempted to introduce a Western alphabet to combat the difficulty of memorizing characters, but the campaign was not effective on a widespread basis.

LITERATURE

Chinese literature has the longest unbroken tradition of any secular literature in the world. The earliest Chinese work of literature, the *Shih ching* (*Classic of Songs*), contains poems which may date back to 1100 B.C., while the most ancient specimens of Chinese writing (found on the inscribed Anyang oracle bones) are some 500 years older. The *Classic of Songs* is an anthology of 305 poems traditionally assembled by Confucius (551–479 B.C.), but almost certainly in existence as a collection before his time. The poems are essentially anonymous, despite their traditional attribution to various sage rulers of antiquity. They are a heterogeneous lot: ballads and folk songs, court poems, political satires, and religious odes, with a time-span of at least four centuries.

From the two centuries following the death of Confucius only philosophical and historical writings have been preserved. Besides the works which became a part of the Confucian Classics, the *Kuo yü* (*Conversations from the States*) and the *Chan kuo ts'e* (*Intrigues of the Warring States*) deserve mention as examples of tendentious history enlivened with a large admixture of pure invention. Among the numerous philosophical writings of the 4th century B.C., the one most unmistakably a work of literature is the *Chuang tzu* (*Musings of a Chinese Mystic*, 1909), a text of the Taoist School ascribed to one Chuang-tzu, of whom nothing is known that cannot be gleaned from the book itself. Probably not the work of a single author, the *Chuang tzu* contains rhapsodic passages of great poetic power and unforgettable parables that mark the beginning of imaginative fiction in Chinese.

Poetic Forms

After the *Classic of Songs* with its predominantly four-beat meter and short stanzas, the next poetry to appear was new in form, manner, and subject. Generically it is called the *sao*, from the title "Li sao" (often rendered as "Falling into Trouble") of the best-known poem by Ch'ü Yuan (fl.300 B.C.), China's first known poet. The "Li sao" is a long (187 lines), allegorical poem written in the first person. The "I" of the poem alternately complains about the fickleness of his ruler and describes in rhapsodic terms an imaginary quest through space and time. The new genre was imitated by a school of poets associated with Ch'ü Yuan's native state of Ch'u; an anthology of their works, the *Ch'u tz'u* (*The Songs of the South*, 1959), contains examples of *sao* poetry through the 2d century A.D.

The descriptive aspect of the *sao* was further developed in the *fu*, using an irregular meter with obvious similarities

to that of the *sao*, but permitting even more freedom of variation, so that the *fu* is sometimes mentioned as a prose genre ("rhyme prose"), despite its regular use of rhyme and definite, though variable, meter. The most famous early *fu* writer was Ssu-ma Hsiang-ju (d.117 B.C.) whose versified descriptions of royal hunting parks were much imitated. Such imitations were a characteristic of the genre, which continued to develop through the 6th century, becoming more regular metrically and more mannered and artificial in its use of language. A marked tendency toward regular couplet structure became the invariable rule in the *fu* by the end of the 2d century A.D., facilitating and reinforcing the use of grammatical parallelism, which peculiarity was strictly observed in the *fu* through the T'ang Dynasty (618–906). During the Sung Dynasty (960–1279) writers of *fu* developed a new type, called the prose *fu*, which reverted to the free meters and more lyric manner of an earlier period and introduced a large element of plain prose. In the hands of Su Shih (1036–1101) and Ou-yang Hsiu (1007–72) the prose *fu* became an important literary form. After the 12th century the *fu* lived on chiefly as an exercise in versification.

Popular ballad verse reappeared in the Latter Han Dynasty (1st and 2d centuries A.D.) with a few anonymous specimens of uncertain date. These seem to have inspired a revival of lyric poetry toward the end of the 2d century A.D. under the leadership of the Ts'ao family, which produced the founder of a new dynasty (the Wei) in addition to three outstanding poets. The most famous, Ts'ao Chih (192–232), wrote lyrics and political satires in both ballad meters and the new five-beat form which was to remain the most popular meter for traditional poetry (*shih*). Through the Six Dynasties (222–589), a period of political division, lyric poetry developed in subtlety and refinement, but tended to follow the lead of the *fu* in becoming stereotyped and obsessed with purely verbal dexterity, of which parallelism was an obvious symptom. An exception even in his own time to this trend was T'ao Ch'ien (365–427), the greatest poet of this period. More representative were Hsieh Ling-yün (385–433), noted for his marvelous landscape descriptions in verse, and Yü Hsin (513–81), whose name is synonymous with technical mastery and linguistic difficulty. In the 8th century under the T'ang Dynasty occurred a tremendous renaissance of lyric poetry which revitalized a tradition already 500 years old. Li Po (701–62), Wang Wei (701–61), and Tu Fu (712–70), some of the best-known names in Chinese poetry, wrote under the rule of Emperor Tang Hsüan-tsung (Minghuang), himself a minor poet and a great patron of all the arts. The T'ang is the great period of classical poetry (*shih*) in both the five- and seven-beat meters.

Later periods produced important poets, among them Su Shih, Ou-yang Hsiu, Huang T'ing-chien (1045–1105), Kao Chi (1336–74), and Yuan Mei (1716–97), to name only a few. But the *shih* was not usually the most important vehicle for lyrical expression, and in the Sung Dynasty the song (*tz'u*) is the more viable form. The song has affinities with the ballad (*yüeh-fu*), both historical and prosodic, but is a distinct genre. The earliest preserved examples come from the 8th century, and by the middle of the 9th century it had become common, if still not quite respectable. The early association of the song with the brothels and entertainment centers accounts for its prevailing theme of sentimental love as well as the reluctance with which it was admitted into the canon of serious poetry. Su Shih was the first major poet to use the new form for a wider variety of themes. In so doing he helped bring about its divorce from music, so that in time the song became a purely literary verse form independent of any musical setting; in fact most of the tunes to which words have been written were lost. The Sung Dynasty is the golden age of the song. Liu Yung (fl.1045), famous for the psychological subtlety of his love songs, Ch'in Kuan (1049–1100), a romantic poet of the same school, and Hsin Ch'i-chi (1140–1207), a major poet who enriched the form with new themes of heroism and philosophy, are all known chiefly for their poems in the song form. The major *shih* poets—Ou-yang Hsiu, Su Shih, Huang T'ing-chien, and Lu Yu (1125–1209)—are also important song writers.

Prose Forms

Chinese prose in the written language is used for a number of literary genres, of which the essay may be taken as representative. Like its English counterpart, it is in good part an exercise in style. Prose styles range from the plain to the ornate, and each extreme has enjoyed a few centuries of popularity. The euphuistic style known as parallel prose (*p'ien t'i wen*) makes use of all the prosodic devices of poetry and remains prose only by avoiding any of the prescribed verse rhythms. Literary language prose is also used for short fiction. The earliest examples are the parables and exemplars of the pre-Han philosophers, but other early models were the biographies of outstanding men and women, some of them scarcely historical, in the early *Shih chi* (Historical Records) of Ssu-ma Ch'ien (145–?90 B.C.) and *Lieh nü chuan* (Biographies of Famous Women) by Liu Hsiang (77–6 B.C.). Anecdotes, ghost stories, and travelers' tales contributed to the development in the T'ang Dynasty of the tale of the marvelous (*ch'uan ch'i*), tales which often made no pretense of being anything but fiction. After the T'ang Dynasty there are few first-rate stories in the literary language until P'u Sung-ling (1640–1715) wrote his *Liao-chai chih-i* (Liao-chai Stories), containing over 400 stories and sketches, all written in a masterly prose.

The mainstream of fiction in Chinese is in the vernacular. The literary language was until modern times the universal written medium of communication among the educated. Although close to speech at one time, its natural conservatism resulted in a divergence of the two until by the 1st century A.D. the written language no longer used living speech patterns. Phonological simplification finally resulted in its being quite unintelligible to the ear, even of the educated writer of the language. By the 12th century attempts to write in the vernacular had produced the beginnings of a popular language literature. The vernacular language story was first of all an imitation of the oral story teller's story, using the same materials and techniques, and the first novels were similar imitations of his sequel narration dealing with historical subjects.

MUSIC

History

Generally speaking, Chinese music history can be divided into four major periods with regard to style: (a) early antiquity (c.5000 B.C.–5th century A.D.), from primitive times through the Chin (Tsin) Dynasty (265–420), when aboriginal Chinese music was most prevalent; (b) late antiquity (4th–10th century), from the Southern and Northern Dynasties (386–581) to the T'ang Dynasty (618–906), when an international music was flourishing under the influence of Indian, Iranian, and Central Asian musical importations; (c) the middle age (10th–20th century), from the Five Dynasties to the Ch'ing Dynasty (1616–1911), when national music developed with less influence from abroad; (d) the modern age, after the Republic of China Revolution (1911), when so-called "world music" began to be created under the influence of European music.

Early Antiquity. Most traditional sources on the origin of Chinese music are unreliable, except for a few; from these, historical facts can be presumed with the assistance of archeological materials and sociological observations. In the Shang (Yin) Dynasty (c.1500–1000 B.C.), when both stone and bronze were in use, music and dance were related to shamanism, and musical instruments were made under the influence of animism, and totemism. Among various instruments of this age, including primitive pipes, flutes, zithers, and drums, the stone-chime (*ch'ing*) is noteworthy as a remnant of the Stone Age. In the Chou Dynasty (c.1000–221 B.C.), especially in its second half, when Confucius established the idea of *Li* and *Yüeh* (Rites and Music), the bronze bell (*chung*) became the basis of temperament, or interval tuning, and other instruments developed in various styles. In the Han Dynasty (202 B.C.–220 A.D.), the Confucian music called *ya-yüeh* became the music of national ceremonies. About 25 kinds of instruments, such as bronze bell-chimes, stone-chimes, long zithers (*ch'in* and *se*), pipes, flutes, the mouth-organ (*sheng*), panpipes (*hsiao*), various drums (small and gigantic), percussion instruments (*yü* and *chü*), among others, formed a large orchestra and accompanied the warrior and civil dances, which, in the case of the emperor's ceremony, were performed by 64 dancers. Until the end of the Chin Dynasty, this Confucian ceremonial music and Chinese popular music, of which the *ch'ing-shang-yüeh* was the most important, were predominant.

Late Antiquity. From the time of the Southern and Northern Dynasties, western music (Indian, Iranian, and Central Asian) streamed steadily eastward into China, where it had a remarkable effect. However, in the Han Dynasty Iranian music had already begun to move into China, as is evident from instrumental names: for instance, the four-stringed lute (*barbat*) became the *p'i-p'a*, and the angular harp (*qungqua*) became the *k'ung-hou*.

In the T'ang Dynasty (7th–10th century A.D.), the most flourishing period of late antiquity, over 30,000 slave musicians and singing-girls belonged to the court and the government, performing foreign and Chinese music. In the *li-yüan* (pear garden) of the capital (Changan) there was a music school in which the Emperor Hsüan-tsung himself taught. (Chou Wen-chü's scroll-painting, owned by the Art Institute of Chicago, represents the female musicians' orchestra of this time.) The *shih-pu-chi* (Ten Kinds of Music) was a type of large suite consisting of music of various nations, such as *T'ien-chu* (India), *Kuei-tzu* (Kucha, in Chinese Turkestan), *K'ang-kuo* (Samarkand, in Russian Turkestan), *Kao-li* (Korea), and so on. The *ya-*

CHINESE MUSIC

THREE CHINESE MUSICAL INSTRUMENTS

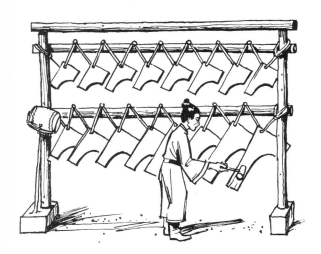

The Chinese four-stringed lute (p'i-p'a), based on an instrument from Iran, dates back to the Han Dynasty (202 B.C. — 220 A.D.)

One of the oldest Chinese musical instruments is the stone-chime, an ancient form of which was in use during the 2d millenium B.C.

The long zither, like the ch'in above, is the oldest stringed instrument of China. It is played horizontally.

yüeh (Confucian music) and popular music were also part of the main repertory of T'ang music.

The development of instrumental music was most important in this period. For instance, a large orchestra of over 30 kinds of instruments, of which the mouth-organ, lute, zither, and harp produced the ancient style of harmony, performed the dance piece which was called yen-yüeh and which was composed by the order of the Emperor Kao-tsung (of the T'ang Dynasty). It should be noted that in the same period the main body of European art music consisted of monophonic (single-part) chanting (Gregorian chant).

The Middle Age. From the Sung Dynasty (960–1279 A.D.) on, Chinese music changed its style from the international and aristocratic to the national and popular. The major genre was the Chinese opera, which appeared first as the tsa-hsi in the Sung Dynasty, developed into the yüan-ch'ü of the Yüan (Mongol) Dynasty (1260–1368), then into the k'un-ch'ü of the Ming Dynasty (1368–1644), and took final form as the ching-hsi of the Ch'ing Dynasty (1616–1911) and of the present day. Various other types of popular music, as for example, narrative style songs (ta-ku) and numerous folksongs were performed in theaters, singing-girls' houses, and at folklore festivals open to the public. In the court and government, the Confucian music was still preserved, the feast music including music of surrounding nations was presented to Emperors, and the opera, which was enjoyed by the people, was also given on the stage of the big theater in the court.

Even in this period of national music there were some important influences from abroad. Of these, Islamic instruments were most prominent; thus, for instance, the san-hsien (three-stringed lute with a long stick) derived from

the qupuz or setar, and the hu-ch'in (two-stringed viol) from the rebab.

Style Characteristics

The present condition of Chinese traditional music shows a continuous development from the music of the middle age. The music of the T'ang Dynasty was quite different from it. In contrast to T'ang music, which is characterized by large instrumental ensembles, ancient-style harmony, and a seven-tone scale, the music of the middle age features monophony, the five-tone scale, and vocal music.

In the later Chou Dynasty (1027–220 B.C.) the 12-tone system existed. One bamboo pipe, nine Chinese-inches long (23cm.), determines the basic note of this system. By cutting off one-third of the pipe, the note one-fifth higher is obtained; then, by adding one-third of the second note (that is, by adding one-third of the new pipe-length), the third note is obtained (a major second above the basic note). By repeating 12 times the alternate cutting and adding by ⅓, 12 semitones are obtained in an octave. Later, in the Han Dynasty, this procedure was executed on a string. The method of calculation is exactly the same as that used for the Pythagorean 12 tones. Both appeared almost at the same time, but no historical connection can be proved.

The seven-tone scale was used from the Chou Dynasty on, and in the T'ang Dynasty the tonality system resembling the 24 major and minor tonalities came into use. However, since the middle age pentatonic scales have become common. Each note of these 12-tone and five- or seven-tone scales has its old name; thus, the basic note of the 12 tones is called huang-chung (yellow bell), and the five tones are kung, shang, chiao, ch'ih, and yü, the etymology of which is unknown, except for the *kung* which means "palace" or "main house." The five tones are connected with the philosophical idea of *wu-hsing* (five fundamental elements, wood, fire, earth, metal, and water).

As to melody, it should be noted that following the Sung Dynasty melodic patterns became highly important. The extreme example is the composition of opera, in which the text is written to ready-made melodies. The ancient style of harmony, which was based on the intervals of the fifth and the fourth and on the simple idea of sounding all tones of the seven-tone scale at one time (which bears some resemblance to the impressionism of Debussy's harmony), was used in the instrumental music of the T'ang Dynasty. However, from the Sung Dynasty on, Chinese music has been monophonic. Furthermore, the rhythm has been comparatively simple and mechanical.

Sensitivity to timbre is keen, but timbre is not so rich in variety as in the case of European instruments. The most characteristic timbre is found in the voice of the male singer who assumes female roles in the opera. The voice sounds like a keen falsetto, which is related to the sharp tone of the *hu-ch'in* (viol). Musical form varies according to the genres of music. In comparison to Western music, Chinese musical forms are not very sophisticated, but simple and stereotyped in each genre. The main genres of traditional music preserved today are the opera, instrumental ensemble, solo music of the *ch'in*, *p'i-p'a*, and *sheng* instruments, among others, and the narrative style of story-singing, folksong, and dance.

Distribution

In late antiquity the distribution of Chinese music was most remarkable. Korean music in the Three Dynasties (1st–7th century) and Silla Dynasty (7th–10th century) was strongly influenced by Chinese music. Confucian music and the feast music in the court of the Sung and Ming dynasties still exist in Korea today. Japanese *gagaku* (Imperial Court Music) is a living tradition of the feast music of the T'ang Dynasty. The Imperial Treasury of the Shosoin in Nara preserves about 80 musical instruments which were used in the big Buddhist ceremony at the Great Buddha in Nara (752 A.D.). Later in the middle age Chinese music spread, with modifications, to Vietnam and Mongolia. The *san-hsien* was introduced to Japan through Okinawa and became the *shamisen*, one of the representative instruments of Japan.

PHILOSOPHY

CHINESE PHILOSOPHY. Possessing a long history and a rich heritage, the philosophy of China developed in three main periods: the ancient period of indigenous philosophy; the medieval period, when it was stimulated by Buddhism; and the modern period, when Western ideas reached China.

Ancient Period (to 400 A.D.): Indigenous Chinese Philosophy

Before the dawn of philosophy religion controlled the minds of men in Chinese antiquity. The world of men was closely related to the world of spirits. The Shang Ti, or Supreme Lord, ruled over the numerous spirits, and the departed ancestors acted as intercessors between men and the spirits. When the Chou replaced the Shang on the throne (c.1027 B.C.), the new ruling clan contributed its belief in T'ien, or Heaven. This supplemented the concept of Shang Ti at first and replaced it eventually.

Broadly speaking, the coming of the Chou Dynasty initiated a gradual transfer of emphasis from divine direction to human endeavor in human affairs. With the passing of time, the well-defined feudalistic hierarchy set up at the beginning of the Chou Dynasty began to decay and crumble, and there arose a class of impoverished noblemen, who became scribes, petty officials, teachers, and philosophers. The best known among them was Confucius.

The Six Schools (c.550–c.200 B.C.). Confucius ushered in the most vigorous and creative period in the history of Chinese philosophy. This period is known in the West as the period of classical Chinese philosophy, but in China it is usually referred to as the period of "the hundred philosophers." The hundred philosophers were eventually classified into six schools—the Confucianists, the Moists, the Taoists, the Logicians, the Diviners (*yin-yang*), and the Legalists.

Confucianism. Confucius (c.551–c.479 B.C.) is revered among the Chinese as their "Supreme Sage and Foremost Teacher." His system of teaching introduced the unitary principle of *jen* ("love" or "benevolence"). "*Jen* is to love all men."

In the teachings of Confucius, *jen* is the common denominator among men and, therefore, the essence of humanity. *Jen* is both the innermost nature and the highest ideal of true manhood. It is the measure of the greatness of an individual, and it is the mark distinguishing man from animal. A superior man is said not to act contrary to *jen*, but to hold himself true to it under all circumstances. And when necessary, the man of *jen* would choose to preserve his *jen* rather than his life. So central is the concept of *jen* in this teaching that Confucianism might be said to be the way of benevolence, human-heartedness, and love.

Moism. In the philosophy of Mo-tzu (c.470–c.391 B.C.) the cause of misery in the world might be summed up in one word, partiality. To rectify the situation, he taught the doctrine of universal love. He was critical of the Confucian *jen*, because *jen*, he thought, was graded love, leading easily to partiality. Mo-tzu also believed there is a Heaven, that Heaven has a will, and that the will of Heaven is to be obeyed by all men.

Taoism. The central theme of this system of thought is the *Tao*. *Tao* means literally "path," or "road," but in the philosophical context it has come to signify the basic principle that pervades man and the universe. Taoism teaches the lesson of humility, quietude, and calm and the folly of force, pride, and self-assertion. Taoism is a philosophy of letting things alone, of "to live and let live." Taoism urges everyone to keep the original simplicity of nature and human nature, and the gifted ones to achieve complete union and identity of the individual with the whole, that is, the *Tao*, in an experience of naturalistic mysticism.

The School of Logicians. On the whole, the Chinese thinkers have paid little attention to logic as a systematic discipline, and the school of Logicians has only a minor importance. The term "logic" is here used in a very broad sense. Logicians dealt with the problems of the one and the many, thing and its attributes, the nature of knowledge, the function of names, and so on.

The School of Diviners. The Diviners included the philosophers who taught the *yin-yang* and those who taught the Five Elements. Both of these concepts represent early attempts at working out a metaphysics and a cosmology. *Yin-yang* meant originally the shady and sunny sides of a valley or a hill, and developed into a pair of fundamental elements described in terms of female-male, cold-hot, wet-dry, and so forth. The Five Elements consisted of metal, wood, water, fire, and earth. In either case, these elements are to be understood as forces, powers, or agencies, rather than as material entities.

Ascendancy of Confucianism (c.150 B.C.–c.200 A.D.). The period of "hundred schools contending together" came to an end in the 3d century B.C. with the reunification of the Chinese Empire. During the ensuing centuries until the introduction of Buddhism, Chinese philosophy developed along two main lines: the synthesis of the schools and the ascendancy of Confucianism.

Taoist Renaissance (c.200–c.400 A.D.). When the Han Dynasty came to an end at the beginning of the 3d century A.D., the Chinese Empire fell into a state of disorder and dismemberment, with the northern parts of the country held under barbarian rule for several centuries. In such a condition of turbulence Taoism advanced to the intellectual foreground while Confucianism receded to the background, a pattern that was to repeat itself time and again throughout Chinese history.

Buddhism (3d–10th Centuries A.D.). Down to the 3d century A.D. the history of Chinese philosophy had been an indigenous development. However, from that time on, Buddhism, which had been introduced into China a couple of hundred years earlier, began to play an increasingly important role in Chinese philosophy. For the several centuries that followed, the best Chinese minds were attracted to Buddhism, and it was not until the 10th century A.D. that the Confucianists finally succeeded in reinstating Confucianism to its position of national predominance in the form of Neo-Confucianism.

Several schools of Buddhism were brought into China from India and several more were developed by the Chinese. In all, there were some 13 major schools, representing the Hinayana as well as the Mahayana branch of Buddhism. The most significant Chinese contribution was the Ch'an school. (*Ch'an* is the Chinese transliteration of the Sanskrit term *dhyana;* Japanese, *zen.*) While originating in certain teachings of the Buddha, Ch'an was, for the most part, a philosophic-religious creation of the Chinese mind. It was Buddhism with a distinctly Taoist accent, and it exercised a profound influence on Chinese art and literature, as well as Chinese attitudes toward life and the universe. Insofar as Buddhism became a part of Chinese philosophy, it underwent assorted transformations in the direction of simplicity, practicality, and catholicity. The doctrine of universal salvation over individual salvation, for one, was strongly stressed by the Chinese Buddhists.

Neo-Confucianism (10th–17th Centuries A.D.). Buddhist teachings continued to intrigue the Chinese mind until the establishment of Neo-Confucianism in the Sung Dynasty. Neo-Confucianism is Confucianism revived and revised in response to the problems and propositions presented by Buddhism. The result is a more sophisticated version of Confucianism, with definite traces of influence from Buddhism and also, to some extent, from Taoism.

Chu Hsi (1130–1200) is regarded as the principal spokesman for Neo-Confucianism. He proposed a pair of concepts regarding the world of existence, namely, *Ch'i* (Ether or concrete Matter) for the physical world, and *Li* (Reason or abstract Law) for the metaphysical world. *Ch'i* is tangible but not intelligible, whereas *Li* is intelligible but not tangible. *Li* is the intrinsic nature of all things, but in actual existence *Li* and *Ch'i* are never separated. The metaphysical interest shown here had evidently been inspired by Buddhism. In ethics, the Neo-Confucianists followed more the traditional Confucianist lines. The central concept of *jen* in Confucianism became a kind of cosmic compassion.

THEATER

Chinese classical theater—or "opera," as it is more widely known in the West because of its amalgam of spoken dialogue, song, dance, and acrobatics—is called *ching hsi,* the theater of the capital (Peking). Although *ching hsi* is the major type of drama of the entire Chinese nation and popular throughout the whole of China, its purest and most traditional forms and its finest artists have for centuries been found in Peking.

The first historical references having a direct connection with classical Chinese theater as it is known today date from the T'ang Dynasty, when by imperial decree a college of dramatics was founded (720). To this day actors are sometimes referred to as "people of the Pear Garden," an allusion to the poetic name for this first place of instruction. During the Yüan Dynasty in the 14th century, theater reached its height. The Mongols invaded China from the north and, with the capture of Peking, took over the administration of the country. A large number of scholars who had been employed as officials of the government were forced into idleness. They turned to the theater and wrote plays, partly out of amusement and partly as a means of livelihood; the best surviving texts—in fact, the only literary masterpieces of Chinese dramatic writing—date from this period.

The actual crystallization of the classical theater in its present form took place in the 19th century during the rule of the Manchus. In order to ensure their control over the capital, the Manchus restricted the right to leave Peking, and as a result public and private theaters flourished as an antidote to boredom. It is this precise theater that is still seen today with its deafening music, dazzling costumes, grotesque make-up, vertiginous acrobatics, and mixture of high tragedy and grossly comic interludes.

Classical Dramatic Types and Characteristics. Theater in China is divided, not into tragedy and comedy, but into military (*wu*) and civil (*wen*) plays. Military plays are heroic in nature, full of loyal generals, glorious emperors, and wise government officials, all of whom struggle against traitorous opposing forces. Civil plays concern themselves with domestic joy or sorrow, filial piety, marital fidelity, and the effect of ghosts and spirits on the lives of ordinary people. All the plots are drawn from historical events or incidents from classical novels. The story outlines are fairly uniform. In a military play, good is pitted against evil in combat, and after some stratagem, evil is destroyed. In a civil play, A abuses or deceives B; as a result B suffers; C appears and resolves the wrong.

The normal program at the theater consists of isolated scenes rather than full plays and presents them as vehicles for the actors without reference to context. As a result the greatest moments of classical theater are scarcely more than highlights—the concubine parting from her general who performs a sword dance in farewell, the junior wife who gets drunk while her husband spends the night elsewhere, the general who tricks his opponents by leaving the city gates open and thereby leading them to believe he is more powerful than he is, the fickle young widow who goes to her husband's grave to pray but flirts with a government official en route, the scholar who stays all night in the rain outside a pavilion in order to avoid compromising a virtuous woman by speaking to her. Some scenes are merely pantomimes, for which the Chinese are celebrated—the picking up of a jade wristlet or the rowing of a ferryboat across a river. The total repertoire of still extant and regularly performed scenes numbers over 500.

All characters fall into rigid classifications: the military hero (*wu-sheng*); the handsome young man or scholar (*hsiao-sheng*); the "painted face" (*hua-lien*) or "blackhead" (*hei-t'ou*), who may be very brave or very evil (emperors, generals, landowners) according to the design painted on his face and the color of his long beard; old man (*lao-sheng*); comedian (*hsiao-ch'ou*), whose nose is always painted white; the "flower" (*hua-tan*), a vivacious and attractive girl, concubine, second wife, or young widow; the "subdued dress" (*ching yi*), a faithful wife or dutiful daughter; the comic maidservant (*ya-tou*); and the old woman (*lao-tan*), usually a mother or mother-in-law, and sometimes an elderly queen.

Traditionally, all roles have been played by men and boys, and in the 18th century the Emperor Ch'ien-lung formally barred women from the stage. In impersonating women, male actors speak and sing in a shrill falsetto, and as "flowers," they wear "golden lilies," tiny wooden shoes designed to give the impression of daintiness. Early in the 20th century, women began to appear on the stage, though great male actors such as Mei Lan-fang continued to keep the art of female impersonation alive.

Chinese classical theater abounds in stylized conventions. All entrances are made at stage left and all exits at stage right. During a scene of combat, the man who exits first is considered defeated. The actor always opens an imaginary door and takes a high step to indicate that he is entering a room. If an actor carries a riding crop, he is on horseback. A general's rank is immediately recognizable from the number of flags he wears on his shoulders. Wind, clouds, sunshine, and the moon are indicated to the audience by stage attendants who wave various colored flags. A ricksha or chariot is signified when the actor whirls two flags held in either hand while he glides on or off stage.

The traditional performing area is an open stage whose scenic effects are expressed through properties rather than Western-style décor. An important part of the performance is music supplied by an orchestra on stage.

TRADITIONAL MEDICINE

CHINESE TRADITIONAL MEDICINE, that form of medicine practiced by Chinese physicians prior to the advent of Western-type medicine. The earliest known records of Chinese medicine are *The Herbal*, and the *Nei Ching*, or *Classic of Internal Medicine*. *The Herbal*, shrouded in mysticism, is a three-volume work said to have been written in the 27th century B.C.; the style of writing, however, places it more accurately in the 1st century B.C. This book classifies over 300 drugs and has been constantly revised. The table of contents lists many unusual items such as tiger bones and bat's dung, and also includes some drugs used in modern medicine, such as chaulmoogra oil and ephedrine. The *Nei Ching*, although thought to have originated in the 26th century B.C., was probably written about 1000 B.C. There have been no major changes in traditional Chinese medicine since this book was written. The *Nei Ching* is still venerated by many Chinese physicians.

According to the *Nei Ching*, there were two major forces controlling the state of the body: Yang and Yin. These two forces represented complete opposites such as life and death, or light and dark, and existed in a complicated state of flux; perfect harmony means health, disharmony brings disease. These two vital forces were thought to be contained in 12 main ducts coursing through the body. The ducts were usually imbedded deeply in the muscles, but rose to the surface at 365 distinct sites. Depending on the disease, the physician directed his therapy to one or more of these locations.

Two ancient forms of therapy, still in use today, were acupuncture and moxa, or moxibustion, both used to correct the imbalance of Yang and Yin. In acupuncture long needles were driven into the body, either manually or with a mallet. The number of needles, sites used, duration and depth of penetration, as well as the direction in which the needle was rotated, all depended on the nature and severity of the illness. Moxa, the ignition of small cones of combustible material placed on the skin, was of actual value only as a counterirritant.

Because of the belief in the sacredness of the human body, cadaver dissection was prohibited; this led to a fanciful concept of the anatomy and physiology of the human body.

The most important part of the patient's examination was the taking of the pulse, which was thought to be in direct communication with various internal organs; hence diseases could be diagnosed without further investigation. The *Nei Ching* listed many rules for this, including the time of day the pulse was to be taken, the effect of seasonal changes, and the position of the stars.

Surgical procedures were virtually unknown, yet the ancient Chinese physicians discovered a form of smallpox vaccination as far back as the 11th century A.D.

At the present time, many hospitals on the Chinese continent are divided into two units, the modern and the traditional, with patients assigned alternately to each division. This practice insures the preservation of Chinese traditional medicine in spite of modernization.

PEOPLE, PLACES, AND TERMS

BUDDHISM. An important event for Buddhism was the introduction of Mahayana in about 65 A.D. into China, where it was patronized by some Emperors, persecuted by others, yet continued to fructify into a number of sects. Some famous Chinese pilgrims visited their Holy Land of India, in particular Fa-hsien (4th century), and I-tsing and Hsüan-tsang (7th century), who visited Nalanda. Their accounts remain valuable records.

The *Madhyamikavada* of Nagarjuna formed the basis of several sects in the Far East, and Mahayana Buddhism soon spread beyond China to Annam (3d century), and to Mongolia, Korea, and Burma (4th century). Around 400 A.D. the devotional White Lotus Sect (forerunner of the Pure Land School) was founded in China by Hui-yüan. From the *Vijnanavada* school of the 4th and 5th centuries there developed other *tsung* (sects) in China. The mystical *dhyana* (contemplative) side of *Yogacara* was introduced by Bodhidharma from South India, who founded in 520 A.D. the Ch'an Tsung. During the second half of the 6th century Chih-i started the T'ien-T'ai Tsung. From Korea, Buddhism was taken to Japan, around 550 A.D.

In the 5th century the Magadhese monk Buddhaghosa visited Ceylon, where he composed the *Visuddhimagga* and other commentaries on the Pali canonical books. At the same time, Mahayana was being introduced into Cambodia and Siam, and thence, in the 6th century, into Sumatra and Java. Around 640 A.D. the Tantric Buddhism of Bengal was taken to Tibet by the Indian saint Padmasambhava, the virtual founder of Lamaism. In Burma during the 8th century Mahayana gave way to the orthodox Hinayana of the Theravada sect.

CHAMPA [chăm′pə], **KINGDOM OF,** long-enduring southeast-Asian kingdom of the Cham people, centered upon Hue in modern Vietnam. According to uncertain Chinese records, the Champa kingdom was founded in the year 192 A.D. by a native official, who revolted against the collapsing Chinese Han Dynasty, the previous rulers of the area. The history of Champa is one of almost incessant warfare, usually provoked by Cham aggression. Time and again, whenever China was experiencing dynastic crisis, the Cham kingdom attempted to expand into the areas of what is now North Vietnam. In addition, the Cham rulers were constantly embroiled with neighboring Cambodia and, from the 10th century on, with the new northern kingdom of Annam. Interestingly, the apogee of Cham power occurred in the 14th century when Che Bong Nga, the last king of the 12th dynasty was able not only to threaten Cambodia but to sack the Annamese capital of Hanoi (1371). One hundred years later, Annam achieved the final conquest of Champa, which survived until 1720 only as a tributary of Annam.

Throughout its existence, Champa was under Chinese political influence and Indian cultural domination. While the former fluctuated with the military power of China, Champa remained firmly within the Indian culture area throughout its history. In the early period, the dominant religion was Shiva worship, but it soon shifted to an acceptance of Mahayana Buddhism, which reached its peak in the 9th and 10th centuries. During this same period, close cultural contact with Java exerted much influence on Cham artistic development.

CH'IN [chĭn] **DYNASTY** (221–207 B.C.), short-lived but powerful Chinese dynasty. As a state within the Chou Kingdom, it developed a highly organized, centralized

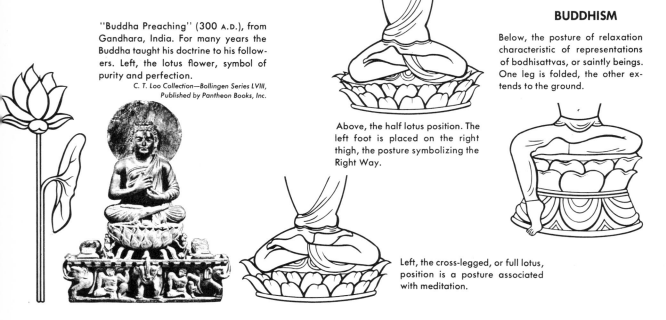

"Buddha Preaching" (300 A.D.), from Gandhara, India. For many years the Buddha taught his doctrine to his followers. Left, the lotus flower, symbol of purity and perfection.
C. T. Loo Collection—Bollingen Series LVIII, Published by Pantheon Books, Inc.

Above, the half lotus position. The left foot is placed on the right thigh, the posture symbolizing the Right Way.

BUDDHISM

Below, the posture of relaxation characteristic of representations of bodhisattvas, or saintly beings. One leg is folded, the other extends to the ground.

Left, the cross-legged, or full lotus, position is a posture associated with meditation.

government, much as was envisioned by philosophers of the Chinese Legalist school. It enforced rigid laws, encouraged military exploits, practiced private land ownership, and held all people liable to law and taxes.

In time, the Ch'in Dynasty annexed all its surrounding states, overthrew the Chou Dynasty, and unified China under a totalitarian central government. Feudalism was replaced by a centralized government which appointed Governors to newly created prefectures. Titles and positions were made nonhereditary, and the government maintained tight control over the life of the people. It unified all laws, currencies, and measurements.

Freedom of thought, however, was greatly restricted, and all books of a political or controversial nature were burned. Many learned men who refused to conform to the philosophy of the new regime were killed. As a part of his program of thought control the first Ch'in Emperor collected all former noblemen and influential people of China at his capital, Hsien-yang. Merchants were also subjected to harsh oppression. The Great Wall of China, about 1,500 mi. long, was completed, chiefly through the use of forced labor. The Ch'in Dynasty collapsed after only 14 years because of intrigues at the court and a serious lack of popular support.

CHOU [jō] **DYNASTY** (c.1027–256 B.C.), ancient Chinese dynasty, whose reign has come to mean the first golden age to the Chinese people. The dynasty first flourished under Chou Wu-wang (King Wu) who, with his brother Chou Kung (Duke of Chou), established a virtuous kingdom celebrated in Chinese history and philosophy. During the next four centuries, the Chou Kings lost power to the great vassal lords who had once been their subjects. By the 6th century B.C., the *de facto* control of the Chou court was reduced to a small territory on the North China Plain, which was bounded by its larger and more significant vassal states of Ch'in, Chin, Ch'u, Yen, Ch'i, Lu, and Sung.

The political organization of these states resembled European feudalism in many respects. The latter part of the Chou period, known as the Eastern Chou, is divided historically into two parts—the Spring and Autumn period (722–481 B.C.) and the Warring States period (403–221 B.C.), so named because of its continuous warfare, both of which are named for historical works dealing with the periods. After centuries of war the state of Ch'in eventually conquered the other states, unified China, and created an empire (221 B.C.).

In the realms of literature and philosophy, the Chou period produced outstanding works. It was during this era that the Chinese classics were written, that Confucius, Lao-tzu, Mencius, and many other great Chinese sages lived and taught. The times were also marked by economic progress. Towns and commerce grew, and iron replaced bronze as the chief metal. It was during this period that jade, mirror, lacquer, and chopsticks came into use.

The agricultural people of the Chou period were the first in the world to dress in trousers. The eight centuries of the Chou, with their contending influences of civilization and barbarism, have exerted an enduring influence on the Chinese way of life.

CHOU KUNG [jō' gŏong'] **or DUKE OF CHOU** (d.1105 B.C.), ancient Chinese statesman. The younger brother of Emperor Wu-wang of the early Chou Dynasty, Chou Kung became the Emperor's chief counselor and assistant. Soon he proved himself to be an exemplary statesman, selflessly dedicated to public service. True to the feudal law he supposedly drafted, Chou Kung refrained from taking over the Empire after the death of Chou Wu-wang, and supported the legitimate heir, who was a child at the time. The regency of Chou Kung was much admired by Confucius, and it has often been held up by the Chinese as the exemplar of true statesmanship.

CHUANG-TZU [jwäng'dzŭ'], **or CHUANG CHOU** (c.369–c.286 B.C.), ancient Chinese philosopher, poet, and mystic. He is best known as a founder with Lao-tzu, who lived two centuries earlier, of the important system of Taoism. Born in the district of Meng, in what is now Honan Province in Central China, Chuang-tzu briefly held a minor local government post. He soon lost all interest in fame and fortune and became a recluse. His teachings consisted mainly of the relativity of knowledge, equality of things, and absolute truth and freedom in the *Tao*. He presented his ideas through imagery, anecdote, and parable, as well as the allegory and parody of the *Chuang-tzu*. Written in poetic prose, several of the 33 chapters of this work are considered to be literary masterpieces. The characteristic humor, charm, and detachment of the work are evident. For example, in the well-known piece, the "Butterfly Dream," on waking, Chuang-tzu wondered "whether it was Chuang Chou dreaming that he was the butterfly or the butterfly dreaming that it was Chuang Chou," and concluded dryly, "between Chuang Chou and the butterfly presumably there is a difference."

CHU-KO LIANG [jōō'gŭ' lyäng'] (181–234), Chinese statesman and strategist of the period of the Three Kingdoms (220–65). Serving as Prime Minister of the Kingdom of Shu, Chu-ko reformed the civil administration and sought unsuccessfully to restore the Liu family to the throne which was usurped by Ts'ao Ts'ao, who had seized northern China. Although regarded by historians as a typical statesman in the Confucian tradition, Chu-ko has enjoyed lasting fame as a shrewd strategist and has been revered by poets and writers of succeeding generations as one of China's greatest heroes. One of the popular works on Chu-ko Liang's exploits is the historical novel *San-kuo-chih yen-i* (*The Romance of the Three Kingdoms*) written by Lo Kuan-chung during the Ming Dynasty (1368–1644).

CONFUCIUS [kən-fū'shəs] (551–479 B.C.), most revered philosopher, teacher, and sage of China. Confucius was born in the small feudal state of Lu (now Shantung Province). K'ung was his family name and Ch'iu his personal name; Confucius is the Latinized form of K'ung Fu-tzu, or "Grand Master K'ung," the title commonly used among the Chinese in referring to their sage. At the time Confucius was born, his family, which was probably of the lesser aristocracy, had long since seen its better days, and his father died while Confucius was still a young boy.

Though he had to earn his living early in life, he managed to have a period of study and travel. His itinerary included a visit to the Imperial Capital which still stood as the cultural center of the Empire even though the political authority and military might were being increasingly usurped by the powerful feudal lords. As Confucius grew in stature and reputation, young men of all stations of life came to him to seek instruction. With the conviction that "in education there is no discrimination," (*Analects*) he taught everyone with equal enthusiasm. Eventually he was said to have had 3,000 pupils, of whom 72 had mastered the six arts. As the first professional teacher in Chinese history, Confucius symbolized popular education in China, his birthday being celebrated as Teachers' Day by the Chinese.

However, Confucius did not consider teaching his primary mission in life. He wanted to be a man of action even more than a man of learning and wisdom, and he had a public career in his native state of Lu. Records show that Confucius was a capable and successful administrator, and his rise on the official ladder was quite rapid—from county magistracy to acting premiership of the state government within a few years. As eager as he was to be of service to Heaven and mankind and to bring order out of chaos in the world, he would not compromise his integrity and principles in order to cling to his esteemed position. Situations soon arose which made him feel honor bound to relinquish his post at Lu, and he started to travel from state to state in the quest of a feudal ruler who might be more sincerely receptive to his politico-educational program.

His wanderings lasted some 13 years and were filled with disappointment, privation, and even danger. While Confucius was received with due respect and courtesy by most rulers, none wanted to entrust his government to an idealistic visionary in an age dominated by political intrigue and military strife. A small group of disciples remained devoted to the master, and the sage himself acquired a more penetrating understanding of man and nature and the will and mission of Heaven.

Confucius finally returned to Lu at the invitation of the reigning lord. He was then nearly 70. With a feeling of frustration, he resignedly devoted his remaining years to the instruction of his disciples and the editing of literary collections including the *Classic of Poetry*, the *Classic of History*, and the *Classic of Changes*. He also compiled and wrote a year-by-year history of the state of Lu covering the period of 722–481 B.C. which eventually became the *Classic of Spring and Autumn Annals*.

Although Confucius died in 479 B.C., his influence grew with each succeeding age and generation. His tomb and his temple have made Ch'ü-fu, Shantung, a mecca for all educated Chinese. A Confucian temple, of less pretentious proportions, stands in almost every county seat throughout China. The Chinese revere him as their "Supreme Sage and Foremost Teacher." The Chinese way of life, when limited to a one-word description, is the Confucian way, and this overwhelming Confucian influence has spread to China's neighboring countries such as Korea, Japan, and Vietnam.

After Confucius' death, notes of his discourses, conversations, and travels were collected by his disciples. Known as the *Analects of Confucius*, this work consists of 20 books and 496 chapters. It is the most reliable source on the life and teachings of Confucius, and is regarded by his followers as the scripture of Confucianism. Numerous commentaries have been written on the *Analects* by scholars through the ages, and translations of the work have been made and published in many languages.

FOOT BINDING, form of feminine mutilation practiced in China from about 600 A.D. It was supposed to have arisen as a custom because of the desire of the women of the imperial court to emulate the small feet of one of the Emperor's favorite concubines. The feet of females of the Mandarin class were compressed in infancy by extremely tight swaddling so that they were permanently stunted and walking became painful. This operation was performed, of course, only upon the children of the upper classes as a sign of social status and of their not having to work. Thus the custom forms an extreme instance of what the American economic philosopher Thorstein Veblen called "conspicuous leisure," a badge of socially consecrated waste, in this case waste of feminine work-value. The custom went out of fashion in the late 19th century and virtually disappeared in the 20th.

GREAT WALL, ancient China's greatest engineering feat. It was built to defend the country against barbarian invasion. The first Ch'in Emperor, Shih-huang-ti (259–210 B.C.), initiated the project which linked all the separated walls previously erected by various vanquished states. It stretched from Kiayükwan near Kiuchüan in Kansu Province eastward to Shanhaikwan in Hopeh Province on the Gulf of Chihli. With a length of 1,500 mi., the wall was built by labor conscripts and 3,000,000 soldiers.

Section of the Great Wall of China, conceived by Emperor Shih-huang-ti in the 3d century B.C. Construction of the 1,500-mile wall required the work of millions of soldiers and other laborers.

Fernand Gigon—Pix

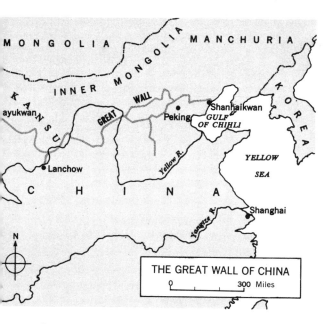

THE GREAT WALL OF CHINA

0   300 Miles

Constructed mainly of earth and stone, it is covered by a brick facing. Its height varies from 20 to 50 ft., and its thickness at the base fluctuates from 15 to 25 ft., tapering at the top to 12 ft. Passages 3 and 4 ft. wide run between indented parapets on the wall's ridge. Square watchtowers 40 ft. high were erected as sentry posts every 200 yd. and 9 soldiers guarded every mile of the wall. Land near the wall was given to the soldiers to provide them with food.

The wall in the west, built only of earth, has deteriorated, and its history illustrates its vulnerability to successive invasions from the north. There were numerous historical writings, poems, and songs in China depicting the toil of wall building and the battles against barbarians which resulted in heavy casualties. "White skeletons" were said to have piled up to match the wall's height. Today, the usefulness of the wall is retained in two ways: the Chinese government collects toll revenue at a few, closely watched passes, and the well-preserved sections near Peking provide dramatic attractions for tourists.

HAN DYNASTY (202 B.C.–220 A.D.), ruling house of ancient China. Rulers of one of the most glorious periods in Chinese history, the dynasty was established by Liu Pang who reigned under the title of Kao-tsu. During the 400 years of Han rule, which was interrupted briefly by the Hsin (New) Dynasty (9 A.D.–23 A.D.), the Chinese empire extended itself from Korea in the northeast to northern Vietnam in the southwest, and Chinese military might reached through Central Asia to the border of the Roman Empire. The Western (or Early) Han (202 B.C.–9 A.D.) is marked by the preoccupation of Kao-tsu (reigned 202–195 B.C.) with pacifying his enemies on the frontier. Wu-ti (reigned 140–87 B.C.) allied himself with other central Asian peoples against his enemies, thereby establishing and maintaining contact with western Asia. Colonization and exploration as far as the Indian Ocean mark this period of the Han whose population (some 59,000,000) and territorial expanse exceeded that of Rome at its peak.

Established at this time was a system of governmental bureaucracy based on the results of civil service examinations. Thus learning became essential to those desiring official positions, and from the 2d century there existed a college of doctors at the national capital, Loyang, eventually attended by over 30,000 students. Confucianism, Buddhism, and Taoism, the systems of thought that were to dominate China throughout history, were established. Extensive use of the writing brush and ink, the production of paper (c.105 A.D.), the flourishing of poetry and historiography, and the compilation of the first encyclopedic history of China were some of the material and intellectual developments. The mingling of native Chinese elements with borrowings from contacts outside its border enriched its science, art, music, and industry.

After ruling for two centuries, the Han was weakened by political intrigue to the extent that Wang Mang, a court minister, was able to institute an interregnum called the Hsin (New) Dynasty (9 A.D.–23 A.D.). His rule is noted for its radical reform, including the nationalization of land. Natural disasters, such as the Yellow River floods, and rebellions in South and Central Asia, necessitating the forfeiture of Chinese colonies in both regions, weakened his regime.

After Wang's death, anarchy reigned until the establishment of the Eastern (or Later) Han (25 A.D.–220 A.D.) by Liu Hsiu who reigned under the title of Kuang-wu-ti. Under him the Han court was moved eastward from Changan to Loyang. The government concerned itself both with pacifying internal China and recovering its former possessions including Tongking, Annam, and Hainan Island. For a while the Han exerted power in Afghanistan, India, southern Manchuria, and parts of Korea. The decline of the emperors, initiated by the intrigues of eunuchs and empresses, was intensified by the rebellion of dissatisfied peasants, notably that of the Yellow Turbans (Huang-chin) in the 2d century. In 220 the deposition of its virtual emperor brought the once magnificent Han Dynasty to an end.

HUANG-TI [*hwäng'tē'*] (Chin., "the Yellow Emperor") prehistoric legendary ruler of China. He is said to have consolidated northern China for the first time by making an alliance with other chieftains to defeat his archenemy Ch'ih Yu. He is recognized as having regulated the calendar and having improved commerce. Under his direction 11 notes of music were discovered by cutting a pitch pipe. He is said by some to have had a harem of 1,200 women, while others claim that his one wife was the first cultivator of silkworms. Folklore has attributed much credit to Huang-ti for the founding of the Chinese nation.

HUI-TSUNG [*hwā'dzŏŏng'*], personal name Chao Chi (1082–1135), emperor of China in the Sung Dynasty. He reigned from 1101 until 1126, when he was forced to abdicate by the Chin Tatars. An accomplished painter, Hui-tsung supported during his period of imperial rule a thriving painting academy. He enforced his ideal of accurate depiction upon his court artists and practiced it in his own works, which are meticulous representations of birds and plants. Notable among the many paintings ascribed to him are the "Two Small Birds in a Blossoming Wax Tree"

(Palace Museum Collection, Taiwan) and "Five-colored Parakeet" (Museum of Fine Arts, Boston).

KAO-TSU (247–195 B.C.), temple title of Liu Pang, founder of the Western (Earlier) Han Dynasty and the first commoner to rule China. In 209 B.C., almost immediately after the death of the founding emperor of Ch'in, the first unified empire of China, rebels arose in many areas of the nation. Liu's final victory over his rival insurgents in 202 B.C. placed him as the emperor of a new dynasty. As a ruler, Kao-tsu revived the old feudal system, after the collapse of the centralized authority of the Ch'in.

Although the new nobles came from origins as humble as his own, in time they grew in strength, endangering the central government. The Hsiung-nu (Huns), a tribe belonging to a Turkish language group which founded the first steppe empire in the 3d century B.C., also presented a perennial menace to the new Han empire. Nevertheless, Kao-tsu secured for China great influence and prestige in neighboring lands and set the pattern for empire that was to last for more than 2,000 years.

KUAN-YIN [kwän′yĭn′], also known as Kuan-shih-yin, the most popular Buddhist deity in China. A goddess, she was derived from the Indian male divinity Bodhisattva Avalokitesvara. In the 7th century the Chinese transformed him into the female Kuan-yin, which means "the seer of the sound of suffering." It is written that when she was about to enter into her Buddhahood, Kuan-yin turned back to listen to the cry of suffering which arose from the earth and vowed to postpone her deification until the level of existence of her own sublime elevation had been achieved by all other living creatures. She is regarded as the chief deity of Chinese Amidism, the Buddhist sect which claims that the only road to salvation and of escaping the torments of Hell is to be reborn in the marvelous Sukhavati (Paradise), or what the Chinese call Hsi-t'ien (Western Heaven). As a substitute for Gautama, who preaches the arduous life of abstention and contemplation, Amidism praises Amida, the Buddha of Boundless Light who is the ruler of Sukhavati. In order to achieve Buddhahood one must invoke the name of Amida and must worship and follow the precepts of Kuan-yin by devoting one's whole life to benevolence toward all men. In the mind of the Chinese, Kuan-yin thus became known as the compassionate Goddess of Mercy, who is the giver of male descendants and the guardian of children and womanhood.

KUAN YÜ [kwän′yōō′] (?219 A.D.), Chinese general of the Three Kingdoms period and folk hero. He was an able soldier who fought and died in the unsuccessful attempt to restore the fallen Han Dynasty. Kuan is also a famous legendary Chinese hero, partially as a result of the image created in the popular historical novel *The Romance of the Three Kingdoms*. He was respected not only for his valor, but also for upholding the principle that a man's personal loyalty to his friends is no less important than his allegiance to the regime. After his death he was deified.

LAO-TZU [lou′dzŭ′] or **LAO-TSE** (c.575–c.485 B.C.), philosopher of ancient China and founder of Taoism. The life of Lao-tzu is enshrouded in greater obscurity than that of most of his contemporaries, partly because of his own preference for anonymity. According to tradition, Lao-tzu was a man of Ch'u (now Honan Province), which at the time was regarded as South China. His family name was Li and his given name, Erh; "Lao-tzu" was an affectionate epithet, equivalent to the phrase "elderly master." It is said that he served the Chou court as the keeper of the imperial archives. A legend relates that Lao-tzu, who believed that forms and ceremonies were practically useless, advised the ambitious young Confucius to forget his grandiose plans for world order. Evidently, Lao-tzu did not take students nor did he leave a record of his doings and sayings, as was the custom with thinkers of the day.

The traditional story of Lao-tzu in his old age riding to the Western Pass and into oblivion beyond the pale of civilization gave rise to the popular pictorial representation of his riding on the back of an ox. It is told that when Lao-tzu stopped at the pass, the keeper implored the Old Master to write down his teachings for the keeper's benefit. If tradition is to be believed, "Thereupon Lao-tzu wrote a book in two parts consisting of some five thousand words, in which he discussed the meaning of the *tao* and the *te*." The book which actually came to be written bore his name, the Lao-tzu. It was subsequently also called the *Tao Te Ching* (Classic of the Way and Power), and is the all-important text of Taoism. Consisting of 81 brief chapters, this small classic is not only the shortest, but also one of the most provocative and inspired works in all Chinese literature. Much speculation has been directed to its authenticity, literary style, and date of composition, as well as to related information concerning its purported author. Presumably the book was completed in the 4th and possibly even 3d century B.C., but some of the ideas and teachings, held perhaps by the hermit philosopher himself, might well have been of an earlier origin.

Lao-tzu and the *Tao Te Ching* advocated the importance and supremacy of the *tao*, an over-all principle pervading nature and man, which could be grasped better through intuition than understood through the intellect. This element of mysticism in Taoism was later seized upon by occultists, and Lao-tzu was made a saint of the Taoist religion and the *Tao Te Ching* its primary scripture.

LI PO [lē bō′] (701–62), renowned Chinese poet of the T'ang Dynasty. Born in west China (modern Szechwan), he left his native province when he was about 20 and spent the next 20 years living off the bounty of relatives and patrons scattered throughout the country. Introduced to the Emperor Hsüan-tsung in 743, he became a royal favorite for a few years, writing occasional poems and joining in the dissolute life of the court. The rest of his life was spent in further travels around the country, in the course of which he married for the fourth and last time. He finally returned to central China, where he died of illness, not, as tradition would have it, by drowning when drunk as he tried to embrace the reflection of the moon in the water.

Living in the golden age of Chinese poetry, Li Po is by common consent one of the two greatest poets of the period. His poetry is characterized by a vigor and exuberance that reflect the character of the man. He wrote relatively little in the highly restricted verse form (*lü shih*, "regulated verse") that was popular with the T'ang poets, but seemed to find more congenial the freer forms of rhapsody, ballad, and song. Over 1,000 poems by Li Po survive; of these only a small part has been translated into English.

MENCIUS [měn′shē-əs] (c.372–c.289 B.C.), ancient Chinese philosopher and most important follower of Confucius. The Chinese revere Confucius as the Supreme Sage and Mencius as the Second Sage. Mencius was born in Tsou in what is now Shantung Province, eastern China. His family name was Meng and his personal name, K'o. He studied with a disciple of Tzu Ssu, the well-known philosopher grandson of Confucius, and like Confucius, Mencius spent a number of years traveling among the states and interviewing their rulers. He urged them to forsake the "tyrant way" in favor of the "kingly way" and to conduct their government on the basis of love and commiseration, not by force and profit. At a time historically known as the period of Warring States, Mencius was the most outspoken champion of the cause of the common people and their right to good government.

In his philosophical teaching, Mencius emphasized the inborn character of the basic Confucian concepts of magnanimity and righteousness, and declared that human nature was originally good. He advocated a "commiserating government from a commiserating heart," and placed much importance on the material well-being of the people. Also, he called attention to man's native power of intuition and claimed that in the mind of man one could find the truth and reality of all things. This phase of Mencius' teachings eventually became the basis of Neo-Confucianism, which flourished from the 10th to the 18th century.

Mencius spent his disillusioned old age teaching students and writing a record of his sayings and doings. The *Book of Mencius*, consisting of seven books, was elevated to the ranks of the classics around the year 1000, when it became a part of the *Four Books*.

PO CHÜ-I [bō′ jü′ē′] (772–846), Chinese poet of the T'ang period. He had a successful career in government service, holding responsible positions both at court and in the provinces. During his lifetime he was the most famous living Chinese poet, and his popularity has endured both in China and in Japan. He strove for directness and simplicity in his writing and tried to make his poetry the vehicle for social criticism. His best-known works are two long poems in ballad form, *Ch'ang-hen ko* (Song of Everlasting Remorse), 806, and *P'i-p'a hsing* (Lute Song), 816. Some of his ballads read more like moral tracts than poetry, but his position as one of China's major lyric poets is secure.

SHIH-HUANG-TI [shĭr′hwäng′tē′] (259–210 B.C.), the first Emperor of the Ch'in Dynasty (221–207 B.C.) and architect of the first centralized empire of ancient China. As King of the state of Ch'in (246–221 B.C.) in northwestern China, he conquered six feudal states and established a centralized government to replace the feudal system of the previous Chou Dynasty (1027–256 B.C.). The empire was at first divided into 36 provinces, later into 41, which were

subdivided into prefectures of differing sizes and governed by salaried, appointed officials.

Determined to make the unity of the new empire complete and enduring, Shih-huang-ti was as attentive to changing the people's customs as to eradicating the power of the feudal aristocracy. Under his absolutist reign the old states were suppressed and the Ch'in code was enforced throughout the realm. Differing standards of weight and measurement were abolished and the standards of the Ch'in were substituted. Another important reform, the unification and standardization of Chinese script, made the written language intelligible throughout China.

In addition, all weapons of war not required by the armies were collected, transported to the capital, and melted down, thus decreasing the threat of internal revolt. To form a barrier against the incursion of nomads from the north, Shih-huang-ti linked up the many walls built by former states into a Great Wall running about 1,500 mi. Trunk roads stretched from the capital to the farthest frontiers of the empire and the building of "the marvelous canal" facilitated water transportation from the Yangtze to the Si (West) River.

Inspired by his adviser, Li Ssu, the Emperor injudiciously established unity by suppressing differing modes of thought. His order to burn all books (213 B.C.) except those dealing with medicine, divination, agriculture, and Ch'in history proved an irreparable catastrophe for the Chinese people and resulted in the execution of 460 scholars who defied the decree. Dissatisfaction with the 14-year tyrannical Ch'in rule was expressed in the murder of Shih's son three years after the Emperor's death and by the establishment of the Han Dynasty (202 B.C.–220 A.D.).

SUI [swī] **DYNASTY** (581–618), a short but remarkable Chinese dynasty. It reunited China in 589 A.D. after a period of disunity which began at the end of the Han Dynasty (202 B.C.–220 A.D.). During the reign of its founder, Wen-ti (reigned 581–605), Sui was able to reestablish Chinese power in central Asia, and through adept administration it accumulated much wealth for the national coffers. Soon after Yang-ti (reigned 605–16) was enthroned, he embarked the nation on an ambitious building program, the successful completion of which set the pattern of Chinese national transportation for centuries.

Within a short period of 10 years a network of canals and 1,000 mi. of imperial highways were opened to commercial traffic connecting North and South China. During Yang-ti's reign Sui also established a civil service examination system through which officials of all ranks were selected. But extravagance and three unsuccessful military expeditions to Korea brought financial ruin to the government and poverty to the people. Rebellions caused Yang-ti's assassination and the downfall of the dynasty two years later.

SUNG [sŏong] **DYNASTY,** Chinese imperial house spanning the three centuries (960–1279) in between the Five Dynasties and the Yüan. Sung was actually made up of two periods, the Northern Sung (960–1127) and the Southern Sung (1127–1279). The former had its national capital in Kaifeng and the latter in Hangchow. Chao K'uang-yin, founder of the Northern Sung, came to power amid great political chaos, when North China underwent successive changes of five dynasties and South China was divided into ten small kingdoms. Before his death in 976, however, he conquered all but two states, Wü-yüeh in the South and Northern Han in the North. These were annexed (in 978 and 979 respectively) by his brother and successor, T'ai-tsung. China was then again unified.

In terms of military strength, Sung never matched the Han or the T'ang. Even at the time of founding, Sung faced a threat, first of the Liao (Khitan) from the North and Northeast, and later of the Hsi-hsia (the Tangut Tibetans) from the West. Peace was maintained precariously by an annual Sung tribute to both. The sixteen northern prefectures lost to the Liao and the humiliating vassal treatment were two strong motives for revenge by the Sung. In the Tungusic Jurchen people they found an ideal ally. In 1114 the Jurchen rebelled against the Liao, and the following year adopted Chin as the name of a new dynasty. An agreement was concluded between Sung and Chin to attack the Liao jointly. The Jurchen conquered the Liao in 1125, while the Sung scored little success. Argument between the two led to Chin's southward advances, which resulted in the capture of Kaifeng in 1126.

Meanwhile, a scion of the Sung Dynasty continued the struggle in the face of Chin invasion, which reached as far south as Hangchow and Ningpo. The sudden death of the Chin emperor, coupled with local topography unfavorable to their cavalry, induced the Chin to withdraw to the north. In 1135 the Southern Sung established the national capital in Hangchow. Sporadic battles between the Sung and Chin followed, but in 1141 peace was concluded. Sung agreed to pay a yearly tribute under the name of a vassal.

Unmindful of the earlier mistake by the Northern Sung of raising the Chin against the Liao, the Southern Sung

"Bare Willows and Distant Mountains" (12th-13th century) by Ma Yüan, a painter of the Sung Dynasty. (MUSEUM OF FINE ARTS, BOSTON)

repeated the error by joining the Mongols against the Chin. As a result, the Mongols conquered the Chin in 1234, captured Hangchow in 1276, and destroyed the last organized Sung resistance in 1279.

The lack of military prowess, however, was more than compensated by the prosperity during the Sung period of fine arts, literature, philosophy, and general technology. The population increased sharply, and metropolitan cities grew up as commercial centers, particularly under the Southern Sung in the lower Yangtze valley, where economic development was advanced. Large-scale commerce with nations of the South China Sea also increased, resulting in an unusual prosperity for such coastal cities as Chüanchow and Canton. The tea and cotton industry expanded, and the introduction of a new species of rice greatly increased rice production in the south. Improved porcelain was exported to Oriental as well as Occidental nations in large quantities. With the expansion of trade came greater demands for currency, both hard coinage and paper money, which the Sung provided. Richer and easier life, in turn, demanded the diversification of literary works, resulting in the creation and refinement of such new genres as *tz'u* poetry, professional storytelling, and colloquial drama. Greater demand for books stimulated the printing industry, one product of which was the "Sung edition," highly prized then as now. Similarly, the availability of fine silk increased both the durability and the popularity of Chinese paintings.

Sung also produced many famous scholars, among them Chu Hsi (1130–1200), the most important Neo-Confucian philosopher, Wang An-shih (1201–1086), a renowned man of letters and fearless social reformer, and Ou-yang Hsiu (1007–1072), an eminent statesman-scholar. The group of distinguished Sung scholars also included Ssu-ma Kuang (1018–1081), once a prime minister and the author of the first general history of China, and Su Shih (1036–1101), a versatile poet, essayist, painter, and calligrapher. Differences between scholarly groups, however, deepened partisan struggles, which ultimately weakened the political and military system of the Sung.

SU SHIH [soo' shih'], pseudonym of Su Tung-p'o (1036–1101), Chinese poet and statesman. A native of Ssuchuan, he was the son of Su Hsün and the brother of Su Che, both outstanding prose writers of the Sung Dynasty. His political career alternated between periods of favor and disgrace. Because he belonged to the conservative party that opposed the reforms and innovations proposed by Wang An-shih, Su Shih was demoted to undesirable provincial posts. Later he returned to favor and became Governor of Hangchow. A prolific writer, Su Shih ranks first among the poets of the Sung Dynasty, particularly in the lyric (*shih*). He also was a master of prose, writing outstanding essays and criticism, and was one of the greatest calligraphers of the Sung period.

T'AI-TSUNG [tī'dzoong'], posthumous title of Li Shih-min (601–49), second Emperor (reigned 627–49) of the T'ang Dynasty (618–907) of China. Largely responsible for the establishment of the T'ang, T'ai-tsung was enthroned as

Emperor when his father, Li Yüan, abdicated. Even before his installation T'ai-tsung had proceded to lay the foundation for a new political and social order which inaugurated one of the most powerful and prosperous eras of Chinese history. During his reign, known as the Chenkuan period, Chinese rule was extended west to Turkestan, north to Mongolia as far north as Lake Baikal, east to Manchuria, and south to Annam. Thus direct contact with Iran and India was achieved. Under him even secluded Tibet was brought under Chinese sovereignty. T'ai-tsung became known as the "Heavenly Khan" to the Turkish peoples and he reigned splendidly as both Emperor and Khan.

Being one of the most enlightened Chinese rulers, T'ai-tsung encouraged the study of Confucian classics. A complete commentary on the Five Classics was published under his decree. More than 200,000 books were collected in the Royal Academy. A new examination system without discrimination on the basis of social esteem or wealth was inaugurated to enable any qualified Chinese to serve in the government.

During his reign the Chinese people enjoyed greater freedom of worship and of speech. The capital, Changan, became a metropolitan city where foreign students of different tongues and foreign missionaries of various faiths lived side by side. Buddhists, Zoroastrians, Muslims, Nestorians, Manichaeans, and the native Taoists had their churches or temples built throughout the country.

One of T'ai-tsung's most admirable qualities was his ability to accept criticism. One of his favored ministers, Wei Cheng, was once very critical of his private life. The Emperor had Wei's criticism recorded on a wall screen as a personal reminder. His 22-year reign brought peace, unity, and prosperity to China and fostered the great art and the literary achievements of the T'ang period.

T'ANG [täng] **DYNASTY** (618–907), ruling house of China. Generally regarded as the most glorious of all Chinese dynasties, it was founded by Li Yüan, a general stationed in Shansi during the chaotic years of the Sui. He was assisted in his many military campaigns and political maneuvers by his able son, Li Shih-min (better known as T'ai-tsung) who succeeded him after liquidating his own brothers. The reigns of T'ai-tsung (627–49), and Hsüan-tsung (713–56) are traditionally considered the golden periods of the T'ang, whose rule extended from North Korea to North Vietnam and westward beyond the Pamirs. To exercise effective control over distant kingdoms, the T'ang created the system of four administrative protectorates, each located in a strategic area.

Administratively, the T'ang maintained and further strengthened the three basic divisions of government, the imperial secretariat, the imperial chancellery, and the secretariat of state affairs. Under the last-named were the six boards: personnel, revenues, rites, war, justice, and public works. In addition, there was the board of censors, which served as the "eyes and ears" of the emperor. Improved competitive examinations served to recruit educated officials. The government structure, with its many distinctive features, was faithfully copied by adjoining states, as it also was by other Chinese dynasties in the next 13 centuries.

Gunpowder and block-printing came into being during the T'ang. Glazed ceramic products became articles of lasting aesthetic value. The increase in maritime trade led to improvements in the shipbuilding industry, as well as the use of the magnetic compass.

During the T'ang period, Buddhism began to be assimilated into Chinese life, resulting in the establishment and popularization of many sects. Chinese Buddhist monks, such as Hsüan-tsang and I-ching, even took long and tedious pilgrimages to India by land or sea. The prosperity of Buddhism in China, in turn, molded new trends in architecture, sculpture, and portrait painting.

In the field of literature, the T'ang achievements were no less impressive. Poetry in its five-character and seven-character forms, written in either "broken-off" or "regulated" style, reached maturity, as amply demonstrated in the works of Li Po (701–62), Tu Fu (712–70), Po Chü-i (772–846), and many others. Tz'u poetry also made its debut in the closing years of the T'ang. As prose and historical writers, Liu Chih-chi (661–721), Han Yü (768–824), and Liu Tsung-yüan (773–819) are literary immortals.

The rebellion of An Lu-shan (755), who was responsible for the capture and devastation of Changan, is interpreted as the turning point of T'ang history, but other events around the same time contributed to the decline. In 751 the Nan-chao of Yunnan defeated the T'ang forces, and in the same year the Arabs won a military victory over a T'ang general in Central Asia, signifying the collapse of the Chinese hegemony in that region. The monopoly of power by regional commanders inevitably led to warlordism, and the factionalism in government as well as the ever-present conspiracy between bureaucrats and eunuchs further shattered the solidarity of the political system. The deterioration of the T'ang eventually led to the complete breakup of the nation into divided kingdoms and contending regimes of the ensuing period of the Five Dynasties and Ten Kingdoms.

TAOISM [dou'ĭz-əm, tou'ĭz-əm], system of Chinese philosophy and religion.

Philosophy. Philosophical Taoism is known as the system of the hermit philosophers, and it can best be described as a philosophy of "live and let live." Lao-tzu (c.575–c.485 B.C.) is traditionally regarded as its founder, and Chuang-tzu (c.369–c.286 B.C.) its chief exponent. The Tao Te Ching (attributed to Lao-tzu) and the Chuang-tzu (by Chuang-tzu) are its basic texts. The central theme of this system of thought is the "Tao." Not unlike the English word "way," which is often used to translate it, Tao means literally "the path" or "the road," but in the philosophical context it has come to signify the basic principle that pervades man and the universe. Thus the Tao is eternal and absolute, infinite and immutable. Hence Taoism expounds the doctrine of inaction, or wu-wei. "The Tao does nothing and yet there is nothing left undone," says the Tao Te Ching. The final goal of this system of naturalistic mysticism is the complete union and identity of the individual with the whole of nature. In this mundane world everything is relative, whereas only in the world of Tao is there absolute freedom and complete equality.

Religion. The beginnings of Taoism as a religion go

back to the latter half of the 2d century A.D. Amidst widespread political and social unrest a scholar named Chang Ling became the leader of a fast-growing politico-religious community. Eventually the sect became known as the Taoist religion, and the leadership of the religion remained in the Chang family until 1927. The Taoist religion claimed Lao-tzu as its founder, absorbed the folk religion of nature worship, and borrowed heavily from Buddhism. For example, it is not always easy to tell a Taoist temple from a Buddhist temple. A notable feature of the Taoist religion is its stress on various rituals which would result in long life. Taoism is ranked with Confucianism and Buddhism as one of the three "religions" of China.

On the whole, Taoism as a religion is popular only among the uneducated. But as a system of philosophy and a way of life, Taoism has challenged and attracted the best of Chinese minds throughout the ages. The importance of Taoism is only second to Confucianism in setting the pattern for Chinese life and culture. The stamp of its charm of serenity and detachment is unmistakable in such expressions as Chinese landscape painting, nature poetry, and the development of the branch of Buddhism now internationally known as Zen.

THREE KINGDOMS, THE (221–65), name of a Chinese dynastic period linking the Eastern (Later) Han and the Western Chin. The Three Kingdoms comprised the Wei in the Yellow River valley, the Shu Han on the central and upper Yangtze, and Wu on the lower Yangtze. The foundation of the Wei was laid by Ts'ao Ts'ao, a northern warlord. But it was his son, Ts'ao P'ei, who proclaimed himself first emperor of the new dynasty in 220 A.D., the year of his father's death. Liu Pei, a distant scion of the imperial house of Han, took over the province Shu in 215 and became the first emperor of Shu Han in 221, one year after the founding of Wei. Sun Ch'üan, the founder of Wu, enthroned himself in 222. Despite unceasing warfare between the three, Shu Han and Wu often were close allies dealing jointly with the more powerful Wei.

The period lacked the glamor and military prowess of the preceeding Han. However, each of the Three Kingdoms was noted for its territorial expansion. Wei made a northeasterly thrust into Manchuria and Korea. Shu Han conquered some aboriginal tribes in the southwest, while Wu won control over mountaineers within its border and exercised authority over Vietnam. A steady process of colonization of the Yangtze valley and a simultaneous southwestward movement were thus under way. In the field of traditional scholarship, the period was not as outstanding as the Han either. But there were a great number of men of letters, well remembered in later periods for their achievements. This group included the Ts'ao brothers, P'ei (188–226) and Chih (192–232).

Shu Han was the first of the Three Kingdoms to fall. It was conquered by the Wei in 263. Two years later, however, Wei was usurped by Ssu-ma Yen, founder of the succeeding Western Chin Dynasty. Wu was the last to vanish, in 280, again absorbed by the Western Chin.

TU FU [tōō'fōō'] (712–70), Chinese poet of the T'ang Dynasty. Having failed in 736 to pass the examinations for a governmental position, he nevertheless was appointed to a nominal literary post in 755. In the course of the An Lu-shan rebellion he was captured by rebels, but he escaped with his family to the imperial court. An unsuccessful courtier, he was demoted and then served in a minor provincial office until his resignation in 759. His last years were spent in poverty and wandering. Tu Fu's poems, of which more than 1,400 survive, exhibit metrical dexterity, richness of texture, and a note of personal sincerity that have established him as one of China's greatest poets.

WANG WEI [wäng' wā'] (699–759), Chinese poet of the T'ang Dynasty. He occupied a position in the imperial court until his capture during the An Lu-shan rebellion, when he was forced to serve under the rebel government. He is best known as a pastoral poet who finds in natural scenery a serenity peculiarly Buddhist. He was also a painter and musician. Toward the end of his life he retired to a Buddhist monastery.

WU [wōō] (625–705), Empress of China (690–705), only female sovereign of her nation. Of humble origin, she was taken into Emperor T'ang Tai-tsung's harem at the age of 12 and was retired into a Buddhist nunnery at his death in 649. By a series of intrigues, including the murder of her own baby, she forced Emperor Tang Kao-tsung to banish his wife. He then made her Empress, and was dominated by her during the latter part of his reign. After his death in 684, she promptly displaced the crown prince. Six years later she changed the dynastic title from T'ang to Chou and styled herself as Empress God Almighty. An arrogant and overbearing woman, she ruled China with a firm hand, securing peace at home and overawing the frontier tribes. She later fell under the influence of court favorites. Shortly before her death, she abdicated in favor of the crown prince.

WU-TI [wōō'tē] (156–87 B.C.), the most dynamic and militant emperor of the Chinese Han Dynasty. During his long reign (141–87 B.C.), China underwent a change from dynastic consolidation to territorial expansion. The first steppe empire founded by the Hsiung-nu of the Turkish language group in the third century B.C., had made deep inroads into northern China. The early Han emperors were much too preoccupied with other problems to deal with the Hsiung-nu. Wu-ti undertook a series of long-drawn-out battles, which finally brought them into subjugation. In the course of these campaigns the Chinese army reached as far as the Gobi desert and established Chinese authority in Central Asia, through which the "silk route" stretched to the Roman Empire. Because of the many costly campaigns, public works, and expanded bureaucracy, Han China approached exhaustion toward the end of Wu-ti's reign. No succeeding Han emperor was able to recapture his military brilliance and grandeur.

EGYPTIAN CIVILIZATION

ARCHITECTURE

EGYPTIAN ARCHITECTURE was simple in structure and material. The arch, though known and used in brick, was not favored by the Egyptians, who supported their roofs and doorways with posts and lintels. Materials used included wood, brick, and stone; mud was used as a mortar for brick, and a mixture of gypsum and sand for stone masonry. In the latter case the mortar served, not as a binding material, but as a lubricant in moving heavy blocks, and sheer mass was generally all that held a building together.

Houses. The house was the beginning of Egyptian architecture. The temple was the house of god; the tomb was man's eternal house. The temple and tomb were more important and generally built of stone, whereas the house for the living man was of brick and wood.

Most of what is known of Egyptian houses is derived from the city of Tell el-Amarna built during the Empire, or New Kingdom (1573–c.1085 B.C.). There the house stood in a courtyard and had a flat roof and small windows. A central living room was surrounded by an open-sided loggia and suites of rooms for masters, wives, and guests. In the courtyard also were a garden with a household shrine and a pool, kitchens, stables, storebins, and a well.

In earlier periods this style of house was often provided with a colonnaded portico overlooking the court. This portico was derived from an open-fronted tent house, the columns being derived from the tent posts. Several other types of one-room houses were also used in the earliest eras: round houses of mud and wattle, rectangular houses of mud brick or latticework with flat roofs, and wood-frame houses with low vaulted roofs. Many features of later temples, shrines, and even coffins were derived from these primitive house forms. The Egyptians were conservative and the shapes of their buildings retained in stylized form architectural elements that had long ceased to be used.

Town houses of three or four stories were built from the Middle Kingdom (1991–c.1778 B.C.) onward. Kitchens,

The Metropolitan Museum of Art

Reconstruction of the temples of King Mentuhotep (11th Dynasty) and Queen Hatshepsut (18th Dynasty) at Deir el-Bahri. The queen's temple (*foreground*) was modeled on the temple of Mentuhotep (with pyramid roof).

living rooms, and bedrooms were on the ground, second, and third floors respectively, and the flat roof was used as extra sleeping space or for storebins.

Artisans constructing the royal tombs were provided with barracks near the Great Pyramid at Giza and with walled villages at Kahun during the Middle Kingdom, and at Deir el-Medina and Tell el-Amarna during the New Kingdom. The houses were simple three- or four-room buildings laid out in rows along narrow streets, but more elaborate houses were provided for officials and overseers. Palaces differed from the better-class houses only in size and luxury.

Tombs. Abundant evidence of tomb architecture has survived from all periods. The Egyptians believed that the body must be preserved so that the soul could return to it in afterlife. The body was therefore mummified, and food and other offerings were deposited in the tomb both during and after the funeral. The tomb thus required storage chambers and an offering chapel in addition to the burial chamber. The offerings attracted tomb robbers, and in time the tomb was made larger and stronger to thwart them.

The tomb began as a mere pit in the ground. As the pit became larger and deeper it was found necessary to line the sides with mud brick. As the offerings increased in quantity and variety, the pit was divided by crosswalls into an increasing number of separate chambers. The excavated material formed a mound on the surface, and this was enlarged and made rectangular with mud brick. Offerings after the funeral were at first simply placed on the ground, but soon a special niche was built to receive them. This niche became larger and more elaborate until it formed a chamber built into the superstructure.

As technology advanced, the animal skins and basketry that protected the earliest burials were replaced by rectangular coffins in the shape of houses, and the simple pit became a brick tomb. Finally, by the beginning of the Old Kingdom (c.2780–c.2254 B.C.), Egyptian craftsmen had the skill and tools to make stone masonry sufficiently economical for the construction of tombs and temples.

The first all-stone building was the Step Pyramid of King Zoser, a notable King of the 3d Dynasty (c.2780–c.2680 B.C.), at Sakkara. This elaborate complex of buildings consisted of the pyramid tomb itself, plus its funerary temple and a series of special shrines for the royal ceremony held every few years for the renewing of the king's power. This is the earliest example of free-standing masonry with regular courses and fine joints, lintels and roofing blocks, decorative attached columns and false arches, all of stone. The uncertainty of the architect in his material is reflected by the employment of small-size blocks, by the columns not being free-standing, and by the constant use of decorative and structural features derived from earlier brick and wood forms.

Within four generations, by the beginning of the 4th Dynasty (c.2680–c.2565 B.C.), Egyptian stone masonry had reached its apex. Monolithic blocks were used—some weighing up to 30 tons. The casing blocks of the Great Pyramid of Khufu (Cheops) at Giza show amazingly close joints of a ten-thousandth of an inch. Even private tombs were of stone, grouped around the pyramid tombs of the Pharaohs, and consisting of a nearly solid rectangular superstructure, or mastaba, over a burial shaft. The chambers in the mastaba were decorated with painted relief scenes of daily life and the preparation and presentation of offerings. One wall in the offering chamber was in the form of a false door through which the dead man could pass to receive these offerings.

Remains of the entrance hall to the funerary temple of King Zoser, near the Step Pyramid at Sakkara.

Marburg—Art Reference Bureau

Pillars with papyrus (*background*) and lotus motifs in the 18th Dynasty temple of Amon at Karnak.

Court built by Rameses II (13th century B.C.) in the temple of Luxor. The 80-ft.-high obelisk is covered with hieroglyphs.

After the Old Kingdom, tombs were generally cut into the cliffs, with a concealed burial chamber, small storage chambers, and a pillared offering chamber decorated with wall paintings. In the New Kingdom, rock-cut tombs were built at Thebes, the new capital, for both royal and private burials. Many private tombs had a small brick pyramid over the entrance; others had open forecourts with decorated façades cut in the rock face. However, royal tombs with no superstructure were hidden away in some remote valley to avoid attracting robbers. The private tombs were decorated with painted scenes of daily life, but the royal tombs had religious scenes.

Temples. Egyptian architectural style is best seen in the temples. Funerary temples were a development of the offering niche in the tomb. The Old Kingdom examples, attached to the pyramids, generally had an open court with statues of the King, one or two pillared halls, and a sanctuary with a cult statue of the King and a false door. Mentuhotep I of the 11th Dynasty (c.2134–1991 B.C.) had a rock-cut tomb and a temple in the form of a dummy pyramid surrounded by a colonnade built on a terrace in front of the cliffs at Deir el-Bahri in Western Thebes.

In the New Kingdom, when royal tombs were hidden away in the Valley of the Kings, the funerary temples were built separately along the edge of the desert. That of Queen Hatshepsut at Deir el-Bahri took as its prototype the nearby terraced temple of Mentuhotep. A processional way led from a valley temple, where the mummifi-

cation took place, along a causeway to a walled forecourt, and up ramps to two terraces fronted by colonnades. On the upper terrace were the sanctuary, cut into the cliff face, an open colonnaded court, and subsidiary shrines. Sphinxes and statues of the Queen lined the way and stood in the court and sanctuary.

The cult temple housed the statue of the god, to whose daily worship and service the temple was devoted. The earliest probably consisted merely of a covered sanctuary and an open forecourt. Few traces remain until the New Kingdom. The Temple of Khons at Karnak, built by Rameses III, may be regarded as a typical temple. It is free of the usual additions and alterations of later Kings, and is thus simple in plan. A processional way lined by sphinxes leads to the pylon, a gateway flanked by two large rectangular towers. The pylon has walls that are battered, that is, they slant back slightly. They are surmounted by a concave cavetto cornice and have round torus moldings on the corners. Its form is derived from that of a primitive wall made of bound reeds that was strengthened by bundles at the corners, allowing the tops of the reeds to wave free. Behind the pylon is an open forecourt surrounded by a colonnade with capitals in the shape of papyrus buds. Next is the pillared hypostyle hall with four pairs of columns. The two center pairs have papyrus-head capitals and are higher than the outer two pairs, which have papyrus-bud capitals. This difference in height permits the hall to be lit by clerestory grill windows.

Model of the hypostyle hall in the temple of Amon at Karnak. The roof is supported by 134 columns arranged in 16 rows. The central columns are 69 ft. high and are topped by capitals 11 ft. high.

Beyond the hypostyle hall is the sanctuary, in this case open at both ends and surrounded by an ambulatory. Here rested the boat shrine containing the figure of the god. The sanctuaries in other temples sometimes had only one door and housed a small shrine containing the divine statue.

Statues of the King usually stood in the forecourt of the temple and before the pylon, in the latter case often of colossal size. A pair of monolithic stone pillars, or obelisks, stood on either side of the gateway, and tall flag staffs were fastened in grooves in front of the pylon.

The temple of Rameses II at Abu Simbel is of this type, but instead of being free-standing it is entirely carved from the solid rock of a cliff face. The great Temple of Amon at Karnak has all these features repeated several times by different kings, who added to the work of their predecessors.

A special type of temple known as the peripteral temple, consisting of a small central chamber open at both ends and surrounded by a colonnade, was used principally as a resting house for the statue of the god during religious processions.

Most Egyptian temples have been partly or completely destroyed by people seeking building material or treasure, and many were used by the Christian Egyptians, or Copts, as churches. Much damage to reliefs is due to the religious fervor of the Copts against the earlier pagan religion and to the plundering of modern Egyptians.

ART

During a period of over 3,000 years, Egyptian art changed remarkably little in style. The Egyptians were a conservative people, living in a land of few natural features, and virtually isolated from their neighbors. Life was simple and constant, following a regular rhythm of birth, life, death, and rebirth in step with the yearly inundation of the Nile.

Statues, reliefs—either incised or standing out slightly from the ground and originally painted—and paintings were created mainly to satisfy religious needs. A statue was one guarantee of immortality, because it could house a man's spirit after death if the embalmed body were destroyed. It did not have to be an exact representation, as the name of the man was inscribed on it for identification. Therefore, most statues were idealized portraits showing their subjects as the types of men they were in their prime. A relief or painting was capable of perpetuating the actions or objects depicted. Either one could be used in a tomb to supply the man with provisions and ensure the continuance of his normal life after death, or in a temple to assist in the divine ritual.

Archaic Period and Old Kingdom. By the 1st Dynasty (c.3000–c.2980 B.C.), the relief style had developed, as in the slate palette of King Narmer (Egyptian Museum, Cairo). The decorated area is divided into registers, within each of which there is a balance of mass and movement.

Front and back views of the slate palette of King (Narmer) Menes, a ruler of Egypt during the 1st Dynasty.

In private tombs reliefs were at first in the form of steles, or panels of limestone, with a scene showing the deceased seated before an offering table piled high with food and other gifts. Later the walls of the offering chamber were decorated with additional scenes showing the preparation of these gifts—the butchering of the meat, growing and harvesting of the grain and grapes, and so forth—and their presentation by servants and priests. As time passed, scenes from the life of the dead man were added—hunting, playing games, or viewing cattle—and later still, scenes of the funeral.

In the temples attached to the royal pyramids and in the causeways leading to them similar scenes were represented along with religious scenes of the King worshiping various gods. The chambers of the pyramids were not decorated until the end of the 5th Dynasty (c.2565–c.2420 B.C.), and then only with inscriptions.

A 4th Dynasty statuary group found at Giza depicts King Mycerinus (*right*) with the seated goddess Hathor and a local deity.

Museum of Fine Arts, Boston

The standing figures stay on the base line and are shown in typical Egyptian manner—all of the body is in profile except the shoulders and eye, which are full face. The most important figure in the scene, the King, is shown much larger than the rest, and there is the typical visual symbolism of the hawk handing over the Delta people to the King. A close relation between the scene and the written word creates the impression that the figures are really only enlarged hieroglyphs to be read as part of the inscription.

By the end of the 2d Dynasty (c.2780 B.C.), statuary had also developed along typical Egyptian style and conventions. The 2d Dynasty slate statue of King Khasekhem seated on a throne (Egyptian Museum, Cairo) and the 3d Dynasty (c.2780–c.2680 B.C.) standing statues of Sepa and his wife Neset (Louvre, Paris) show the frontality common to Egyptian, Mesopotamian, primitive Greek, and other preclassic styles. The figure faces directly to the front and the limbs are held close to the body. There is little undercutting, and where limbs protrude they are connected together or to a back pillar with bridges of stone for strength. The eyes, the eyebrows, and the anatomy of the body and limbs are treated in a conventional instead of naturalistic manner—for example, Sepa's two staffs are held in unnatural positions so that the sculptor could carve them in relief against the body instead of in the round. The impression given is of solidity and endurance, which is exactly what the Egyptians sought.

Egyptian tempera painting was at first generally employed on reliefs, but it early developed as a separate art form. The tomb of Atet in Medum, dating from the beginning of the 4th Dynasty (c.2680–c.2565 B.C.), contained painted scenes of farming, hunting, and the like, among which was the famous panel showing geese (Egyptian Museum, Cairo). In technique, style, and subject matter these paintings are in the finest Egyptian tradition and use a wide palette of colors—black, white, gray, brown, yellow, red, orange, and green.

Fresco in 18th-Dynasty King Tutankhamen's tomb portrays him embracing Osiris, god of the dead. At right, Tutankhamen is shown with Nut, goddess of the sky.

Red granite statue of the 18th-Dynasty Queen Hatshepsut, found at Deir el-Bahri.

In private tombs statues depicting the buried man, sometimes accompanied by his wife and family, were generally hidden away for safety in an enclosed chamber, called the serdab, close to the offering chamber. Special portrait heads of the deceased were carved during the 4th Dynasty. These are known as reserve heads and served in case all other representations of the deceased were destroyed. They are among the few true portraits in Egyptian art.

Royal statues stood in the funerary temples and include portraits of the King alone or with his consort, for example, the statue of Mycerinus and his Queen (Museum of Fine Arts, Boston), and groups showing the King accompanied by one or two deities under whose patronage he ruled. An example of the latter, also in Boston, is the group depicting Mycerinus with the goddess Hathor and another local goddess. These statues display a greater interest in anatomy and musculature.

In the Old Kingdom (c.2780–c.2254 B.C.) works of art were created in the royal workshops near the capital of Memphis. They have been found in the tombs and temples of Giza, Sakkara, Medum, and Abu Sir. Toward the end of the period a livelier, more naturalistic style began to develop. At the end of the Old Kingdom, when royal power waned and Egypt began to split up into separate provinces, several local art styles developed—at Aswan on the southern frontier, at Dendera and nearby Coptos, and at Thebes. These styles are more powerful, more formal, and at first cruder and less sophisticated than the northern Memphite style, which continued.

Middle and New Kingdoms. Though most Middle King-

dom (1991–c.1778 B.C.) relief was in the Memphite tradition, the statuary stayed more formal and abstract. Statues of the Kings, as those of Senusret III, have a stern, forceful expression, a broad face, high cheekbones, and thick lips. Statues of nonroyal personages also tended to follow this style of portrait, were smaller than in the Old Kingdom, and carved in hard stones instead of limestone.

The conquest of Egypt by the Hyksos, ending the Middle Kingdom, and the creation of the Empire, or New Kingdom (1573–c.1085 B.C.), brought a new outlook to Egypt. The country became wealthy from foreign tribute and was in closer contact than ever before with its neighbors in western Asia, Crete, and Nubia. The army became professional, the priesthood, which was organized under the leadership of the priests of the god Amon, grew wealthy, and a bureaucracy developed.

Art became extremely varied in character—sometimes feminine and luxurious or monumental and overpowering, sometimes spiritual and emotional or traditional and formal. Tremendous building programs were undertaken, especially in Thebes, the new capital, where many funerary temples, cult temples, and palaces were built. Hundreds of statues were also created for these temples. The funerary temple of Hatshepsut at Deir el-Bahri contained many sphinxes and standing, kneeling, and sitting statues of the queen, a selection of which can be seen in the Metropolitan Museum of Art in New York.

The rockcut tombs at Thebes were decorated with paintings rather than reliefs, and most of the finest Egyptian paintings came from these 18th- (1573–c.1349 B.C.) and 19th-Dynasty (c.1349–c.1197 B.C.) tombs. In the pri-

Annan Photo Features

Bas-relief from the temple of Hathor at Dendera, built in the Ptolemaic Period (332–30 B.C.). Hathor, the goddess of love, mirth, and social joy, is shown at center left.

The most famous of all Egyptian portraits is of Queen Nefertiti, carved about 1370 B.C.

Marburg—Art Reference Bureau

vate tombs the artists were under less formal restraint and developed a freer, livelier, and even humorous style.

After the New Kingdom Egyptian traditions began to fall into decay, being replaced by foreign, especially Greek, modes. There were still brief periods when, by consciously imitating the past, the artists created masterpieces in the pure Egyptian style, but soon Hellenistic and later Muslim traditions prevailed.

Sculpture. With the rise of great civilizations in ancient Egypt, Mesopotamia, and the Aegean area (4000–500 B.C.), sculpture developed rapidly to serve religion and glorify godlike kings. Although artists learned to carve human and animal forms in skilled techniques with increasing fidelity to nature, true naturalism was thwarted by their strange disregard of three-dimensional space. This led sculptors to ignore its action in changing the appearance of objects seen at different distances. A sort of spatial blindness therefore hampered all early artists, binding them with three rigid conventions—the so-called "laws" of frontality, fractional rendering, and vertical perspective.

The "law" of frontality required every figure carved in the round to be posed bolt upright and facing front. The "law" of fractional rendering demanded that all figures in painting or bas-relief be formed of parts related in an unnatural manner. Each part was shown in its most easily recognized shape: feet and legs in profile, torso and arms from the front, head and face in profile, the eye in frontal view. The "law" of vertical perspective controlled scenes with many figures. It caused groups of people and objects, supposedly one behind another in depth, to be shown one above the other in flat, horizontal rows. Fractional rendering and vertical perspective imposed on all such compositions a characteristically flat, rectangular design.

EGYPT. Portrait sculpture originated in Egypt because of the belief that images of the dead aided the soul's survival. Outstanding examples from the Old Kingdom (c.2780–c.2254 B.C.) include the standing "Sheikh el-Beled," of wood, and the enthroned "King Khafre," of diorite (both, Egyptian Museum, Cairo). Famous New Kingdom portraits (1573–c.1085 B.C.) are the beautiful polychrome "Queen Nefertiti" (Staatliche Museum, Berlin) and the colossal rock-cut figures of Rameses II at Abu Simbel. Temple walls were richly adorned with reliefs of gods and worshiping kings (Temple of Seti I, Abydos), and tomb-chapel walls were spread with colorful scenes of every sort of activity.

DANCE

Six thousand years ago the Egyptians honored such gods as Hathor, Isis, and Apis with dancing. Although the Egyptian word *hbj* means both "dancing" and "to be joyful," there were mourning dances for the dead which date back to 5000 B.C. Remnants of this ceremonial are known to have survived as late as 1880 B.C. The movements were austere and mystic: the long strides of the dancers were meant to overstep death and win eternal life for the deceased.

There were many other dance-ceremonials: a folk dance of the wine press, performed 4,000 years ago; the death and resurrection of the god Osiris in the dance-play festivals at Abydos (in the Middle Kingdom during the 19th century B.C.); mimed dances, such as the feminine trio of "The Wind" dance (shown on a wall painting of the Middle Kingdom, 12th Dynasty, c.1900 B.C.); and the astral circle dances of whirling priests or women (still in existence today as the triple-circle whirling dervish dance of the Middle East).

EGYPTIAN HISTORY

The aristocracy had for a long time maintained a class of professional dancers; as a result, weather-charm, birth-magic, and other ritual dances became "theater." Dancers were imported; Pygmies especially were prized. By about 1500 B.C. Asian *bayaderes* had brought a new concept of feminine dance into Egypt. The long stride, the high kick, the back-bend disappeared, and the "speaking hands" (hand gestures) with quiet feet, typical of Asia, took their place.

During the centuries of Arab domination in Egypt, the broad movements and angular lines of the ancients gave place to the plastic curves of Arabia. The convulsive abdominal dance, once an austere ritual of birth, became a vehicle of sexual excitement. This *danse du ventre* (belly dance) is called by the Arabs *mesri*, a word which also means "Egyptian." It is believed that the Gaditans performed the *mesri* in ancient Rome. Toward the end of the 19th century it was believed that certain of the ancient Egyptian ritual dances still existed (for example, among the almes of Isna).

The dancing seen in Cairo, Port Said, and Alexandria today is almost purely Arabic. The feet stay close to the ground, the body moves sensuously, and the hands and face are highly expressive and generally pantomimic. There are some acrobatic movements, such as the back-bend from the knees. In the nonimitative dances, *chinchines* (finger-cymbals) are often used. Dances are improvised on the spur of the moment, and the watchers throw money to the performers.

HISTORY

In ancient times Egypt was called *To-meri* (Gr. Timuris) and *Kemet*, "the Black Land." The name "Egypt" itself was never used by the Egyptians, being derived from *Aigyptos*, the Greek form of *Hut-ka-Ptah*, an ancient name of Memphis. Herodotus' description of Egypt as "the gift of the Nile" accurately characterizes the country's total dependence on the great river which both formed it and nourished it and without which Egyptian civilization would not have come into being. The narrow alluvial strip along the banks of the Nile, averaging only about 2–3 mi. in width, extending 600 mi. from the Mediterranean to the First Cataract, and totaling approximately 12,000 sq. mi., in fact comprised the entirety of Egypt in earliest antiquity. By Roman times, it was made to support a population of 6,000,000. Egypt's borders were gradually pushed southward to the Fourth Cataract in Ethiopia and eastward from Sinai to the Euphrates River, although the oases of the western desert were not controlled or exploited until relatively late in Egyptian history.

Egypt's resources included limestone, sandstone, granite, gold, copper, and turquoise, but its principal wealth was the rich black silt deposited annually by the Nile, and the fertile acreage of the multibranched Delta region in the north. Egypt's confinement to a long, attenuated valley and the consequent necessity of controlling the unruly and inconstant river therefore to a remarkable degree determined the course of its history and shaped its technical and cultural development. Government itself prob-

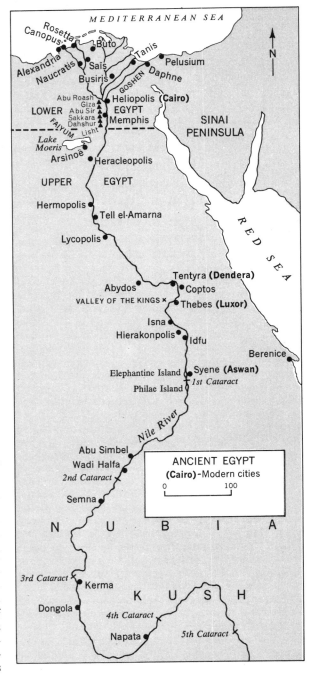

ably originated in the need for co-operation demanded by the gigantic task of organizing the use of floodwaters. The advantages to be gained from the effective administration of large areas for the purposes of irrigation must have early encouraged centralization.

Chronology and Historical Periods. The ancient Egyptians did not use any system of era dating, nor have any complete outlines of their ancient history survived. The earliest method of dating was by naming a year after some important event, a method succeeded in the 2d Dynasty by reckoning according to the biennial cattle census. It was not until after the 6th Dynasty that dating by the regnal years of individual Kings was developed. The modern system of dynasties is due to Manetho (3d century B.C.), an Egyptian priest who lived during the reigns of Ptolemy I and II, and wrote a history of Egypt in Greek. Only a summary of this work and some fragments have survived, but, although his earlier dates are too high, his division into 31 dynasties is approximately correct and his work is a convenient and valuable aid. All those sources, however, would not have permitted the drawing up of a reliable chronology if there had not also been astronomical data. The Egyptian civil year of 365 days was supposed to begin on the traditional day of the rising of the Nile (July 19, Julian calendar), which was also the day of the heliacal rising of Sothis (the Dog Star, Sirius). The discrepancy of approximately a quarter of a day between the Egyptian civil year and the true year resulted in a cycle of 1,456 years before the two years, if not corrected, would coincide again: this is the Sothic Cycle. Egyptian references to the rising of Sothis enable us to fix certain events within a margin of four years: thus the beginning of the 12th Dynasty can be fixed at 1991 B.C., that of the 18th at 1573 B.C., and dead reckoning carries the beginning of the 11th Dynasty to about 2133 B.C. All earlier dates are subject to an increasing degree of uncertainty and modern estimates of the 1st Dynasty vary between 3400 B.C. and 2850 B.C. It is probable that 3000 B.C., or very slightly later, may ultimately prove the more realistic date.

The duration of the Predynastic Period cannot be accurately estimated, and no dates at all can be assigned to the different cultures. Even the new carbon-14 method of dating is of very limited use. For the Upper Egyptian series of cultures an ingenious system of Sequence Dates (S.D.) has been evolved in which each date represents a step in a cultural sequence, but not a date in terms of our era. According to this system, S.D. 64 is roughly contemporary with the beginning of the 1st Dynasty. It is highly improbable that any of the Predynastic cultures could have been permanently settled on the floor of the Nile Valley before 5000–4500 B.C.

As a matter of convenience the history of Egypt is now usually divided into a number of periods: Predynastic (before 3000 B.C.); Archaic, or Protodynastic (1st and 2d Dynasties, c.3000–2780 B.C.); Old Kingdom (3d to 6th Dynasties, c.2780–2254 B.C.); First Intermediate Period (7th to 11th Dynasties, c.2254–1991 B.C.); Middle Kingdom (12th Dynasty, 1991–1778 B.C.); Second Intermediate Period, including the Hyksos domination (13th to 17th Dynasties, 1778–1573 B.C.); New Kingdom (18th to 20th Dynasties, 1573–1085 B.C.); the Late Dynasties (21st to 31st Dynasties, 1085–332 B.C.); Ptolemaic Period (332–30 B.C.); and Roman and Byzantine Periods (30 B.C.–642 A.D.).

Predynastic Egypt. Men of the Old Stone Age (Paleolithic) had settled on the desert margins of the Nile Valley, but their Neolithic successors descended to Upper Egypt (southern Egypt) and developed three known Predynastic cultures. The oldest of these is the Badarian (before S.D. 30) whose settlements and cemeteries are almost exclusively confined to the district of Badari. Next is Naqada I, or Amratian (S.D. 30–38), found between Badari and the First Cataract, with its center at Naqada. Of Naqada II, or Gerzean (S.D. 38–64), cemeteries are found near the entrance to the Faiyum, and from Badari deep into Lower Nubia, with an outpost at the Second Cataract. All these groups used copper to a limited extent, and produced excellent handmade pottery, which was sometimes painted. They buried their dead in cemeteries apart from the settlements. Their graves were oval or circular, in Naqada II tending to become rectangular concurrently with the introduction of the sun-dried mud brick. The dead, accompanied by a few simple grave goods, were usually buried in a contracted position, resting on the left side, head to the south, though the attitude tends to vary in Naqada II. Walled towns or settlements built of brick are known from Naqada II at the latest. Naqada II also sees increased production of stone vessels as a consequence of easier access to copper supplies. Little is known of their religious beliefs, apart from the fact that they obviously believed in an afterlife, and that their principal deity may have been the mother goddess.

Other groups have since been found in places outside Upper Egypt proper. The earliest of these is the Faiyum A, a very primitive agricultural people who lived on an ancient lake level in the Faiyum. They did not know metal, produced some rough pottery, and had an important flint industry. Their cemeteries have never been found. Another community at Merimde-Beni Salaam, on the desert edge about 40 mi. northwest of Cairo, has often been hailed as the oldest Predynastic culture in Egypt, largely because it was exceedingly primitive and "neolithic" in type. The archeological evidence suggests that it was more likely to have been a backward group, without knowledge of copper, that existed toward the end of Naqada II. The characteristic of Merimde is of a compact village with burials in the settlement, either in the streets or houses.

Protodynastic, or Archaic, Period. Though Egypt, as a unified entity, can claim a longer recorded history than any other modern nation, its unrecorded history goes back many centuries further. It is during this so-called prehistoric period that the gradual transition from small isolated communities to ever-larger groupings took place and that the foundations of mature Egyptian civilization were laid. At the end of the Predynastic Period, Egypt was divided into two kingdoms, that of the Delta (Lower Egypt) with its capital at Buto, and that of Upper Egypt with its capital at Hierakonpolis. Also, in the final stages of the Predynastic era, a small and new racial element entered Egypt. The newcomers, though not themselves Sumerians, brought in various ideas and influences from Sumeria, including the idea of writing, the cylinder seal, a number of artistic motifs and techniques, and a new architectural style. The Upper Egyptian kingdom under Menes conquered the Delta and thus founded the united Egyptian kingdom, which was thereafter called the kingdom of "the Two Lands." The 1st Dynasty had its capital at Memphis. Practically nothing is known of the political history of the first two dynasties, though in the mid-2d Dynasty unity was temporarily disrupted by the so-called Seth Rebellion and the situation was only restored under the last King of the dynasty. Nevertheless, it is certain that these were times of very rapid growth, in which most of the permanent and characteristic features of Egyptian culture manifested themselves. Writing developed slowly; the 365-day calendar was introduced; easier access to the copper of Sinai led to a veritable copper boom, which in turn led to increased exploitation and working of stone; superb stone vases were made; and the first experiments in using stone in building were made. The royal tombs of the 1st Dynasty at Sakkara show a magnificent and exciting architecture in brick. Trade flourished, timber was imported from Syria, and trading or exploring parties penetrated at least as far south as the Second Cataract.

Old Kingdom. The preparatory work of the first two dynasties reached its fruition in the 3d Dynasty and is epitomized by the Step Pyramid of Sakkara, the tomb of Zoser, the first King of that dynasty. It was the first pyramid to be built and the first monumental building in stone. Thereafter, there was very rapid economic and cultural progress that reached its peak in the 4th Dynasty and is exemplified by the three great pyramids of Khufu, Khafre, and Menkaure and the Great Sphinx at Giza. The 5th Dynasty saw the triumph of the cult of the sun-god Ra (or Re) of Heliopolis, but the decline in the size and quality of the pyramids testifies to changing ideas, to increasing economic stress, and to a progressive decline in the power of the crown. In the 6th Dynasty military campaigns were conducted in Asia, while trade and exploration in Nubia and the Sudan were vigorously pushed. Decentralization, however, inevitably decreased the power of the King while increasing that of the nomarchs, or provincial governors, and a combination of this with economic distress and the infiltration of Asiatics into the Delta led eventually to a social upheaval and collapse. The Old Kingdom was a time of brisk foreign trade with Africa and Asia, and the first high-water mark in architecture and in statuary and relief.

First Intermediate Period. After less than 50 years of weak rule by Kings of the 7th and 8th Dynasties during a period of confusion, control was seized by the princes of Heracleopolis, who formed the 9th and 10th Dynasties. The short-lived 9th Dynasty had at first probably lost the Delta, but eventually appears to have regained some measure of control. On the other hand, they had at least nominal rule over all Egypt as far as Aswan. But this was only of short duration and was ended by the rise to power of a family of Theban princes. In the north the 10th Dynasty succeeded in regaining the Delta, whose eastern frontier they secured with military works and colonies, and resumed trade with Syria. In the south their rule did not extend much south of Asyut and there ensued a long war of fluctuating fortune with the Theban Kings of the 11th Dynasty. In this war the Thebans were finally successful (c.2040 B.C.) and Egypt was once more united under a single ruler, Mentuhotep II. The First Intermediate Period saw a disastrous decline in art, but the production of some of the best Egyptian literary works. It saw the triumph of the cult of Osiris, god of the dead, and the partial democratization of the hereafter; that is, the privileges of eternal life were extended to the nobles. In spite of civil war and confusion, there was a considerable level of material prosperity, and wealth appears, according to the evidence of the cemeteries, to have been more widely distributed.

Middle Kingdom. After about 40 years of peace the 11th Dynasty collapsed in renewed civil war and confusion, and the throne was seized (1991 B.C.) by Amenemhet I, formerly chief minister of Mentuhotep IV. Thereafter, for over 200 years, Egypt was ruled by an energetic and remarkable line of Kings who formed the 12th Dynasty and raised Egypt to its second period of greatness. In Syria-Palestine the political and economic influence of Egypt was dominant, and in Nubia an aggressive policy was pursued. Lower Nubia was conquered and secured by a remarkable fortress system, and a trading post was maintained at Kerma, south of the Third Cataract. The principal energies of the rulers were concentrated on internal affairs and reform. Vast irrigation schemes were carried out and the country raised to a high level of prosperity. Art, especially jewelry and statuary, flourished, and the Middle Kingdom is the classical period of Egyptian language and literature.

Second Intermediate Period. For about 100 years following the end of the 12th Dynasty, relative peace and prosperity were maintained in Upper Egypt by the 13th Dynasty, but there was a gradual decline. Gradually groups of Semites, now known collectively as the Hyksos, infiltrated into the Delta and by c.1674 B.C. they controlled to a greater or lesser degree all Egypt and Nubia. This extensive rule did not long endure. Nubia asserted its independence and the princes of Thebes (the 17th Dynasty) began a long and eventually successful war of independence. The Hyksos were by no means the barbarians that the Jewish historian Josephus and later Egyptian tradition would imply, and during their sway the horse, chariot, composite bow, and other innovations were introduced into the country.

New Kingdom. The final stages of the war against the Hyksos occupied the first few years of the reign of Ahmose I of Thebes, founder of the 18th Dynasty. After a relatively brief period to reorganize the country and to regain and extend control over Nubia, Egypt embarked on an aggressive policy in Asia. The Kassite invasions had produced a temporary vacuum in Western Asia and Egyptian policy was primarily directed toward breaking or containing its only rival, Mitanni, in northern Mesopotamia, and toward removing as far as possible any threat to its frontiers. This policy, apart from the peaceful and prosperous reign of Queen Hatshepsut, culminated in the 17 successive campaigns of Thutmose III in Asia. As a result of these campaigns, Egyptian control and influence were extended from the Euphrates to beyond the Fourth Cataract in the Sudan. This was the furthest extent of the Egyptian Empire.

In the second half of the dynasty this policy was drastically changed. The resurgence of the Hittites and the rise of Assyria threatened both Egypt and Mitanni, and the two were forced into alliance. This, however, failed to save Mitanni. Egyptian Asia was now assailed by Hittite intrigues and pressure, and by the infiltration of the Khabiri in the east. Amenhotep III, indolent, pleasure-loving, and occupied with building operations at Thebes,

The first all-stone building of Egypt was the Step Pyramid of King Zoser (3d Dynasty; c.2780–c.2680 B.C.) at Sakkara. Designed by the architect Imhotep, it was the prototype of the true pyramids of the next dynasty.

did not meet the threat. His son, Akhenaton (Amenhotep IV), with Akhenaton's wife, Nefertiti, was preoccupied with religious and artistic innovations and the building of a new capital at Tell el-Amarna, and neglected his imperial responsibilities. Akhenaton's attempt to introduce a form of monotheism, the worship of the Aton, or Sun's Disk, moreover, rent and weakened Egypt, and Egyptian influence in Asia sank to a new low. After the collapse of Atonism, Harmhab, the last King of the dynasty and himself a usurper, restored order at home, but was able to do little to reassert Egypt's position in Asia. In spite of internal friction and external losses, Egypt's still great wealth at this period is attested by the splendid funerary furnishings that were placed in the tomb of even a minor Pharaoh such as Tutankhamen.

The 19th Dynasty, from its capital Tanis in the northeastern Delta, attemped to regain Asia, but met with only very limited success. Seti I recaptured Palestine and Syria, but the drawn battle of Kadesh (1286 B.C.), between his son Rameses II and the Hittites, spelled the end of any larger hopes. The growing pressure of the great ethnic movement of the so-called Peoples of the Sea eventually impelled the conclusion of an Egypto-Hittite alliance (1270 B.C.). This gave Egypt a brief respite. The first attack of the Peoples of the Sea, which occurred in the reign of Merenptah, was not repulsed until it had nearly reached Memphis, but the main onslaught did not come until the reign of Rameses III, in the 20th Dynasty. A struggle that lasted six years saw the final defeat of the Sea Peoples, but also the exhaustion of Egypt and the end of its imperial power. The rest of the 20th Dynasty is the story of almost uninterrupted decline, of economic distress, internal weakness, and priestly intrigues.

Late Dynasties. Some years before the death of Rameses XI, a Prince of Tanis established a new dynasty. After Rameses' death this 21st Dynasty ruled the whole country, but it was in turn overthrown by the descendants of Libyan mercenaries who had been settled near Heracleopolis. Sheshonk I, the first King of the 22d (Libyan) Dynasty, conducted a successful campaign in Palestine, but the later years of the dynasty were contemporaneous with the 23d Dynasty at Thebes and the 24th Dynasty in the north, and the country was rent by civil war. Thus the Ethiopian King Piankhi (25th Dynasty) had little difficulty in invading the Thebaid (730 B.C.), and eventually he and his successor, Shabaka, extended Ethiopian rule over the whole land. Egypt was now directly threatened by Assyria, but the Ethiopian Kings were torn between their homeland and Egypt. Their generalship was frequently inept, and in 664 B.C., the Assyrians finally conquered Egypt and sacked Thebes.

Under the Assyrians, control of Egypt was left in the hands of a council of Princes, whose leader, Psamtik I, in due course asserted his independence and founded the 26th, or Saite, Dynasty. Under the Saite Kings, Egypt, for 140 years, enjoyed a final era of peace, prosperity, and artificial revival. The dynasty depended primarily on a picked force of Greek mercenaries. It promoted economic revival by encouraging Greek traders at Naucratis and Daphne, and by building a strong navy and commercial fleet, while it claimed the allegiance of the Egyptians by deliberately fostering a spirit of nationalism in harking back to the glories of the past. Toward Asia the dynastic policy was one of maintaining the balance of power, and for long Egypt used its naval and economic power astutely and successfully to implement this policy.

EGYPTIAN HISTORY

But eventually Cambyses conquered Egypt, which thus came under direct Persian rule in the 27th Dynasty (525 B.C.). The new masters were at first mild, but the increasing harshness of the later Persian Kings provoked constant native revolts, and at last the country regained its freedom (404 B.C.). For 63 years, during the 28th to 30th Dynasties, Egypt maintained an uneasy independence, due less to its inherent strength and merits than to Persian preoccupation elsewhere. Finally, in 341 B.C., under the 31st Dynasty, there came the second Persian conquest which, in turn, came to an abrupt end with the victory of Alexander the Great at Issus (333 B.C.).

Ptolemaic Period. With the victory of Alexander, the history of Egypt merges with that of the Hellenistic world. Alexander was welcomed as a liberator and in turn treated Egypt well and with imagination. He founded Alexandria, which was to become the commercial and intellectual center of the Mediterranean world. On his death (323 B.C.) the empire was divided into a number of satrapies and Egypt fell to Ptolemy, who in 304 B.C. made himself King as Ptolemy I Soter. The dynasty founded by Ptolemy lasted until 30 B.C. Though the Egyptians salved their pride by treating the Ptolemies precisely like native Pharaohs, the Ptolemies remained completely Greek, hardly entering into Egyptian life. It was not until Ptolemy V (reigned 205–180 B.C.) that one of them was crowned by Egyptian rite at Memphis, and the last of the line, the great Cleopatra, was the first to have any knowledge of the Egyptian language. The Ptolemies developed Egypt, but also exploited it for their own ends; still, the country was prosperous and at first relatively peaceful.

The victory of Ptolemy IV at Raphia in Palestine (217 B.C.), over Antiochus III of Syria, had, however, important consequences. Egyptian troops had been employed for the first time and acquitted themselves well. This in turn inspired the first of the native revolts, which thereafter were almost incessant, especially in Upper Egypt, until Ptolemy VIII destroyed Thebes in 85 B.C. The corruption and dynastic quarrels of the Ptolemies steadily weakened the regime until in 55 B.C. Ptolemy XI had to be restored by Roman legions, and it was clearly only a matter of time before Egypt fell completely into Roman hands. This duly came to pass as the result of the defeat of Antony and Cleopatra at Actium and Cleopatra's subsequent suicide (30 B.C.).

Roman and Byzantine Period. Under Rome, Egypt had a special position in, but apart from, the empire, and was governed on behalf of the Emperor by a prefect. Rome considered it judicious to follow the Ptolemaic policy toward the native religion, and at first paid the same outward attention to the old gods. But Egypt was ruinously exploited for its grain and consequently became impoverished; and as time went on it reflected the growing weakness and strains of the empire. When the capital of the empire was transferred from Rome to Constantinople (330 A.D.), Egypt entered the Byzantine Period, and became virtually Coptic, or Christian, Egypt.

Traditionally, Christianity was brought to Egypt by St. Mark, and grew rapidly, in spite of many persecutions, the most savage and notorious being those instituted under Diocletian. With the coming of Christian Emperors, the pagan cults in their turn were assailed. Theodosius I (reigned 379–95 A.D.) declared Christianity the religion of the empire and ordered the closing of the temples. But the old religion was a long time dying, especially in the more remote parts—the temple of Isis at Philae was not closed until 543 A.D., in the reign of Justinian. The Egyptian Christians, monks, priests, and patriarchs, were a turbulent people, possessed by an intensely nationalistic and bigoted spirit, and their violence and theological controversies only weakened the country still further, so that the Arabs under Amr ibn al-As had relatively little difficulty in finally conquering the country in 642 A.D.

People and Society. The Egyptians were a black-haired, dark-skinned, short and slender people of the Eastern Hamitic division of the Mediterranean branch of the Caucasoid race. Though class distinctions were not rigid in ancient Egypt, there were vast differences between the royal family, nobles, priests, scribes, and government officials, at the top of the social scale, the artisans, craftsmen, and merchants in the middle, and the workers at the bottom. In the Old Kingdom almost all men were free. Little slavery existed and there was no rigid caste system. But a kind of serfdom developed as a result of the deterioration in economic conditions toward the end of the period. In the Middle and New Kingdoms some slaves were created as a punishment. But even in the New Kingdom the vast majority of slaves were prisoners of war. It is only with the general decline in the later dynasties that the number of native slaves increased and the institution of voluntary servitude developed. At all times the rights of slaves were strictly defined by law, and slaves could even own property.

Women in ancient Egypt enjoyed an exceptionally high and respected position. They were free, unveiled, and there was no system of purdah (seclusion of women). Marriage appears to have been a legal contract rather than a religious ceremony. The rights of women and children in marriage and divorce were strictly guarded. A woman could even reign as Pharaoh. She could also own property

Model of a carpenter's chest and tools, found in a tomb at Asyut. The equipment was for a servant's use in afterlife.

Metropolitan Museum of Art, Gift of Edward S. Harkness, 1916–17

and buy, sell, inherit, and dispose of it at will; and she could engage in commerce and trade in her own right, and testify in court. Except in the royal family, brother-sister marriages, though permissible, were rare. Monogamy prevailed except for the plural marriages contracted by Kings.

Economy and Daily Life. The peasants, who comprised the mass of the people, were engaged in agriculture—barley, flax, and emmer wheat being the chief crops. A smaller proportion of the people engaged in minor industries and crafts, and in mining, building, and quarrying (especially prisoners). Merchants sailed all over the eastern Mediterranean to exchange Egyptian copper, grain, linen, papyrus, and stone for the goods of foreign nations, especially timber, and to ports on the Red Sea and the east coast of Africa to barter for the gold, ivory, hides, ostrich feathers, and other exotic products of Somaliland. Egyptian caravans were also active in the Sudan. Under the *corvée* system, all men, unless otherwise exempted, were liable to be called upon to perform any manner of forced duties. It was men levied for the *corvée* who built the gigantic pyramids of Giza in the Old Kingdom.

The average, or poor, Egyptian lived in a small hut built of mud or sun-dried brick, covered with palm leaves or straw, with palm-trunk beams supporting the flat roof. His furnishings were minimal. Rich Egyptians, on the other hand, enjoyed more spacious homes of brick and wood construction, which were luxuriously furnished and decorated.

The diet of the poor included barley bread, fish, vegetables, and beer. The wealthy, in addition to these staples, had beef, veal, antelope and gazelle meat, fruit, and a variety of sweets.

Men's clothing at first consisted only of a loin cloth; later this developed into a pleated skirt or apron. Women wore long tight dresses attached by shoulder straps and made extensive use of cosmetics, darkening their eyebrows, outlining their eyes with black kohl and green paint, applying lip rouge, and dyeing their fingernails. Wealthy Egyptian women also wore heavy black wigs made of human hair or sheep's wool both to adorn themselves and to protect themselves from the heat.

For recreation Egyptians played games, such as an ancient form of backgammon, and hunted, fished, and participated in athletic contests.

Government. The Egyptians believed that the world order was instituted at the beginning of time when the first god-king came to earth bringing the kingship with him. Their view of the cosmos was thus an essentially static one, encompassing a world made perfect once and for all by the gods, in which there was little change apart from the normal seasonal fluctuations, the change from day to night, or the annual flooding—a world of small, regular, and regulated change occurring in an immutable frame. The kingship was the keystone of Egyptian civilization. It alone explains the extraordinary stability and longevity of the Egyptian state and way of life. At the heart of the concept of kingship lay the idea of truth and justice. Maat, goddess of truth and justice, was the daughter of the sun-god Ra, the first god-king, and came to earth with him. Thereafter, gods, kings, and men were all bound by the law and could not break it. The king himself was a god. Although he differed in many ways from the

gods, he was in a very real sense divine and elevated above other men. The idea of the divinity of the king was weakened seriously as time went on, but throughout Egyptian history the fiction was steadfastly maintained, for without this central, unifying, and comfortable belief, the whole fabric of society would have fallen apart. The earthly king was the living Horus, the last member of the dynasty of gods, and owed his position less to primogeniture or physical prowess than to the belief that, as Horus, he was the dutiful and legitimate son of Osiris, whose legitimacy and succession to his father's throne had been confirmed by a divine court of law. As leader and shepherd of his people, the king alone, in theory, initiated all activity. Theoretically, he owned all Egypt, though in practice individuals could own and dispose of land and property without restriction. Technically, he was the chief priest and the sole officiant in every service in every temple. He led the army in war and inspired and promoted all peaceful enterprises. He was the source of all legislation, and at the same time subservient to the law. His health and well-being were essential to the prosperity of his land and people.

A long, narrow country such as Egypt has always been difficult to hold together and rule, especially in antiquity, when communications were slow and poor, and much depended on the personal energy and drive of the ruler. In practice, of course, there had to be delegation of authority and an efficient administrative machine. In the Old Kingdom, and even in the Middle Kingdom, to a lesser extent, social organization and administration were essentially amateur. The hereditary principle began to develop only toward the end of the Old Kingdom, largely because of the need to make permanent provision for the service of funerary endowments. Earlier, any official was liable to be nominated to lead any type of undertaking, whether military, religious, economic, or administrative. Not until the New Kingdom was there a more comprehensive professional organization in the army, priesthood, and administration, but even then one man could perform many and diverse functions. The chief minister under the King was the vizier. In the New Kingdom there were separate viziers for Upper and Lower Egypt, a practice that may already have existed at the end of the Old Kingdom. The vizier was the supreme judge and was responsible for finance, taxation, justice, agriculture, public works, custody of the archives, and the administration of the army and navy. Under him served a vast army of provincial governors and administrators, inspectors, controllers, and a multitude of subordinate officials and scribes. In the New Kingdom the rich and important province of Nubia was under a separate official, the viceroy of Nubia, answerable to the King. Throughout Pharaonic times Egypt was divided into nomes, or provinces, the standard number being 22 nomes in Upper Egypt and 20 in Lower Egypt.

Until the New Kingdom no standing army existed. Men were summoned for military service on a provincial basis. The foreign wars of the New Kingdom necessitated the formation of a professional army, which, in time of war in the field, consisted of the chariotry (the crack section of the army), the infantry, and mercenaries, and was organized into four divisions.

Religion. The ancients were profoundly impressed by the religiosity of the Egyptians, by their strange gods and sacred rites and practices. They were led to invest Egyptian religion with a far deeper mystery and significance than it really possessed—a view that has not died out even today. Egyptian religion was intensely parochial; although one may at times speak of a state cult, there was no such thing as a national religion, and a man's allegiance was primarily to his local god. This explains the immense number of gods who often differ from each other in little more than name. It was thus relatively easy for a local god to become attached to one or another of the more powerful gods.

Local loyalties were strengthened by the innate conservatism of the Egyptians which rendered them disinclined to abandon any belief or practice they had once possessed. It is the parochial nature of Egyptian religion that probably explains the family and domestic nature of the gods, their worship and festivals. This in turn accounts for the mildness of Egyptian religion, the absence of blood baths and excess in any form. Thus in matters religious the Egyptian was tolerant. His own local loyalties prevented him from seeking to impose his own local cult, whose efficacy in any event would be restricted to a particular locality, on those who lived outside its range. Hence, although there are abundant religious books in Egypt, there were no sacred books, and consequently no dogma and no heresy hunts.

Religious life in Egypt was less a matter of belief or of revealed truth than of cult, and the essential requirement was the absolutely correct performance of the ritual, accuracy of the spoken word, and the strictest ritual purity. It was only in the late period that the people in general, largely as a reaction to foreign domination, in a sense turned inward and gave passionate and exaggerated devotion to those simpler elements that were most typically Egyptian and most sharply differentiated from the beliefs and practices of foreigners.

There is good reason to believe that the earliest gods were nature gods—birds, mammals, fish, reptiles, and so forth—worshiped because they appeared to represent forces that were feared, loved, or admired. Although in the beginning they were worshiped in their animal form, the majority were soon anthropomorphized. Probably equally primitive were certain sacred inanimate objects, whose precise origin is uncertain but is likely to be found in purely local conditions. Somewhat later were the cosmic gods who represented the great forces of nature. Inevitably such gods tended to be universal in character, but they were soon localized and were usually worshiped in human or animal form, or in a combination of the two.

From time to time certain human beings, other than Kings, were deified because of special qualities they had displayed during their lifetime. Such cults were normally short-lived and confined to a fairly restricted locality. The two most famous exceptions were Imhotep and Amenhotep. Imhotep, the chief minister and architect of Zoser, was deified and worshiped as a god of wisdom and medicine, being regarded as the son of Ptah, and later identified by the Greeks with Asclepius. Amenhotep, son of Hapu, a favorite and official of Amenhotep III, became a god of wisdom. Animal worship was always a typical feature of Egyptian religion and was particularly popular in the late period. These animal cults were on the whole local,

all members of a particular species being worshiped in a specific district. Less common were the animals of which only one, distinguished by special markings, was worshiped and mummified and buried in special cemeteries. The most famous of the latter class were the bull cults, especially Apis at Memphis, Mnevis at Heliopolis, and Buchis at Armant. Also included in the Egyptian pantheon were genii, or familiar spirits, and a certain number of foreign deities that were mainly, but not exclusively, Asiatic in origin.

In order to explain their world and its creation the Egyptians elaborated three theological systems. The first and most widespread was that of Heliopolis, which from the 5th Dynasty dominated the sacred ritual. According to this system, Atum emerged out of primeval chaos and produced from himself Shu ("air") and Tefnut ("moisture"). These in turn produced Geb ("earth") and Nut ("sky"), whose children were Osiris, Isis, Seth, and Nephthys. These nine gods, with the fusion of Atum and Ra, formed the Great Ennead.

At Memphis there was formulated a different theory. Ptah at Memphis was declared to be an older god than Ra of Heliopolis, and the Memphite system seems, in part at least, to have been elaborated to combat the rising solar theology. According to this system Ptah created eight other gods who were in essence only aspects of himself. For example, Atum was his thought, Horus his heart, and Thoth his tongue. The central idea of this system was the creative Word, the world's earliest formulation of the doctrine of the Logos. As a system it was more advanced than the other theologies, but for this reason it never became popular, though it retained its appeal and force for a small minority of priests throughout the course of Egyptian history.

The third system was that of Hermopolis, which was built up around a group of eight gods, the Ogdoad. According to this system, out of the inert primeval ocean emerged four pairs of beings, four frogs (male) and four snakes (female) who represented Night, Darkness, Mystery, and Eternity. From an egg which they created at Hermopolis emerged the Sun (Atum), and it was he who created men and organized the world.

The form of solar monotheism called Atonism, associated with Akhenaton (reigned c.1369–1353 B.C.) and the Tell el-Amarna Period, is entirely distinct from the religious systems sketched above. It introduced one god only, the Aton, or Sun's Disk, more particularly the life-giving power of the sun. This system also attempted to close the temples of the old gods, to abolish all the ancient gods and cults and even the word "gods." It was exclusive and intolerant. The typical Aton temple was completely different in type from the normal cult temple. It contained no cult image and was composed of a series of courts, all of which were open to the sky. In spite of these differences, there is no justification for attempting to seek a foreign, still less a Semitic, origin for Atonism; its seeds lie solely in Egypt. It is doubtful whether the movement was purely religious. The explanation of the revolution is probably to be sought more in politics than in religion, and can be seen as an attempt to curb or break the Amon priesthood which had become too powerful, and as an attempt to establish a common religion for the whole Egyptian Empire, in Egypt, Asia, and Nubia.

Since solar worship was always somewhat remote from ordinary people, the new cult was given immediacy by linking the Aton very closely with the person of the King. Though he was the son, disciple, and high priest of the Aton, at times the King and Aton were almost identical. The movement failed. After sweeping away the old religion, including Osiris and the deeply rooted funerary beliefs of the Egyptians, as well as all the moral ideals and sanctions that were connected with them, it supplied nothing in their place and merely created a spiritual vacuum. Atonism was frankly amoral; its much vaunted "teaching" was nonexistent apart from a beautiful hymn to the Aton. Although it retained traditional funerary practices, it cast off the underlying funerary beliefs. Under it there was no celestial or underworld hereafter, no judgment of the dead. Instead, the dead, like the living, slept at night, and by day emerged from their tombs to maintain a rather forlorn existence near their former homes or in the temple of the Aton and near the King. Atonism failed to gain popular support and died with Akhenaton.

Apart from the theological system sketched above, the family triad of Osiris, Isis, and Horus enjoyed wide popularity in the funerary religion of the Egyptians. Originally a local god of Busiris, Osiris came to the fore in the First Intermediate Period and was worshiped throughout Egypt. He was therefore accounted for in the principal theologies. He was primarily the god of the dead: the human appeal of his story and the hope of eternal life in the other world that was extended to his devotees account for his great popularity.

Temples. The temple played a dominant role in Egyptian culture. More than a religious institution, it was also a center and patron of learning, and attached to it would be a "house of life," for writing and copying religious and learned books, and a staff of doctors, astronomer priests, and scribes. There were three types of temple in Egypt: (1) the normal cult temple, with its specialized subtypes, the funerary temple, and the rock-cut temple; (2) the peripteral temple, essentially a kiosk on a rectangular base, whose primary purpose was to serve as a temporary stopping place for the god at certain festivals; and (3) the solar temple, which differed from the normal cult temple in that it contained no sacred image, or idol, and that both the temple and all ceremonies performed within it were open to the sky.

Very little is known about the ordinary cult temples of the Old and Middle Kingdoms because they were destroyed to provide space and building materials for later temples, and it is only those of the New Kingdom and, still more, those of the Greco-Roman period that have been relatively well preserved. The temple was surrounded by a great brick wall, to insure both protection and privacy. In the space thus created were a sacred lake, storehouses, workshops, kitchens, administrative offices, and quarters for the priests. The temple itself was approached through a monumental doorway between massive pylons, and in the face of the latter were grooves for tall flagstaffs, and before them a pair of obelisks. The temple consisted of one or more open courts, and at least one pillared, or hypostyle, hall. Its central aisle was higher than the rest to facilitate illumination of the hall by clerestory lighting. At the rear, surrounded by a varying number of other rooms, was the sanctuary. The sanctuary and rear of the temple were devoid of any illumination. The progressive darkening from entrance to sanctuary promoted a sense of mystery and awe, an effect that was enhanced by the simple device of lowering the level of the roof and slightly raising the level of the floor the nearer one approached the sanctuary in which the god resided.

The temple was linked by processional ways to a quay on the river or canal side and to other temples in the same town. The temple was entered by priests only, and the sanctuary by a single priest, the officiant. The public was not admitted to the temple, but provision was made at the gate in the temenos wall for ordinary people to offer prayer and gifts, and to make their petitions. It is important to note that the temple and all within it were in a very real sense considered to be alive. At the dedication ceremony, repeated annually on New Year's Day, the temple as a whole—every relief on its walls and every sacred image that was kept in it—underwent the ceremony of "Opening the Mouth," which had the effect of filling the temple and its reliefs with latent life. How very real this idea was is eloquently demonstrated in both Coptic and Muslim Egypt by the care taken to "kill" the reliefs before using the rooms of the temple for purposes other than those for which it was built.

The type of temple thus briefly described was admirably designed to serve the purposes of the two types of worship: the daily service celebrated in all intimacy in the sanctuary, and the processional festivals that took place either inside or outside the temple. The ordinary daily worship consisted of services at dawn, midday, and sunset. The elaborate dawn service was in essence a dramatization, in a religious context, of daily life. The god, resting in the sanctuary, was awakened by the morning hymn sung by the temple choir. The officiant, in theory the King, but in practice his deputy, entered the sanctuary alone, disrobed the god, performed his toilet, and offered him a meal. After all this had been completed, and after the cotemplar gods had been awakened and fed in similar but simpler fashion, the offerings were removed and a double reversion of offerings was celebrated. The first reversion was celebrated within the temple for the benefit of the royal ancestors, and was succeeded by a second reversion of offerings outside the temple to the priests. In all these ceremonies the people in general took no part. There was no congregational worship of any description.

In addition to these daily services, every temple had its own calendar of festivals which varied in length from a day to a whole month. In the 18th Dynasty the temple of Karnak had over 50 such festivals each year. The majority of these festivals were processional, some within the temple, but others outside the temple to other temples in the same town or to more distant towns. The great calendar festivals that involved processions outside the temple area, such as the Feast of Opet, were the occasions that offered the mass of the people direct contact with the official state religion. They were accompanied by popular rejoicing, free food, drink, and even side shows. Some festivals included dramatic performances somewhat akin to the medieval mystery or morality plays.

It is inevitable from the fact that almost all our knowledge of Egyptian religion, other than funerary religion, is derived from the temples, temple reliefs, and surviving temple rituals, that we should have the impression that the only religion in Egypt was that recorded on the monuments. It could hardly be otherwise, since the mass of the people were illiterate and rarely left any hint of their own beliefs. On the other hand, it would be wrong to conclude either that the people were only devotees of the state religion or that they had no religious beliefs at all. It is probable that the common man was largely unaffected by the state religion. Of course, he could participate in the excitement of a great processional festival and could, on occasion, adore or have an attachment to one of the great gods. But it seems that the religion of the mass of the simple, unlettered people was of an entirely different and more elemental order: a religion of genii, spirits, and folk-type divinities. Thus the workers of the Theban necropolis personified and worshiped as their patroness the great peak that rises at the head of the Valley of the Kings and in whose body, so to speak, their daily bread was earned.

There was no proper professional priesthood until the New Kingdom. At all times the King, in theory, was the sole officiant at all temple services. But in practice he was forced to delegate these religious duties—in the New Kingdom, to the high priest of the appropriate temple; in earlier times, to nomarchs, officials, and other laymen. Professionalism began to enter the priesthood at the end of the Old Kingdom because of the need to make permanent provision for the celebration of the funerary cult. The temple priesthood was divided into four companies, each of which served in the temple for a month at a time. Priests could fill secular posts, even the highest in the land, and could marry and engage in commerce. Appointment to, and installation of, at least the high grades was the personal act of a king; payment was in kind. Great emphasis was laid on the strictest ritual purity. The usual role of women in the temple was as musician-priestesses, but in certain circumstances they could hold higher offices. During the New Kingdom certain priesthoods grew so rich and powerful that they became, at one time, the dominant force in the state.

Funerary Beliefs and Practices. By far the greater part of our knowledge of the ancient Egyptians is due, directly or indirectly, to their remarkable funerary beliefs and practices. So prominent do tombs, death, and preparations for death appear to be in Egyptian life, that it is easy to imagine that the Egyptians were a morbid people, with an almost pathological preoccupation with the problem of death. Such an impression is completely false. The intense interest in and preparation for death were due fundamentally to an intense passion for life. The Egyptians believed that a man only really and finally died if the last thing in which his soul, ba, could find food, drink, and shelter was destroyed. The funerary cult was therefore a vast insurance policy to avoid the ultimate disaster of dying the "second death," and its basis was

the imperative need to make that permanent provision for the soul's needs on which survival depended.

From earliest times this idea of survival appears to have been linked with the preservation of the material body, or, in the last resort, some substitute for it. This idea appears to have originated in the accidental discovery in Predynastic times that the dead, when buried in shallow graves in the dry desert climate, did not necessarily decay. Thus there developed side by side with the provision for the material needs of the dead attempts to preserve the body. Mummification is attested at least as early as the 2d Dynasty, possibly even in the 1st. Mummification at first was reserved for those few who could afford it, but in the Middle Kingdom it became more widespread. The true art of mummification, however, was not acquired until the New Kingdom. Mummification at its best consisted of the dehydration of the body, after the removal of the brain and the entrails (except for the heart), and then the elaborate wrapping of the body. The vital organs were placed in four canopic jars which accompanied the dead to the tomb. Normally, dehydration required 40 days, wrapping 30 days. The body was then buried after the Opening of the Mouth ceremony (which was supposed to restore to the dead man his vital functions) had been performed over the mummy at the entrance to the tomb. In the tomb were placed food, clothing, furniture, and even *ushabti*, or images of servants, to wait upon the deceased. The walls, bearing scenes of daily life and offerings, had a practical function, for since the Opening of the Mouth had been performed over all these as well, they were deemed capable of serving the needs of the dead man indefinitely. Magical spells and incantations, known as Pyramid Texts, were from the 5th Dynasty onward carved on the walls of certain royal pyramids to aid the dead in his journey toward the next world. In the late First Intermediate Period, Coffin Texts were inscribed inside the coffins of nonroyal people. In the 18th Dynasty a collection of spells written on papyrus, now called the Book of the Dead, was often placed inside the coffin of royalty.

In the earliest times, it can reasonably be inferred, there were two main ideas of the next world: one of an underworld in the west, and one that postulated a stellar hereafter, in which the deceased became a star, more particularly, one of the circumpolar stars. The dominance of the solar cult throughout most of the Old Kingdom had as a natural consequence the popularity of a solar hereafter. The dead supposedly ascended to the sky in one of a variety of ways and hoped to remain evermore in the company of the sun-god in his journeys across the sky and under the earth. He even had to submit to some form of trial in the presence of the sun-god. Osiris does not begin to emerge as the god of the dead until the late Old Kingdom, his rise being increasingly reflected in the Pyramid Texts. The triumph of Osiris in the First Intermediate Period meant that henceforth it was the Osirian concept of the hereafter that prevailed. The picture is not a simple one. On the one hand there were the Elysian fields where the crops grew more luxuriantly than on earth. On the other, the kingdom of Osiris was quite clearly the underworld, a dark, dismal place that could depress even Osiris himself as a passage from the Book of the Dead

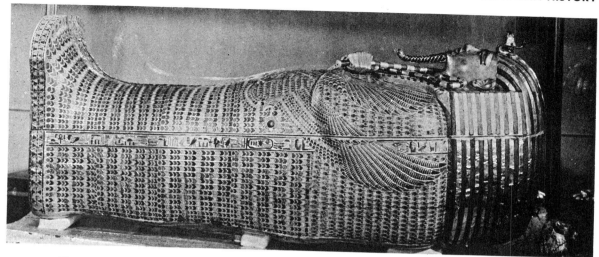

Annan Photo Features

The gold coffin of King Tutankhamen (18th Dynasty) is painted with a likeness of the young King. The tomb was discovered in 1922 in the Valley of the Kings near Luxor by the British archeologist Howard Carter.

clearly shows. The sole comfort that the hapless dead received was the mighty passage of Ra through the 12 divisions of the underworld.

The dead man could not be admitted to the next world without passing a test to prove that he had lived a blameless and exemplary life. This test consisted of a trial before Osiris and a court of 42 assessors. The heart of the dead man was weighed against a feather, the symbol of truth, and a Denial of Sin—often, but more inaccurately, known as the Negative Confession—was made to the gods. The Osirian judgment set a moral standard and embodied a high ethical ideal. But unfortunately, magic completely nullified it, for if one could recite the Denial of Sin accurately and correctly speak or act the other prescribed measures, even the greatest sinner could avoid the consequences of his evil-doing. Failure to pass the test was annihilation, and the sinner was devoured by a monster; but, naturally, this ultimate disaster was always avoided.

Science and Learning. Life in ancient Egypt, and above all, orderly, civilized life, would have been impossible if its people had not acquired certain skills. The supreme challenge and stimulus was the river, and the problem of water. The annual inundation brought water and fertility to the land, but it also swept away landmarks and destroyed property. Administration was impossible, taxes could not be levied, or government function unless, after the floods, the land could be surveyed. On the solution of the problem of the storage, control, raising, and distribution of water, the very existence of the whole people depended. Thus the Egyptian was inevitably a practical man, who was forced to acquire a knowledge of engineering, arithmetic, geometry, surveying, and mensuration. It is typical of the Egyptian that once having acquired this knowledge and having thereby been enabled to attain his immediate end, he never felt any impulse, or stimulus, to carry this knowledge further or to develop it theoretically. The Egyptian was literal; he did not indulge in hypotheses, philosophy, or metaphysics. It was left to the Greeks, who learned much of their mathematics and medicine in the valley of the Nile, to take the forward steps that Egyptians never seemed to have envisaged.

Egyptian mathematics was essentially a decimal system, originally finger numbering, but the decimal point, the cipher zero, and positional numbering were unknown. Hence there was a cumbersome system of notation and a barbarous system of fractions that used only the numerator 1. In spite of these handicaps, Egyptian mathematics was surprisingly efficient. Any problem involving areas or volumes, contents of buildings, or arithmetical or geometrical progressions could be successfully tackled, and the Egyptian approximation to the area of the circle and the value of pi was more accurate than that of any other ancient civilization.

The Egyptians produced elementary geographical maps and star maps, and used a simple form of theodolite. They were the first to discover the 365-day year. They divided the year into 12 months, each of 30 days, or three "weeks" consisting of ten days each, and at the end of the year added five extra, or epagomenal, days. This Egyptian calendar is the direct ancestor of our modern calendar. The discovery of the 365-day year was due primarily to the Nile flood. Without any advanced knowledge or apparatus, the mean of not more than 50 years' observation of the flood would have given the true length of the year. The approximate length could have been obtained in an even shorter period.

Egyptian doctors and medical schools enjoyed a high reputation in the ancient world. Doctors were apparently attached to the court or to the temples, and included not only general practitioners but also specialists. Egyptian medicine was of two kinds: folk medicine and magic, and true scientific medicine. Medicine and magic walked hand in hand. The successful magician inevitably developed into the doctor who dealt with those cases whose cause was known or could be seen; while the magician dealt with those complaints which had no obvious cause. No operative surgery was practiced in Egypt, though one or two instances of trepanning and one case of draining an abscess by drilling a hole in the lower jaw are attested. It is noteworthy that Egyptian anatomical terms are derived from animal anatomy. In spite of practicing mummification, it is evident that they had little real knowledge of human anatomy and that that little was only derived from morbid anatomy. There must have been some taboo that prohibited the cutting of the living body or the dissection of the dead body. Yet through mummification the Egyptians were accustomed to handling and cutting corpses and hence the Greeks found in Egypt the one place in which they could dissect and study anatomy with impunity.

LANGUAGE AND LITERATURE

Language and Literature. The language of the hieroglyphic inscriptions is largely Semitic, but with some notable divergencies in grammar and, to some extent, in vocabulary; and it still preserves traces of an earlier Hamitic system, presumably the language of Predynastic Egypt. This Semitic language and the idea of writing were introduced into Egypt approximately at the end of the Predynastic Period by people who had been influenced by Sumeria, but were not themselves Sumerians. Egyptian writing was in origin picture writing and always retained some of this pictorial element. Unlike the Sumerians, the Egyptians never developed syllabic writing and never used any vowels. Hieroglyphic is purely consonantal and is a mixture of picture signs, phonograms (picture signs used for their phonetic value only), determinatives, or signs indicative of the meaning of words, and a number of uniliteral signs resulting from certain short words being reduced by normal phonetic processes to a single strong consonant. The Egyptians did not possess a true alphabet since they had no vowel signs; but all alphabetic systems of writing are ultimately derived from Egyptian. Three scripts were used: Hieroglyphic is the monumental pictorial writing carved on stone or wood. Hieratic is a cursive form of hieroglyphic, the result of drawing hieroglyphs on papyrus, linen, or other soft materials with a reed brush dipped in ink. Demotic is a still more cursive script in which the vernacular of the Late Period (from about the 5th century B.C.) was written. Finally, the latest stage of the Egyptian language, which employed Greek characters, including vowels, and seven characters borrowed from demotic, formed Coptic, the language of Christian Egypt. Demotic continued in use until 452 A.D., and Coptic was written up to the 10th century, giving Egypt the longest continuous linguistic record in history.

The written records of Egypt cover an immense and varied field. They include history and biography, business and legal texts, letters private and official, medical and mathematical papyri, a dream book, lexicographical texts, and an immense religious literature which includes hymns, rituals, and numberless funerary papyri and texts. All these, however, are of little or no literary value. In addition to them there are many genuine literary works, both religious and secular, which may conveniently be grouped in four classes: drama, the short story, verse, and the didactic, reflective, or pessimistic literature. Some of these works were produced for political purposes, others served the ends of the official religion, but, nevertheless, the Egyptians were the first people to cultivate literature for its own sake, without thought of religion, politics, or commercial profit. The Egyptians were also the first consciously literary people in history, the first to value and appreciate style in writing.

Drama seems to have been essentially religious, though there is slight and inconclusive evidence of the existence of strolling players. The extant plays and fragments, and the stage directions that accompany them, indicate that there was no characterization, that the actors declaimed and ranted rather than acted, that very frequently a chorus played a big part, and that the dialogue was linked by continuous narrative read by a lector.

Egypt was the home of the short story, and from the Old Kingdom onward many have survived. These short stories include tales of adventure and travel, of magic and folklore, an allegory, a fragmentary detective story, and two incomplete ghost stories. The *Contendings of Horus and Seth* describes the foibles and weaknesses of the gods in a way that is almost Homeric. The *Story of the Eloquent Peasant* is less a tale than a treatise on eloquence and a tract on social justice. As a literary form the short story may justly be claimed as an Egyptian invention. It is typically simple, direct, and factual. There is no real attempt to draw character or to set a scene, but the *Story of Sinuhe* and the *Misadventures of Wenamun* demonstrate that some Egyptians at least saw, though they never developed, the possibilities of psychological treatment.

Egyptian poetry is characterized primarily by a pronounced rhythm, or beat, a tendency to use a strophic arrangement, and the employment of such literary devices as parallelism of members. There is an enormous mass of religious verse of very little merit, marked mainly by interminable and tedious puns and endless mythological allusions. Among the few exceptions is the outstanding religious hymn, the beautiful *Hymn to the Sun* of Akhenaton, which is noteworthy for its freedom from mythological allusions and its delight in nature. In complete contrast to the state and religious poems is a considerable body of lyric poetry which includes not only snatches from the songs of the people but also many charming love poems. Many of the latter are of considerable merit and worthy of inclusion in any world anthology.

Perhaps the most characteristic of all Egyptian literary works, however, are the didactic works, or wisdom literature. These were immensely popular throughout Egyptian history. All are much of the same pattern, and most are in verse. They are strictly practical and utilitarian works of counsel on such matters as honesty, moderation, behavior at table and toward superiors—in short, how to succeed in life. One of these works, the *Teaching of Amenemopet*, has been widely accepted as the direct source of Proverbs (12:17–13:11) and some other sections of Hebrew wisdom literature.

MUSIC

A fairly comprehensive view of ancient Egyptian music and its millennial history can be obtained from present research and analysis of archeological, pictorial, and hieroglyphic material. The first traces of this music are revealed by prehistoric findings. Music later played an important role in the lives of Egyptians under the Pharaohs. Although it has not been possible to reconstruct ancient melodies, the indirect evidence on hand seems to certify that the strongly traditional music of ancient Egypt had developed its own characteristic traits. Notwithstanding repeated cultural importations, from the Old Kingdom on it differed from that of its Asian and African neighbors. Traces of it can still be found in the Coptic liturgy and in the folk music of modern Egypt. In the latter case this is evident in the manner of rhythmic handclapping, in the use of many of the same instruments, in the same old folk tales (the cat and the mouse), and so on.

Musical Style

Musical Notation and Conducting. Ancient Egyptians did not possess a musical notation like the modern Western one. Music was learned and passed on by purely oral tradition. However, starting with the Middle Kingdom (c.2000 B.C.) they sometimes attempted to denote musical details with the familiar means of hieroglyphic symbols, repetitions of the same letter, or other signs. Very similar means and signs were later used for the same purposes in the music of the Christian churches. Musical instruments of this time included clappers, rattles, all kinds of jingles, sistral, vessel-pipes, long flutes, double clarinets, hemispheric drums, harps, and newer instruments such as the barrel drum, castanets, and asymmetrical lyre.

Another ancient method of representing music visually was used by the chironomists, as shown in the painted and sculptured music scenes from the 4th Dynasty on (c.2723–c.2563 B.C.). The chironomists were singers or special professionals communicating hand signs to the musicians. Singers and chironomists were designated by the same term in the Old Kingdom (c.2780–2254 B.C.), but from the Middle Kingdom on a distinction was made between "singers" and "singers with the hand." Chironomic signs are occasionally used in the contemporary Coptic Church.

The Egyptian signs can be classified into two series, one of rhythmic and one of melodic meaning. The rhythms have scarcely been explored, but it has been possible to interpret some of the melodic signs denoting tones and intervals.

Scales. An analysis of the instruments preserved and of the chironomic art representations seems to prove that the scales used in the Old and Middle Kingdoms had large intervals which progressively diminished during the New Kingdom (c.1573–c.1085 B.C.). The reconstructed scales show a structure in principle resembling the tetrachordal system of ancient Greece, namely, two movable notes within the frame of a fourth. The scales often contained intervals smaller than a semitone.

Harmony. Although Egyptian music was essentially a monodic (nonharmonic) art, melismatic (ornamented), and chanted, a kind of primitive polyphony (harmony) can be proved to have already existed in the music of the Old Kingdom (c.2700). Soloists were often accompanied by a vocal or instrumental drone (a continuous note or notes) which could consist of the fundamental note of the scale as well as its fifth and octave (for example C-G-C). It seems certain that heterophony (the simultaneous performance of the same melody model by several musicians with individual variants) was also practiced.

Vocal and Instrumental Styles. Singing was more highly appreciated than instrumental performances. Scientific analysis of the facial expression in art representations of singers proves that they sang with a nasal timbre resembling that of modern singers of the Near East and of the Coptic Church.

Representations of vocal and instrumental solos are rare. Singing was usually accompanied on the harp, and the male and female singers were as a rule also harpists. The accompaniment was occasionally enriched by a lute, lyre, flute, and various rhythm instruments. During the New Kingdom many new instruments were imported from Asia: double and single oboes, bronze drums, round tambourines, ladle-shaped, boat-shaped, angular, and semicircular harps of different sizes, giant lyres, and long- and short-necked lutes. Silver and gold trumpets have been found among the many relics in the relatively intact tomb of Tutankhamen.

Melody and Form. It is evident that ancient Egyptian music consisted largely of variations of traditional melody models—a practice customary in the music of the whole Orient today and in ancient Greece. Antiphonal singing (alternating choirs) in temples and accompanied solo performances are documented for the Old Kingdom. The rondeau form, consisting of solos with a refrain, became popular at least from the Middle Kingdom on. A more developed form of the rondeau, resembling the modern Arabian *dor*, which is a variation suite composed of solos and instrumental and ensemble parts, was known from the beginning of the New Kingdom. In addition, ancient Egyptians had hymns, strophic (verse form) and dance songs, and other special types of solo and ensemble music.

Professional Musicians. Musicians, particularly those attached to temples and to the court, were highly honored in ancient Egypt. The known musicians of the Old Kingdom were usually functionaries and holders of high administrative posts, or priests. They were among the confidants of the Pharaoh and were also the private music teachers of the royal family and the nobility. (The first professional musician known to music history was Khufu-Ankh, chief of the royal singers and flutists, who died c.2560).

The professional career of a gifted musician would consist of the following stages: singer in the royal choir, then assistant choir leader, later royal music director, and, at last, superintendent of court music. Music instructors were known from the Old Kingdom on, and during the New Kingdom there existed schools for temple musicians in Memphis. Specialists in the different branches of music were organized in corporations under an "overseer," who was usually one of the higher-ranking musicians at the royal court.

From the 21st Dynasty on (c.1085–c.950 B.C.) there are accounts of touring virtuosos of international reputation. The very rich documentary sources of the Saite (c.1085–332 B.C.) and of the Greco-Roman (332 B.C–359 A.D.) periods show that musicians and other artists signed regular contracts with their employers and that a breach of contract would usually end with a lawsuit.

EGYPTIAN TRANSPORTATION

Finally, the existence of amateur musicians and connoisseurs should be noted, a fact documented from the beginnings of the Old Kingdom on. This is one of the striking parallels among the musical phenomena of ancient Egypt revealed to those of later cultures and of our modern civilization.

TRANSPORTATION

Ancient Egyptian Transport. The greatest advance in land transport after the sled was the invention of the wheel, probably first invented in the Tigris-Euphrates valley some time before 3500 B.C. That the ancient Egyptians took little or no part in this invention was no doubt due to the fact that water transport was more important than land transport in Egypt. Egypt is a thin ribbon of green beside the Nile, surrounded by desert. The Nile is a perfect highway, and, as a result, transport in Egypt was much more closely tied to the river than it was in Babylonia, where a system of irrigation canals had pushed out settlement far into the plains. At all events, water transport in Egypt far outstripped land transport. The great blocks of stone which went to make the pyramids were floated on barges down the Nile River and then moved

ically significant inscriptions and reliefs, including one representing the Battle of Kadesh, are found inside the temple. Construction of the Aswan High Dam has caused the site to flood, and a vast international effort was crowned in 1966 when the two temples were cut into blocks and trucked to a nearby location above water level. The temples are the largest of the many Nubian monuments saved.

ABYDOS, ancient cemetery of Upper Egypt, situated on the west bank of the Nile at El-Araba el-Madfunah in the province of Girga, about 50 mi. northwest of Thebes. Remains include the tombs (possibly cenotaphs) of many kings of the first two dynasties. After the Middle Kingdom, one of these was considered the tomb of the god Osiris, and pilgrims came from all Egypt to attend the Osiris Mysteries. To be buried or to erect a funerary monument in the sacred area was greatly desired, and chapels or temples attributed to a number of kings from the 12th to 20th dynasties have been found there. The temple and cenotaph of King Seti I (19th dynasty) are especially noteworthy for the fine quality of their reliefs. To the north the ruins of an important temple, eventually dedicated to Osiris, can be traced from the 1st to the 30th dynasty. The district around Abydos had political significance during

In Egypt slaves dragged heavy loads on sleds that ran on rollers. Great statues and stones for pyramids were transported this way.

overland on sleds running on rollers. Wall pictures sculptured in Egyptian temples show clearly the method used. Gangs of slaves dragged the blocks of stone by means of large ropes, while other slaves at the rear of the sled picked up the rollers over which the sled had passed and hurried around to place them in position at the front. To raise the blocks of stone to their positions in the pyramids, the Egyptians built ramps, extending long distances, when necessary, to give the required grade.

PEOPLE, PLACES, AND TERMS

ABU SIMBEL [ä′boo sĭm′bĕl], also called Ipsambul, site on the bank of the Nile River near the southern border of Egypt, some 33 mi. northeast of Wadi Halfa, Sudan. It is the location of two famous temples, hewn from a sandstone cliff by order of Rameses II (c.1250 B.C.). The entrance to the larger, known as the "Great Temple" and dedicated to Re-Harakhti and other Egyptian deities, is flanked by four colossal statues of Rameses, about 65 ft. high. Histor-

Entrance to the Great Temple at Abu Simbel before removal to save it from flooding. The head of the second figure, broken off by an earthquake centuries ago, was placed in the same position in the reconstruction. (GUNTER R. REITZ—PIX)

One of the great statues of Rameses II as the face is about to be lifted. The colossal figures were cut into blocks weighing from 20 to 30 tons each, then reassembled at a new site. (GUNTER R. REITZ—PIX)

the first two dynasties as the home of the kings and again in the 6th dynasty, when King Pepi I married two daughters of an influential family, members of which continued to hold high office through the 8th dynasty.

AHMES PAPYRUS [ä′mēz pə-pī′rəs], an Egyptian document, also called the Rhind Papyrus, dating back to about 1650 B.C. It contains many mathematical problems and their solutions in hieratic script, a written form of hieroglyphics. The decipherment of the papyrus has provided much of the present knowledge of early Egyptian mathematics. The document, which is an 18-ft. long roll, begins with the words, "Accurate reckoning. The entrance into the knowledge of all existing things and all obscure

secrets. . . It is the scribe A'h-mosé (Ahmes) who copies this writing." The name Rhind refers to A. H. Rhind who acquired the papyrus and gave it to the British Museum.

AKHENATON or AKHENATEN [ä-kə-nä′tən], Egyptian King of the 18th dynasty, reigned 1369–1353 B.C. Son of Amenhotep III and Queen Tiy, he began his reign as Amenhotep IV. After abandoning the traditional Amon worship of Thebes for that of the solar disk, Aton, he changed his name to Akhenaton and destroyed the monumental inscriptions of the other gods. He established a new capital at Akhetaton (modern Tell el- Amarna) where he and his wife, Nefertiti, devoted themselves to art and literature. His neglect of imperial responsibilities led to the loss of Syria and Nubia, and his monotheistic fanaticism alienated the powerful priesthoods, who succeeded in destroying the Aton cult soon after his death.

AMASIS [ə-mā′sĭs] **II** (c.570–527 B.C.), fifth Pharaoh of the 26th dynasty in Egypt. He defended the country against Nebuchadnezzar and Cyrus the Great, and cultivated friendly relations with the Greeks, particularly their rulers and philosophers. He assigned the harbor of Naucratis to Greece. He was an able ruler, and under him Egypt enjoyed considerable prosperity.

AMENEMHET [ä-mən-ĕm′hĕt], name of four Egyptian Pharaohs of the 12th dynasty, of whom the most important were the following. **AMENEMHET I** (reigned 1991–1961 B.C.), founder of the dynasty, ushered in a new era by re-establishing the authority of the Pharaoh, centralizing the government at Thebes, and subjecting the feudal nobles to the state. In his reign the god Amon first came into prominence. **AMENEMHET III** (reigned 1840–1792 B.C.) extended the irrigation system, reclaiming about 27,000 acres, established the first Nilometer.

AMENHOTEP [ä-mən-hō′tĕp], meaning "Amen (Amon) is satisfied," the name of four Pharaohs of the Egyptian 18th Dynasty. **AMENHOTEP I** (reigned 1546–1526 B.C.), son of Ahmose I, furthered his father's domestic political and building policies. He carried the reconquest of Nubia as far south as the Second Cataract, and campaigned against the Libyans and in Palestine-Syria. **AMENHOTEP II** (reigned 1450–1425 B.C.), the successor of Thutmose III, vigorously maintained his father's Asiatic conquests. The reign of **AMENHOTEP III** (1417–1379 B.C.), son of Thutmose IV, marks the height of Egyptian dominion and magnificence. His extensive building program included the rebuilding and expansion of the temple of Amon at Luxor and the creation of two enormous seated statues of himself. Known as the Colossi of Memnon, the statues flanked the entrance to his mortuary temple at Thebes. The dissolution of the Asiatic empire began in the latter part of his long reign and went unchecked in the reign of his son, **AMENHOTEP IV,** who changed his name to Akhenaten (q.v.).

AMON [ä′mən], **AMEN, or AMUN,** an ancient Egyptian god ("the Hidden One"). Of obscure origin, Amon was unimportant outside the Theban district before the rise of the Middle Kingdom at Thebes. Then in the 15th and 13th centuries B.C. he became "king of the gods" and the paramount divinity of the Egyptian empire through the benefactions of the great 18th Dynasty pharaohs who credited Amon with their huge conquests. They and their successors enriched the priesthood of Amon with sizable gifts of land, gold, and booty. Of the many temples erected in Amon's honor, the most notable are Luxor and Karnak, the latter repeatedly enlarged by the additions of several monarchs. So powerful did the high priests of Amon become through their wealth and the use of oracles that they were able, by the end of the 11th century, to make themselves kings. Although Amon's supremacy in Egypt ended with the Assyrian destruction of Thebes (664 B.C.), he became the chief god in Ethiopia. His oracle at the Siwa oasis in the Libyan desert received a visit from Alexander the Great in 332 B.C.

Originally a god of the air, Amon was also a fertility god. The local mother-goddess, Mut, was his consort and Khonsu, the moon-god, his son. Under the name Amon-Re, he was associated with the sun-god, Re, and became a universal deity for whom great hymns of praise were composed. He was depicted in human form or as a ram-headed figure.

ANUBIS [ə-nū′bĭs], jackal-headed god of the ancient Egyptians. As Osiris' usher, he conducted the dead into the presence of the sovereign judges before whom he then weighed their souls. In this capacity he was later identified with Hermes. The son of Nephthys and Osiris, he was abandoned by his mother and brought up by his aunt, Isis. As a man, Anubis accompanied Osiris on his conquest of the world and buried him after his murder. He presided over embalments and funerals.

APIS [ā′pĭs], sacred bull of the ancient Egyptians. He was Osiris' sacred animal and believed to be his reincarnation. He was housed and worshiped at Memphis, where vast underground chambers containing mummified bodies of sacred bulls buried in immense sarcophagi were discovered in 1850. The funeral cult of the dead bull was celebrated in a temple above the galleries.

BUBASTIS [bū-băs′tĭs], ancient Egyptian city, in the eastern Nile Delta. Once important, its site is now marked only by the ruins of Tell Basta near modern Zagazig. It was the seat of the worship of Bast, a cat-headed deity whose festival is described by Herodotus as a time of drinking and revelry. Excavations have disclosed the Great Temple of Bast and her cemetery of sacred cats. Bubastis was the home of the kings of the 22d dynasty.

CANOPIC JARS, modern designation of four stone or pottery jars usually included in the burial equipment of ancient Egyptians. They contained the carefully wrapped internal organs which had been removed from the corpse before mummification. Each jar represented one of the god Horus' four sons, whose responsibility it was to protect the dead from hunger and thirst. The lids—at first plain, then human-headed—eventually represented a human (containing the liver), a baboon (the lungs), a falcon (the stomach), and a dog (the intestines).

The Metropolitan Museum of Art, Gift of J. Pierpont Morgan, 1912

Canopic jars found in a tomb in the ancient city of Abydos, Egypt. They are believed to date from 650–350 B.C.

CHARIOT, one of the earliest forms of two-wheeled vehicle, used first for warfare and later for racing. Known among the Babylonians before 2000 B.C., chariots were introduced to Egypt by Hyksos invaders about 1700 B.C.

The Metropolitan Museum of Art, Rogers Fund, 1921

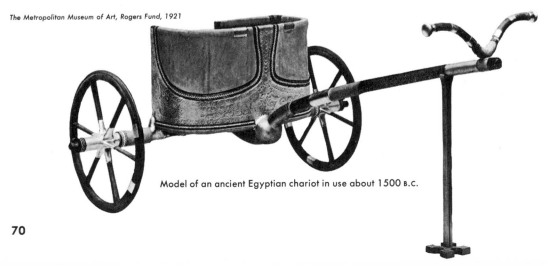

Model of an ancient Egyptian chariot in use about 1500 B.C.

Use of these vehicles spread over the Near East, and later they became widely distributed throughout Europe, North Africa, and Asia—from the British Isles to China. In its day, the chariot was a deadly war weapon comparable to the armored knight of the Middle Ages or to the modern tank. It is probable that the need for such a weapon led in the first place to the development of the wheel in transport, and then to further improvements, such as the spoked wheel, which added to the speed and maneuverability of chariots. Chariot racing became a highly developed sport in ancient civilizations; Roman racing chariots were drawn by two, three, or four, and sometimes even six, eight, or ten horses.

CLEOPATRA [klē-ə-păt′rə, klē-ə-pä′trə], a common Hellenistic name. The most famous Cleopatra (c.69–30 B.C.) was Queen of Egypt, the seventh Ptolemaic princess to bear that name. On the death of her father, Ptolemy XII Auletes, in 51 B.C., the 20-year-old Cleopatra ascended the throne with her 13-year-old brother, Ptolemy XIII, whom she had married according to Ptolemaic practice. The King was persuaded to exile his ambitious sister in 49 B.C. when Julius Caesar arrived and captured him. Tradition has it that Cleopatra was smuggled into Caesar's presence rolled up in a carpet and charmed him over to her cause. His restoration of Cleopatra caused the Alexandrians to revolt and the Romans were besieged from Oct. 48 B.C. until Mar. 47 B.C., when reinforcements arrived. The King was released and died in the flight of the Egyptian forces.

Cleopatra now reigned with a new husband, her 11-year-old brother, Ptolemy XIV. The captivated Caesar

Cleopatra, as depicted in a sandstone frieze from the Temple of Hathor at Dendera, Egypt. (EGYPTIAN MUSEUM)

spent the rest of the winter with her before resuming his conquests. In 46 B.C. Cleopatra and her son by Caesar, Ptolemy Caesarion, joined Caesar in Rome where the Dictator's attentions to the Egyptian queen aroused Roman suspicions. When Caesar fell to assassins in 44 B.C., Cleopatra returned to Egypt, poisoned her consort, and made Caesarion co-ruler.

In 41 B.C. Cleopatra was summoned to Tarsus by Marcus Antonius (Mark Antony), Roman commander in the East, who intended to demand money from her to pursue his campaigns. She arrived dressed as the goddess Aphrodite and entertained him aboard her pleasure barge, with the result that Antony got his funds and Cleopatra arranged the murder of her sister Arsinoë (q.v.). Antony spent the winter with Cleopatra in Egypt, but they did not meet again until their public and illegal marriage in Antioch in 37 B.C. Antony now had the resources for a Parthian campaign and Cleopatra gained the hope of control over Rome's eastern territories. This marriage, the failure of the Parthian war, Antony's recognition of Caesarion as Caesar's son and heir, and his refusal to allow Octavia, his legal wife and Octavian's sister, to join him aroused public opinion in Rome against him.

The final breach between Octavian, who became the first Roman emperor five years later, and Antony came in 32 B.C. when Antony formally divorced Octavia. Octavian, not wishing to appear to start a civil war, declared war on Cleopatra. A decisive naval battle was fought at Actium (31 B.C.). When Cleopatra fled, so did Antony, assuring their defeat. Octavian attacked Alexandria in 30 B.C. and when a false report of Cleopatra's suicide reached Antony, he took his own life. Unwilling to be captured by Octavian, Cleopatra chose death from the bite of an asp. Caesarion was put to death, as was the eldest son of Cleopatra and Antony. Their daughter, Cleopatra Selene, married Juba II of Mauretania. The death of Cleopatra VII ended the dynasty of the Ptolemies, and Egypt became a Roman province.

Not as beautiful as tradition or the plays of Shakespeare and G. B. Shaw would portray her, Cleopatra was an intelligent, charming, and able woman, the only Ptolemaic ruler able to speak the native Egyptian language.

DENDERA [děn′də-rə] (anc. *Tentyra*), in antiquity, capital of the sixth district of Upper Egypt, on the west bank of the Nile, opposite Qena. It was renowned for its great temple to the goddess Hathor, built on a site that had been hallowed since early dynastic times. Begun in the 1st century B.C., the temple still stands. The ceiling of the Outer Hypostyle Hall is covered with astronomical scenes, and the staircases depict processions of Hathor. Forming the ceiling of one of the smaller chambers was the only surviving Egyptian circular zodiac, now in Paris. The sacred area also included temples to Isis, Horus, and others, a sacred lake, and a sanatorium. Secular remains include graves of the early dynasties and large tombs of the late Old Kingdom. Pop., 17,000.

EBERS [ā′bərs] **PAPYRUS,** one of the best-preserved Egyptian medical documents, which contains instructions for the treatment of virtually every disorder known to the ancient Egyptians, including headaches, heart trouble, and crocodile bites. The papyrus was discovered in Thebes in 1862 and came into the hands of the German Egyptologist Georg Ebers in 1873. It is believed to have been compiled about 1550 B.C. About one ft. wide and 68 ft. long, the document contains instructions for the preparation of salves, gargles, and inhalations, and includes a headache preparation which contains "berry-of-the-poppy-plant," apparently an Egyptian reference to opium.

EGYPTIAN [ĭ-jĭp'shən], the language of ancient Egypt. It constitutes a branch of the Afro-Asiatic family of languages. Egyptian was in active use from an unknown length of time before the beginning of Dynasty I (c.3200 B.C.) until the 17th century A.D. As a "dead" language it is still preserved in the liturgy of the Coptic Church. During its long life the language changed extensively, undergoing five stages: Old, Middle, and Late Egyptian, Demotic, and Coptic. All of these can now be understood, but only Coptic can be pronounced, since vowels are not expressed in the writing of the other forms.

EGYPTOLOGY [ē-jĭp-tŏl'ə-jē], the study of the archeology and culture of ancient Egypt in all its aspects, such as art, architecture, history, language, literature, and religion. In considering Egypt before the beginning of the historic period, about 3000 B.C., Egyptology naturally merges with general prehistory. Greek influences and artifacts postdating the conquest by Alexander (332 B.C.) are usually studied as part of Hellenistic culture. The coming of Christianity, about 200 A.D., ends the period with which Egyptology is concerned. However, the Coptic language, a direct descendant of the earlier tongue, belongs to the field of Egyptian philology.

Early Egyptology. At the beginning of the Renaissance, Western knowledge of ancient Egypt was confined to the writings of a number of classical authors, including Herodotus, Diodorus Siculus, Strabo, Ptolemy, Plutarch, and Horapollon; to references in the Bible and remarks by the Jewish historian Josephus; and to ancient Egyptian monuments collected by the Romans, especially obelisks.

By the middle of the 17th century Europeans began to publish accounts of travel in Egypt. The British astronomer John Greaves (1602–52) was in Alexandria in 1637–38, traveled as far as Memphis, and in 1646 wrote *Pyramidographia*, thoroughly reviewing ancient writings and giving his own careful observations and measurements of the pyramids of Giza. Coptic manuscripts began to be brought into Europe at the beginning of this century, and Athanasius Kircher (1601–80) produced, from 1636 onward, scholarly studies of this language. In the next century many Europeans traveled in Egypt and published accounts of their journeys. But a systematic study of Egyptian antiquities really began with Napoleon. Napoleon took with him on his expedition to Egypt in 1798 a great number of scientists, scholars, and artists. One of them, Dominique Vivant Denon (1747–1825), published his own account, but the group concentrated on the publication of *Description de l'Égypte* (1809–28), including five large folios of engravings of the antiquities.

The Decipherment of Hieroglyphs. Kircher had attempted to interpret the hieroglyphic inscriptions, but had followed the lead of Horapollon in believing that the signs were wholly symbolic. In the 18th century many others followed the same course. The Danish Coptic scholar Georg Zoëga (1755–1809) and the French professor of Syriac, Joseph de Guignes (1721–1800), though wrong on other points, had guessed that the cartouches contained the names of royalty. The Swedish diplomat Johan Åkerblad (1760–1819) in 1802 identified about half the alphabet used in the demotic section of the Rosetta Stone; 12 years later the British physician and scientist Thomas Young (1773–1829) read several royal names and made other advances toward decipherment. In 1822 Jean François Champollion (1790–1832), working on the Ro-

Excavation of the tomb of Mentemhet at Luxor. Mentemhet was a high priest and governor of Upper Egypt during the 25th Dynasty.

H. Wright—Birnback

Workers excavating the temple of Queen Hatshepsut at Deir el-Bahri use a derrick to hoist pieces of stone statuary into position.

The Metropolitan Museum of Art, Egyptian Expedition

setta Stone, read the name of Rameses from another monument and realized that the hieroglyphic characters and the cursive writing of the same, hieratic, were phonetic renderings of the language, and not symbolic.

Excavation. Most of the major monuments of Egyptian antiquity had never been lost to view, but many others were sites of later villages or individual dwellings, and all had to be cleared. In the ancient necropolis of Memphis and elsewhere the low structures were covered by desert sands. The expedition of Napoleon disclosed that there was an almost inexhaustible supply of antiquities, and for the rest of the century much excavation was merely the collecting of booty. Of those early engaged in such collecting, one of the most careful was Giovanni Belzoni (1778–1823). In general, records of origin were carelessly kept, if at all, and crude methods of excavation were employed. Unwanted objects were cast aside and often destroyed. Frequently the local inhabitants were the actual discoverers of antiquities, and even today some surreptitious excavations continue. Many of the great museum collections of Egyptian antiquities were acquired through these early unscientific excavations.

In an effort to control excavation, Auguste Mariette (1821–81) was appointed Conservator of Monuments in 1858, and in 1899 the Department of Antiquities was organized under Gaston Maspero (1846–1916). Mariette also founded the first Museum of Antiquities in Cairo. At present all archeological activities in Egypt are under the control of the Department of Antiquities. Permits for excavating are given only to experienced scholars representing institutions of learning. The majority of objects found and all unique pieces are retained by the Egyptian Museum.

Mariette began excavating Sakkara in 1850, systematically exploring the Serapeum, the burial complex of the Apis bulls. Later he uncovered many mastabas (tomb superstructures) of the officials of the Old Kingdom. Just before his death in 1881 he found the inner chambers of the Sakkara pyramids, with walls covered with Pyramid Texts. These earliest religious writings are the foundation for any study of Egyptian religion. Various excavators working for the Department of Antiquities have excavated the mud-brick mastabas of the first two dynasties, the temple complex of the Step Pyramid of the 3d Dynasty, and an unfinished step pyramid.

The Giza pyramids were examined and measured by Richard Howard-Vyse and John Shae Perring in 1837–38. In 1880 Flinders Petrie (1853–1942) made more exact measurements. The tombs of the officials of this area were excavated by Selim Hassan for the Egyptian University, Hermann Junker for the Austrian Academy of Science, and George Reisner for the Boston Museum of Fine Arts and Harvard University. Reisner found in 1925 the hidden tomb of Hetepheres, mother of Khufu (Cheops). Through careful observation and removal of the disintegrated remains it was possible to reconstruct the gold-inlaid furniture. In 1954 a dismantled solar ship belonging to Khufu was found in a pit alongside the Great Pyramid, and is being reassembled.

Many tomb chapels of Tell el-Amarna were known to early travelers. The town site first came to attention in 1887, when natives offered for sale clay tablets with

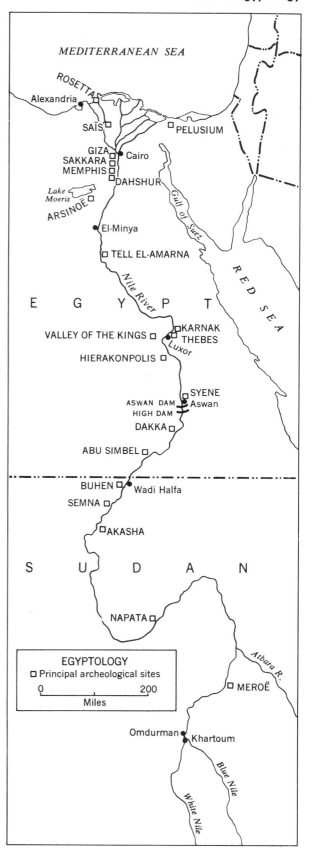

cuneiform writing. Wallis Budge of the British Museum purchased many. They proved to be the official correspondence of Asiatic princes with Amenhotep III and Akhenaton. Petrie excavated here in 1891–92. The best of the Amarna sculpture, including the painted head of Nefertiti, was found by Ludwig Borchardt (1863–1938) of the German Oriental Society in excavations from 1907 to 1914. From this area comes much knowledge of the Amarna religious revolution.

Most of the burials from the vicinity of ancient Thebes were robbed in ancient times, and records of the trials of the thieves are extant. In 1871 a local inhabitant discovered a cache containing mummies of some of the Kings of the 18th-20th dynasties, and ten years later these came to the attention of the authorities. No unrobbed royal tomb was known until 1922, when Howard Carter (1873–1939) found the burial chamber of Tutankhamen, which showed the splendor of the funerary equipment of even a minor Pharaoh.

Collecting the Records. When Champollion deciphered the hieroglyphs there was no body of Egyptian texts available. He sought to remedy this by his copies. Systematic recording of the monuments began with the Prussian expedition of 1842–45 under Karl Richard Lepsius (1810–84), which completed 12 giant folios. Standards of accuracy improved, and reliable copies of a great number of inscriptions are now available. The French Archaeological Institute has been copying temples of the Ptolemaic and Roman periods. The Egypt Exploration Society of London has published, in *Archaeological Survey of Egypt*, descriptions of many tomb chapels throughout Egypt. Norman de Garis Davies (1865–1941), who did

much of this, also made records for the Metropolitan Museum of Art in New York. Since 1924 the Oriental Institute of the University of Chicago has produced copies of the scenes and inscriptions of the temples of Ramesses III about Luxor.

In 1897 the Prussian Academy of Science inaugurated a project for a hieroglyphic dictionary under the editorship of Adolf Erman (1854–1937). To collect material, leading Egyptologists gave their assistance for the next 15 years, copying inscriptions in museums and in Egypt. Especially able was Kurt Sethe (1869–1934), whose copies have formed the basis of many publications by himself and his pupils. The dictionary began to be published in 1926, the last volume of references appearing in 1953.

Papyri are other sources of information. On them are written stories, historical records, letters, accounts, and religious literature, including the Book of the Dead. The most important documents have been well published.

Linguistic Studies. For almost 60 years after Champollion there was no real understanding of the grammar of ancient Egyptian, but with Erman's analysis of Late Egyptian in 1880 a systematic examination was begun. As Erman continued to make advances, other scholars supported him. His methods provided a firm foundation for futher research on the structure of the language, and modern translations have a high degree of accuracy. Among the leading contemporary grammarians are Sir Alan Gardiner of England and Elmar Edel of Germany.

Centers of Egyptology. The largest collection of Egyptian antiquities, including the Tutankhamen treasure, is in the Egyptian Museum, Cairo. In Europe outstanding collections are in the museums of Berlin, Leiden, Turin,

Part of the outstanding collection of Egyptian antiquities on view at the British Museum, London. In the foreground is the massive sarcophagus of an ancient scribe. (ART REFERENCE BUREAU)

the Louvre in Paris, and the British Museum. In the United States the Museum of Fine Arts, Boston, the Metropolitan Museum of Art and the Brooklyn Museum, and the University Museum, Philadelphia, contain the largest collections; an excellent smaller one is at the Oriental Institute, Chicago.

The Department of Antiquities of Egypt is now foremost in excavation. In Cairo are the French Institute of Oriental Archaeology (founded, 1881), the German Archaeological Institute, the Swiss Archaeological Institute (a private institution), and several smaller centers. The Egypt Exploration Fund, later the Egypt Exploration Society, of London, has been working since 1882 recording inscriptions and excavating. The Oriental Institute of Chicago has permanent headquarters in Luxor.

HATHOR [hăth'ôr], ancient Egyptian sky-goddess, identified by the Greeks with Aphrodite. Her principal temple was at Dendera, but in her various aspects she was worshiped throughout Egypt. Her origin is traced to the worship of the sistrum, a metallic jangling instrument, which became one of her chief symbols. In myth she was a cow-goddess, and in Thebes, a funerary goddess in the form of a cow living in the western cliffs. As a tree-goddess she gave drink to the dead. Her marriage to Horus was celebrated annually at Idfu, where her son Harsomtus was conceived. She was goddess of women, love, song, dance, music, and drink, and also of foreign lands, particularly Byblos, Sinai, and Punt.

HATSHEPSUT [hăt-shĕp'soōt], Egyptian Queen of the mid-18th Dynasty (reigned c.1490–1469 B.C.), daughter of Thutmose I, and wife of her half brother Thutmose II. After the death of the latter Thutmose III should normally have succeeded to the throne, but Hatshepsut was coregent with him for two years and was then virtually sole ruler until her death 20 years later. Her reign was one of profound peace and prosperity, celebrated for an expedition to the land of Punt (Somaliland) to acquire incense and other exotic products, and for her superb mortuary temple at Deir el-Bahri.

HELIOPOLIS [hē-lē-ŏp'ə-lĭs], ancient Egyptian city, the Biblical On, 6 mi. northeast of Cairo. A center of higher learning, it was the city of the sun-god Re-Harakhti-Atum, and contained one of the oldest and richest temple complexes in Egypt. The nine gods (*Ennead*) of its creation myth were venerated throughout the land. The priests of Heliopolis were accounted very learned and exercised a continuous influence on the crown, as coronation by Atum was essential from early dynastic times for assuming effective rule. Akhenaton's "heresy" may have originated in the apprehension of Re-Harakhti's priests over the growing power of the Theban god Amon. Town and temples were devastated before the time of Strabo and have served as quarries since. The earliest dateable fragments are from a temple of Zoser (27th century B.C.); the only standing relic is an obelisk of Senusret I (20th century B.C.).

HIEROGLYPHS [hī'ər-ə-glĭfs], oldest and most formal of the writing signs employed by the ancient Egyptians. The name is derived from the word *hieroglyphikos* (Gr. *hieros*,

"sacred"; *glyphein*, "to carve") applied by the Greeks to this script, which in their time was used principally for inscriptions on temple walls. Hieroglyphs are pictures, and by extension the word "hieroglyphic" has come to be applied to any picture writing (for example, Cretan, Hittite, and certain pre-Columbian scripts of the Western Hemisphere). Egyptian hieroglyphs were in use for about 3,500 years: the earliest inscriptions are legends on monuments of the late predynastic period (c.3100 B.C.). The latest inscription is dated in the year 394 A.D. and comes from the island of Philae.

Although the ability to read them was lost for many centuries, hieroglyphs early attracted the curiosity of scholars such as Herodotus, Diodorus, Tacitus, Plutarch, Clement of Alexandria, and finally Horapollon. Most of these writers were especially interested in the ideographic aspects of hieroglyphic writing and either were ignorant of, or disregarded, the fact that many signs were used phonetically. As a result, post-Renaissance efforts at decipherment proceeded on a purely symbolic level. A serious attempt along these lines was made in the mid-17th century by the Jesuit Athanasius Kircher, whose principal lasting contribution to the subject lay in his idea that the language expressed by hieroglyphs was ancestral to Coptic. Actual decipherment was achieved only in the early 19th century after the discovery of the Rosetta stone. Of the persons associated with this achievement, Jean François Champollion is usually given most credit. He went on from his first discoveries to establish the values of most of the phonetic signs, compile a dictionary, and write a grammar of ancient Egyptian.

Hieroglyphs are small pictures, sometimes exquisitely carved and colored. As already suggested, they function in two distinct ways: (1) as word signs with direct, derived, or determinative meanings, and (2) as phonetic symbols used to indicate the consonantal skeleton of words, some signs standing for one, others for two or three consonants. Vowels are not written. Biconsonantal and triconsonantal signs are often accompanied by one or more monoconsonantal signs, which repeat some or all of the consonants. The determinatives help to distinguish words spelled with identical consonants but having different meanings.

Hieroglyphic inscriptions may be arranged in columns or in horizontal lines; the writing may proceed from right to left—the most frequent arrangement—or from left to right. In cases where symmetry was desired, as around a doorway, an inscription was sometimes divided into two or more parts, each part having a different direction. The orientation of the signs shows the direction in which to read: one always proceeds toward the faces of human and animal figures. Within columns or lines the signs were grouped in rectangles, and the columns or rows were separated by carved or painted lines. On walls of buildings explanatory legends were planned as integral parts of the sculptured decoration; sometimes it is chiefly the size of the figures that enables one to tell where pictorial representation ceases and writing begins.

Hieroglyphic writing was only one of several scripts employed in ancient Egypt. For writing in ink on papyrus, the detailed drawings were usually replaced by a simplified script termed *hieratic*. Over the centuries this became increasingly cursive until it was a kind of shorthand. This

Jean François Champollion, noted for his contributions to the translation of hieroglyphs. The accompanying hieroglyphs, with English pronunciation and meaning, show the complexity of ancient Egyptian writing.

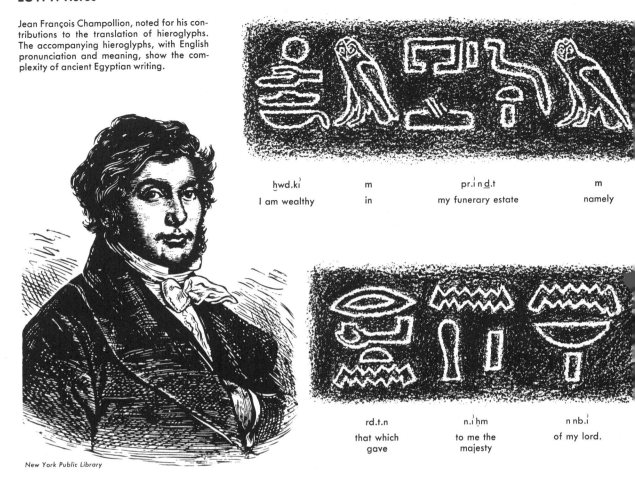

hwd.kı	m	pr.ı n d̠.t	m
I am wealthy	in	my funerary estate	namely

rd.t.n	n.ı ḥm	n nb.ı
that which gave	to me the majesty	of my lord

New York Public Library

last script, *demotic,* was the one in ordinary use during the Greek and Roman occupations of Egypt, and bore little resemblance to the hieroglyphs from which it was derived. Because it was so difficult to read, the scholars who translated the Bible into Egyption in the 3d and 4th centuries A.D. rejected it and employed the Greek alphabet, supplemented by a few signs to render Egyptian sounds not found in Greek. This kind of writing and the stage of Egyptian it records are called *Coptic.*

Hieroglyphic Hittite, in use from about 1500 to 700 B.C., is as yet incompletely deciphered, though bilingual inscriptions in Hittite and Phoenician found at Karatepe in Turkey in 1947 largely confirm previous interpretations. The hieroglyphic writing used in Crete from about 2000 to 1700 B.C. still resists decipherment.

HORUS [hō′rəs], in Egyptian religion, ancient sky-god whose eyes were the sun and the moon, worshiped in the form of a falcon. As Re-Harakhti he was also a sun-god. Originally, Horus was probably an Upper Egyptian deity who extended his control over Lower Egypt. His war with his wicked brother Seth ended in a lawsuit over the sovereignty of Egypt, in which Horus was triumphant. From the 1st Dynasty he was considered the divine ancestor of the Pharaohs; thus his lawsuit became the legal foundation of the kingship. He was later connected with the Osiris cycle, and as the son of Isis and Osiris, avenged the murder of Osiris by warring against Seth.

HYKSOS [hĭk′sōs, hĭk′sŏs] (Egyptian, "rulers of foreign countries"), Asiatic Semites who settled in Egypt and eventually ousted the weak kings of the late Middle Kingdom (c.1730 B.C.). They established a capital at Avaris in the eastern delta and for a time ruled all of Egypt. Direct information about them comes either from the hostile Theban rulers who gradually displaced and finally drove them out (c.1570 B.C.), or from later nationalistic writers, who recalled them as a scourge. Contemporary evidence suggests that they fostered and assimilated Egyptian culture. Certainly they brought valuable new ideas and implements: the vertical loom, the composite bow, and the horse and chariot. Furthermore it was through their domination that Egypt was forced to awareness of the world beyond her borders.

IMHOTEP [ĭm-hō′tĕp], ancient Egyptian, chief minister of Zoser (c.2650 B.C.), and architect of the step pyramid of Sakkara, the first stone building. He had a great reputation as craftsman, architect, wise man, and doctor, and was later deified as "Imhotep the great, son of Ptah." Scribes made libations to him before beginning to write. In later times he was worshiped primarily as a god of medicine and was identified with Asklepios (Aesculapius); healing miracles were effected at his principal cult centers.

ISIS [ī′sĭs], ancient Egyptian goddess. Originally the personification of the royal throne, she was regarded as the sister and wife of Osiris and mother of Horus. As a funerary goddess she was one of the protectors of the coffin, and from her function as protectress of the youthful Horus developed her special skill and reputation in magic. In Greco-Roman times Isis and her mysteries became a world religion, she herself being the universal mother goddess. Her cult was preserved until 560 A.D.

JEWELRY, earliest surviving was made by the ancient Egyptians, who did their best work in the Middle Kingdom (1991–1778 B.C.). Egyptian women wore circlets or tiaras over wigs, hair rings fastened to locks of hair, necklaces, bracelets, finger rings, and narrow girdles of beads round their hips. Gold and silver, almost the only metals used, were set with stones such as carnelian, amethyst, turquoise, lapis lazuli, feldspar, beryl, garnet, jasper, hematite, and rock crystal, as well as glazed steatite. Beads were frequently made of blue or green Egyptian faïence (essentially glazed powdered quartz) mainly as a substitute for more costly stones. Colored glass was also known. Egyptian jewelry depended for its effect on shape, design, and combinations of color, stones being used for their hue and not for their intrinsic value. At a certain stage even gold was given a reddish-purple bloom by the addition of iron. Gold and silver ball- and barrel-shaped beads were hollow; they were molded in two halves and soldered together. Circlets were made of fine twisted gold wire and rosettes of beaten gold. Among the more magnificent specimens were gold pendants to which were soldered narrow gold strips set on edge to form the outlines of the design. The compartments thus formed were inlaid with pieces of colored stone ground to exact shape and fixed with cement. Finger rings were often mounted with scarabs. These were originally tied to the finger with a loop of cord—the origin of the modern finger ring.

During the New Kingdom (1573–1085 B.C.) earrings were more commonly worn than before. They were either passed through a perforation in the lobe of the ear or made in the form of a cleft ring and clipped onto the ear. Shell, bone, carnelian, jasper, faïence, gold, and bronze were the materials used. From this period date signet rings, mostly of copper, but also of gold, electrum, and bronze. Other finger rings were made of faïence, gold, carnelian, and bronze. The later jewelry of the Egyptians showed an increased use of floral and vegetable design motifs, such as rosettes, palmettes, leaves, petals, and small fruits.

Mycenaean jewelry (c.1800–1100 B.C.) was mainly decorated with embossed designs of circles, spirals, rosettes, palmettes, and figures of lions, goats, and sphinxes. The designs were unevenly punched in relief into thin sheets of gold laid on a yielding substance such as pitch; spirals were perhaps produced by hammering over wires. Some use was made of inlaid glass paste. The jewelry took the form of strips of gold foil, earrings, pins, rings, necklaces, and pendants. It was not cast solid except when the nature of the article demanded solidity.

From about the 9th to 7th centuries B.C. the designs on Mycenaean jewelry showed Assyrian influence, for example, in the use of rosettes. At the same time much use was made of granulation, a technique brought to a high standard of perfection by the Etruscans in about the 7th to 5th centuries B.C. Granulated work consists of small metal globules soldered onto a plain surface of the same metal. Etruscan jewelry of about the 7th century B.C. was sometimes decorated with friezes of lions, chimeras, and palmettes—motifs that betray Oriental influence. Cylindrical earrings and fibulae (clasps) were common.

KARNAK [kär′năk], tiny village in Upper Egypt, noted for its ancient temples, lying just east of the Nile about 1¼ mi. north of Luxor (q.v.) and occupying part of the site of Thebes. The temples are grouped in three walled areas, with the center area containing the temple of Amon-Ra, King of the Gods. Though chiefly built during the New Kingdom, these temples were under construction for more than 2,000 years, beginning before the Middle Kingdom and ending in the Roman period.

The main temple of Amon is an aggregate of separate elements and chiefly renowned for its size: the length along the main axis is nearly a quarter-mile; the front pylon is 370 ft. wide and 142 ft. high; the great hypostyle hall, measuring 388 ft. by 170 ft., is supported by 134 columns arranged in 16 rows, the central columns being 69 ft. high, 11¾ ft. in diameter, and topped by capitals 11 ft. high. An avenue of sphinxes extends the quarter-mile south from the main temple area to the walled enclosure of Mut, Amon's consort. Just north of the Amon precinct is that of Montu. Numerous additional temples are in the area.

Rameses III built this part of the temple of Amon-Ra at Karnak. Its massiveness and symmetry are typical of Egyptian architecture.

Since the New Kingdom Pharaohs lived and warred under the standard of Amon, records of their achievements were inscribed at Karnak, thus leaving a rich treasury for historians. Excavation and recording are making available the information contained on thousands of square yards of decorated wall surface and on decorated blocks found as reused in foundations and in the fillings of the 10 pylons.

KHAFRE [käf'rā], Greek name Chephren, fourth King (reigned c.2556–2526 B.C.) of the 4th Dynasty of ancient Egypt, brother or son of Khufu. He was the builder of the Second Pyramid of Giza. The Sphinx at Giza is probably a gigantic portrait of him. His superb diorite statue, in the Egyptian Museum, Cairo, is one of the greatest masterpieces of Egyptian art. His reign marks the peak of the materialism and royal absolutism of the Old Kingdom.

KHUFU [koo'foo], Greek name Cheops, second King of the 4th Dynasty of ancient Egypt (reigned c.2598–2568 B.C.). son of Snefru. He was the builder of the Great Pyramid of Giza. Its size and the massive stone blocks used in its construction well illustrate the power and technical competence of the dynasty. Khufu worked the alabaster quarries of Sinai and exploited the diorite quarries in Nubia. Later traditions of the cruelty, tyranny, and impiety of Khufu and Khafre, probably inspired by the obviously colossal effort of pyramid building, are without any foundation in fact.

LUXOR [lŭk'sôr] (Arab. **EL-UQSOR**), city in Egypt, located on the east bank of the Nile, 415 mi. by rail south of Cairo at the site of ancient Thebes (q.v.), and today the tourist center for Upper Egypt. Its Arabic name derives from "Castra," the name applied by the Romans, who had two camps there.

Luxor's chief monument is a temple to Amon, Mut, and Khons. The ruins are of structures erected mainly by Amenhotep III (early 14th century B.C.) and expanded by Rameses II (13th century B.C.). The building was at first a normal New Kingdom temple, with pylon, forecourt, hypostyle hall, anterooms, sanctuary, chapels, and storerooms. Amenhotep III began enlarging it by erecting a second hypostyle hall before the pylon, but only the center colonnade was completed. Its 14 beautifully proportioned columns, each nearly 52 ft. high beneath its abacus and architrave, are among the most awesome sights in Egypt. Rameses II is responsible for the larger court in front of this colonnade, as well as for numerous colossi, two imposing obelisks before the main entrance, and many other additions or repairs.

The temple was called the "southern harem" (that is, of Amon) and was connected with the Karnak (q.v.) complex by a paved road bordered by recumbent rams. Once a year during the Festival of the Harem, representations of Amon and his family were brought by river from Karnak for a formal visit to this temple.

A mosque now occupies part of the court of Rameses II, and a Coptic church the first anteroom behind the original hypostyle hall. Pop., 34,555.

MEMPHIS [mĕm'fĭs], ancient capital of Egypt, beneath modern Mit Rahineh some 12 mi. south of Cairo. More generally Memphis includes the ancient cemeteries from Abu Roash to Medum, where the number and splendor of the monuments give substance to traditions concerning the glory of the lost city. Royal tombs or cenotaphs of the 1st Dynasty, what are probably substructures of 2d-Dynasty royal tombs, and the undoubted royal cemeteries of the 3d through 10th Dynasties (see PYRAMIDS) are known. A great temple of Ptah (New Kingdom) was the third largest in Egypt. From the Old Kingdom on the goddess Hathor had a shrine here; and from the New Kingdom on the Apis bulls were buried at Sakkara in extensive catacombs.

Memphis supposedly was founded when Menes, the

Elliott Erwitt—Magnum

The Colossus of Rameses II, gigantic statue at the entrance to the temple of Luxor. In the background is one of a pair of obelisks that once stood at this site. The other was taken to Paris in 1831.

Restored columns of the temple of Luxor.

United Arab Republic Tourist Office

first King of the 1st Dynasty, built a fortress, the White Wall, at this place, and the royal residence was usually in the area until the 18th Dynasty. Even when the capital was elsewhere, Memphis was of crucial military importance; Ethiopians, Assyrians, Persians, and Macedonian Greeks boasted of its conquest. In the time of Alexandria it was still an imposing and cosmopolitan city. Its downfall began with the destruction of the temples by order of Theodosius the Great, and the buildings were dismantled for stone by the builders of medieval Cairo.

MENES [mē'nēz], traditionally, first King (c.3000 B.C.), of the 1st Dynasty of Egypt, which united Upper and Lower Egypt. He founded Memphis and built the temple of Ptah and an antiflood embankment around the city. No certain examples of his name exist before the 19th Dynasty. He was probably identical with Narmer and the immediate predecessor of Aha, second King of the dynasty.

MENKAURE [mĕn-kou'rā] **or MENKURE** [mĕn-ko͞o'rā], Greek name Mycerinus, Egyptian King of the late 4th Dynasty (reigned c.2525–2508 B.C.), son of Khafre. He built the Third Pyramid of Giza, much smaller than its predecessors but notable for the greatly increased use of granite in its construction.

MERENPTAH [mĕr-ĕn-tä'] **or MERNEPTAH** [mər-nĕp'tä], Egyptian Pharaoh (reigned c.1223–1211 B.C.), 13th son and successor of Rameses II. In the fifth year of his reign he defeated a Libyan invasion which had penetrated deeply into the Delta. He probably campaigned in Palestine, as a stele records "Israel is desolated," the only mention of Israel in hieroglyphic. The long-standing supposition that he was the Pharaoh of the Exodus is without foundation.

MUMMIFICATION [mŭm-ĭ-fĭ-kā'shən], the process of embalming or artificially preserving dead bodies, especially as practiced by the ancient Egyptians. The Egyptians of antiquity are widely known for their success in embalming the dead; and their characteristically wrapped, embalmed corpses, called "mummies," are to be found in many museums. The word "mummy" is of uncertain origin; it may be derived from Persian *mummia*, "bitumen," because of the mistaken idea that bitumen was an essential element in the embalming process.

The earliest sure evidence of mummification comes from the early 4th Dynasty (c.2600 B.C.), the latest from the 5th century A.D. Our knowledge of the process comes in part from Greek authors, especially Herodotus and Diodorus Siculus, and in part from modern medical and chemical studies of mummies. No Egyptian treatise on the embalming of humans has been found, but there is one on the embalming of sacred bulls. Errors in the Greek accounts can be corrected on the basis of the modern studies, and the general procedure can be outlined.

An incision was made in the left side of the abdomen or, later, the pelvic region, and through this the internal organs, with the exception of the heart and sometimes the kidneys, were removed. Sometimes the brain was removed through the nostrils. The internal organs might also be left in place or else removed by allowing them to dissolve in oils or unspecified liquids injected through the anus and

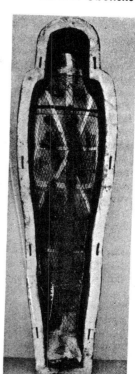

The Metropolitan Museum of Art, Museum Excavations, 1922–23; Rogers Fund, 1923

The mummy in the coffin at the right was found near the ruins of ancient Thebes, Egypt. At left is the painted coffin lid.

later drained off. If removed, the viscera were washed, treated with palm wine mixed with spices, wrapped in linen, and stored in canopic jars or, less commonly, in the body itself. More often the body cavity was stuffed with resin, resin-impregnated linen, a mixture of sawdust and resin, or the like.

Next the body was desiccated by being covered for several months with solid natron, a naturally occurring soda consisting of a mixture of impure sodium carbonate and sodium bicarbonate. Then the body was washed, anointed with special oils and ointments, and rubbed with fragrant materials. Finally it was wrapped in strips of fine linen, first each digit and limb separately, and then, with wider strips, the entire corpse. The wrappings near the skin were arranged so that they imitated body contours; those outside were often arranged in intricate geometric patterns.

The entire embalming process, from the day of death to that of burial, occupied 70 days. It was essentially a religious rite to preserve the body in which the spirit was thought to reside in the afterlife. The place of embalming was called the "place of purification." Aided by the extremely dry climate, the measures described were sufficient to preserve the dead, at best in a fair degree of lifelikeness, at worst as bundles of bones covered with blackened skin.

The word "mummy" is also applied to bodies buried in predynastic times in Egypt and to bodies of various American Indians which have been naturally preserved by the dryness of the climate.

OBELISKS [ŏb'ə-lĭsks] are tapering monolithic shafts of stone, square in cross section, topped by a pyramidion.

Red granite obelisk (c.1950 B.C.) of Senusret I at Heliopolis, Egypt.
(MARBURG—ART REFERENCE BUREAU)

They were first used in ancient Egypt, and their significance is not surely known. The typical large obelisk was of granite, its pyramidion covered with electrum or copper. On the shaft were inscribed the names of the ruler who commissioned the monument and the god to whom it was dedicated. In the New Kingdom, when most of the existing large examples were erected, it was usual for a pair of obelisks to stand before the pylons of important temples.

The earliest obelisks discovered date from the 5th and 6th Dynasties. They are less than 3 ft. tall and were associated with tombs. Possibly related but somewhat more squat obelisks characterized the 5th-Dynasty sun temples. These had a masonry base, probably more than 60 ft. high, which was provided with an internal ascending corridor to reach the platform on which the obelisk stood.

The earliest surviving large obelisk is one erected by Senusret I (12th Dynasty) at Heliopolis. Only four others are still standing in Egypt, though a number have been moved elsewhere, to İstanbul, Rome, Paris, London, and New York. Rome alone contains 12. The 69-ft.-high red granite obelisks, known as Cleopatra's Needles, brought to London and New York in the 19th century, were originally erected by Thutmose III c.1475 B.C. in Heliopolis. The largest obelisk ever projected was abandoned in the quarry after the stone was discovered to contain a number of serious faults. It would have measured 137 ft. and weighed 1,168 tons. The feat of detaching monuments of this scale from the quarry, moving them to their eventual destination, and erecting them—without steel tools, pulleys, or winches—was a considerable one.

OSIRIS [ō-sī'rĭs], Egyptian god of the dead. He was the oldest son of Geb (Earth) and Nut (Sky), his wife being his sister Isis. He was usually depicted as a mummy wearing a tall crown flanked by two feathers, and holding the crook and flail, emblems of kingship; his face and hands were usually green because he had been mummified.

His was a complex nature. He was a dead king and royal god. He was a nature and vegetation god, maker of corn, identified with the Nile and its inundation, that rose from his body and fertilized the land, and identified also with Orion and the moon. He was also god of the dead.

His earliest cult center was Busiris in the Delta, where he supplanted and absorbed Anzeti, an early hero-god. But later his principal center was Abydos, where he absorbed the earlier local god Khentamentiu, "Chief of the Westerners." No complete Egyptian version of his myth has survived, but Plutarch's account is evidently based on sound traditions.

The myth represents Osiris as a good and beneficent king, murdered by his brother Seth. Isis finds his corpse, only to have Seth dismember it. But she buries the scattered limbs (hence the local relic cults throughout Egypt), and Anubis mummifies the body. Isis conceives and bears a posthumous son, Horus, who avenges his father and is declared by the gods to be the legitimate king and heir of Osiris after a long lawsuit. Thereafter Osiris became king of the dead and Horus king of the living. Worship of Osiris may be traced back to the 1st Dynasty, but he only emerged into prominence as god of the dead in the late Old Kingdom and finally triumphed in the First Intermediate Period. Henceforward every man aspired to become an Osiris, and, after successfully surviving a trial before Osiris, to live eternally in his kingdom. Worship of Osiris became particularly popular in the later dynasties, largely as a reaction to foreign domination.

PAPYRI [pǝ-pī'rī], documents written on a kind of paper made in Egypt as early as the 1st Dynasty (c.3000 B.C.). This paper was exported from Egypt to the entire Mediterranean world, where it continued in use until at least the 11th century A.D. Papyrus can be made from freshly picked stems of the reed *Cyperus papyrus*, which are cut into uniform lengths, sliced into thin strips, and laid in rows on a linen-covered slab, their edges overlapping. A second layer is placed on the first with strips at right angles, and the whole covered with linen and beaten for about two hours. The sheets so formed are dried under pressure and polished with a stone until the surface is perfectly smooth.

In antiquity the color of good-quality new papyrus was nearly white. Sheets were of standard sizes, and 20 sheets were pasted together to make a roll. A number of rolls were pasted together for especially long works. The writing medium was black and red ink. Until the 3d century B.C., when coarse reed pens were adopted, the ink was applied with a fine rush brush. Until about 2000 B.C. the writing was arranged in columns; after that time horizontal lines arranged in sections or "pages" became the rule.

In Egypt all documents of more than passing importance, including memorandums, letters, religious, literary, and scientific works, court records, oracles, and architects' plans were written on papyrus. Rolls were stored in wooden boxes or pottery jars. Temples had special rooms, or libraries, where rolls were stored.

Some of the most important Egyptian papyri include

The Turin Papyrus, a 19th-Dynasty papyrus which gives a complete list of the legitimate rulers of Egypt up to the time of its composition; the *Papyrus Abbott*, edited by T. Eric Peet (1930), which deals with a 20th-Dynasty inspection of royal and other tombs stated to have been robbed and with events arising from this; the *Papyrus Harris*, translated by J. H. Breasted in *Ancient Records of Egypt* (1906), a detailed statement of Rameses III's benefactions during his reign, which is of enormous importance for the economic history of Egypt; and *The Edwin Smith Surgical Papyrus*, edited by J. H. Breasted (1930) and *Papyrus Ebers*, translated by B. Ebell (1937), which shed considerable light on Egyptian medical knowledge and practice.

PHARAOH [fâr'ō, fā'rō], the Old Testament rendering of a circumlocution meaning "great house," employed in ancient Egypt to refer to the king, as "the White House" is used to mean "the President." By his subjects the pharaoh was viewed as a god—during his lifetime as an incarnation of Horus and at death as Osiris, King of the Dead. According to dogma, pharaoh's plans were perfect and everything he ordained came to pass; he assured the well-being of his subjects, while striking terror into the hearts of his enemies. It was believed that the king's death might cause cosmic, as well as political, chaos but that the coronation of a new king restored order to the universe.

PHILISTINES [fĭ-lĭs'tĭnz], major group of non-Semitic people in antiquity whom the Egyptians called the "Peoples of the Sea." The name comes from the Hebrew *Pelishtim* (Egyptian *Pulesati*, Assyrian *Palastu*), a people who settled along the coast of southern Palestine c.1150 B.C. after an unsuccessful attempt to invade Egypt. During the 13th century B.C., Egyptian inscriptions speak of Sea Peoples who were both invaders and mercenaries. In the reign (c.1175–1144 B.C., according to a "low date" chronology) of Rameses III Egypt was invaded from land and sea by several groups of them over a six-year period. Defeated, some of them fell back on Palestine, where they served nominally as mercenaries of Egypt, preserving Egyptian monuments in a Beth-shan temple, for example, long after Egyptian power in Palestine had come to an end. About this time, in coastal towns especially, a new pottery suddenly appeared which imitated 13th-century Greek (Mycenaean) models. This fact, in addition to various literary allusions, makes it certain that the Philistines came from the Aegean world.

In Palestine the Philistines organized themselves under five "lords" in five main cities (Gaza, Ashkelon, Ashdod, Ekron, and Gath), where they became Israel's worst enemy between c.1150 and 1000 B.C. Their greatest victory was when they captured Israel's sacred Ark, destroyed the central shrine of Israel's tribal league at Shiloh, and took control of the central hill country (I Sam. 4–6; 13:19–23; Jer. 7:12–15). This forced Israel to abandon its loose tribal confederation and turn to a monarchical government. Under the first Israelite kings, Saul and David, the Philistines were defeated and were never again a serious threat. In the 8th century B.C. the Philistine federation, which had become a series of city-states, was conquered by Assyria.

POTTERY. During its long history, many kinds of pottery were made by artisans in Egypt. The earliest and most distinctive have been found in graves of the predynastic period (c.4000 to c.3000 B.C.). These wares are handmade with rounded or pointed bases and have a turned-over rim of double thickness for strength. They seem to have been fired upside down in an open fire, the rims resting in about an inch of ashes, which effectively prevented the oxidation of iron substances in the part of the vessel so protected. In the firing the shiny, red body thus acquired a shiny black band at the rim, producing a plain though pleasing decoration. The Egyptians were the first to convert residual clay into a slip, that is, clay mixed with enough water to thin it to a liquid. Slip can be used for painted decoration that turns white on firing. This kind of ornament adorns later Egyptian wares.

A type of ceramic peculiar to Egypt is the ware known as faïence. A lightly fired body of sand mixed with a small quantity of clay was covered with a thick glaze made from sand and natron, fused and colored in a range of turquoise and green colors by the addition of copper oxide. Small figures, charms, beads, vessels, and other objects were made in this ware from the 1st Dynasty (c.3000 B.C.) to the Ptolemaic period (332–30 B.C.).

Some extremely important developments in pottery appear to have originated in the area called Mesopotamia, between the Tigris and Euphrates rivers. Bowls, vases, and cups with footed stems dating from c.3500 B.C. have been found, usually painted with geometric designs and conventionalized animals in brown or red. A long-spouted vessel was introduced c.3000 B.C. Other vessels of the same period show evidence of having been made on a turntable, the earliest form of potter's wheel. The great advantage of this was that the potter had both hands free to fashion his pot quickly and symmetrically as it rotated on the wheel, spun probably by a helper. During the Babylonian period (3d millennium to 539 B.C.) kilns were used to bake building bricks, although sun-hardening also continued. The great innovation of the Assyrian period (3d millennium to 612 B.C.), was the development of a glaze made white and opaque by the addition of tin oxide. Glazes similar to those of Egyptian faïence were also used, especially on wall bricks that formed large-scale lion and beast figures in low relief.

The general stirring of creative impulse in pottery in the 3d millennium B.C., which has been noted in Egypt and Mesopotamia, is also reflected in finds from Crete, Cyprus, and the Cyclades. Baked clay figures were common, and terra-cotta and pottery vessels were widely used. Trading contacts were established by these islands with both Egypt and Mesopotamia in the 3d millennium B.C., and it is probable that the use of the kiln and wheel had spread to all other pottery-making regions by the end of the millennium.

PSAMTIK [săm'tĭk] **I,** first King of the 26th (Saite) Dynasty of Egypt (reigned 663–609 B.C.). A leader of the group of nobles whom the Assyrians left to rule Egypt after the defeat of the Ethiopians, he eventually gained independence and control over Egypt. An astute and able King, he laid the foundations of the Saite revival. This was based on an army of Greek mercenaries, encouragement of Greek traders, and an appeal to Egyptian nationalism linked with a deliberate archaism.

PTAH [ptä], in Egyptian religion, the god who created the universe. In the Memphite theological system he was usually represented as a bearded, standing, mummiform man. The world was made by his heart (thought) and tongue (word). As patron of arts and crafts he was identified by the Greeks with Hephaestus.

PTOLEMIES [tŏl'ə-mēz], name of all the Macedonian kings who exercised power in Egypt from 323 to 30 B.C. They never attempted to become one with their Egyptian subjects, though they diplomatically patronized the native religion and were active builders of temples. The last ruler of the dynasty, the great Cleopatra VII, was the first to have any knowledge of the Egyptian language. Egypt in general was treated as their private domain, to be ruthlessly, and sometimes efficiently, administered and exploited. Although many valuable legal, economic, and agricultural reforms and innovations were introduced, the corruption of the royal family and incessant civil wars after the death of Ptolemy III entailed the progressive weakening and impoverishment of Egypt.

PTOLEMY I SOTER I (reigned 304–283 B.C.), son of Lagus, a Macedonian, born c.367 B.C. One of Alexander's seven companions and one of his most competent generals, Ptolemy became, on the death of Alexander in 323, Satrap of Egypt, nominally ruling in the name of Alexander's successors. He astutely brought the body of Alexander to Egypt, and in 304 he proclaimed himself King. His main concern was to establish himself in Egypt and create an adequate buffer state in Asia, but he was inevitably involved in the wars and quarrels of the other satraps. He succeeded in conquering Palestine and Cyprus and in acquiring wide territories in the Aegean and Asia Minor. He was responsible for drawing up the main lines of the Ptolemaic administrative, legal, and military system. He originated the cults of Alexander and Serapis in Egypt and founded Ptolemais in Upper Egypt. He was a patron of the arts and sciences. After 285 B.C. he took no active part in affairs.

PTOLEMY II PHILADELPHUS (283–246), son of Ptolemy I and Berenice I, born in 308. In 285 he was elected joint ruler with Ptolemy I. By his marriage c.276 to Arsinoë II he acquired most of her Aegean possessions. He campaigned with varying success in Asia. It was in his reign that much of the Ptolemaic financial administration was organized. Greek settlements were founded, especially in the Faiyum, which was developed and turned into the Arsinoites nome. The ancient canal linking the Nile with the Red Sea was reopened, and Red Sea trade was actively promoted. He introduced the Ptolemaic ruler cult and built the Pharos lighthouse, the Museum and Library (founded by Ptolemy I), and enhanced other institutions of Alexandria. During his reign the Jewish colony of Alexandria, founded by his father, completed the translation of the Septuagint.

PTOLEMY III EUERGETES I (246–221), son of Ptolemy II and his first wife Arsinoë I, born between 288 and 280 B.C. His marriage in 247 to Berenice II, daughter of Magas of Cyrene, united Cyrene with Egypt. His reign marks the peak of Ptolemaic power and expansion, and his campaigns in Syria against Seleucus II added much to Egypt's foreign possessions.

PTOLEMY IV PHILOPATOR (221–205), son of Ptolemy III and Berenice II, born c.244. He married his sister Arsinoë III in 217. He decisively defeated the attempts of Antiochus III of Syria to invade Palestine at the battle of Raphia in 217. Here, for the first time, native Egyptian troops served in the Ptolemaic army. This was a great stimulus to Egyptian nationalism and sparked off the first of a long series of native revolts. From 208 to 186 most of the district around Thebes was under Nubian kings.

PTOLEMY V EPIPHANES (205–180), son of Ptolemy IV and Arsinoë III, born c.210. He was a child on the death of his father, which was apparently concealed for some time, and was not declared of age until 197. He married Cleopatra I, daughter of Antiochus III, in 193. The great Theban revolt that had broken out under Ptolemy IV was not suppressed until the 19th year of his reign. Most of Egypt's foreign possessions were lost under combined attacks by the Seleucids and Macedonians. The Rosetta Stone, principal key to the decipherment of the hieroglyphs, was inscribed in his honor in 196.

PTOLEMY VI PHILOMETOR (180–145), son of Ptolemy V and Cleopatra I, born c.186. He succeeded Ptolemy V as joint ruler with Cleopatra I, who died in 176, and married his sister Cleopatra II in 175. As a result of a successful invasion by Antiochus IV, who took Philometor prisoner in 170, joint rule with his brother Ptolemy VIII and Cleopatra II was established. In 164 he was expelled by Ptolemy VIII, but, with Roman help, returned the following year and continued as joint ruler with Cleopatra II, in spite of his brother's intrigues, until his death in battle against the Syrians.

PTOLEMY VII NEOS PHILOPATOR (145–144), son of Ptolemy VI and Cleopatra II, born c.162. He was murdered at the instigation of Ptolemy VIII after the latter had returned from exile.

PTOLEMY VIII EUERGETES II (144–116), son of Ptolemy V and Cleopatra I, born c.182. After many years of intrigue against his brother, Euergetes became King again in 144. He married his sister and brother's widow Cleopatra II, but two years later married her daughter Cleopatra III, without divorcing Cleopatra II. After a troubled decade, an Alexandrian revolt led by Cleopatra II in 132 compelled Euergetes and Cleopatra III to flee to Cyprus; Cleopatra II remained in power in Egypt. Ptolemy recaptured Alexandria in 127 and for the remainder of his reign ruled jointly with both Cleopatras. His will bequeathed all power to Cleopatra III. An earlier will, drafted in Cyrene, where he had reigned from 163 to 145, had bequeathed his possessions to Rome.

PTOLEMY IX SOTER II (116–108 and 88–81), eldest son of Ptolemy VIII and Cleopatra III, born c.141. The reigns of Ptolemy IX and his younger brother Ptolemy X were bedeviled by the ambition and hatreds of their mother, who apparently supported her younger son. On the death of Ptolemy VIII, Soter was elected joint ruler with Cleopatra III, who, after several attempts, forced him to flee. He thereupon took over his younger brother's kingdom of Cyprus. During his exile Egypt was ruled by this brother, Ptolemy X, first with Cleopatra III and later (101–88) with

Cleopatra Berenice. After Ptolemy IX regained the throne in 88, revolt broke out in the Thebaid; Thebes was captured and destroyed in 86. Until his death he ruled jointly with Cleopatra Berenice, his daughter, who remained sole ruler for a short time afterward.

PTOLEMY X ALEXANDER I (108–88), younger brother of Ptolemy IX, born c.140. He was supported by his mother against his brother. After the death of Cleopatra III in 101 he married Cleopatra Berenice, daughter of Ptolemy IX. Expelled by a rebellion, he tried repeatedly to regain the throne but died in a naval battle in 88.

PTOLEMY XI ALEXANDER II (80), son of Ptolemy X, born c.100. Forced by Sulla to accept Cleopatra Berenice, his stepmother, as joint ruler, he married her, then murdered her 19 days later. But he was in turn killed by the outraged Alexandrians. His will, of doubtful authenticity, bequeathed Egypt to Rome. He was the last legitimate male member of the Ptolemaic family.

PTOLEMY XII AULETES (80–51), son of Ptolemy IX and one of his mistresses, born between 116 and 108. Forced to flee to Rome in 58, he was restored by the Syrian proconsul Gabinius in 55. He then had his reigning daughter Berenice killed.

PTOLEMY XIII (51–47), son of Ptolemy XII and brother of the celebrated Cleopatra VII, born in 63. He married his sister Cleopatra VII in 51, and ruled jointly with her at first but soon expelled her. Forced by Julius Caesar to take Cleopatra back in 48, he threw in his lot with the revolt against Caesar in the Alexandrine War and was drowned in the Nile.

PTOLEMY XIV (47–44), another brother of Cleopatra VII, born c.59. Appointed King of Cyprus by Caesar in 48, he became joint ruler and husband of Cleopatra VII in 47, at the command of Caesar. When Cleopatra followed Caesar to Rome, he remained in Egypt as sole ruler. He was poisoned by Cleopatra on her return in 44, after Caesar's assassination.

PTOLEMY XV CAESARION, son of Cleopatra VII and Caesar, born in 47. Joint ruler with Cleopatra from 43, he was murdered by Octavian's orders in 30, following Octavian's defeat of Antony and Cleopatra and their suicides. Upon his death Egypt became a Roman province.

PTOLEMY [tŏl'ə-mē], also known as Claudius Ptolemaeus (c.100–170), Egyptian astronomer, mathematician, and geographer. Probably born in Ptolemais, Egypt, he spent much of his life in Alexandria. Little is known of his life other than that he made many astronomical observations between 127 and 151 A.D.

Ptolemy's major contribution was his great work called the *Almagest*, in which he compiled both his own astronomical findings and the knowledge of earlier observers, especially the Greek astronomer Hipparchus. The *Almagest* includes 13 books, the first of which contains the principles of astronomy and spherical trigonometry. The second lists the zones into which Ptolemy divided the earth, and it explains the rising and setting of the sun. The third gives the length of the year and sets forth a theory of solar motion. The fourth gives the length of the month and explains lunar motion.

In the fifth book are listed the distances of the moon from the sun and from the earth, as well as details of the instrument that Ptolemy used in his observations. The sixth explains the conjunctions, oppositions, and eclipses of the sun and moon. The seventh and eighth books are a catalogue of 1,028 fixed stars, based on the work of Hipparchus, and they include a discussion of precession. In the remaining books is the explanation of planetary motions that has come to be called the Ptolemaic System, although the theory is not entirely Ptolemy's. Generally accepted until the time of Copernicus, the Ptolemaic System assumes that the moon, sun, planets, and stars all revolve around a central earth

Originally written in Greek, the *Almagest* has been translated into several languages. Its title is an Arabic contraction of the original Greek title.

In his *Geography* Ptolemy included descriptions and maps of what was known of the inhabited world. His concept of latitude and longitude, though inaccurate, was the main basis of geographical knowledge until the great explorations of the 15th and 16th centuries.

PYRAMIDS [pĭr'ə-mĭdz], in architecture, monumental structures having a rectangular, usually square, base and triangular sides meeting in a point. Pyramidal buildings are best known from ancient Egypt, where they were used primarily as royal tombs. The earliest true pyramid is the "northern stone pyramid" at Dahshur, a few miles south of Sakkara. This is thought to have been built by King Snefru, the first king of the 4th Dynasty (c.2600 B.C.). Several 3d-Dynasty kings, of whom the best known is King Zoser, covered their tombs with structures often called "step pyramids." Probably the last of these, at Medum, was finished by King Snefru as a true pyramid. Snefru also built a third tomb of modified pyramidal shape, the "bent" pyramid at Dahshur. This differs from a true pyramid in that the sides slope upward very steeply for about half the vertical height and more gradually thereafter.

From the 4th until the 17th Dynasty, the pyramid was the favored form of royal tomb and the remains of some 80 exist on the west bank of the Nile in Lower and Middle Egypt. From the New Kingdom (1573–1085 B.C.) on, kings generally built less conspicuous tombs, although the Nubians who ruled Egypt in the 8th and 7th centuries B.C. erected small pyramids with steeply sloping sides in their cemeteries in the Sudan. During the New Kingdom the nobles at Thebes built small brick pyramids on top of their rock-cut tombs.

From the 3d to the 6th Dynasty, pyramids were built by adding successive, relatively thin coverings of masonry to a stone core. In the step pyramids the stones comprising these coverings (or skins) sloped downward toward the center of the monument; in the true pyramids they were laid flat. In the 12th Dynasty pyramids were built by filling sand and rubble around radial stone or mud-brick walls. Most Egyptian royal pyramids were faced with stone, generally fine limestone, though some granite was used. The apex was a single pyramidal block.

The slope of the step pyramids is steeper than that of true pyramids (angle of elevation about 75° as compared to about 52°). The entrance was generally in the north face of the pyramid, sometimes at ground level, sometimes above. Long passages, equipped with great blocking

Ed Drews—Photo Researchers

Pyramids of King Khufu (*right*) and King Khafre at Giza, Egypt. In the foreground is a Muslim cemetery.

stones or concealed exits, or both, led eventually to a burial chamber in or under the monument. In the 5th, 6th, and 7th dynasties, the walls of the burial chamber were covered with liturgical texts (the so-called Pyramid Texts), which may have been used for royal funerals and at the presentation of offerings to the dead ruler.

Throughout its use as a royal tomb, the pyramid was only part of the mortuary complex. This also contained (1) an entrance building or "valley temple" at the desert edge; (2) a causeway, sometimes hundreds of yards long, ascending from the entrance building to the pyramid-plateau; (3) a mortuary temple for the worship of the dead king and the presentation of offerings for his perpetual nourishment; (4) a small "ritual" pyramid of which the purpose is not known; (5) one or more small pyramids for the burial of the queen or queens; and (6) mastabas for the burial of other members of the royal family and high officials. Most of the buildings on the plateau were surrounded by a wall. Near this wall, or at the side of the causeway, some of the 4th- and 5th-Dynasty complexes had two or more cavities in the shape of boats. (Such a pit to the south of the wall surrounding the Great Pyramid was found on excavation in 1954 to contain a large cedar boat.) The walls of the entrance building, the causeway, and the mortuary temple were generally covered with painted reliefs of great beauty.

Construction of Pyramids. The methods used in constructing the pyramids are still a matter of dispute. However, it is agreed that the stone was quarried and dressed with stone and hardened-copper tools, and raised into position without pulleys through the use of earth embankments or ramps, sledges, and levers. The surface of the stones was dressed after laying. Labor was conscripted, and the men were paid in clothing, food, drink, and oil (to prevent their skin from cracking painfully in the dry Egyptian air). They were housed in barracks or walled towns near the pyramid complex on which they were employed. All stages of the project were supervised by high officials of special competence.

The best-known Egyptian pyramids are the three at Giza. These were built in the 4th Dynasty by King Khufu (Cheops) and his sons Khafre (Chephren) and Menkaure (Mycerinus). The Great Pyramid of Khufu is the largest: its base is about 756 ft. on a side and covers 13.1 acres. When complete the pyramid was 481.4 ft. tall. Individual blocks weigh as much as 15 tons, yet the preserved facing blocks are finished so accurately that the cracks between them are nowhere wider than 1/50 in.

RA [rä] **or RE** [rā], in Egyptian religion, the sun-god. His principal center was at Heliopolis. Supposedly he sailed across the sky by day and through the underworld in another boat by night. Prominent from the late 4th Dynasty, he triumphed in the 5th Dynasty, and his liturgy thereafter was the basis of the daily temple ritual. In the Old Kingdom he was judge and lord of the royal hereafter. He was later superseded by Osiris. But a New Kingdom compromise made Ra and Osiris virtually two aspects of one divine being.

RAMESES [răm′ə-sēz] **II,** 3d King of the 19th Dynasty of Egypt (reigned 1290–1224 B.C.), son of Seti I. His attempt to restore the Egyptian Empire in Asia was checked by the Hittites at the drawn battle of Kadesh in 1286. He concluded peace with the Hittites in 1270 and married a Hittite princess in 1257. A prodigious builder throughout Egypt and the Sudan, he was also adept at appropriating the monuments of others. His principal buildings include the temple at Karnak, the Ramesseum opposite Thebes, and the rock temple at Abu Simbel. Under Rameses II, Egyptian civilization reached its height of prosperity and splendor, though bearing within itself the seeds of decay. A much married man, Rameses fathered more than 110 sons and 55 daughters. His mummy is in the Egyptian

The wedding of Rameses II and a Hittite princess, from an ancient copy of the original carving on the rock temple at Abu Simbel.

Oriental Institute, University of Chicago

Museum in Cairo. The Exodus probably took place in the first half of his reign.

RAMESES III, 2d King of the 20th Dynasty of Egypt (reigned 1198–1167 B.C.). The first 11 years of his reign were occupied in bitter warfare against invasions of Libyans and the Peoples of the Sea. Though Rameses finally triumphed, Egypt was exhausted. His internal economic troubles were exemplified by the strike of the Theban necropolis workers. He died as a result of a harem conspiracy.

RAMESSEUM [răm-ə-sē'əm], mortuary temple built by Rameses II on the west bank of the Nile, opposite Thebes. It is near the present village of El-Qurna. The temple consisted of two courts, each about 140 by 180 ft. The front court still contains the remnants of the colossal statue of Rameses that it housed and that is estimated to have weighed nearly 1,000 tons. It was built from a single block of granite. The columns of both courts are magnificent specimens of Egyptian architecture. The mural sculptures are especially noteworthy. One of the murals depicts Rameses' battle with the Hittites. A small adjacent chamber is noted for its ceiling covered with astronomical symbols.

SAIS [sā'ĭs] (modern **SA EL-HAGAR**), ancient Egyptian city, formerly on the Canopic branch of the Nile delta, now on the Rosetta branch. It was the chief cult city for the goddess Neith, who was closely connected with the kingship and the Lower Egyptian crown. It was also the home of the Kings of the 26th Dynasty, the first of whom (Psamtik I) ended the Assyrian domination of Egypt in 664 B.C.

SENUSRET [sĕn-ŭs'rĕt], name of three Egyptian Kings of the 12th Dynasty. SENUSRET I (reigned 1971–1928 B.C.), son of Amenemhet I, with whom he was coregent for 10 years, campaigned in Libya and conquered Nubia. There he initiated the great Nubian fortress system, which possibly extended Egyptian control to the Third Cataract.

SENUSRET II (reigned 1897–1879 B.C.), son of Amenemhet II, possibly initiated the irrigation works in the Faiyum which were completed by his grandson Amenemhet III. SENUSRET III (reigned 1879–1841 B.C.), son of Senusret II, reconquered and pacified Nubia, established the frontier at Semna, and dug two canals at the First Cataract. He also campaigned in Palestine. Suppressing the provincial nobles, he centralized the administration under the crown.

SETH or SET, ancient god of Upper Egypt, identified by the Greeks with Typhon. At first the partner and rival of Horus, Seth, under the influence of the Osiris religion, became the brother and murderer of Osiris, and the epitome of evil. He was the god of the Hyksos and enjoyed brief official popularity in Ramessid times (20th Dynasty). Later he was universally execrated as the god of evil.

SETI or SETHI [sĕ'tē] **I,** second King of the 19th Dynasty of Egypt (reigned c.1303–1290 B.C.), son of Rameses I. He restored Egyptian influence in Asia by defeating the Hittites and concluding a peace treaty with them. He campaigned against Libya and was also active in Nubia. His cenotaph at Abydos and his tomb at Thebes are among the finest artistic masterpieces of Egypt.

SHESHONK [shē'shŏngk] **I,** the Biblical Shishak, Egyptian Pharaoh, founder of the 22d (Libyan) Dynasty (reigned 950–929 B.C.). Descended from Libyan mercenaries who had settled at Heracleopolis, he seized power and eventually ruled all Egypt. He invaded Palestine, where, profiting from the troubles that followed the death of Solomon, he sacked Jerusalem. An active builder, especially at Karnak, he was mainly concerned with internal reforms and administration.

SNEFRU [snĕf'rōō] **or SNOFRU** [snŏf'rōō], Egyptian King (reigned c.2613–2590 B.C.), founder of the 4th Dynasty. A wise and beneficent ruler, Snefru campaigned successfully in Libya and Nubia. He was deified and worshiped from the 4th Dynasty until Ptolemaic times. His pyramid is at Medum.

The sphinx at Giza, most famous of the Egyptian sphinxes.

SPHINX [*sfingks*], a composite creature with leonine body and human head, which probably originated in Egypt, where it was known as early as the 4th Dynasty (2650–2500 B.C.). Most examples show the features of a pharaoh, who thus appears embodying the power of a lion. By the 6th Dynasty (2350–2254 B.C.) the sphinx was represented as a protective power trampling Egypt's enemies underfoot. Later pairs of recumbent sphinxes guarded doorways, and long lines of them bordered processional avenues. Although there are examples with women's (or rams') heads, the typical Egyptian sphinx was masculine, with royal headdress and false beard. When shown in relief the creature often had wings folded along its back.

The most famous Egyptian sphinx is that carved from an outcrop of rock east of the pyramids on the Giza plateau. Probably a likeness of Khafre, the builder of the second pyramid, this colossal figure was set on a carved rock pedestal, with a temple adjoining it on the east. It was worshiped as the god Horus-in-the-Horizon (Harmachis), and several small New Kingdom temples, as well as many votive figures and steles honoring him, have been found in the vicinity. The cult was continued into Roman times. The face of the Giza sphinx was deliberately disfigured by an Arab iconoclast in the 14th century A.D.

Sphinxes also appear in the art of most pre-Christian cultures of western Asia and the Aegean, and the word is Greek. Non-Egyptian sphinxes are generally female with spread wings. Characteristically, they are pictured in a sitting position. In Greek mythology the sphinx was cruel.

TELL EL-AMARNA [*tĕl′ ĕl ə-mär′nə*], Egyptian site of the town built by King Akhenaton about 1360 B.C. on the east bank of the Nile just south of Sheikh Said. Having for religious and political reasons rebelled against the authority of the priests of Amon, Akhenaton left Thebes to establish a new capital, which he called Akhetaton ("the horizon of the sun disk"). The city was deserted after less than 20 years, when Tutankhamen moved the court back to Thebes. Most of Akhetaton's temples and public buildings were destroyed by zealots. However, the structures that escaped and have been excavated provide our only comprehensive view of an ancient Egyptian city, and most of our knowledge of secular, nonfunerary architecture.

In 1887–88 about 400 tablets inscribed with the foreign correspondence of Amenhotep III and Akhenaton were found, adding immeasurably to the knowledge of international relations in the 14th century B.C. The name "Amarna" is frequently used to designate the particular artistic style fostered under Akhenaton. The term is also applied to his religious teachings, which neglected most of the ancient gods to center worship on the sun disk, one aspect of the god Ra.

THEBES [*thēbz*], ancient Greek name for the entire fourth district of Upper Egypt. It now designates only the area from Luxor (q.v.) north to Karnak (q.v.) on the east bank of the Nile, and from Medinet Habu north to El-Qurna on the west bank. The city between the two temples on the east bank was known to the Egyptians as the City of Amon. It is believed to have had no importance until the 11th and 12th Dynasties (from about 2100 B.C.) when the kings, whose home was nearby, honored the gods of the district by building important temples. Several centuries later Thebes regained prominence when two of its princes, Kamose and Ahmose, broke the power of the Hyksos kings. Thereafter, for nearly 300 years, when Egypt was a thriving imperial power, Thebes was the political and religious capital of the land, its magnificence renowned throughout the ancient world.

Its decline began when Seti I and Rameses II built a new capital at Tanis, and was accelerated when the kings of the 21st Dynasty discontinued the custom of building tombs and funerary temples on the west bank. However, Thebes retained religious prominence until it was sacked by the Assyrians in 664 B.C. Five centuries later the Theban temples prospered again under the Ptolemies. Today, because its extant ruins are extensive as compared with

The Temple of Queen Hatshepsut (18th Dynasty) at Deir el-Bahri is part of the complex of temple ruins of Thebes, Egypt.

(NAT & YANNA BRANDT—PHOTO RESEARCHERS)

those of Memphis and Heliopolis, which have virtually disappeared, Thebes is perhaps the best place to study the material remnants of ancient Egyptian culture.

Besides the great temples on the east bank and the royal tombs in the Valley of the Kings, in the desert, Thebes has a long series of royal mortuary temples on the west bank. Most of them date from the New Kingdom (for instance, those at Medinet Habu and Deir el-Bahri, and the Ramesseum). In addition, the western cliffs contain the tombs of hundreds of Middle Kingdom and New Kingdom nobles. These are famous for their wall paintings, which picture the rites performed to secure eternal life and also many activities and arrangements undertaken to make that life one of luxurious ease.

THOTH [thōth, tōt], in Egyptian religion, a god who was scribe of the gods. He was the patron of writing, reckoning, and magic. His principal cult center was Hermopolis. His sacred animals were the ibis and baboon. He was regarded as the heart of Ra and the tongue of Ptah, that is, the divine thought and creative word. Assimilated with the Greek Hermes, as Hermes Trismegistus he played an important role in Neoplatonic Hermetic literature. He was originally, perhaps, a moon-god in ibis form.

THUTMOSE [thŭt′mōz, thōot-mō′sə], name of four Egyptian Kings of the 18th Dynasty. **THUTMOSE I** (reigned c.1526–1508 B.C.), son of Amenhotep I by a concubine. By his

campaigns in Asia he reached the Euphrates, and in Nubia he extended Egyptian control to between the third and fourth cataracts. He was the first King to be buried in the Valley of the Kings. His son and successor, **THUTMOSE II** (reigned c.1508–1490 B.C.), married his half sister Hatshepsut and campaigned in Asia and Nubia. **THUTMOSE III** (reigned c.1490–1436 B.C.), son of Thutmose II by a concubine. He was proclaimed King on the death of his father, but all power was exercised by Hatshepsut (his stepmother and aunt) till her death in 1469 B.C. Immediately thereafter Thutmose began his imperial wars. Seventeen annual campaigns in Asia and others in Nubia resulted in the creation of an empire extending from the Euphrates to beyond the fourth cataract in the south. He raised Egypt to a peak of power and prosperity. He was an active builder in Egypt, especially at Karnak, and in Nubia. His statue is in the Egyptian Museum, Turin, Italy. **THUTMOSE IV** (reigned c.1411–1397 B.C.), son and successor of Amenhotep II, married a Mitannian princess, thus allying with Mitanni, a former rival, against the new Hittite threat.

TUTANKHAMEN or TUTANKHAMUN [tōōt-ängk-ä′-mən], Egyptian King (reigned c.1353–1345 B.C.). The successor of Akhenaton, he came to the throne at the age of 10.

Trans World Airlines

Gold mask portraying Egyptian King Tutankhamen in the Egyptian Museum, Cairo.

Though his exact parentage is unknown, he was certainly of royal blood and very probably a son of Amenhotep III and his daughter Sitamun. Tutankhamen's wife was the third daughter of Akhenaton. At first, under the influence of Nefertiti (Akhenaton's Queen), Tutankhamen maintained the Aton faith at Amarna. But between the second and fourth years of his reign he abandoned Amarna, returned to the former capital, Thebes, and restored the old religion, changing his name from Tutankhaton to Tutankhamen. His virtually intact tomb was discovered in the Valley of the Kings by Howard Carter in 1922, and yielded fabulous treasures, which are now all in the Egyptian Museum in Cairo. He was succeeded by a usurper, Ay, who married his widow after murdering the Hittite prince who had been sent, at her desperate appeal, to marry her.

The entrance to King Tutankhamen's tomb, discovered in 1922 by Howard Carter in the Valley of the Kings, near Luxor.

GREEK CIVILIZATION

ARCHITECTURE

Greek architecture is a style of building that arose during the 7th century B.C. in eastern Mediterranean countries. It evolved not only in continental Greece and the Aegean islands, but also in coastal areas of western Asia Minor, southern Italy, and Sicily, regions which in ancient times were inhabited by Greek-speaking peoples. Its culminating phase, in the 5th century B.C., represents the most perfect development and highest artistic expression of column-and-lintel construction. The system of design, novel types of buildings, and the enduring beauty of Greek masterpieces aroused the admiration of later ages and inspired such important styles as those of ancient Rome, the Renaissance, and modern times.

Formative Influences and Stylistic Periods

Because of primitive construction with sun-dried brick and wood on rough foundations, few traces of the earliest Greek buildings remain. They were clearly influenced, however, by traditions surviving from Aegean architecture in its final, or Mycenaean, phase. The typical plan of the early Greek temple repeats that of the great hall (megaron) of the Mycenaean palace. Monumental entrances (propylaea) to sacred enclosures such as the Athenian Acropolis were inspired by similar, but more simple, gateways to enclosed courts before Mycenaean palaces. As structural methods improved in the early 6th century B.C., temples were built of ashlar masonry, that is, of squared stone blocks laid in horizontal courses. Stone columns and entablatures replaced the primitive wooden elements. Beautiful Greek marbles became the preferred building material in the early 5th century B.C., and were used thereafter in almost all religious and civic structures.

Since the evolution of Greek architecture was essentially a process of refining and perfecting a few traditional types and elements of design, its successive stylistic phases are less obvious than in other great styles. Four main periods are usually distinguished: (1) the Archaic and Transitional period (c.550–c.450 B.C.); (2) the Culminating period (c.450–c.400 B.C.); (3) the period of Decline (began c.400 B.C.); and (4) the Hellenistic and Greco-Roman phases (which may be dated after 323 B.C., the year of Alexander the Great's death). In the last stage many Greek designs were used in modified form throughout the classic world.

This period ended with the Roman conquest of Greece in 146 B.C.

Elements and Principles of Design

The fundamental elements of Greek architecture were three types of columns and entablatures, called "orders": Doric, Ionic, and Corinthian. Doric and Ionic, thought to have evolved from primitive wooden prototypes, are much the oldest; Corinthian was created in the late 5th century B.C. Their distinctive features are as follows:

Doric Order. The column lacks a base and rises directly from the pavement (stylobate). Its sturdy, tapering shaft is diversified by 20 vertical flutes and crowned by a capital. The latter consists of a spreading, cushionlike form (echinus), topped by a square block (abacus). Resting on

The Parthenon, begun in 447 B.C., at the summit of the Acropolis of Athens. It was a temple to Athena, patron deity of the city.

Louis H. Frohman

The Acropolis at Athens. Left of the Parthenon is the Erechtheum, a small temple to Athena. Farther down the hill is the propylaea, gateway to the Acropolis. Below it stands the small Temple of Athena Nike. The theater was originally constructed in the 4th century B.C., reconstructed c.143 A.D. by Herodes Atticus, and rebuilt again for the Olympic games in 1896.

Charles Rotkin—P.F.I.

the columns is the entablature. It consists of a plain, functional lintel (architrave), a decorative frieze of alternating triglyphs and metopes, and overhanging eaves (cornice). The square metopes were sometimes decorated with relief sculptures. The Doric order played a leading role in Greek architecture because of its sturdy simplicity, its clear-cut rational design, and its beautifully proportioned forms.

Ionic Order. The column stands on a circular molded base. Its slender shaft is relieved by 24 deeply cut vertical flutes; its capital is distinguished by graceful spiral volutes and delicately carved ornament. The entablature is in three parts: the functional architrave, its face carved with three overlapping strips (fasciae) and an ornamental molding; the frieze, usually plain, but sometimes adorned with ornamental moldings and sculpture in relief; and the richly carved cornice. Because the Ionic order originated in western Asia Minor and adjacent islands, it reflects Oriental influence in its slender, graceful proportions and delicate ornament. Although rarely used in the Culminating period, it became popular in later centuries.

Corinthian Order. It differs from the Ionic only in its capital, which has an inverted bell-shaped core, carved with two ranges of acanthus leaves, and with slender spiral volutes rising to the four angles of the abacus. Although seldom used in classic Greece, its elaborate capital and enriched ornament made it popular with Hellenistic and Greco-Roman architects.

The principles of design that inspired Greek architecture and set it apart from all earlier styles may be expressed in general terms as simplicity, clarity, rhythm, unity, and harmony. The last two were achieved by careful subordination of parts to the whole, so that an impression of balanced symmetry and perfection might result. Although the operation of these principles is clearest in architecture, they underlie all forms of Greek art and in large measure explain the unique reputation for formal beauty it still enjoys. They are best illustrated in the temple.

The Temple

The temple's function was to house and protect a divine image, not to provide space for congregational worship or elaborate ritual. Therefore, its only essential element was a completely enclosed room (cella), entered through a single doorway. Because the earliest temples adopted the form of the Mycenaean megaron, they were rectangular structures with a simple entrance portico formed by two columns between extensions of the lateral walls. The building was covered by a double-pitched roof with gables at front and back. Almost all later temples elaborated this primitive nucleus by adding exterior columns, at first across the ends, then in freestanding ranges on all four sides. Two ranges of interior columns were introduced in the cellas of large temples to support the heavy, tiled roof. Sculptural decoration was confined to exteriors, where the two end-gables (pediments) were filled with sculptured groups, the friezes of the entablatures with figures and scenes in relief.

Architects directed their greatest effort toward refining, enhancing, and perfecting the visual impact and aesthetic effect of the temple. They determined its proportions on the basis of a selected unit (modulus), yet varied them continually by minor adjustments of part to part and of parts to the whole. To counteract geometrical coldness and vitalize the over-all design, they introduced so-called optical refinements—subtle rising curves in seemingly horizontal steps and stylobate, slight bulges in the profile of columns, and minor departures from geometric regularity throughout the temple. These efforts culminated in the Parthenon (begun 447 B.C.), designed by Ictinus and Callicrates, and built on the Acropolis in Athens. It ranks among the masterpieces of world architecture.

The usual cella was replaced in the largest temples by

an open courtyard with a roofed shrine at back. Double ranges of columns surrounded the exterior walls. The Olympieum (174 B.C.–132 A.D.) in Athens was of this type. Most famous of irregularly shaped temples is the late-5th-century Erechtheum on the Athenian Acropolis. The entablature of one of its three porticoes is supported by sculptured maidens (caryatids).

Other Architecture

The monumental entrance, or propylaea, is best represented by the famous gateway to the Athenian Acropolis. It was begun in 437 B.C. by Mnesicles, but was never completed according to his original plans.

Greek architects, designing for a drama that had begun with the choral dance, created the classic type of open-air theater. Its finest surviving example is the theater at Epidaurus (4th century B.C.).

For the famous Olympic Games, Greek architects originated the typical stadium, now best seen in the Stadium of Delphi (4th century B.C.).

City planning, with regular blocks of houses about an open marketplace (agora), also evolved in Greece. The typical agora was surrounded by columned porticoes for shops and was often adorned with statues and fountains.

In the Greek democracies, or oligarchies, the citizen lived less for himself than for the state. Its business was his business, and its temples his own offering to Zeus or Hera, Athena or Apollo. As such he had free but individual access to these shrines. The citizens did not meet in groups within the temple, as Christians gather for worship in their churches. The single interior chamber, the cella, housed the cult statue, but the sacrifices were performed outside the building. Hence the colonnaded exterior of the Parthenon with its wealth of sculpture was rather more important than the small interior. The complete unity of the Parthenon and particularly its clearly defined shape bespeak the love of the Greek for the tangible, his hatred of the amorphous, just as the human scale of his temples suggest his anthropocentric mind. The largest Egyptian temples are overwhelming in size, like the unlimited power of the pharaohs; the Greek temple is linked to the individual. The Greek's love for drama called theaters into existence with nearly circular tier upon tier of seats rising around the orchestra. Colonnaded stoas provided meeting places for business purposes. Living as he did largely in public, the Greek had a modest home that contrasted sharply with his public buildings.

ART

Greek art is the style of artistic expression that flourished in continental Greece and other parts of the Mediterranean area inhabited by Greek-speaking peoples from the 7th to 2d centuries B.C. It is distinguished from earlier styles by its ideal beauty, its concern with human values, and its creative approach to the expressive possibilities of the human figure. Although hampered at first by stereotyped forms inherited from Egypt, its progressive spirit gradually eliminated traditional restrictions. In search of more vital inspiration, its artists concentrated on a study of nature. The popularity of athletics, and the long-established custom of Greek athletes to train and compete in the nude, provided artists with an abundance of living models. This

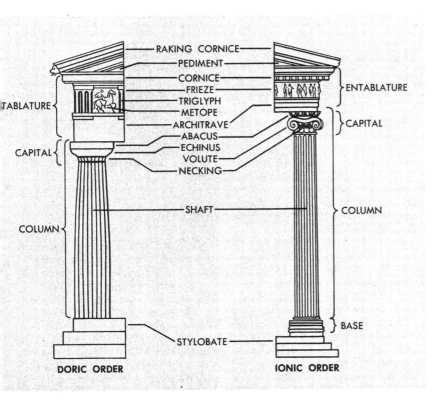

DORIC ORDER — IONIC ORDER

RAKING CORNICE
PEDIMENT
CORNICE
FRIEZE
TRIGLYPH
METOPE
ARCHITRAVE
ABACUS
ECHINUS
VOLUTE
NECKING
SHAFT
STYLOBATE
ENTABLATURE
CAPITAL
COLUMN
BASE

Left, the Doric and Ionic orders. Below, plan of the Parthenon, which represents the climax of the Doric temple. A statue of Athena stood in the long cella. The smaller room behind it was for storing temple treasures. Most Greek temples were similar in plan.

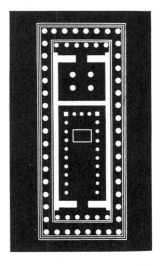

Archaic kore (late 6th century B.C.), now in the Acropolis Museum, wears the slight smile typical of sculptured figures of the period.

The Bettmann Archive

Roman copy of the lost "Discus Thrower" (c.460–450 B.C.), by Myron of Athens, the leading sculptor of the Transitional period.

enabled them continually to correct and improve the rendering of the human form.

Principles and Evolution

The principles of design that inspired all forms of art as well as Greek architecture can be stated generally as simplicity, clarity, rhythm, unity, and harmony. Naturalism and idealism, two other qualities supremely characteristic of sculpture and painting, were unique contributions of Greece to the history of art. The direct study of nature as an essential basis for representation originated with the Greeks. But their art descended to literal and realistic imitations of natural forms only in its decadent phase. It strove consistently for ideal values, stressing the typical and universal aspects of its chosen themes. Its highest aim was to improve on nature by eliminating imperfections and trivial details. Because realism is enhanced by a specific background and setting, figures and groups of the greater periods were always shown against a neutral ground. This device, by eliminating definite connotations of time and place, gave them universal and timeless significance. It was used most effectively in religious and mythological contexts.

The evolution of Greek art was marked throughout by a consistent naturalistic trend. As artists realized that the renderings of nature in works by earlier masters were awkward and inadequate, they strove continually to correct and improve them, especially when dealing with the human form. Their interest in the natural world, however, rarely extended beyond the human. Hence, they never attempted the visual representation of remoter aspects of nature. Instead, they personified rivers, springs, forests, and mountains as mythological beings of graceful human form.

Since the Greek genius developed along rational, intellectual lines, it attained its greatest triumphs in the arts of form—architecture and sculpture. Because of its fundamental concern with man, its favorite and most typical art was sculpture. Therefore, the history of Greek art can be traced most clearly in sculpture.

Four main periods are generally recognized: (1) the Archaic and Transitional Period; (2) the Culminating Period; (3) the Period of Decline; and (4) the Hellenistic and Greco-Roman Period.

Sculpture

Archaic and Transitional Period (7th century B.C.–c.450 B.C.). Among the earliest extant works are individual figures, life-size or larger, carved in limestone or marble. Created as dedications to honor the gods, they follow the stiff, unnatural traditions of Egyptian sculpture. The most popular type, a nude male figure (*kouros*, s.; *kouroi*, pl.)

Greek Information Service

"The Charioteer from Delphi" (c.475–470 B.C.), erected as a votive offering after a chariot race victory.

The Bettmann Archive

The "Laocoön" group (2d century B.C.), a work that illustrates the dramatic themes popular during the Hellenistic period.

perhaps representing Apollo, stands rigidly erect with left foot advanced. A well-known example is the Apollo of Tenea (Glyptothek, Munich). Similarly posed female figures (*kore*, s.; *korai*, pl.) are clad in clinging, schematized draperies that model the form beneath. A third type is represented by enthroned figures heavily draped.

During the Transitional phase (c.500–c.450 B.C.), great advances were made in rendering anatomy, and important temples were adorned with famous pedimental groups and with metopes, the blocks that form part of the Doric frieze, sculptured in relief. In the pediments of the Temple of Aphaea at Aegina such groups showed combat scenes of the Trojan War. Their active, athletic figures (c.490 B.C.) have been reassembled in the Glyptothek, Munich. In Olympia the sculptures of the Temple of Zeus (c.480–c.460 B.C.) present mythological themes in a more dignified and imposing style. The leading sculptor of this period was Myron of Athens. Although none of his original bronzes survive, his most famous work, the "Discus Thrower," is admired in marble copies of later date.

Two notable anonymous bronzes from this period have survived in the original: "The Charioteer from Delphi" (Museum, Delphi) and a heroic figure of Poseidon or Zeus (National Museum, Athens).

Culminating Period (c.450–c.400 B.C.). The great masterpieces of the Culminating Period, now known only through later marble copies and contemporary descrip-

tions, were judged in antiquity as the climax of Greek art. Phidias, of Athens, gained undying fame with two colossal chryselephantine (gold-and-ivory) figures: the Athena Parthenos (finished c.438 B.C.), which stood in the Parthenon on the Athens Acropolis; and the Olympian Zeus, which stood in the Temple of Zeus in Olympia. The dignity and perfection of Phidias' style still may be glimpsed in the marble figures and reliefs of the Parthenon (begun 447 B.C.), carved by skilled assistants under his general direction. Particularly admired works are preserved in the British Museum, London. Among them are a magnificent male figure, sometimes identified as Theseus, the mythical founder of Athens; a group of seated female figures, perhaps representing the Three Fates; beautiful reliefs depicting the Panathenaic procession, from the frieze that runs around the cella wall; and the sculptured metopes of the exterior frieze, the best-preserved of which depict a battle of centaurs and Lapiths.

Polyclitus, the most famous sculptor of athletes, is known only through later marble copies of his bronze Spearbearer, Diadumenus, and Amazon. The Spearbearer was considered perfect in bodily proportions.

Other outstanding works survive in fragmentary friezes and reliefs from various temples, such as the Erechtheum and the Temple of Athena Nike on the Athens Acropolis. The frieze from the Temple of Apollo at Bassae is also famous.

93

The Bettmann Archive

A chariot scene is painted in delicate detail on a black-figured hydria made in the second half of the 6th century B.C.

Period of Decline (c.400–c.323 B.C.). Having thoroughly mastered the human form, sculptors abandoned the earlier dignified modes and turned to styles of greater emotional appeal. Praxiteles was noted for his nude Venus of Cnidus and for male figures in graceful, relaxed poses. A marble group of "Hermes with the Infant Dionysus," discovered in Olympia and now in the museum there, was perhaps carved by his own hand. His other masterpieces are known in later copies. Scopas pioneered in depicting emotion through facial expression and violent movement. Lysippus excelled in slender, athletic figures of bronze.

Hellenistic and Greco-Roman Period (323–146 B.C.). Highly dramatic, pathetic, and erotic themes became popular during the Hellenistic period. Extremes of pathos and drama were rendered in the "Dying Gaul" (Capitoline Museum, Rome), the famous "Laocoön" group (Vatican Museum, Rome), and the frieze of the Great Altar of Pergamum (Pergamum Museum, Berlin). Other renowned works are the "Venus of Milo" and the "Winged Victory of Samothrace" (both Louvre Museum, Paris).

Painting, Ceramics, and Minor Arts

Mere fragments of painting survive, but descriptions of great frescoes in Athens and Delphi indicate that painters followed the lead of sculpture until Hellenistic times. Thereafter, they gave attention to many aspects of nature and even attempted landscape. A mosaic from Pompeii, "The Battle of Issus" (National Museum, Naples), reflects a style of the 4th century B.C.

The history of painting appears most clearly in ceramics, where thousands of painted vases document its evolution. The Greeks raised the art of vasemaking to a high level, both in the development of the various types (the basic ones of which are shown in the accompanying diagram), and in their decoration. Polychrome Corinthian vases (7th–6th century B.C.), decorated with elaborate rosettes and fantastic monsters, reflect Oriental influence. Black-figured vases (6th century B.C.), with figures and scenes in black silhouette on the reddish clay, were perfected in the vicinity of Athens. Although products of commercial art, they reflect the great styles of their day. The Culminating Period, in Athens, produced red-figured vases (5th century B.C.). Artists outlined mythological scenes and incidents of daily life in a precise, but delicate, linear style. Arrangements of scenes and ornament were beautifully designed to harmonize with the shapes of the vases.

Many terra-cotta figurines and representations on coins and engraved gems throw additional light on the unique attainments of Greek art.

Sculpture

Classic Greek sculpture, throughout its history, served religion with statues of gods. It adorned Greek temples with marble groups and friezes. It created few portraits before the time of Alexander the Great (d.323 B.C.), because military and athletic victors were usually commemorated indirectly by representing the legendary exploits of mythical heroes. Greek-carved ornament, however, influenced many later decorative styles by its formal beauty and delicate charm.

GREEK VASE SHAPES

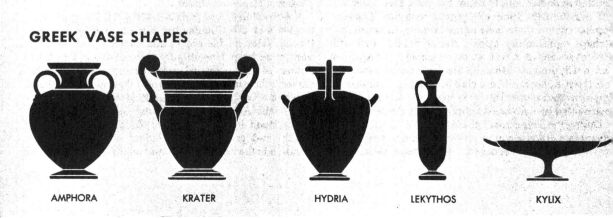

AMPHORA KRATER HYDRIA LEKYTHOS KYLIX

"Dying Gaul" (3d century B.C.) exemplifies the naturalism and emotional themes of late Greek sculpture.

Alinari—Art Reference Bureau

Although pioneer Greek sculptors inherited Egyptian conventions, their keener perception and more rational methods inspired persistent efforts toward correcting and improving the rendering of human forms. The body was shown not in awkwardly joined fractions, but with all parts correctly articulated and naturally disposed in space. These advances appear (7th–5th centuries B.C.) in the increasing naturalism and vitality of early frontal figures such as "Apollo of Tenea" and, more clearly, in the free and active warrior groups from Aegina (both, Glyptothek, Munich). Few traces of archaic conventions remain in marble copies of Myron's famous "Discus Thrower" (Museo Nazionale Romano, Rome). The idealized naturalism and grave beauty of Greek sculpture culminated c.450–400 B.C. in Phidias' great chryselephantine statues of "Zeus" and "Athena," in the sculptures of the Athenian Parthenon created under his direction, and in famous statues of athletes by Polyclitus.

Sculptors of later centuries (c.400–146 B.C.) turned to more emotional themes after thoroughly mastering

Roman copy of the lost "Venus of Cnidus" of Praxiteles.

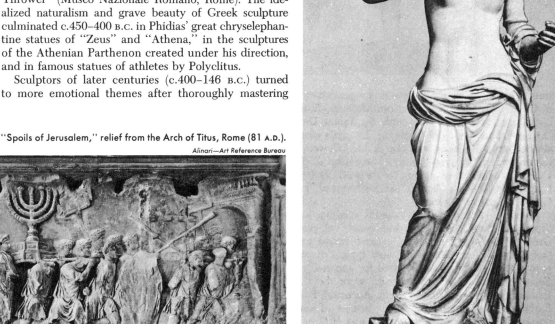

Alinari—Art Reference Bureau

"Spoils of Jerusalem," relief from the Arch of Titus, Rome (81 A.D.).

Alinari—Art Reference Bureau

95

human anatomy. Praxiteles created his seductive "Venus of Cnidus" (a copy in the Vatican Museum, Rome) and his famous group "Hermes with the Infant Dionysus" (Archeological Museum, Olympia). Lysippus excelled in slender athletic figures, and one of his followers carved the renowned "Winged Victory of Samothrace" (Louvre, Paris). To a final phase belong the pathetic "Dying Gaul" (Capitoline Museum, Rome) and the tortured "Laocoön Group" (Vatican Museum).

Roman sculpture (c.200 B.C.–4th century A.D.), although influenced by the ideal beauty of plundered Greek works, soon developed a more varied and individual style. Portraiture, the most typical Roman art, grew out of death masks required for ancestor worship. Earlier portraits (1st century B.C.) were therefore unsparingly realistic ("Roman with Ancestral Portraits," Barberini Museum, Rome). Later images of emperors, however, were often ennobled by traces of Greek idealism ("Prima Porta Augustus," Vatican Museum; "Equestrian Marcus Aurelius," Capitol, Rome).

Sculptors also excelled in beautiful naturalistic ornament. More impressive are the great historical reliefs, created to glorify emperors by recording their conquests and glittering triumphs. In Rome the Arch of Titus reliefs (81 A.D.) reveal a new depth with true atmospheric perspective, and the continuous spiral of scenes encircling the huge Column of Trajan (113) gives a full account of an important military campaign. Works of this type developed a novel method of visual narration, in which the chief actors reappear in successive events against a changing scenic background. This Roman system of continuous pictorial narration was later adopted by Christian artists and enriched with symbolic religious meaning. It is still used in the modern comic strip.

DEMOCRACY

Ancient Greece. From the very beginning, "democracy" has been used in two quite distinct, although related, ways. It has had both a specific, political meaning and a general, sociological meaning. The first of these is very clearly implied in the Greek roots of the word *demokratia: demos*, "the people," and *kratos*, "rule." In this sense, democracy is a form of government in which political power is regularly exercised by the citizenry. This definition is intended, among other things, to distinguish democracy from anarchy in the sense of absence of government, or the rule of each person by himself. The paradox that the rulers and ruled in a democracy are in a real sense the same people fascinated and perplexed the ancient Greeks, who may be said to have invented not only the word but the reality of democracy as well.

For several centuries the history of the Greek city-states was the story of the long and bitter conflict between the forces of democracy and those of oligarchy, the rule of the few. Both within the individual states of Greece, especially Athens, and in the recurrent wars between Athens and Sparta, this struggle was the overwhelming fact of Hellenic political existence. As has been so often the case in human affairs, these bloody attempts to find some political form to replace the traditional aristocratic government of the city-state were inconclusive. By the 4th century B.C. all

the participants were materially and spiritually exhausted, and the city-state itself had virtually ceased to exist. But this does not mean that the struggle was without meaning or importance. Above all, it formed the background and the stimulus for the most thorough and sophisticated discussions of the theory and practice of government, democratic as well as oligarchic and aristocratic.

To appreciate the Greek philosophers' views of democracy it is necessary to know something of the actual practice of Athenian democratic government. Two facts stand out. In the first place, widespread slavery was not only tolerated by the Athenian form of democracy but was essential to it. It has been estimated that in Athens a citizen population of roughly 30,000 was supported by the labor of some 100,000 slaves. In the second place, for the Athenians democracy meant the direct participation of the mass of the citizenry in the processes of government. Laws were made by vast popular assemblies, officials were chosen by lot and served on a rotating basis, even lawsuits were decided by direct vote after a theatrical trial. This meant, of course, that a very substantial amount of the time of every Athenian citizen was devoted to public affairs; political life was a matter of such personal concern as has perhaps never again been equaled. Indeed, so strong was this commitment to personal involvement in politics that the Greeks were unable to imagine anything resembling representative government. In describing his "best possible" state Plato fixed the proper number of citizens at exactly 5,040. It was argued that the territory of a state should never be so large that a man could not walk across it between dawn and dusk. In view of these facts, it is not surprising that Aristotle should have defined man as the "political animal." But the continuous participation of the citizen in politics that is the hallmark of Athenian democracy was possible only because the citizens' leisure was bought by the labor of tens of thousands of slaves.

Generally speaking, the great Athenian philosophers were profoundly suspicious of democracy and often openly hostile to it. Plato's account of decadent democracy in *The Republic* is among the most scathing ever written. Contrasting democracy with the rule of an aristocracy of the truly wise and virtuous, he can find little to say in its favor. Similarly, Aristotle tends to consider democracy as a perverted form of government, one in which the selfish interests of the poor predominate over the general good of the community. But it should be noted that this is his judgment of direct, mass democracy—a judgment perhaps not unlike that which would be made by a modern American confronted with the same phenomenon. For it is perfectly clear that Aristotle found much to admire in the notions of equality and self-rule that were implicit in the Athenian ideal of democracy. It may be argued that Aristotle's difficulty in reaching a clear judgment of the merits and demerits of democracy resulted from his inability to dissociate the term from the facts of Athenian political life. Although he approved of the participation of the citizenry in the government and of at least partial political equality, Aristotle was repelled by the disorder and internecine strife that so often accompanied democratic processes. If this is the case, it may also be said that Aristotle's dilemma has had to be faced by the supporters of democracy in the two millenniums since his day.

In the writings of both Plato and Aristotle we find clear evidence that from the very beginning democracy has meant more than simply a particular form of government. With their keen appreciation of the social and economic context of politics, the Greek philosophers were quick to realize that governmental institutions at once reflect and shape communities and their inhabitants. Thus democracy, like aristocracy, oligarchy, and the rest, is a way of life as well as an ordering of public offices. The democratic ideal, in these terms, is a society of free and equal citizens; a society in which the worth of each individual is recognized and cherished; a society unmarked by special privilege of birth, wealth, or status. It is interesting that the same historic experience that produced Plato's hostile criticisms of democracy should also have produced what has come to be regarded as perhaps the most eloquent statement of this democratic ideal, the Funeral Oration that is attributed to Pericles in Thucydides' *History of the Peloponnesian War.* Speaking at the grave of the Athenians who had died in the struggle against Sparta, the statesman contrasted the two societies, the military despotism of Sparta and the democracy of Athens. Although Athenian democracy died, the glorious image of Athenian democracy pictured in the Funeral Oration has remained an inspiration to later ages.

EDUCATION

Ancient Greece and Rome. The history of education in ancient Greece and Rome stretches from the foundations of those societies, the Greek story going back before 1000 B.C., the Roman to 500 B.C. The history of the two cultures becomes combined after the fall of Greece to Roman armies in 146 B.C. and terminates with the collapse of the Western Roman Empire, traditionally dated at 476 A.D. It should be noted, however, that many aspects of Hellenistic (Greco-Roman) education were maintained in Byzantium for centuries after the fall of the Western Empire. These became fused with Islamic knowledge after 620 A.D. and were reintroduced into the stream of Western culture toward the end of the Middle Ages.

As with all societies in the early phases of their development, education in Greece and Rome was originally centered in the family. There were no formal schools and parents were responsible for the education of their children. A characteristic of Roman education was the way boys and girls learned by observing and doing as they helped their mothers and fathers in their daily duties. As societies become more complex, mounting responsibilities take the father from the home and from family duties. More highly specialized skills and knowledge are also in order, hence formal schooling is introduced by parents. A family servant or slave may be assigned to teach or a tutor may be hired. Eventually teachers, usually men, establish schoolrooms in their homes, or a group of prosperous parents may set up a school and employ a schoolmaster. In this manner formal schools eventually arose in ancient Greece and Rome. Many centuries later, on the American frontier, the first formal schooling was often provided in much the same manner.

Generally, in Greece and Rome, only the children of the citizens were schooled beyond the early years of child-

hood education handled by the family. Thus only a minority of the total population was literate. Most girls, except for isolated instances as in Sparta, received no formal schooling. The peasants, the landless working classes in the cities, and slaves also went without education.

Throughout much of the Greco-Roman period those boys who were educated usually went to the homes of their teachers. Often they were accompanied by household slaves known as pedagogues. The boys might spend time first with a grammarian for literary and writing instruction, then journey to a music or elocution teacher. and end the afternoon at a gymnasium. They had no books, just wax tablets on which they inscribed letters or words with a stylus. They counted on their fingers. Most teaching consisted of lecturing, and the ability to memorize was the prime need of the pupil.

Gradually, formal schools at various levels were established. By 150 B.C., small Roman boys would go for a few years to the elementary school, the *ludus;* then those who went on would train with a Greek or Latin grammarian who taught beyond the fundamentals previously instilled. A limited number of able upper-class boys would move on to the rhetorical school for oratorical training as well as advanced studies in other areas. This school was adopted from the Greeks, the first such school of rhetoric having been opened by Isocrates in Athens c.392 B.C. The Romans also borrowed the bulk of their curriculum, methods, and even their teachers from Greece. However, Rome had few institutions of higher education to match the apex of the Greek educational ladder, the philosophical schools such as those at Athens founded by Plato and Aristotle. Even at the height of the Empire, young Romans went abroad for their final education—to Hellenistic schools at Athens, Rhodes, Pergamum, and to the famous library and museum at Alexandria.

The Greek curriculum blended effectively emphases upon the intellectual, the aesthetic, and the physical. The traditional offerings that emerged from the Greek experience were modified and extended by the Romans. These evolved into the liberal arts—the subject matter fit for the upbringing of a young freeman. Down through the centuries in many other nations, particularly at secondary and higher levels, the content of a curriculum that met the needs of an elite minority in ancient Greece and Rome came to be the prototype of what was educationally proper.

Among the great Greek teachers was Socrates (469–399 B.C.), the self-styled "gadfly of Athens." For his questions and activities he was sentenced to death, thus providing one of the first examples of a problem of academic freedom, that is, of the right of the teacher and pupil to pursue the truth as they see it. Socrates' greatest pupil was Plato (429–347 B.C.). Plato's influence can be traced in educational theory from his own day to the 20th century. Although he presented a plan for education in his own world—the emphasis being on the training of philosophers as leaders—his impact on education was even greater in other lands and times than in ancient Athens. Aristotle (384–322 B.C.), a student in Plato's Academy, became another of the world's most influential philosophers and an unequaled systematizer of scientific knowledge. His works formed the most important part of the courses of study in medieval universities a thousand years after his death.

GAMES

The Olympic Games, the most celebrated of the ancient Panhellenic athletic festivals, were held every four years in late August or early September at Olympia in connection with rites honoring Zeus. In earliest times, funeral games had taken place at Zeus's oracle, and in legend the foundation of the games was attributed to Hercules. Supposedly half-forgotten during the troubled centuries after the Trojan War, the Olympic Games were renewed about the 9th century B.C. as a peace move. A truce was established which demanded safe conduct for all Greeks traveling to and from the Olympic festival and forbade wars during that season. This remained an unalterable law throughout Olympia's existence.

No reliable victor lists were kept for the first 27 celebrations (108 years) after the renewal; these began officially with the games in which Coroebus won the foot race (776 B.C. by modern chronology). These games were thus erroneously called Olympiad I by ancient compilers. Already in the 7th century B.C. the games were immensely popular throughout the Greek world and embodied a mixture of business, social, religious, and athletic events. By 472 B.C. the new city of Elis, 34 mi. from Olympia, became the administrative center of the festival.

The date, duration, and athletic events of the Olympic Games were altered from time to time, but by the early 5th century B.C. the festival probably required five days. Aspiring athletes had to arrive in advance for a month's pitiless training under special Olympic rules and under trainers quick with the punishing stick. Events were open only to men of strictly Greek parentage and of certain proven ages: 17–20 for junior events, 20 plus for senior events. After a colorful procession of all participants from Elis to Olympia, the athletes took part in religious rites and lot-drawing for positions. They then swore before Zeus regarding their Greek parentage, unblemished character, and adherence to training rules for the previous 10 months. This was followed by the swearing of the umpires.

Athletic contests in the 5th century B.C. included foot racing for 200 yd., 400 yd., and 3 mi. or more; the pentathlon (foot race, jumping, discus throwing, javelin throwing, and wrestling); wrestling; boxing; the pancratium (ground wrestling with no holds barred); racing in armor for 400 yd.; and chariot and horse racing. Victors were awarded wild olive wreaths at Olympia in the temple of Zeus. Sacrifices, parades, and singing of traditional triumph songs followed and culminated in a complimentary dinner for victors in the public hall. Champions received, in addition, valuable gifts and privileges upon their return home.

The Olympic Games, after a history of almost 1,200 years of recorded victor lists, ceased about 400 A.D. as a result of Christian edicts against the Zeus temple at Olympia and chaotic conditions throughout Greece.

HISTORY

Prehistory (c.3500–800 B.C.). Under this heading is included the record of the whole span of human habitation around the Aegean Sea before the use of alphabetic writing. Although the term "prehistoric" usually refers to periods for which no written documents are available, Mycenaean clay tablets, written in the so-called Linear B script, are now being deciphered, thus pushing back the frontiers of the historical era at least to the 13th century B.C. For prehistory we must rely chiefly on the data derived from the work of archeologists.

Neolithic Stage (c.3500–2800 B.C.). The earliest certain inhabitants of Greece were Neolithic men who settled first in the northeast and then gradually penetrated most of the peninsula.

Bronze Age (c.2800–1100 B.C.). Invaders from Asia Minor who probably spoke a non-Indo-European tongue ushered in the Bronze Age, or Helladic period, as it is called in mainland Greece, by introducing copper smelting and the use of metal weapons. About 1900 B.C. these Early Helladic people were conquered by new, warlike invaders. The Middle Helladic newcomers burned and destroyed many towns, and built over the ruins or on new sites. Arriving in east-central Greece, apparently by sea, they radiated out south and west, carrying with them their distinctive gray Minyan pottery. They may have used an early form of the Greek language. The Late Helladic period began c.1550 B.C., although there does not seem to have been an invasion or distinctive cultural change to mark the transition. For some time overseas trade and local population had been increasing rapidly. A strong wave of Cretan, or Minoan, influence affected the mainland, and was especially noticeable for several generations after 1550. Possibly Cretan artists and workmen lived in mainland towns, but there is no evidence to prove Cretan political domination.

The Late Helladic is often called the Mycenaean period, because Mycenae was clearly the largest and richest population center. The Mycenaeans, also known as Achaeans, occupied most of the good agricultural land and controlled all the best harbors in southern, central, and northeastern Greece, as well as the Ionian Islands and some in the vicinity of Rhodes in the southeastern Aegean. Agriculture and herding of domestic animals were still the main occupations, although manufacturing and sea-borne trade were becoming increasingly important. The Mycenaeans gradually drove Minoan traders from the seas and finally occupied Knossos, the Cretan capital. In the 14th and 13th centuries B.C. Mycenaean shipping dominated the eastern Mediterranean. Their pottery and trading stations are found from Sicily and southern Italy in the west, to Rhodes, Cyprus, and Syria in the east.

The Homeric poems, particularly the *Iliad*, preserve echoes of Mycenaean society. Homer's "bronze-clad Achaeans" were a restless, proud, and hospitable people who loved war, hunting, sport, feasting, song, and oratory. Their leaders occupied fortified acropolises, lived in beautifully decorated and furnished palaces, and were buried in great domed royal tombs. Clay tablets from palace archives list the royal wealth in slaves, land, goods, and produce. It was a highly centralized and bureaucratic society, with religious, military, and civil functions tightly organized under the King's control. Independent Late Helladic kingdoms included Mycenae, Pylos, Thebes, Orchomenus, Athens, and Sparta.

Dorian Invasion. Toward the end of the 13th century

B.C., the Achaeans won the Trojan War, but soon afterward were themselves under attack by the Dorians. The Dorian invasion was not, however, a single massive attack. In its earlier stages it seems to have involved a series of sea-borne raids originating in the northern Adriatic and aimed at individual centers. Throughout the 12th century B.C. the great Mycenaean capitals, together with lesser towns, were systematically destroyed and their inhabitants scattered or killed. Some refugees founded or reinforced Achaean colonies west and east of the Greek mainland. Tradition relates that exiles, especially from Pylos in the southwest, made their way to Athens, which the Dorians never captured.

The Dorian invasion has long been equated with the beginning of the Iron Age. In addition to the invincible iron weapons, Dorians were supposed to have introduced cremation burial and the Geometric style in pottery decoration. Actually, all three of these cultural innovations were gradual developments and not the product of sudden and forcible change.

Early Iron Age (c.1100–800 B.C.). The period from the fall of Mycenaean power to the earliest alphabetic writing is often called the "dark age" of Greek history. Settlements were scattered, isolated, and sparsely populated. Culture and commercial exchange was sporadic. Shipping and trade were controlled mainly by the Phoenicians from c.1000 until well after 800 B.C. But a Greek revitalization appeared about 950 B.C. in and around Athens. By c.800 B.C. the distinctive Geometric tradition in art had been carried by trade, mostly sea-borne, over central and southern Greece and the Aegean Islands. This period saw the first great migrations from Greece to the Asia Minor coast. Distinctions of race, dialect, and origin among the colonists are confused in later tradition. Even the motivation is obscure. Invasions at the end of the Bronze Age may have pushed the northeast Achaeans across the Aegean to occupy the so-called Aeolian area south of Troy. Survivors of the southern Mycenaean kingdoms participated in the settling of the central Ionian area opposite central Greece. And the Dorian invaders gave their name to the most southerly group of colonies.

Early History (c.800–550 B.C.). The colonies in Asia Minor prospered. Fertile soil was far more abundant than at home, and there were new opportunities for trade with the interior and with Syria and Egypt. Ionian colonies rapidly became the pace-setters in economic prosperity and in cultural advance. Their contributions to literature, science, philosophy, and art were basic to the brilliant developments all over the Greek world in the following centuries. They no doubt built on what they had retained from the Bronze Age, but they also absorbed much from the older cultures of their neighbors in Asia Minor and from Phoenician contacts.

Homeric Age. Sometime between 900 and 700 B.C. the Homeric poems were unified and written down in approximately their present form. Scholarly opinion still disputes their exact origin and date, though Ionia is the most likely home of the final stages. Since the basic subject matter and even the language of the poems were highly traditional, the result, which incorporated details reflecting the contemporary conditions of several periods, must be treated cautiously as a historical document.

The political institutions described in the *Iliad* and the *Odyssey* in the main reflect the status of the earliest colonial settlements. The King was still the leader in war, as well as chief priest, judge, and executive. But his power was not absolute. A council of aristocratic Princes was beginning to gain in prestige, and an assembly of warriors could, at least, express its approval or disapproval on military, political, and legal questions.

Rise of the City-State. Social identity originally depended on family or tribal ties. Gradually small towns, for reasons of economic advantage or political security, united into larger political entities. The largest or best-situated town within each natural geographic unit became the capital, and the smaller towns and villages, along with the total territory, comprised the state. The Greek word "polis" refers to both, and is often translated "city-state." Personal loyalties gradually shifted from ties of family to pride in the independent and sovereign state. Political power shifted to the aristocratic council, and the King lost nearly all his prerogatives except for certain religious duties.

Every state had its own government, laws, army, and patron deity. As good land was scarce and the populations were increasing, quarrels often developed over markets and disputed boundaries. Interstate rivalry in every area of community life led to tremendous competitive efforts. This fragmented nationalism both contributed to Greek greatness and to the weakness which ultimately made foreign domination inevitable.

In spite of an intense desire for local independence the Greeks were conscious of their national identity as opposed to the alien *barbaroi* around them. Their common heritage was clear in their language, religion, and past achievements recounted in myth and literature. Some states, for example, Boeotia, formed political leagues around a powerful leader; others, like the Ionian states, around a famous sanctuary. Another kind of interstate organization which did not entail any surrender of individual sovereignty was the amphictyony (association) of states organized to administer and protect the sacred shrine of Apollo at Delphi. The Panhellenic games were also continuing reminders of all that Greeks had in common.

Second Colonial Era (c.750–550 B.C.). The poet Hesiod suggests the motivation for a new wave of emigration. Farmers had increasing difficulty making the stony Greek soil produce enough food for a growing population. A wider gap had developed between farmers and a new-rich trading class which had begun to supplant the old land-owning aristocracy in political power. Interest rates were high, and debts often resulted in farmers losing their lands and even being enslaved. Thus, the prospect of greater political and economic freedom provided a powerful impetus for individual colonists. The location of many of the new settlements indicates that they were deliberately planned as depots to facilitate trade operations in new territory.

A colony was usually sponsored by a single metropolis ("mother state"). Although the two maintained close ties, the colony enjoyed complete political independence. Some of the most prolific colonizing states were Miletus, Chalcis, Eretria, Corinth, and Megara. The main areas of expansion were the north Aegean coast, the Black Sea coast, and Magna Graecia, that is, southern Italy and central and eastern Sicily.

Greek trading towns also sprang up all the way from

Naucratis in the Nile Delta and Cyrene on the Libyan coast to Massilia (Marseilles) in southern France and Tartessus in Spain. Food and raw materials flowed from the colonies to the older states, and the new states provided a market for processed and manufactured goods. The struggle against natural difficulties and hostile natives was often grim, but traders had scouted the best sites and most colonies prospered.

Age of Tyranny. The new frontiers only temporarily mitigated popular resentment against the ruling oligarchs and aristocrats. In addition to poverty and debt, ordinary citizens had other grievances, including a lack of written laws and the state's failure to protect the liberties of its citizens. As a result, an ambitious aristocrat often proclaimed himself the champion of the people and with their support took over the government.

Because the Greeks had a deep distrust of unconstitutional government and because such a man, who was called *tyrannos*, occasionally turned out to be oppressive, the word acquired the unpleasant connotation which the English "tyrant" has inherited. Actually, tyrants usually did much to lessen tensions and to increase the prosperity and prestige of their states. They carried out ambitious programs of public works, founded or enlarged popular religious festivals, and generously patronized artists and writers. Some of the better-known early tyrants were Cypselus and Periander of Corinth (c.655–585 B.C.), Cleisthenes of Sicyon (fl.600–570 B.C.), and Polycrates of Samos (fl.540 B.C.). The first-generation tyrants were almost always able men, genuinely concerned with improving conditions. Most, however, wanted to found dynasties, and their sons and grandsons were usually repudiated.

The 6th Century B.C. During this period Athens and Sparta attained leadership in their respective areas. The two states achieved prominence in radically different ways, and it is instructive to trace the process and observe the result.

The Spartans were a conquering minority who ruled over a very much larger pre-Dorian group living in the area called Laconia, in the southeast Peloponnesus. At first they seem to have resembled their neighbors in other states. Encouraging poets, musicians, sculptors, and painters, they enjoyed a variety of cultural interests. Toward the end of the 8th century B.C. they had conquered Messenia to the west, thereby more than doubling their territory. About 650 B.C. the Messenian serfs, under the leadership of Aristomenes, rebelled, and the Spartans barely succeeded in suppressing the revolt. This crisis apparently shocked them into a deep sense of insecurity and a determination to let nothing interfere with preparedness for war. Lycurgus, the lawgiver, is said to have planned the new regime. Some modifications continued until the mid-6th century B.C., but thereafter Spartan institutions changed very little. The Spartans were in fact the arch-conservatives of Greece.

Sparta was governed by two Kings who originally were, probably, the heads of two tribes. Their main duties involved leadership of the army. An aristocratic council, the *gerousia*, was composed of the Kings plus 28 elders, representing noble clans, who had to be over 60 years of age and were elected for life. The assembly of all citizens over 30 years of age could merely shout approval or disapproval, as in Homeric times. Finally, a board of five ephors (magistrates) was elected annually and gradually became the chief executive power. A middle class of noncitizens, called *perioeci*, carried on limited commerce, although coined money was prohibited. The serfs, or helots, worked the land for their Spartan masters, who were thus free to devote their lives to developing physical endurance and military prowess. Spartan home life, business, and intellectual or artistic interests were closely regulated and even discouraged. Education was strictly utilitarian. Obedience, simplicity, conformity, and bravery were encouraged as the highest virtues. At home Spartans practiced absolute ruthlessness in dealing with opposition among their subjects, and abroad, their military might overawed every state in the Peloponnesus except Argos. Allied states were organized into a loose confederacy, called the Peloponnesian League, under Spartan leadership. The menacing line of heavy-armed Spartan hoplites was for three centuries the invincible power in mainland Greece.

The Athenians. The record of the Athenian political evolution is, in contrast, one of flexibility and responsiveness to change. Critics then and now have insisted that policy decisions were dangerously subject to popular whim. At first, a landowning aristocracy controlled the government through the judicial council of the Areopagus and an executive board of nine magistrates, or archons, chosen annually. The assembly was not open to poorer citizens. Popular pressure resulted in the publication in 621 B.C. of the first written code of laws, drafted by Draco. The laws, however, were harsh and did little to correct political and economic inequality. The aristocratic poet and lawgiver Solon realized that further concessions had to be made to prevent a violent revolution, and in 594 B.C. the Areopagus granted him extraordinary power to inaugurate necessary reforms. Solon's wisdom and caution are reflected in the criticism he received from both rich and poor. On the political level he made property rather than noble birth the qualification for high office, and he admitted all but the poorest class of citizens to the assembly. He set up a new council of 400 members (boule) to prepare business for the assembly, instituted new popular law courts, and also a court of appeal against decisions of the magistrates.

His economic reforms included prohibiting enslavement for debt, encouraging trade and manufacturing, stimulating the export of olive oil, forbidding the export of grain, and, perhaps, certain restraints on extensive landholdings. Solon's main purpose was to strengthen the position of the merchant class and to effect a shift in the Athenian economy from an agricultural to a commercial basis. In the latter he was permanently successful, but the economic improvement was not felt by the common people in time to prevent an interval of tyranny.

Pisistratus, an aristocrat who had failed in two previous attempts, finally seized firm control of the government in 545 B.C. Many of the nobility went into exile, and their property was redistributed among the landless. Pisistratus set the people to work on new temples, civic buildings, and an improved water supply. Poets were honored, and the celebration called the Panathenaea in honor of the

ANCIENT GREECE

0 — 50
Miles

patron goddess Athena was given new importance. Pisistratus also established or reorganized the famous dramatic festival called the Greater Dionysia, which became one of the chief cultural ornaments of Athens.

Pisistratus' actions have been explained as schemes to divert attention from the illegal origin of his power; but there is little doubt that he was genuinely patriotic. Athens owed much of its future brilliance to his encouragement of artistic and cultural excellence. Pisistratus' attempt to found a dynasty failed, however. One son, Hipparchus, was assassinated, and the other, Hippias, was driven out in 510.

Sparta had helped expel the tyrant Hippias, expecting a return to oligarchy. But the Athenians insisted on moving in a democratic direction, and again, in 508, an aristocrat, Cleisthenes, led the popular party in liberalizing the constitution. He reorganized the voting system by forming ten tribes, which were artificial units containing representation from various sections of the state. This made impossible the former divisive voting and action by factions and families which had facilitated Pisistratus' coup. Another precaution against a recurrence of tyranny was

the institution of ostracism (temporary banishment by popular vote). Since it was not utilized until the early 5th century B.C., however, there is some question whether it should be attributed to Cleisthenes.

In Cleisthenes' reorganization, the assembly, or ecclesia, became unquestionably the sovereign legislative body, and all magistrates were ultimately responsible to it. Every adult male citizen had the right to attend, cast his vote, and otherwise directly express his opinion. Solon's popular council of 400 was enlarged to include 50 members elected annually from each of the ten new tribes. This new council of Five Hundred (boule) became the chief administrative body, controlling finances and actions of all magistrates. Quotas of infantry and cavalry were levied by tribes, and each tribe elected a general. The ten generals, or *strategoi*, and especially their president, gradually became the supreme officials in the state.

By the end of the 6th century B.C. Athenian and Spartan systems of government were radically different. Repeated attempts by Sparta and other conservative states to interfere on behalf of aristocratic minorities in Athens and elsewhere only augmented their differences.

The 5th Century. At the beginning of the century Athens had barely launched its democratic experiment. In the succeeding 20 years the free Greek states, under the leadership of Athens and Sparta, successfully defended Europe against the absolutism of the Persian Empire. By mid-century the prosperous Greek states were forced into a choice, often involving violence, between Athenian or Spartan leadership. By the end of the century the exultant glow following the Persian Wars had disappeared and Greece lay exhausted from a bitter internal war which had racked it for almost 30 years.

Persian Wars. From the earliest colonial expansion Greek states had ringed the whole Asia Minor coast. Their freedom and prosperity challenged any absolutist regime which controlled the interior. The Lydians, with their capital at Sardis near the Ionian coast, were generally friendly to the Greeks, and the two peoples developed an extensive cultural interchange. But in resources and military strength the Greeks were at a disadvantage; thus the last Lydian King, Croesus, gained political control of every Greek state in Asia Minor except Miletus.

In 546 B.C. Cyrus the Great conquered Lydia. The Greeks found the Persians harsher masters than the Lydians, and in 499 B.C. the Ionian states, led by Miletus, revolted. To their request for aid from the Greek city-states, only Athens and Eretria responded favorably. The revolt spread all the way from the Black Sea to Cyprus, but was finally crushed. Following that, the Persian King Darius in 492 B.C. organized an invasion of European Greece. He advertised it as a punitive expedition against the two states which had dared to help the Ionians, but probably realized that his control of the Eastern Greeks would not be secure while their countrymen across the Aegean retained their freedom.

The first expedition collapsed after most of the Persian fleet was wrecked in a storm off Mount Athos in Thrace. Darius, however, assembled a larger striking force and meanwhile sent heralds demanding surrender. A fair number of states, including Thebes, were frightened into submission. In 490 the fleet crossed directly to Euboea and destroyed Eretria. The next objective was Athens, and for this purpose the army disembarked at Marathon on the east coast of Attica, intending to march overland. But a small force of Athenians and Plataeans under Miltiades hastened to Marathon, charged down on the Persians, and with slight losses cut the enemy to pieces, driving them into the sea. As a result of the victory, Athenian prestige soared.

Darius' war plans were inherited by his son, Xerxes, who prepared a vast land and sea force. The attack came in 480 B.C. A gallant stand under Spartan leadership at the Pass of Thermopylae and an action by the allied fleet at Artemisium off northern Euboea slowed but did not stop the advance. The Persian army swept into Attica, and the Athenians abandoned their homes rather than surrender. The Greek fleet would also have given up Attica if Themistocles, the talented Athenian admiral, had not insisted on remaining and fighting in the Straits of Salamis southwest of Athens. In the previous ten years, at Themistocles' urging, Athens had concentrated her resources on building a powerful fleet, using the income from the rich silver mines at Laurium. As a result, more than half of the Greek triremes at Salamis were Athenian. Since the Greeks were trained to maneuver in cramped quarters, they thoroughly defeated the far superior fleet of the Persians.

Salamis broke the force of the Persian attack. The Persian army remained in central Greece until the following year when a Greek army under Spartan leadership defeated it at Plataea. The Persians never again attempted a direct attack on European Greece. From this point on the tide turned, and it was the Greeks under Macedonian leadership who invaded Asia a century and a half later.

Another Greek victory was won, according to tradition, on the same day as Salamis. Under the leadership of Syracuse, the Sicilian Greeks defeated the Carthaginians at Himera. In this action another encroachment on Europe by a great power was stopped. The Carthaginians were not driven out of western Sicily, however, and they and the Greeks maintained an uneasy balance of power there until both came under Roman control more than two centuries later.

Delian League and Athenian Empire. With the Persian defeat in 480–479 hope rose among the Greeks in Asia Minor. Within a few days of the battle of Plataea, a Greek fleet landed at Mycale and destroyed an important Persian military base. The Greek fleet was commanded by a Spartan, Pausanias, but before long Sparta withdrew from the lengthy operations which led to the liberation of the Aegean Islands and the Asia Minor coast. Distant expeditions were not to its taste, and Spartan leaders, in spite of iron discipline at home, often proved morally weak in an alien environment. So Athens was left to carry on the offensive overseas.

The Aegean states formed a league (478) with headquarters on the island of Delos. Aristides of Athens was in charge of the first assessment of each member's share in the common task of protecting commerce and wearing down Persian power. The larger states normally supplied ships and crews for the allied fleet, while the smaller states contributed money. Each member was free to manage its internal affairs and was represented in league deliberations on foreign policy. But from the first Athens contributed the largest number of ships and provided the commander of the allied fleet. In the early years Cimon was commander. As leader of the conservatives, he stood for co-operation with Sparta. Themistocles, his democratic counterpart, after outwitting Spartan opposition to the fortification of Athens and its harbor Piraeus, gradually lost ground and was ostracized in 471 B.C.

Before long a difference of opinion arose within the league over the need for maintaining the fleet. Some felt that Persian power was no longer a real threat. Others resented the financial drain or the slight limitations on their sovereignty. Members began to refuse to meet their commitments. For some years members had been converting their contributions from ships to money, which Athens used to build and maintain more ships. As the dissolution of the league would have meant a drastic cut in Athenian maritime power, Athens, when faced with secession by league members, chose to use the fleet to force them to maintain their obligations. Besides having a conviction of the continuing need for the league, Athens must have been affected in its decision by the knowledge that allied contributions indirectly subsidized the expensive Athenian democratic innovations. But once force was applied to member states, the league, in reality, became an Athenian empire.

Cimon's policy of co-operation with Sparta suffered a severe reverse in 462 B.C. when an Athenian relief force, sent to aid the Spartans put down a helot revolt, was rebuffed. After its return, Cimon was ostracized. The anti-Spartan reaction strengthened the democratic faction, whose leadership passed to Pericles. A direct descendant of Cleisthenes, he was, with few exceptions, annually elected one of the ten generals until his death (429), and his unique power of persuasion made him the unquestioned leader of the state. One of his first acts was to build parallel walls joining Athens and Piraeus, an ominous recognition that Athens might have to depend on food from abroad in case of a siege.

From this time on the attitude of Athens and its maritime allies hardened toward Sparta and the Peloponnesian League, supported by Thebes, Megara, and other states in central Greece. Open war broke out in the middle years of the century, and Athens lost considerable territory in central Greece which it had won by conquest and alliance. Also, a large Athenian fleet sent to support a revolt against Persian control in Egypt was totally defeated. This reversal on sea provided an excuse for transferring the league treasury from Apollo's shrine on Delos to Athena's temple on the Acropolis (454 B.C.). This step can be regarded as the formal break between a free coalition and an empire maintained by force. From then on Athens considered the contributions of other states as tribute which was its to spend as it saw fit. Pericles began plans for a great building program and instituted (451) pay for the large Athenian juries which now handled cases involving allies as well as Athenians.

Realizing that Athenian ambitions had led to overextension both on land and sea, Pericles negotiated two peace treaties. By the Treaty of Callias (c.449) Persia granted independence to all Greek states in Asia Minor. The Thirty Years' Peace (445) with Sparta provided that Athens give up almost every claim to mainland territory outside of Attica; in return, Sparta recognized the Athenian maritime empire. Each promised to respect the other's alliances, and trade was to be free.

Peloponnesian War (431–404 B.C.). The Thirty Years' Peace did little to bridge the deep political, economic, and cultural differences between Athens and Sparta. The immediate cause of new hostilities was the insistence by Corinth and Megara that the Peloponnesian League stop Athens from ruining Megara's trade and interfering with Corinth's relations with its colonies, particularly Corcyra and Potidaea. As with a struggle between an elephant and a whale, each protagonist was superior in its own element. The Spartan allies included almost all of the Peloponnesian and central Greek states; the Athenian empire was almost entirely maritime and concentrated around the shores of the Aegean. The early campaigns consisted mainly of land invasions of Attica and sea raids on the Peloponnesian coast and certain maritime allies of Sparta. Athenian life was seriously disrupted, since the invasions destroyed crops and farms and forced the

inhabitants of Attica to move inside the walls of Athens. There was no possibility of starving out the Athenians as long as the sea lanes were open to their shipping. But an unpredictable event seriously hurt Athens at the very start. "Plague" broke out in 430 B.C. and in two years killed some 10% of the total population, including Pericles himself. Crowded and unsanitary conditions inside the walls certainly intensified, if they did not actually cause, the epidemic.

Passions ran high as the struggle progressed. Plataea, the traditional ally of Athens in Boeotia, was captured and the whole surviving garrison executed. Cleon, who succeeded Pericles, persuaded the assembly to vote the death penalty for the whole population of the state of Mytilene on the island of Lesbos when they tried to revolt. They were barely saved by a last-minute reprieve. Off Pylos in the southwest Peloponnesus a force of Spartans was besieged on the island of Sphacteria and eventually surrendered (424). This unheard-of feat greatly encouraged the Athenians and impressed the Greek world. But in the same year Athens lost an important battle at Delium in Boeotia, and the Spartan general Brasidas began to threaten empire territory on the north Aegean coast. In 421 B.C., after both Brasidas and Cleon had been killed at Potidaea, the way was open for Nicias, leader of the Athenian conservatives, to negotiate another peace treaty.

Owing in part to the aggressive alliances and intrigues of Alcibiades, the peace was broken. In 415 B.C. Athens, in an apparent attempt to extend its empire westward, sent a large fleet to Sicily under the command of Nicias and Alcibiades. Nicias had opposed the Sicilian expedition from the start, and Alcibiades, during the voyage, escaped to Sparta to avoid being tried on a charge of sacrilege. The attempt to capture Syracuse was stalemated, and a second fleet sent to assist. Due mainly to Nicias' incompetent generalship and superstition, the campaign failed disastrously in 413. No ships and very few men ever returned home. The Sicilian affair was a heavy blow to Athenian resources, prestige, and confidence in the judgment of the sovereign assembly. Attempts at revolt increased among member states and internal disagreements led to a brief and bitter period of oligarchic rule by a committee of Four Hundred (411 B.C.).

The main action was now at sea and centered upon the Athenian lifeline from the Black Sea. Democratic government was restored in Athens, and Alcibiades, who was pardoned, led the fleet in several successful actions. But Persia was now actively helping the Spartans financially, and an able Spartan admiral, Lysander, at last appeared. Athens' last fleet was surprised and completely defeated in 405 B.C. at Aegospotamos, inside the entrance to the Hellespont. After months of siege and starvation Athens was forced to relinquish all possessions outside Attica and pull down its fortifications. But Athens did retain its independence, and it is to Sparta's credit that it resisted demands by its own allies to destroy Athens completely. An oligarchic government of 30, later referred to as the Thirty Tyrants, proved so vindictive against democratic leadership that even Spartan support could not keep them in office. A popular revolution led by Thrasybulus restored the democratic constitution in 403.

The 4th Century. Sparta emerged from the Peloponnesian War as the most powerful state in Greece, but its subsequent leadership was shortsighted and tactless. Reactionary governments were encouraged everywhere and liberal regimes suppressed. Resentment spread, and Athens' former allies began to join a second Athenian League. To check Athenian recovery, Sparta continued to intrigue with the Persians, and by the treaty of Antalcidas (386) control of all the Greeks in Asia Minor was ceded to Persia. Thebes emerged as a third power after successfully resisting Spartan interference (379). Its massed heavy infantry under the able direction of Epaminondas thoroughly defeated the Spartans at Leuctra (371 B.C.). All of Greece except Laconia itself shook off Spartan control, and buffer states like the new foundation of Megalopolis in Arcadia were encouraged to keep Sparta off balance. But within ten years Thebes, too, was unpopular, and with the death of Epaminondas at the battle of Mantinea in 362 B.C. its power declined. Clearly no one Greek state was strong enough to force the rest to unite, and voluntary efforts at "peaceful coexistence" never got far. For the time being an uneasy balance of power prevailed, with Sparta, Athens, Thebes, and Argos the strongest states.

Macedonian power was meanwhile growing in the north. King Philip II, using gold from nearby Mount Pangaeus to recruit a large and efficient native army, bought off opposition to his seizure of territory and pressure on the Chalcidian League in the north Aegean. Although Greek in race, the Macedonians were regarded by their peninsular kinsmen as semibarbarians. Yet Demosthenes of Athens was one of the few who warned that resistance must be planned immediately to check the expansionist Macedonian policies. The second Athenian League tried to act, but a revolt of allied states, the so-called Social War (357), diverted it. Then the Sacred War (356) between members of the Delphic Amphictyony gave Philip an excuse to intervene in Greek politics. He marched down and punished the Phocians who had plundered Apollo's treasure.

When Olynthus, capital of the Chalcidian League, was destroyed (348) and its inhabitants enslaved, there could no longer be any doubt of Philip's intentions. He accepted another invitation to use his army in central Greece in 338, and Demosthenes was able to persuade Athens and Thebes to organize resistance. In the battle of Chaeronea Philip, in effect, won control of all Greece. He organized the formerly independent city-states into the Corinthian League, bound to him as commander in chief. Athens was treated with special favor, while Sparta was excluded. The individual states were allowed to retain their institutions and a semblance of self-government, but genuine political liberty, which the Greeks were the first to achieve, disappeared in its own birthplace and was not recovered there for over 21 centuries.

Philip immediately prepared to invade Asia Minor and free the eastern Greeks from Persian control. This was his long-standing ambition and one which the Athenian orator Isocrates had recently advocated as a means of uniting the Greek states. Philip, however, was assassinated in one of the frequent Macedonian court intrigues (336), and his 20-year-old son Alexander, later to be known as "the Great," inherited his throne and incomplete plans.

Alexander the Great (356–323 B.C.). Before his death 13 years later, Alexander had made an impact on world history and men's imaginations rarely equaled before or since. Quickly suppressing the widespread unrest and revolt which erupted following his father's death, Alexander ruthlessly destroyed Thebes (335) as a warning to other potentially rebellious states. In 334 his army moved on Asia Minor. After defeating a Persian army at the Granicus River, he marched through Asia Minor with little opposition, then defeated a large Persian army commanded by Darius at Issus (333), which controlled the routes into Syria. He next won control of the Syrian coast by the siege of Tyre (332), then conquered Egypt and founded the city of Alexandria at the mouth of the Nile, soon to become the greatest city in the ancient world, and, along with at least 75 other new foundations, a center for spreading Greek culture throughout the East.

In his greatest and most decisive battle Alexander defeated a huge Persian army at Gaugamela (331), which opened up the Persian Empire to him. The capture of Babylon, Susa, and Persepolis, with its royal treasure, followed soon after. In the next six years the army penetrated as far as Afghanistan and northwestern India, conquering regions not previously included in the Persian Empire itself. Back in Babylon (325), Alexander began to organize the vast territories he had conquered, inspired by the ideal of a fusion of east and west with Greek culture as the binding medium. He encouraged intermarriage between Greeks and Asiatics, transferred populations, and promoted equality in political and military status, measures which proved unpopular with his Macedonian troops who did not share his grand international conception. But on the brink of further expeditions, Alexander died suddenly in 323 B.C.

Hellenistic Age (323–146 B.C.). Shock, disbelief, and confusion followed Alexander's death. Quite characteristically, he had designated no one to take over central authority. The political history of the next two centuries is a complex web of alliances, intrigues, and wars among his various successors, the *diadochi*, and their heirs and rivals. A revolt of nearly all mainland Greece was suppressed by Antipater, the Macedonian Governor, and the instigators, including Demosthenes, were sentenced to death. Ptolemy, the Governor of Egypt, kept control there. Before the end of the century, Cassander had established himself as King in Macedonia, Seleucus in Syria, and Lysimachus in western and central Asia Minor. The more remote eastern areas failed to recognize Greek rule almost from the first.

Antigonus Gonatas founded the Antigonid kingdom in Macedonia and played a decisive role in Greek affairs from 287 to 239 B.C. In the mid-3d century B.C. a small independent kingdom under the Attalid Dynasty was established at Pergamum in Asia Minor. From the mid-3d century on, Rome increasingly involved itself in Greek wars and intrigues until finally each independent monarch had to bow to the new and more thorough unification.

In Greece itself, below the level of Macedonian control, the chief political power gravitated to two federal leagues, the Aetolian League and the Achaean League. Although formed originally on the basis of close religious, ethnic, and local ties, the leagues expanded rapidly in periods of power vacuum. Every league member preserved its autonomy except for decisions on foreign policy, war, certain laws, standards of coinage, special taxes, and the like. Thus, only when it was too late, did the Greeks evolve the federal principle of a number of states appointing or electing representatives and surrendering individual sovereignty in carefully defined areas.

The first clashes with Rome resulted from Greek provocation. In 280 B.C. King Pyrrhus of Epirus invaded Italy to aid Rome's enemies, particularly the Greek state of Tarentum. He was, with great difficulty, driven back across the Adriatic, and there was little direct contact until 215 B.C. when King Philip V of Macedon made a treaty with Hannibal. Rome was not then in a position to undertake serious punitive action against Philip's considerable power. But soon after the end of the Second Punic War (200 B.C.) Rome was persuaded by Philip's enemies to declare war. The issue was decided at the battle of Cynoscephalae in Thessaly (197 B.C.).

The federal leagues and nearly all of the Greek states which Philip had controlled were pleased by the Roman intervention, particularly so when the Roman general Flamininus announced at the Isthmian games that Philip must confine himself to Macedonia and that all the Greek states were to be free (196 B.C.). But only five years later Roman legions were back in Greece to suppress a disturbance of the peace instigated by the Aetolian League and King Antiochus III of Syria. Antiochus was forced to withdraw his army, and the league was stripped of much of its territory (189 B.C.). Friction continued between Rome and Macedon, until at Pydna (168 B.C.) the Romans defeated Perseus, son of Philip, and replaced the Macedonian kingdom with four independent republics. Finally, in 146 B.C., Roman suspicions concerning the aggressive policies of the Achaean League in the Peloponnesus led to its forcible dissolution, the destruction of Corinth, and the enslavement of its total population.

Roman Control. By the settlement of 146 B.C. Macedonia became a Roman province and most of the remaining states were allowed limited self-government under conservative administrations. The Greeks were beaten and helpless. Their deep resentment became manifest when many supported King Mithridates of Pontus in his rebellion against Rome, 88–84 B.C. The Roman general Sulla severely punished Mithridates' Greek supporters, and the war left central Greece in a ruinous condition. Again in the Roman civil wars (48–31 B.C.) fought on Greek soil between Caesar and Pompey and later between Brutus and Antony and Octavian (Augustus), Greece was the loser whoever won. Augustus converted central and southern Greece into a second Roman province called Achaea with its capital at the newly rebuilt Corinth. Many favored states such as Athens and Sparta retained nominal freedom. But if the Greek provinces were better treated than most in the empire by governors and tax collectors, it was because there was little to rob, except art treasures.

In general, the empire period marks a steady decline. Special favors from philhellenes like the Emperors Nero and Hadrian could not turn the tide. Threatened invasions from the north culminated in a Gothic raid (267 A.D.) which penetrated the peninsula as far as Athens. Perhaps the year 394 A.D. might serve as an arbitrary terminus for ancient Greek history. In that year the Emperor Theodosius suppressed the Olympic Games as part of a systematic discouragement of paganism. At any rate, it is interesting that the traditional date for the founding of the games (776 B.C.) was often regarded (erroneously) by the Greeks themselves as the beginning of their recorded history.

Looking back over a span of 1,170 years, the period of "approach to greatness" seems relatively short, less than 300 years. But its roots reached back at least 700 years into the Late Bronze Age. The acme, or flowering, of Greek civilization also seems short—200 years at most. The decline was long, though from time to time there were flashes of the former inspiration and brilliance. Most important, perhaps, is the fact that the Roman conquerors had a healthy respect for Greek culture, and the long decline gave them time to assimilate it. Thus the whole Greco-Roman tradition was firmly established before it was exposed to the erosion of much less civilized, but often deeply receptive, peoples from northwest Europe.

LITERATURE

Ancient Greek literature, source of most of the forms of Western literature, probably owes its own origins to Mycenaean-Minoan prototypes transmitted orally. Little is known of this early tradition, but it culminated in the flowering of the great epic poems ascribed to Homer: the *Iliad* and *Odyssey*. Probably composed (perhaps not by a single author) in Ionia in the 8th century B.C., but not committed to writing until the 6th, these epics of the Trojan War and its aftermath were regarded by later Greeks as a treasury of ideas of beauty, morality, and truth: beauty in the verse (dactylic hexameter), with its lovely similes, its touches of brutality, lyricism, and tenderness; morality in the poetic justice of the tales embodied; truth in the realistic portrayal, as seen by the early Greek, of the now comic, now tragic relationship between man and man, and between man and his gods. The influence of these epics on Greek writing cannot be overestimated.

Poetry. Heroic epic poetry, which in part reflected the ideas of a decaying feudal aristocracy, soon found a complement in the didactic epics of the lesser poet Hesiod (probably late 8th century). A native of Boeotia, he sang in his *Works and Days* of the hardships and virtues of the small farmer. His *Theogony* established for centuries a nearly standard mythology.

In the 7th and 6th centuries a number of new poetic genres were invented or perfected, all strongly indebted to Homer, but based on different attitudes and emotions. While Homer and Hesiod were in a sense the spokesmen of their societies, the poet of the new era tended to speak for himself as an individual. This change of outlook was prompted by the breakdown of the feudal system, colonization, and the growth of a mercantile class. The new art assumed four major forms: (1) the elegiac couplet, related metrically to the dactylic hexameter of Homer and originally designed for recitation to the accompaniment of the flute; (2) iambic poetry, closer than others to the rhythms of ordinary speech; (3) monodic lyric poetry, that is, poems sung by a single voice and accompanied by the lyre; (4) choral lyric, performed by a choir of as many as 50 singers.

None of these forms was exclusively devoted to any single kind of subject matter, but narrative, military exhortation, and philosophical reflection were especially the province of elegy. The most noted masters of elegy were Archilochus (fl. early 7th century) and Mimnermus (fl.630) in Ionia, and Tyrtaeus (fl.640) and Theognis (fl.540) in mainland Greece. The iambic genre, apt for satire and invective, was first and brilliantly used by Archilochus. Sappho and Alcaeus (fl. early 6th century), both of Lesbos, created monodic lyrics of exceptional beauty, their subject matter ranging from love to politics. Somewhat later, Anacreon (c.570–485) added in lighter vein to the tradition of love poetry. Choral lyric appropriately concerned itself with public religion and civic celebration. Only small fragments of the genre survive from the 7th and 6th centuries, especially from Alcman (fl.630) and Stesichorus (fl.580), but we possess fine examples from the 5th century in the epinician odes celebrating athletic victories written by the Theban Pindar (518–438), a poet whose flights of dazzling images belie the notion that ancient Greek poetry is direct and simple. Simonides of Ceos (c.556–468) and Bacchylides (c.520–c.450) also excelled in this medium.

Drama. With these exceptions, the 5th century saw the decline of lyric poetry and the maturing, particularly in Athens, of the drama, a Greek invention and a poetic art admirably suited to the expression of the clash between traditional values and the democratic values of the rising city-state. The semilegendary Thespis (fl.534) is said to have created the art, at first based on the interplay between a lyric chorus and a single actor, but its true originator and first great practitioner was Aeschylus (525–456). Sophocles (c.496–406) and Euripides (c.485–c.406) soon produced tragedies of comparable stature. The plays of all three dramatists are deeply, if indirectly, concerned with the course of Greek politics and with the condition of man, both as an individual and as a social and metaphysical being. Yet in spite of these basic similarities of interest, the reader of the plays is struck by the great variations in attitude and form which characterize these poets as individual, original artists. Later tragedy (none survives) tended to become imitative, and probably never reached the heights attained by the masters of the 5th century.

Comedy was developed in the early 5th century, both in Sicily and in Athens. The Attic branch, known as Old Comedy, was notable for its freedom of expression, often directed to personal attack and political and social satire, and for its frank earthiness, imaginative plots, and soaring lyrics. All these qualities are reflected at their best in the only extant comedies of the period, those by the Athenian Aristophanes (c.450–c.385), a poet of astounding versatility and inventiveness. In the 4th century Middle Comedy succeeded the Old. The only surviving example, the *Plutus* of Aristophanes, corroborates secondary sources in indicating that it increasingly avoided the personal invective and open physical humor of its predecessor.

Prose. The 5th century also saw prose literature rise to importance, especially in the developing areas of science, philosophy, history, and oratory. Little remains today of the earlier writings of the first two categories, though we fortunately possess several treatises by the physician Hippocrates and brief fragments from the works of the philosopher-scientist Democritus. With both writers, literary polish is subordinate to the quest for a forceful clarity. History, an art which traces its origins to lost Ionian Greek works of the 6th century, is a different matter. The earliest extant example of the genre is the *History* of Herodotus of Halicarnassus (c.485–c.425), a work which delights the student of literature while providing the historian with invaluable information about the eastern Mediterranean world in the period leading to and including the Persian Wars. The *History* is in a sense a prose epic recounting the fate of nations, infused with a feeling of tragedy, and studded with digressions and anecdotes which attest the author's universal curiosity and his skill as a teller of tales. Rigorous skepticism and scrupulous observation, the only qualities appropriate to a historian that are not fully developed in Herodotus, are prominent characteristics of the works of his successor, Thucydides (c.460–c.400) of Athens. Indeed, his *History of the Peloponnesian War* appears to borrow from the empirical techniques of Hippocratic medicine. Yet Thucydides is an artist as well, in both the style and the dramatic structure of his work. One cannot say as much for Xenophon (c.430–c.354), who, in the *Hellenica*, set out to continue the history of Thucydides. The result is much less satisfactory, since Xenophon could not compete with the latter, either in objectivity or in literary style. He is more interesting when dealing with persons and matters directly involving his own life, as in his *Memorabilia* of Socrates and in the *Anabasis*, which recounts the retreat of the Greek mercenaries after the death of Cyrus the Younger.

Philosophy. The *Dialogues* of Plato (c.429–347) are the earliest philosophical writings preserved in extent. Inspired by the personality and teaching of Socrates, the *Dialogues* are brilliant prose conversations which owe much in their form to poetry and drama. The dialogue form also fully embodies the essential Platonic philosophical method of dialectic, which works, by intellectual exchange, from lower hypotheses toward what Plato saw as higher truths. His influence, in thought and style, on later literature from the ancient period to the present is inestimable.

Plato's pupil Aristotle (384–322) rivaled his master in philosophical insight, and surpassed him in encyclopedic scientific activity, but was no match for him in literary expression. Many of his important treatises, such as the *Metaphysics*, are made more difficult by a terse, crabbed, even awkward style. Indeed, some of his works are thought to represent the notes of a lecturer, perhaps somewhat revised but not at first designed for publication. This stylistic aridity does not, of course, detract from the monumental stature and influence of Aristotle's system. The *Poetics*, with its seminal analysis of tragedy, is of special interest to the student of literature; in effect, it is the earliest work to deal exclusively with literary theory, though Aristophanes in the *Frogs* and Plato (particularly in the *Ion*, *Republic*, *Phaedrus*, and *Symposium*) had paved the way for this new branch of philosophy.

Oratory. From the mid-5th through the 4th century, realization of the role of public persuasion in the functioning of the democratic state brought the long tradition of oratory to new heights. The Sophists were instrumental in forging it into the self-conscious, sophisticated art which was the core of their revolutionary educational curriculum. Of the many orators famous in antiquity, Lysias, Isaeus, Isocrates, Aeschines, and Demosthenes are exceptional, both because many of their speeches survive and for their obvious mastery of their craft. Isocrates and Demosthenes are notable for the role played by their rhetoric in Greek politics. Their words express with clarity and vigor the divergent tensions of thought in an era which proved to be a turning point in Greek culture.

Hellenistic Age

The Hellenistic age which followed, commonly dated from Alexander's death in 323 to the complete loss of Greek independence in 146 B.C., wrought enormous changes in the form and content of literature. When large national states superseded the small city-state, formerly the focal point and foundation of all values, the writer was no longer able to achieve any sense of identification with his fellow citizens in the massive new political structures. Feeling that his voice could no longer significantly influence the course of affairs, he now turned to genres of limited popular appeal, to light themes or esoteric subjects, to descriptive realism, or escapist romanticism. Nonetheless, Greek literature remained energetic and creative, though more exclusively dependent for its effect on brilliance of style than on penetrating analysis of universal human problems.

Poetry. Under the patronage of the Ptolemies, the city of Alexandria, Egypt, became the center of much of the literary activity of the Hellenistic age. This international city, with its vast library and museum, fostered not only science and scholarship, but poetry as well. Callimachus (c.305–c.240), head librarian and virtually literary dictator of his age, was a prolific, clever poet who set the standards of taste for much of the 3d century. With their inclination to break away from tradition and to seek originality, the poets of the period found two older genres (learned elegiac poetry and the epigram) and one new one (the pastoral) especially congenial forms of expression.

Learned elegiac poetry, descended in form but not attitude from earlier elegy, was directed to erudite mythological subject matter (for example, the *Aitia*, or *Origins*, of Callimachus) and to science (as in the *Phaenomena*, an astronomical work by Aratus of Soli). The epigram, a relative of elegy, was a short poem, often of only two lines. In its origins, of great antiquity, it was functional as a near-ritual form employed largely for sepulchral inscriptions and dedications to deities. In the 5th century it became an art form in the hands of poets such as Simonides of Ceos, who composed superb epigrams for many public monuments. By the 3d century the epigram had become a purely literary form, in most cases detached from its earlier functions. Though sometimes pretending to serve

in the same veins as its precursors, it now broadened its scope to include love, satire, and wit. A vast collection of epigrams, of uneven quality and ranging from the earliest literary period to the high Byzantine era, is preserved in the *Greek Anthology*, a compilation much admired and imitated by Continental and English poets of the Renaissance.

Pastoral poetry was an outgrowth of the crude but inventive songs of the shepherds of Sicily and other islands settled by Greeks. Theocritus (c.310–250) of Syracuse molded this lively material into a new, artistic genre that was colorful, escapist, and highly melodic; Bion and Moschus, poets of the 2d century B.C., modeled their bucolics on those of Theocritus. The works of all three pervasively influenced subsequent pastoral, even as late as the 19th century.

Epic poetry was generally avoided by the Alexandrians because of its ties with tradition. Only one major Hellenistic work in this genre exists, the *Argonautica* of Apollonius of Rhodes (c.295–after 247). This is a romantic poem, with many of the virtues, as well as the vices, of the period. Apollonius displays descriptive power and psychological insight, but his obsession with mythological erudition often overburdens the flow of the plot.

Drama. Of the traditional genres, drama remained active in the Hellenistic age, at least till the 2d century, though no tragedy of the period is extant, and the quality of the plays is conjectural. We know considerably more of Hellenistic comedy, commonly termed New Comedy. Continuing trends begun in the 4th century, this new form owed more to the romantic plays of Euripides than to the satiric gusto of Aristophanes. Basically, it is a comedy of manners and wit, in which the chorus plays little integral part. Preoccupation with local issues was replaced by an urbane concern with social relationships, as between father and son, and lover and mistress, set in complex romantic plots. Diphilus and Philemon were acknowledged masters of the genre, but their works are known today only indirectly, through the adaptations of the Latin poets Plautus and Terence. Menander (342–291), perhaps the greatest exponent of New Comedy, is represented by several major fragments and by the only complete play of the era, the *Dyskolos*, or *Curmudgeon*.

Prose. Little Hellenistic prose of major literary interest has come down to us, though there is much of great value to the scholar. For example, the *Universal History* of Polybius (c.203–c.120) shows that writer to be of high rank as a historian, but little better than mediocre as a stylist, while the fragments of the works of the great philosopher Epicurus are devoid of literary grace. Theophrastus (c.372–c.288), the successor of Aristotle, wrote lucidly on scientific matters, and shows, in his satirical *Characters*, a dryly witty style. But the bulk of Hellenistic prose demands treatment in an essay on intellectual history, not on literature.

After the Greek world submitted to Rome in 146 B.C., the center of literary creation gradually moved to the new Mediterranean capital, and Latin literature infused the Hellenic heritage with a new vitality. Nonetheless, Greece was still to offer much of value to Western literature, especially in the fields of literary criticism, the satiric dialogue, the novel, and biography. Longinus, in his treatise *On the Sublime*, deplores the loss of creativity in his own era (1st century A.D.?), but at the same time presents us with a work of literary criticism which rivals the *Poetics*. The satiric dialogues of Lucian brought new verve to the old Greek spirit of witty skepticism. While seeds of the romantic novel may be found in the 2d century B.C., the fully developed form seems not to have appeared until the 1st century A.D. or later, with such authors as Longus, whose *Daphnis and Chloe* is based on a plot resembling those of New Comedy.

But it is perhaps in the moralist and biographer Plutarch (c.46–after 120 A.D.) that one finds most of the finest qualities of the Greek character in a world ruled by an alien power. Conscious of the gifts of peace and security provided by Rome, Plutarch nevertheless looked back, in his *Parallel Lives*, to the glories of his own tradition, and in those moralized biographies commemorated for later ages the aspirations of mind and soul which had led Greece to her pinnacle of cultural achievement.

A literature of such long tradition and diversity does not readily invite summary. Yet one may discern within that tradition, from the time of Homer, certain almost constant characteristics. These include a rare consciousness of the virtues of both precision and connotative suggestion in language; the love of balanced, almost architectural style; a tendency toward spareness and understatement without sacrifice of delicacy and emotive richness; and an abiding, active curiosity concerning the nature of man and his place in the universe.

PHILOSOPHY

The Ionians or Milesians. European philosophy began early in the 6th century B.C. at Miletus, a large and flourishing Greek trading colony on the Ionian coast of Asia Minor. Economic prosperity and numerous foreign contacts had induced a worldly and secular outlook among the people there, and, in some men at least, a burning curiosity about the nature and origin of the world around them. In one generation these thinkers completely rejected the hitherto universal belief in the agency of personal and capricious gods and started a process of objective inquiry into nature and causality which was the beginning of both science and philosophy. Unconsciously they may have been influenced by certain earlier cosmogonic ideas of a "separation" from an original fusion in which "earth and heaven were one," which occur in Greek as in Hebrew and other mythologies; but their conscious minds were astonishingly free from any mythological preconceptions.

These earliest philosophers were Thales (c.624–546), Anaximander (c.610–545), and Anaximenes (c.560–c.500). They assumed the existence of a single, everlasting substance (water, air, or some indeterminate matter) with an internal power of motion, and hence in a sense alive and "divine," though quite remote from the popular notion of the gods. The movement of this substance led to a "separation" (Anaximander) or a process of condensation and rarefaction (Anaximenes) by which the cosmic order was produced.

Pythagoreans. For Pythagoras (c.570–490), who migrated from Samos to southern Italy, philosophy was not merely the satisfaction of curiosity but the intellectual foundation for a way of life. He founded a religious brotherhood and taught the kinship of all nature and the transmigration of the soul. Philosophically he turned from matter to form, and diverted thought into more abstract and mathematical channels.

Heraclitus and the Eleatics. All these ancient philosophers were dependent on speculation rather than scientific observation and experimentation, because as yet they had devised no other means of getting below the surface of things.

Heraclitus (c.544–484), was the first to question the witness of the senses, because, as he maintained, the senses show a different world to each individual. For him the hidden law of nature was conflict, and he saw the whole world in terms of a continuous cycle of flux and change, made up of things which are never the same from one moment to another. Nothing is ever at rest. In his view there was, however, the logos, a mysterious force involving a law of regularity and measure within change. And since purely spiritual being had not yet been imagined, the logos was thought of as the highest form of matter, namely fire, in which this regulating law is embodied.

Heraclitus was a lonely thinker, but opposed to him was a philosopher whose impact upon other thinkers was tremendous. This was Parmenides of Elea (born c.510), the founder of the Eleatic school. In him and his school the purely speculative approach to science and philosophy reached its climax. He also denied the witness of the senses, and starting with the Milesian assumption that ultimately only one thing existed, he showed that logically it could not become many, and that there could be no movement because there was no empty space for anything to move into. The physical world of plurality and movement was therefore an illusion. Thus Parmenides, as it were, brought the world to a standstill, by showing up the contradictions involved in the naive assumption that there was only one basic substance, and by demanding that motion be explained and not merely assumed.

His successors accepted the dictum that nothing can come-to-be, either from what is not or from what is; but they were not so sure that ultimate unity was a necessary postulate. Given more than one primary substance, and with motion restored, the visible world might be produced by processes of mixture and separation. Hence Parmenides' successors offered various forms of pluralism.

Empedocles, Anaxagoras, and the Atomists. Empedocles (c.495–435) posited four elemental substances—earth, water, air, and fire—all everlasting, and producing the phenomena of nature by their interaction. He also introduced love and strife, two semiphysical forces of attraction and repulsion, respectively, as motive causes. In the Italian tradition, he linked his physics with religious and moral teaching, including transmigration. The doctrine of Anaxagoras (500–428), that matter consists of an infinite number of qualitatively different "seeds," was a kind of halfway house to atomism. Anaxagoras called the motive cause "mind" but employed it purely mechanically to start the cosmic revolution. He was prosecuted for atheism. Pluralism culminated in Leucippus (5th century

B.C.) and Democritus (c.460–370), with their theory that reality consisted of tiny particles (Gr. *atomoi*, "indivisibles") differing only in size and shape. Everything was composed of aggregates of these, and sensible qualities were purely subjective. Leucippus and Democritus provided no separate moving cause, but by asserting the existence of the void, which had been denied by Parmenides as "what is not," they set matter free to move.

All these thinkers from Parmenides on belong to the 5th century, in the middle of which a major change of emphasis occurred. Athens was at this time the intellectual center of Greece, and the 5th century saw her rise to political leadership and unprecedented prosperity. The establishment of extreme forms of democracy gave every citizen the chance not only of voting but of taking a personal part in government. The atmosphere of the times was unfavorable to theoretical speculation, and moreover the conclusions of the natural philosophers seemed to suggest that the "real" world had little to interest the ordinary man. The world of his experience was very different, and its practical demands were pressing. Interest shifted from macrocosm to microcosm.

The Sophists took full advantage of this situation. They were itinerant teachers, sufficiently familiar with the subtleties of Eleatic logic to employ it in ridiculing natural philosophy. In place of natural philosophy they gave instruction, principally in rhetoric, needed for practical success, especially in politics. From this instruction they earned high fees and considerable influence. The Sophists believed in no absolute standards of truth or conduct. Empiricists in philosophy and opportunists in practice, they taught, in the words of Protagoras (c.490–420), the greatest of them, that "man is the measure of all things."

Socrates. This was the world of Socrates (469–399). Later antiquity exaggerated in making him solely responsible for the new spirit in philosophy, but at least one may say that in him the new spirit found its first genuine philosopher. Against the Sophists he upheld the absolute character of moral standards and claimed that understanding of the true nature of goodness would lead men inevitably to seek it. Thus "virtue is knowledge." He was a moral teacher, not a metaphysician, and he bequeathed some intractable intellectual problems to his successors; for in his teaching he seemed to assume by faith rather than reason (a) that absolute goodness exists, (b) that the human mind can know what it is, and (c) that this intellectual grasp will be sufficient in itself to ensure right action in practice.

Plato (429–347), his greatest pupil, tried to justify these claims. Goodness is real because it is supreme among the "forms." These are perfect entities existing beyond space and time, constituting models for the impermanent and imperfect manifestations of truth in ethical, mathematical, and other spheres which we meet in this world. Knowledge is possible because the human soul is immortal and between its many incarnations has been face to face with the realities of the other world. By intellectual and moral self-discipline we may use our earthly experience to reawaken the memory of this revelation. The soul has three parts: appetitive, spirited or impulsive, and rational. Each directs *eros* ("desire") to a different object. In the philosopher's soul the lower two are kept within strict bounds, and his *eros* is canalized, and flows in greater strength toward the objectives of reason: namely, knowledge and goodness. From this psychology springs Plato's aristocratic and authoritarian political system, with its three distinct classes and its philosopher-rulers. In his later years he devoted more attention to the underlying problems of knowledge and logic, but he never abandoned the doctrine of "forms."

Aristotle (384–322) was for 20 years a member of Plato's Academy. Its influence on him was permanent but was modified by a more scientific temperament. He substituted immanent for transcendent form and by his division of existence into potential and actual finally laid the ghost of Parmenides: becoming proceeded neither from being nor from not-being but was the actualization of potential being. Everything in nature had an innate urge to realize its proper form in so far as the limitations of matter allowed. This impulse was activated by God, the Unmoved Mover, who, as pure form and intellect, by his mere existence filled all nature with the desire to emulate his perfection. With the abandonment of the Platonic forms, ethics and politics were confined to the contingent sphere and became a matter of empirical rules. On this basis Aristotle worked out his doctrine of each separate virtue as a mean between two extremes. A great part of his achievement is scientific, particularly zoological, and, with his pupils, he may be said to have founded natural science, in the sense of careful and systematic observation and classification, of which the speculative Greek genius had been somewhat impatient hitherto. Formal logic also owes its origin to Aristotle's painstaking classification of syllogisms and introduction of symbols.

Aristotle was the tutor of Alexander the Great, whose transformation of the Greek world set men's thoughts in a new direction. Large kingdoms began to replace the autonomous city-states. Learning, science, and technology flourished, particularly in Alexandria under the enlightened patronage of the Ptolemies. But the old zest for speculation on cosmic questions and the nature of reality was dimmed, and in political theory the world of Plato's *Republic* and Aristotle's *Politics* was gone forever. They had based their thinking on the permanence of the city-state of a few thousand citizens as the largest political unit. In this, the individual knew his place and had his definite rights and duties. Society was small, comprehensible, organic, and purposeful, like Aristotle's universe. In the new order, the individual was more like a Democritean atom, aimlessly drifting in an infinite void. This produced a sense of unease and loss of direction, a situation in which the inevitable accidents of life—poverty, slavery, loneliness, death—loomed larger and more alarming.

One result was that mystery-religions, from Egypt and Asia, as well as from Greece, bringing promises of salvation in one form or another, increased enormously in popularity. In philosophy, also, the new systems attempted to fulfill the new needs, the demand for *ataraxia* ("freedom from worry") or *autarkeia* ("self-sufficiency"). Chief among them were the Stoic and Epicurean, both of which accepted as their physical basis a modification of pre-Socratic cosmologies and concentrated on the human situation.

Socrates (469–399 B.C.)

Plato (429–347 B.C.)

Aristotle (384–322 B.C.)

Epicurus (341–270 B.C.)

Epicureans. For Epicurus (341–270) the source of spiritual sickness was religion, with its fear of the gods and of punishment after death. He therefore adopted, with modifications, the atomic theory of Democritus, which excluded the possibility of divine agency in either the origin or the present working of the world. Gods existed, but it was blasphemous to suppose that they lived otherwise than in perfect bliss and peace, which would be impossible if they concerned themselves at all with terrestrial affairs. Their abode is in the vast spaces outside the worlds. The goal of life he named "pleasure," but it is more accurately described as absence of pain. He was no voluptuary, but taught that indulgence in sensual delights was inimical to the bodily and mental calm desired by the wise man, whereas a prudent and righteous life conduced to it. Cicero remarked that Epicurus proved pleasure to be the highest good only by giving it a meaning which no one else would recognize. Yet, the Epicurean life, though harmless, was egocentric, and excluded participation in public affairs and responsibilities as destructive of inner calm.

Stoics. Stoicism made the greater appeal, and may be called the characteristic philosophy of the Greco-Roman world. Although almost incredibly austere in its highest form, it managed to exist at different levels for different classes of people. Its founder, Zeno (332–262), a Phoenician from Cyprus (his nationality seems itself a symbol of the new cosmopolitan age), revived the mind-matter complex of Heraclitus. The ruling power or God is the logos, materially embodied in fire. The universe is the product of this divine mind, which yet is immanent in it. In this materialistic pantheism, divinity pervades everything, but only in the outer heaven is it pure. On earth only man possesses it in the form of logos, or reason, and hence, though his body is animal, he shares part of his nature with divinity. The sage knows that everything must strive to live according to its own highest nature, and that therefore only this inner self matters. All external circumstances are strictly speaking indifferent, though our animal side may justify us in putting some things before others. With this knowledge, the sage is perfectly self-sufficient and will be "happy even on the rack."

The most difficult Stoic doctrine was that virtue, equated with wisdom, is an absolute like straightness. There are no degrees between wisdom and folly, virtue and vice. "All sins are equal," for a man is drowned just the same whether his head is several fathoms or only a few inches below the surface. Here again, however, most Stoics agreed that in practice some imperfect actions might be preferred to others.

The doctrines of logos, as a universal human attribute,

and of the unity of virtue led the Stoics to a great innovation: all were by nature free and equal, and wisdom might be found in women or slaves as well as in free men. The Stoic teacher Epictetus (c.55–135 A.D.) was himself a slave and wrote that "virtue invites all, nobles, slaves, kings, or exiles." All are "kinsmen by nature, children of God." It is not surprising that St. Paul should have cited Stoic doctrine in commending the Gospel to a Greek audience. The universal community and the brotherhood of man were Stoic ideals.

Stoicism proved readily adaptable to the life and ideals of the Roman ruling class, which was introduced to it by Panaetius of Rhodes, friend of the brilliant Scipio Aemilianus, in the 2d century B.C. He emphasized the application of Stoic principles to practical affairs and saw the ideal constitution as a mixture of autocracy and democracy, to which the Roman republic was the nearest approach. From now on the theoretical aspects of Stoicism became less important than the practical. Under the early Empire, Seneca (d.65 A.D.) and other Stoics exercised considerable influence; in the 2d century Emperor Marcus Aurelius (121–180) was himself the leading Stoic thinker.

Other schools—Academic, Peripatetic, Skeptic—continued in the shadow of the Stoa. The Academy turned to Skepticism under Carneades (213–128 B.C.), an opponent of Stoicism; but its later head, Antiochus (d.68 B.C.), described by his pupil Cicero (106–43 B.C.) as "almost a Stoic," maintained that its differences with the Stoics were verbal rather than substantial.

RELIGION

Until the final suppression of pagan worship by the Emperor Theodosius in 392 A.D., Greek religion had a continuous history of some 2,000 years. Homer (c.8th century B.C.) provides the earliest literary evidence, but archeological discoveries, notably the excavations of Heinrich Schliemann at Mycenae in the 1870's, of Sir Arthur Evans in Crete, from 1900 on, and the decipherment of the Linear B tablets by Michael Ventris and John Chadwick in 1953, reveal that Greek religion was essentially a product of the richly creative Mycenaean period (c.1600–1100 B.C.). The familiar gods of classic Greece prove to be of diverse origins. Zeus and Hestia are of the same Indo-European stock as the Greek-speaking invaders, but Athena derives from the household snake goddess of Minoan Crete, Aphrodite from the Semitic Astarte (via Cyprus), and Apollo probably from northern Europe (via the amber route), to cite only the clearer examples. Already in Homer, and probably even in Mycenaean

Greece, the major gods are fully anthropomorphic, though more primitive concepts persisted even into late classic times in the cult of rough stones, sacred trees, and such hybrid figures as the horse-headed Demeter of Phigaleia.

If Homer's gods were ideally human—a fact of great importance for the development of Greek art—they differed from man in being both immortal and more powerful. Morality as such was not a basic aspect of divinity, and even in later times it was chiefly Zeus or "the gods" collectively to whom a concern for moral values was ascribed. All things, both good and evil, came to man by will of the gods. There was, therefore, no devil. The gods, though unpredictable, were not unconcerned with human affairs, and man normally approached them not in awe or abject dread, but as superior beings of kindred nature. Priests existed, but there was no professional priestly caste, and in general any man was competent to perform the basic ritual of sacrifice. After death all men alike went to the common underworld abode of the dead, the "house of Hades," but the psyche, or soul, had no meaningful existence apart from the body.

The Homeric picture, though incomplete in itself and subjected to criticism by succeeding poets and philosophers, established the norm for all later Greek paganism. Homer's most striking omission was the cult of heroes, a unique feature of Greek religion. Heroes, by definition, were common or uncommon men who, after death, because of proven supernatural powers, received a local cult at their tombs. Though most heroes belonged to a shadowy past, many historical figures, including the poet Sophocles, received heroic honors. Significant development of the mystery cults, which gave scope to aspirations for a happier afterlife, was perhaps post-Homeric, as were certainly the esoteric doctrines that are loosely associated with the name of Orpheus (q.v.). On the other hand, the ecstatic cult of Dionysus (q.v.), which provided an outlet for pent-up emotions, was perhaps ignored as alien to the taste of Homeric nobles. The last major addition to the native Greek pantheon was Asclepius, god of healing. Though not accepted in Athens until 420 B.C., his cult gained steadily in popularity in succeeding centuries.

Greek religion was at no time bound by fixed creeds, and although each citizen was expected to participate in the religious observances of the state, he was free to interpret these in the light of his own highest insights. Apart from household and family cults, the characteristic form of worship in the city-state was the festival (normally annual). The ritual, often archaic, varied with the divinity and the occasion concerned, but most included processions, sacrifices, hymns, and dancing; in many there were musical and athletic contests, as well. Athletics were, in fact, the staple of the four great Panhellenic festivals.

Oracles were generally held in high repute, especially that of Zeus at Dodona and of Apollo at Delphi. To these, and to many lesser ones, both individuals and states turned to seek divine guidance. Magic, superstitious practices, and fears of the supernatural were not, of course, unknown, but on the whole Greek religion in the classical period was, to apply the phrase of William James, a "religion of healthy-mindedness."

The troubled times after Alexander the Great saw both an influx of foreign cults, chiefly Oriental, and the development of popular philosophies, notably Stoicism and Epicureanism, which for many persons supplemented or supplanted the traditional patterns of belief. This age also saw the rise of the ruler cult, and the creation of numerous private mysteries of Dionysus. By the beginning of the Christian era, astrology, also borrowed from the East, had gained wide acceptance, even though its deterministic doctrines were fundamentally incompatible with a belief in omnipotent deities. Yet through all the complexities of later paganism, the Olympic gods retained, for the majority of men, their effective appeal, until the final victory of Christianity in the 4th and 5th centuries.

THEATER

CLASSICAL THEATER. The Western European theater arose in the classical stage of ancient Athens. The word "theater" ("a place for seeing"), together with many other basic technical terms ("proscenium," "scene," and "orchestra"), derive from this source. The ultimate origin of both theater and drama was the singing of a hymn or ode to the god Dionysus by a choral group standing beside an altar. Gradually the leader of the chorus separated himself from the group and became an individualized actor (a development traditionally associated with Thespis). Then a second actor was introduced, followed by a third, and by the employment of mutes (such as guards and servants).

At the same time three dramatic genres came to be sharply differentiated—tragedy, comedy, and the satyric play (ancient burlesque drama employing a chorus of satyrs). These plays were presented at one of three great state festivals, attended by the entire citizenry of Athens, when prizes were awarded for the best dramas and productions. Comedies were given separately, but it was the custom to associate three tragedies together in a trilogy, adding to them a satyric drama (which thus completed a tetralogy). The whole atmosphere surrounding the theater was thus dignified, religious, and patriotic. The priest of Dionysus was present at all the productions; the entire festival was superintended by an archon, and the office of choregus, or "producer," was an honored one.

Aeschylus (525–456 B.C.), of whose more than 70 plays only seven have come down to us, was responsible for establishing the tragic form. This was enriched and mellowed by Sophocles (496–406 B.C.), of whose 130 plays we also possess seven; while Euripides (484?–406 B.C.), of whose 92 dramas 18 are extant, by stressing pathos and theatrical devices, tended to lower its majestic dignity. After him, Greek tragedy had little or nothing to offer.

During the early years the typical comic style was that of the "Old Comedy" as expressed by Aristophanes (c.448–c.380 B.C.), author of 54 plays, of which we possess 11. The fantastic, exuberantly lyrical quality of this "Old Comedy" gradually declined, giving place to a "Middle Comedy," more social in character, and to a "New Comedy," of which Menander (343?–?291 B.C.) is the master and which turned to depicting manners in a more realistic way.

Early Greek Theaters. For the very first dramatic performances no more was required than a large circular area (the "orchestra") with an altar at its center around which

Performance of Sophocles' *Electra* in the ancient amphitheater at Epidaurus, Greece.

Herbert—Frederic Lewis

spectators might stand to listen to the hymns and to watch the chorus' dancing. Later the orchestra was set on a level tract near a hillside on which wooden seats might be set up; and soon this arrangement was made more permanent by the construction of stone seats, divided by passageways, sweeping round one-half of the orchestra and fanning out diagonally at the sides so as to embrace an area somewhat larger than a semicircle. Magistrates and other dignitaries occupied reserved places in the front rows. At the same time a structure known as a "skene" (Gr., "scene-building") was erected opposite to these seats at the orchestra's other side; this served the double purpose of giving dressing-room space and of providing stage and background. Simple at first, the skene gradually became more elaborate. Its stage was long and narrow; the columned wall behind it was broken by large entrance doors. Above, an upper platform could be used for the appearance of deities and for the installation of such machinery as, for example, elevated Socrates in Aristophanes' *The Clouds* to a position between heaven and earth.

The characteristic early Greek theater was thus marked by a clear separation of auditorium, circular orchestra, and skene, and its formation soon came to develop various conventions, such as the use of the central doorway to indicate the entrance to a palace, of the two side doorways to represent other localities, and of the passages at the sides to signify entrance of characters from abroad. Of scenery in the modern sense there was none, although some painted effects, no doubt symbolic, are ascribed to Sophocles' invention, and frequent use was made of machines, of which the most important was a turntable placed within the central doorway.

The principal actors in serious dramas were heavily dressed in formal robes, with massive masks over which towered special headdresses, and with the high-soled boots, or cothurni, which became a kind of symbol of tragedy. In comic performances grotesque masks were also employed, together with padding that emphasized the ridiculous. The tragic chorus, because of their dance evolutions, were more lightly clad; the chorus in the "Old Comedy" often wore fantastic garments (as in Aristophanes' *The Birds* and *The Frogs*). In view of the fact that the performances were festive seasonal affairs, it is natural that the actors remained for the most part amateurs, although we must note that the training given to them was careful and precise, and that, as years passed by, they came to organize themselves into a formal guild.

As the function of the chorus began to decline both in tragedy and in comedy, changes in the general arrangement of the theater's three main parts began to creep in. During the so-called Hellenistic period there was thus a tendency for the skene to encroach upon the orchestral circle, bringing the stage nearer to the auditorium, while at the same time the stage itself was modified now that the focus was placed upon it rather than upon the orchestra. None of these modifications, however, were sufficiently great to alter the essential "Greek" form handed over as a model to Rome.

PEOPLE, PLACES, AND TERMS

ABYDOS [ə-bī'dəs], ancient Greek city on the Asiatic side of the Hellespont opposite *Sestos*, colonized from *Miletus*. There Xerxes spanned the narrowest part of the strait with a bridge of boats for the passage of his army into Europe. From Abydos, too, Leander swam the Hellespont nightly to visit his beloved Hero, priestess of Aphrodite in Sestos.

ACADEMY, THE, school founded by Plato about 385 B.C., so called because it was situated in the precinct of the hero Academus in Athens. Plato, deterred from active politics, first by the oligarchic terror, and then by the action of the restored democracy in executing Socrates, turned instead to the education of statesmen. Owing to his ideal of the "philosophic ruler," the curriculum included philosophy, mathematics, and astronomy, as well as political science; and important advances were achieved in all these subjects. Among the most accomplished members of the Academy were Aristotle and the astronomer and mathematician Eudoxus, who evolved the earliest scheme for reducing the paths of the planets to a complex of purely circular motions.

The Academy was legally constituted as a religious institution, dedicated to the cult of the Muses, like the college of an English university, with its chapel dedicated to a saint or to the Holy Trinity. Methods of instruction included lectures and informal discussion with questions and answers.

Under Plato's immediate successors—his nephew Speusippus and Xenocrates—the Academy remained a center of scientific and mathematical research. But later, under Arcesilaus in the 3d century B.C., the so-called Middle Academy changed its character and became the chief representative of skepticism. It could still claim to be in the tradition of Socrates, who professed that he knew nothing; but the skeptical impulse came from a reaction against the extreme dogmatism of the Stoics, who claimed that certain perceptions were infallible. Arcesilaus, an able dialectician, refuted this certainty and contended that knowledge was impossible. Theory thus became less important than conduct, which could be based on common sense or "the reasonable." The skeptical attitude continued with Carneades, founder of the so-called New Academy in the next century; but he, while continuing to deny certainty, developed a theory of probability.

A notable Academic of the 1st century was Antiochus, the teacher of Cicero, an eclectic who tried to prove that Academic, Peripatetic, and Stoic philosophies were fundamentally in agreement. After this the Academy lapsed into obscurity; but it was still in existence in the 5th century A.D. as a home of Neoplatonists, some of whom (Proclus, Simplicius, Damascius) were the authors of valuable commentaries on the works of Plato and Aristotle. The end came in 529, when the Emperor Justinian closed the pagan philosophic schools of Greece. The Athenian Neoplatonists, however, did not give up, but migrated to the court of Khosrau of Persia.

ACHAEA [ə-kē'ə], province of ancient Greece on the northern coast of the Peloponnesus, between *Elis* and *Sicyon*. The name derives from the Achaeans, who, traditionally, migrated here when driven out of other parts of the Peloponnesus by Dorian invaders. *Sybaris, Croton,* and *Metapontum* were colonized from Achaea. Settling in 12 cities, the Achaeans formed the Achaean League, a loose association for mutual protection, assembling at *Helice* until 373 B.C. and later at *Aegium*. The state was not influential in Greek affairs until Hellenistic times, when a reinvigorated Achaean League controlled the whole Peloponnesus and became the chief political power in Greece. As a Roman province, Achaea comprised the entire peninsula and much of central Greece.

ACHAEAN [ə-kē'ən] **LEAGUE,** ancient Greek federation of northwestern Peloponnesian states, organized in 280 B.C. The shrine of Zeus Amarius at *Aegium* had been a common religious center for 12 Achaean towns, but in the early 3d century B.C. the original Achaean League was reorganized and non-Achaean states were admitted to membership on an equal basis. States in the federation retained practically complete self-government except in the area of foreign policy. The primary league assembly, open to all adult citizens from allied states, decided major policy such as declarations of war, but business matters, such as taxation and legal and monetary affairs, were handled by another assembly, which may have been composed of elected representatives. A council of 120 delegates appointed from the local councils of member states prepared the agenda for the assemblies. An elected group of 10 magistrates presided over league assemblies and acted as an advisory board to the chief magistrate. He was commander of the league army and was eligible for reelection, but not in successive years. Since all offices were unpaid and much time and travel were involved, participation in league government was restricted to the wealthier citizens even more than in individual states. The league produced several fine statesmen, such as Aratus, Philopoemen, and Polybius. It was a steady defender of the cause of Greek liberty against Macedonian and Roman power. At the time of its greatest prestige (c.191 B.C.) the league counted as voluntary members practically every Peloponnesian state. Opposition to Roman policy led to its defeat and practical dissolution in 146 B.C.

ACHAEANS, one of the four traditional ethnic divisions of the Greeks (the others being Aeolians, Dorians, and Ionians). In historical times the name designated the inhabitants of Achaea Phthiotis in southeast Thessaly, and those of the other district of Achaea on the north coast of the Peloponnesus. The Greeks remembered in their tradition a time when Achaeans had occupied a much wider territory. Homer used the name *Achaioi* for Agamemnon's army, important people from communities in almost all parts of Greece, and it seems probable that the Achaeans were leading figures in the civilization of the Late Bronze Age that we call Mycenaean. Mycenae itself, Tiryns, Pylos, Thebes, and Orchomenus were among the chief centers. The form of writing used there, which is also found at Knossos in Crete, is a syllabic script known as Linear B. Its recent decipherment showed that the language was an early form of Greek, related to the Arcado-Cyprian dialect, and this fact has lent further strong support to the identification of Homer's Achaeans with Mycenaean Greeks.

In later times it was believed that the Achaeans were an aboriginal people who migrated to the Peloponnesus from their home in Thessaly. Modern speculation about their remote origins has been fruitless, but they seem to have been a natural growth and development from Indo-European peoples who entered Greece at various points and in several stages in the Middle Bronze Age.

113

The names *Ahhiyava*, in Hittite records of the late 14th and 13th centuries B.C., and *Akaiwasha*, in Egyptian archives around 1221 B.C., may well be references to Achaeans whose activities brought them into conflict with the imperial powers in this period when new pressures were unsettling the balance of the Mediterranean world.

ACROPOLIS [ə-krŏp′ə-lĭs], "high city," or citadel, of ancient Greek cities, selected for its defensibility. Fortified from earliest times, it was later devoted mainly to the sanctuaries of the patron gods of the city, although it could still be used as a fortress in case of emergency. The Larissa at Argos, Acrocorinth at Corinth, and Cadmea of Thebes are familiar examples, but the best known is the Acropolis of Athens whose summit is about 1,000 by 500 ft. There is evidence that its slopes were inhabited during neolithic times, and the hill itself was a great Mycenaean fortress with a palace during the Late Helladic period. After this latter period and until the 6th century B.C. there is little physical evidence of habitation, although fragments of brightly colored porous sculpture seem to belong to pediments of early temples now vanished. There remain the foundations of the Old Athena Temple of the Pisistratean period and also those of the early-5th-century predecessor of the Parthenon.

The entire area was sacked and burned by the Persians in 480 B.C., and the earlier Parthenon was abandoned in favor of a more splendid marble structure, the present Parthenon, dedicated in 438 B.C. The pedimental sculptures and frieze, executed under Phidias, are one of the great treasures of the British Museum, and the architectural "refinements" carried out by the architect Ictinus are considered more successful than those of any other temple. The 5th century, under the statesman Pericles, also saw the building of the monumental gateway, or Propylaea, by the architect Mnesicles, at the western approach; the Erechtheum on the north, on the site of the old Mycenaean palace; and Callicrates' exquisite little Ionic temple of Athena Nike. In addition to these, there were buildings on the Acropolis that housed many other cults, and the dedicatory offerings and statues were numberless. Among them was the huge bronze Athena Promachos, whose spearhead was visible far out to sea.

The Acropolis suffered heavily in postclassical times, the Parthenon becoming successively a Christian church, Turkish mosque, and powder magazine; the Propylaea, the Turkish governor's palace; and the Erechtheum, a private house. Located outside the walls, on the south slope of the Acropolis, were the Theater of Dionysus, the Asclepieum, the stoa of Eumenes and the Odeum of Herodes Atticus.

AEGEAN CIVILIZATION, general designation for the various cultures that flourished in and around the Aegean Sea during the Bronze Age (c.3000–1100 B.C.). Archeological investigation has shown that cultural developments in the area were centered in four geographic regions: the mainland of Greece, Crete, the Cyclades islands, and the coast of Asia Minor. The first of these cultures to achieve eminence arose and matured on the island of Crete and exercised influence over a wide area. In 1900 it was named Minoan by Sir Arthur Evans, the excavator of Knossos,

1 Temple of Athena Nike Apteros, sometimes called Nike Apteros.

René Burri—Magnum

Alison Frantz—Amer. Sch. of Classical Studies, Athens

Blackened areas above show where the Propylaea (*left*) and the Statue of Athena once stood on the Acropolis.

3 The Parthenon, temple of Athena on the Acropolis.

Alison Frantz—Amer. Sch. of Classical Studies, Athens

2 The Caryatids of the delicately detailed Erechtheum.

after Minos, the legendary king of Crete. The cultures which developed on the Greek mainland are called Helladic, after Hellas, the Greek name for Greece. The term Cycladic refers to the culture known mainly from the Cyclades islands, located between Greece and Crete. Finally, there are the Troadic cultures of the northwestern corner of Asia Minor, an area known as the Troad, after Troy. While it was affected by contact with the other Aegean civilizations, the Troadic development was related more to the cultures of Asia Minor than to those of the Aegean region.

Excavations in the Aegean area have shown that Minoan, Cycladic, and Helladic cultural development proceeded at different paces, so that their individual phases frequently overlapped. A system has been devised which distinguishes the phases culturally and chronologically. Since absolute dates for the Bronze Age Aegean civilizations are generally quite uncertain, it is customary to employ such terms as Early Minoan, Middle Minoan, or Late Helladic. Still finer phase distinctions are Early Helladic I, Middle Minoan III, and so forth. These terms are determined on the basis of archeological investigation. Occasionally the Aegean world can be linked chronologically with the more precisely established dates for various stages of Egyptian civilization. Such linkage is possible when objects of Egyptian manufacture are discovered in Aegean sites or when the tombs of Egypt contain or depict artifacts made in the Aegean region.

Minoan Civilization. The extensive excavations of Sir Arthur Evans on Crete in the first three decades of this century brought to light evidence that Crete was the center of an impressive and influential civilization in the period c.2600–1400 B.C. The origins and early stages of this culture remain a matter of speculation, but Evans' work indicated that the Middle Minoan period (c.2000–1600 B.C.) was marked by the building of new cities on Crete, by the construction of elaborate palaces and villas, and by the expansion of overseas trade. The latter took Minoan merchants to the mainland of Greece, to many islands of the Aegean Sea, to Egypt, and to the commercial cities along the coast of the eastern Mediterranean. At Knossos, the chief city of Crete, the immense palace of Minos has been laid bare by the archeological shovel. Its size and complexity reflect the cultural and commercial attainments of the period. The height of prosperity was reached in the Late Minoan period (c.1600–1400 B.C.). Late Minoan II (c.1450–1400) is known only from Knossos and is thought by many scholars to reflect Mycenaean Greek control of the city, before it was sacked and burned by unknown forces in about 1400 B.C.

The chief evidence for this brief period of Mycenaean domination is linguistic. The Minoans employed a syllabic writing system of pictographic origin, called Linear A, or Minoan Linear, by modern scholars. Although attempts are made continually, Linear A has not yet been deciphered, but the language does not appear to be Greek or any other Indo-European tongue. At Knossos, in Late Minoan II, this script was supplanted by one now called Linear B, or Mycenaean Linear. In 1952 Michael Ventris, an English scholar, deciphered the Linear B script from clay tablets and demonstrated that it was used to write Greek. These inscribed tablets were accidentally baked and preserved in the fire that destroyed Knossos. They suggest that Linear B was brought to Knossos by Mycenaeans. A majority of the Linear B tablets have been unearthed on the Greek mainland, and some predate the

Most animals held religious significance for Minoans. *Left,* sacred bulls on a sealstone found near Knossos, and (*right*), the ivory Snake Goddess in typical Cretan costume. The slender gypsum throne, used by ancient kings, is shown below. At far left, ornate jars in one of the labyrinthine palace's many rooms.

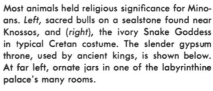

Marble figure of a woman from the Cyclades.
(THE METROPOLITAN MUSEUM OF ART)

Reconstructed dolphin fresco in the palace at Knossos.
(ALISON FRANTZ—AMER. SCH. OF CLASSICAL STUDIES, ATHENS)

Clay tablet inscribed in Linear B, a late Minoan script. Tablets were accidently baked and thus preserved. (MUSEUM OF HERACLION, CRETE)

This Middle Minoan vase pictures the octopus. At far left, one of the 3,500-year-old, gold Vaphio cups, found near Sparta in 1889.
(MUSEUM OF HERACLION, CRETE)   (NATIONAL MUSEUM, ATHENS)

Knossos tablets. This writing system continued in use until the end of the 13th century B.C. in Greece.

Architecture on Crete is represented chiefly by large, complex and luxurious palaces, such as those at Knossos, Phaistos, and Mallia. The palaces were built on a multi-level plan, with some sections arranged about open courtyards. The throne rooms, private shrines, workrooms, living rooms, storage areas, and the many corridors of the palace at Knossos lead some scholars to suspect that it was the famous mazelike Labyrinth of later Greek tradition. Ventilation and drainage were provided for, but the cities probably lacked fortifications. During most of their history, the Minoans could rely on their sea power for protection. Large temples have not been found, indicating that there was a tradition of outdoor religious observances.

Collections in the museums of Crete and Greece attest to the brilliance of Minoan artistic achievement. Vivid frescoes adorned the walls of palaces and the villas of wealthy Minoans. Panels and friezes depict scenes of religious life, court ceremonial, soldiers, acrobats, hunters, lithe young men, and fashionable women. Life in the sea and in the woods provided rich inspiration for wall painting and the decoration of fine pottery. The minor arts are well represented by finely carved steatite vessels, terra-cotta figures, bright faience, ivory objects, jewelry, and miniatures. The themes are mainly Minoan inventions, but there is evidence of the influence of Egyptian ideas, acquired in the course of Minoan trade with the Nile Valley. Minoans and their merchandise appear in some Egyptian private tomb painting of the 18th dynasty (c.1475 B.C.).

Royal Minoan tombs consist of several chambers, reminiscent of Egyptian rock-cut tombs of the New Kingdom. There are also some *tholoi*, or circular tombs, more commonly associated with the Greek mainland. Pit and shaft graves used large jars and terra-cotta tubs as sarcophagi.

The chief deity of the Minoans appears to have been a "mother-goddess," associated with the snake. The bull also seems to have played an important role in Minoan ritual. Minoan religious influence is revealed by the quite frequent mention of Crete in Greek myths.

The end of Minoan power (c.1400 B.C.) did not significantly alter the prosperity or daily life of Crete, but signaled a shift of power in the Aegean world from Crete to the Greek mainland.

The Cyclades. The earliest settlers in the Cyclades probably came from southwestern Asia Minor at the end of the fourth millenium B.C. They were followed by more immigrants from their homelands during the early Bronze Age (c.2600–2000 B.C.). These latecomers merged with their predecessors and developed a culture whose distinctive features were subjected to influences from Crete, Syria-Palestine, and Asia Minor. Highly stylized marble figurines and vases, typical of Cycladic material culture, were found in burials. Some also made their way to Crete through trade. Among the Cyclades, the island of Melos was of considerable trade importance, because of its relatively large deposits of the highly prized obsidian (volcanic glass). While archeological investigation in the Cyclades has not been very extensive, certain features of the culture have emerged from the work already done.

Excavations on the isle of Syros show that the inhabitants of early Cycladic cities fortified their citadels. The Middle Cycladic period (c.2000–1600 B.C.), roughly coeval with Middle Minoan, is best represented by the second of three levels excavated at Phylakopi on Melos. It yielded Kamares pots from Crete and a flying-fish fresco, reminiscent of the Minoan marine scenes. Minyan ware from the Greek mainland has been found in several Cycladic sites, and Cycladic ware has been unearthed in such mainland sites as Lerna. The uppermost level at Phylakopi is Late Cycladic and reflects strong Late Helladic (Mycenaean) influence. The city at Phylakopi was encompassed by massive walls and gates on the Myce-

The Lion Gate at Mycenae, one of the notable art works of the Aegean civilization on the Greek mainland. The tapered column reflects the Minoan culture of Crete.
(ALISON FRANTZ—AMER. SCH. OF CLASSICAL STUDIES, ATHENS)

naean model. Mycenaean chamber tombs and settlements have been found on a number of the Cyclades, such as Ceos and Amorgos. The Cycladic culture lost its distinctive qualities after c.1400 B.C.

The Greek Mainland. Shortly before 3000 B.C., a people already possessing a well-developed neolithic culture settled in mainland Greece. The Early Helladic period (c.2600–1900 B.C.) saw the arrival of two important new groups. Agricultural people, perhaps from Asia Minor, came first, attracted by the fertile coastal plains, such as that at Tiryns. Mainly through the agency of these folk, the Bronze Age came to Greece. Occasionally violent, their settlement and merger with the earlier population was generally peaceful, as at Lerna. The mature, Early Helladic culture showed great development in architecture, typified by a large and complex building at Lerna, the so-called House of Tiles. Protected by a double ring of fortifications, the structure was probably a royal palace. Also of interest from this age is the great round building at Tiryns. Early Helladic sites have yielded samples of worked objects of copper, stone, and bone, together with much pottery.

A second and most important wave of invaders, the last for some 800 years, ushered in the Middle Helladic period. Ventris' decipherment of Linear B makes it clear that these people were Greek-speakers, the first to penetrate Greece proper. They are called Achaeans, the name most commonly applied to the Greeks by Homer. The name serves to distinguish the Bronze Age Greeks from those of the later Classical era. The term Mycenaeans refers to the Achaeans of Mycenae in particular but is more widely employed because of the preeminence of Mycenae among the Greek cities.

The Achaean settlement was accompanied by some violence. The mingling of the new people with the earlier,

apparently non-Indo-European population, is reflected in some later Greek myths which blend Greek and pre-Greek ideas. Many sites offer evidence of a gradual transition, rather than a sharp cultural break. The older apsidal houses continued to be built alongside new ones which anticipate the later megaron style. Minyan ware, a soapy, gray (later yellowish) pottery of Achaean manufacture was introduced in this period. Minoan influence was strong and undoubtedly quickened Greek cultural development in the growing cities of Orchomenus, Athens, Thebes, Pylos, and Mycenae.

At the beginning of the Late Halladic period (c.1600–1125 B.C.), the shaft grave, a new type of royal tomb, was adopted at Mycenae. Burial equipment continues to show strong influence from Crete. By exploiting natural resources and becoming involved in trade, especially in competition with the Minoans, the cities of Greece, particularly Mycenae, became wealthy and powerful. The cultural presence and influence of Mycenae can be detected in a great number of sites throughout the eastern Mediterranean. This Late Helladic period is usually called Mycenaean now, because both archeological evidence and the tradition of the Homeric epics indicate that by 1450 B.C. Mycenae had become the most important city of Hellas. It is Agamemnon, king of Mycenae, whom Homer describes as "most kingly." Agamemnon leads the fabled expedition against Troy, and all the other kings were subordinate, but not necessarily subject, to him.

The discovery of ancient Mycenae's site was a second triumph of determination for Heinrich Schliemann, who had demonstrated the basic historicity of Homeric tradition by locating the site of Troy in 1873. In 1876 this untrained German businessman began the excavations which revealed the glory of Mycenae.

About 1500 B.C., a new dynasty came to power in

Mycenae. There is a dramatic change in the type of royal burials from the shaft grave to the *tholos* tomb, an immense beehive-shaped structure approached by an unroofed causeway (*dromos*). In 1450 the Mycenaeans acquired the support of many of the Greek rulers. Taking advantage of the dislocations caused by a severe natural calamity—earthquake or volcanic eruption—on Crete, the Mycenaeans descended on that island c.1450 B.C. They captured Knossos and were able to hold it for about 50 years. Both Minoan power and Mycenaean control of Knossos ended in about 1400 B.C., when the city was seized, possibly by pirates. There are no subsequent Mycenaean settlements on Crete, but Mycenaean culture and influence spread elsewhere. It would seem that the Mycenaeans, who dominated the Aegean world until the Dorian "invasion" of the late 12th century B.C., did not destroy Knossos and other Cretan cities. Mycenaean culture has been traced to the islands of the Aegean, the coast of Asia Minor, and to the Levant. It has even been suggested that the Trojan War had its roots in Trojan-Mycenaean trade rivalry.

The work begun by Michael Ventris and John Chadwick on Linear B has been continued by numerous scholars. Painstaking scholarship has made it possible to extract considerable information about the Mycenaean world from the surviving inscribed tablets, even though they tend to be brief and of limited content. The majority are accounts, palace records, inventories, offering lists, and so on. No literary texts or royal correspondence has yet come to light, and there is reason to think that such documents were not composed. The texts seem to be "bookkeeping" records, limited in detail and time span. They do suggest that the political structure was rather like that reflected in the *Iliad* and *Odyssey*. Each city had a king (*wanax*) advised by a council of military chiefs. There may have been an assembly of warriors that approved major decisions. There was a complex, well-organized bureaucracy and a record-keeping scribal class. The documents refer to landholding, revenues, storehouses and their contents, and reveal a high degree of specialization in the crafts. Many are mentioned: weavers, masons, nurses, bakers, and the like. There were priests who led the religious observances for gods such as Poseidon, Hermes, and Zeus, names well known from later Greece.

The tablets inform us that the royal palace was the nerve center of the economy and administration of the Mycenaean city. Excavation also shows the palace to be the most prominent physical feature of the Mycenaean city. Built on the *acropolis* (citadel) and protected by the city's "Cyclopean" walls, the palace was a complex structure, built about a central portion called a *megaron*, basically a large room with a forecourt. The so-called Lion Gate at Mycenae still shows the extent of artistic development, while the advances in architecture can be seen in the corbeled roofs of the *tholos* tombs. Tomb equipment and pottery are rich testimony to the Mycenaean ability to absorb Minoan influences, reshape them, and blend them with Greek motifs. Vases from Mycenae depict warriors, both foot soldiers and charioteers, ships, animals, and plants. The famous dagger from Mycenae is inlaid with a scene of warriors carrying their great "figure eight" shields, hunting lions. Schliemann found a large quantity of gold in one of the *tholos* tombs, which he named the "Treasury of Atreus." The gold masks, pendants, and vessels now on display in the National Archaeological Museum in Athens attest to the wealth of Mycenaean Greece.

While direct Mycenaean control was probably limited to the nearer parts of the Aegean area, the Greeks of this period were widely known in the eastern Mediterranean. Their crafts were known to the Pharaohs of Egypt and to the far-traveling Phoenician merchants. Achaean rulers were in a position to conduct diplomatic negotiations and correspondence with the rulers of the Hittite empire in eastern Anatolia (modern Turkey). All of this ended with the "Dorian invasion" of the 12th century. The Mycenaean decline was rapid. Hesiod, a later Greek poet, lamented the passage from the age of Bronze to that of Iron, but the Mycenaean achievement was not entirely lost. Some aspects of Mycenaean culture were preserved throughout the dark period that separated the glories of Mycenae from the flowering of Classical Greece. Not a small share of the credit goes to the epic bards, the greatest of whom the Greeks called Homer. This poetic genius of the dark ages of Greece brought together the strands of the tradition of Greece's past and wove a tapestry peopled by heroes and gods which gave the Greeks a sense of their history. Although the *Iliad* and the *Odyssey* include elements of Homer's own age, they also preserve important aspects of Minoan and particularly Mycenaean civilization.

AEOLIANS, one of the four major ethnic divisions of the ancient Greeks (Aeolians, Ionians, Achaeans, and Dorians), named after the mythical hero Aeolus. They originally settled in Thessaly and Boeotia, but according to ancient tradition, many fled the invasions of Greece from the north in the 12th century B.C. Taking the direction followed generations later by the Ionians, the Aeolians went eastward and found new homes along the northwestern coast of Asia Minor, in the area known as the Troad. They also settled on islands of the Aegean Sea, such as Lesbos and Tenedos. Comparatively unimportant in the larger scheme of Greek affairs, the Aeolians contributed two of the finest writers of Greek lyric poetry, Alcaeus and the poetess Sappho. Both came from Lesbos and flourished c.600 B.C. The language of Homer contains some traces of the Aeolic dialect and Hesiod was descended from Aeolic stock.

AESCHINES [ĕs′kĭ-nēz] (390?–314? B.C.), Athenian orator, and chief rival of Demosthenes. After a brief acting career, Aeschines entered public life as clerk in the Athenian assembly. He supported co-operation with Macedon and opposed Demosthenes, against whom his three extant speeches are directed.

AESCHYLUS [ĕs′kĭ-ləs] (525–456 B.C.), the earliest of the great Greek tragic dramatists, was born in Eleusis, near Athens. In his youth he witnessed the expulsion of the tyranny and the growth of the new Athenian democracy. His plays suggest that he was profoundly moved by this development, and strongly favored it. In 490 he fought as a foot soldier against the Persians at Marathon, and in 480 probably took part in the victorious naval action at Salamis. Pride in the military achievements of Athens is openly reflected in the *Persians*, which describes the battle of Salamis in realistic detail. The same patriotic feeling is an indirect but strong undercurrent in his other extant works.

His first tragedies were apparently produced in the first two decades of the 5th century. Then, or soon after, and through the rest of his career, he was well established as the foremost Greek playwright, though he was soon to encounter competition from the brilliant young Sophocles. His reputation spread far beyond Athens, as attested by his two visits to Sicily, where he produced plays under the patronage of the tyrant Hiero I. He died at Gela, in Sicily.

Of some 80 plays written by Aeschylus, only seven survive. These more than suffice, however, to confirm the high esteem in which the ancient world held his art. Modern critics have justly termed him the "father of tragedy." The dramas he saw in his youth were cantatalike performances by a chorus and a single singer or actor. Aeschylus took the decisive step of adding a second actor, thereby creating the possibility of conflict, the essence of tragic drama. His earliest extant historical tragedy, the *Persians* (472), explores this new form's potentialities for the opposition of idea and personality. The *Seven Against Thebes* (467) develops genuine dramatic conflict still further by projecting it into the mythical world of the house of Oedipus. The lyrical *Suppliants* (464?) and the spectacular *Prometheus Bound* (date unknown) exhibit both the poet's versatility and his deepening concern with the problem of the relationship among God, man, and the human civilization created by the two. This problem is the subject of the *Oresteia* (458), a trilogy comprising the *Agamemnon*, *Choephoroe*, and *Eumenides*. Undoubtedly the masterpiece of Aeschylus, the *Oresteia* summarizes his main beliefs, at the heart of which are a profound religious commitment which verges on monotheism, and an optimistic faith in the future of man. It also displays in maturest form his typical dramatic and poetic techniques, including the creation of majestic, "larger than life" characters, and the forging of an original poetic language which, in its grandeur and sheer emotive power, has rarely been equaled.

AESCULAPIUS [ĕs-kū-lā′pē-əs], Greek god or hero, son of Apollo and Coronis, and patron of physicians. Taught medicine by the Centaur Chiron, he became so skilled that he raised men from the dead. Therefore Zeus killed him with a thunderbolt. In the myth he was a hero who died; but he may have been an ancient deity, first worshipped in Thessaly, and especially venerated in later times at Epidaurus, site of his greatest shrine. His Greek name is Asklepios.

AESOP [ē′səp] (fl.6th century B.C.), Greek author of beast fables. A rich and often contradictory opinion clustered about his name in antiquity. Although many elements in this tradition should be assigned to popular imagination, there is no reason to doubt that behind this mass of invention lay a real figure of the 6th century B.C. By the 5th century B.C., Aesop's name was clearly associated with the beast fable, and to this original nucleus many fables were later added. The resulting collection exerted an immense influence on subsequent authors, for example, La Fontaine in his *Fables*.

Coin portrait of Alexander the Great. (AMERICAN NUMISMATIC SOCIETY)

ALEXANDER THE GREAT (356–323 B.C.), Macedonian King, conqueror of the Persian empire, and one of the greatest leaders in history. Son of Philip II and Olympias, who traced her ancestry back to Achilles, Alexander derived outstanding traits from both parents—diplomatic astuteness and military ability from his father, and a fiery and imaginative temperament from his mother. He received the best education obtainable, including instruction in riding, hunting, and fighting from his father, and in natural science, literature, and moral philosophy from the great Aristotle. He became expert in every skill befitting an aristocrat. Boldly handsome, courageous to the point of rashness, personally magnetic, and intensely loyal, Alexander was at the same time imperious and subject to sudden fierce anger and resentment. His favorite author was Homer, and he imagined himself a second Achilles.

Alexander led the impetuous attack at the battle of Chaeronea, which ended the era of the independent Greek city-state. Two years later his father was murdered (336 B.C.), leaving to him his throne and his almost-completed plans for an expedition to free the Greeks of Asia Minor from Persian control. At Philip's death rebellions broke out in the south, north, east, and west. Although only 20, Alexander handled the trouble with characteristic energy. A prompt show of force intimidated Thebes and checkmated the plans of Demosthenes and others at Athens. At a meeting of the so-called Corinthian League, Alexander, like his father, was named commander in chief of the allied Greek army for service against Persia. The next year (335 B.C.), while he campaigned in the north against Thracian and Illyrian tribes, a rumor of his death prompted a second rebellion by Thebes. Alexander returned suddenly, took the city, destroyed every building except the temples and the house where Pindar had lived, and killed or enslaved the entire population. This fearful lesson kept the Greeks in line for years afterward when he was far off in the East.

The following spring Alexander crossed into Asia Minor with an army of about 40,000, of whom perhaps half were Macedonians. He first visited the site of Troy and there paid tribute to the heroes of Homer. He may at first have intended no more than the capture of the eastern coastal area of the Aegean, or perhaps also the Persian naval bases in Phoenicia and Egypt, but his rapid and relatively

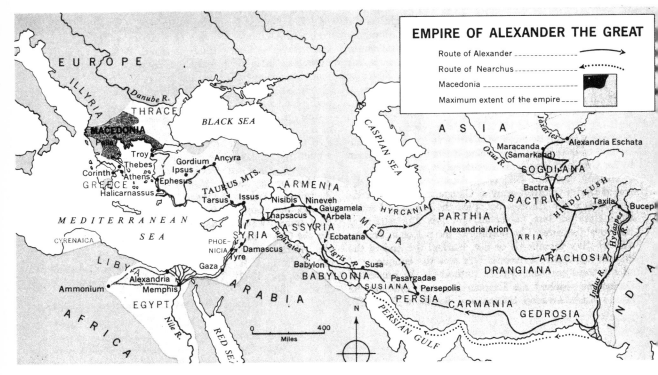

easy success must have encouraged him to raise his sights continually. As he overcame hardships and risks, his egotism grew. His interest in geography and scientific exploration also drove him on, and he was genuinely convinced (as were all Greeks) that he was conferring a benefit on Asiatics by introducing them to Greek culture.

His first major victory, at the Granicus River, exposed Asia Minor. Alexander's use of cavalry under his personal command was the deciding factor in this and other engagements. Passing through the Cilician Gates, he defeated the Persians at the battle of Issus (333 B.C.) in northern Syria, and this opened the way to the heart of the empire. After the capture of his family, King Darius offered to negotiate, but Alexander refused. He turned south to secure the eastern Mediterranean coast, but was delayed seven months by the siege and capture of Tyre (332 B.C.), his greatest military feat, and by the resistance of Gaza. Egypt surrendered without a struggle, as did most Persian subjects. At the mouth of the Nile Alexander founded the greatest of the many new cities to be named after himself; this Alexandria soon became the main link between the Western and Eastern worlds. In Egypt he also journeyed into the western desert to the shrine of Zeus Ammon, and was there supposedly greeted as the god's own son. As divine kings were common in the East, such a claim strengthened Alexander's position with his new subjects. But he seems also, either from policy or conviction, to have insisted on being treated as superhuman by his Greek soldiers. This they deeply resented.

Turning eastward (331 B.C.), Alexander met and defeated Darius' greatest army at Gaugamela, in the northern Tigris plain. He then occupied the principal Persian cities, Babylon, Susa, Persepolis, and Ecbatana, with their vast royal treasures. The burning of the palace at Persepolis, whether intentional or not, marked the end of the Persian monarchy. Alexander was now the conqueror of all southwestern Asia; yet he pushed on. In pursuit of Darius, he reached the Caspian Sea, and crossing the Hindu Kush, invaded Bactria and Sogdiana (330–327). After fierce resistance, this area acknowledged his sovereignty, which was perhaps lightened somewhat by his marriage to their beautiful princess Roxana. In the next three years he broke into northwestern India, defeated the gallant King Porus on the Hydaspes River, founded Buchephala to honor his horse, who had died in the battle, overran the Punjab, and was only prevented from pressing further, perhaps to find the fabled "eastern ocean," by a determined mutiny. He returned west along the Indus River and from its mouth sent a fleet under Nearchus to explore the sea route to the head of the Persian Gulf, while the army proceeded through the desert to Babylon. Both army and fleet reached their destination (324 B.C.), after great danger and privation. The military results were negligible, but from then on trade flowed in increasing volume between the Mediterranean and India.

Back in Babylon, which he apparently intended to make his capital, Alexander devoted himself with the same concentration to the organization of the conquered territories. He wished to make Greeks and Asiatics partners in civil administration, and even in the army. This policy caused resentment among the conquerors, especially when Alexander insisted that his officers follow his own example and marry Persian women.

But Alexander's interests and abilities lay more in conquest and exploration than in administration. Preparations were made for an Arabian expedition. Representatives at his court included envoys from the western Mediterranean, and there was speculation that he might turn his restless energies in that direction. But in May or June, 323 B.C., Alexander was stricken with a fever and in 11 days was dead. Only 32, he had reigned less than 13 years. His resistance had been weakened by continuous overexertion, wounds, fierce fits of anger, and heavy drinking. He had not provided for a successor, although it is said that at the last he handed his ring to his second-in-command, Perdiccas. Probably not even Alexander himself could have long held together the vast territory he had conquered. Certainly it rapidly disintegrated without him, to be fought over by his generals. Yet large areas of Asia remained for centuries under Greek political control, and Alexander's dream of a common Greco-Asiatic culture was at least partially realized. Perhaps no single individual in ancient times had so great an impact on world events as did Alexander. It is only natural that time should have magnified and distorted his fame into a legend which history can hardly match. Already legendary during his lifetime, Alexander passed into the literature of many nations after his death, adopted by Arabic-Persian tradition under the name Iskander, and becoming especially popular in the romances of the Middle Ages.

AMPHICTYONIC *[ăm-fĭk-tē-ŏn'ĭk]* **COUNCILS** , administrative and judicial bodies which administered the affairs of certain ancient Greek shrines, notably that of Apollo at Delphi. Amphictyony refers to an organization of amphictyonies (literally "those who live around"), that is, neighboring states. The original motives may have included trade, defense, and close ethnic relationships, but in historical times, the main purpose of the amphictyonic leagues was to insure the independence of religious centers of international scope. Little is known of the history of organization of any except those of Apollo's famous shrines at Delos and Delphi.

The Delphic league was, from the early 6th century B.C., associated with that of Demeter at Anthela near Thermopylae. Members were originally 12 tribes of central Greece, but more distant kinsmen later gained representation. An elected council met twice a year at both shrines. Its regular duties included administration of the god's real estate and treasure; maintenance, adornment, and, when necessary, rebuilding of the temple; protection of pilgrims; upkeep of roads; and conduct of the Pythian games. In matters as serious as the declaration of a sacred war, the decision was referred to the league assembly in which all citizens of allied states had voting rights. The Delphic league was potentially a powerful force for international law and arbitration, as is indicated by the oath of membership forbidding the destruction of a member city or cutting it off from running water. But selfish members, ambitious outsiders like Philip of Macedon, and groups like the Aetolian League, often subverted the amphictyonic purpose to their own interests.

AMPHIPOLIS *[ăm-fĭp'ə-lĭs]*, ancient Greek city in Thrace, on the Strymon River. It controlled most of the trade with inland Thrace, particularly the export of gold from the Pangaean mines. Miletus attempted to colonize it in 497 B.C., and Athens in 465; but both were repelled by the native Thracians. The Athenians succeeded in 437. The gold trade was hotly disputed in the Peloponnesian Wars,

with the city finally falling to Sparta. After a short time as a free city, it was conquered by Philip of Macedon in 357. It became Roman in 168 B.C., and was visited by St. Paul during the 1st century A.D. Deserted today, it contains the remains of an ancient acropolis and town, as well as the colossal Lion Monument of the 4th century B.C., which was re-erected in modern times.

ANACREON *[ə-năk'rē-ən]* (6th century B.C.), Greek lyric poet from Teos in Ionia. A wanderer, Anacreon lived many years at Samos under the protection of the tyrant Polycrates, but spent his last days in Athens. The author of poems on old age and love, he treated these themes with wit and detachment. He was also capable of fierce satire, as his poem on Artemon shows. There exists a collection of poems, the *Anacreontics*, whose themes parallel Anacreon. By general agreement, however, these are of a much later date, and are not by Anacreon himself.

ANTIGONIDS *[ăn-tĭg'ə-nĭdz]*, Macedonian dynasty founded by Antigonus I, called the one-eyed (c.382–301 B.C.). Having served in the army of Alexander the Great, he was assigned Phrygia, Lycia, and Pamphylia in Asia Minor in the partition of Alexander's empire. But his unswerving aim was to reunite the empire under his own control, and he perhaps had a better chance than any of the other successors. His exploits finally caused the formation of a hostile coalition (315) between Cassander in Macedonia, Lysimachus in Thrace, and Ptolemy in Egypt. But Antigonus was only temporarily stalemated. His son, Demetrius Poliorcetes, won notable success in the Aegean and Greece, and Antigonus assumed the title of King in 306. Finally Seleucus joined Cassander, Lysimachus, and Ptolemy in an all-out counter effort, and Antigonus was defeated and killed in the battle of Ipsus in Phrygia in 301.

Antigonus II Gonatas (c.320–239 B.C.), son of Demetrius Poliorcetes, assumed the title of King of Macedonia after his father's death (283), but for several years his control was interrupted by attacks, especially by Pyrrhus of Epirus. With Spartan help, however, he decisively defeated Pyrrhus when he invaded the Peloponnesus in 272. Thereafter, Antigonus's power extended as far south as Corinth. His later years were chiefly occupied with naval campaigns against Egypt. Athens and Sparta, with Egyptian help, launched the unsuccessful Chremonidean War (267–262) against his control. Antigonus was a conscientious ruler, who helped re-establish Macedonian prestige. A person of culture, he encouraged philosophy and the arts.

Antigonus III Doson (c.263–221 B.C.), whose father was half-brother to Antigonus II, became guardian to Philip, the heir of Demetrius II (229). Assuming the title of King in 227, he somewhat revived Macedonian prestige in the Aegean by an expedition against Caria. When the Achaean League was unable to resist King Cleomenes of Sparta, Aratus invited Antigonus to intervene (224). He freed the central Peloponnesus, occupied Sparta, and organized the Greek states and leagues in a confederacy presided over by himself. The power of the Antigonids was crushed by the Romans in the reigns of Philip V and Perseus.

ARCADIA *[är-kā'dē-ə]*, province of ancient Greece in the center of the Peloponnesus, traditionally known as the home of Pan. It was a remote region, and preserved into classical times a Greek dialect spoken before the arrival of the Dorians. It is mountainous country but well-watered by the river Styx, popularly identified as the river of the underworld. The land is ideal for pasturage, and many bronze figurines representing shepherds, dating back to the 6th century B.C., testify to the prevailing occupation of its inhabitants. Arcadia was unimportant politically, although often unwillingly allied with its powerful neighbor Sparta, and, in addition, providing a rich source of mercenary soldiers for other warring states. The Arcadian League, formed in the 4th century B.C., proved an ineffective organization and joined the Achaean League in 234 B.C. The principal Arcadian deities were Hermes, Pan, and Despoina (a form of Demeter). The principal cities were Mantinea, Megalopolis, Arcadian Orchomenus, and Tegea. The name has long signified a life of idyllic simplicity.

ARCHILOCHUS [är-kĭl'ə-kəs] (fl.7th century B.C.), Greek lyric poet from the island of Paros. One of the first poets in Greek literature to employ the personal lyric, Archilochus speaks with a force and flamboyancy which can only cause lament for the almost total loss of his poetic output. A poet of great verbal power and metrical versatility, he used both traditional forms (elegy) and others (epode), most likely invented by himself, to create a vivid, almost violent, portrait of his life as a mercenary soldier. In a world he clearly considered uncertain, Archilochus raised the momentary emotion and impression to the level of absolute validity. He openly proclaimed with fierce honesty his moods of drunken abandon, anger, and cowardice. In the imagination of later antiquity Archilochus became the embodiment of implacable hatred.

ARCHIMEDES [är-kə-mē'dēz] (287–212 B.C.), Greek mathematician. Little is known factually about his personal life, except that he was born in Syracuse and was killed there when the city fell to the Romans. Legend has attributed to him the personality of an absent-minded genius who ignored food, drink, and clothing when occupied with problems in mathematics. On discovering a basic law of hydrostatics, namely that a floating body apparently decreases in weight by an amount equal to that of the liquid it displaces, he is said to have run naked through the streets shouting "Eureka, eureka!" (I have found it, I have found it!)

His achievements in pure mathematics and applied mathematics are well established. He constructed a planetarium imitating the motions of the heavenly bodies; he designed a hydraulic organ and invented the Archimedean screw used in irrigating the Nile valley; he launched a large ship by means of levers and pulleys and boasted that he could move the earth if given a lever sufficiently long; and he contrived engines of war with which the Romans were kept at bay for two years.

Archimedes is said to have regarded such achievements as unworthy of attention as compared with the theoretical treatises he sent to friends at Alexandria. These latter works included *On the Equilibrium of Planes* (on the lever and centers of gravity); *On Floating Bodies* (containing his hydrostatic principle); *Quadrature of the Pa-*

Brown Bros.

ARCHIMEDES

rabola (showing that the area of a segment is four-thirds the area of a triangle in which it is inscribed); *On the Sphere and Cylinder* (proving that the volume and area of a sphere are two-thirds the volume and area, respectively, of a circumscribed cylinder); *The Sand Reckoner* (a calculation of the number of grains of sand required to fill the universe); *On Conoids and Spheroids* (with the determination of volumes of segments); *Measurement of the Circle* (a determination of the value of π), and, most sophisticated of all, *On Spirals*.

In 1907 there was published a long-lost treatise, *Method*, in which Archimedes showed how he had discovered many theorems through the use of infinitesimal methods akin to the integral calculus. Arabic and Greek commentators mention other Archimedean works not now extant.

ARCHIMEDES' SCREW, type of water pump, invented by the Greek mathematician Archimedes (287–212 B.C.). Usually housed in a hollow open cylinder or pipe, the "screw" consists of a strip that is spiraled around a central axis. When the lower end of the cylinder is placed in the water and the screw is turned, the water rotates to the top of the cylinder and out into the collecting area. Such pumps were used in irrigation and drainage operations.

ARCHON [är'kŏn] (Gr. "the ruling one"), ancient Greek magistrate. As government changed from monarchy to aristocracy, the archons inherited the king's various duties. In Athens there were at first three archons: the *basileus* (king), the *polemarch* (leader in war), and the chief archon. The king archon was responsible for most state-administered religious matters. The chief archon was in charge of civil affairs. As his name was used to designate the year in which he held office, he was later titled *eponymos*. At first the office of king archon was hereditary and the other two were appointed for ten-year terms. In the early 7th century B.C. six thesmothetae (lawgivers) were added, making up a board of nine, and the term was shortened to one year. Archons were chosen by the council of the Areopagus from men of like background, who became members of the Areopagus after their term. As democratic institutions developed, the archonship was gradually opened to almost all citizens and selection was by lot. In the course of the 5th century B.C. other officials, notably the generals, gradually overshadowed the archons in importance.

ARGOLIS [är′gə-lĭs], ancient Greek province (originally Argos, denoting both town and state) comprising the easternmost peninsula of the Peloponnesus. Peopled as early as Neolithic times, it was the center of the Bronze Age culture described by Homer. The chief deity was Hera, whose extensive sanctuary near Argos has been excavated, as have other principal sites: Mycenae, Tiryns, Epidaurus, Hermione, Asine, Lerna, Nemea, and Troezen. Argolis flourished under the tyrant Pheidon in the 7th century B.C., and later joined the Achaean League. It came under the Romans in 146 B.C.

ARGOS [är′gŏs], ancient Greek city of the Peloponnesus, located in a fruitful plain about 3 mi. from the Gulf of Argos. The site was occupied before 2000 B.C., and has never been abandoned since, though the town has suffered many vicissitudes. During the Late Bronze Age it was a flourishing community, with its own citadel. Apparently dominated earlier by Mycenae, Argos, after the Bronze Age, became the chief city of the Argive Plain. Under King Pheidon (probably 7th century B.C.) it became a first-rate power. In the classical period Argos' foreign policy was shaped by its traditional hostility to Sparta, and in Hellenistic times it belonged to the Achaean League.

ARISTOPHANES [ăr-ĭs-tŏf′ə-nēz] (c.450–c.385 B.C.), Greek dramatist, one of the greatest comic poets of the ages. He was probably of Athenian parentage, though his association with the island of Aegina, where he lived or owned property, caused his citizenship to be questioned by Cleon. His life spanned the most vibrant period of Athenian history—from the brilliance of the Periclean Age to the destruction of the Athenian Empire and the fall of the democracy at the end of the Peloponnesian War; his comedies, with their mordant satires on current politics and politicians, war, philosophy, science, education, literature, and theology, reflect to a remarkable degree the temper of the times, and serve as a primary source for an understanding of 5th-century Athenian culture. As the only representative of Old Comedy whose works are still extant, Aristophanes also provides us with invaluable data on the development of comic drama from its earliest origins in Dionysiac ritual.

The popularity of Aristophanes is attested by his success in winning prizes at the festivals honoring Dionysus, the god of wine, to whom the plays were dedicated. Of the 54 plays ascribed to the poet, only 11 have survived. These are usually divided into three periods, the first from 425 to 421, the second from 414 to 405, and the third from 391 to 388.

In the first, Aristophanes concentrated his satire on the political situation. In *The Acharnians* (425) and *The Peace* (421), he attempts to win converts to the cause of peace with Sparta and Panhellenic unity. In *The Knights* (424) —one of the most violent and undisguised political attacks known to literature—he continues his virulent assault on Cleon, radical leader of the popular faction, begun in an earlier lost play, *The Babylonians;* and in *The Wasps* (422) he satirizes the Athenian love of litigation and the outsized popular courts which were a mainstay of demagoguery. Unique in this period, *The Clouds* (423) lampoons the new spirit of intellectual inquiry popularized by the Sophists and grossly caricatures Socrates as the representative of the new trends in physical philosophy and rhetoric.

The plays of the second period, written after Athenian hopes had been crushed and the political climate was no longer ripe for harsh political satire, retreat into fantasy, as with *The Birds* (414), or are concerned with literary criticism, Euripides providing a fine target for parody in *The Thesmophoriazusae* (411) and *The Frogs* (405). *Lysistrata* (411) is an exception in which the poet's last moving plea for peace is embedded in high-spirited ribaldry.

From the last period following the Peloponnesian War come *The Ecclesiazusae* (391), satirizing current communistic theories, and *The Plutus* (388), written in the style called Middle Comedy, which recounts the results of restoring the sight of Plutus, the blind god of wealth.

The censorial function of Old Comedy and its foundation in Dionysiac religion permitted Aristophanes' genius unparalleled license and scope. As a poet, his lyrical choral passages place him immediately in the front rank, and as a dramatist he is unrivaled in comic inventiveness, satire, parody, wit, pun, burlesque, and farce. His only weaknesses lie in plot construction and character portrayal, though he brilliantly depicts types. His power is in his intellect and soaring imagination, rather than in his emotions. No translator can do justice to the cumulative hilarity, brilliance, and force that mark his plays.

ARISTOTLE [ăr′ĭs-tŏt-əl] (384–322 B.C.), philosopher and scientist from Stagira in northern Greece. His father, Nicomachus, was physician to Philip of Macedon, father of Alexander the Great. Aristotle came to Athens in 367, and for 20 years was a member of Plato's Academy. After Plato's death in 347 he joined a circle of Platonists in Asia Minor under the patronage of Hermeias, King of Atarneus, who eagerly embraced the Platonic ideal of the philosopher-ruler, until his capture and execution by the Persians in 341. There and in the neighboring island of Lesbos, Aristotle taught and carried on research in biology. In 343 he was appointed tutor to the young prince Alexander (later to be called "the Great") at Pella. When Alexander, after his accession, set out for the conquest of Asia (334), Aristotle returned to Athens and founded his own school. Its atmosphere was as much scientific as philosophical, and pupils collected material on which to base studies of separate subjects, such as medicine (Meno) and botany (Theophrastus). To this category belongs the collection of 158 political systems, of which the Athenian, written by Aristotle himself, was rediscovered on papyrus in 1890. The rest are lost. This amassing of scientific data was in striking contrast to the speculative character of earlier philosophies. In the outburst of anti-Macedonian feeling after Alexander's death in 323, a charge of impiety was brought against Aristotle and he retired to Chalcis in Euboea, where he died a year later.

Aristotle's Philosophy

Aristotle, like Plato, wrote dialogues which won high praise in antiquity for their literary form and style. These however have perished. What survives is for the most part either lecture manuscripts or research notebooks, compiled for school use only. They range from disjointed jottings to more or less finished treatises, and some show evidence of frequent revision and additions.

Twenty years of association with Plato left an indelible impression on Aristotle's thought; but since his own philosophical temperament was very different, it is inevitable that a note of conflict should be discernible at the heart of his philosophy. Intensive study of the chronological order of his works, a feature of 20th-century scholarship, does not indeed bear out the oversimplified theory that he progressed continuously away from Platonism. Psychologically, it is also more probable that an initial strong reaction was succeeded by more moderate views. But change and development there was, and modern research has dispelled forever the Scholastic idea of his mind and system as rigid and unchanging.

Temperamentally he sympathized with the common-sense view that the world of experience is real and must be explained by internal causes. His less metaphysical mind had no use for a realm of transcendent entities (the Platonic "Ideas") which he saw only as a visionary duplication of the natural world, impossible to bring into causal relation with it save by "poetic metaphor." He admired his fellow northerner, Democritus, and it is conceivable that, had it not been for Plato, the atomic view of the world as an undesigned accretion of particles might have undergone remarkable developments in his keen and scientific brain. As it was, he retained through life, from his Academic inheritance, both a teleological outlook, and a sense of the supreme importance of form, which sometimes led to difficulties in his own interpretation of nature.

Matter and Form. Every natural object is a compound of matter and form: "matter" in its absolute sense meaning, not physical body (which in itself possesses some degree of form), but a wholly unqualified substratum, with no independent existence, but logically necessary, as that in which form inheres. Immanent form replaces the transcendent forms of Plato. Plato's problem of how to acquire philosophical knowledge of an ever-changing world is solved by saying that though concrete objects change continually, analysis reveals the permanent principles underlying that change: the substratum and pairs of contrary forms which qualify them in turn.

Everything has an indwelling impulse toward the development of its own specific form, seen most clearly in the organic process of seed to plant, or embryo to adult. This process in Aristotle's terminology is from potentiality to actuality, and in the division of existence into potential and actual lies his answer to the Eleatic denial of change on the ground that nothing can come to be out of either what is or what is not.

At the apex of the *scala naturae* exists pure form (or "act") which, as perfect Being, has no part in matter or potentiality: that is, God. His existence is necessary on the principle that potentiality can only be actualized by the presence of an already actual being. In physical generation, a seed drops from a mature plant, a child must have a father. (The hen comes before the egg.) On this plane, actual and potential are only relative, whereas to sustain the teleological order of the whole Universe calls for a perfect and absolute Being. Aristotelian teleology implies the actual existence of the *telos*, an ultimate final-efficient cause for the whole, as well as the relative final causes working within each separate species.

The Idea of God. God is pure mind or intellect, the highest type of existence and the only one conceivable as existing apart from matter. He is no deliberate creator, since concern for the world of forms-in-matter would detract from his perfection and involve him in the potential. But his existence suffices to keep in motion (not "set in motion," for Aristotle's world is eternal) the whole world order by activating the internal impulses toward form. Everything, that is, is striving to imitate within its natural limitations the perfection of God, the Unmoved Mover. Physically, his existence leads directly to the circular motions instigated by the intelligences that move the heavenly bodies, which in turn activate the processes of terrestrial life. From this angle mankind is at many removes from God, but the possession of reason gives us a unique position, a kind of direct line of communication. Hence it is by his intellectual life that man fulfills his proper nature. It is natural for everything to develop the activity of its highest part, thus realizing its proper form. For man, alone of earthly creatures, this means cultivating a divine spark within him.

Ethics. Not even a philosopher can do this all the time. In his ethical theory we see most clearly the effect of Aristotle's common-sense outlook and the abandonment of transcendent models. The absolute character of the Platonic virtues meant that answers to moral questions were bound up with metaphysical knowledge. Conduct must be founded on fixed principles, imparted by the philosopher, who through his training has recovered his prenatal knowledge of reality, of the changeless forms of the virtues, which are but dimly reflected in earthly behavior. Now, however, moral virtue and rules of conduct lie entirely within the realm of the contingent. In the *Ethics* he repeatedly asserts that scientific precision is out of place in this study, which is purely practical in aim: "not to find out what virtue is, but to become good men." For Plato and Socrates there was no such distinction. For Aristotle virtue lies in a mean between two extremes, which are its perversions. Thus courage, for instance, lies between cowardice and foolhardiness, generosity between meanness and extravagance. There is no golden rule: the correct mean must be found in each case by experience and common sense.

The Soul. In psychology, Aristotle defined soul (life) as, in his technical sense, the "form" of the body: that is, the highest manifestation of the particular compound of form and matter, which is a living creature. This does not imply an epiphenomenalist view. Form is the prior cause and in no way dependent on matter. It does, however, exclude Plato's doctrine of transmigration. Aristotle seems to have believed in the survival (not necessarily individual survival) of *nous* (intellectual intuition), our link with the divine, the only part of us which "comes in from outside."

Science. A great part of Aristotle's achievement was scientific. He excelled in the descriptive and classificatory work of natural history, and in the surviving zoological writings the extent of factual knowledge and the soundness of his method still excite the admiration of his modern successors. The identification and description of species was, of course, a task particularly suited to the genius of the philosopher who still, like his master, saw reality in form, yet discovered this form in the natural world instead of banishing it beyond space and time. He and his school founded the natural sciences as separate disciplines, though the doubtful advantage of an admitted cleavage between science and philosophy still lay far in the future.

Logic. In logic, which he regarded not as a part of philosophy but as a preparatory discipline, he stood on Plato's shoulders to a greater extent than is sometimes appreciated. Yet here, as elsewhere, his genius for system and order took him far beyond the mere rearrangement of other men's ideas, and he is entitled to his place as the founder of formal logic and scientific method. His great merit was to carry his distinction of form and matter into the sphere of language and argument. To exhibit the formal aspect of arguments necessitates the use of symbols or variables, and the introduction of variables is one of his best achievements, and contains the germ of modern symbolic logic. Both the Stoics in the next century and the medieval Scholastics made further logical discoveries, but so great was the authority of Aristotle that their importance passed unnoticed until comparatively recently. His reduction of all argument to the form of the categorical syllogism was accepted until the 19th century, and it is only in the last hundred years or so that Aristotelian logic has been seen to be, not erroneous, but inadequate to cover all the forms of argument which are in common use.

ATHENS. For the earliest history of Athens we must rely on much later authors, the most reliable being Thucydides of the 5th century B.C. and Aristotle of the 4th. The monarchic period, which probably dates back to Mycenaean times in the 2d millennium B.C., is adorned with the names of many legendary kings, beginning with Cecrops. The many scattered settlements in Attica, politically independent of Athens, were gradually amalgamated into a loose alliance (synoikismos) by the hero-king, Theseus. Under these kings were the noble clans, the Eupatrids, and the populace, who belonged to four Ionian tribes composed of phratries (brotherhoods); judicial authority was vested in the Areopagus, the equivalent of the Homeric Council of Elders.

In the 8th century B.C. the office of archon (or leader) was instituted. The king (basileus) was reduced to *archon basileus*, and put in charge of traditional religious ordinances. With the addition of the *archon polemarchos* (military leader) and *archon eponymos* (civil leader) the executive and judicial duties of the monarch were absorbed. In the early 7th century B.C. the number of archons was increased to nine, and their term shortened to one year. During this period aristocracy of birth began to give way to that of wealth. The state was organized into property-classes based on financial ability to supply military equipment: the highest were the knights (mounted cavalry), the second the hoplites (heavy-armed infantry), the third the thetes (light-armed foot soldiers).

As Athenian affairs grew more complex, Draco undertook in 621 B.C. to codify the laws, which had previously been unwritten and subject to the arbitrary interpretation and administration of the powerful. Though the code was harsh, it at least enabled people to know what kind of legal judgment to expect and eliminated the tendency to inconsistency and oligarchical bias.

The plight of debt-ridden and half-enslaved farmers who, for the most part, depended on a meager grain crop became so acute under the aristocracy of wealth that Solon was given power (c.594 B.C.) to relieve it. One of his successful financial measures to enable repayment of commercial debts was the devaluation of the coinage; he also forbade in future the pledge of one's person as security, and encouraged specialization in olive and viticulture as well suited to Attic soil. He instituted the Council of the Four Hundred, 100 from each tribe, and improved the political position of the thetes, the lowest class of property-holders, by allowing them to participate in the assembly and serve as jurors. Continued dissatisfaction among the populace and strife among the Eupatrids led in 560 B.C. to the assumption of power by Pisistratus, a benevolent despot whose prosperous rule ended after his death with the assassination of one son, Hipparchus (514 B.C.), and the expulsion of the other, Hippias (510 B.C.). A political reorganization was demanded, and Cleisthenes redistributed the citizens into ten new tribes, based on an ingenious geographical arrangement rather than on heredity, thus making Solon's Council of Four Hundred a Council of Five Hundred; according to tradition he also invented the useful practice of ostracism, a method of banishing "dangerous" citizens by popular vote. With Cleisthenes we have the real beginning of Athenian democracy.

Increasing prosperity among the Greek States, particularly in Asia Minor, brought them into conflict with the Persian Empire. After the defeat of the Ionian cities (494), which had revolted against Persia, Athens began a long struggle in which she successively defeated Persia at Marathon (490 B.C.) and Salamis (480 B.C.), although the city of Athens itself was sacked. The naval victory at Salamis was achieved by Themistocles' clever interpretation of the Delphic Oracle's advice to the Athenians to rely on their "wooden walls" as meaning that the navy should be strengthened and the Persians be met at sea rather than on land. The final defeat of the Persians was, however, on land—at Plataea in 479 B.C. As a result of his continued demands for arms and support against Persia, Themistocles was ostracized in 471 B.C. His successor, Cimon, urged Athens to ally with Sparta against Persia, but he too suffered ostracism in 461.

Pericles followed as political leader, and it is to him that we can attribute the conversion of the Delian League, first formed in 477 B.C. as a protective alliance against the Persians, into an Athenian Empire. Though Athens realized an almost perfect democracy at home, her aggressive championship of democratic governments throughout

J. L. Hamar—Frederic Lewis

The Tower of the Winds was built about 40 B.C. Called the Clock of Andronikos, for its designer, it was equipped with a water clock, a weather vane, and numerous sundials. The octagonal shape derives from the "eight winds," or major compass points.

Greece led to an imperialism that approached tyranny. The treasury of the league was removed to Athens in 454, and the contributions of member-states, much to their annoyance, were largely devoted to a spectacular building program on the Acropolis and to other improvements at Athens. It was during this era, often called the "Golden Age of Pericles," that Greek literature and art reached its peak, with the tragedians Aeschylus, Sophocles, and Euripides, the comic poet Aristophanes, the historians Herodotus and Thucydides, the philosopher Socrates, the architects Ictinus and Callicrates, and the sculptor Phidias.

Athenian power, however, was soon to dwindle in the protracted struggle with Sparta for hegemony in Greece, starting as early as the Athenian defeat at Coronea in 447 B.C. The Peloponnesian War began on a grand scale in 431 B.C., and Athenian suffering from Spartan attack was greatly increased by the Great Plague (430 B.C.) in which Pericles died. The fortunes of war fell alternately to Athens and Sparta until the ill-fated Peace of Nicias brought hostilities to a temporary halt. Alcibiades, the brilliant commander and adopted son of Pericles, probably neither hurt nor helped Athens by his alternate victories and defeats, defections and returns. Athens was finally crushed by Sparta at Aegospotamos in 405 B.C. and never again regained political supremacy, though she re-

mained the cultural leader of Greece throughout antiquity.

Anger over the defeat caused the overthrow of the democratic government by the Thirty, who carried on a one-year tyranny until ousted by the prodemocratic Thrasybulus in 403 B.C.

The 4th century B.C. saw an economic revival and produced the philosophers Plato and Aristotle, the historian Xenophon, the sculptor Praxiteles, and the orators Lysias, Isaeus, and Isocrates. Although siding with one state against another during the first half of the 4th century, Athens was at last aroused to the common danger posed by the rise of Macedon. The great debates on this subject between Aeschines and Demosthenes were settled by the defeat of Athens at the battle of Chaeronea in 338 B.C. Immediately after, however, Lycurgus managed to restore Athens to some semblance of independence and prosperity.

The 3d century B.C. found Athens the home of the playwright Menander, the scientist and satirist Theophrastus, and the center, if not the birthplace, of Stoicism and Epicureanism. In the larger and more cosmopolitan world that followed the death of Alexander the Great, Athens was embroiled in the feuds of his successors and inevitably came into conflict with Rome. First subjugated in 146 B.C., she was thoroughly destroyed by Sulla for siding with Mithridates in 86 B.C. Under Imperial Rome Athens enjoyed an honorable place, and many a well-born Roman was proud to have studied there. The disorders in the Roman Empire in the 3d century A.D. permitted Athens to be overrun by the barbarian Herulians in 267 A.D., and the city gradually sank into obscurity. Although the Apostle Paul had preached from the Areopagus in 51 A.D., the city's pagan glory was not completely extinguished until the conversion of the temples into Christian churches, and the closing of the Schools of Philosophy by the Edict of Justinian in 529 A.D.

ATTALIDS [ăt'ə-lĭdz], a Hellenistic dynasty which ruled the kingdom of Pergamum (Pergamon) in western Asia Minor. Founded in 263 B.C. by Eumenes, the local Seleucid governor, its rise in prestige and prosperity began with **Attalus I Soter** (reigned 241–197 B.C.). His votive statuary, including the "Dying Gaul," commemorated his victories over the Gauls and Galatians. He set two precedents firmly adhered to by his successors: a staunch pro-Roman policy and extensive support of literature, philosophy, and the arts. **Eumenes II,** eldest son of Attalus I, reigned from 197–159 B.C. He expanded Pergamene territory by his participation in the Roman victory over Antiochus at Magnesia (189 B.C.), for which the Romans rewarded him with Chersonese (Thrace), Mysia, Lydia, and Phrygia. He established a famous library at Pergamum. **Attalus II Philadelphus** (reigned 159–138 B.C.), brother of Eumenes II, continued his predecessors' policies. He gave Athens a stoa (portico), which stands reconstructed amid the ruins of the Agora. **Attalus III Philometer** (reigned 138–133 B.C.), nephew of Attalus II, wrote treatises on agriculture (used by Pliny) and botany. He willed his kingdom to the Romans, giving them control of most of Asia Minor and a foothold for further conquest in the East.

ATTICA [ăt'ĭ-kə], a mountainous peninsula in southeastern Greece, approximately 1,300 sq. mi. in area, jutting out into the Aegean Sea and bounded on the north by Boeotia and the Megarid. Named, according to legend, after Atthis, daughter of an early local king, Attica was inhabited as early as the Neolithic period. During the Bronze Age, Athens developed as the chief city. Cut off from central Greece by Mounts Cithaeron and Parnes, Attica's Ionian population was spared the Dorian invasion of the late 12th century B.C. By the 7th century all Attica had been incorporated into the Athenian city-state, an achievement attributed to Theseus. After 594 B.C., its thin soil was devoted mainly to the cultivation of olives and grapes, although wheat continued to be grown. The chief port is Piraeus although there were also good ports at Marathon and Phaleron. The district had marble and silver, fine clay for pottery, and was famous for the honey from Mt. Hymettus. The Attic dialect was considered the most highly cultivated of Greek dialects.

BOEOTIA [bē-ō'shə], ancient province of central Greece, bounded by Attica, Megaris, and the Corinthian Gulf on the south, by Phocis on the northwest, Locris on the north, and the Straits of Euboea on the east. Except for the southerly mountains—Parnes and Cithaeron—and the Copaic Basin, then a swamp, Boeotia was mostly farming country. Boeotians were regarded by Athenians as boorish rustics, though Hesiod, Pindar, and Plutarch were all natives of Boeotia. Excavations show extensive habitation in Neolithic times and in the Bronze Age (now associated with the legendary Minyans), and the Homeric Catalogue of Ships cites 29 Boeotian cities; their dialect suggests that the historical Boeotians were migrants from Thessaly. The powerful Boeotian League was administered by elected boeotarchs, or military magistrates. Thebes dominated the league with two boeotarchs to the other cities, one each. Other important cities were Chaeronea, Coronea, Orchomenus, Plataea, Tanagra, and Thespiae. Their common sanctuary was the temple of Itonian Athena at Coronea where the Pan-Boeotian Games were held. Always intensely hostile to Athens, Thebes aided the invading Persians and also supported Sparta against Athens in the Peloponnesian War. In the 4th century the Boeotian League under Epaminondas expelled the Spartans from central Greece (Battle of Leuctra, 371 B.C.) and several times invaded the Peloponnesus. After the defeat of Chaeronea in 338 B.C. Boeotia never again recovered its prosperity. The league soon dwindled and was finally dissolved with the rise of Rome in the mid-2d century B.C.

BOULE [bōōl], the political council in ancient Greek city-states. It gave advice (boulê) to the supreme legislative authority, whether the system of government was monarchic, aristocratic, or democratic. In Homeric times the heads of noble families formed a council to consult with the king. Its authority reflects a stage when monarchy was yielding to aristocracy and the king was not much more than "first among equals."

In states with aristocratic or oligarchic governments membership in the council depended on noble birth or wealth or both. The Athenian council of the Areopagus (q.v.) represents this stage. The aristocratic councils were usually quite limited in total membership, the term of office was usually indefinite, the councilors served without pay and were likely (or required) to be elderly men.

Councils in states with democratic constitutions were quite different in qualifications for membership, tenure, size, and to some extent in function. Any citizen in good standing was normally eligible, appointment or election was for a limited time, the number of councilors was large, the council acted as a committee of the popular assembly, and they were paid for their services (at least in Athens from Pericles' time). The Athenian council of 400 instituted by Solon (q.v.) had 100 representatives from each of the four original tribes. Its number was increased to 500 by Cleisthenes (q.v.), with 50 members chosen annually by lot from each of the 10 new tribes. The 50 councilors from the same tribe made up a *prytany* and each *prytany* sat in continuous session for one-tenth of the year. The president of the current *prytany* was also president of the *ecclesia* or assembly. The council prepared all business and made recommendations for consideration in the assembly. It also had major administrative and judicial responsibilities. Council meetings were usually held in a special council house (*bouleuterion*) and were normally open to the public.

CITY-STATE, term used to describe an independent urban community governing itself and, usually, surrounding rural lands. City-states began with civilization, and their contribution to its progress was enormous. The oldest city-states of which we are well informed grew up in the ancient Near East—in Sumeria, the region of lower Mesopotamia between the Tigris and Euphrates rivers—sometime between 4000 and 3000 B.C. These cities (we know of some 14, the most famous being Ur) were founded originally by Sumerian and later Semitic immigrants to the fertile Mesopotamian plain and were able to maintain their independence for about 1,000 years. Each city-state was ruled by a god and by the god's special servants, priests, and kings. The god owned the surrounding agricultural lands, made highly productive by a complicated system of irrigation. A huge temple and its tower (ziggurat) characteristically dominated the landscape. Some of these cities had over 20,000 inhabitants, and were centers of long-distance trade, which gave them a strongly cosmopolitan character. The administration of lands, the maintenance of the complex irrigation system, and the active trade provided effective incentives for the development and use of written records (cuneiform tablets) and for the use of standardized weights and measures and mathematical calculations. Literature and art also developed in the wealthy, cosmopolitan atmosphere.

Greece and Rome. The second great center of city-state civilization was Greece. The Greek peninsula, geographically divided into many semi-isolated areas by hills and sea inlets, gave ample opportunity for small, independent urban communities to grow up (c.1000–500 B.C.). These city-states, usually including the surrounding agricultural villages, were free to experiment with a great variety of political constitutions. Athens, for example, developed the model democracy. Not surprisingly, the variety of words used today to describe governments—democracy, oligarchy, aristocracy, tyranny—are not only largely Greek in derivation, but actually characterized various city-state constitutions. Intense civic pride and the rivalry among these independent cities also served as strong stimuli to cultural development, as each city tried to outdo the others in the beauty of its temples and the skill of its athletes and artists. Still, while each Greek city-state was free to experiment, each continued to share a common culture and each could easily know of and adopt the successes of a neighbor. Diversity, rivalry, and freedom to experiment, superimposed upon a fundamental cultural unity, helped the ancient Greek city-states to develop one of the most brilliant of world civilizations.

COMEDY [kŏm′ə-dē], major dramatic form. Along with tragedy and the satiric play (burlesque drama with a chorus of satyrs), comedy was one of three such forms recognized in the Greek theater. The term "comedy" derives from the Greek words *kōmos* (a ritualistic revel concerned either with scurrilous fertility celebrations or with a kind of masquerade in which the participants wore animal masks and costumes) and *ōidē* (a song).

Evolution of types. Unquestionably the form known as Old Comedy, represented in the plays of Aristophanes, was based primarily upon such revels, but it also incorporated other elements from a species of burlesque performances, possibly improvised, that is known to have existed at an early date in Sparta and elsewhere. In the typical Old Comedy a fantastic story is introduced, followed by a debate conducted largely through the chorus, with a final parabasis, or "coming forward," of the chorus, which then directly addresses the audience. The stories themselves were all extravagant and impossibly imaginative—the building of a city-state in the skies (*The Birds*), a sex strike designed to stop a war (*Lysistrata*), the descent of Dionysus, dressed as Hercules, to the nether regions (*The Frogs*)—but always there was clear satiric pertinence to existing political problems, together with barbs directed at living persons. This comedy was like a more vigorous, bawdy, and more lyrical Gilbert and Sullivan opera.

The Old Comedy gave way, toward the close of Aristophanes' lifetime, to Middle Comedy, less lyrical, more narrative in style, and although still political, less personally satiric. In turn it gave way to the New Comedy, of which Menander was the chief exponent; the chorus had disappeared, the plots became romantic stories, and intrigue was highly developed. Although in Roman times the plays of Plautus often betray a debased kind of Aristophanic fantasy, it was this New Comedy, imitated and polished by Terence, which became the prime model for the early modern drama in the 16th and 17th centuries.

CORINTH [kôr′ĭnth] (Gr. **KÓRINTHOS**), ancient Greek city on the Isthmus of Corinth, controlling from its harbors on the Corinthian and Saronic gulfs the trade routes from the Peloponnesus to central Greece, and from Italy to Greece and the East. The abundant water and fertile plain of Corinth attracted settlers as early as Neolithic times, and it was continually inhabited throughout the Bronze Age, particularly on the lower slopes of the Acrocorinth, its 1,900-ft.-high citadel, until laid waste around 1000 B.C., presumably by the Dorians. After the Dorian conquest it was subject to Argos, then ruled in the 8th century B.C. by a local oligarchy, the Bacchiads, who founded the important colonies of Corcyra and Syracuse in 734. Under the benevolent Tyrant Cypselus (reigned c.657–625), who had overcome the aristocracy, and his son Periander (reigned 625–585), Corinth reached a peak of mercantile prosperity, and became famous for its love of luxury and pleasure. It took little part in the Persian Wars of the early 5th century B.C., and rapidly lost ground to Athens as a naval power, even losing control of its own colonies. Corinth's dispute with Athens over Potidaea and its war with Corcyra precipitated the disastrous Peloponnesian War in 431, in which it sided with Sparta. It abandoned Sparta in 395, however, allying with Athens in the Corinthian War (395–387). Subjected to Philip with the rest of Greece, the city received a Macedonian garrison in 335. Liberated by Aratus in 243 and incorporated into the Achaean League, Corinth became the seat of the league in 196. Its revived wealth and political importance

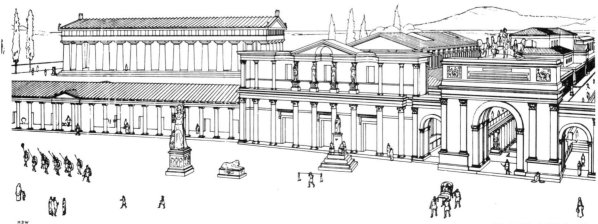

Excavations and discoveries at Corinth, Greece, by the American School of Classical Studies provide the basis for this line drawing. Scene is of the north side of the market place during the period of Roman rule.

American School of Classical Studies, Athens

Ruins of the Temple of Apollo.

American School of Classical Studies, Athens

aroused the jealousy and cupidity of Rome, and led finally to its merciless destruction by Mummius in 146. A new city was built and repopulated by order of Julius Caesar in 44 B.C.; Corinth became the capital of the Roman province of Achaea, and recovered much of its ancient prosperity. St. Paul preached there in 51–52 A.D., later writing his Epistles to the Corinthians. In the same period Nero attempted to cut a canal across the Corinthian Isthmus, a feat not completed until modern times. Sacked by the barbarian Heruli in 267 and by Alaric in 395, Corinth was periodically ravaged until, in the 6th century A.D., the city retired to its acropolis, Acrocorinth. It was successively occupied by Byzantines, Crusaders, Venetians, and Turks, until it again became Greek (1822) in the War of Independence. The modern town, 3 mi. northeast of ancient Corinth, dates from 1858, when Old Corinth was destroyed by an earthquake. The city was again destroyed by an earthquake in 1928.

The lower city is dominated today, as in antiquity, by the Doric temple of Apollo of the 6th century B.C., but the main city, as excavated by the American School of Classical Studies, is almost entirely Roman, testifying to the thoroughness of the Roman destruction. The city walls, connecting Corinth with its harbor Lechaeum, have been traced; and an impressive agora with shops and stoas, the great fountains of Pirene and Glauke, a theater, and a sanctuary of Asclepius have been uncovered. Excavated outside the walls are a potters' quarter, the north cemetery, and a tile factory. Besides being famed for its painted pottery, terracottas, and bronzes, which were widely exported, classical Corinth was known for its coinage (the head of Athena in Corinthian helmet on one side, the winged Pegasus on the other). There are medieval remains, including an imposing Crusader castle, on the Acrocorinth. Pop., 17,728.

CUMAE [kū′mē], ancient Greek city of Italy, in Campania, about 10 mi. west of Naples. Founded by Euboean Chalcis, perhaps with Cyme, about 740 B.C., it was the first Greek colony in Italy. As the most northerly Greek colony, it was the gateway for Greek trade to the north, and transmitted Greek letters and arts to the Romans and Etruscans. Cumae itself founded other colonies, notably Zancle (Messina) and Neapolis (Naples), the latter of which robbed it of much of its trade. In 474 B.C., aided by Syracuse, Cumae defeated the Etruscans and Umbrians, but was conquered by the Samnites c.420 and by the Romans c.340; the city then became a Roman *municipium*, and rapidly fell into decline. It was destroyed by the Saracens in the 9th century A.D. and again by Naples in 1207. The remains of ancient Cumae are impressive: on the Acropolis, which preserves traces of 5th-century walls, are temples of Apollo and of Zeus, both later converted to Christian churches; a necropolis containing tombs from pre-Hellenic to Imperial times has been excavated; and the celebrated cavern of the Cumaean Sibyl, a long trapezoidal tunnel illuminated by lateral vents, made famous by Vergil, has been completely cleared.

CYRENE [sī-rē′nē], ancient Greek city, located in northeast Libya, 8 mi (13 km) from Apollonia. It was the chief city of the Kingdom of Cyrenaica. An important stopover for trade between Egypt and Carthage, it exported silphium (a medicinal herb), grain, wool, dates, and fine horses. It was founded by Dorians from Thera and Crete (c.631 B.C.) whose leader took the name Battus ("king" in Libyan), and initiated the Battiad Dynasty which ruled Cyrene for eight generations. Colonists from the Peloponnesus arrived in the following century when Cyrene alternately battled against and was allied with Egypt. In 525 Cyrene submitted to Cambyses. Around 450 a revolution established a democracy. In 331 Cyrene was allied with Alexander of Macedon, becoming part of Egypt under his successor Ptolemy I. It was bequeathed to Rome in 96 B.C. and combined with Crete to form one province. The city was a center of Greek learning and culture, and the birthplace of Callimachus, Carneades, Aristippus, and Eratosthenes. Excavations, first by Americans, then by Italians, have uncovered a temple of Apollo of the late 7th century B.C., which was rebuilt in the 4th century, and again in the 2d century A.D. in Roman style. There is also a large temple of Zeus, with a peristyle 8 by 17 columns, dating from about 540 B.C., in which fragments of a copy of the Zeus of Phidias at Olympia were found.

DELIAN [dē′lē-ən] **LEAGUE**, ancient confederacy of free maritime Greek states formed in 478 B.C. Its initial purpose was to suppress piracy, encourage sea-borne commerce, and guard against further attacks from Persia; but successful actions by league fleets soon challenged Persian control of Greek states along the Asia Minor seaboard. The league synod met at the shrine of Apollo on Delos under the presidency of Athens. Each member had a single vote, but an Athenian admiral was in charge of the allied fleet. Support quotas in ships or money were originally fixed by the Athenian statesman Aristides, whose popularity with the allies stimulated the formation and early success of the league. The first annual assessment was set at 460 talents, to be paid to the treasury on Delos. Athenian preponderance in prestige and resources posed a problem of balance from the first.

With the sweeping successes of the fleet under Cimon,

immediate danger of Persian attack soon passed, and the intensely individualistic tradition of Greek politics began to reassert itself. States which objected to providing fleet quotas could alternately convert to monetary contributions, but this merely increased the imbalance by indirectly subsidizing the Athenian fleet. Outright refusal by Naxos (c.467 B.C.) to continue any support was the crucial challenge. The league decision, no doubt under strong Athenian pressure, was to enforce allegiance. When Thasos attempted secession, she also was subdued. Right or wrong, this policy seemed irreconcilable with the concept of an alliance of free and equal states. The league gradually evolved into an Athenian empire, symbolized by the transfer of the treasury to Athens in 454 B.C. Athens' defeat in the Peloponnesian War ended the empire.

DELOS [dē′lŏs], Greek island in the Aegean Sea, smallest of the Cyclades, with an area of 2 sq. mi. It was the legendary birthplace of Artemis and Apollo and site of the great Ionic sanctuary of Apollo. From earliest times it was a religious center for the Island Amphictyony, first protected by Naxos, then dominated by Athens. The Persians respected the sanctity of the island in 490 B.C., and in 477 it became the center of the Athenian maritime confederacy, the Delian League, whose treasury was removed to Athens in 454 B.C. Unwillingly subject to Athens thereafter, Delos regained autonomy in 314 and prospered remarkably, especially when, after Rome declared it a free port in 166, it became the center of the slave trade. Mithridates of Pontus sacked the island in 88 B.C., and Delos became increasingly both a prey and stronghold for pirates, until in the 2d century A.D. only the guardians of the sanctuary remained. French excavations since 1873 have uncovered the imposing sanctuary, extensive market places, temples, the Lion Terrace, well-preserved Hellenistic houses with fine mosaic floors, and many historically important inscriptions.

DELPHI [dĕl′fī], ancient Greek sanctuary in central Phocis on the south slopes of Mount Parnassus, 2,000 ft. above the Gulf of Corinth, renowned for its oracle of Apollo. It was a sacred spot as early as 1600 B.C. and was considered the center of the earth. In legend, Apollo seized the oracle from the earth-goddess Gaea, slew her dragon Python, and later battled with Heracles over the prophetic tripod. In the inner sanctum of the temple a priestess (Pythia) gave incoherent responses (once thought to have been inspired by fumes emanating from a crevasse), which were interpreted by temple officials in verse. The pronouncements on religion, politics, education, literature, art, colonization, and commerce wielded enormous influence throughout the ancient world. Delphi early accepted the cult of Dionysus, and in later classical times during three winter months Dionysus was believed to be in charge of the shrine. Although Delphi was theoretically the independent center of a religious league, controlled by the Amphictyons (representatives of the member states), in practice, the oracle often sided with one state against another.

During the Persian invasion of 490–479 B.C., Delphi fearfully supported the Persians, yet Greek victory thank-

offerings for the defeat of the Persians at Marathon and Salamis were dedicated there. Embroiled later in Greek internecine wars, the shrine nevertheless received the trophies of the conflicting states. Delphi itself took arms in three Sacred Wars—the first (600–590 B.C.) against neighboring Crisa; the second (355–345 B.C.) when the Phocians seized and fortified the sanctuary; and the third (339–338 B.C.), which precipitated the onslaught of Philip of Macedon, who restored the Amphictyonic administration.

Sacked by Rome in 86 B.C., and plundered by the earlier Roman emperors, in later imperial times Delphi flourished until despoiled by Christian emperors for the beautification of Constantinople. The oracle finally fell silent under the Edict of Theodosius in 390 A.D.

French excavations at Delphi begun in 1892 have revealed a considerable Mycenaean settlement with religious offerings. From the late 8th and 7th centuries B.C., there are substantial dedications—first bronze caldrons and tripods, later statues. The ancient sanctuary was filled with splendid offerings of kings and princes and entire city-states, but ancient depredations have left only a fraction. Nero alone is said to have carried off 500 statues. The bronze "Charioteer" and the "Dancing Women of the Acanthus Column" are some of the finest preserved works found.

Within the walled sacred precinct (temenos) above the ancient town are the Sacred Way, a large number of state treasuries which housed offerings, including the Siphnian Treasury, with its archaic Caryatids, and the Athenian Treasury, its walls inscribed with words and music for hymns to Apollo, and a theater. In the center is the tem-

The theater and the temple of Apollo, at the ancient Greek sanctuary of Delphi, site of the famous Delphic oracle.

Alison Fran

ple of Apollo itself, now poorly preserved. It burned down in 548 B.C.; was rebuilt by the Alcmaeonidae in the late 6th century; was destroyed by earthquake in 373 B.C. and gradually rebuilt. As excavated, it contains remnants of all its periods, including sculptural fragments from the late 6th-century B.C. temple. Outside the sacred enclosure lie the sanctuary of Athena Pronaia with a round marble building, the stadium where the Pythian Games were held, and the celebrated Castalian Spring.

DEMOSTHENES [dĭ-mŏs′thə-nēz] (384–322 B.C.), most celebrated orator of antiquity and leader of Athenian opposition to Macedon. In order to recover property embezzled by his guardians, Demosthenes, on coming of age, subjected himself to a rigorous study of rhetoric and law, perhaps under the direction of Isaeus. The series of suits which he prosecuted on his own behalf secured him a livelihood as a writer of speeches for others, many of which survive. Beginning with *Against Androtion* (355 B.C.), he was asked to write speeches in cases of political significance, and with *Against Leptines* (354) he first personally undertook a political prosecution. His earliest deliberative speech, *On the Symmories* (354), was followed by a great series including the four *Philippics* and the three *Olynthiacs* (349). Demosthenes at first supported the pacifist policy of Eubulus (c.405–330). However, he became increasingly alarmed at the growing strength of Philip II of Macedon and tried to arouse his fellow citizens to the threat to their liberty, urging them to strengthen their forces and seek alliances, even with traditionally hostile Thebes. Despite his efforts the Greeks were decisively defeated at the battle of Chaeronea in 338 B.C.

In *On the Embassy* (344), Demosthenes had accused the rival orator and politician Aeschines of having been bribed by Philip to conclude a dishonorable peace, thus initiating a life-long political enmity. His greatest speech, *On the Crown* (330), was delivered in defense of his right to a crown awarded for his services to Athens. Aeschines questioned the legality of the award and in an extant speech attacked Demosthenes' whole career. The latter replied with a lengthy justification of his actions and won an overwhelming victory. The end of his life was clouded by charges of receiving bribes from Alexander's treasurer Harpalus. Unable to pay a heavy fine, he went into exile, but was recalled after Alexander's death, in 322 B.C. With the defeat of the Greeks by Antipater in the ensuing Lamian War (322), he fled to the island of Calauria and there drank the poison hidden in his pen.

Demosthenes was a patriot who refused to believe that Athens' day was past. Though he gained the glory of a martyr, he unnecessarily embittered political change and was led by expediency and emotion to irresponsibility and excess. His success was as an orator rather than as a statesman. In his two constant themes—the greatness of Athenian traditions and the need for action to preserve them—he succeeded more than any other Greek in imparting to the spoken word a fiery earnestness. He was scrupulous in the details of style; for example, he avoided using more than three short syllables in succession. Though he shows some influence of the rhetorician Isocrates, he had a much greater variety of style at his command than any other Greek orator. The basis of his power was in thought

Vatican Museum and Galleries

"Demosthenes," Athenian orator and patriot. This statue is believed to be a Roman copy of a Greek original by Polyeuctus.

rather than words. His influence on other orators, especially on Cicero, has always been great.

DIONYSIA [dī-ə-nĭs′ē-ə], ancient Greek festivals celebrated in honor of the god Dionysus. In Athens there were, besides the Anthesteria, three distinct festivals called the Dionysia. (1) The Rural Dionysia was celebrated in the local townships of Attica in the month Poseideon (Dec.-Jan.). The rites comprised a phallic procession, a sacrifice, and a *komos*, or masked revel, out of which Athenian comedy probably developed. (2) The Epilenaea Dionysia, or Lenaea, was held a month later in Athens. The name (from *lenai*, "madwoman") suggests that the rites were emotional, concerned with Dionysus as the god of ecstasy. (3) The City Dionysia, a relatively late creation (6th century B.C.), was held in spring. The five-day celebration included, on a grander scale, the elements of the ancient rural festival, but is chiefly famous as the major occasion for dramatic performances. Both tragedy and comedy arose in Athens as part of the cult of Dionysus and were always regarded not as mere entertainment, but as religious ceremonies in his honor. Plays were also presented at the Lenaea, and at least in later times at the Rural Dionysia as well.

DIONYSUS [dī-ə-nī′səs], also known as Bacchus, Greek god of fertility and vegetation, especially of the vine. His Roman name was Liber. Until recently scholars believed that he was originally Thracian, but it now seems probable that he was an early Greek deity. The historic Dionysus, however, was a composite of various origins—Greek, Cretan, Thracian, and Anatolian. His worship, accompanied by wine drinking, was often ecstatic and orgiastic. The great Greek dramas were presented at the Dionysiac

Dionysus with Satyrs and maenads as depicted on a Greek vase (5th century B.C.). (THE METROPOLITAN MUSEUM OF ART, ROGERS FUND, 1907)

festivals of Athens. He also had important cults in Thebes and Delphi, and, in fact, was worshiped nearly everywhere. His favorite plants were the grapevine and ivy; his sacred animals, whose shapes he could assume, the goat, bull, snake, panther, and lion.

DORIANS [dôr′ē-ənz], one of the four traditional ethnic divisions of the Greeks. In historical times the most important communities of the Peloponnesus, the southern Aegean Sea, and the south coast of Asia Minor were considered Dorian settlements. These included Megara, Corinth and her many colonies, Argos, Sparta, Aegina, Melos, Thera, Halicarnassus, and many cities of Crete. The inhabitants of these communities were believed to have had a common physical and cultural heritage, and evidence for this kinship was found in their related dialects, political institutions, personality traits, and art forms. There is greater validity in the evidence adduced from the common Doric dialect than from the other similarities, since many Dorian communities differed extensively in matters of tribal divisions, political forms, social outlook, and temperament.

The traditional homeland of the Dorian peoples who

migrated to the Peloponnesus and beyond was a small district in central Greece called Doris, to which they came, probably from farther north, under the leadership of Dorus, son of Hellen, the son of Deucalion. The ancient Greeks associated the movement of these Dorians into southern Greece with the conquest of most of the Peloponnesus by the descendants of Hercules, which they dated about 80 years after the Trojan War. However the "Dorian invasion" seems to have covered a considerable period of time, perhaps 100 years, and occurred in multiple stages over various routes. This movement was probably stimulated by disturbances and pressures farther north. In their search for better and safer territories the Dorians became the agents of destruction of the major sites of the Mycenaean Greeks about 1200 B.C., with the exception of Atticá, which was apparently by-passed.

ECCLESIA [ĭ-klē′zē-ə], the political assembly of ancient Athens and many other Greek city-states. The Athenian ecclesia included all adult male citizens. Summoned regularly by the boule, it met on the Pnyx Hill just west of the Acropolis and Areopagus. Special meetings were also convened here and elsewhere. The ecclesia was the sovereign administrative body, controlling domestic and foreign policy as well as the selection and supervision of all elective officials. It passed decrees, but not laws in the strict sense. An agenda was prepared by the current subcommittee (prytany) of the council, or boule, and all measures were first discussed in, and recommendations made by, the council.

The president of the ecclesia was the citizen to whom the chairmanship of the current prytany had rotated on that particular day. Every member of the ecclesia had the right to debate as well as to vote on proposals. In addition, any member could propose an amendment or call for introduction of a particular topic at a subsequent meeting. Strict provisions existed for challenging proposals which contravened existing laws. A simple majority of those present was enough to carry all ordinary measures. While in principle this system was thoroughly democratic, it had weaknesses. Clever orators could persuade the voters to support unwise and even disastrous measures which took effect immediately, and even in a small state many eligible voters, particularly farmers, could not attend regularly.

EPICUREANISM, philosophy developed by the Greek philosopher Epicurus in the late 4th century B.C. It presented "pleasure" as the highest good, but defined it as merely the absence of pain, a sort of peace of mind and body which could be achieved by avoiding the disturbing situations of life and enjoying the simple satisfactions which even the poorest life affords in some small measure. In the Hellenistic and Roman worlds it was the rival of Stoicism. Frequently today the term "Epicurean" is mistakenly used as a synonym for a gourmet or one who enjoys the satisfaction of luxurious living.

EPICURUS [ĕp-ĭ-kū′rəs] (341–270 B.C.), Athenian philosopher. His doctrine that pleasure was the highest good gave a misleading impression of his tastes and habits. Pleasure to Epicurus meant the absence of mental turmoil, a peace of body and mind, to be attained by avoidance of all external sources of disturbance or anxiety, including public life, marriage, and the begetting of children. "To live hidden" was the ideal. He had a rare gift for friendship, lived with his disciples (including women) a retired and simple life, and died after a long and painful illness, which he bore with exemplary fortitude.

Holding that the worst enemy of spiritual peace was fear of death and of the gods, he adopted as the physical basis for his ethics the materialistic atomism of Democritus. Only sensation is infallible; all other knowledge is inference based on sensation and may be wrong. Objects are constantly giving off films of atoms which affect the sense organs by direct contact. Only atoms and the void are real. Unlike Democritus he endowed single atoms with an arbitary and incalculable power to swerve from their direct course. This accounted for their collisions and entanglements, and also provided an escape from the mechanical necessity governing the Democritean universe. Death brought dispersal of the soul-atoms and cessation of all consciousness.

Gods exist, but are material, like human souls and everything else. Space is infinite and contains innumerable worlds; and the gods dwell in the intervals between the worlds, where they enjoy a life of untroubled blessedness, unconcerned with the actions of men.

His philosophy was a natural product of the postclassical age, when Alexander's conquests had disturbed the compact unity of city-state life and religion. His school continued after his death, but made little change in the doctrine. The most famous preacher of Epicureanism was the Roman poet Lucretius, who infused intense passion into his attack on religion and the afterlife.

EPIDAURUS [ĕp-ĭ-dô'rəs], ancient Greek city-state on the east coast of the Peloponnesus, on the Saronic Gulf. Politically independent throughout the history of ancient Greece, it was famed for its sanctuary of the healing god Asclepius, which lay 5 mi. outside the city. The sacred enclosure, entered by a colonnaded portico of the 4th century B.C., contains a temple of Asclepius, a fine marble tholos (rotunda) designed by the Argive Polyclitus the Younger and built c.360–330 B.C., and other buildings for patients and priests. Beyond are a beautifully preserved theater (also by Polyclitus) with remarkably fine acoustics, a stadium, gymnasium, and other buildings, all excavated by the Greek Archaeological Society. Epidaurus was at the peak of its prosperity in the 4th century B.C., but was still much frequented in Roman times.

ETHICS, the philosophical study of the nature of good, virtue, right, and other morally relevant terms. In Western culture, reflection on the nature of morality began in ancient Greece with the Sophists in the fifth century B.C. The Greeks were aware of the different moral customs of other peoples, as well as of differences existing between the Greek city-states. The awareness of diversity among customs led them to consider whether any moral practices could be regarded as better than others. Is there any possibility of disputing the correctness of opposing moral beliefs? The Sophists generally were moral skeptics because their professional posture precluded an absolutist position.

They were basically teachers who sometimes advertised their talents by claiming that they could teach one to demonstrate the moral acceptability of any cause whatsoever. The teaching of success, in argument or life, was their main aim. One of the philosophical articulations of this aim is that "justice is the interest of the stronger," or, "might equals right."

The Early Greeks

Socrates (470?–399 B.C.) was the chief opponent of the Sophists. His views are presented in the early dialogues of his most famous pupil, Plato (427?–347), who portrays him as a good man in search of truth, regardless of the consequences of his pursuit. Indeed, Socrates was finally condemned to death because many believed his views were corrupting the youth of Athens. He did not have a completely defined conception of virtue, good, justice, or truth. He spent his energies in showing that those who felt they knew the truth about these subjects were really ignorant. He was willing at all times to confess his own ignorance. His wisdom consisted in showing that others were equally ignorant without knowing that they were. His most general belief was that virtue is knowledge.

Plato accepted Socrates' position on the relation of virtue and knowledge, arguing that there really must be entities rightly called "virtue" or "courage," which are distinct from individual acts of virtue or courage. These are the Ideas or Forms of the various moral qualities, and they enjoy a timeless and nonsensible existence. Through training and contemplation, a man may come to grasp the Form of the Good, enabling him actually to *be* good. Plato demonstrates the connection of justice and knowledge in his *Republic*, where he divides the soul into three parts—rational, spiritive, and passional. This division of the soul is patterned after a division of social classes, where a laboring, guardian, and governing class may be distinguished. The just society is one in which each class tends to its own business, everyone benefiting from a division of labor. Such a society must be governed by someone with a knowledge of how the labor should be divided. A state run on the basis of anything other than knowledge of the Good is bound to suffer from some defect. Similarly, a soul governed by passion is destined to suffer. The soul must be organized by reason, and this means that the just man is necessarily acquainted with truth. The great majority cannot attain knowledge and, consequently, cannot be personally just. However, by following their leaders who know the truth, they can be socially just. Plato's argument has been used to justify the subordination of subjects to their rulers.

Plato was not opposed to a life of pleasure, though he did not identify the good life with the pleasurable life. He argued that there were good and bad pleasures, and that the latter were based upon false judgment. The pleasures to be pursued are the pure ones, such as those of sight and hearing. Apprehending beautiful sights and sounds does not involve any admixture of pain. The more intense the pleasure, the greater likelihood of pain. Pleasures are rejected in accordance with their tendency to produce pain.

Aristotle (384–322 B.C.), Plato's most famous pupil, adopted many of his teacher's views, though his philosophical method was different. This difference is best illustrated in his critique of Plato's notion of the Good. Plato had argued that there must be some *one* thing which made all the individual acts which are rightly called "good," good. Aristotle rejected this argument, maintaining that there are many different ways in which the term "good" is used. Some things are good in themselves, others are good as means, and there are variations within these categories. It is wrong to suppose that some one thing makes all things good, though generally the realization of human purposes may be considered good. Building houses, growing food, producing clothing is all good as a means to preserving and protecting man. Happiness is the only thing which is not pursued as a means but solely as an end, though it is difficult to specify exactly what happiness is.

As a keen biological observer, Aristotle was aware of the importance of functional explanation in the understanding of organic activity. Accordingly, he felt that happiness for man must consist in the realization of the function a man has insofar as he is a man, and not some unique individual. Man shares almost every function—life, nutrition, sensation—with plants and animals. Man's unique function is reason, and since every function may be exercised well or badly, it was Aristotle's contention that happiness for man involves the proper exercise of reason. It was his view that it is impossible to define any one mode of activity as virtuous. Courage, for example, is different for every man. The reckless man is easily foolhardy, the cautious man is easily cowardly. Courageousness is a mean between foolhardiness and cowardliness, but it differs for each man. Aristotle's analysis of the distinction between voluntary, involuntary, and nonvoluntary acts still stands as a deft piece of philosophical analysis, having both theoretical and practical import.

Stoics and Epicureans. The last movements in Greek ethics were Stoicism and Epicureanism, both of which manifested themselves as ways of attaining control over one's response to living conditions in the world. While the Stoics felt that a life lived in accord with the processes of nature was good, they also distinguished certain unhealthy aspects of life. They thought that dependence upon the material conditions of life was to be avoided. Through training and discipline, they believed that one could attain spiritual independence. The Epicureans dedicated their lives to the pursuit of pleasure, though in such a fashion as to minimize pain. Desire itself is depreciated because the never-ending cycle of desire, fulfillment, desire, fulfillment, produces a continuously unsettled state. The Epicureans identified pleasure more with tranquillity than with any positive emotional state.

EUCLID [ū′klĭd] (fl. 2d half of the 4th century B.C.), Greek mathematician and author of a famous comprehensive treatise on geometry, the *Elements*. The material in the *Elements*, which effectively displaced all earlier textbooks in the field, was not entirely original with its author, much of it being taken from earlier work by the Pythagoreans, Hippocrates of Chios, Eudoxus, and others. The logical structure, however, is presumably due to Euclid. Although the bulk of the work is made up of geometrical propositions, there are sections on a sort of geometrical algebra

and three books (VII, VIII, and IX) on the theory of numbers, including a proof that the number of primes is infinite, a formula for perfect numbers, and the "Euclidean algorithm" for finding the greatest common divisor of two magnitudes. The *Elements* is divided into 13 "books," the last of which contains the proof that there are five and only five regular solids. The so-called 14th and 15th books are spurious.

EURIPIDES [ū-rĭp′ə-dēz] (c.485–c.406 B.C.), last of the three great Athenian tragic poets, born in Athens of a re-

Culver Pictures, Inc.

Bust of Euripides, in the National Museum, Naples.

spected family. Few details of his life are known; but it seems clear that, unlike Sophocles, he was not prominent in Athenian politics. While his dramatic career was long and successful, he did not equal Aeschylus and Sophocles in public recognition; only about a fifth of his offerings were awarded first prize in the theater. After 408 B.C. he retired from Athens to the patronage of the tyrant of Macedon, possibly in disillusionment over the moral deterioration in Greece caused by the Peloponnesian War. Soon after his death, his tragedies received the highest acclaim. Throughout later antiquity he was the most popular of the tragic poets. Nineteen of his 92 plays survive.

Though he was highly conscious of, and indebted to, the tradition of the tragic art, Euripides restlessly and skillfully experimented with it, even to the point of creating new dramatic forms which cannot be wholly contained within the Aristotelian or modern definitions of tragedy. *Alcestis* (438) and *Ion* are tragi-comic, *Iphigenia in Tauris* almost pure (and superb) melodrama, and *Helen* (412) is both comic and melodramatic. Such works were to become instrumental in shaping later Greek comedy. Yet the poet could masterfully adopt the true tragic tone, as in *Medea* (431), *Herakles*, *Hippolytus* (428), *The Trojan Women* (415), and *Bacchae* (c.405).

Among the innovations associated with Euripidean theater are the elaboration of the the melodic structure of lyrical passages, the use of stylized rhetorical debates inspired by the law courts, and the lessening of obvious relationship of the choral odes to plot. His contemporary critics charged that he often relied on pathos for effect, and lowered the dignity of tragedy by presenting certain of his "heroic" characters in shabby clothing and squalid settings.

This departure from tradition was undoubtedly a calculated element of his repeated attack on the emptiness, for his time, of the values embodied in the old heroic myths from which he drew his plots. A discerning critic, he exposed with wit and irony both the inefficacy of the lingering, outmoded aristocratic standards, and the fraudulent educational methods of the more extreme Sophists of the era. Most of all he deplored unrecognized ascendancy of the irrational, which he felt to be the ruling force in his world. This criticism of his society is adroitly conveyed through realistic psychological analysis of the complex motivations of his heroes and heroines.

Despite his preoccupation with social criticism, Euripides seldom permitted the moralist in him so to intrude into his art as to make it didactic rather than dramatic. Even his lesser plays easily demonstrate that he belongs in the small, select company of the world's great playwrights.

HELLENISM [hĕl′ən-ĭz-əm], in its original sense, refers to the cultural and social ties (language, religion, and education) which united the Greeks (Hellenes) and distinguished them from others. In its immediately postclassical sense it refers to the general dispersion of Greek language and culture throughout the East which followed upon Alexander the Great's conquests. In modern times Hellenism refers generally to Greek culture and ideals and more particularly to the humanistic tradition which is based on the values explicit and implicit in classical Greek literature and art.

As early as the 2d century B.C., sensitive Romans were developing an intense admiration for Greek artistic and literary accomplishments. They tried to emulate the people they had conquered, particularly in such fields as sculpture, architecture, oratory, philosophy, and literature. The earliest postclassical wave of Hellenism occurred in the Renaissance, when Greek culture was rediscovered in Western Europe. Writers and artists were tremendously stimulated by Greek models, but in general used them with much greater freedom and originality than had the Romans. The period of most intense enthusiasm for Hellenism began with the writings of Johann Joachim Winckelmann in the 18th century. The romanticists of the 19th century tended to idealize Greek culture as the perfect expression of human aspiration and achievement. The prevailing notion was that later artists and writers could never fully attain this standard but should concentrate on close imitation of Greek models. The vogue for everything Greek at times approached a cult and spread far beyond the ranks of the arts. Greek political ideas loomed large in the democratic revolutions of the time. Philhellenism showed continued vitality in Western sympathy for the Greek War of Independence in the early 19th century and in the curricula of schools

and colleges. It was powerfully reinforced by the exciting archeological discoveries of Heinrich Schliemann toward the end of the century. Since then, the influence of Hellenism has gradually waned, though it still remains a powerful force in the work of some modern artists, thinkers, and writers. The Greek contribution to the general framework of Western thought, ideals, and values is by now a massive and inescapable fact.

Various features of classical Greek culture contribute to the composite "image" which in Western eyes represents Hellenism. A synopsis is difficult, certain to be oversimplified, and can be misleading, but a few generalizations can perhaps be defended. The qualities which seem to have made the greatest impact fall into two complementary categories. On the one hand we note a pervading curiosity, originality, ingenuity, and rationality; on the other, an instinct for simplicity, moderation, balance, and order. Greek intellectuals refused to accept unquestioningly their ancestors' or neighbors' solutions to problems which concerned man and nature. They insisted that each individual use his own intellect to search for new approaches. The Greek atmosphere discouraged conformity. At the same time Greeks were interested in organizing and channeling this surge of creativity and new knowledge into something that was manageable, comprehensible, and capable of transmission. Greeks tried to approximate in human affairs the admirable "tidiness," regularity, and dependability which they observed and explored in nature.

All through the Greek experience runs this instinct, or at least search, for equilibrium, for a middle way between superstition and atheism, tradition and change, bareness and lushness, freedom and responsibility, imagination and restraint, emotion and reason, law and duty. It is the measure of their inevitable weakness that the Greeks ultimately yielded to extremes, and the most rational among them were the most painfully aware of a proneness to excess.

HELOTS [hĕl′əts, hē′ləts], serfs in ancient Sparta. The name apparently connotes "captives." Helots lived in Laconia in the southeast and Messenia in the southwest of the Peloponnesus. Both groups were ruled by Sparta, the Messenians as a result of a historical conquest, the Laconians perhaps from the time of the Dorian invasion at the end of the Bronze Age. In Laconia the helots at least equaled the Spartans and *perioeci* ("dwellers-around") in numbers. They were not owned outright by their masters but were bound to the land which they cultivated for them, and paid a proportion of the produce to the Spartan landowners. They could be set free only by the state and could not be sold out of the country. In war helots served as light-armed troops. In both peace and war they were often personal servants of the Spartans. Desperate helot rebellions attest to repressive conditions, but Spartan secret police (*krypteia*) kept them under constant supervision and an annual declaration of war against them legalized the harshest measures.

HERMAE [hûr′mē], in ancient Greece, square pillars surmounted by busts of Hermes or other deities and decorated by phallic representations midway up the column.

135

These statues were publicly placed as sacred markers. The blasphemous mutilation of the Hermae in 415 B.C. rocked Athens politically on the eve of the ill-fated Sicilian expedition and led to Alcibiades' banishment.

HERODOTUS [hĭ-rŏd′ə-təs] (c.484–c.425 B.C.), Greek historian, called "the father of history." Born in Halicarnassus in Caria, he left his native city for Samos while still young because of opposition to the tyrant Lygdamis. He may have returned, but at any rate, he soon began to travel. His travels took him to the coast of Asia Minor and the northern Greek islands, to the shores of the Black Sea and Scythia, to Phoenicia, Mesopotamia, and Egypt, where he journeyed up the Nile as far as Elephantine. In 447 he was in Athens, and in 443 he helped found the Athenian colony at Thurii in southern Italy. Very little else is known of his life.

Where and when he wrote his celebrated *Histories* is disputed. The theme of the work is the Persian Wars, though of the nine books which compose it, only the last three give a systematic account of the wars between Greece and Persia. The first six describe the countries subject to or connected with Persia. Herodotus begins by narrating the history of King Croesus of Lydia. Croesus' attempt to find allies among the Greeks in his war against Persia in turn permits the author to digress at length on Athenian and Spartan history. He also describes in this first book the customs and history of the Medes, the Persians, and the Assyrians. The second book deals with the customs and beliefs of the Egyptians. Books III–VI concern Persian history, the peoples of the Persian Empire, and begin the story of Darius' expedition against the Greeks, which ended with the Persian defeat at Marathon. The last three books give a detailed account of Xerxes'

Bust of Herodotus, Greek historian of the 5th century B.C. The bust is in The National Museum, Naples.

preparations for his campaign against Greece, the Greeks' counterpreparations, the Greek victory at Salamis, and the final victory over the Persians at the Battle of Plataea. As a historian Herodotus has many faults. He depended perforce on informants and traditions which may have been unreliable, but he states frankly that he reports what is said, and that he is not obliged to believe it all; nor are his readers. His digressions on geography, ethnology, sociology, and religion, for which he was formerly criticized, are, in fact, of the greatest interest to modern readers, and show Herodotus to have been a pioneer in cultural and social history. Where later historians limited their view to Athens or Greece, Herodotus included all the peoples of the eastern Mediterranean in his investigations, showing high respect for non-Greeks. Though recognizing divine intervention in human history, he was primarily concerned with motivations and actions of his human characters. His *Histories*, written in the Ionic dialect, in a simple, apparently artless and easy style, remains one of the great classics of Greek literature, and Herodotus continues to delight the reader with his charm, wit, innumerable anecdotes, and encyclopedic interests.

HESTIA, in Greek religion, the deified hearth, central figure of household worship and guardian of domestic life. She was daughter of Cronus and Rhea. She was called Vesta by the Romans.

HIPPARCHUS [hĭ-pär′kəs] (c.190–c.125 B.C.), greatest of the ancient Greek astronomers. He was born in Nicaea in Bithynia (now part of Turkey). Little is known of his life, other than that he lived in Rhodes, where he founded an observatory, and in Alexandria, where he made many astronomical observations. Except for a commentary in three books (140 B.C.) on the *Phainomena* of Aratus and Eudoxus, none of Hipparchus' writings have survived. His contributions have been preserved through the writings of Ptolemy, notably in the *Almagest*.

By observing the sun's apparent motion, Hipparchus was able to determine the length of the seasons—the intervals into which the year is divided by the solstices and the equinoxes. He made a table giving the sun's position for every day of the year. He also catalogued and gave coordinates for more than 800 stars, which he divided into the six magnitudes visible to the naked eye. Comparing the positions of these stars with positions given by other observers 150 years before, Hipparchus discovered that their distances from the equinoctial points had changed. He realized that these points had moved, thereby discovering the phenomenon known today as precession of the equinoxes. Because of his improved theories of the motions of the sun and moon, Hipparchus was able to predict solar and lunar eclipses more accurately than did his predecessors. He is credited with discovering the use of trigonometry, which he used in his calculations. Hipparchus also devised the system of longitude and latitude by which points on the earth's surface are located.

HIPPOCRATES [hĭ-pŏk′rə-tēz] (c.460–c.377 B.C.), Greek physician known as "the father of medicine." Hippocrates lived during the Golden Age of Greece and was a contemporary of Pericles, Socrates, Plato, Aristophanes, and other famous figures.

He left a large number of writings, which have been collected and incorporated in the Hippocratic Corpus, a collection of medical treatises, some written by himself, others by his colleagues, pupils, and later disciples. From these writings we form our estimate of Hippocrates and understand why he has been called the father of medicine. Three reasons are clear.

First, he separated medicine from the priests who claimed to be in direct association with the gods who sent disease. At that time epilepsy was called the "sacred disease" since it was supposedly caused by divine displeasure. Hippocrates taught that no disease was sacred and that disease resulted from natural causes. He also drew a clear distinction between physicians and philosophers. Many of the great philosophers of the time were also physicians and maintained that all physicians should be philosophers. Hippocrates answered this argument by saying curtly that the function of the physician is to heal, not to spin philosophical theories.

Secondly, Hippocrates set a high moral standard for the practice of medicine, as stated in the Hippocratic oath and in numerous other places in his writings. He never ceased to stress that a good physician must love his fellow man.

A third outstanding characteristic of Hippocrates was his professional skill. His descriptions of disease are so accurate that we can make a diagnosis today, two thousand years later, by reading the case history. His descriptions of pulmonary tuberculosis, puerperal septicemia, epilepsy,

Bust of Hippocrates, "the father of medicine," in the Capitoline Museum, Rome, is dated from the 3d century B.C. (BETTMANN ARCHIVE)

tetanus, and malaria, with a few minor alterations, could be incorporated in a textbook of medicine.

His method of diagnosis still has a modern ring. First, he took the history, paying special attention to hereditary diseases in the family, the patient's occupation, where he lived, and where he had traveled; next, he inspected the patient and in certain cases practiced percussion (thumping) and auscultation (listening). Then he examined the excreta.

Hippocrates was a skilled surgeon as well as a physician. He understood the treatment of fractures, devised methods of traction in fractures, and understood the complications of skull fractures. The memory of Hippocrates is regularly invoked today in the Hippocratic oath, which is sworn to by modern physicians upon graduation from medical school.

HIPPOCRATES OF CHIOS [kī'ŏs] (fl.450–430 B.C.), Greek mathematician who wrote the first known textbook on geometry. He discovered the quadrature of certain lines and reduced the problem of duplicating the cube to one of finding two mean proportionals between one line segment and another twice as long. He may possibly have invented the method of *reductio ad absurdum* and the method of exhaustion.

HIPPODROME [hĭp'ə-drōm], in ancient Greece, an oval track for chariot and horse racing, with tiered seats for spectators. A barrier down the middle divided the area in two, and the starting-finish end was slanted, so that the holders of inner positions would travel the same distance as those on the outer. The most famous Greek hippodrome was at Olympia. Later famous hippodromes at Constantinople, Antioch, and Alexandria were actually representatives of the Roman *circus*, translated as "hippodrome" in Greek. In modern times the word has been applied to variety theaters such as the old Hippodrome on Sixth Avenue in New York and the London Hippodrome.

HOMER [hō'mər], first and foremost of the Greek poets, author of the two earliest and greatest European epics, the *Iliad* and the *Odyssey*. Nothing is known, or indeed was known in antiquity, of Homer's life, though in ancient times legends about him abounded. He was traditionally said to be blind; and his birthplace was claimed by seven cities, of which Smyrna and Chios are the most likely contenders. The literary type of Greek used, Ionic with Aeolic admixtures, at any rate, points to an Ionian origin. Opinions on Homer's dates vary widely, but today the 8th century B.C. is generally accepted as the most probable.

Until recent years many critics believed that the poems were not composed by a single author. In 1795 Friedrich August Wolf published his *Prolegomena ad Homerum* (Preface to Homer) which advanced the theory that the Homeric epics were not two complete poems, but were put together from separate, shorter lays already in existence. Wolf held that such long poems must have been composed in writing, and that writing was unknown in early Greece. An alternative theory upheld by the historian George Grote(1794–1871) proposed an original author for the epics, but stated that the poems had been so suc-

The Bettmann Archive

The Trojan horse, described in Homer's *Iliad,* from a painting by Henri Motte. Greek soldiers concealed in this wooden horse brought about the destruction of Troy after unsuspecting Trojans pulled it into the city.

An ancient conception of Homer, Greek epic poet.

cessively expanded and altered by various hands as to culminate in a final product twice the length of the original.

These theories have since been generally abandoned in the light of new evidence. It has been shown, for instance, that even in our own day, very long poems have been composed orally by bards unable to read or write. The "oral" poet has in mind a store of decorative epithets, formulas, and set phrases for describing actions which recur, such as fighting, feasting, and the like, and inserts these at appropriate places while continuing to compose his narrative. These characteristics of oral composition may persist even after the introduction of writing.

In view of the careful construction of the *Iliad* and the *Odyssey,* however, it seems probable that Homer actually composed his poems in writing while using oral techniques; and since the decipherment of the Minoan Linear B script by Michael Ventris in 1953, we know that Greek was in use and could be written centuries before the earliest possible date for Homer. Thus, the chief arguments against single authorship have been removed. Inconsistencies and anachronisms in the poems can easily be explained by the fact that the author was writing of an age (Mycenaean) already remote in his own day. Interpolations, additions, and linguistic modifications there certainly were, but these are now thought to be of a minor nature and cannot detract from the underlying unity of plot and action.

The principal question remaining today is whether Homer was the author of both poems. The similarities between the two works, however, outweigh the differences, and such differences as there are can be attributed to the fact that the background of the *Iliad* is war, while that of the *Odyssey* is peace, or simply to the passage of time between the composition of the two.

The personality of the author can only be surmised from the poems. It is probable that Homer composed for an aristocratic audience; certainly his heroes and heroines, his heroic code of morality, and his conception of the gods, are aristocratic; yet in his similes, the images are drawn from the humble daily life of farmers.

It has often been said that Homer's emphasis on the Olympian gods, as opposed to the primitive earth-deities, created classical Greek religion. His heroes were worshiped throughout Greece, and his poetry formed the basis of Greek literature and education. Together the *Iliad* and the *Odyssey* embody the epic prototype. Their rich, complex language, simplicity of style, brilliant characterizations, dramatic narrative, and nobility of thought inspired the emulation of all subsequent classical poetry and even on later ages left a mark so pronounced that their influence on Western culture can hardly be measured.

ILIAD [ĭl′ē-əd], Greek epic by Homer (q.v.), in 24 books of hexameter verse. Centering upon a single episode in the 10th year of the Trojan War—the wrath of Achilles—the poem tells of Achilles' withdrawal from the war in anger over Agamemnon's theft of the captive maid Briseis, whom Achilles had won as a prize of war. Without Achilles' help the war goes badly for the Greeks. It is only after Patroclus, who has borrowed Achilles' armor, is slain in battle by Hector that Achilles rushes into battle and kills Hector to avenge the death of his friend. Thus Achilles is reconciled with the Greeks. The poem ends with the funeral games held in honor of Patroclus and the ransoming of Hector's body by the aged Priam.

IONIA [ī-ō′nē-ə], in antiquity, the coastal strip of western Asia Minor extending from the Hermus River to the Maeander valley, settled by Greeks c.1000 B.C. Recent investigation at Miletus suggests a Minoan settlement of the 2d millennium, and Colophon may have been a Mycenaean foundation. The Greeks who later settled this coast were,

ANCIENT IONIA

finally put down at the battle of Lade in 494. After the Persian defeat at Mycale (479), Ionia was freed from Persian rule; most of the cities joined the Delian League and subsequently became subject-allies of Athens. With the King's Peace in 386, Ionia was returned to Persian rule, under which it remained until its liberation by Alexander of Macedon half a century later.

IONIAN SCHOOL, three Greek philosophers—Thales, Anaximander, and Anaximenes—of the Ionian city Miletus in the 6th century B.C. They were the first Greeks to seek rational, instead of mythical, explanations of the origin and composition of the world, which they supposed to have evolved from a single basic substance.

ISTHMIAN [ĭs′mē-ən], **GAMES,** Greek athletic festival celebrated in honor of Poseidon on the Isthmus of Corinth. Organized in 582 B.C., the games were held every second and fourth year of each Olympiad and were managed by Corinth. From 475 to 200 B.C. the prize was a wreath of wild celery; later it was a crown of either pine or celery. Under Rome the restored Corinth built an elaborate setting for the games, but the moral tone of the festival deteriorated. The Isthmian Games were always popular due to the attractions of nearby Corinth.

KNOSSOS [nŏs′əs], chief city of ancient Crete, located near Candia, about 3 mi. from the north central coast. The first excavations at the site were made by Sir Arthur Evans from 1900 to 1908, and later continued by the British School at Athens. A 25-ft.-deep Neolithic deposit indicates that this period was long and relatively prosperous. The population appears to have been non-Indo-European, with cultural affinities to southwestern Asia Minor. Knossos was an important center of Bronze Age Minoan civilization until the mid-15th century B.C. In about 1450 B.C., after a severe earthquake, Mycenaean Greeks captured Knossos and held it for about 50 years. With the destruction of Minoan power around 1400 B.C., Knossos gradually declined in importance.

The most impressive remains on Crete are those of the great Palace at Knossos, called the Palace of Minos. Because of consolidations of pre-existing buildings of the Early Minoan period, repair of earthquake damage, and successive additions, the palace represents the work of several periods after 2000 B.C. The great complexity of this structure, which covers more than 6 acres, probably accounts for the Greek legend of the "Labyrinth" at Knossos. The palace grew from a series of structures surrounding a very large central court. Workshops, scribal quarters, storerooms, bathrooms, throne rooms, and domestic quarters were added to this core. Generally, the walls of the building were constructed of brick or rubble covered with stucco. The walls of the various rooms and corridors were richly decorated with brilliant frescoes, which took as their themes life in the sea, animals, flowers, and athletic and religious ceremonies. The palace seems to have lacked extensive fortifications.

Near the palace were found the remains of smaller but impressive palaces and villas, presumably belonging to members of the royal family or the nobility. Certain throne rooms, more martial pictorial representation, and fluted columns date to the period of Mycenaean rule of

according to tradition, refugees from the Dorian invasion of the homeland, led by Neleus and Androcles, sons of Codrus, King of Athens. The Ionian tribal names indicate early links with Attica. The immigrants seem to have settled first on the islands of Samos and Chios, spreading thence to the mainland, where they occupied easily defensible sites on promontories and offshore islets. The native Carians and Lydians in the south and east, however, and the earlier-established Aeolian cities to the north confined the Ionians to a narrow coastal area. The climate was favorable, the soil fertile, and the many sheltered harbors invited trade, so the land prospered. It lacked mineral resources, however, and by 700 B.C. the population had so increased that an agricultural economy did not suffice to support it. The Ionians were forced in turn to send out colonists, who settled the coasts of the north Aegean, the Hellespont (Dardanelles), the Propontis (Sea of Marmara), and the Euxine (Black Sea).

Twelve Ionian cities—Phocaea, Clazomenae, Erythrae, Teos, Lebedos, Colophon, Ephesus, Priene, Miletus, and Myus from north to south, plus the two island cities of Chios and Samos—were loosely linked in a religious league centered at the Panionium, a sanctuary of Poseidon Heliconius on Mount Mycale. This Poseidon, the national deity of the Ionians, remained purely Hellenic, uncontaminated by local native cults (unlike Artemis of Ephesus and Apollo at Claros and Branchidae). The league, established by the 8th century, seems to have played no part in politics in the 7th and 6th centuries, which were troubled by Cimmerian raids and which saw the consolidation of the Lydian kingdom. Under Gyges, Alyattes, and Croesus, Lydia attacked and subjugated several of the Ionian cities, including Old Smyrna. The conquests of Cyrus the Great in 546–545 placed all of Ionia under Persian control, and most of the cities were governed by tyrants who favored the Persian King and were supported in power by him. The league served as a rallying point during the Ionian revolt of 499, which was

The throne room in the Palace of Minos at Knossus.
(MARBURG—ART REFERENCE BUREAU)

Knossos. Some of the well-known Mycenaean "bee-hive" tombs and many clay tablets bearing texts written in the Linear B script, first deciphered in 1952 by Michael Ventris, also date to this period.

KOINE [koi-nā'], common language of the Greek world, formed about the 4th century B.C. by a merging of various dialects, with the Attic dialect as a base. By extension, it denotes any common language similarly formed.

LESBOS [lĕz'bŏs], Greek island in the Aegean Sea off the western coast of Turkey, at the entrance to the Gulf of Edremit. This mountainous island has an area of 623 sq. mi., and two large bays cut deep into its southern and eastern sides. The fertile soil of Lesbos produces wheat, olives, fruit, vegetables, and wine. There is sardine and sponge fishing offshore.

Occupied toward the end of the second millennium B.C. by Aeolians who migrated from the Greek mainland, Lesbos developed commercial and cultural contacts with Egypt and Asia Minor. In the late 7th and early 6th centuries B.C., the island became a center of Aeolian culture under such men as the statesman-poet Pittacus (ruled c.585–75 B.C.). The poets Terpander, Alcaeus, and Sappho were Lesbos' great contributions to the development of Greek lyric poetry. The 4th-century philosopher Theophrastus was also born there.

LYSIAS [lĭs'ē-əs] (c.459–c.380 B.C.), Attic orator. Born in Athens, Lysias became a colonist in Thurii, returning in 412 to Athens as a resident alien. There he manufactured shields. His property was confiscated by the Thirty Tyrants in 404 B.C., but he himself escaped to Megara. After the fall of the Thirty, Lysias again returned to Athens and became a professional writer of speeches for others. All or part of 34 speeches survive. As an orator, Lysias is characterized by a clear and elegant style and by great facility in subtly suggesting the character of the litigant who was to deliver the speech.

MAENADS [mē'nădz] (Gr., "madwomen"), also called Bacchae, Bacchantes, Bassarides, and Thyiades, in Greek religion, frenzied women-worshipers of Dionysus, or Bacchus, represented as clothed in animal skins, adorned with wreaths, and carrying the thyrsus. They experienced raging states of sacred madness, during which they tore apart wild animals with their nails and teeth (devouring their flesh raw). Possessed by Dionysus, they tore apart Orpheus and, in Euripides' *Bacchae*, rent the limbs of the sceptical King Pentheus.

MAGNA GRAECIA [grē'shə], ancient section of southern Italy, so called because of its heavy colonization by the city-states of Greece proper, beginning in the 8th century B.C. The earliest and most northerly colony was Cumae, west of modern Naples; other important Greek cities were Neapolis, Paestum, Elea, Rhegium, Locri, Croton, Sybaris (later Thurii), Heraclea, Metapontum, and Tarentum. Their greatest prosperity was from the 7th to the 5th century, when they served as intermediaries who brought the products of Greece and Asia Minor to the less advanced Italian tribes and the Etruscans. Greek influence on the art of these peoples was profound, and it may be that the Etruscans and Latins borrowed their alphabet from the Greek colonies. Disputes among themselves, with the indigenous populace, and with the Greek cities of Sicily (especially powerful Syracuse) contributed to their gradual decline; and involvement in the Punic Wars between Rome and Carthage brought their independence to a close. In the 2d century B.C. most of the Greek cities became *municipia* or *coloniae* of the Roman Republic.

MENANDER [mĭ-năn'dər], (c.342–292 B.C.), Athenian poet, the principal writer of Greek New Comedy. The nephew of Alexis, one of the chief writers of Middle Comedy, Menander studied under Theophrastus, who succeeded Aristotle as head of the Peripatetic school. Menander's plays owe much to Aristotelian philosophy and classical tragedy, particularly Euripides, but they deal realistically with the upper middle-class world of his time. Plays such as *Perikeiromene* (*The Girl Who Gets Her Hair Cut Short; or, The Rape of the Locks*), *Samia* (*The Girl From Samos*), and *Epitrepontes* (*The Arbitrants*) bring about the eventual reconciliation of lovers, or husbands and wives, who have been separated. Menander's plots often turn on the recognition of someone who had been exposed to die as a baby. There is little of the supernatural in the plays, although abstract characters, such as "Misapprehension," may speak the prologues. His plays optimistically affirm an underlying justice in the world. Extremely popular in his time, most of them survive only in fragments. A whole play, *Dyskolos* (*The Misanthrope*), was discovered in 1958. Menander's plays were reworked by the Roman comic writers Plautus and Terence, and through them deeply influenced the subsequent history of comedy.

MYCENAE [mī-sē′nē], city of ancient Greece, located in the northeastern Peloponnesus. In 1876 Heinrich Schliemann began excavations at Mycenae. With his earlier discovery of Troy, the excavations demonstrated that the Homeric epics and related Greek legends of the House of Atreus were based, in part at least, on historical foundations. Subsequent work at the site was carried out by Chrestos Tsountas between 1886 and 1902, A. J. B. Wace from 1920 to 1923, and others.

Mycenae was inhabited as early as the Neolithic period, but nothing is known of its Stone-Age or early Bronze-Age settlers. By the beginning of the Middle Helladic period, c.1900 B.C., a new people, the Greeks, had entered mainland Greece. Mycenae's growth in population, wealth, and importance is reflected in its material remains and in the Homeric tradition that Agamemnon, king of Mycenae, led the Greeks against Troy. Scholars today apply the term "Mycenaean" to the civilization that flourished on the Greek mainland from the 16th to the 12th centuries B.C. During this period, Mycenaean Greece reached the peak of its power. It enjoyed extensive commercial relations with many cities of the eastern Mediterranean and with Egypt, especially after the collapse of Minoan power in about 1400 B.C. Shortly after 1200 B.C. Mycenae and many other Greek cities were violently destroyed by still unidentified invaders. Mycenae was partially reoccupied after this. A temple is known to have been built on its acropolis in the 7th century B.C., and a contingent of Mycenaean troops fought against the Persians at Plataea in 479 B.C. Depopulated by Argos and then revived briefly in the Hellenistic period, Mycenae was finally abandoned in Roman times.

Mycenae consisted of a citadel occupied by the royal palace, and the surrounding countryside occupied by the populace. The early kings were buried in shaft graves grouped in circles and surrounded by a double ring of stone slabs. Out of some of these rock-cut tombs, Schliemann recovered a dazzling array of gold and silver cups and jewelry, bronze-inlaid daggers and swords, stone vessels, and clay objects. Many of them are on display in the National Museum in Athens. Kings of the subsequent period were buried in nine monumental *tholos* or "beehive" tombs. The largest of these round, domed chambers is the so-called Treasury of Atreus and shows the considerable skill of the Mycenaean engineers.

While virtually nothing remains of the earlier palaces, large parts of the late Helladic III palace, built by 1400 B.C., are preserved. A grand staircase leads to an antechamber and then to the throne room. Beyond another court lies the large *megaron*, which had a central hearth and walls decorated with vivid frescoes of martial and hunting scenes. The entire complex is enclosed by massive stone walls termed "Cyclopean" by amazed later Greeks. The chief entrance was the famous Lion Gate. There is a sally port in the east bastion and remains of a postern on the north. Foundations of large, complex houses have been found on the plateau to the west. The fires which consumed Mycenae preserved many clay tablets inscribed in the Linear B script, first deciphered by Michael Ventris in 1952.

MYRON [mī′ron] (fl.5th century B.C.), Greek sculptor. He was from the town of Eleutherai on the boundary between Attica and Boeotia and according to tradition was a pupil of Ageladas. He worked mainly in Athens. None of his works have survived, but Roman copies give an idea of his style. The *"Discobolus,"* or "Discus Thrower," exists in a number of copies, one being in the Museo Nazionale Romano in Rome. A Roman version of his "Marsyas," a group that includes Athena as well as the satyr Marsyas, is in the Lateran Museum in Rome. It is difficult to evaluate his achievement since he worked mainly in bronze and all the copies of his sculptures are marble adaptations, but his position as a genius of Greek sculpture is well assured.

NAXOS [năk′səs], ancient Greek city on the east coast of Sicily, founded by Chalcis in 735 B.C., the oldest Greek colony on the island. It was completely destroyed by Dionysius the Elder of Syracuse in 403 B.C.

NEOPLATONISM [nē-ō-plā′tən-ĭz-əm], dominant school of philosophy in late antiquity. Besides Platonism, it absorbed elements from the Pythagoreans, Stoics, and Peripatetics. Its founder was Plotinus (205–70), who taught in Rome, and whose *Enneads* remained the basis of the system, in which, however, three stages may be discerned. First was the period of Plotinus and his own pupils Porphyry and Amelius. Second was the Syrian period, when, under the leadership of the Syrian Iamblichus (c.250–325 A.D.), a pupil of Porphyry, the religious side was developed into a systematic theology of pagan polytheism in open opposition to Christianity. To this period belongs also a compendium of Neoplatonic theology, *On the Gods and the World*, by Sallustius. Third was the Athenian school of the 5th and 6th centuries, which concentrated on the interpretation of early Greek philosophy and a return to Plato and Aristotle. The chief figure of this last period was Proclus (c.412–87), head of the Academy and author of commentaries on Plato's dialogues and of many other works. This was the age of the great commentaries on Aristotle, notably those of Simplicius. They oppose the fantastic and ultramystical side of Neoplatonism and are an invaluable source of Greek philosophic and scientific thought.

From St. Augustine onward Neoplatonism powerfully affected Christian philosophy through the Middle Ages and the Renaissance to the present day. Compare, for instance, the Cambridge Platonists in the 17th century and a modern Platonist like the late W. R. Inge.

OLYMPIA [ō-lĭm′pē-ə], ancient Greek sanctuary in Elis in the northwest Peloponnesus, at the junction of the Alpheus and Cladeus rivers. It is famous as a very early sanctuary of Zeus and as the site of the Olympic Games, the greatest Panhellenic festival of classical antiquity. The origins of the sanctuary and games are anterior to history, but it is known that the games were reorganized in 776 B.C., a date which marks the first Olympiad. Chronology by four-year Olympiads was later accepted throughout the Greek world, since local systems of dating were hopelessly at variance. Research at the site began as early as the 18th century, the French Expédition de Morée did some work there in 1829, and large-scale clearance by the German Institute began in 1874 and still continues. The earliest structures, dating from before the 6th century B.C., were grouped at the foot of Mount Kronion within a large walled enclosure called the Altis (600 by 500 ft.). These were administrative buildings, the heroa of Pelops and Hippodamia, the Heraeum, and a great altar of Zeus.

The Altis also contained the great temple of Zeus (finished 457 B.C.), the 6th- and 5th-century treasuries of wealthy Greek city-states, and other buildings, in addition to numberless votive statues and dedicatory or commemorative inscriptions. In the temple of Zeus was the colossal gold and ivory statue of the god by Phidias, whose workshops with his tools and molds have recently been found on the site. The architectural temple sculptures are much admired as beautiful examples of the early classical style. The excavators also unearthed the 5th-century Nike of Paeonius and the statue of Hermes attributed to Praxiteles. East of the Altis lay the stadium.

In early Hellenistic times Olympia flourished and was embellished by various Macedonian dynasts and Ptolemaic potentates, but in the 2d century B.C. it began to decline. Sulla ravaged it in 86 B.C. and under the early Roman emperors Olympia was systematically despoiled, particularly by Nero, who, however, compensated for his depredations by building himself a palace and a triumphal arch there. Many baths and gymnasiums of the Roman period have also been found. The Olympic Games, one of the last survivals of pagan antiquity, were finally abolished by Theodosius I in 394 A.D., and the temple was closed by his successor in 426 A.D. The monuments were much damaged by earthquakes in the 6th century A.D., and disappeared increasingly under landslides and river inundations until brought to light in the present period. The most valuable finds are exhibited in a small museum at the site.

OLYMPIAD [ō-lĭm′pē-ăd], in ancient Greece, the four-year interval between two successive Olympic festivals. Timaeus (352–256 B.C.) was the first to date events with reference to the listing of Olympic victors, available from 776 B.C. Thereafter, until Olympic records ceased (394 A.D.), Olympiads were used as units of chronology.

ORACLES [ôr′ə-kəlz], prophetic shrines at which the ancients sought either divine guidance or foreknowledge of the future. The word is also applied to the responses thus received. Oracles played a major role in classical antiquity, both on the personal level and in public affairs. Of the numerous oracles in Greece, the most famous was that of Apollo at Delphi. This became in effect the religious center of Greece, the final authority on questions of morality, ritual, purification from blood-guilt, the founding of new cults, and even on such practical matters as colonization. Little is known of the actual methods of consultation. Some responses were obtained by drawing lots, others were uttered by the Pythia, the inspired priestess, in a trance and interpreted by the temple officials. At the oracle of Zeus at Dodona, the message was somehow indicated by the rustling of leaves in a sacred oak tree. At oracular healing shrines, like that of Asclepius at Epidaurus, "incubation" was the usual practice: the patient, after offering sacrifice, slept in the sacred precinct (often on the skin of the victim) and the god's advice was given in a dream.

The consultation of oracles was only one of many forms of divination. There were individual seers and prophets. Omens could be drawn from the flight of birds, from the vital organs of sacrificial victims, and from celestial phenomena (for example, lightning, meteors, eclipses). Dreams were normally regarded as of supernatural rather than of psychological origin, and a whole literature developed on their interpretation.

Outside of Greece there were, among others, important oracles of Amon at Siwa in Egypt, of Apollo at Claros and at Didyma in Asia Minor, of the Sibyl at Cumae (q.v.), near Naples, and of Fortune at Praeneste near Rome.

PAPPUS [păp′əs] **OF ALEXANDRIA** (fl.300 A.D.), Greek mathematician who sought to revive interest in classical geometry. His chief work, the *Synagoge* (Mathematical Collection), was in eight books, all of which survive except Book I and the first part of Book II. It includes two theorems, which still bear the name of Pappus, relating areas, centers of gravity, and volumes of solids of revolution. He also wrote a commentary on Euclid's *Elements* and another on the *Almagest* of Ptolemy.

PARMENIDES [pär-mĕn′ĭ-dēz] (born c.510 B.C.), Greek philosopher of Elea, in southern Italy. He was the first philosopher to rely on deductive reasoning without reference to external facts. In the absence of any established logical or linguistic theory, this led him to reject the perceptible world and pose a dilemma for subsequent Greek thinkers. Taking the premise of the Ionian school that one thing exists ("it is") and assuming only one sense (the existential) for the verb "to be," he denied that this basic reality could ever be differentiated. Change and movement involve "what is" becoming what or where it is not; but to say of what is that "it is not" is impossible (the earliest statement of the law of contradiction). Reality, then, is a timeless, changeless, motionless, homogeneous mass. Since it does not appear so, appearances deceive, and must give way to logic.

He thus set the Greeks on the path of abstract thought, which they were only too ready to follow, at the expense of observation and experiment; yet he deserves recognition as the founder of logical method. In deference to human weakness he also described a conventional cosmology, with the explicit warning that it contained not truth but "seeming."

PARTHENON [pär′thə-nŏn], most famous Greek temple,

The Parthenon, a marble temple (5th century B.C.) dedicated to Athena, dominates the Acropolis in Athens.

built 447–438 B.C. on the Acropolis, in Athens, by Ictinus and Callicrates. The work on carvings and decorations continued until 432 B.C. Dedicated to the city's patron goddess, Athena Parthenos (The Maiden Athena), and unequaled in beauty of proportion and the nobility of its sculptures, it ranks as a masterpiece of world architecture.

Constructed throughout of costly marble from Mount Pentelicus, the temple stands on a three-stepped foundation and is surrounded by a single range of Doric columns, eight at front and back and seventeen on each of the longer sides. It measures 101 ft. by 228 ft. on the top step; the columns are 34 ft. high; and the ridgepole was about 65 ft. above the ground.

Behind the eight columns of each entrance portico another range of six columns formed a vestibule enclosed with metal gratings. The eastern enclosure guarded rich offerings and protected the huge gold-and-ivory statue of Athena, a renowned masterpiece by Phidias, which stood in the main cella or sanctuary. The cella, the larger of the two interior rooms, had a single eastern doorway and was divided into a broad nave and surrounding aisles by two-storied Doric colonnades. The smaller room, to which the name "Parthenon" was originally restricted, served as a treasury. It had a single western doorway and its ceiling was supported by four Ionic columns.

The Parthenon, badly damaged and stripped of most of its sculptures, is being restored. A full-scale reproduction of the building, made of modern concrete, stands in a park in Nashville, Tenn.

PERIPATETICS [pĕr-ĭ-pə-tĕt′ĭks], name given the students of Aristotle from their habit of conducting discussions while pacing up and down a covered walk (Gr. *peripatos*) on the grounds of the Lyceum at Athens. A center of scientific research under Aristotle's successors Theophrastus and Strato, the peripatetic school later declined. There was a revival of Aristotle's own philosophy, however, from Andronicus (1st century B.C.) onward, when the great body of Aristotelian writings was edited in the form in which it has passed through medieval to modern times.

PERSIAN WAR (499–479 B.C.). The struggle between the

143

Persian Empire and mainland Greece can be said to have begun with the revolt of the Ionian Greek cities of Asia Minor against Persia and ended only with the conquest of Persia by Alexander the Great 170 years later. But the end of the first phase (known as the Persian War) is marked by the repulse of the most serious direct Persian attack on European Greece in 480–479 B.C.

The flourishing Greek states on the Asia Minor coast resented even indirect Persian interference with their political autonomy. Under the leadership of Aristagoras of Miletus they revolted and called on their mainland kin for help. While there was considerable sympathy for the insurgents, only Athens and Eretria sent tangible aid. This was provocation enough, however, to harden King Darius' intention to subjugate Greece.

When the Ionian revolt had been suppressed (494 B.C.), the Persian general Mardonius conquered Thrace and Macedonia (492 B.C.). Then a powerful fleet under Datis and Artaphernes crossed the Aegean in 490 B.C., captured Eretria, and proceeded to attack Athens. Probably on the advice of the exiled tyrant Hippias, who accompanied them, the Persians landed at Marathon on the east coast of Attica, intending to march on the city overland. Spartan aid did not arrive in spite of Pheidippides' 150-mi. run to notify them of the threat, and the Athenian army faced the Persians with no allies except 1,000 soldiers from Plataea. The battle of Marathon was won through the bold strategy of the Athenian general Miltiades. The victory resulted in a great surge of self-confidence in Athens. Themistocles began building a powerful fleet. Efforts at Panhellenic co-operation were now more seriously undertaken, for there was no doubt that Persia would try again.

Xerxes, the new King, launched a diplomatic offensive which neutralized much of northern and central Greece. Then in 480 B.C. he mounted a huge attack by land and sea. Units of the Greek army under King Leonidas of Sparta attempted to hold the pass of Thermopylae, while the fleet engaged the Persians at the nearby straits of Artemisium. The Greeks were defeated in both engagements; the Greek army retreated to the Isthmus of Corinth, while their fleet evacuated the whole population of Athens and took up its position in the straits of Salamis. There Themistocles, the Athenian admiral, forced a decisive sea battle, perhaps by falsely warning the Persians that the Greeks intended to slip away. In a confined area the superior maneuverability of the Greek ships and discipline of their crews overwhelmed the Persians.

Xerxes' surviving ships fled and the King retreated by land with most of his troops, leaving Mardonius in command of a still formidable force. The next year a large Greek army commanded by the Spartan King Pausanias invaded central Greece and routed the Persians at Plataea in Boeotia. Concurrently the Greek fleet invaded east Aegean waters and (by tradition on the same day as Plataea) defeated the Persians off Cape Mycale. This action initiated a series of Greek counterattacks on Asia Minor which continued until the mid-5th century and which secured independence for the Asiatic Greeks. Greek success in exploding the myth of Persian invincibility had a profound psychological effect. Henceforth Persian prestige gradually deteriorated and a balance of power was barely maintained through Persian exploitation of rivalries among the Greeks themselves.

PHALANX [fā′lăngks], ancient Greek infantry formation. Although used as early as Homeric times, the phalanx reached its peak under Philip of Macedon and Alexander the Great. It consisted of 8 to 16 close-packed parallel ranks of heavy-armed foot soldiers (hoplites) whose main offensive weapon was a long lance or pike (*sarissa*). The principal advantage of the formation was its massed weight and stability, but maneuverability was limited and cavalry protection was needed on flanks and rear. It became obsolete after the Roman victory over Perseus' Macedonian army at Pydna in 168 B.C.

PHIDIAS [fĭd′ē-əs] **or PHEIDIAS** [fī′dē-əs] (c.500–c.432 B.C.), Greek sculptor, considered the greatest ancient artist. Although his masterpieces are known only through contemporary descriptions and late copies, they were judged in antiquity as the climax of Greek art. His famous statues of classic deities, distinguished by grandeur and purity of conception allied with technical excellence, established an ideal for the representation of divinity that influenced later religious art even into Christian times.

Among his earliest recorded works were a colossal bronze "Athena Promachos" that stood in the open on the

Roman copy of a head believed to be from the "Lemnian Athena" by the Greek sculptor Phidias.

Alinari—Art Reference Bureau

Acropolis in Athens, and another figure, the "Lemnian Athena," also on the Acropolis. Phidias became chief director of all artistic activity at Athens under the statesman Pericles, who was his personal friend. This included general oversight of the sculptures of the Parthenon, and creation of the colossal chryselephantine (gold and ivory) "Athena Parthenos" that stood in this temple. More famous was his statue of "Zeus" installed in the Temple of Zeus, in Olympia. In each of these colossal figures the draperies were of beaten gold, the flesh surfaces incrusted with ivory.

Apart from richness of material and elaborate adornment, Phidias relied for effect upon simplicity of pose and calm dignity of expression. This appears in a small copy of the "Athena Parthenos" known as the "Varvakeion Statuette" (National Museum, Athens). His masterpiece, the "Olympian Zeus," was a majestic bearded figure seated on a magnificent throne and clad in a mantle rich with sculptured decorations. It ranked in ancient times among the seven wonders of the world.

Tradition says that Phidias was accused of sacrilege for representing himself and Pericles on the shield of his "Athena Parthenos," and that he fled from Athens and died in Olympia, after completing his statue of Zeus there.

PHOENICIA [fə-nē'shə] (from Gr. *phoinix,* "purple"), ancient Greek name for the land of the Canaanites (q.v.) in the area of modern Lebanon. The Phoenicians, who called themselves "Canaanites" (*Kinahni, Kinahhi*), were natives of the eastern Mediterranean coast land during the 3d and 2d millenniums B.C. They occupied the coastal region and the mountainous hinterland which is Mount Lebanon, its northern extensions into Syria as far as the Orontes River, and its southern foothills in the central hilly ridge of Palestine. During the 13th and 12th centuries B.C. they were thrust out of much of this area by a series of invaders. These included the Israelites, who seized the hill country of Palestine in the 13th century, the Peoples of the Sea (the Philistines) from the Aegean area, who took control of the coast during the 12th century, and the Aramaeans, who moved into areas east of the coastal mountains at approximately the same time.

During the Iron Age, after 1200 B.C., they were largely confined to the area of modern Lebanon, west of the Lebanon ridge. Here their main cities were developed along the coast: on the two islands, Tyre and Arvad (Ruad), and in the shore line areas, Sidon (Saida), Beirut, and Byblos. Following the treaty between the Egyptian Pharaoh Rameses II and the Hittites about 1270 B.C., the border between these two empires was fixed across the narrow waist of Lebanon by Arvad; north of that point Hittite city-states came into being.

Language and Literature. The Phoenicians belonged to the Semitic family of peoples whose language is generally described as Northwest Semitic. Biblical Hebrew is one dialect of this linguistic branch, and Aramaic is another. Wherever Phoenicians spread, they took their language with them, and inscriptions dating from as early as the 9th century B.C. are found as far away as Karatepe in southern Turkey, Cyprus, Sardinia, and Tunisia. The earliest witness to the language is an inscription found at Byblos in a special script, dating from the late 3d millennium B.C. But the Semitic names of the city-states of the Early Bronze Age (dating back to the 4th millennium B.C.) also attest to the language.

The recovery of Canaanite classical literature began in 1929 with the excavation of Ugarit (modern Ras Shamrah) on the northern Syrian coast. There, in a library associated with a temple, a number of mythological texts and legends were recovered, dating from c.1400 B.C. Excerpts from a later work on Phoenician mythology, written by one Philo Byblius, who in turn claimed to have obtained his information from a Phoenician named Sanchuniathon, are quoted by the Church Father Eusebius. The Ugaritic tablets are written on clay in cuneiform signs specially devised to write alphabetically. The Phoenicians invented alphabetic writing in the early 2d millennium B.C. The earliest examples of it are small plaques from Shechem and Gezer in Palestine, dating from c.1600 B.C. The Greeks borrowed and adapted this Phoenician alphabet c.800 B.C., and it subsequently spread all over the world.

History. The basic political organization of the people before 1200 B.C. was the city-state, and large numbers of them came into being in Early Bronze I, beginning shortly before 3000 B.C. Within four centuries the best known of these city-states, Byblos, was already being used by Egypt as a trading center for various Asiatic imports, especially the coveted cedars from Lebanon. Between c.1675 and 1570 B.C., when Syria-Palestine was ruled from Egypt by the Hykos, a high level of prosperity was achieved. When native Egyptian rulers regained the throne and took over the empire, the prosperity was dissipated by the militarism, poor administration, and greed of the Egyptian rulers.

Following the great destructive events during the transition from the Bronze to the Iron Age c.1200 B.C., a Phoenician state developed with its capital at Tyre c.1000 B.C. Possessing fine harbors but little hinterland, Phoenicia, like Lebanon today, became the most prosperous area of the eastern Mediterranean, serving as the trading center for east and west. Beginning in the 10th century, Phoenician ships ranged so widely over the Mediterranean that it became virtually a Phoenician sea. Great merchant ships known as *tarshish* ships were built, made possible in part by the newly available iron, the term *tarshish* evidently referring to smelting operations. Phoenician refineries were in operation by the 9th century on Sardinia and perhaps also in the area of Tartessus, in southwestern Spain. Trading colonies were established at these and many other points, the most famous of which was Carthage, founded in 814 B.C.

In the 10th century B.C., Israel, having no architectural and artistic traditions of its own, made a commercial treaty with King Hiram of Tyre to provide materials and artisans for government building in Israel. The most famous structure so built was the Temple of Solomon in Jerusalem, begun c.959 B.C. A similar arrangement existed in the next century with the father of Jezebel, Ethbaal of Sidon. Archeological as well as scriptural evidence confirms such Phoenician influence. Phoenician art was a creative amalgam of Egyptian, Mesopotamian, and Hittite motifs, with the Egyptian, superficially at least, furnishing a delicacy and chasteness of line, motif, and color in the finest work. Between the 15th and 7th centuries B.C., Phoenicians excelled in metallurgy; glass-making; weaving; the production of the ancient world's most coveted dye, Tyrian purple; and ivory carving for inlay work in fine furniture and boxes. With the failure of the ivory supply in the upper Euphrates, Phoenician artists turned to fine silverwork.

Beginning in the 8th century B.C., Phoenician power was restricted by Assyrian supremacy in western Asia, and in the 6th century Nebuchadnezzar of Babylonia laid siege to Tyre for 13 years without taking it. After 538 the Persians controlled the Phoenician fleet, and one purpose of their attempt to capture Greece was to keep that fleet supreme in the Mediterranean. Its defeat at Salamis in 480 B.C. marked the beginning of the decline of Phoenician naval supremacy, but the end of Phoenician hegemony did not come until the destruction of Tyre by Alexander the Great after a seven-month siege in 332 B.C. In 64 B.C. Phoenicia passed from Seleucid to Roman rule, becoming part of the province of Syria.

Religion. Phoenician religion was typical of ancient polytheism, an interpretation of life in the setting of nature, the powers of which were personified as gods on whom life was dependent. Inasmuch as there was never one unified theological control by a particular priesthood over religious practice, the historian is faced with a bewildering variety of data which defies simple systematization. Not only were there many shifts of emphasis during 2,000 years of traceable history, but there were also differences in various geographical areas. A few generalizations, however, are possible: "El," the common noun for god, was also the name of the chief god of the Canaanite pantheon; his consort was Asherah, the mother goddess. The second-in-command was the storm-god Baal (q.v.), whose consort was the fertility goddess known as Anath in northern Syria and Astarte in southern Canaan. "Baal" was also used as a common noun for god or master. Beginning in the 10th century, the mother goddess, Asherah, was given particular attention, and figurines supposed to resemble her were frequently found even in Israelite homes.

From both Biblical and classical sources one would judge that the problems of fertility and reproduction were a central concern in religious worship. The chief festivals, accordingly, were based on the cycle of nature: the revival of nature in the spring, the drought of the summer, and the return of the rain in the fall. This was celebrated as the spring mating of Baal and the fertility goddess, the killing of Baal by Mot (Death), and Anath's slaying of Mot in the fall followed by the resurrection of Baal. The people of Israel reacted strongly against this phase of Phoenician religion and were particularly shocked by its orgiastic excesses, involving human sacrifice and ritual prostitution. On the other hand, the Canaanite creation myth is frequently referred to metaphorically in the Old Testament. In it, the chief threat to life was conceived to be chaos, symbolized in the uncontrollable force of the sea and given form as a dragon with various names such as Yam ("Sea"), Rahab,

and Leviathan. Creation was conceived as Baal's slaughter of Yam, a victory that had to be yearly renewed.

The influence of Phoenician religion on Greece was undoubtedly considerable. It can also be said that the religion of Israel, which was to have such great influence on civilization, developed both in dependence upon, and in radical reaction to, Phoenician culture and religion.

PINDAR [pĭn′dər] (518–438 B.C.), the acknowledged master of Greek choral lyric poetry. He was Boeotian by birth. Though he lived through the great Greek victory in the Persian War, he represented the aristocratic ideals of an earlier age and was unsympathetic to the rising democracy of Athens. His four extant books of epinician ("victory") odes contain elaborate poems to be sung and danced by large choruses in honor of victors at the Olympian, Pythian, Isthmian, and Nemean games. These poems were commissioned by members of princely houses, in various parts of the Greek world, who participated in the games. Pindar not only believed in the prerogatives of aristocracy but was also convinced of his own inspiration and high dignity and insisted on his superiority to his rivals. His work in other forms, amounting to 17 books, is known only from fragments and allusions.

The Pindaric odes are spacious in structure and sublime in language. They are normally built of large triads (strophe, antistrophe, epode) in varying numbers, with intricate metrical patterns and striking vocabulary and syntax. The victor, his family, and the occasion are brought in almost incidentally, in connection with some relevant myth, and the story is presented through glimpses of high points rather than in orderly narrative. The effect is one of gleaming brilliance, high prowess, and impressive lordliness.

PLUTARCH [plōō′tärk] (c.46–after 120 A.D.), Greek philosopher and biographer, born in Chaeronea in Boeotia. He studied in Athens and spent some time in Rome, where he enjoyed high respect. Later he retired to his native town and lived there quietly as a teacher and writer, a municipal official, and a priest of neighboring Delphi. He seems to have conceived his mission to be the propagation of the cultural values of Hellenism. He himself knew, and in a sense summarized, all the Greek past, and his attractive and perennially popular writings have been a principal channel for communicating knowledge of classical antiquity to Europe.

His work falls into two parts. Most familiar is his *Parallel Lives*, paired biographies of Greek and Roman soldiers and statesmen of comparable careers, with comparisons between the two following the biographies. Typical pairs are Alexander and Caesar, Demosthenes and Cicero, Alcibiades and Coriolanus. There are 50 lives extant—23 pairs and four individual lives. Plutarch's general purpose in writing the *Lives* was to instruct by means of the moral implications of his character portrayals. His particular purpose was to show the Romans that the Greeks had ability in warfare and statesmanship as well as in literature and the arts. As a biographer he insisted that his work was individual portraiture rather than history. His primary interest is in fact psychological and ethical, and with this purpose in mind he makes generous use of anecdotes.

The second and longer part of Plutarch's writings are the *Moralia*, a collection of miscellaneous dialogues and essays ranging over a wide variety of subjects. Some of the most attractive concern philosophy and religion; for example, *Isis and Osiris*, *The Oracles at Delphi*, and *On the Delay of Divine Retribution*. Some are ethical, as *Can Virtue be Taught?*, *Control of Anger*, and *Brotherly Love*. Others are collections of anecdotes and literary studies. As compared with his predecessors of the classical period, Plutarch is notable for his amiability and kindliness and his sympathy for women, children, and animals.

PLATO [plā'tō] (c.429–347 B.C.), Greek philosopher. One of the great minds of the world, Plato exerted a profound influence on the development of Western thought, both through his own teaching and through that of his foremost pupil, Aristotle.

Plato's Life

Plato's father, Ariston, according to tradition, was descended from the ancient kings of Athens. His mother, Perictione, was the sister of Charmides and the niece of Critias, both of whom were prominent in the oligarchy which governed Athens briefly at the end of the Peloponnesian War (404 B.C.). On his mother's side he was descended from Dropides, who was a friend and kinsman of Solon (c.640–c.560 B.C.), the great Attic legislator. Dropides' father, another Dropides, was archon in 644 B.C. Plato had two older brothers, Adeimantus and Glaucon, and a sister, Potone. After the death of Ariston in Plato's childhood, Perictione married her uncle, Pyrilampes, who had been a close friend of Pericles and a distinguished supporter of Periclean policies. As a result of this marriage, Plato had a younger half brother named Antiphon.

Thus Plato was brought up in a family which had for generations been influential in the political life of Athens. He was proud of these connections and in his youth looked forward to a political career himself. But the oligarchy of which his mother's brother and uncle were a part disgusted him with its corruption, and the democracy which succeeded it distressed him by its senseless execution of Socrates.

Undoubtedly the greatest influence in Plato's life was his acquaintance with Socrates, whom he must have known as long as he could remember, since his uncle Charmides and his great-uncle Critias were intimate associates of Socrates before Plato was born. It is unlikely that Plato was one of the inner circle of Socrates' friends, but he was a youthful admirer of Socrates and was closely associated with him for some 10 years or more before his death. Plato was present at Socrates' trial, but illness prevented his being present at his death, which occurred when Plato was about 30.

Certainly Socrates was the inspiration of Plato's earlier dialogues, in which he was the leading figure, and which presumably set forth Socratic ideas in conversations which were based on discussions which had actually taken place in Socrates' life. These earlier writings ended with the *Republic*.

When Plato was 40 he visited Italy and Sicily, probably

The Bettmann Archive
Roman copy of a Greek bust of Plato, in the Vatican Museum, Rome.

to meet the Pythagoreans, who were forming a new school there under Archytas of Tarentum. It was perhaps at this time that he first made the acquaintance of Dion, the son-in-law of Dionysius I, then Tyrant of Syracuse.

The next 20 years of Plato's life were spent in organizing and directing the Academy, which was the distinguished forerunner of all medieval and modern universities. This was pre-eminently a place where science (principally mathematics) and philosophy were studied as a basis for a career in public service.

In 367, when Plato was over 60, he was invited by his old acquaintance Dion to come to Syracuse, as Dionysius I had died and left as his successor his son Dionysius II, a young man of 30. The young Tyrant's education had been sadly neglected, and Dion thought Plato was the one who could remedy this unfortunate circumstance. Plato was not at all optimistic about the prospects of success; but the invitation was a challenge to apply his theories to a situation where wise political leadership was of the utmost practical importance. The rising power of Carthage threatened the independence of the Greek states in Italy and Sicily, and Syracuse was the natural leader of a defensive coalition.

So Plato undertook the assignment and at first met with some success. Dionysius became attached to Plato, who prescribed a rigorous course in geometry for him, and geometry for a time was the fashion at the Syracusan court. But Dionysius' interest in serious study soon lagged and he grew jealous of Dion and banished him. Plato then returned to Athens. But Dionysius corresponded with him, and in 361–360 Plato, then about 68, returned to have another try at helping Dionysius measure up to his serious responsibilities. Meeting with failure again, and being in some personal danger from Dionysius' barbarian guards, Plato, with assistance from Archytas of Tarentum, returned to Athens.

The year Plato first went to Syracuse, 367, was the year Aristotle entered the Academy. From 360 to his death, some 12 years later, Plato must have written his later dialogues, ending with the *Laws*.

It is well to remember that Plato was born about the time of the death of Pericles (c.429 B.C.), during the opening years of the Peloponnesian War (431–404 B.C.), and that he was about 25 when the war ended with the disastrous defeat of Athens. He died just before the end of the Third Sacred War (355–346 B.C.), which gave Philip II of Macedon (reigned 359–336) the foothold in Greek affairs which led to his complete mastery of Greece with the fall of Athens and Thebes at Chaeronea in 338.

Plato's Philosophy

Plato's writings, all extant, consist of some 26 dialogues (including the *Apology*, or defense of Socrates at his trial) and 13 letters, whose authenticity is disputed. The seventh, probably genuine, at least contains trustworthy historical material.

The Socratic Dialogues. The earlier dialogues aim largely at dramatic portrayal of Socrates, his method of tireless questioning, and his insistence that "virtue is knowledge." No one can be consistently just, brave, and wise without understanding what justice, courage, and wisdom are: that is, being able not only to enumerate instances of these virtues but to state the common "form" or the definable essence of the specific instances. Socrates did not claim this knowledge for himself, but invited his companions to seek it with him. Consequently some of these dialogues conclude with apparent failure: the method is demonstrated, but the definitions suggested by Socrates himself, as well as by others, are rejected as inadequate (*Hippias Major, Laches, Lysis, Charmides*). In the *Protagoras*, dramatic considerations take first place, with an elaborately drawn setting, and vivid, ironic character sketches of Sophists and Athenian citizens. But its moral is similar: that one cannot determine an attribute of virtue (whether it can be taught) without knowing what virtue is.

The Doctrine of Ideas or Forms. Socrates' search for definitions raised a philosophical difficulty: Is the search legitimate? Everyone recognizes just acts, but where is there a thing called "justice" apart from them? Is it a reality, and if not, why waste time trying to define it? This deeper problem Plato faces in his maturer works. He accepted from the Heracliteans that the world grasped by man's senses (sight, hearing, and so forth) was in a continuous state of change. From Parmenides he accepted the belief that the object of knowledge must be something immutable and grasped by the mind, not the senses. These influences, and his interest in Pythagoreanism, determined his answer.

It was not in him to abandon faith either in the existence of absolute moral standards or in the possibility of scientific knowledge. Therefore his only possible solution was to suppose that the definable objects of knowledge could not be identified with anything in the perceptible world. The Socratic "form" (Gr. *idea*) of a thing became for him a transcendent entity beyond space and time. These "Platonic Ideas" differ from "ideas" in our sense by existing independently of the mind which knows them. They resemble them by being what we call the "idea" or "concept," say of goodness or equality, which enables us to use the same word in talking of *good* work or *good* wine, *equal* triangles or *equal* chances. Particulars, he says (using metaphors to express a relationship which eludes rational argument), "imitate" the forms, or, alternatively, share in their nature.

To account for our awareness of these transcendent forms, Plato adopts the Pythagorean doctrine that the soul is immortal and undergoes a series of incarnations (*Phaedo, Phaedrus, Republic*). In the other world, before and between earthly lives, it has been vouchsafed a vision of "reality." Genuine learning is a process of "recollection" of these forgotten truths (*Meno, Phaedo*). This perpetuates Socrates' identification of soul with rational and moral consciousness, and his exhortation to "tend" it as the most precious part of man. For Plato the soul has three parts: reason, appetite, and between them the spirited, or willing faculty, which should be obedient to reason against appetite.

The Republic. The political organization of the *Republic* rests on this psychological basis. Few men exhibit perfect balance of the parts. Those who do, with passion subserving reason, are the natural rulers. The "spirited" natures make ideal soldiers, and those in whom appetite prevails are debarred from political or military activity and will attend to the city's material needs. Only this class may hold private property. The first rulers are selected at an early age. They have the traditional education until about 17, then three years of physical and military training, ten studying advanced mathematics and five devoted to philosophy. Those who complete the course can "recollect" the Ideas up to the supreme Idea of the Good, and will interpret all earthly problems in the light of this knowledge. For such men government will be a burden undertaken solely for the good of the community. They live communally like Spartans, and procreate anonymously at fixed festivals. No child knows its own parents.

Plato's answer in the *Republic* to the Socratic question, "What is justice (or righteousness)?" is that it is this state of "harmony," or right ordering of the parts of the soul in the individual, and of classes in the state. Politically, Plato's instinct is for order and regulation under the rule of the expert. Democracy comes low in his constitutional order of preference. The reason lies partly in himself, partly in history. Democracy as restored in Athens in 403, after defeat by Sparta in the Peloponnesian War, was far from what it had been under Pericles, and moreover had the blood of Socrates on its hands.

Epistemology and Logic. In his later period Plato returns to the problem of knowledge with more developed critical weapons. The *Parmenides* subjects the doctrine of Ideas to a rigorous criticism. In the *Theaetetus* the question "What is knowledge?" is asked in Socratic form, and three possible answers are examined and rejected. The first, that knowledge is sense perception, introduces a critique of the relativism of Protagoras and Heraclitus. Next comes true judgment, which involves a discussion of how false judgment is possible, and finally, true judgment plus "logos," the ability to give an account or explanation of one's judgment. The conclusion, as in the early dialogues, is negative; but the Platonic Ideas have been entirely left out of account. This may be deliberately done to show that knowledge is inexplicable without them.

In the *Sophist* the chief speaker is, significantly, an Eleatic. It discusses the meaning of "not-being," which Parmenides had declared an impossible concept, and of the propositions *A is B* and *A is not B*. Plato posits five universal Forms: being, motion, rest, sameness, otherness. It is then a question of deciding which of these can combine. Motion cannot "share in" rest, but can in being: "motion exists." Everything shares in identity and otherness, being identical with itself and other than everything else. *A is not B* does not mean that *A* has any share in not-being (which was what Parmenides mistakenly supposed), but only in otherness. The Eleatic dilemma is thus resolved. The dialogue develops the method of "division" introduced in the *Phaedrus*, a forerunner of definition by genus and differentia as developed by Aristotle. This dialogue and the *Theaetetus* mark a great philosophic advance.

Ethics and Cosmology. The *Philebus* considers the claims of knowledge and pleasure to be the good, and concludes that neither is adequate alone. The *Timaeus*, perhaps the most remarkable of Plato's dialogues, describes the origin and present constitution of the world and mankind in a tremendous sweep of myth, logical argument, and factual detail. There are three ultimate and independent entities. These are the Creator who is intelligence, the realm of Forms which is his model, and the Receptacle, or unformed chaos, which he reduces to order so far as he can, shaping it into a universe of elements based on the five geometrical solids. (The influence of Pythagoreanism is marked.) Chaos is the realm of "necessity," an independent disorderly force, which the creative mind can only partially subdue.

In the *Laws*, his last and longest work, Plato modifies the *Republic* and brings it down to earth with a plethora of legislation covering every aspect of life. He also re-emphasizes the need to believe that the whole cosmos is divinely regulated.

We learn from Aristotle that Plato's oral teaching, especially a famous lecture on "The Good," contained difficult doctrines of a mathematical nature omitted from the dialogues. For instance, there is a class of mathematical entities intermediate between Ideas and particulars, the identification of the Ideas with numbers, and their theoretical construction out of the One and indefinite quantity (called the Indefinite Dyad, or the "great and small").

Plato's thought cannot be adequately summarized; to appreciate it needs direct contact with the dialogues. They are not treatises, but literary masterpieces blending philosophy with drama, religion, humor, and reminiscence. Feeling is not suppressed but is sublimated in the doctrine of Eros—the emotional and aesthetic impulse which combines with intellect to lead the philosophic soul upward from awareness of earthly beauty to the beauty of moral ideals and learning. Finally it attains the vision of the supreme Idea in which beauty coalesces with truth and goodness visible to the eye not of the body but of the mind.

POLYBIUS [pə-lĭb'ē-əs] (c.203–c.120 B.C.), Greek historian of Rome. Born in Megalopolis, Polybius played an active role in the politics of the Achaean League and was transported to Rome as a political hostage after the Greek defeat at Pydna in 168 B.C. In Rome he acquired an intimate knowledge of the people and institutions that were to govern the known world for the next 500 years. Convinced that his Greek countrymen should possess an accurate account of their Roman conquerors, Polybius set about composing a history of the Greco-Roman world from the time of the Second Punic War to the destruction of Carthage and Corinth. This history, originally in 40 books of which five are extant, avoided the rhetorical fashions of the day and is a masterpiece of ancient historiography.

POLYCLITUS, POLYCLEITUS [pŏl-ĭ-klī'təs], **or POLYCLETUS** [pŏl-ĭ-klē'təs] (fl.450–420 B.C.), Greek sculptor. His fame rivaled that of his contemporary, Phidias. He was particularly renowned for the ideal bodily proportions achieved in his statues of nude athletes. Because his works were usually made of costly bronze, the originals are lost and now known only through copies of later date.

His most famous statue, honored in ancient times as the "Canon of Polyclitus," became the influential standard of proportions for countless subsequent works. It exists in several marble copies, of which the finest, known as the "*Doryphorus*" ("Spearbearer"), stands in the National Museum, Naples. The "*Doryphorus*" illustrates the sculptor's preference for heavy, muscular, square-headed athletic types. Other marble copies reproduce his "*Diadumenus*," an athlete binding a fillet about his head, and also a clothed female "Amazon." Ancient writers mention a chryselephantine (gold and ivory) statue of the goddess Hera, made by Polyclitus for her temple in Argos.

POTTERY. On the mainland of Greece the art of pottery developed independently in Neolithic times, and by c.2500 B.C. shared the general characteristics of the island cultures previously mentioned. The earliest distinctive group of Greek pottery emerged c.1000 B.C. in Attica. Pots of extremely large size, sometimes as much as 5 ft. high, were covered with painted decoration strongly angular in character. A later variant of these, found in the Dipylon cemetery near Athens, shows combinations of stylized human and animal figures with geometric ornament.

The unique pottery style of Corinth and Athens, which has preserved a pictorial record of life in Greece during its greatest period, was fully established by 600 B.C. Large markets gained in Italy and eastern Mediterranean countries by the black-figured wares were later maintained by red-figured ware. This trade was severely damaged by the Peloponnesian War, but the style lasted in a degenerate form until the mid-3d century B.C.

The pots were made in a few standard shapes that were not only severely practical and symmetrical but inherently more refined than any previously made. They are still considered among the masterpieces of ceramic achievement of all time. The clay was carefully washed, sieved, and kneaded to remove impurities and secure a close, even-textured substance free of air bubbles. The pots were then thrown, that is, fashioned on the wheel. The plasticity and tension of Athenian clay in particular allowed daring, wide-spreading shapes to be made, as well as more conservative vase and urn forms. When dried to a state of leather-hardness, the wares were recentered on the wheel and trimmed to their final chaste perfection, probably with metal-smoothing tools. Handles were added at this stage, being literally stuck on with diluted clay. In the firing the pots turned a handsome red-brown and the handles became firmly attached. Many Greek pots of this type bear the potter's name.

Black-figured wares, which developed c.600 B.C., were decorated with mythological scenes whose figures were painted in silhouette in a shiny black. Any interior lines needed to render the forms understandable were scratched through the black, allowing the red body to show through. In red-figured wares, made between c.525 and 350 B.C., the black coating covered the background and the figures were represented by the red of the uncoated body. Details were added in black, purple, or white. Mythological, everyday, and historic scenes were depicted. Funerary vases in which the background is white instead of black have also been found. Some vase painters signed their work. The Greeks also excelled in making terra-cotta figurines, the best coming from the Tanagra district of Boeotia and dating from the 4th century B.C. on.

PRAXITELES [prăk-sĭt'ə-lēz] (fl.370–330 B.C.), Greek sculptor. His statues were the first to embody the graceful personal charm reflected in many later phases of Greek art. In his sculptures of deities he replaced the lofty and austere idealism of earlier masters with a more human and even subjective tone. Through relaxed, sinuous poses and facial expressions that produce an effect of dreamy revery, he gave to his creations an intimate personal quality that made them very popular in later centuries.

Among some 50 works ascribed to him by ancient writers, the most famous was his marble "Venus of Cnidus." Of several extant copies, the best (Vatican Museum, Rome) shows the goddess standing nude and conscious of her beauty, but without coquetry or shame. A marble group, "Hermes with the Infant Dionysus," discovered in the ruins of a temple in Olympia and now in the museum there, is thought by some critics to have been carved by his own hand. Other masterpieces of Praxiteles that are still admired in extant copies include "Apollo Sauroctonus," or "Apollo the Lizard-Slayer" (Vatican Museum), "Silenus and Dionysus" (Louvre, Paris), and the "Young Satyr" (Capitoline Museum, Rome). The last was celebrated in Hawthorne's romantic novel *The Marble Faun*. His famous "Eros of Thespiae" has been lost.

Roman copy of Praxiteles' "Venus of Cnidus" (Vatican Museum).
(ANDERSON—ART REFERENCE BUREAU)

PYTHAGORAS [pĭ-thăg'ə-rəs] (c.570–490 B.C.), Greek philosopher and religious teacher. Born in Samos, he immigrated to Croton in southern Italy. There he founded a brotherhood which wielded political power until dispersed in the latter part of the 5th century B.C. Pythagoras' life is overlaid with legend, and his own thought was a mixture of rationality and superstition. His philosophy is a way of life. All nature is akin, the soul is immortal and undergoes a series of incarnations, both human and animal. Knowledge assimilates the knower to its object, hence philosophy (the understanding of the living, divine cosmos) is the path to salvation. But purity must also be sought by observance of such taboos as abstention from meat and beans.

Pythagoras' cosmology seems to have originated in his discovery that the then recognized musical intervals were based on ratios of the numbers 1 to 4. Their sum, the decad, represented by a triangular arrangement of dots, became a sacred symbol ("tetractys"). This musical discovery was extended to all nature, which he regarded as ordered according to laws of harmonious proportion. It is exemplified in the theory of the "harmony of the spheres," based on a supposed ratio between the distances of sun, moon, and planets. Number, geometrical figure, and body were identified (unit-point-minimum body); hence the dictum that "things are numbers."

In spite of the primitive residue in his thought, his mathematical conception of the universe opened up fruitful possibilities, and by turning Greek philosophy from its preoccupation with the matter of the world to a study of its form, he paved the way for Plato.

PYTHAGOREANS [pĭ-thăg-ə-rē'ənz], followers of the Greek philosopher Pythagoras (c.570–490 B.C.). They were active, particularly in southern Italy, from the 6th to the 4th century B.C., and there was a Neopythagorean revival in the Greco-Roman age which merged into Neoplatonism. Unlike the scientific Ionians, the Pythagoreans regarded philosophy as a way of life, with a strong religious side based on the mystical properties of number and harmony and a belief in the kinship of all nature.

PYTHEAS [pĭth'ē-əs] (late 4th century B.C.), Greek geographer and explorer. Born in the Greek city of Massilia (Marseille), Pytheas sailed up the Atlantic coast past Portugal and France, circumnavigated Britain, visited Thule (Norway or Iceland), and penetrated the Baltic Sea. His own account of these explorations is lost, but later geographers such as Strabo and Pliny drew from it descriptions of these lands and peoples. Pytheas' work was also an important source for later Greek map makers.

PYTHIAN [pĭth'ē-ən] **GAMES,** in ancient Greece, national festival held at Apollo's shrine in Delphi every fourth August to commemorate Apollo's slaying of the Python. Originally held every eight years, the festival at first included a one-day musical competition for the best hymn to the god composed with a lyre accompaniment. Reorganized c.582 B.C. under the direction of the Amphictyonic Council, the festival added games on the Olympic plan to the music contests. The brilliance of the chariot races and equestrian events soon almost eclipsed Olympia. Victors received laurel wreaths. The Pythian Games were still held as late as 361 A.D.

SAPPHO [săf'ō] (fl. early 6th century B.C.), Greek lyric poet from Lesbos. Born into the aristocratic society of Mytilene, which was being challenged in the social upheavals of her day, Sappho fled her native island and took refuge, with her family, in Sicily. Returning to Lesbos in more peaceful times, she became the mistress of a small college of women, a thiasos, which was dedicated, under the auspices of Aphrodite, to the perfection of young womanhood and to a preparation for marriage. This college became the center of Sappho's poetic life. Her poems, in Aeolic dialect, express adoration for this or that young pupil, jealousy, grief at parting, scorn for the mistress of a rival school, the ambivalent feelings of a young student about to be married, and a host of other emotions which were the product of her intense involvement.

Her lyric poems originally formed nine books. Most of these were lost, and Sappho was known only through quotations in other ancient writers until 1900, when considerable fragments of her work began to be found on papyrus in Egypt. Sappho's verse is characterized by simplicity, a careful control over meter, a lively use of epithet, and a matchless lyricism. In the opinion of ancient Greek critics she was the greatest woman poet.

SCEPTICISM [skĕp'tə-sĭz-əm], school of philosophy which questions the possibility of knowledge in various areas. Scepticism in the modern sense had a long history in Greek thought. Xenophanes (c.570–475 B.C.) ridiculed the contemporary belief in gods with human form and human failings and emphasized the limitations of human knowledge. The trend was carried further by the Sophists (5th century B.C.), especially Protagoras (c.490–420 B.C.) with his religious agnosticism and theory of the relativity of perception. But the term "sceptic" (meaning "thoughtful" or "inquiring") was applied only to Pyrrho (died c.275 B.C.) and his school about a century later, and to

its revival under Aenesidemus (1st century B.C.) and Sextus Empiricus (2d century A.D.).

Pyrrho saw the aim of life in perfect tranquillity of mind, and considered that this could be best attained by a silent suspension of judgment about all things. His attitude was a natural reaction against the extreme dogmatism of the Stoics and was agnostic rather than denying. Sextus in his *Outlines of Pyrrhonism* and *Against the Dogmatists* sets out the system, and his criticism of other schools provides incidentally one of the most valuable sources of information on earlier Greek philosophy. More openly destructive was the scepticism of the later Academy (q.v.) from Arcesilaus (c.315–240 B.C.) to Carneades (213–128 B.C.).

SCOPAS [skō'pəs] (fl.4th century B.C.), Greek sculptor renowned for originality in depicting emotion through facial expression and violent bodily movement. Twenty-five masterpieces were ascribed to him by ancient writers, about half the number recorded for his contemporary Praxiteles. None has survived, however, even in the form of clearly recognizable copies. Yet the powerful expressive qualities and widespread influence attributed to Scopas' works have justified the recognition of his distinctive style in many antique sculptures. Chief among them are fragmentary marble heads (National Museum, Athens) discovered in the ruined Athena Alea Temple at Tegea. Because Scopas is reported to have designed this temple and to have carved figures for it, and because the heads themselves embody the intense emotion said to have characterized his style, they are perhaps his work. Probable copies of masterpieces by Scopas are "Ludovisi Ares" (Terme Museum, Rome) and "Meleager" (Fogg Museum, Cambridge, Mass.).

SELEUCIDS [sĭ-loo'sĭdz], Hellenistic dynasty ruling in the Near East, centering on Syria and Mesopotamia, from 312 B.C. until the establishment of a Roman province in 64 B.C. After the death of Alexander the Great, his huge empire gradually split up into a number of separate kingdoms. The successors (*Diadochi*) were among Alexander's officers, and the story of their rivalries and alliances is a complex one. It required almost 50 years for the political map to assume reasonably stable shape.

SELEUCUS I, called Nicator ("Conqueror"), (c.358–280 B.C.) received the satrapy of Babylonia in 321 B.C., was displaced, and finally succeeded in establishing himself permanently in 312. Thereafter he rapidly extended his territory eastward as far as Bactria. His new capital, Seleucia on the Tigris River, replaced Babylon as the main trading center for caravans linking the Far East and the Mediterranean world. Seleucus joined in the opposition to Macedonian supremacy, and after the victory at Ipsus in 301, Syria was ceded to him. From then on this vital link between Egypt and Asia was a bone of contention between the Seleucids and the Ptolemies. In his later years Seleucus' main interest was increasingly in the west. He founded a second great capital city at Antioch on the Orontes River in 300, and in 293 made his son, Antiochus, associate ruler, with headquarters at Seleucia. Cilicia became part of his empire in 295, and Seleucus' victory over Lysimachus at Corupedion in Lydia in 281 gave him control of Asia Minor. While pressing on across the Hellespont he was assassinated in 280.

ANTIOCHUS I (324–261) succeeded his father in 280 and followed his example by making his own son Seleucus coruler in the east. Antiochus made peace with Macedonia in 279 and gradually lost much of Asia Minor. His greatest military exploit was the defeat in 276 of Gallic tribes invading Asia Minor. From this victory he took the title "Soter" ("Saviour"). Antiochus I was succeeded in 261 by his second son, **ANTIOCHUS II** (c.287–247 B.C.), who was distinguished by the title "Theos" ("God"). Early in his reign (260–255) he recovered from Egypt much of the territory in Asia Minor and Syria which his father had lost. But weakened by long wars, he lost Parthia and Bactria in revolt.

SELEUCUS II (c.265–226), became King in 247. Throughout his reign he was in difficulties with family intrigues, internal revolts, and attacks from outside the empire. He lost most of the Seleucid territory in Asia Minor, and during his reign the rival Kingdom of Pergamum was founded. Control over the eastern part of the empire had always been insecure, but Seleucus II lost Bactria for good and faced the encroachment of the new and menacing Parthian Empire. His eldest son, **SELEUCUS III** (d.223), reigned only three years and was followed in 223 by a younger brother, Antiochus III (q.v.) called the Great. Antiochus had spectacular success in restoring Seleucid prestige, until he collided with Rome. His campaigns in the east (212–206), as far as Arabia and India, earned him the same title which Alexander had held. Bactria and Parthia were made Seleucid vassals, Armenia was annexed, and Syria was recovered from Egypt (202–198). Asia Minor, the Aegean islands, and the European mainland were threatened, but appealed for Roman help. Although he had made a secret treaty with Philip V of Macedon, Antiochus did not join him in resisting Rome. An attack on Thrace in 196 brought on long and inconclusive negotiations with the Roman senate. On the advice of Hannibal, who had taken refuge with him after the Second Punic War, Antiochus invaded Greece to encourage the resistance of the Aetolian League. Defeated at Thermopylae in 191 and the next year at Magnesia in Asia Minor, he was forced to agree to the peace of Apamea (188 B.C.), by which he had to pay Rome a heavy indemnity. His western boundary was set at the Taurus Mountains, and thus Seleucid ambitions in the Mediterranean area were permanently checked.

Antiochus' son, **SELEUCUS IV** (c.218–175), called Philopator, succeeded in 187 B.C., but after a brief reign was followed in 175 by a younger brother, Antiochus IV (q.v.), called Epiphanes. His attack on Egypt would probably have resulted in annexation if the Romans had not objected. Antiochus was extremely unpopular among the Jews of Palestine, whom he ruthlessly attempted to Hellenize, and his use of force there led to a massive resurgence of Jewish nationalism. Antiochus was killed in resisting a renewed Parthian threat in the east. The only King of any note among the later Seleucids was **ANTIOCHUS VII** (reigned 137–129), called Sidetes. He, too, died in battle against the Parthians, whose pressure continued to be a major threat to the eastern empire even after the Romans succeeded the Seleucids. The Seleucid line continued to exercise nominal sovereignty until 64 B.C., when Pompey overthrew **ANTIOCHUS XIII** and organized Syria as a Roman province.

The Seleucid Kings, especially Seleucus I, Antiochus I, and Antiochus III, were among the most gifted administrators of the Hellenistic age. They followed Alexander's precedent in founding new cities and inducing Greek veterans and immigrants to settle in them, side by side with indigenous Asians. Their enlightened rule had much to do with the prosperity of the Near East in the centuries around the beginning of the Christian Era.

SIMONIDES [sĭ-mŏn'ə-dēz] **OF CEOS** [sē'ŏs] (c.556–468 B.C.), Greek lyric poet. Simonides, who lived to be nearly 90, was highly esteemed as a poet by his contemporaries and was the intimate of some of the great rulers of his time. His compositions, today extant only in fragments, embraced most of the types of ancient lyric poetry. In addition to victory odes, dirges, dithyrambs, and drinking songs, Simonides composed magnificent funereal dedications to the Greeks who died in the Persian War. The epitaphs in which he celebrated the dead of Marathon and Thermopylae were renowned and imitated throughout antiquity.

SLAVERY. Among the Greeks slavery can be traced back to prehistoric times. The poems of Homer indicate that it was the expected fate for prisoners of war. Female slaves are portrayed as domestic servants, concubines, and workers in household industries, while the males worked chiefly in agriculture. Slavery was, according to Homer, limited in extent. Masters were kind, and slaves were loyal and affectionate. Later, however, slavery increased in importance, and slaves constituted a considerable portion of the population of the Greek city-states. When the Greeks colonized the shores of the Mediterranean and the Black Sea, the demand for the product of their handicraft industries multiplied enormously, and slave labor became increasingly important. In general, slave status was not regarded as degrading among the Greeks, nor was the treatment of slaves particularly harsh, though evidence of abuses is not lacking.

SOCRATES [sŏk'rə-tēz] (469–399 B.C.), Athenian philosopher. The son of Sophroniscus, he was strikingly ugly, physically strong, and indifferent to comfort, and possessed great physical and moral courage and a personal magnetism inspiring extraordinary devotion. Late in life he married Xanthippe, notorious for bad temper. He was condemned to death on a charge of corrupting young men, denying the city's gods, and introducing new divinities.

Believing in the living interchange of ideas in conversation, he wrote nothing, and his teaching lives through the work of pupils and friends, especially Plato and Xenophon. In Plato's dialogues he is often the chief speaker, and it is sometimes uncertain how much is historical.

Concern with Ethics. His passion was for moral reform, and he abandoned an early interest in natural science as irrelevant to questions of conduct and the purpose of life. He was fond of illustrating his teleological viewpoint from the crafts. A shoemaker must know what a shoe is and what it is for before he starts to work. Similarly, if, as everyone agreed, there is any general human virtue or ex-

Bust of Socrates, in the Capitoline Museum, Rome.
(ANDERSON—ART REFERENCE BUREAU)

cellence, there must be a function or purpose for a human being as such. Only by knowing what this is can we hope to live rightly: "therefore virtue is knowledge."

He laid no claim to this knowledge. His advantage lay only in awareness of his ignorance. He wished to persuade men to seek it with him, but was hindered by their delusion that they already possessed it. Hence his first task was destructive, to convince men of their ignorance. The Athenians classed him with the Sophists, who also said that men were ignorant, but there was an essential difference. The Sophists believed knowledge to be impossible, but Socrates saw it as an attainable goal.

Most men when asked what justice or courage was replied by enumerating instances. Socrates then pointed out that this was only the first of two necessary stages. To discover what justice is, instances of agreed just acts must first be collected, and secondly, examined, to discover the common quality by right of which they are called just. This, the "form" of justice, expressed in a definition, will be the answer to the question: "What is justice?" The method is inductive, and its outcome was to reduce all virtues, including justice, to an understanding of the true nature of good and evil. Armed with this understanding, Socrates believed, men would automatically choose the right: "No one errs voluntarily." Strength or weakness of will is ignored, an omission which Plato tried to remedy, and which was undoubtedly due to Socrates' own intrepid character.

His constant exhortation was to "care for the soul"

(*psyche*), and he introduced a novel conception of the soul as the whole rational and moral personality. The body is only its instrument. With this high estimate goes naturally a belief in its immortality. After his condemnation he argued that death was no evil, since it must be either a dreamless sleep or else a translation to a new life. He states both alternatives, but he would scarcely open his inner heart in a public speech, and Plato's *Phaedo* is evidence for his real conviction. Its arguments for immortality are those of Plato, but he would hardly have put them in Socrates' mouth if Socrates had denied the fact.

His Condemnation. The charge of irreligion was only sustained by harking back to his early interest in natural philosophers such as Anaxagoras. He worshiped the established gods and encouraged others to worship them. The charge of "introducing new divinities" relied on his "divine sign," an inward voice which he claimed to hear warning him against embarking on wrong courses of action. But he himself believed that this was the way in which one of the recognized gods chose to reveal his will to him, as he might to others through the accepted channels of oracles or omens. There was no question of introducing new divinities.

In fact, there was little substance in any of the charges brought against him. He had little difficulty in demonstrating that they were the fruit of long-standing prejudice, arising from his ceaseless probing of accepted ideas and values, and also from the fact that some of his youthful associates, such as Alcibiades, had earned just hatred for their political acts. His own insistence that good government demanded expert knowledge was itself unfavorable to democracy.

His uncompromising attitude at his trial made the death sentence inevitable. Afterward his friends planned to smuggle him across the state borders, but he refused on the grounds that since he had enjoyed the protection of Athenian law all his life, duty demanded that he abide by its decree now. A state, he argued, is doomed when individuals start flouting the laws because it suits them.

SOLON [sō'lŏn, sō'lən] (c.639–c.559 B.C.), Athenian statesman and poet. His name has become synonymous with impartial arbitration of civil disputes. Of a noble but not wealthy family, he moderated between aristocratic rights based on birth and property and the claims of landless and needy commoners. Surviving fragments of his poetry reflect wisdom, fairness, and intense patriotism.

He apparently first rose to prominence about 600 B.C. as a leader in the dispute with the neighboring state of Megara over control of the island of Salamis. In 594, when tension between rich and poor in the Athenian state had reached the breaking point, Solon as chief archon was granted extraordinary power to mediate the outstanding political and economic differences. How fairly he acted may be gauged by the fact that both sides criticized his reforms.

In the economic sphere he aimed to balance the power of the landed aristocracy by encouraging the growth of a new merchant middle class. To this end he encouraged trade and manufacturing, reformed the coinage, and offered citizenship to foreign artisans. He forbade loans on the security of the borrower's personal freedom, limited interest rates, encouraged the production and export of olive oil, and prohibited the export of grain.

His constitutional reforms became the basis of the Athenian democracy, although temporarily obscured by the succeeding tyranny of Pisistratus. The major magistracies and the aristocratic council of the Areopagus retained their steadying conservative force, but were now opened to wealthy businessmen. This power was counterbalanced by the institution of a new and more democratically controlled council (boule) of 400 which prepared and introduced business in the sovereign assembly (ecclesia), now opened to all freemen. Commoners gained the right of appeal to the popular courts (Heliaea) against the judgments of magistrates, and the severity of the earlier Draconian laws was moderated in other respects. According to tradition, Solon then left Athens to travel extensively in the east, partly to avoid pressure to modify his reforms.

SOPHISTS [sŏf'ĭsts], **THE,** itinerant educators who toured the cities of Greece in the 5th century B.C., lecturing and speaking for fees. Individual teachers rather than a school, they shared a common outlook—empirical, practical, and sceptical— and had great influence with the rising generation in the new democracies. Their denial of moral standards and absolute truth brought them into sharp conflict with Socrates and Plato. Among them Protagoras concentrated on the art of political success, Gorgias on rhetoric, and Prodicus on language; whereas Hippias was a Jack-of-all-trades, with his own memory-training system. In the Roman Empire the word became restricted to rhetoricians.

SOPHOCLES [sŏf'ə-klēz] (c.496–406 B.C.), Greek poet acclaimed since his own time as a dramatic genius of the highest order. He was born in Colonus, a suburb of Athens. After receiving the finest traditional and aristocratic education, he embarked upon a remarkably successful career in the theater. Twenty-four of his tetralogies (groups of three tragedies and a satyr play, presented in a single day) were awarded first prize in the dramatic competitions. Thus 96 of the 123 plays he is said to have written were publicly honored by his fellow Athenians. He was moderately prominent in the political life of the city as well, being twice elected to the high office of general, in which he appears to have served with no particular distinction.

A generation younger than Aeschylus, Sophocles was deeply influenced by the works of his great predecessor. Before his 40th year, he had achieved fame as a poet and had effected decisive changes in the form of Attic tragedy. Perhaps the most important of these was the addition of the third actor, which made possible a greater complexity of plot and subplot than was available in the two-actor Aeschylean theater. (It should be noted that Aeschylus, in the *Oresteia,* adopted this Sophoclean innovation.) Sophocles also abandoned the magniloquent diction of Aeschylus, turning to a style that was somewhat more colloquial, yet rich and dignified.

Only seven complete plays are extant, all written after his middle age. The earliest, the *Ajax* (c.445), exhibits a theme which repeatedly occupied the dramatist—the clash of traditional values with the new attitudes of the Athenian enlightenment. The same concern appears, in varying forms, in the *Antigone* (441), the *Trachiniae* and

Alinari—Art Reference Bureau

Antique bust of Sophocles, in the National Museum, Naples, Italy.

Electra (dates of both uncertain), and in the *Philoctetes* (409). *Oedipus Tyrannus* (c.428) is commonly regarded as his greatest play, largely because of its superbly tight dramatic structure, its masterful use of irony, and its psychological insights, from which Freud was to find inspiration. The *Oedipus at Colonus* (posthumous production, 401) strives to resolve the moral and religious problems posed in the earlier play, by proposing a mystic, divine reward for Oedipus, the sinner who had erred in ignorance but had suffered cruelly for his guilt.

Sophocles, reputed to be a pious, conservative Athenian, sees human nature as a basically good but fallible constant set against the backdrop of a regular, but mysterious, almost impersonal divine order which countenances no transgressions, however motivated. This constriction, stern as it is, is an indispensable condition of human greatness. It puts man to the ultimate test, in which he inevitably meets physical defeat, but is spiritually, and therefore tragically, victorious.

SPARTA, ancient Greek city-state, in Laconia, in the southeast Peloponnesus, occupying the valley of the Eurotas River. It is separated from Messenia to the west by a mountain range which includes Mount Taygetus (about 7,900 ft.). Argolis and Arcadia lie to the north.

The Spartans proper of historic times were limited to citizens of Sparta itself and of four neighboring villages who had full civil rights. The perioeci ("dwellers around") were ruled by Sparta and were liable for army service, but had no civil rights. They engaged in trade and industry, which was forbidden to Spartans. The helots were serfs attached to the soil, who tilled it for the Spartans. They were little better than slaves, though they, too, were drafted for military duty. These three groups together made up the Lacedaemonians.

Mycenaean remains have been found at nearby Amyclae and Therapne. In Homeric tradition Sparta was a Bronze Age kingdom ruled by Menelaus, husband of Helen, though it was no doubt dominated by powerful Mycenae in the Argolid. The advent of the Dorians at the end of the 2d millennium B.C. submerged the native Achaean population, many of whom probably became helots.

The Spartan constitution, remarkably similar to that of other Dorian cities, notably Gortyn in Crete, was ascribed to the lawgiver Lycurgus, of the late 9th century B.C. This date has been thought to be too early, but recent research supports it. There were two hereditary kings, with little power except as military commanders in the field, the Gerousia (Council of 28 Elders plus the two kings), the Apella (Assembly of all citizens over 30), and five powerful ephors (overseers elected annually by the citizens). The official list of magistrates goes back to 757 B.C.

Sparta in the 9th, 8th, and 7th Centuries. The prosperity of Sparta in the 9th, 8th, and 7th centuries is attested by the rich finds of this period from the great sanctuary of Artemis Orthia, excavated by the British. The First Messenian War (c.743–724 B.C.) led to the annexation of neighboring Messenia and the subjugation of its population as helots. About the same time, Tarentum, Sparta's lone overseas venture, was founded in Italy. Sparta flourished particularly in the 7th century, and poets and musicians, such as Terpander, Alcman, and Tyrtaeus, flocked there from all parts of the Greek world. Laconian pottery was highly prized and widely exported.

A massive helot revolt brought on the Second Messenian War (c.645–628 B.C.). The helots were put down with such difficulty that it became clear to the Spartans that if they were to keep their mastery they must eschew luxury and become a military state. It was then that a "Spartan" regime was imposed on every citizen. At the same time, gold and silver coinage was prohibited in favor of age-old iron. This put Sparta at a great disadvantage commercially and artistically. From then on Spartans became increasingly provincial and culturally backward in comparison with both the older Greek states and the burgeoning new ones.

Military Supremacy. The first part of the 6th century was mostly spent at war with Argos, but in 564 B.C., after the "Battle of the Champions," Sparta decisively defeated Argos and became unquestionably the greatest military power in the Peloponnesus. She then allied herself with Croesus of Lydia against the Persians and generally caused trouble for the Persian Empire. Sparta also tampered with the internal politics of other Greek states, expelling tyrants and installing oligarchies.

In the first Persian invasion of Greece a religious festival prevented the Spartans from fighting at Marathon, but in the second (480 B.C.) they reluctantly joined in at Salamis, after their heroic but unsuccessful stand at Thermopylae. At the decisive battle of Plataea (479 B.C.) they were pres-

ent in force and turned the tide of battle for the Greeks. In 464 B.C. Sparta was devastated by earthquake, and the helots, with some perioeci, took the opportunity to revolt, again being put down with difficulty, this time only with the aid of Athens.

By 457 B.C. the expansion of Athens had led the Spartans to ally themselves with the Boeotians and this alliance defeated Athens at the battle of Tanagra. The Thirty Years' Peace of 445 B.C. was ineffectual in resolving the rivalry between Athens and Sparta. Their rivalry culminated in the Peloponnesian War (431–404 B.C.), in which both sides had allies. The war ended with the total defeat and temporary ruin of Athens, and with Sparta the mistress of Greece. Sparta's ascendancy lasted until the rise of the Boeotian League, which defeated Sparta at Leuctra in 371 B.C. and freed Messenia from Spartan control. Sparta was again defeated by the Theban Epaminondas at Mantinea in 362 B.C., and Spartan supremacy was forever ended.

Decline. Under King Agis III, Sparta resisted the Macedonians, but was defeated at Megalopolis in 331. By the 3d century, wars and emigration had reduced the citizen population to a reported 700, and economic difficulties led Agis IV to a redistribution of the land. But he was executed by the ephors in 241 B.C. for exceeding his authority and his reforms were nullified. This redistribution and other reforms were later achieved by Cleomenes III, who admitted loyal perioeci to full citizenship, extending the citizenry to 4,000. But Cleomenes was overthrown at Sellasia in 222 B.C. by the Achaean League, allied with Macedon.

Sparta was concurrently involved in the wars of Alexander's successors, allied first with the Aetolian League, then with the Achaean League. In 148 B.C. Sparta seceded from the Achaean League. The constant intrigues, disorder, and open warfare in the Peloponnesus brought Roman intervention in 146 B.C., and Sparta became part of the province of Achaea. Sparta was finally destroyed by Alaric in 396 A.D. Its ruins were excavated by the British School, 1906–10 and 1924–29.

Spartan Constitution. The Spartan constitution and social system were regarded even in antiquity as political curiosities and have left no legacy in the West today. As developed, it was a kind of socialistic despotism, in which the state controlled, by common consent, the property, conduct, and even the lives of its full citizens. Among many strange institutions, perhaps the most striking was the isolation of all male citizens from the age of seven in military barracks (married men over 30 were allowed to sleep at home) and the common mess halls where they shared their frugal meals. Part of the boys' training was in stealing food for these meals—perhaps as training in foraging during campaigns—and flogging was the penalty for detection. Women suffered the same rough education until marriage, when they gained a degree of comfort and freedom. The plain of the Eurotas today yields much more than it did under the ancient regime and produces citrus fruits, raw silk, honey, and olive oil. The modern town of Sparta was built in 1834.

FREEDOM OF SPEECH. The Greek attitude toward freedom of speech was poignantly defined in Pericles' funeral oration. He declared, "Instead of looking on discussion as a stumbling block in the way of action, we Athenians think it a desirable preliminary to any wise action at all." In the Athenian democracy of the 5th century B.C. freedom of speech was upheld as a fundamental right of the citizen. There were few laws of libel or slander. Consequently political debates were often vehement and vituperative, an extreme which the Greeks acknowledged and allowed. This tendency had its dangers, as illustrated by the careers of such tyrants as Cleon and Hyperbolus, who utilized political demagoguery to manipulate the emotions of the populace. Demagoguery, the Peloponnesian War, and other factors eventually contributed to the destruction of freedom of speech.

Socrates' plea before the jury that eventually convicted him remains one of the most eloquent defenses for freedom of speech:

> If you offered to let me off this time on condition that I am not any longer to speak my mind in this search for wisdom, and that if I am caught doing this again I shall die, I should say to you, "Men of Athens, I shall obey the God rather than you. While I have life and strength I shall never cease to follow philosophy and to exhort and persuade any one of you whom I happen to meet. For this, be assured the God commands . . ." And, Athenians, I should go on to say, "Either acquit me or not; but understand that I shall never act differently, even if I have to die for it many times."

STOICISM [stō'ə-sĭz-əm], philosophical school founded at the end of the 4th century B.C. by Zeno of Citium and named after the hall (stoa) in Athens where he taught. The history and development of Stoicism falls into three periods. The chief figures in the early period are Zeno, Cleanthes, and Chrysippus. The middle period is represented by Panaetius and Posidonius (2d and 1st centuries B.C.), and the late period by Seneca, Epictetus, and Marcus Aurelius in Roman imperial times.

Stoicism is based on a materialistic pantheism adapted from Heraclitus (c.500 B.C.). A Logos (reason), related to fire, pervades the universe as God or fate, and man as human reason. Man must grasp the workings of this natural principle and live in harmony with it. Hence, as with Socrates, "virtue is knowledge." This is the only good. The sage is indifferent to external circumstances ("happy on the rack"), though it is admitted that certain things (for instance, health) will be preferred to others (for example, pain) if the choice is consistent with virtue. Knowing that pain and death are not evils, and pleasure not a good, the sage possesses all virtues: courage, temperance, justice. All other men are fools.

Panaetius, friend of Roman statesmen and admirer of Roman government, modified this rigidity in more practical directions and admitted degrees of progress toward virtue. In the Roman Empire, Stoicism became almost entirely concerned with conduct and practice. The most important literary monument of this time is the *Meditations* of Marcus Aurelius (121–180 A.D.). In logic the Stoics made an important advance on the syllogistic logic of Aristotle by creating the logic of propositions.

THALES [thā'lēz] (fl.6th century B.C.), Greek philosopher of Miletus, founder of the Ionian School. He taught that everything comes from water (or moisture in general), that the earth floats on water, and that everything is "full of gods." This probably meant, as Aristotle thought, that he regarded moisture as the principle of life and the whole universe as animate ("hylozoism"). One of the Seven Sages of Greece, he was credited with achievements, for instance in mathematics and astronomy, which were scarcely possible until later. But the story that he predicted an eclipse in 585 B.C. is well attested by Herodotus.

THEBES (modern **THEVAI**), ancient Greek city in Boeotia, located on the ridge dividing the region. During the greater part of its history it was one of the major cities of Greece. It was the scene of a cycle of myths, such as that of Oedipus, from which many Greek tragedians drew the plots of their plays. According to legend, Cadmus, King of Phoenicia, was its founder. He consulted the Delphic oracle, which told him to follow a certain cow and found his city where the cow lay down.

The oldest discovered remains of habitation are from the early Bronze Age. After about 1600 B.C. the city expanded in extent and power. A loose confederation of Boeotian cities under Theban leadership was formed some time in the 6th century B.C. About 560 Thebes shared in the foundation of Heraclea in Pontus. During the Persian invasion of 480–479 Thebes helped the Persians, losing control of the Boeotian League as a result of their defeat. But in 457, allied with Sparta against Athens, Thebes regained leadership of the League. Thebes fought on the Spartan side again in the Peloponnesian War. During the Corinthian War (395–387 B.C.), Thebes turned against Sparta, and under the peace treaty of the Spartan general Antalcidas, most of the Boeotian cities were freed from Theban domination. Sparta further undermined the position of Thebes in 382 when a Spartan commander seized its citadel, the Cadmea. This was recovered in 378 by the Theban general Pelopidas.

At the battle of Leuctra in 371 Spartan power was finally destroyed, and Thebes regained its position as head of the now powerful Boeotian League, under Epaminondas. When he was killed at the battle of Mantinea in 362 B.C., Theban power again declined. Thebes was defeated at Chaeronea in 338, fighting against Philip of Macedon. In 336, after Philip's death, it tried to break away from the Macedonians, but Alexander the Great destroyed most of the city in retaliation, massacred 6,000 inhabitants, and sold 30,000 into slavery. Quickly rebuilt, Thebes again suffered serious damage at the hands of the Roman general Sulla in 87 B.C. in punishment for siding with Mithridates. Insignificant in Roman times, Thebes became an important city in the Middle Ages, when it was noted for its silk manufacture. Excavations have revealed relatively few monuments. The most important is the Palace of Cadmus, which dates from the Bronze Age.

THEOGNIS [thē-ŏg'nĭs] (fl.6th century B.C.,), Greek elegiac poet from Megara. Living in an age of social unrest, he defended the values of a dying aristocracy. Theognis' poetry is characterized by an earnest and bitter tone of exhortation, most often addressed to his young friend Cyrnus.

THEOPHRASTUS [thē-ō-frăs'təs] (died c.287 B.C.), Greek philosopher. He succeeded Aristotle as head of the Peripatetic school. Keenly interested in natural science, he wrote extensively on botany, as well as a history of philosophy and a treatise on the nature of religion.

THURII [thū'rē-ī], ancient Greek city near Sybaris in southern Italy, founded about 452 B.C. by fugitives from Sybaris who were expelled by neighboring Croton. It was refounded by Athens in 443. Here Herodotus wrote the major part of his history of the Persian War. Later the city was an insignificant Roman colony. The ancient site has not been precisely located.

TRAGEDY [trăj'ə-dē], one of the principal forms of drama. It is of Greek origin, having begun in the ancient Greek theater, where it became the chief dramatic form.

Early History and Development. Tragedy derived from the Greek choral lyric—specifically from the chorus of worshipers who sang and danced round the altar of Dionysus. The form, originally choral, was gradually modified to assume a dramatic structure. Thespis, Greek poet of the 6th century B.C., is credited with having been the first to introduce an actor in addition to the chorus and its leader. Later a second actor was added (by Aeschylus) and then a third. In the plays of Aeschylus, Sophocles, and Euripides may be traced the monumental early development of tragedy, the rich expansion and the first traces of decline in the Greek style. It was largely from a study of the first two that Aristotle drew his conclusions concerning tragedy in the *Poetics* (see below). In this period the tragic performances were closely associated with religious celebrations, and for the most part the playwrights confined themselves to the treatment of a limited range of legendary material.

After the fall of Athens, numerous lesser writers of the ancient world essayed the tragic form, taking Euripides as their chief model, but these produced nothing of worth. Following their efforts, the Roman Seneca penned a series of tragedies imitative of the Greek form but more rhetorical and sensational. These were destined to prove a potent influence in Italian, French, and other theaters from the 16th century until the close of the 18th. In France, Pierre Corneille and Jean Racine refined and invigorated the classical style in the 17th century. Toward the end of the 18th century the Italian Vittorio Alfieri invested it with a fresh psychological content. Most of the works of their contemporaries, however, were uninteresting. These authors (1) tended to narrow the content of their tragedies to the theme of "love and honor" and (2) relied on a declamatory rhetoric that lacked life and fire.

The fact that tragedy is a dramatic form not limited to the Greek model was demonstrated by the Elizabethan theater. Undoubtedly Seneca's works influenced writers of the English tragic dramas, but basically these took their inspiration from native sources. For the most part the English works abandoned the restricted range of legendary subjects to which the majority of the classically inclined authors confined themselves. Despite this, the essential spirit of Shakespearean romantic tragedy is markedly akin to that of Sophocles' classical dramas. The Shakespearean form exerted a profound influence during the romantic period, although, apart from a few plays—notably those of Goethe and Schiller—it did not produce much of real value.

The Essential Nature of Tragedy. The correspondence between the spirit of Shakespearean and Sophoclean tragedy indicates that the tragic style is expressive of a basic human experience. This experience has been much discussed by critics since the time of Aristotle. Although a firm, positive definition of tragedy is impossible, certain basic qualities inherent in it are evident. One obvious element is the serious nature of the theme.

TROY [troi], in literature and legend, the city of King Priam, besieged for 10 years and finally taken by the Achaean army under Agamemnon. In archeological terms, it is a citadel of the Bronze Age in northwestern Asia Minor, some 3 mi. from the mouth of the Hellespont, or Dardanelles, near the modern village of Hissarlik. The site was found and first excavated by Heinrich Schliemann (q.v.), who worked there intermittently from 1870 to 1890. He was joined in 1882 by Wilhelm Dörpfeld, who collaborated with him and carried on the excavation in 1893 and 1894 after Schliemann's death. In annual campaigns (1932–38) the site was re-examined stratigraphically by an expedition from the University of Cincinnati, under the direction of Carl W. Blegen.

Situated on the crest of a natural scarp and looking out over the plain of the Scamander and Simois rivers toward the Hellespont, Troy had a commanding position. Through much, if not most, of its history, it was a fortified stronghold, the seat of a ruler with military power and authority. In times of danger the inhabitants of undefended villages in the district could take refuge within the walls.

A few of these villages were, indeed, settled in the Neolithic Period, before 3000 B.C., earlier than Troy itself. The first occupation of the principal site occurred in the early Bronze Age, when the working of metals was known, probably near the beginning of the 3d millennium. The people seem to have been hardy, conservative, and tenacious. A strong element of continuity and individuality is evident throughout the long history of Troy, although there were many changes, some of them violent and sudden. Dörpfeld distinguished nine principal periods of occupation. The Cincinnati excavations defined many phases in each of these chief settlements.

Troy I. Scarcely 100 yd. in diameter, the stronghold was surrounded by a massive wall with gates and towers. Some of the houses were relatively large (one measuring 22 by 60 ft.), rectangular or with apsidal ends. Objects found include a stone stele with human features carved in low relief; implements of copper, stone, bone, terra cotta; handmade pottery, chiefly gray and black, and a few pieces of imported Early Helladic wares.

Troy II. A citadel like the first but bigger, the area was enlarged three times by extension of the circuit walls. One of the gates was approached by a broad ramp. A great megaron occupied the central position and was surrounded by other buildings. Toward the end of the period, small houses encroached on the palace area as more people lived within the walls. This settlement was destroyed in a tremendous conflagration. In the ruins Schliemann found the "Great Treasure," comprising jewelry and ves-

Ruins of Troy's eastern wall and a tower. The fortifications, which are from Troy VI, were repaired in Troy VIIa.

sels of gold and silver. He thought that this level must represent the city of Priam. The mistake was corrected later. Troy II flourished in the 3d millennium B.C., the early Bronze Age, as is proven by the types of imported pottery and other objects, as well as by the relative stratigraphy.

Troy III–V. The site was resettled soon after the great fire, probably by the same people. The houses were small, clustered in irregular blocks that were divided by narrow lanes. It is not certain that major buildings existed or that the settlements were fortified. Household furnishings, however, were of traditional Trojan types. A jar assignable to Troy IV has been found in a context of Early Helladic III (c.2100–2000) at Lerna in the Argolid.

Troy VI. With the sixth settlement there is a change. There is little evidence of violent destruction in the remains of Troy V, but its characteristic features, which were still those of the early Bronze Age, are now replaced by others. Gray Minyan ware appears, locally made but identical with that of Middle Helladic settlements in Greece. Bones of the domestic horse are found for the first time. Clearly a new people had arrived and occupied the site (probably in the 19th century). Some of the old Trojan qualities persisted, but there was now a vigorous and orderly progress toward greater accomplishments.

About the time when the late Bronze Age began in Greece (16th century) the people of Troy VI were build-

ing the first of their fortifications, and these were gradually developed into a mighty system of defenses. The walls, some 16 ft. thick, were of solid masonry to a height of 20 ft. or more, and were topped with battlements of crude brick. The outer face had a slight batter and was divided into offset panels. At intervals there were massive towers which guarded the gates. Inside were concentric rings of streets and houses rising on terraces toward the center, where the palace presumably stood. The higher parts of the hill were cut away in later times, and no trace of them remains. Basements of the buildings that were spared are very large. Some have stone bases for the wooden columns that supported the upper stories of the buildings.

In the late stages of Troy VI the dead were cremated, and their ashes were buried in jars, a practice that occurred occasionally in Hittite lands but not in Mycenaean Greece. Yet the foreign contacts of the Trojans were with the Aegean rather than with central Anatolia. Late Helladic pottery was imported in considerable quantities, especially in the 14th century. Around 1300 the citadel was rocked and largely demolished by a violent earthquake.

Troy VIIA. The town was rebuilt after the disaster, the great circuit walls being restored to use, but the spacious buildings were replaced by much smaller and more crowded houses. Storage jars were sunk below the floors to hold extra provisions, suggesting that the people feared a siege. Local pottery was essentially like that of late Troy VI, but imports from Greece became scarce. Insofar as they can be dated, the latest pieces seem to belong to a time around 1250. Then, only a generation or two after the earthquake, Troy was utterly destroyed in a great fire. This presumably followed its capture by enemy forces, and may be equated historically with the taking of Troy by the Achaean armies of Agamemnon.

Troy VIIB. Again reoccupied by survivors who had escaped, the town continued its independent existence for a time, and then was overrun by immigrants or invaders. A barbarous people using peculiar handmade pottery, they may have come from the Balkans: They were not Phrygians, but were perhaps displaced in the upheavals which brought that race into central Asia Minor.

Troy VIII. Between 1100 and 700 (including the time when Homer lived) Troy was uninhabited. A small settlement was founded in the archaic Greek period.

Troy IX. In Hellenistic and Roman times there was a thriving town, called Ilium, or Ilion. It received patronage from Alexander and his successors because of its heroic past, and again from the Julian Emperors, who traced their descent from Aeneas. It survived until the 4th century A.D.

ZENO OF CITIUM [sĭsh′ē-əm] (332–262 B.C.), Greek philosopher, founder of Stoicism. Semitic by race, he left his home in Cyprus for Athens when 22. Cynicism first attracted him, but later he studied Plato, Aristotle, and earlier philosophies and finally evolved a systematic philosophy of his own, divided into logic, physics, and ethics. His teaching filled a contemporary need and drew large audiences, and his admirers included the Macedonian King Antigonus II.

ZENO OF ELEA [ē′lē-ə] (born c.490 B.C.), Greek philosopher. A pupil of Parmenides, he upheld the Eleatic thesis of the unity of being by attacking the notions of plurality, motion, and time as themselves absurd and contradictory. His famous paradoxes are directed against the hypotheses that magnitudes (and intervals of time and space) are either (1) infinitely divisible or (2) composed of individual units or moments. An example that treats space as infinitely divisible is the story of Achilles and the tortoise. Achilles can never overtake a tortoise that has started ahead of him, because when he reaches its starting point, it will have advanced to a farther point. When he reaches that point, it will have gone a little farther, and so ad infinitum. An example for the second paradox is that of the flying arrow. At any given moment the arrow occupies a space equal to its own dimensions, but a body which does this is at rest. Therefore the arrow is both moving and at rest. This example assumes motion like that on a cinema screen, composed of innumerable momentary "stills." Some of Zeno's other arguments aimed at showing that if there is a plurality of objects, they must be simultaneously finite and infinite in both number and size. Aristotle called Zeno the first dialectician, dialectic being defined as the art of arguing from opponents' premises.

HEBREW CIVILIZATION

HISTORY

JEWS, HISTORY OF THE. Jewish history is a complex phenomenon that resists a simple and concise summary. Its beginnings are to be traced back to the early civilizations of the ancient Near East; while its development involves an interaction with many empires and civilizations. It displays a bewildering array of contradictory manifestations that defy facile generalizations. Jewish history is the history of a people, living in its own land and enjoying independence; it is also a history of a people living on its own land, but subject to the sovereignty of powerful empires. It is the history of religious communities affirming their

viability in a world-wide diaspora (dispersion), long after the land of Israel had ceased to be a major area of Jewish settlement. Yet it is also the history that includes the emergence of the modern state of Israel. Wherever one turns, Jewish history confronts the historian with diverse and contradictory phenomena. Jews have created tribal, monarchical, theocratic, aristocratic, oligarchical, republican, and democratic forms of self-government. They have espoused innumerable religious formulations: prophetic, priestly, pharisaic, rabbinic, rationalistic, mystic; they have spawned heresies: they have embraced secularistic

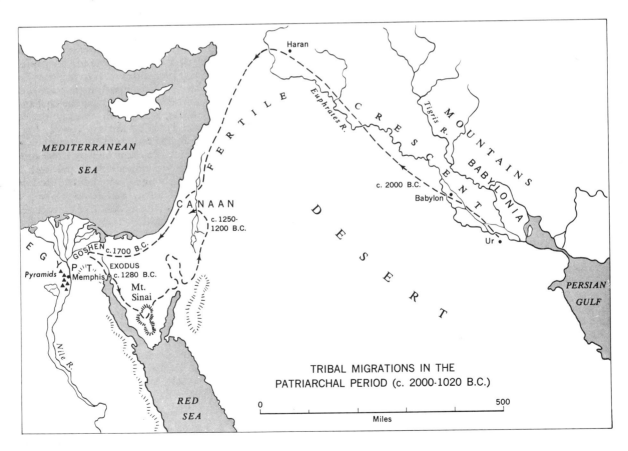

TRIBAL MIGRATIONS IN THE
PATRIARCHAL PERIOD (c. 2000-1020 B.C.)

"The Procession" (1957), by El-bert Weinberg. The man leading carries a Torah, or scroll of the law. Behind him walk three men, one carrying a prayer book and another a holy seven-branched candelabrum, or Menorah.

Frank J. Darmstaedter—Jewish Museum

and nationalistic ideologies. Jews have been nomads and peasants, shepherds and craftsmen, warriors and scholars, statesmen and pariahs, slaveowners and slaves, creditors and debtors, capitalists and proletarians, rich and poor. They have been literate and illiterate, provincial and cosmopolitan, naive and sophisticated, rationalistic and mystical, legalistic and moralistic, heretical and traditional, liberal and reactionary, nationalistic and universalistic. Such a welter of diverse and conflicting manifestations would present formidable problems for the historian even if they followed one upon the other, but they almost defy generalization when they are continuously intermingling, resisting neat classifications and categories.

To find our way through this bewildering maze, we shall approach Jewish history as a process displaying two major features: (1) An evolution of interdependent forms in the direction of greater and greater complexity. This evolution accounts for the differentiated character of Jewish history—that which makes it distinct and separate, and which justifies the giving of a single name, Jewish, to so contradictory a process. (2) A relationship with larger societies, cultures, and civilizations which is so interlocked in character that every phase in the history of the Jews bears the ineradicable stamp of these larger units. Yet the impress of the larger world is so absorbed and reworked

by the prevailing Jewish forms that the end result is the maintenance of a distinctively Jewish pattern. Jewish history can thus be thought of as a process that elaborates ever more complex and interdependent forms through an intellectually selective interaction with the larger social, cultural, and civilizational complexes within which this history developed.

Ancient Near Eastern Phase (2000–332 B.C.)

Patriarchal Period (2000–1020 B.C.). The history of the Jews had its origins in the migration of seminomadic Amorite tribes into the Fertile Crescent, c.2000 B.C. Some of these tribes, under their patriarchal chief Abraham, maintained their tent-dwelling culture in Canaan (Palestine), a land viewed as promised to them by their protector-God, El-Shaddai.

Compelled by famine to seek food in Egypt (c.1700), some of the tribes settled in Goshen. Reduced to servile status, they responded to the leadership of Moses, fled from Egypt c.1280, and at Mount Sinai covenanted themselves to Yahweh, the God whom Moses identified with Shaddai. They swore exclusive loyalty to Him and accepted legislation that Moses promulgated in His name.

Taking advantage of the weakening of Egyptian imperial control in Canaan, the tribes, under the leadership of Joshua, conquered a considerable part of Canaan c.1250–1200. A century of semianarchy followed these exploits. It was marked by occasional coalitions against external enemies, led by military chieftains, such as Gideon, called Judges.

Monarchical Period (1020–587 B.C.). The emergence of an agricultural-urban society transformed the seminomadic tribal structure, and ushered in a monarchical order. Confronted by the Philistine menace and the need for dependable state power, the prophet-priest Samuel first selected Saul (1020–1005 B.C.) and then David (c.1004–965) to unify the tribes under a monarchical system. David's son Solomon (c.965–926) consolidated the structure through heavy taxation, a bureaucratic hierarchy, a mercenary army, and an elaborate cultus in the Temple that he built at Jerusalem.

Resentful of this despotic system, the 10 northern tribes rebelled in 926 and established the kingdom of Israel. In contrast to the stable Davidic dynasty of the kingdom of Judah, the kingdom of Israel's history was marked by violent dynastic changes.

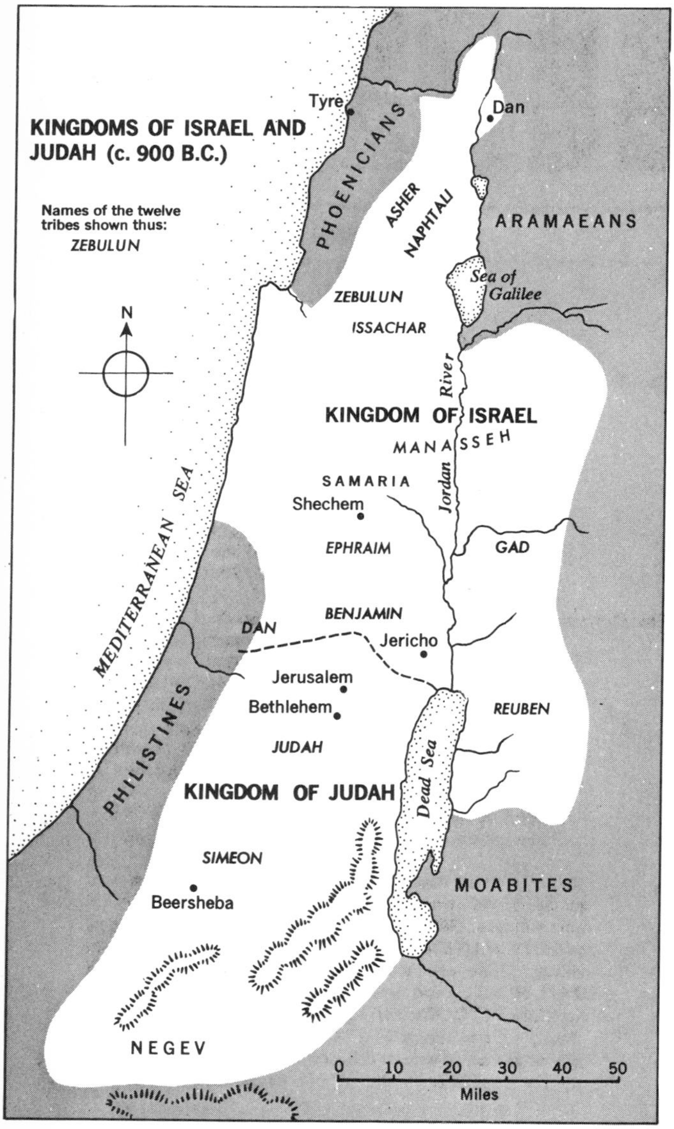

The cementing of commercial relations by the dynasty established by King Omri (882–871) with Tyre evoked the wrath of Elijah, who denounced Ahab (871–852) for introducing the Tyrian Baal. Elijah's insistence on the exclusive worship of Yahweh bore fruit when his successor Elisha supported Jehu's bid for the throne.

The Elijah-Elisha type of guild prophet was gradually superseded by a new kind of prophet. Amos was the first of these. Dissatisfied with the limited vision of the Yahweh exclusivists, he denounced the elaborate Yahwistic cult patronized by Jeroboam II (787–747) of Israel. He insisted that Yahweh was the God of justice, who abhorred the exploitation of the lower classes, and who would punish both Judah and Israel. The new prophetic message was spread in Israel by Hosea (c.747–735) and in Judah by Isaiah (c.740–701), Micah (745–700), and Jeremiah (626–c.585).

The rise of Assyria brought an end to the kingdom of Israel in 721, while the triumphant Babylonians destroyed Jerusalem and its Temple in 587. The Judaeans, however, were spared the fate of the lost Ten Tribes, for though exiled to Babylonia, they were not annihilated.

Since these catastrophic events had been predicted by the new prophets, the Jews accepted them as evidences of Yahweh's anger and not His weakness.

Exile and Restoration (587–445 B.C.). This notion was fortified by Ezekiel (c.592–c.570) who interpreted the destruction and exile as deserved punishment for disloyalty to Yahweh and for the profanation of His house by an impure priesthood. He prophesied a glorious reconstruction of the Temple cult. The Second Isaiah (c.550), however, placed greater emphasis on the cosmic power of Yahweh and conceived the restoration as an opportunity to spread His teachings throughout the world.

Persia's imperial successes were followed by Cyrus's permission for a restored Judaea in 538 B.C. Although the Temple was rebuilt around 516, the restored society remained unstable until a durable system—associated with the leadership of Nehemiah and Ezra and based on the canonization of the Pentateuch—was achieved (c.445).

Persian Domination (445–332 B.C.). As Persian imperial governor, Nehemiah set up a society that was centered around the Temple priesthood. Power was concentrated in the hands of the Aaronide priesthood, presided over by a high priest of the Aaron-Eleazar-Phineas-Zadok line, which sought its support from a free peasant class.

The authority for such far-reaching structural changes was the canonized Pentateuch. This remarkable document has for millenniums been accepted as divine revelation by Jews, Christians, and Muslims. Although modern scholars hold it to be a composite consisting of at least three distinct strata, it functioned from the time of its canonization (445 B.C.) as a unified work. As such, it stresses the efficacy of a sacrificial cultus, and it accords the Aaronides supreme authority. Though never attaining the rank of the Pentateuch, other writings, such as those of the prophets, were also venerated.

The newly established hierocracy proved to be a very

KINGDOMS OF ISRAEL AND JUDAH (c. 900 B.C.)

Names of the twelve tribes shown thus:
ZEBULUN

N

PHOENICIANS
Tyre
Dan
ASHER
NAPHTALI
ARAMAEANS
ZEBULUN
Sea of Galilee
ISSACHAR
Jordan River
KINGDOM OF ISRAEL
MANASSEH
SAMARIA
Shechem
EPHRAIM
GAD
MEDITERRANEAN SEA
BENJAMIN
DAN
Jericho
Jerusalem
Bethlehem
REUBEN
JUDAH
Dead Sea
PHILISTINES
KINGDOM OF JUDAH
SIMEON
Beersheba
MOABITES

NEGEV

0 10 20 30 40 50
Miles

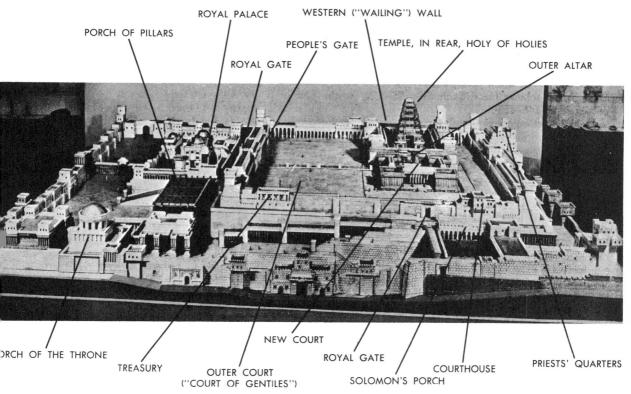

PORCH OF PILLARS   ROYAL PALACE   WESTERN ("WAILING") WALL

PEOPLE'S GATE   TEMPLE, IN REAR, HOLY OF HOLIES

ROYAL GATE   OUTER ALTAR

PORCH OF THE THRONE   NEW COURT   ROYAL GATE   PRIESTS' QUARTERS

TREASURY   OUTER COURT ("COURT OF GENTILES")   SOLOMON'S PORCH   COURTHOUSE

Frank J. Darmstaedter—Jewish Museum

Model of the great Temple built in Jerusalem by King Solomon (reigned c.970–930 B.C.). The Temple was destroyed in 587 B.C., when Jerusalem was conquered by the army of King Nebuchadnezzar of Babylon.

durable system till the reign of Antiochus IV Epiphanes (175–163 B.C.).

Greco-Roman Phase (332 B.C.–425 A.D.)

Hellenistic Domination (332–142 B.C.). Alexander the Great and his successors, the Ptolemies and the Seleucids, radically transformed the structural patterns of the Near East, primarily through the introduction of the Greek city-state and the Greek culture that accompanied it. Though the Aaronide hierocracy easily accommodated itself first to Alexander (336–323) and later to the Ptolemies (323–197) and the Seleucids (Antiochus III, 197–187), it could not but be affected by the quickened tempo of trade, commerce, urbanization, and cultural change. The integrity of the priesthood was severely undermined when Hellenistically oriented priests (Jason, Menelaus) vied with one another to buy the high priestly office from Antiochus IV Epiphanes. Favoring the extension of Hellenistic forms, Antiochus attempted to obliterate Judaism in 168 B.C. The majority of the Jews, however, were stirred to revolution, and rallied around the priest Mattathias, the Hasmonean. Under the effective military leadership of his sons Judas Maccabeus, Jonathan, and Simon, they were able to purify the temple and secure independence in 142 B.C.

Hasmonean Dynasty (142–63 B.C.). Simon the Hasmonean, in becoming high priest and ethnarch, ushered in not only a period of independence, but also a new high priestly dynasty. This was a momentous change, for hitherto the high priest had been from the family of Zadok, which traced its rights to Phineas, to whom God (Num. 25:10–13) had promised the high priesthood as an everlasting possession.

The legitimists (that is, Zadokites, whence "Sadducees") at first rejected the Hasmonean line, but subsequently they modified their opposition and supported the Hasmonean John Hyrcanus (135–104 B.C.) when he broke with the Pharisees.

The Pharisees were a revolutionary scholar class that had supported the claims of the Hasmonean high priesthood. This they were able to do because they posited the ultimate authority of an oral law that had been revealed by God simultaneously with the written law. Since this affirmation of an oral law subordinated the Zadokite hierocracy to a non-Aaronide scholar class, it was rejected by the Sadducees, who denounced these *Sopherim* ("scholars") as *Perushim* ("separatists," "heretics"; whence the name "Pharisees").

The masses, however, enthusiastically supported the Pharisees, the oral law, and the legitimacy of the Hasmonean high priesthood. Indeed, they sided with the Pharisees when the rupture occurred with John Hyrcanus, and they violently resisted Alexander Jannaeus' (103–76) attempt to consolidate a monarchy with Sadducean support. Only after Salome Alexandra (76–67) restored authority to the Pharisees and their oral law did the masses acquiesce in the monarchy. Thenceforth the Pharisees and their successors, the rabbis, were sovereign in the realm of Jewish law.

Roman Domination (63 B.C.–425 A.D.). Judaean independence was brief (142–63 B.C.). The collapse of the Hellenistic monarchies enabled Rome to take over the Near East, and Rome maintained imperial control over Palestine after the destruction of Jerusalem, either through puppet kings (Hyrcanus II, 63–40; Herod, 37–4 B.C.; Agrippa I, 41–44 A.D.), procurators (7–36 A.D., 44–66), through the scholar class (Sanhedrin, 70–132), or the patriarchate (145–425).

Heavy taxation coupled with provocative acts by the Roman authorities twice threw the Jews into bloody rebellion (66–70 A.D. and 132–35 A.D.). The first of these ended with the destruction of the Second Temple.

The turbulent years 7 to 70 A.D. encouraged a variety of dissident movements within Judaism, one of which grew up around Jesus of Galilee (c.4 B.C.–c.30 A.D.), who preached the imminent coming of the kingdom of God, and was himself deemed by his most devoted disciples to be the Messiah. Although the Procurator Pontius Pilate crucified Jesus (c.30) for the challenge to Roman sovereignty that a messianic "King of the Jews" implied, a small handful of Jesus' disciples, led by Peter, believed that he would return to usher in the kingdom. The movement made little headway among the Jews, but Paul, by rejecting the law, offered the message of the redemptive power of Christ, which had great appeal to the Gentiles. This rupture with Judaism, however, could not eradicate the historical consequences of the umbilical relationship.

Triumph of Oral-Law Judaism (70 A.D. on). The destruction of the Temple ended once and for all the cultus and the power of the Aaronides, and elevated to supremacy the Pharisaic scholar class. In the following centuries the majority of the Jews accepted the leadership of the scholar classes, whose authority was rooted in the concept of a twofold law, written and oral. Also, the synagogue form of religious expression made the cultus unnecessary.

The leadership of this scholar class was recognized by Rome when it permitted the reconstitution of its legislative body, the *Beth Din Ha-Gadol* (now called Sanhedrin), under the aegis of Johanan ben Zakkai (70 A.D.). Although the participation of some members of the scholar class in the unsuccessful Bar Kokhba revolt against Hadrian (132–35 A.D.) induced Rome temporarily to declare illegal the ordination of scholars, the Antonine emperors underwrote the authority of a strong patriarch, Judah ha-Nasi ("the Prince") (170–217). The latter effectively curbed the independence of individual members of the scholar class by curtailing ordination and by promulgating in the Mishnah an authoritative rendition of the oral law. Although the Mishnah, the patriarch's lawbook, bears—in its systematization and its logical-deductive mode of thought—the impress of Greco-Roman forms, it came to enjoy a sanctity almost equal to that of the Pentateuch.

The patriarchal absolutism of Judah ha-Nasi coincided with the last decades of Roman imperial splendor. The disastrous 3d century spelled not only mighty changes for the structure of empire but also for the viability of Palestinian Jewry. Although the patriarchate continued under Judah's progeny until the 5th century, it held sway over growing poverty and disintegration. The development of Rome into a Christian state encouraged further deterioration. Palestinian leadership steadily eroded, so that the Palestinian Talmud, unlike the Mishnah, never came to enjoy uncontested authority. With the abolition of the patriarchate, Palestinian Jewry played a relatively insignificant role until the Islamic period.

The Diaspora or Dispersion (from 586 B.C.)

With the decline of the patriarchal system in Palestine in the 3d century A.D., the history of the Jews shifts to other parts of the world. Indeed, except for very brief interludes (in the 10th, 16th, and 17th centuries), Palestine is only peripherally involved in Jewish history until the emergence of the Zionist movement at the turn of the 20th century.

As early as the destruction of the First Temple in 587 B.C., viable Jewish communities were set up by exiles in Babylonia and refugees in Egypt. With the Hellenization of the Near East, Jews settled in all the major cities. An especially virile community developed in Alexandria under the Ptolemies which produced a durable literature (for instance, the Septuagint, the Letter of Aristeas, and Philo) and enjoyed a vigorous life until the pogroms of the

Ruined synagogue at Capernaum on the northern shore of the Sea of Galilee. According to Luke 7:5, Jesus preached and performed miracles here. The synagogue was destroyed by earthquake.

Roman period (38 A.D.). By the time of Paul's journeys, Jews were living throughout the cities of the Roman and Parthian worlds.

Jews in the Sassanian World (225–650 A.D.). The Babylonian Jewish community of the Sassanian period, however, was the first Diaspora Jewry to dominate Jewish historical development for any substantial length of time.

Two Babylonian Jewish scholars, Rav (219–47) and Samuel (219–54), brought back with them from Palestine the patriarchal lawbook, the Mishnah, and adopted it as the fundamental law for the Babylonian Jewish scholar class. The decline in Palestinian fortunes, coupled with the favor shown the Jewish scholar class by the Persian Sassanian Emperor Shapur I (241–72 A.D.), enabled Rav and Samuel to free themselves from Palestinian authority, establish academies for the thorough study of the Mishnah, and determine the laws by which Babylonian Jewry was to be ruled.

The disintegration of Sassanian power brought with it deterioration of Jewish status, and led two scholars, Rav Ashi (375–427) and Rabina (474–99), to collect all the discussions (called Gemara) of the Babylonian Jewish scholar class into a massive work known as the Babylonian Talmud—no simple lawbook like the Mishnah, but a compendium of everything that the scholars had uttered. Though the Mishnah serves as its text, the Talmud contains not only complex legal debates over the meaning of the Mishnah but also homilies, folklore, anecdotes, and much else. Though never meant to be a code, the Talmud attained an authority among Jews paralleled only by the Mishnah and the Bible.

KINGDOM OF ISRAEL (722 B.C.)
0   Miles   30

KINGDOM OF ISRAEL

ISRAEL, KINGDOM OF, political establishment of the main body of the Hebrew people, known as Israelites. The chief power of this group resided in the two great northern tribes, Ephraim and Manasseh. The tribe of Judah was probably not originally considered a member of the group, a conjecture which is strengthened by its omission from the Song of Deborah (Judg. 5). Though they had a common religion, the Israelite tribes were at first politically independent, forming coalitions only in times of common danger (Book of Judges). But the attempt of the Philistines to subjugate Israelite territory (I Sam. 4:1–2) made necessary a greater unity, and Saul of the tribe of Benjamin was chosen King over all Israel (I Sam. 11:15). Thus the first Kingdom of Israel came into being, and its ruler took the field against the Philistines. In the war certain families from Judah, including that of Jesse, co-operated with the Israelites (I Sam. 17:12–19). After the defeat of Saul and the destruction of his family, David, who in the meantime had become King of an independent Judah, was invited by the Israelites to become their ruler also (II Sam. 5:3–5). Toward the end of his reign, during the rebellion of Absalom, the two parts of the Kingdom split apart, and David, after the rebellion had been put down, had difficulty achieving unity again (II Sam. 19:8–15, 40–43; 20:1–22).

Solomon, his son and successor, was an oppressive ruler, and when he died after a long reign, the resentment of the Israelites against a ruler from Judah came to the surface again. They assembled in Shechem, demanded relief from the oppressions of Solomon, and forced Rehoboam, Solomon's son and successor in Judah, to appear before them and give an answer to their demands. When the answer was unsatisfactory, the 10 northern tribes rebelled, and Rehoboam was forced to flee for his life to Jerusalem. Immediately, the Israelites chose as their king Jeroboam I, a former rebel against Solomon. Thus, about 930 B.C., the two parts of the Kingdom were separated, never to be joined again.

Israel, the northern Kingdom, in the period after Solomon, had about three times as much territory as Judah and twice as many people, in addition to greater natural wealth and economic advantages. But externally, it was more exposed to military attack, and internally, seeds of dissolution began to appear in the form of widespread disloyalty to the religion of Yahweh, coupled with bad social conditions, particularly an ever-growing disparity between rich and poor. The lack of a religious center like the Jerusalem Temple and of a political rallying point like the Davidic Dynasty were keenly felt. A number of dynastic changes were brought about by assassinations, sometimes provoked by prophets in the hope that the new king would prove more religiously loyal. The kings seldom had a clear foreign policy, often relying instead on playing off the great powers of the time, Assyria and Egypt, against each other. The foreign entanglements and internal weakness brought the final downfall of the Kingdom of Israel at the hands of Assyria in 722–21 B.C., leaving Judah as the sole surviving Hebrew nation. Through exchange of populations by the Assyrians, the former territory of Israel came to be inhabited by a culturally mixed people called the Samaritans, who were despised by the Jews, as the people of Judah came to be called (II Kings 17; Ezra 4:1–3; Neh. 4:1–2; John 4:9). Some of the more prominent Kings of Israel were Omri, Ahab, Jehu, and Jeroboam II.

KINGDOM OF JUDAH

JUDAH, KINGDOM OF, political establishment based on the (southern) tribe of Judah as distinguished from the main (northern) body of the Hebrew people known as Israel. While Judah had always been somewhat separate from the tribes of Israel, in the defensive war against the Philistines, David and other sons of Jesse, from Bethlehem in Judah, fought in the army of Israel under King Saul (I Sam. 17:12–15; 18:2–5). It was the expulsion of David from the Israelite ranks through Saul's jealousy that finally led to the establishment of a separate kingdom of Judah. After the defeat and death of Saul, David established himself in Hebron, and was there proclaimed king of Judah (II Sam. 2:1–7). Thus the kingdom of Judah came into being and grew steadily stronger (II Sam. 3:1). Later, the leaders of the tottering kingdom of Israel also placed themselves under David, thus bringing into being a united kingdom of Israel and Judah (II Sam. 5:1–5).

When the northern tribes seceded after the death of Solomon, the kingdom of Judah once more stood alone, only part of Benjamin having been wrested from Israel. Though Israel had more territory, more people, and more natural wealth, Judah had definite advantages in its retention of the Davidic dynasty and the city of Jerusalem, with all their political and religious prestige. It was also more secluded from the main routes of invading armies of the great powers of the time, and its primitive pastoral economy saved it from some of the internal social upheavals that plagued the northern kingdom. These factors enabled Judah to survive for more than a century after the fall of Israel. But political folly and religious apostasy finally contributed to the fall of Judah to the Chaldeans in 587–586 B.C. Unlike Israel, however, Judah experienced a limited restoration after deportation and exile. This revival was fortunately more religious than political, having the effects of preserving the spiritual heritage of Judaism, which in turn provided a basis for Christianity and Islam.

PALESTINE

PALESTINE [păl'ĭs-tĭn], a 10,000-sq.-mi. area connecting three continents at the eastern end of the Mediterranean.

Great Britain governed Palestine as a League of Nations mandate after World War I and in 1948 the mandate was replaced by the state of Israel.

The Land

Palestine has a varied topography and contains several climatic zones. Winter resorts on the Sea of Galilee (also known as Lake Kinneret and Lake Tiberias), almost 700 ft. below sea level, are an hour's drive from the summer resorts on the top of neighboring mountains and in cities such as Safad. Deserts, plains, mountains, seas, and the lowest place on earth at the Dead Sea (almost 1,300 ft. below sea level) are within easy reach in this land only slightly larger than New Hampshire.

Landforms. Wedged between sea and desert, the land of Palestine contains four parallel bands of contrasting landforms. On the west is the Mediterranean littoral broken by the Carmel range at Haifa and the Plain of Esdraelon (also known as the Plain of Jezreel). The coastal plain gradually widens southward to approximately 20 mi. at Beersheba. Traders and armies could easily move up along the coastal plain through the Megiddo pass into the wide and fertile Plain of Esdraelon to the Sea of Galilee, and from there on to Damascus and points east. The second band is the central range of Judaea, Samaria, and Galilee, broken by the Plain of Esdraelon. The third band is the sunken Jordan and Wadi Araba rift, or fault, which extends the length of the land from Dan to the Red Sea—and beyond into Africa. The fourth band is the eastern range of Transjordan.

Climate. Jerusalem and the Galilee mountains occasionally get snow. The rainy season begins in late October and extends through March. The remaining seasons are dry, and the summers are hot, with temperatures at the Dead and the Red seas climbing up to 120° F. Galilee receives more than 25 in. of rain, but southward the fall gradually diminishes. The northern Negev at Beersheba receives about 6 in., while Eilat (Elath) on the Red Sea receives little or no rain.

Cultivation of the Land. The history of Palestine is recorded in its soil. The ancient "land of milk and honey" was alternately tended and trampled, cherished and forsaken. The Nabataeans, in the Roman and Byzantine periods, cultivated even the wadis in the Negev desert. Shifting trade routes and selfish empires exploited the land and demoralized resourceful inhabitants until the hills were barren and the valleys useless.

History

The Roman and Byzantine Periods. In 135 A.D. the Roman Emperor Hadrian stamped out the determined and heroic Bar Kokhba rebellion in Judaea. He destroyed Jerusalem (or what remained of it after it had been laid waste by Titus in 70 A.D.) and began building on the ruins a new Roman city called Aelia Capitolina. Jews were forbidden to enter the new city; a pagan temple to Jupiter was built on the Temple site; and the name of the province was changed from Judaea to Syria Palestina. From then until the establishment of the state of Israel in 1948 "Palestine" was the geographical designation of the area.

The Bar Kokhba defeat was so overwhelming that it

made it impossible for Jewish independence to be realized until the modern era. The synagogue, an institution already 200 or more years old, became the center of worship, and the Jewish people prayed hopefully for the day of return and restoration.

The dispersion of the Jews under the Romans was never total, but there was a brief period of complete exile from Jerusalem. (They were permitted to return to Jerusalem by Empress Eudocia, d.460, widow of Theodosius II). Galilee became the center of Jewish population and learning; Tiberias, the seat of the Sanhedrin and the patriarchate. The synagogue plus the religious literature of the Jews (the Torah, the Mishnah, and the Jerusalem and Babylonian Talmuds) formed the basis for a strong spiritual and intellectual life.

Religious conflict and tension became characteristic of this Holy Land in which matters of religion did not easily yield to compromise. Rome, devoted to its pagan cults, faced first a resolute Judaism and then a determined Christianity. Both were considered threats to the Roman Empire and called for repressive measures. Unsuccessful efforts to destroy the Jewish religion, the soul of the Jewish people's resistance to Rome, took the form of forbidding circumcision, the observance of the Sabbath, the teaching of the Torah, and proselytizing. Jewish leaders and scholars—among them, Ishmael and Akiba—were martyred defying the ban.

Christianity in its early years freed itself from the land of its origin and became a faith with a universal concern and a zealous missionary outreach. Since its most aggressive impact was made elsewhere in the Empire, Rome's repressive measures and persecution were not as frequent or as violent in Palestine. However, the Holy Land had its share of martyrs, including the somewhat legendary St. George of Lydda.

Rome was interested more in tranquillity and prosperity than in uniformity of belief, especially in the provinces. Despite periodic upheavals, general prosperity prevailed in the eastern provinces. Cities east of the Jordan, such as Damascus and Heliopolis (Baalbek) of Lebanon, became wealthy trading cities. Palestine, too, reflected a measure of this prosperity.

Under the Emperor Constantine I (reigned 306–37), Christianity became a tolerated, then a favored, religion. Theodosius the Great (reigned 379–95) made Christianity the state religion by declaring that the creed worked out at the Council of Nicaea, at the insistence of Constantine, was to be the only accepted belief of the Empire. After Christianity and the state were thus joined, Christians became a privileged people, but Jews faced new hostility for refusing to accept Christianity. Emperor Julian (reigned 361–63), called the Apostate by Christians because he sought to restore paganism, wanted to help the Jews and even wished to rebuild the Temple. Ironically, these efforts not only came to nothing, but they precipitated violence against the very people he wished to assist. The Jews were denied public offices. They were not permitted to build synagogues, and many old synagogues were converted into churches. In 611, when Khosrau (Chosroes) II, King of Persia, invaded Syria and Palestine, the Jewish people gave him support, hoping to overcome their misfortunes and second-class status. Khosrau conquered Jerusalem and destroyed the Church of the Holy Sepulchre. His destructive rule lasted 15 years. The Byzantine Emperor Heraclius (reigned 610–41) retook the area, and there followed a massacre of Jews.

PEOPLE, PLACES, AND TERMS

AARON [âr′ən], in the Biblical account, elder brother of Moses, and progenitor of Israel's priests. The name is Egyptian and there is no reason to doubt that Aaron was a historical figure, the ancestor of a priestly family serving in the Israelite sanctuary of Bethel, where God was worshipped as riding on a bull. Later Old Testament writers regarded this worship with disapproval and considered it

PALESTINE

----- Present-day country boundaries

Miles
0   50

Beirut
Sidon
Tyre
Mt. Hermon (9,232')
Dan
Safad
Acre
GALILEE
SEA OF GALILEE
Haifa
Tiberias
CARMEL RANGE
Nazareth
PLAIN OF ESDRAELON
MEGIDDO PASS
Yarmuk R.
MEDITERRANEAN SEA
SAMARIA
ISRAEL
Tel Aviv-Jaffa
Jerusalem
Bethlehem
Gaza
JUDAEA
DEAD SEA
Hebron
Beersheba
NEGEV DESERT
COASTAL PLAIN
CENTRAL RANGE
WADI ARABA RIFT
EGYPT
SINAI PENINSULA
GULF OF AQABA
Eilat
Aqaba
JORDAN

a sin (Exod. 32). Aaron himself may never have been in Bethel, living rather in the south of Palestine, where tradition recorded his tomb on Mount Hor in Edom (Num. 20:22–29). In the growth of Israelite tradition Aaron was linked with Moses and Miriam as their brother, and after the exile of 586 B.C., when Bethel ceased to be an accepted sanctuary, Aaron's descendants were the sole legitimate priests of Jerusalem.

ABRAHAM [ā'brə-hăm], traditional progenitor of the Hebrews, a historical figure from antiquity who migrated with his family from Mesopotamia to Palestine (Gen. 11:31). No exact date for his life can be fixed, though the story of Abraham's battle against a confederacy of kingdoms in Genesis 14 contains the names of historical kings. None, however, can be certainly identified. Abraham lived a seminomadic life, with flocks and herds, settling for brief periods when pasture was good, then moving elsewhere. He received a revelation from God (Gen. 15:1ff.), who became known as "the Shield of Abraham," in which he was promised numerous descendants and permanent possession of the land where he pastured his flocks. Abraham lived in the south of Palestine, near Hebron, where the later Calebite clan remembered him. With the permanent settlement of Israelite tribes after the conquest of Canaan, the traditions were enlarged with stories of Beersheba, Shechem, and Bethel, and the divine promise was extended to include all the land of Canaan. Other tribal ancestors were then related to Abraham to present a picture of the family of the Patriarchs. Abraham thus came to be regarded as the father of all Israelites. David's kingdom was thought to be the divine fulfillment of the original promise to Abraham, and the Shield of Abraham was identified with Yahweh, the God of Israel. With the breakup of the kingdom, a renewed fulfillment of the promise was looked for in the future. The New Testament resumes the theme of God's promise to Abraham, but stresses that Abraham was righteous through faith (Gen. 15:6), and that those who show a similar obedience of faith, whether Jews or non-Jews, are the true heirs of Abraham and of the promises to him (Rom. 4).

ABSALOM [ăb'sə-ləm], third son of David, noted for his handsomeness and reckless ambition. By procuring the murder of his elder half brother Amnon, he both avenged a wrong done to his sister, Tamar, and made himself heir to the throne. Fearing David's wrath, he fled to the court of his grandfather, Talmai, King of Geshur (II Sam. 13:20–39). After three years he was allowed to return to Jerusalem, but was excluded from David's presence for two more years. A reconciliation followed; but Absalom took advantage of it to plot to obtain the throne.

After four years of this, Absalom raised the standard of revolt, and David was forced to flee. Ahithophel, a former counselor of David, advised Absalom to pursue the old King and strike him down before he could regroup his forces. But Hushai, secretly loyal to David, successfully counseled delay. When the rival forces met east of the Jordan, the rebel army was defeated. Absalom, fleeing, caught his hair in the branches of a tree and was dispatched by Joab.

AHAB [ā'hăb], King of Israel. Influenced by his Phoenician wife Jezebel, he introduced Baal worship into Israel. His corrupting innovations were strongly opposed by the prophet Elijah. For coveting Naboth's vineyard and causing his death, Ahab incurred divine retribution and his line was prophetically sentenced to extermination. In his foreign policy, he allied Israel with Phoenicia and Judah to counter Assyria, but, fulfilling the prophecies, met his death in a campaign against Syria (I Kings 16:29–22:40).

ASA [ā'sə], third King of Judah (c.917–876 B.C.). Blockaded by Israel's forces, he sought help from Benhadad, King of Syria. Criticized for this, he is yet praised by the Chronicler for his zeal in abolishing the foreign altars and heathen practices from Hebrew worship (II Chron. 14–16).

BAR COCHEBA or BAR KOKBA [bär kōкн'bä], **SIMON** (d.135), Hebrew hero and pretended Messiah, leader of the fanatical Jewish revolt against the Romans in Palestine (132–35 A.D.). The rebellion, which was touched off by Emperor Hadrian's decision to establish the Roman colony of Aelia Capitolina at Jerusalem and replace Yahweh's Temple with Jupiter's, destroyed over 500,000 people and 1,000 strongholds, and accelerated the Diaspora.

BENJAMIN, an Israelite tribe, settled in southern Palestine, noted for its military skill (Judg. 20:16). From them arose Israel's first King, Saul, and in their territory were the famous cities of Jerusalem, Jericho, and Bethel. In the later tribal history Benjamin was reckoned as Jacob's youngest son.

BETHEL, town in ancient Palestine, 12 mi. north of Jerusalem. Archeological excavation indicates that it was founded about 2000 B.C. as the main village of the area, replacing the 3d-millennium town, Ai, which had been destroyed. Heavily fortified as a Canaanite city-state (17th–13th centuries B.C.), it was destroyed by the invading Israelites and promptly reoccupied by them. It became the chief religious center of the northern kingdom of Israel (9th–6th centuries B.C.), chosen because of its close association with patriarchal traditions. (Gen. 28:10–19; 35:1–15; Josh. 12:16; I Kings 12:26–33). The site of Bethel is occupied by the village of Beitin, Jordan.

BRAZEN SERPENT, brass image God commanded Moses to erect to save the Israelites from the poisonous "fiery serpents" He had sent among them as punishment for their rebellion near Mt. Hor (Num. 21:4–9). The story reflects both a primitive belief in magic and the existence of a serpent cult in ancient Hebrew worship. The Brazen Serpent was popularly worshiped as a symbolic idol, called Nehushtan, until its abolition by King Hezekiah (II Kings 18:4).

COVENANT [kŭv'ə-nənt], **ARK OF THE,** wooden chest (described in Exod. 25:10–22) in the Tabernacle of Moses, and later, in the Temple of Solomon. It was made of acacia wood, approximately 3 ft. 9 in. long, 2 ft. 3 in. wide, and 2 ft. 3 in. deep. The wood was overlaid with gold, and the lid was of pure gold. The lid was termed "the mercy seat"; Yahweh was understood to dwell between the two golden cherubim on top of it. Hence, the ark was enshrined in the innermost sanctuary, the Holy of Holies. The ark originally contained the two tablets of stone on which were written the Ten Commandments, and other cultic objects were also placed in it for a time (Heb. 9:4). It was carried at the front of the Israelite host in the wilderness; and after some vicissitudes in Canaan (including capture by the Philistines) it was enshrined at Jerusalem during David's reign, before being placed in Solomon's Temple. Its later disappearance is a mystery, though it was probably stolen by Nebuchadnezzar's troops, who destroyed the Temple in 587 B.C.

COVENANT, BOOK OF THE, originally the legislation of Exodus (20:22–23:33), which, with the Ten Commandments (Exod. 20:2–17), listed Israel's obligations to Yahweh under the terms of the divine covenant. Many of its enactments are similar to sections of the Code of Hammurabi. How much of this legislation really dates from the time of Moses is impossible to say, but it undoubtedly had its beginnings then. It is, in fact, a commentary on the Ten Commandments, which in their earliest, abbreviated form were almost certainly Mosaic. Later the term was applied to the whole "Law of Moses."

DAN, Israelite tribe originally settled in west-central Palestine, but forced by the Philistines to migrate to the extreme north of the land. Their ancestor was claimed to be a son of Jacob.

DAVID, son of Jesse and second ruler of the united kingdom of Israel and Judah. Our knowledge of the historical David is considerable, information being found almost continuously from I Sam. 16 through I Kings 2. The youngest of eight brothers, he early attracted the attention of King Saul, either by slaying the Philistine giant Goliath, or by playing the lyre for Saul and thus soothing his depressions. For a brief time the young musician and warrior stood high in the favor of Saul and the Israelites. He excelled in battle, developed a deep friendship with Jonathan, Saul's eldest son, and married Michal, Saul's younger daughter. But Saul became increasingly jealous of David and sought to kill him.

David took refuge in the wild lands of southern Judah, gathering around him a retinue of freebooters, and living an outlaw existence. But Saul continued to pursue him so closely that he was forced to ally himself, temporarily, with the Philistines. When the latter moved northward for their final battle with Saul, they left David and his men behind, fearing their defection to the Israelites. After Saul was defeated and killed, David appeared in Hebron and was proclaimed King of Judah, which had never been strongly attached to Israel. As the result of losses in the war, followed by a series of assassinations, partly engineered by Joab, David's commander, the Israelites were soon left without either royal family or military leaders. They then turned to David and offered him the kingship of Israel in addition to that of Judah.

David's first act was to capture Jerusalem, the last town remaining in Canaanite hands, and make it his capital,

Alinari—Art Reference Bureau

"David with the Head of Goliath" by Caravaggio, in the Borghese Gallery, Rome.

since it was strategically located between the two parts of the kingdom. Then followed the expulsion of the Philistines, his former allies, from his new territory. The Ark of the Covenant was brought to the capital to make it the religious as well as the political center of the kingdom. The new king then embarked on a highly successful military conquest of the little kingdoms to the east and north. It was during a campaign against the Ammonites, carried on by Joab while David remained in Jerusalem, that the adulterous affair with Bathsheba took place. Bathsheba's husband, Uriah, was killed and the woman herself was incorporated into the King's harem. The most serious threat to the kingdom during David's long rule was the revolt of his son Absalom, who was killed in battle. As a result of the influence of Bathsheba, her son Solomon, rather than Adonijah, the eldest remaining son of David, succeeded to his father's throne.

David is said to have reigned 40 years (c.1010–970 B.C.). His ability in war was greater than his skill in civil affairs. Yet he was on the whole very able and deeply religious, leaving a mark for all time on Biblical history and religion. He has been idealized in the Books of Chronicles, is connected by tradition with the Book of Psalms, and is often referred to in the Bible as the prototype of the Messiah (Jer. 33:15; Ezek. 34:23–24; John 7:42; Rev. 3:7).

ELIJAH [ĭ-lī′jə], one of the great prophets of the Old Testament, who exercised his stormy ministry in Israel during

169

the reigns of Ahab and Ahaziah (869–849 B.C.). He is known from the record of his activity in the books of Kings (I Kings 17–19, 21; II Kings 1–2). A gaunt figure of forbidding appearance and fierce conviction, he fought for the distinctiveness of the Mosaic faith when it was threatened by the cults of Canaan (I Kings 18:17–40; II Kings 1:1–17) and for social justice when it was threatened by royal tyranny (I Kings 21). Standing in the tradition which runs from Moses to Amos, he earned the title "Troubler of Israel" (I Kings 18:17) and knew the burden of his prophetic commission (I Kings 19:4–8). His reputation became legendary in Jewish tradition. He was expected to return before the coming of the Kingdom of God (Mal. 4:5) and is regarded in the New Testament as the typical Old Testament prophet (Mark 9:4).

EPHRAIM [ē'frē-ĭm], Israelite tribe settled in the central highlands of Palestine, named after the mountain range there. Their ancestor later came to be regarded as a son of Joseph.

ESSENES [ĕs'ēnz], a group of Jewish ascetics who flourished from about 200 B.C. to 100 A.D. The name has been variously derived from Hebrew, Aramaic, and Syriac words covering a wide range of meanings. As described by such ancient authors as Josephus (in the *Antiquities* and *Wars*), and Philo (in the *Apology for the Jews*), they lived for the most part among, but separated from, the larger community, observing their own interpretation of the laws of ritual purity with great vigor.

"They shunned pleasures as a vice and regarded temperance and the control of the passions as a special virtue. Disdaining marriage, they adopted other men's children" (Josephus). They lived a communal existence, in which all possessions were owned jointly, and elected officers to attend to the interests of the community. The communal meal was an important function in the life of the group. They were devoted to charity and to study. Entrance into the group was preceded by a strict period of probation; infringement of its rules resulted in expulsion. The doctrine of the soul's immortality was strongly affirmed.

Since the discovery of the Dead Sea Scrolls at Qumran in 1947, there has been renewed interest in the Essenes. A number of scholars have identified the community of Qumran with them, and have used the writings of that group to explain long-standing mysteries concerning the Essenes. The occurrence of the name Hasidin (*see* HASIDIM) in one document revived the identification of the Essenes with the Assideans of the Maccabean period.

EXILE, THE, also called the Babylonian Captivity, the period following Nebuchadnezzar's conquest of Judah in the 6th century B.C., during which the leaders of the Jewish community were exiled in Babylon. The first deportation occurred after the devastation of Judaean towns in 597 (II Kings 24) and the second deportation after the destruction of the Temple and city of Jerusalem in 587 (II Kings 25). The return of the exiles began fitfully after Cyrus the Persian conquered Babylon in 539 and issued his edict of religious toleration (Ezra 6:3–5). He appointed Sheshbazzar to restore the sacred vessels to Jerusalem and lay the foundations of the Second Temple (Ezra 1:7–11;

5:14–16). A larger number of Jews returned home with Zerubbabel, a Davidic prince appointed Governor of Judah, some time before 522, and in conditions of great difficulty (Hag. 1:1–11) the new Temple was completed in the spring of 515 (Ezra 6:13–18). The Jews in Babylon during the "Captivity," so far from being prisoners, lived in their own communities (Ezek. 3:15; 33:30–33) and were free to develop such distinctive religious observances as the Sabbath and Circumcision. Many families settled and prospered in their new surroundings (Jer. 29:5–13) and never returned to Palestine. Although Jewish religious life was maintained amid the ruins of Jerusalem throughout this period (Jer. 41:5), the Exile was the most decisive turning point in Old Testament history. It brought to an end Israel's existence as an independent state, and with it the institution of the Davidic monarchy. It inaugurated the priestly and scribal community of postexilic Judaism.

FAMILY LIFE. Many modern family patterns originated among the ancient Hebrews, Greeks, and Romans. In all three of these groups the family was patriarchal in character and women were under the legal control of their husbands. Hebrew women, for example, could not inherit property or indulge in commercial or political activities. They were forced to dress conservatively, to make sure that their bodies were well covered, and to wear veils. Whereas the husband could procure a divorce for whatever reason suited him, the Hebrew wife had no legal right to divorce. Although the Hebrew patriarch had extensive familial power, the community expected him not to abuse his authority. Along with his patriarchal privileges went responsibilities; that is, he was expected to be a good husband and father, to provide food and shelter for his family, and to protect them from danger. Husbands who did not fulfill their familial obligations faced public criticism. Although the husband had the right to divorce his wife for any reason, the community did not look kindly upon men who procured a divorce on trivial grounds. Unless the cause was considered a just one, such as adultery or sterility, the husband would not receive the support of the community. Sterility was considered a serious ground because family names were important. Childbearing was a sacred obligation, and it was considered sinful to let family names die out; in fact, barrenness or sterility was interpreted as an omen of God's disapproval. The ancient Hebrews practiced tribal endogamy, or marriage within the group.

Adultery was considered a heinous offense by the Hebrews, particularly on the part of the wife; the death penalty was prescribed, although it is not clear how often it was actually imposed. Sex relations on the part of single people was also considered a sin, though it is referred to much less often in the Old Testament than is adultery. Nevertheless, virginity was practically mandatory on the part of a bride-to-be, and violators received harsh punishment; the death penalty might even be imposed. For virtually all sex offenses, violations by the female were considered more serious than those committed by the male. This double standard of sexual behavior has existed at all times among virtually all peoples.

GAD (Heb., "good fortune"), an Israelite tribe settled in the central region of Palestine, east of the River Jordan. It claimed as its tribal ancestor a son of Jacob (Gen. 30:11).

HASIDIM [hä-sē'dĭm] (Heb., "men of steadfast love," plural of *hasid*), name applied to three distinct Jewish groups: (1) Strict observers in the time of Judas Maccabeus who joined in the revolt against the Seleucids (167–162 B.C.); (2) mystics in the Rhineland at the end of the 12th century; and (3) members of a mystical pietist movement called Hasidism (q.v.) that began in the 18th century.

HASMONEAN [hăz-mə-nē'ən] **DYNASTY** (167–29 B.C.), Jewish dynasty founded by the Maccabees. They were descendants of Mattathias, the priest who led the revolt against the Seleucid King, Antiochus IV Ephiphanes (176–163 B.C.). The victory over the Syrians, achieved by Judas Maccabeus and his brothers Jonathan and Simon, resulted in independent status within the Seleucid empire. The family took the high priestly office (152 B.C.). Simon became ethnarch and high priest in 140 B.C., and his son, John Hyrcanus, transformed Judaea into a Hellenistic princedom. Under Alexander Jannaeus (d.76 B.C.) the kingship was restored, but his two sons, Aristobulus and Hyrcanus II, engaged in a civil war which resulted in the intervention of Rome and Pompey's taking of Jerusalem (67 B.C.). The dynasty was now reduced to the status of petty Hellenistic princelings. Hyrcanus II was overthrown by his nephew Antigonus in 40 B.C.; Antigonus was in turn removed by the Romans in 37 B.C. The rule was then entrusted to Herod, son of Antipater, appointed procurator of Judaea by Julius Caesar. Herod, who had married Mariamne, the granddaughter of Hyrcanus II, entered upon a systematic destruction of the family, ending with the death of the last survivor in 25 B.C.

HEBREW, a member of the Canaanite division of the Northwest Semitic branch of the Semitic subgroup of the Afro-Asiatic family of languages. Hebrew originated in the general area now partly occupied by the state of Israel, and may have descended from earliest Ugaritic.

The basic characteristic of Hebrew, as well as of all other Semitic languages, is that the words have roots consisting of three consonants. Inflectional changes in tense, mood, person, or number are indicated by interpolated vowels, added prefixes or suffixes, and doubling of the root consonants, in accordance with strict rules. In its original form, the Hebrew verb had two quasi-tenses, loosely termed "past" and "present," which denoted complete and incomplete action respectively.

The 22 letters of the alphabet are all consonants. The language is written from right to left without vowels.

HEBREW LITERATURE, the literature in the Hebrew language, together with literature pertaining to the Jewish religion written in other languages.

Old Testament and Apocrypha. The Old Testament contains writings from more than 3,000 years ago to the 2d century B.C. Some of the books excluded from the Biblical canon and some works in Biblical style of later origin (up to c.100 A.D.) were preserved (mostly in Greek translation) in the Apocrypha and in the Pseudepigrapha.

Hellenism. The spread of Greek civilization generated contacts between Judaism and Hellenism, especially in Ptolemaic Egypt. In the 3d century B.C. the Pentateuch was translated into Greek. The Greek version of the Bible, known as the Septuagint, of which this translation of the Pentateuch was the first part, was intended both for Greek-speaking Jews and for intelligent heathen. The Apocryphal Wisdom of Solomon (2d century B.C.) fused Judaic with Greek ideas. Philo Judaeus, also known as Philo of Alexandria (c.30 B.C.–c.40 A.D.), advocated a synthesis between Hebrew and Greek wisdom. Flavius Josephus (38–c.100 A.D.), of Jerusalem and Rome, described the Judaeo-Roman war of 66–73 A.D. (*The Jewish War*) and wrote a history of his people (*Jewish Antiquities*) and a treatise in defense of Judaism (*Against Apion*), all in Greek.

The Dead Sea Sect. Since 1947 we have possessed some of the writings of the Essenes (fl.2d century B.C.–1st century A.D.). The Scroll of Discipline records the rules by which they lived; the Thanksgiving Hymns, their devotional life; and the War of the Sons of Light with the Sons of Darkness, their Messianic beliefs.

Rabbinism and Biblical Scholarship. After the destruction in 70 A.D. of the Second Temple and with the rise of new centers of Judaism (for example, in Babylonia), more and more emphasis was placed on exegesis of the Bible, interpretation of the Law (as originally given in the Torah, or Pentateuch), and study of the classical traditions. The basic record of these investigations is contained in the Palestinian and Babylonian versions of the Talmud, which were completed in the 4th and 5th centuries, respectively. Nonlegal, theological, historical, and legendary materials are contained in numerous Midrashim, homiletic works of the same period. The post-Talmudic Geonim, heads of academies in Babylonia, wrote *Responsa*, or scholarly answers to legal inquiries. In the Gaonic period (589–1038), too, a uniform Biblical text (the Masorah) was established.

HEROD THE GREAT (73–4 B.C.), King of the Jews (37–4 B.C.). His father, Antipater, of Idumean Arab descent, was chief minister to Hyrcanus II, Hasmonean high priest who ruled under Roman control. Herod began his career successfully at the age of 26 as Governor of Galilee. After his father's murder, he and his brother Phasael were made Tetrarchs (Princes) by Mark Antony. Invasion of Palestine in 40 B.C. by the Parthian general Pacorus forced Herod to flee to Rome for help, and the senate made him King of the Jews. Three years later he was able to take Jerusalem, and at that time married Mariamne, daughter of Hyrcanus II.

Herod showed great skill in ruling his kingdom, with its mixed Jewish and pagan population. He was loyal to Augustus, as he had been to Antony. He brought order to the country east of the Jordan, and in times of famine reduced taxes and provided food from his private fortune. In non-Jewish cities such as Sebaste (Samaria) he built temples to Augustus, and he provided Caesarea with a splendid harbor. Jerusalem was adorned with public buildings and the Jewish Temple was begun in 19 B.C. A patron of Greco-Roman culture and literature, Herod also tried to promote the honor and welfare of the Jewish religion, but he never understood its spirit.

He had always ruled severely and with the help of secret police. In his later years there were court intrigues involving his various wives and children. He had several of these, including his wife Mariamne, executed. Herod died in Jericho of a loathsome disease just after condemning to death a group of Jewish zealots who had torn down the golden eagle which had been placed over the entrance to the Temple. The story of his massacre of the children around Bethlehem is told only in the New Testament (Matt. 2:16) but is in character.

HEZEKIAH [hĕz-ə-kī′ə], 14th King of Judah (c.715–687 B.C.). He inherited subservience to Assyria from his father, Ahaz, but sought to break away. Foreign religious practices were eliminated from the temple in Jerusalem as part of this policy. Isaiah warned against an alliance with Egypt, but Hezekiah disregarded his pleas, and in 701 Sennacherib besieged Jerusalem. Hezekiah paid a heavy indemnity and the Assyrians withdrew after ravaging the country around the city.

ISAIAH [ī-zā′yə] **I**, aristocratic citizen of Jerusalem, son of Amoz, called to a prophetic ministry which lasted from about 742 to 701 B.C. His preaching was distinctively shaped by a series of international crises. In 735–733 B.C. Judah was being coerced to join an Aramaean-Israelite coalition against Assyria. Ahaz, the King of Judah, wished, rather, to take his stand with Assyria, but Isaiah strenuously opposed dependence on foreign alliances (Isa. 7:1–8:4). The people's trust should be in God alone (30:15). This cardinal conviction led the prophet to denounce a plot to join Egypt in a revolt against Assyria in 714–711 B.C. (20:1–6) and again in 705 B.C. (30: 1–7; 31:1–3).

Although Isaiah was almost certainly brought up to believe in the special sanctity of Jerusalem, he came to expect God's judgment of the holy city (5:1–7; 28:7–13), and it is probable that the oracles which represent Zion as being especially protected for all time (10:24–27; 29:5–8; 31:4–9) present the outlook of his less heroic and less penetrating disciples.

Isaiah was the first to speak of God as "the Holy One of Israel" (1:4). This, like the revealing phrase, "the glory of his majesty" (2:10, 19, 21) expressed the prophet's fundamental conviction that the course of history and the destiny of Israel were in the hands of a righteous Sovereign Power (14:24–27), whom to trust was the only way of salvation.

ISAIAH II, title given to the anonymous poet-prophet to whom we owe Isaiah 40–55. A true successor to pre-exilic prophets like Hosea, Isaiah, and Jeremiah, he lived with the Babylonian exiles, and about 539 B.C. wrote his profound interpretation of their condition and future vocation to meet their bewilderment and threatened loss of faith. Israel, he declared, was called to be God's agent, His suffering servant, in a mission to the whole world. He saw in Cyrus' conquest of Babylon the dawn of a new age, which would see the return of the exiles to Palestine, the restoration of Jerusalem, and the fulfillment of God's age-long purpose which He first disclosed in the creation of the world.

JEHOIACHIN, also called Jeconiah (Jer. 24:1), or Coniah (Jer. 22:24), next to the last King of Judah. Grandson of Josiah and son of Jehoiakim, he had reigned only three months when Jerusalem was taken by the Chaldaeans, and he and his family, and other leaders, were carried into captivity (II Kings 24:8–17). He was succeded by his uncle, Zedekiah.

JEHOIAKIM (d.598 B.C.), originally called Eliakim, King of Judah. Son of Josiah and father of Jehoiachin, he was put on the throne by the Egyptians, who had defeated and killed his father in 609 B.C. When the Chaldaeans defeated the Egyptians in 605, Jehoiakim transferred his allegiance to Nebuchadnezzar, but he rebelled shortly after (II Kings 24:1).

JEHOSHAPHAT [jĭ-hŏsh′ə-făt], fourth King of Judah. Forming an alliance with Ahab, King of Israel, he fought with him against Syria at Ramoth-Gilead, where Ahab was killed. Later he joined Ahab's son, Jehoram (or Joram), in a campaign against Moab. Controlling Edom, he constructed a fleet of merchant ships for trade on the Red Sea, but a storm wrecked the ships and put an end to the project.

JEHOVAH [jĭ-hō′və], modern form of the Hebrew sacred name of God, probably originally "Yahweh." From c.300 B.C. the Jews, from motives of piety, uttered the name of God very rarely and eventually not at all, but substituted the title "Adonai," meaning "Lord," the vowels of which were written under the consonants of "Yahweh." In the Middle Ages and later, the vowels of one word with the consonants of the other were misread as Jehovah.

JEHU [jē′hū], 10th King of Israel. A commander under Joram (Jehoram), the son of Ahab, he fell under the influence of the prophet Elisha, had himself declared King by his men, and then assassinated both his master and the visiting King of Judah, Ahaziah. By further wholesale assassinations, he attempted, unsuccessfully, to eliminate Baalism from Israel (II Kings, 9, 10).

JEREMIAH [jĕr-ə-mī′ə], the most sensitive and intimately known of all the great Old Testament prophets, whose 40 years' ministry coincided with the decline and fall of the kingdom of Judah. Born about 650 B.C., the son of a priest family at Anathoth just north of Jerusalem, he was called to be a prophet in 626, and continued to proclaim the coming judgment of his people until after 587.

Jeremiah's life and work fall into four periods. (1) In the reign of Josiah (626–609), he supported the King's policy of national reform (cf. 22:15f.) and especially the abolition of the idolatrous practices encouraged by his predecessor, Manasseh. (2) In the reign of Jehoiakim (609–598), the unscrupulous despot established on the throne by the Egyptians, Jeremiah castigated the king's social and political behavior (22:13–19), denounced the people's superstitious reliance on the Temple (chap. 7 and 26:1–7) and exposed the fraudulence of the professional prophets (chap. 23). In consequence, he was subjected to ridicule and the threat of death (19:14–20:6; 26:8–24). (3) In the reign of Zedekiah (597–587), a weakling put on the throne by the new power of Babylon after the first attack on Jerusalem, Jeremiah strenuously opposed rebellion against Babylon (21:8–10; 28; 38:17f.), which he regarded as God's agent of judgment on Judah (25:9; 27:6); as a result, he was imprisoned by the nationalists as a defeatist and a traitor to his country (37:11–38:16). (4) After the fall of Jerusalem in 587 B.C., Jeremiah joined the governor Gedaliah at Mizpah (chaps. 40 and 41) and was eventually taken as an exile to Egypt, where he disappears from history (chaps. 42–44).

Through years of physical suffering, intense mental anguish and spiritual isolation (cf. 4:19f.; 11:18–23; 12:1–6; 15:10–21; 17:14–18; 18:18–23; 20:7–18), Jeremiah discovered the reality of an inward relationship with God, which was independent of institutional religion, which was a possibility for the Jewish exiles cut off from Temple and sacrifice in Babylon (chap. 29) and which, he believed, would become the universal experience of all God's people when he established his New Covenant (31:31–34). In Jeremiah, the prophetic faith of Israel found expression in a person.

JEROBOAM [jĕr-ə-bō′əm] **I,** first King of Israel after the division of the kingdom. During the reign of Solomon, Jeroboam became, through great personal ability, an overseer of forced labor in the northern part of the nation. Since he was from Ephraim, the principal northern tribe, disaffected elements began to look to him for leadership. He became involved with the prophet Ahijah in a plot against Solomon and was forced to flee to Egypt, where he remained until Solomon's death (I Kings 11:26–40). Returning to his native land, he assumed leadership of the northern tribes in their demands on Rehoboam. When the latter refused to make concessions, the Israelites revolted and set up their own kingdom under Jeroboam (I Kings 12:12–20). Though he reigned 22 years and carried on incessant war with Judah, Jeroboam disappointed many of his supporters by a religious laxity almost as extreme as that of Solomon (I Kings 12:25–14:20).

JEROBOAM II, 13th King of Israel after the division. His long reign (c.786–746 B.C.) was characterized by a superficial prosperity that served only partially to hide the moral and social evils underneath. It was during this time that the two great prophets, Amos and Hosea, came forward to reveal the true state of affairs and to warn of the consequences.

JERUSALEM. The first mention of Jerusalem is in some Egyptian execration texts of the 19th century B.C. which list certain enemies of Egypt who were to be defeated by magical means. We next hear of it in 14th-century letters from Canaanite kings found in the royal archives of Egypt at Tell el-Amarna. It was at that time one of the leading city-states in southern Palestine, and its King, Abdi-Kheba, complained to the Pharaoh of disturbances and marauders, and begged for troops to assist him in retaining the city under the Pharaoh's rule. In the Biblical book of Joshua (Chap. 10) Israel's invasion of the territory is described, and Jerusalem is listed as the leader of a coalition of city-states formed to resist the invasion (10:3–5), probably in the second half of the 13th century B.C.

Because of heavy fortifications, Israel was unable to capture the city until early in the reign of King David, shortly after 1000 B.C. (II Sam. 5:6–8). It then became "the city of David," that is, the personal property of the Davidic Dynasty. It also became the religious center of the nation, because David reconstructed there the old tent-sanctuary (tabernacle), which in Solomon's reign was replaced by a temple. The latter along with other government buildings was erected in a new area directly north of the old city, aid being secured in architectural design from the Phoenician King, Hiram of Tyre. From this time on the city was increasingly looked upon as a religious center, which one day would be the capital of the world where the rule of God would be acknowledged by all. When the city was destroyed by the army of Nebuchadnezzar of Babylon in 587 (or 586) B.C., hope did not die with its physical destruction.

Between 520 and c.516 a small group of returned exiles rebuilt the temple, and under the leadership of Nehemiah, after 445 B.C., the city was refortified as the center of the small district of Yehud (Judah) in the 5th Persian satrapy. During the wars for Jewish independence in the 2d century B.C., Jerusalem became the capital of the Hasmonean rulers, who forcibly attempted to convert their neighbors, particularly the Idumeans to the south and Samaritans to the north. Under Roman rule the client-King Herod the Great (37–4 B.C.) rebuilt the temple on a grand scale, greatly strengthened the city's fortifications, erected a theater and amphitheater, and attempted to create in the city a cultural center worthy of the Roman world. This was the city that was violently destroyed by the Roman general Titus in 70 A.D. after a Jewish revolt.

The history of the town of Jerusalem throughout the centuries after the time of Christ was one of sieges and conquests by many foreign powers, among them Arabs, Crusaders, Turks, and the British. Although according to the Jewish historian Flavius Josephus all of Jerusalem was destroyed by Titus in 70 A.D., evidence indicates that a surviving section of the town adjacent to the Roman camp was used to quarter the families of the legionnaires. By 130, when Emperor Hadrian visited Jerusalem, the considerable pagan community had erected temples to Bacchus and Serapis and one to Venus on the site of Golgotha. Hadrian's decision to make Jerusalem a Roman colony from which all Jews would be excluded provoked a second Jewish revolt (132) led by Simeon Bar Kokhba. The Jews captured Jerusalem, along with the whole of Judaea, and held it until 135, when the Romans killed Bar Kokhba and suppressed the revolt. On the ruins of Jerusalem the Romans built a new colony, Aelia Capitolina, named for Hadrian's family, Aelius, and the principal Roman deity, Jupiter Capitolinus. Jews were forbidden to enter within its wall, which circumscribed much of the same area as does the wall around the present Old City. This ban was enforced from 135 to 324, during which period Jerusalem was an insignificant provincial city.

In the 4th century, under Emperor Constantine, Jerusalem reassumed both its ancient name and its religious importance, and by the early 7th century, when it was seized by the Persians, it had reached unprecedented prosperity because of the influx of Christian pilgrims and money contributed for shrines. The Temple of Venus was removed from Golgotha and the Church of the Holy Sepulcher was built in its stead. Monasteries, nunneries, hospices, and shrines were erected, and Jerusalem became the only thoroughly Christian city of Palestine. In the mid-5th century, through the efforts of the Roman Empress Eudocia, wife of Theodosius II, the Jews were officially permitted to resettle in Jerusalem. During the reign (527–65) of Justinian I, Emperor of the Eastern Roman (Byzantine) Empire, Jerusalem achieved new splendor. In the 7th century the Persians, supported by the Jews, embarked on war against the Romans in Palestine. The Jews were allowed for a time to re-establish a government and make Jerusalem their religious center. In 614 the Persians seized the city, destroying much, including the original Church of the Holy Sepulcher; shortly afterward, however, they granted control of Jerusalem to the Christians. Roman rule over the city was restored for a brief time in 629 when Emperor Heraclius defeated the Persians and expelled the Jews. So exhausted were both the Roman and Persian armies by this war that in 638 they were defeated by the Muslim Caliph Umar. Umar did not disturb the Christian churches in Jerusalem, and he agreed to allow a number of Jews to return.

JESHUA, Jewish high priest who accompanied Zerubbabel and returning exiles from Babylon to Jerusalem in 537 B.C. He assisted in the rebuilding of the altar (Ezra 3:2) and the Temple (Ezra 4:3).

JESSE [jĕs′ē], in the Old Testament, father of David, and a prosperous owner of lands and flocks in Bethlehem of Judah. When his three eldest sons joined the army of Saul, Jesse sent food to them by David, his youngest son (I Sam. 17:12–18), whom Samuel had anointed to be king (I Sam. 16:1–13).

JETHRO, father-in-law of Moses (Exod. 3:1), also called Reuel (Exod. 2:18). He was a priest of the Midianites, from whom Moses learned to know Yahweh.

JEZEBEL [jĕz′ə-bĕl] (9th century B.C.), Phoenician wife of Ahab, King of Israel. As related in I Kings 16:29–II Kings 9:37, she was the daughter of Ethbaal, King of Tyre and Sidon. Omri, the father of Ahab, had brought about the marriage as an exercise in statecraft. However, the Princess soon showed herself to be an ardent advocate of her Baal religion as opposed to the religion of Yahweh, whose chief representative at the time was the prophet Elijah. A great struggle ensued. Jezebel outlived Elijah, but was finally killed in the bloody purge of Jehu, instigated by Elisha, Elijah's successor.

JONATHAN [jŏn′ə-thən], in the Old Testament, the eldest son of King Saul, famous for his friendship with David. He served as a commander under his father, and became so popular that the people would not let Saul slay him for having unknowingly broken a vow (I Sam. 14:1–45). When David entered Saul's service, Jonathan protected him from Saul's insane jealousy (I Sam. 20), and was even willing to renounce the kingship in favor of David (I Sam. 23:16–18). He perished with his father and brothers in their final battle with the Philistines on Mount Gilboa (I Sam. 31) and was mourned by David (II Sam. 1:17–27).

JONATHAN, Jewish military leader and high priest (152–142 B.C.), son of Mattathias and brother of Judas Maccabeus, whom he succeeded (161). In 152 he led a further revolt against the Seleucid empire, enlarged the boundaries of his principality, and later made peace with the central government. His brother Simon succeeded him.

JOSEPHUS [jō-sē′fəs], **FLAVIUS** (c.37–c.100 A.D.), Jewish military commander, historian, and apologist. Born in Jerusalem of noble priestly stock and of royal Hasmonean lineage, Josephus, after personal investigation of the three contemporary forms of Judaism (Pharisaism, Sadduceeism, and Essenism) became at 19 a Pharisee.

A visit to Rome in 64 A.D. so impressed him with the invincibility of Roman power that, on his return to Jerusalem, he sought to deter the people from rebellion in 66. Failing, he joined the rebels and was appointed military commander of Galilee, where he played the dual role of rebel leader and Roman sympathizer. Captured by Vespasian at Jotapata in 67, Josephus openly threw in his lot with the Romans.

After the destruction of the Temple (70), Josephus settled in Rome, where, favored and protected by Ves-

The Jewish Museum

Jewish historian Flavius Josephus, represented in a reproduction of a marble bust (c.100 A.D.).

pasian and Titus, he wrote *The Jewish War* (75–79). This account of the rebellion of 66–70 has historical and literary distinction. Though pro-Roman in sympathy, Josephus neither spares the procurators nor depreciates the courage of his countrymen.

He wrote *The Antiquities* (93–94), a multivolumed history of the Jews from the creation to 66 A.D.; an autobiographical sketch, *Life* (c.100); and *Against Apion* (c.100), a sophisticated apologia for Jews and Judaism against their Greco-Roman detractors.

Josephus skillfully utilized Greco-Roman historiographical models. But for his writings, the history of the Jews in the Hellenistic-Roman period (c.333 B.C.–c.100A.D.) would be virtually unknown. The Christ passage attributed to Josephus is generally considered a later interpolation.

JOSHUA [jŏsh'ōō-ə] (Gr. Jesus; also called Oshea and Hoshea), in the Old Testament, the successor of Moses as leader of the Israelite tribes. He was appointed by Moses to be commander in the battle against the Amalekites, and won a great victory (Exod. 17:8–14). Thereafter he became Moses' personal attendant, even accompanying him to the sacred mountain (Exod. 24:13; 32:17). He was one of 12 sent to spy out the land of Canaan, and upon their return, he and Caleb were the only ones who reported that the land could be taken immediately (Num. 13:1–33; 14:6–9). This idea was rejected, however. As Moses grew old and needed someone to share his responsibilities, Joshua was chosen as his assistant (Num. 27:12–23), and upon the death of Moses, Joshua assumed full leadership (Deut. 34:9). He immediately began the conquest of the Promised Land, as related in the Book of Joshua.

JOSIAH [jō-sī'ə], in the Old Testament, King of Judah (reigned c.640–609 B.C.). He was proclaimed King when only eight years old (II Kings 22:1). In the 18th year of his reign Hilkiah, the high priest, found the book of the law in the Temple (II Kings 22:8) and Josiah began a reform which constituted a purge of all foreign religions (II Kings 23:1–25). When King Necho II of Egypt, in 609, led an army against Assyria, Josiah attempted to stop him and was defeated and killed at Megiddo (II Kings 23:28–30). From that time on the fortunes of Judah rapidly declined (II Kings 24,25).

JUDAISM [jōō'də-ĭz-əm], religion of the Jews. Jewish religious faith and practice are based on the doctrinal and legal content of the Old Testament, as interpreted in the literature of Pharisaic-Rabbinic Judaism, and as developed by legalists and mystics, philosophers and pietists through the ages. In the absence of a supreme ecclesiastical authority recognized by all Jews, at least since the destruction of the Temple and Jewish state in 70 A.D., Judaism, with a few notable exceptions, has not engaged in the formulation and imposition of dogmas. It is thus best approached as a climate of beliefs and opinions which at no time in its long history represents a monolithic structure but rather contains a variety of manifestations: Pharisees, Sadducees, Essenes, in New Testament times; Rabbinites and Karaites, Rationalists and Anti-Rationalists, in the Middle Ages; Orthodox, Conservative, Reform Judaism, at the present time.

JUDAS MACCABEUS [măk-ə-bē'əs] (d.160 B.C.), Jewish military leader, son of Mattathias and his successor in the revolt against the Seleucid Empire. A brilliant general, he took Jerusalem and in 164 B.C. rededicated the Temple. Refortifying the city, he extended his military operations against the royal armies, but was defeated and retired to Jerusalem. He won a peaceful settlement, however, in which Jewish religious law was established as binding for the whole community. When this settlement failed to bring him political leadership, he again revolted. But after initial success, he was defeated and died in battle.

JUDAS OF GALILEE [găl'ə-lē], leader of an armed revolt in Palestine in 6 A.D., when the Roman governor Quirinius took a census for taxation. He was soon captured and executed (Acts 5:37). Judas may have been founder of the extreme nationalist party of Jews.

MACCABEES [măk'ə-bēz], **THE**, alternative name for the Hasmoneans, the priestly family of Mattathias and his sons who revolted against the Seleucid monarchs of Syria in 168 B.C. and established the last Jewish dynasty, one of priestly princes and kings. The name is derived from that given to Mattathias' son Judas, who was called Maccabeus, or the Maccabee, meaning "Hammer." Three of Mattathias' sons led the Jewish forces: Judas, Jonathan, and Simon, who was proclaimed high priest, military chief, and civil governor, and with whom the rule was made hereditary.

MANASSEH [mə-năs'ə], King of Judah, son and successor of Hezekiah. He reigned longer than any other king of Judah (c.697–642 B.C.), and is considered by the editor of Kings the most wicked of his line (II Kings 21:1–18). The Chronicler presents a more charitable interpretation (II Chron. 33:10–20).

MANASSEH, Israelite tribe settled in the central highlands of Palestine, on both sides of the Jordan River. The tribal ancestor appears as a son of Joseph and a grandson of Jacob (Gen. 41:51).

MISHNAH [mĭsh'nə] (from Heb. *shanah*, "to repeat"), compendium of Jewish Oral Law compiled by Rabbi Judah ha-Nasi in the beginning of the 3d century A.D. in Palestine. It ranks second only to the Bible as an authoritative source of teaching for Judaism, and served as the basis of the Gemara, which, together with the Mishnah, forms the Talmud. The Mishnah is divided into six *sedarim* ("orders"): (1) Seeds (*Zeraim*), dealing with agricultural activities and ritual problems; (2) Festivals (*Moed*), treating the laws connected with the Sabbath and festivals; (3) Women (*Nashim*), dealing with the legal aspects of marriage, divorce, and the relations between the sexes; (4) Damages (*Nezikim*), concerned with civil and criminal law; (5) Holy Things (*Kodashim*), containing the laws of sacrifice and the ritual of the Temple; and (6) Purities (*Tohoroth*), presenting the regulations governing ritual impurity. The Mishnah is written in a Hebrew dialect known as Mishnaic Hebrew.

MOSES [mō'zĭs], historical founder of Israel. The name

is Egyptian, and according to the Old Testament account, Moses was born in Egypt among a group of Hebrew slaves who were used for forced labor on national building. Owing to a fortuitous circumstance, he was adopted as a child by Pharaoh's daughter and brought up in Pharaoh's household (Exod. 2:1–10). After killing an Egyptian for smiting a Hebrew, Moses fled to the Sinai Peninsula, where he lived with a Midianite nomad tribe in the desert, married the daughter of its priest, and received a revelation from Yahweh, the god of the area, who identified himself as the God of the Hebrew patriarchs. Yahweh commanded Moses to return to Egypt to deliver his people, and after a conflict with Pharaoh, Moses eventually led the Hebrews out of Egypt and across the Sea of Reeds to the place of his own earlier sojourn in Sinai. There he instituted a rule of law, administered by elders, with the Ten Commandments (Exod. 20:2–17) as its core. Here and in the region of Kadesh, south of Palestine, Moses, serving as prophet and priest, taught the people to interpret their deliverance from Egypt as a gift from Yahweh, and established a covenant between Israel and Yahweh. In this covenant Israel was to be Yahweh's people and was required to worship Yahweh alone.

The personality of Moses left an indelible impression on all subsequent generations of Hebrews. Tradition records that his character was marked by great humility (Num. 12:3), but that he was subject to outbursts of fierce anger (Exod. 32:19). Perhaps his greatest quality as a

Renaissance conception of Moses, Biblical Hebrew leader, by Michelangelo, in the Church of St. Peter in Chains, Rome.

Alinari—Art Reference Bureau

leader was his unselfish identification of his own interest with that of his people (Num. 14:11–19).

The later union of 12 tribes in Palestine was the outgrowth of the religious movement instituted by Moses, whom all the tribes considered as the mediator of Yahweh's revelation to them (Num. 12:7, 8). Few men have exerted a more enduring influence on history.

OMRI [ŏm′rī], sixth King of Israel (reigned c.876–869 B.C.) after the separation of the two kingdoms. The father of Ahab, Omri founded a new dynasty and built the city of Samaria as his capital (I Kings 16:15–28). Modern historical research has shown that Omri was more important than the few verses devoted to him in the Bible indicate.

PATRIARCHS, THE, in the Old Testament, the ancestors of the race, such as Noah, and more particularly of the nation of Israel—Abraham, Isaac, and Jacob. These men were Aramaean seminomads who had migrated from Mesopotamia in the first half of the 2d millennium B.C. and lived in the east and south of Palestine, where traditions of their lives (Gen. 12–50) were kept by the later tribes of Israel who settled there. The Biblical presentation shows Abraham as the father of Isaac, and Jacob as Isaac's son; but originally their lives were separate and their settlements were in different localities. They worshiped God under the form of patron deities who were believed to accompany them on their journeys and were known by the name of the chief of the clan by whom they were worshiped: Shield of Abraham, Fear of Isaac, and Mighty One of Jacob.

With the formation of the 12-tribe confederacy of Israel about 1200 B.C., all the tribes were claimed as descended from Jacob through 12 sons, and Yahweh, the God of Israel, was identified with the gods of the patriarchs. The patriarchs were presented as one family, with Abraham as its head, to whom was promised possession of the land of Palestine.

PHARISEES [făr′ə-sēz], the most important religious division of the Jews in the period preceding the rise of Christianity, developing into rabbinic Judaism in the Christian era. Its origins and name are obscure and have been variously interpreted. The name is related to the Hebrew root *PRSH* ("to separate"), but whether it originally meant self-separation or forcible separation by others is uncertain. The group as an identifiable party was active in the reign (134–104 B.C.) of John Hyrcanus, but its origins are much earlier. There was a connection between Pharisees and the Hasidim of the early Hasmonean period, and also with the "Wise of Israel," a group of lay teachers at the beginning of the 2d century B.C.

Pharisees represented a progressive challenge to the priestly authorities over the right of lay teachers to interpret Scriptures. Eventually confirmed in their right, they developed a notable body of teachings, the Oral Law, composed of interpretations of Scripture and nonscriptural traditions believed to have been revealed along with the Bible. Their goal was the building of a community of faith and observance out of the entire Jewish nation in conformity with their doctrines and practices.

Far from being a reactionary element, they sought new

expressions for Judaism and were responsible for the survival of Judaism after the end of the Jewish state. The New Testament represents them not only as opponents of Jesus but as hypocrites. It has been shown that while there may have been such in the group, on the whole they were pious and learned men, motivated by sincere religious belief and aims.

PHILISTINES [fĭ-lĭs'tĭnz], major group of non-Semitic people in antiquity whom the Egyptians called the "Peoples of the Sea." The name comes from the Hebrew *Pelishtim* (Egyptian *Pulesati*, Assyrian *Palastu*), a people who settled along the coast of southern Palestine c.1150 B.C. after an unsuccessful attempt to invade Egypt. During the 13th century B.C., Egyptian inscriptions speak of Sea Peoples who were both invaders and mercenaries. In the reign (c.1175–1144 B.C., according to a "low date" chronology) of Rameses III Egypt was invaded from land and sea by several groups of them over a six-year period. Defeated, some of them fell back on Palestine, where they served nominally as mercenaries of Egypt, preserving Egyptian monuments in a Beth-shan temple, for example, long after Egyptian power in Palestine had come to an end. About this time, in coastal towns especially, a new pottery suddenly appeared which imitated 13th-century Greek (Mycenaean) models. This fact, in addition to various literary allusions, makes it certain that the Philistines came from the Aegean world.

In Palestine the Philistines organized themselves under five "lords" in five main cities (Gaza, Ashkelon, Ashdod, Ekron, and Gath), where they became Israel's worst enemy between c.1150 and 1000 B.C. Their greatest victory was when they captured Israel's sacred Ark, destroyed the central shrine of Israel's tribal league at Shiloh, and took control of the central hill country (I Sam. 4–6; 13:19–23; Jer. 7:12–15). This forced Israel to abandon its loose tribal confederation and turn to a monarchical government. Under the first Israelite kings, Saul and David, the Philistines were defeated and were never again a serious threat. In the 8th century B.C. the Philistine federation, which had become a series of city-states, was conquered by Assyria.

REHOBOAM [rē-ō-bō'əm], son of Solomon and first King of Judah after the secession of Israel. When he attempted to rule the united kingdom after the death of his father, he was met by a delegation from the northern tribes under the leadership of Jeroboam to demand a lightening of the oppressions practiced by Solomon. He refused the demand and threatened even heavier exactions. The northern tribes immediately seceded (about 930 B.C.). Rehoboam is said to have ruled Judah 17 years (I Kings 14:21; II Chron. 12:13), though some chronologists find an error here and reduce the number to 8.

REUBEN, an Israelite tribe settled in the south of Palestine, east of the River Jordan and the Dead Sea (Num. 32:1–5; Josh. 13:15–23). Supposedly its ancestor was Jacob's eldest son by Leah (Gen. 29:32).

REUEL, alternate name (Exod. 2:18; 3:1) for Moses' father-in-law, Jethro (q.v.).

SABBATH [săb'əth], the seventh day. The observance of the seventh day as holy was considered by the Israelites to date from the creation (Gen. 2:3), and it was re-enacted in the Ten Commandments (Exod. 20:8–11). In the tabernacle and temple ritual, the Sabbath was marked by an extra sacrifice and by the presentation of the shewbread. In later times the Sabbath became the chief day of worship in the synagogue ritual. The principal feature of the day, which in the Jewish calendar extends from Friday evening to Saturday evening, has always been the prohibition of work of any kind. Detailed regulations, defining what is and what is not permissible, have been worked out by the rabbis over many centuries.

The observance of specially holy days was frequent in the ancient world, and the name "Sabbath" probably derives from the Akkadian word *shabattu*. But the ancient days were all of a taboo character. The Biblical interest in the well-being of man and the worship of God is unique.

SABBATICAL [sə-băt'ĭ-kəl] **YEAR,** every seventh year, considered holy by the Hebrews, for whom the number seven had a peculiar sanctity. In that year, the land was to lie fallow, neither sowing nor reaping being permitted (Lev. 25:1–7). The year also served to release Hebrew slaves from bondage and Hebrew debtors from their debts (Deut. 15:1–15). These were well-intentioned economic measures, to restore the earlier status quo. There is occasional historical evidence of the observance of sabbatical years between the time of the 5th-century-B.C. Jewish leader Nehemiah and the 1st-century-A.D. historian Josephus. In modern academic usage the term refers to a paid leave of absence for research or travel granted every seventh year to professors.

SADDUCEES [săj'ŏŏ-sēz], one of the religious divisions of the Jews in the period preceding the rise of Christianity. The name may be derived from a certain Zadok who, in one source, is said to be its founder, or from the phrase "sons of Zadok," referring to the family that controlled the high priesthood after the return from the Babylonian exile (538–438 B.C.). Both the Jewish historian Josephus (c.37–100 A.D.) and the rabbinic sources report the Sadducees' opposition to the Pharisees on the basis of their rejection of the latter's insistence that the oral tradition was of equal validity with Scripture. In addition the Sadducees held a highly transcendent view of God, emphasized the freedom of the human will, and denied retribution and resurrection. Josephus reports that they were "boorish in their behavior" with one another and rude with others. They seem to have been made up of priestly and aristocratic families. After the fall of Jerusalem, in 70 A.D., they lost all influence and apparently ceased to exist as a cohesive group.

SAMARIA [sə-mâr'ē-ə], middle section of ancient Palestine west of the Jordan, between Judea and Galilee. It was about 40 sq. mi. in area and derived its name from the ancient capital of the northern kingdom of Israel, which was in this territory. After 721 B.C. it was inhabited by people from around Babylon, whom the Assyrians settled here and who intermarried with the remnants of the Israelites, most of whom had been carried away in captivity to Assyria. The territory belonged successively to the northern Kingdom of Israel, the Assyrians, Babylonians, Persians, Macedonians, the Maccabean Kingdom, and the Romans.

SAMARIA, city in ancient Palestine, some 45 mi. north of Jerusalem. It was founded by Israel's Omri Dynasty (c.875 B.C.) as the capital of the northern kingdom, which had split with Jerusalem at the death of Solomon a half century earlier (I Kings 16:24). It remained the administrative center of its area under Assyrian, Babylonian, and Persian rule. Alexander the Great in 331 B.C. presented it to certain of his Greek troops, who lived there as a garrison. Herod the Great made it a fine Gentile city, with a theater, stadium, and magnificent temple built in honor of Caesar Augustus. Herod also changed its name to "Sebaste" (a Greek word meaning the same as "Augustus"), a name which survives in the modern village at the site, Sebastiyeh.

One of the great pioneer excavations of modern times was carried out here by Harvard University (1908–10), a work continued in a joint expedition directed by J. W. Crowfoot between 1931 and 1935. The magnificent city walls, palace, and other structures of the Israelite capital, destroyed by the Assyrians in 722–721 B.C., were unearthed, along with other ruins of the Hellenistic and Roman periods, including Herod's temple of Augustus.

SAMARITANS [sə-măr'ə-tənz], one of the national groups of Palestine. Most of the 10 northern tribes of Israel were deported to Assyria in 721 B.C. Those who remained intermarried with Assyrians who settled in the land (II Kings 17:6,24), and the Samaritans were descended from this mixed population. In later times the Jews refused fellowship with them. The break is usually thought to have occurred in the time of Ezra or Nehemiah (458–445 B.C.), but there are indications that it was not complete until 332, when Macedonians settled in the old city of Samaria. The local people who worshiped the God of the Hebrews then made Shechem their center and built a temple on Mount Gerizim. This became a rival of the Jerusalem Temple.

The apocryphal book Ecclesiasticus, written about 200 B.C., exhibits Jewish hostility to the Samaritans (Ecclus. 50:25,26), and the same attitude is attested by the New Testament (John 4:9). Galilean Jews usually tried to avoid Samaritan territory when traveling to Jerusalem, and Jesus was unusual in taking this route and conversing in friendly fashion with Samaritans. In one of His parables (Luke 10:30–37) a Samaritan is the hero. The Talmud in general treats Samaritans as though they were Gentiles, forbidding the eating of their food and intermarriage with them, but in some rulings they are considered almost to be Jews. Christian missionary work among Samaritans began early (Acts 8:4–25).

The Samaritan scriptures contain only the Pentateuch or Torah (the first five books of the Old Testament), traditionally ascribed to Moses. Thus the Jews and Samaritans parted company after the collection of the Torah but before the prophets were canonized. The Samaritan Pentateuch has essentially the same Hebrew text as that used by Jews. It is written in a peculiar alphabet which is older than the square Hebrew character and related to the script used in Old Testament times.

A medieval document shows that the Samaritans believed in the coming of a Messiah or *Taheb*, and this belief probably goes back as far as the beginning of the Christian era (John 4:25). A small community of Samaritans, about 150 in number, still survives at Nablus, in Jordan. It is presided over by a high priest, whose office is hereditary. Their worship includes the keeping of Passover, celebrated on Mount Gerizim with the killing of lambs, as in Biblical times.

SAMUEL [săm'ū-əl], last of the judges in Israel, who was also a prophet and a priest. The circumstances of his birth (I Sam. 1) were similar to Samson's (Judg. 13:2–7) and John the Baptist's (Luke 1:5–25, 57–80). Samuel served an apprenticeship under Eli, the priest in the temple at Shiloh, then became a circuit judge with headquarters at Ramah (I Sam. 7:3–17). His two sons attempted to follow the same profession but proved unworthy (8:1–3). When the people demanded a king, Samuel reluctantly consented and assumed the role of prophet to anoint Saul (8–12). When Saul proved disobedient to the divine will, Samuel rebuked him (13:8–15) and finally agreed to the selection of a new King, David, from a different family (16:1–13). He died while David was in exile (25:1; 28:3). It was reported that after his death Saul spoke with him in a spiritualistic séance with the aid of the witch of Endor (28:3–25).

SANHEDRIN [săn'hē-drĭn], the high council of the Jews, with 71 members recruited from the high-priestly families (the current high priest being president), the scribes, and other lay elders. Its religious influence extended to Jewish communities everywhere, and in Roman times it was the administrative council for Judaea, and was the supreme court. John 18:31 indicates that capital sentences needed confirmation by the Roman procurator. Jesus was arrested on the Sanhedrin's orders, examined by them, and handed over to the procurator on a political charge (Luke 23:2), with the knowledge that crucifixion was the penalty. When St. Paul had offended the Jews by his Gentile associations, he also appeared before the Sanhedrin (Acts 22:30–23:10), whose leaders denounced him to the Romans as an agitator. Their hostility prolonged his imprisonment at Caesarea and determined his appeal to Caesar. The Sanhedrin, abolished with the destruction of Jerusalem in 70 A.D., was later revived by the Jewish community in Palestine but ceased to function by the end of the 4th century A.D.

SAUL [sôl], first King of Israel (reigned c.1030–1010 B.C.). Son of Kish, of the tribe of Benjamin, he is said to have been chosen King by Samuel while still an inexperienced young man (I Sam. 9–10). However, it is more likely that his leadership in the war against the Ammonites gave him the popularity necessary to achieve the kingship (11:12–15). The real test came in the war of defense against the invading Philistines. Saul won an initial victory at Michmash with the aid of his son Jonathan (13–14), but a mental illness began to take its toll.

The hiring of David to soothe the King with music only resulted in intense jealousy and the expulsion of David from the court, though Jonathan remained David's fast friend and advocate (16:14–20:42). Saul even pursued David in person, but in vain (23–24; 26). He then returned to the warfare with the Philistines, but was so dispirited that he entered his final battle under a hopeless handicap. At Mount Gilboa he was disastrously defeated, his sons were killed before his eyes, and he was mortally wounded and fell upon his own sword to avoid being dispatched by the enemy (28:3–25; 31).

The story of Saul's meeting with the witch of Endor in I Samuel 28:3–25 is misplaced. This meeting occurred in the night preceding Saul's defeat and death, and hence the account of it belongs immediately before the final chapter (31). The story of Saul's suicide in this chapter is probably correct. Thus it follows that the claim of the Amalekite in II Samuel 1:6–10 that he dispatched the dying leader as an act of mercy was a lie told with the hope of personal advantage.

SEMITIC [sə-mĭt'ĭk] **LANGUAGES,** subgroup of the Afro-Asiatic family of languages. It constitutes one of the largest and most important world language groups and is the earliest-known language group still in use. The Semitic languages are divisible into four subgroups.

(1) Northeast Semitic includes Akkadian (Assyro-Babylonian), spoken in Mesopotamia from c.3000 B.C. to 500 B.C. and recorded from 2500 B.C. to the 1st century A.D.

(2) Northwest Semitic includes Amorite, Aramaic, and Canaanite (comprising the Ugaritic, Phoenician, Punic, Hebrew, and Moabite languages). Amorite was used in northern Syria from 1900 B.C. to 1500 B.C. The Canaanite dialects were used in Syria and Palestine and from there spread with Phoenician colonization along the Mediterranean coast to North Africa and Spain. Hebrew, used in Palestine from 1200 B.C. to 200 A.D., has been maintained by the Jews as their cultural and religious language. Aramaic was spoken in Syria and Mesopotamia and from 800 B.C. to 300 B.C. was the common language of the Near East.

(3) Southeast Semitic includes Early Arabic, Classical Arabic, and Modern Arabic. Early Arabic consists of dialects known only from inscriptions. Classical Arabic is the language of pre-Islamic poetry, the Koran, and a vast literature written from the 6th century A.D. until modern times. Modern Arabic is the standard language now used for literary and scientific writings, although local dialects of colloquial Arabic differ greatly from region to region in the Arab world. Arabic spread with the Muslim conquests into Palestine, Syria, Iraq, Egypt, North Africa, and Spain. As the religious language of Islam it reached as far east as the Philippine Islands.

(4) Southwest Semitic includes Epigraphic and Modern South Arabic and the Ethiopic languages. Epigraphic South Arabic is known from inscriptions found in South Arabia. Its modern dialects are spoken by a few tribes. Colonizers from South Arabia came to Ethiopia some time in the 1st millennium B.C., and under the influence of native dialects the Ethiopic languages developed. They include Geez, the present church language of Ethiopia; Amharic, the official language of Ethiopia; Tigre; Tigrinya; Gurage; Harari; and Gafat.

The Semitic languages share certain common features of phonology, morphology, and syntax. Important in the morphology of the noun and the verb is the role of the root, which in the verb is modified to express variations of the basic action and in the noun is modified to express variations of the basic meaning. Various scripts have been used for the Semitic languages: cuneiform for Akkadian, Amorite and Ugaritic; the Phoenician script for the Canaanite dialects; and the South Arabic script for epigraphic South Arabic and the Ethiopic languages.

The Semitic languages spoken today are Arabic (spoken from North Africa to Iraq), Ethiopic (in Ethiopia), Hebrew (in Israel), and Aramaic (in remote villages in the Near East). The Semitic languages are related to the Hamitic and to the Cushitic languages.

SOLOMON [sŏl'ə-mən], son of David and Bathsheba and successor of David as King of united Israel and Judah (reigned c.970–930 B.C.). Through the influence of Bathsheba, David on his deathbed was persuaded to designate Solomon instead of the older Adonijah as the next King. After David's death Solomon strengthened his position by ordering the execution of Adonijah and Adonijah's supporter Joab. In like manner Abiathar was deposed from the priesthood (I Kings 1–2).

Solomon's reign was marked by splendor and brilliance. The King was himself a gifted and charming man, noted for his wit and wisdom. He organized his kingdom efficiently, dividing it into 12 districts. He married a number of foreign princesses to improve his nation's relations with its neighbors (I Kings 3:1; 7:8; 11:1–3). He conducted extensive building operations, the most important achievement in this area being the famous Temple at Jerusalem, erected with the help of Hiram, King of Tyre (I Kings 5–8; II Chron. 2–6). The national defense was provided for by the fortification of cities (I Kings 9:15–19) and the development of chariotry (I Kings 10:26; II Chron. 9:25). On the economic side Solomon sponsored maritime trade with Red Sea ports (I Kings 9:27,28; II Chron. 9:21–24) and overland caravan trade with Arabia (I Kings 10:15). He established a copper-smelting plant at the Red Sea port of Ezion-geber, as shown by archaeology. Finally he established a lucrative business as a middleman in the sale and transport of horses and chariots among nearby countries (I Kings 10:28, 29). A corresponding literary development saw the beginning of some of the more important parts of the Old Testament, such as the Books of Samuel, the early sources in the Pentateuch, and Psalms and Proverbs.

But there was also a darker side to Solomon's reign, as may be seen in I Kings 11. The luxurious harem and the easy familiarity with foreigners and foreign religions conduced to a moral and religious laxity contrary to the ancestral traditions of the people. Moreover, Solomon did not have his father's military skill, and surrounding satellite states began to rebel and secede with impunity. Internally the King was compelled to resort to heavy taxes and forced labor to support his vast enterprises (I Kings 5:13; 11:28; 12:4). Jeroboam, an overseer of labor gangs from

"Judgment of Solomon" (Uffizi Gallery, Florence), attributed to the Renaissance painter Giorgione. The King of Israel and Judah determines the true mother of a disputed child (I Kings 3:16–28).

the tribe of Ephraim, plotting revolution, fled to Egypt to bide his time. Upon the death of Solomon the northern tribes (Israel) rebelled, recalling Jeroboam to be their King, while Rehoboam, Solomon's son, retained only Judah as his kingdom (I Kings 12:1–20).

TABERNACLE [tăb'ər-năk-əl], portable shrine used by the Israelites prior to their conquest of Canaan. It or some temporary structure also served for a time after the conquest, until superseded by the Jerusalem Temple during Solomon's reign. The structure and furniture of the tabernacle are described in Exodus 25–27. The structure measured 30 by 10 cubits and consisted of two compartments, the holy place and the Holy of Holies, which were separated by a curtain. It faced west and was surrounded by a court. The most important piece of furniture was the Ark of the Covenant, housed in the Holy of Holies. Other items were the altar of incense, golden lampstand, table of shewbread, and in the outer court the altar of burnt offering and the laver.

Although the description may be idealized and from a later period, the existence of some sort of portable shrine to house the Ark of the Covenant in preconquest times is very likely. Indeed, there are early Canaanite and other parallels. It is also probable that the Temple was modeled on it.

TABERNACLES, FEAST OF (Heb. *Sukkot*), the most joyous festival in the Jewish religious calendar, observed in the autumn for nine days (eight in Israel and among Reform Jews). Its origins go back to the agricultural festivals commemorating the harvest (Exod. 23:16; 34:22; Lev. 23: 34,39; Deut. 16:13,16). It is also connected with the Exodus from Egypt and the wilderness wanderings (Lev. 23:43). During the festival, meals are eaten in a booth (tabernacle) erected out of doors, and, as part of the worship service, palm branches are waved during the recitation of certain psalms. The eighth day is called *Shemini Atzereth* (Eighth Day of Assembly); and the ninth, *Simhath Torah* (Rejoicing of the Teaching).

TEMPLE, JEWISH, center of Jewish worship, in ancient Jerusalem. The first Jewish Temple, superseding earlier temporary structures (tabernacles), was erected in Jerusalem in the middle of the 10th century B.C. It was instigated by Solomon, and the work was largely done under Phoenician supervision (I Kings 5; 6). Throughout Solomon's reign it served as the central sanctuary for the whole Israelite nation, but after his death, when the kingdom had split in two, it was used only by the southern Kingdom of Judah. Though once or twice plundered and damaged, it stood until 587 B.C., when the Babylonian armies under Nebuchadnezzar burned down Jerusalem and the Temple with it (II Kings 25:8–16).

After half a century of exile, when the Jews returned, one of their first concerns was to rebuild the Temple, presumably on the pattern of that of Solomon. This second Temple, however, was far less glorious. Zerubbabel, the Jewish governor, was behind the work, and it was completed in 515 B.C. (Ezra 1–6). This temple, too, had its vicissitudes, but it never suffered destruction. It was desecrated by Antiochus IV Epiphanes in 168 B.C., but was triumphantly rededicated under Judas Maccabeus four years later. Pompey the Great forced his way into it in 63 B.C. but he took no plunder. Herod the Great (37–4 B.C.) decided to rebuild it, but without interrupting the services of worship. He began the magnificent work of renovation and embellishment in 19 B.C. (John 2:20), and the main part of the new building was finished by 9 B.C. All the courts, however, were not completed until between 62 and 64 A.D. This Temple stood until 70 A.D., when the Roman troops under Titus destroyed it by fire at the end of the Jewish War. An Islamic sacred edifice, the Dome of the Rock, now stands on the Temple site.

Description. Cedar wood was the chief material in the first two Temples, though gold and silver were also lavishly used. Herod used huge blocks of white stone. In all three Temples, but particularly in Herod's, there was a complex of buildings and courts, so that the Temple area was sometimes used as a fortress. Jesus and His contemporaries found the courts and colonnades suitable sites for teaching the crowds who frequented the Temple area. One court served for commercial purposes, and Jesus took exception to this, and once or twice ejected the salesmen (John 2:13–16; Mark 11:15–18). But the Temple proper was reserved for the priesthood alone, and only the high priest ever entered the inner sanctuary. The shrine itself consisted of an outer and inner sanctuary, the latter containing the Ark of the Covenant until that most sacred object disappeared. Afterward the innermost chamber remained empty. Another important feature of the several Temples was the entrance porch, which was originally flanked by two great pillars. The entire structure was rectangular, facing east and west.

TEN COMMANDMENTS, known also as the Decalogue, ancient Jewish code. It is the core of the religious and moral teachings revealed by God on Mount Sinai and the basis of God's covenant with Israel. Though modern scholarship has suggested some alternatives, Jewish and Christian tradition finds the authoritative version of the Ten Commandments in Exodus 20:2–17 and Deuteronomy 5:6–21. After God is shown to be the deliverer from Egyptian bondage, there follow religious commandments concerning worship of false gods, misuse of God's name, and the sanctity of the Sabbath. Then came moral commandments concerning parents and prohibition of murder, adultery, theft, perjury, and covetousness. The wording of the Exodus and Deuteronomy versions is at variance, but the contents are essentially the same. However, the sanctity of the Sabbath is motivated in Exodus by the consideration of God's creation; in Deuteronomy, by God's liberation of Israel from bondage. There are variations in the numbering of the Ten Commandments, but their contents have become the foundation of both Jewish and Christian religious teaching.

TEN LOST TRIBES, THE, 10 tribal groups who composed northern Israel in Biblical times and whose nation was destroyed by Assyrian armies from 733 to 732 and from 724 to 721 B.C. Many of the 10 tribes were deported at that time, and many conjectures have been advanced regarding the subsequent migrations of their descendants. But historians do not believe such conjectures are tenable. Judging from the evidence, many of the Israelites were killed and all their cities were leveled by the Assyrian armies. Sargon II, the conqueror of Samaria, recorded that he carried away 27,290 people in 721 B.C. Those that remained mingled with people deported from other parts of the Assyrian Empire into the land, and with them became the later Samaritans. Those whom Sargon deported were settled in Mesopotamia, where cuneiform documents have been found bearing the names of a few of them.

ZEALOTS [zĕl′əts], one of the four divisions of the Jewish community in the period preceding the rise of Christianity. Unlike the Essenes, Pharisees, and Sadducees, the Zealots were not identified by a particular religious position, agreeing, according to Josephus (Antiquities of the Jews, XVII, I, 6), with "Pharisaic notions." Devoted to the struggle for political freedom from Rome, they believed that only through military might could Rome be driven from Palestine and the universal reign of God be established. In their extreme manifestations, they turned against the moderates among the Jews, as well as against the Romans and their sympathizers. They seized control of Jerusalem during the Roman Siege (69–70 A.D.), and even after the fall of the city held out in other strongholds. Many of them finally fled to Alexandria in Egypt, where they fostered anti-Roman insurrections.

ZEBULUN [zĕb′yə-lŏn], an Israelite tribe that lived in the northern highlands of Palestine. The tribe's ancestor appears as Jacob's tenth son and the sixth born to Leah (Gen. 30:20).

ZEDEKIAH [zĕd-ə-kī′ə] or **MATTANIAH** [măt-ə-nī′ə], last King of Judah (c.598–587 B.C.). He was one of the younger sons of Josiah, placed on the throne by the Babylonians after his nephew, Jehoiachin, was deposed and deported to Babylon by Nebuchadnezzar as the result of a revolt by Jehoiachin's father, Jehoiakim (II Kings 24:17). Foolishly, Zedekiah, against the strong opposition of Jeremiah (Jer. 21–39), rebelled against the Babylonians, and Nebuchadnezzar came again to attack Jerusalem. Zedekiah was captured, forced to witness the slaying of his sons, and blinded before being taken, bound in fetters, to Babylon (II Kings 24:20–25:7). Jerusalem and the Temple were destroyed, and the Kingdom of Judah came to a tragic end (II Kings 25:8–21).

ZERUBBABEL [zə-rŭb′ə-bəl], leader of Jewish exiles returning from Babylonia in the 6th century B.C., mentioned in the Books of Ezra, Nehemiah, Haggai, and Zechariah. He urged the rebuilding of the Temple and, after encountering some opposition and delay, resumed laying the foundations in 520 B.C.

HITTITE CIVILIZATION

***

HITTITES [hĭt′ĭts]. The name "Hittites" comes to us from the Old Testament. In the Pentateuch the Hittites figure among the ancient inhabitants of Palestine, but this information is not confirmed by other sources. Later, in the books of Kings and Chronicles, the "kings of the Hittites" rule the country (modern Syria) to the north of Israel, and this has been substantiated by the contemporaneous Assyrian records, which describe wars against the Kings of the "Land of Hatti" from Carchemish to Damascus. However, the clay tablets unearthed near Boğazköy in central Asia Minor have revealed the history and civilization of a much earlier "Land of Hatti," showing that the Syrian region only acquired the name when it became a province of that powerful kingdom in the 14th century B.C. The term "Hittite" is a correlative of the historical Hatti and connotes a distinctive culture, the center of which moved from Asia Minor to Syria during the disturbances at the end of the Bronze Age.

Origins. Certain features of Hittite culture can be traced to the 3d millennium B.C. in Asia Minor, in the tomb treasures of Alaca Hüyük (c.2500 B.C.). However, the fact that the main language of the Hittite kingdom was Indo-European in structure shows that the dominant element in the population had entered the country from the north, probably toward the end of the 3d millennium via the Caucasus. The invaders adopted the culture and the place names, including that of Hatti itself, which they found in the country, contributing at the same time their own more flexible language and their organizing ability. Out of this mixture arose the civilization called Hittite.

History. The Hittite kings claimed descent from one Labarnas, who is said to have made conquests as far as the seacoasts. The earliest texts, however, refer to the reign of his successor, Hattusilis I (1650–1620 B.C.). In the third year of his reign Hattusilis repelled an invasion of Hurrians from across the Euphrates, and for the rest of his reign was occupied with wars in the direction of Syria. Final victory there was left to his successor, Mursilis I, who subdued Aleppo, proceeded on down the Euphrates, and overthrew Babylon itself c.1600. On returning home, however, Mursilis was murdered by his brother-in-law, Hantilis, and for a period of several generations the kingdom was brought to the verge of ruin by a series of palace revolutions.

Order was restored c.1525 B.C. by King Telipinus, who enforced the rule of law both at home and abroad, reforming the laws of the country and entering into treaties with neighboring powers. Upon his death, there ensued an obscure period. There appears to have been a powerful influx of Hurrians from the east, which left a permanent mark on the culture of the country. About 1450 B.C. a new dynasty rose to power, but it was not till the 14th century that the fortunes of the kingdom were restored.

The greatest figure of Hittite history is King Suppiluliumas (c.1380–1335 B.C.). Leading his army eastward, he crossed the Euphrates, passed through the territory of the Hurrian kingdom of Mitanni, and recrossed into Syria, defeating there the army of the King of Kadesh and so acquiring northern Syria for the Hittites. By the end of his reign Mitanni was reduced to vassalage, Hittite princes ruled in Aleppo and Carchemish, and the king of Kizzuwadna in Cilicia had sent his tribute to Hattusas. Suppiluliumas must also have reduced the western kingdom of Arzawa to submission, but the settlement did not outlast his death. The conquest of Arzawa was the main achievement of his successor, Mursilis II, who split up the country into vassal kingdoms.

The next reign, that of Muwatallis, is dominated by the struggle against resurgent Egypt and the indecisive battle of Kadesh. The Egyptians were unable to shake the hold of the Hittites on northern Syria. Under Hattusilis III (1275–1250 B.C.) the two great powers made their peace and with the increasing stability Hittite civilization reached its peak of prosperity. However, the death of Hattusilis was followed by a slow decline. Great movements of peoples were afoot. We hear of new troubles both in the east and in the west, and shortly after 1200 B.C. the Hittite kingdom was overwhelmed by irresistible forces. In the upheaval there was a general movement eastward and immigrants imbued with Hittite culture seem to have founded new kingdoms in what had been the Hittite eastern provinces. These were the Hittite states encountered by the Assyrian and Hebrew kings. Little is known of their history. One by one they succumbed to the mighty Assyrian power, and by 700 B.C. the whole area had become an Assyrian province.

Social Organization. Hittite society was characterized by a sharp division between the nobility and the common people, and by a largely feudal type of organization. At its head stood the king, who appears in the earliest period as

Sculptured stone beast and kneeling figure with an animal head once formed the base of a Hittite column (8th century B.C.).

Pottery vessels like this simply decorated vase (17th century B.C.) from Kültepe were used in the daily life of the Hittites.

the chief executive authority and commander in war. The queen played a remarkably independent role in affairs of state and inherited her position only on the death of her predecessor. In the Old Kingdom (from Labarnas to Telipinus) we hear nothing of divine sanction; each king declared his successor before the assembled nobility, and the appointment of the new king required in practice their assent. This was a source of instability until the succession was regulated by King Telipinus. For the administration of the state the king delegated his authority to his sons and kinsmen. We learn from later texts that most functionaries, from vassal kings to palace administrators, received their offices as fiefs involving a personal oath of loyalty to the king.

A remarkable feature of the Old Kingdom was the right of the nobility to sit as a court of peers, with jurisdiction over their own members and even over the king himself. After Telipinus this right seems to have lapsed. The later kings of the dynasty of Suppiluliumas recognized no such limitation on their power, which they claimed to hold as viceroys of the storm-god. These kings devoted much of their time to their religious functions as chief priest and spokesman for the nation before the divine authority. The nobility, for the most part, possessed large estates, held as fiefs conferred by the king, and it was they who provided the chariotry on which the strength of the Hittite army largely depended.

The common people were occupied mainly in agriculture, but there was a well-defined class of craftsmen, who also held fiefs of land involving duties of service. A labor force was provided by captives deported from conquered territories and by slaves, whose origin and status are not clear. Traveling merchants are mentioned, but trade was probably limited. The organization of the family was patriarchal.

Languages. The official language of the Hittite clay tablets, which we call "Hittite," was known to the Hittites themselves as the language of Kanesh, or Nesa. Closely related to it were Palaic, Luwian, and the language of the so-called Hittite Hieroglyphic monuments, which is as yet incompletely deciphered. All these languages belong structurally to the Indo-European family and preserve archaic features which were lost in the related languages. Luwian was the speech of western and southern Asia Minor, and "Hieroglyphic Hittite," which spread into north Syria after the downfall of the capital Hattusas, is a mere dialect of Luwian. A totally different language, with no known affinities, is called *ḫattili* in the tablets and is known to us as Hattian, or proto-Hittite; it was the language of the indigenous inhabitants and appears to have been no longer spoken in Hittite times. The Hurrian language (*ḫurlili*) was also extensively used in certain cults. The cuneiform script, in which the tablets are inscribed, was borrowed from Mesopotamia and adapted to the Hit-

183

Turkish Information Office

Bas-relief with three human figures (14th-13th century B.C.) from the main gate of Hattusas, capital of the Hittite Empire.

tite language. The "hieroglyphic" script was their own invention and dates from about 1500 B.C.

Religion. Local cults were centered in various cities throughout the country. Prominent among them, as befits a mountainous land, was that of the storm-god, who was worshiped under different names. At Arinna (not located) there was a cult of a sun-goddess. Springs, rivers, and mountains were commonly deified. The priests of Hattusas attempted to centralize the religion and combined the numerous deities into a complicated pantheon. The chief deities of the state were those of the Hattian population; the storm-god of Hatti and the sun-goddess of Arinna were elevated into national deities, whose viceroy and high priest was the king. Kings, and perhaps queens, were deified at death. In the later Empire, Hurrian and Luwian cults were also introduced into the capital. The result is seen at Yazilikaya, where the chief gods and goddesses are represented in bas-relief. The larger temples had large staffs and were the scenes of elaborate ceremonies. Several mythological tales, in most of which the storm-god plays a prominent part, are preserved, but the more elaborate poems are of Hurrian origin. Both inhumation and cremation were practiced concurrently. There was much use of divination for ascertaining the will of the gods, and sympathetic magic was a popular art employed for many purposes.

Architecture and Art. Hittite architectural remains consist characteristically of "cyclopean" masonry, enormous irregular blocks of stone trimmed to fit exactly into place. On this substructure, walls of mud-brick with wooden frameworks were usually erected. Temples consisted of numerous rooms grouped around a central courtyard; the shrine, with its cult statue in precious metal, was usually at one corner and was lit by large windows facing outward. The great defensive wall of Hattusas had huge monumental gateways adorned with massive sculptures; the rampart was penetrated by a postern tunnel. The typical Hittite art form is the bas-relief, carved either on natural rock faces or on orthostats (upright stone slabs) lining a building. The subjects are often religious. Sculpture in the round existed, but all known examples are from the latest period of Hittite civilization. In the art of seal cutting the Hittites also attained considerable proficiency.

Hittitology. The science of Hittitology owes its existence to the discovery of ancient Hittite works of art and inscriptions. Bas-reliefs, such as those at Yazilikaya and Alaca Hüyük, on stone blocks or rock faces, sometimes accompanied by a peculiar pictographic or hieroglyphic script, were recorded by travelers from 1812 onward; but it was not till 1876 that these monuments were first ascribed, by Archibald Henry Sayce, to the Hittites. Many more such monuments were discovered in the following years, notably by the British Museum expeditions to Carchemish in 1879 and 1911–14. But the special study of Hittitology may be said to date from 1906, when a German expedition under Hugo Winckler first excavated the site of the Hittite capital, Hattusas, near Boğazköy, and brought to light thousands of clay tablets inscribed in cuneiform. The language in which most of the texts were written was deciphered in 1915 by Bedrich Hrozný and proved to have Indo-European affinities. E. O. Forrer, a Swiss scholar working in Berlin, did valuable work in extracting and publishing the most important historical information from the tablets; but the systematic evaluation of the material is due to a small group of German scholars. Ferdinand Sommer, Hans Ehelolf, Johannes Friedrich, and Albrecht Götze inaugurated a series of critical editions of the major texts, with such success that in 1933 Götze was able to publish a complete cultural history of the Hittites. Their work has been continued by Hans Gustav Güterbock, Heinrich Otten, Annelies Kammenhuber, Emmanuel Laroche, Sedat Alp, Oliver Robert Gurney, and others. New tablets are continually being excavated at Boğazköy by the German expedition, which was led from 1931 to 1958 by Kurt Bittel. The decipherment of the hieroglyphic script and language made slow progress until 1949, when a Turkish schoolmaster discovered a bilingual text at Karatepe. Thanks to the pioneering work of Piero Meriggi, I. J. Gelb, Helmuth T. Bossert, Emmanuel Laroche, and other Hittitologists, a systematic edition of these texts can now be undertaken.

MESOPOTAMIAN CIVILIZATION

ART AND ARCHITECTURE

MESOPOTAMIAN ART AND ARCHITECTURE include monuments from centers of civilization in Babylonia (the southern part of Mesopotamia) and Assyria (the northern part). From the late fourth millennium B.C. to about the middle of the first millennium B.C., the focus of political power shifted from Sumer in southernmost Babylonia, to Akkad in northern Babylonia, to Assyria, and finally back to northern Babylonia. While architectural forms and styles of art changed during this time, the major monuments were generally created for a temple or a king and were meant to serve religious or political purposes. Therefore, the uses to which Mesopotamian art was put and the historical context in which it was created played an important part in shaping this art.

Sumerian art here refers to the art produced in the centuries from the late fourth millennium B.C. to the end of the third millennium B.C., when political power was concentrated in one or another city of Sumer. The finest works of the first stages of Mesopotamian civilization were remarkable for their high technical level and their inherent monumentality, even in objects of very small size. One such example is the stone figurine of a lioness monster, about 3¼ in. high, in the Brooklyn Museum.

During the third millennium B.C., the Sumerian city-states, or independent principalities, flourished. The wealth of objects discovered in the Royal Cemetery at Ur suggests that the rulers and high officials of the city-states must have lived in great luxury. A typical form of sculpture at this time was the worshiper statuette—a figurine placed in a temple before the statue of a god and intended to substitute for the continuous presence there of the actual worshiper. The large eyes and clasped hands of these figures seem to express a religious fervor or an attitude of pious respect, which is often emphasized by the clearly carved, simple contours.

In the later third millennium B.C., the Akkadians formed the first empire in northern Babylonia. Although the Akkadians were Semitic and not Sumerian-speaking peoples, their art is worth noting for its power, naturalism, and beauty. Life-size stone statues of kings were made, and royal military exploits were pictured in reliefs carved on stelae (large stone slabs).

At the end of the third millennium B.C., Sumerian dominance was restored through the leadership of the kings of Ur. The art of these rulers combined Akkadian forms, such as life-size sculptures and commemorative stelae, with a conservative, religious content. Thus, the final phase of Sumerian art was a revival of earlier Sumerian traditions, expressed in a sophisticated and polished manner.

Babylonian art includes works of the first half of the second millennium B.C., a period when the kings of Babylon dominated Babylonia. A well-known example of Babylonian art is the stele (Louvre, Paris) on which King Hammurabi had his law code inscribed. Above the inscription, the king is shown standing in an attitude of worship before the sun-god, the dispenser of justice. Similar scenes were also carved on cylinder seals, small stone cylinders which were probably used as magical amulets as well as a sort of personal signature. While cylinder seals had been invented in the earliest stage of Mesopotamian civilization, scenes of worshipers standing before deities were characteristic of Sumerian art of the late third millennium B.C. The continuation of this theme in Babylonia no doubt reflects the traditional nature of its art. The style of Babylonian art also owed a great debt to the past. Indeed, the taste for roundly modeled surfaces, evident in the relief on the stele of Hammurabi, can be traced in the art of southern Mesopotamia from Akkadian times in the late third millennium B.C. to the fall of the Chaldean Empire in 539 B.C

Assyrian art, on the other hand, was far more concerned with the present. The kings who established and ruled the Assyrian Empire in the first half of the first millennium B.C. certainly perpetuated Sumerian and Babylonian traditions, but Assyrian art seems to have had more in common with Akkadian art. Although the stone reliefs decorating the walls of Assyrian palaces included some religious scenes, more often there were lively and detailed representations of Assyrian military campaigns and depictions of royal hunts. The emphasis on the accomplishments of the kings and the interest in historical events are typical of both Akkadian and Assyrian art. While Assyrian relief sculptures were usually more flat and less roundly modeled than were Akkadian, Sumerian, and Babylonian reliefs, one feature is shared by the art of all areas of Mesopotamia—an interest in the treatment of

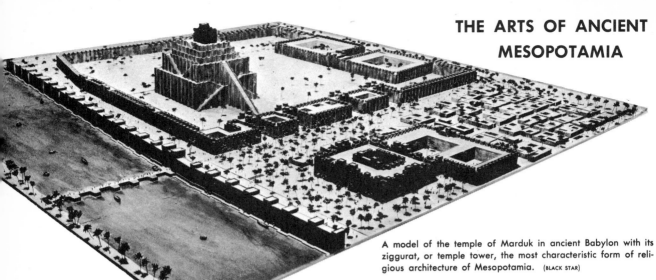

THE ARTS OF ANCIENT MESOPOTAMIA

A model of the temple of Marduk in ancient Babylon with its ziggurat, or temple tower, the most characteristic form of religious architecture of Mesopotamia. (BLACK STAR)

A bull's head, executed in gold foil and lapis lazuli, adorns a harp (c.2600–2400 B.C.) found at Ur. (UNIVERSITY MUSEUM, PHILADELPHIA)

Above, a Sumerian statuette of a standing male figure (c.3000 B.C.). About 1 ft. high, it is made of white gypsum colored with bitumen.
(THE METROPOLITAN MUSEUM OF ART, FLETCHER FUND, 1940)

An Assyrian alabaster wall relief (8th century B.C.) shows a Mede bringing two horses as tribute to Sargon II (reigned 722–705 B.C.). The relief is from the King's palace at Khorsabad (now Dur Sharrukin). (THE METROPOLITAN MUSEUM OF ART)

Royal attendant in a detail from an Assyrian relief (9th century B.C.)
(THE METROPOLITAN MUSEUM OF ART, GIFT OF JOHN D. ROCKEFELLER, JR., 1932)

surfaces of sculpture, whether by modeling, engraving, or inlaying of colored stones.

Chaldean or Neo-Babylonian art was created in the time of the Chaldean Empire, whose rulers conquered Assyria in 612 B.C. and reigned until 539 B.C. An example of Chaldean art is the glazed-brick relief decoration covering the walls of the great procession way in Babylon, the capital of the Empire. Like the earlier art of southern Mesopotamia, Chaldean art was conservative and mainly religious in nature. Babylonia, the cradle of civilization, revered its ancient heritage and preserved its traditions for thousands of years.

Mesopotamian architecture was usually built of mud bricks, since more durable materials like stone and wood were not widely available. Private houses were composed of rooms opening on interior courts, and royal palaces were larger versions of the same kind of plan—complexes of rooms built around courts, with a long, narrow throne room entered from an inside court.

There were several kinds of temples, from small street chapels for the worship of popular deities to huge compounds, where the chief god or gods of the city or palace were worshiped. The temple of Marduk in Babylon is an example of the latter type. The sacred precinct of the principal Babylonian god included a walled temple area and a ziggurat (temple tower) in a separate enclosure.

The nucleus of Mesopotamian temples, both small and large, was a cella, a room in which the statue of a god stood. A further characteristic of Mesopotamian temple architecture was the use of niching, which formed a pattern of recesses on temple facades. For thousands of years niched exterior walls signified a sacred building throughout Mesopotamia. In architecture as in art, traditions were able to unify the diversity produced by changes in population and by shifts in the centers of religious and political dominance.

SCULPTURE. Bound by conventions like those of Egypt, Mesopotamian sculptors developed distinctive

styles in a less religious setting. Although kingly figures in heavy, ornate costumes are stiff and lifeless, the long friezes that decorated palace walls were more naturalistic and colorful. Early Sumerian artists carved from flintlike diorite the dumpy enthroned figure, "Priest-King Gudea" (c.2450 B.C., Louvre, Paris). Assyrian sculptors created the rigidly standing "King Ashur-nasir-pal" (9th century B.C., British Museum, London) and the huge "Winged Man-Headed Bull" (Metropolitan Museum of Art, New York) that guarded the gate to his palace. Vivid bas-reliefs from Ashurbanipal's palace at Nineveh (668–626 B.C.) picture his famous hunts from horseback or chariot (British Museum). Although the horses, gazelles, and savagely struggling lions are beautifully naturalistic, the huntsmen seem strangely stiff and impassive. Ancient Persian sculptors created great friezes of molded brick and tile, brilliantly glazed and colored, such as the "Archer" and "Lion" (6th–5th centuries B.C., Louvre).

ARCHITECTURE. In the valleys of the Tigris and Euphrates clay was plentiful, and an architecture in brick became inevitable. Since brick is not suitable for beams, the arch and the vault became essential. For their pyramidal temple towers, or ziggurats, the Babylonian and Sumerian builders placed one stage or story in solid brick, penetrated by arched drains, on another. Each story was faced in a different color. A small shrine was located on top of the ziggurat.

The other great architectural structures of Mesopotamia were the royal palaces, the best known being those of the great Assyrian rulers. These warrior kings had great platforms of brick constructed as bastions in the city walls. On these they built their one-story palaces, many of whose rooms were narrow corridors with solid, close-spaced walls that presumably carried vaults or arches of brick. It is conceivable that some of the larger state apartments may have been domed. In time, the Mesopotamian cities crumbled into mounds of clay, and only through patient archeological excavation is it possible to glean knowledge of them.

BACKGROUND

MESOPOTAMIA [mĕs-ə-pə-tā′mē-ə] (Gr. *mesos*, "middle," and *potamos*, "river," denoting "the land between the rivers"), the name applied by classical writers to the upper part of the valley of the Euphrates and Tigris. Modern writers use the name to designate the whole region between these rivers, extending from the mountains of Armenia south to the Persian Gulf and from the Syrian Desert east to the Iranian plateau. It is used in this article in the wider sense.

Characteristics. Lower Mesopotamia, from Baghdad southeastward, is an alluvial plain deposited by the two rivers. The old view that the southern half of this plain was created within the last six millenniums is now challenged on geological evidence. North of Baghdad, in the ancient Assyria, are rolling uplands, rising to the north and east through foothills to ranges of 6,000 ft. To the west of Mesopotamia, beyond the Euphrates, lies desert, utilized since prehistoric times by seminomadic sheep-rearing tribes who constantly infiltrate into the more fertile riverine land. The rainfall in northern Mesopotamia is between 12 and 16 in. per year, permitting in favorable years the raising of wheat and barley (perhaps native here) without irrigation. In the south irrigation is indispensable, as rainfall does not exceed 8 in. June to October are rainless, and temperatures of up to 125° F. are recorded during July and August.

Prehistoric Cultures. Northern Mesopotamia, inhabited since the Mousterian period (c.50,000 B.C.), was later one of the regions in which settlement in permanent villages with a food-producing economy began. This transition is shown at the Neolithic site of Jarmo (c.5000 B.C.). The earliest pottery is found at Tell Hassuna near Mosul, which also yields evidence of domesticated animals and cultivated plants, though no trace of metals. This phase is found at sites extending from the Tigris to the Mediterranean. Copper began to be employed c.4500 B.C., in a period known as Tell Halaf, from a site on the Khabur River. Here occurred a wider range of cereals and domestic animals, while technical developments included wheeled vehicles, cobbled streets, mastery of the principle of the vault, and high-temperature kilns.

Occupation of southern Mesopotamia began, contemporaneously with the Tell Halaf period, at Eridu. This was a fishing and farming community, employing primitive irrigation and drainage techniques. The subsequent Al-Ubaid culture, though apparently unacquainted with metals, was an efficient peasant economy. It endured several centuries and eventually spread over all Mesopotamia, a notable site of its northern extension being Tepe Gawra.

About 3000 B.C. a new racial stratum, probably Sumerian, with Erech as its center, began to employ stone in building, introduced the cylinder seal and invented writing.

Excavations of the ancient Mesopotamian city of Samarra, now in north-central Iraq. The city was the capital of the Abbasid caliphs in the 9th century A.D.

The Sumerians and Their Heirs. The following half-millennium (designated Early Dynastic Period) saw the development in southern Mesopotamia of Sumerian city-states. The Sumerians built the canal system which gave agricultural prosperity to southern Mesopotamia until 1258 A.D. They also established much of the framework of Mesopotamian society for the next two millenniums. During this period, Semites were entering Mesopotamia from the western desert, and by c.2350 B.C. the first Semitic empire, centered at Agade, was founded. Though followed by a Sumerian renaissance, this marked the beginning of Semitic racial dominance in southern Mesopotamia, which culminated in the early 2d millennium in the unified kingdom of Babylonia under Hammurabi.

Corresponding racial trends farther north resulted in the rise of Assyria, the most noted ruler being Shamshi-Adad. Subsequently, pressure of non-Semitic peoples from the mountains caused the collapse of Babylonia and Assyria, Assyria sinking to its narrowest limits after the mid-17th century B.C. The Hurrians were the predominant force in northern Mesopotamia and ultimately, under an Indo-Aryan aristocracy, they became the kingdom of Mitanni. Babylon was sacked in 1531 B.C. by Hittites, thereafter falling to the Kassites, non-Semitic invaders from the Zagros Mountains. Assyria re-emerged from Hurrian domination after 1400 B.C., while the Kassites were gradually assimilated, so that by the 12th century native Semitic dynasties again ruled throughout Mesopotamia. There had already begun the rise of Assyria to political supremacy, which culminated in an empire reaching from the Mediterranean (for a short time from Egypt) to Iran. At Assyria's collapse in 612 B.C. its empire

passed to a Babylonian (Chaldaean) dynasty, whose most celebrated king was Nebuchadnezzar II.

Persians and Seleucids. The defeat of Babylonia by Cyrus the Great in 539 B.C. brought Mesopotamia under Persian (Achaemenid) domination. This regime endured until 331 B.C., when it fell to Alexander the Great, who died in 323 B.C., planning a world state centered at Babylon. Alexander's empire disintegrated, the part from Iran to the Mediterranean falling in 301 B.C. to Seleucus, who built Seleucia on the Tigris as a provincial Mesopotamian capital. The most notable Seleucid ruler, Antiochus the Great (reigned 223–187 B.C.), came into conflict with Rome.

The Parthians. Subsequent monarchs failed to integrate the empire. Mesopotamia fell shortly after 141 B.C. to the Parthians from northeast Iran, who opposite Seleucia established a military camp which later became their capital, Ctesiphon. Seleucid efforts to recover Mesopotamia finally failed in 129 B.C. After diplomatic encounters, Rome came disastrously into military conflict with the Parthians in Mesopotamia at Carrhae in 53 B.C. Mesopotamia was henceforward generally recognized for over a century as a Parthian province. The 2d century A.D. saw several clashes in Mesopotamia between Parthia and Rome. Ctesiphon fell temporarily into Roman hands in 115, in 165, and in 198 A.D., northwest Mesopotamia remaining in Roman possession from 165 A.D.

The Sassanians. The Parthian (Arsacid) dynasty was overthrown in 226 A.D. by Ardashir, a Sassanian prince from Fars, who evicted Roman forces from northwest Mesopotamia. After the official conversion of Rome (324 A.D.), Mesopotamia's large Christian population was considered of suspect loyalty, and suffered persecution under Shapur II (309–79). After Shapur's death dynastic rivalries opened the way to Roman advances in northern Mesopotamia. Matters improved under Khosrau I (531–79), who was strong enough to invade Syria and capture Antioch (540). His second successor, Khosrau II (590–628), overran the whole Near East, but was finally defeated at Ctesiphon by the Byzantine Emperor Heraclius.

BRONZE AGE

Defining Bronze Age presents several problems. In the first place, the use of stone tools and weapons overlapped the use of copper and bronze. Moreover, the use of these metals began at different times in different areas. The smelting of copper was probably begun in the Middle East before 4000 B.C. Bronze may have been discovered as early as this, but the casting of bronze tools began about 3500–3000 B.C. in Mesopotamia. Bronze was known in Asia Minor, the Aegean area, and India in the 3d millennium B.C. In Europe, bronze came into use around 2000 B.C. and reached most of Europe in the next few centuries. Bronze continued as the principal metal until iron began to replace it at dates ranging from about 1500 B.C. in the Near East to perhaps 600 B.C. in England.

Thus there is no neatly defined Age of Bronze. Moreover, the use of bronze was not the only important development taking place among peoples who learned metalworking. A more helpful term than "age" might be "age and stage," since the important consideration is a stage in the development of human culture rather than a period of time. During the stage when bronze was in wide use developments in civilization took place that had greater significance than the particular tools that were typical of a time and place. "Bronze Age," or "Bronze Age and Stage" is a convenient designation for a stage in the growth of civilization.

The Urban Revolution. The major development during what is traditionally called the Neolithic Age in the Near East was the establishment of a village-farming community way of life. As a result of this food-producing revolution, during which man learned to raise crops and livestock, food supplies became more assured and settlements more permanent than they were in earlier times. The present article concerns the range of time and cultural activity in the Near East and Europe when—upon the basis of the new way of life developed in Neolithic times—towns and eventually literate city-states began to be established. The story of this urban revolution begins in southern Mesopotamia around 4500 B.C. A reasonably convenient ending for it might be about 1200 B.C., by which time the effects of trade from the eastern end of the Mediterranean—with the Mycenaean Greeks as one group of important carriers—had spread through Europe to affect even Britain and the southern shores of the Baltic.

Mesopotamia. Domesticated plants and animals of the village-farming community way of life, which developed along the grassy hill flanks of the Fertile Crescent within the natural habitat of the domesticated animals in the Neolithic Age, could not immediately be introduced into the hot, dry alluvial plain of southern Mesopotamia. But by 4500 B.C., if not slightly earlier, the first farmers seem to have made their way down along the fertile mud banks of the Tigris and Euphrates rivers, and to have established themselves in the lower alluvial basin. Here, with some attention to irrigation, a fantastically rich agricultural yield was possible. Archeological evidence gives a picture of town-sized establishments with imposing temple structures, trading or market functions and growing specialization and differentiation in occupations, with farmers, craftsmen, clerks, and priests.

The archeological name for the culture of this period and area is Ubaidian (the term comes from an excavated site at Ubaid). Its most brilliant and certainly its focal center was in southern Mesopotamia, where a date of about 4100 B.C. has been established. However, the Ubaidian industrial traditions, especially painted pottery, soon spread over much of southwestern Asia: back into northern Iraq, up into the Anatolian and Iranian plateaus and beyond, toward Baluchistan and the Indus, and to the Mediterranean coast, and even to Palestine. Curiously, few if any metal tools from this period have yet been found in southern Mesopotamia, but copper artifacts have been recovered in various upland Ubaidian contexts.

From this point onward for 2000 years, at least, southern Mesopotamia remained a center of great cultural potential and stimulation. The rise of the Egyptian and Aegean (Cretan) civilizations are to be viewed as having

George Mylonas: Aghios Kosmas

Houses in an excavated city of Aghios Kosmas, Greece, were laid out along a street. The establishment of sizable towns and eventually of complex and powerful city-states was a major achievement of the Bronze Age.

(1) Bronze adz head from Tepe Gawra, Iraq, c.2500–2000 B.C.
(2) Bronze hollow chisel from Tepe Hissar, Iran, c.2000 B.C.
(3) Bronze mattock head from Tepe Hissar, c. 2000 B.C.
(4) Bronze needle from Tepe Gawra, c.2500–2000 B.C.
(5) Bronze lance blade from Tepe Hissar, c. 2000 B. C.

Philadelphia University Museum

Lee Boltin

Goat nibbling at a golden tree, c.2123–2081 B.C., was probably a support for a piece of furniture.

Iranian bronze vessel from Luristan was made c.1200 B.C.

Sumerian copper bull's head da from the 3d millennium B.C.

The Metropolitan Museum of Art, Fletcher Fund, 1

Painted pottery fragment is fr Baluchistan.

American Museum of Natural Hi

The Metropolitan Museum of Art, Chapman Fund, N

been due to an early stimulation of ideas from Mesopotamia (plus more generally southwestern Asiatic ideas), upon which local Egyptian and Cretan patterns developed in time. In Mesopotamia, after the general tone of developments had been set in the Ubaidian period, there followed the Warka period and then the Proto-Literate period, characterized by at least pictographic writing, great competence in the crafts, and notable productions in art and architecture. This developed into the succession of early dynastic Sumerian periods.

Developments to the East are still poorly understood. The brilliant, but short-lived (c.2500–1500 B.C.), Indus Valley civilization, of which Harappa and Mohenjo Daro are key sites, was certainly to some degree dependent on Mesopotamian stimulation; so, too, the civilization on Bahrain Island in the Persian Gulf.

CITIES

CITY, relatively large, dense, permanent settlement of people in nonagricultural occupations.

Origins. Cities developed from a combination of technological, environmental, and social factors. The domestication of plants and animals was the fundamental factor that made it possible for man to live as other than a nomadic hunter and gatherer. In favorable environments with good water supplies and year-round growing conditions, agricultural productivity rose above subsistance levels. This surplus enabled some portion of the population to live without growing its own food and to specialize in crafts and services. Settlements with these conditions could be large and dense. However, this only occurred in conjunction with certain social developments. A new and complex social order had to arise to mobilize the surplus and to integrate the activities of the urbanites, who specialized in crafts and services, with those of the farmers. The urban social order included a written language, mathematics, astronomy, and the sciences. Impersonal media of exchange (money) and the appearance of the state as a focus of loyalty and obligation, in addition to those of family and kin, were other features of urban society. All of these are urban social inventions and indicate why the emergence of civilization is dated from the emergence of cities.

The earliest known cities developed about 3500 B.C. in the floodplain of the Tigris and Euphrates rivers, in an area variously called southern Mesopotamia, Sumer, Babylonia, and, now, southern Iraq. Many of the early cities, such as Ur, Erech, Babylon, and Nineveh, are referred to in the Bible. Cities also emerged relatively early in ancient Egypt, ancient China, and that portion of the Indian subcontinent that we now know as Pakistan. The weight of current evidence suggests that urban development in these areas was at least partly derived from the initial urban inventions in Mesopotamia.

Assyria
(Northern Mesopotamia)

BACKGROUND

ASSYRIA [ə-sĭr′ē-ə], ancient Near Eastern country, covering an area varying in size from time to time, situated within the northern part of present-day Iraq. The name of the country is derived from the city of Ashur (anc. *Ashshur*, modern Qala Sharqat), the capital of a small city-state situated on both sides of the Tigris River, 60 mi. south of the modern city of Mosul. In its farther expansion Assyria included the lands extending east of the Tigris toward the mountains of Iran, especially the lands situated in the river basin of the Upper and the Lower Zab, as well as the territory lying between the Tigris and the Euphrates, called *Hanigalbat* in ancient times. In its farthest expansion in the New Assyrian period, the Assyrian Empire included all of Mesopotamia, Syria, Palestine, and extensive areas in Iran, Armenia, Anatolia, Arabia, and Egypt. At the time of Ptolemy, the geographer, Assyria as a province of the Parthian Empire was again limited to a small area east of the Tigris, surrounded by the provinces of Babylonia, Mesopotamia, Armenia, Media, and Susiana.

The main cities of Assyria were the three cities which, at different times, served as capitals of the kingdom: Ashur, Ninua (the Biblical *Nineveh*, modern Kuyunjik), and Kalhu (the Biblical *Calah*, modern Nimrud). *Dur Sharrukin* (modern Khorsabad) served as capital of Assyria only during the reign of Sargon II. Other important cities of Assyria were *Arbailu* (modern Erbil), *Kakzu* (modern Sadawah), and *Arrapha* (modern Kirkuk), all situated east of the Tigris; and *Mari* (modern Tell Hariri), Haran, and *Nasibina* (modern Nusaybin), situated between the Tigris and the Euphrates.

Prehistory

The basic change from the food-gathering stage to that of incipient agriculture and domestication of animals was achieved about 7000 years ago, perhaps for the first time in the history of mankind, in the area here included under Assyria, mainly in the piedmont area between the Tigris and the mountains of Iran. This change from food collection to food production marks what Gordon Childe calls "the first revolution" in the history of economic progress. The next stage of the village-farming community can be reconstructed at several sites in Assyria, such as Jarmo (near Kirkuk), Hassuna (south of Mosul), and Tell Halaf (on the Khabur River). Men lived in villages composed of mud-built houses. They raised barley and two different kinds of wheat. They certainly domesticated the goat, but the bones of such animals as sheep, cattle, pigs, and dogs do not show sure signs of domestication. They made pottery of clay, and tools, such as sickles and mortars, of stone. In the two successive stages, named Ubaid and Warka after two Babylonian sites where these stages were best represented, a marked social and economic progress can be observed. In these stages larger, townlike settlements appeared, characterized chiefly by the monumental architecture of temples and palaces, the increased use of copper for making tools, of the *tournette* for making pottery, and of stamp seals for the purposes of identification. The Warka stage was followed by the so-called Protoliterate stage, marked by the introduction of writing and of cylinder seals. This is the beginning of the historical age in Babylonia and Assyria.

History

The beginnings of Assyrian history are lost in the mists of antiquity. However, with the help of two Assyrian king lists compiled in the early 1950's by the Assyriologist I. J.

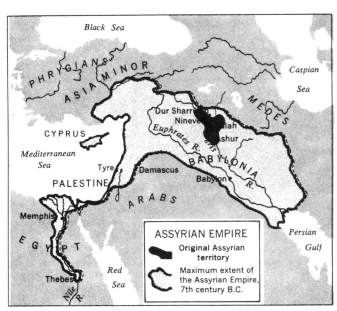

ASSYRIAN EMPIRE
Original Assyrian territory
Maximum extent of the Assyrian Empire, 7th century B.C.

The religion of Assyria evolved from the earlier Sumerian beliefs. Gods and demons were often portrayed as half animal and half man. A winged bull (*left*) from relief at the palace of Ashur-nasir-pal II (883–859 B.C.). Birdheaded deity (*below*) from the palace of Ashur-nasir-pal III (fl.880 B.C.).

Gelb, it is now possible to reconstruct an almost complete sequence of 117 Assyrian kings from the earliest beginnings to the fall of Assyria. Out of this number the names of the first 30 kings are hardly ever attested in any sources outside of the king lists.

Early History. Excavations of Ashur, Mari, and the smaller sites of Chagar Bazar and Brak, as well as information culled from Babylonian sources, indicate that in the Pre-Sargonic and Sargonic periods Assyria stood under the strong cultural and political influence of Babylonia. Culturally, southern influence can be recognized in the use of cuneiform writing and in the form of statuary and monumental architecture. Politically, the inscriptions of Sargon of Akkad (reigned c.2340–2284 B.C.), the first great Semitic conqueror, indicate that he held under his sway Mesopotamia and Syria to the Mediterranean Sea. During the major parts of the Sargonic (c.2340–2159 B.C.) and Ur III (c.2117–2008 B.C.) periods Upper Mesopotamia must have been organized in provinces administered by governors appointed by Babylonian rulers.

The Cappadocian Period. Dating from the period following the fall of the 3d Dynasty of Ur are the first written sources for the Assyrian kings. The most important of these were Ilushuma (fl.1920 B.C.), Irishum I (fl.1900 B.C.), and Sargon I of Assyria (fl.1850 B.C.), known best for their extensive temple-building in the city of Ashur. This is the period of the "Cappadocian" texts, which attest a vigorous Assyrian commercial expansion far into the heart of Anatolia. Thousands of these texts, mainly business letter and economic documents, found at the sites of Kültepe anc. *Kanesh*), Boğazköy (anc. *Hattusas*, the later capital of the Hittite Empire), and Alishar, all situated in central Anatolia (called Cappadocia by the Greeks), give a good picture of the lively trade between Ashur and these Anatolian commercial centers. Commodities traded included textiles, wool, hides, and metals, mainly lead, tin, copper, silver, and gold.

The Mari Period. The period of Cappadocian texts came abruptly to an end due to unknown causes, and was supplanted by a new era, beginning with the rule (c.1813–1781 B.C.) of Shamshi-Adad I. He was probably of nomad Amorite origin. Shamshi-Adad was a great and wise ruler. Knowledge of this king and his period has increased greatly in recent years, thanks to the discovery of the cuneiform archives at Mari. Shamshi-Adad conquered all of Mesopotamia but ruled it indirectly, appointing two of his sons as viceroys in the two main areas of his kingdom, the older son, Ishme-Dagan, in Assyria proper, and the younger, Yasmah-Adad, in Mari. Shamshi-Adad introduced, for the first time, the Babylonian dialect as the language of the court, in place of Assyrian, which had dominated previously.

Hurrians and Mitannians. At the death of Shamshi-Adad, Assyria fell into a total disintegration, which lasted close to 300 years. During the reign of Ishme-Dagan (c.1780–1740 B.C.), both Assyria proper and Mari fell to Hammurabi (reigned c.1792–1750 B.C.), the great conqueror and lawgiver of Babylon. After that, all historical attestation for Assyria ceases, and, with the exception of a brief period around 1500 B.C., nothing more is known about Assyria until the end of the 15th century B.C. Such complete silence cannot be accidental, and it can hardly be explained by the general scarcity of Assyrian historical documents pertaining to the early periods. This silence of sources is as telling as any argument drawn from written materials. It bears eloquent testimony to a great catastrophe caused by invasions of foreign, illiterate barbarians. These invaders must have been Hurrians, who, originating around Lake Urmia in Armenia, under the leadership of Indo-Aryan rulers and nobility, brought in a sort of Middle Ages to large parts of the Fertile Crescent. Establishing themselves first in Upper Mesopotamia, around the headwaters of the Khabur River, in a kingdom named Mitanni, they succeeded in the course of the 15th century B.C., making extended use of horse-drawn chariots, in imposing their military and political control over Assyria, Syria, Palestine, and parts of eastern Anatolia. The greatest period of Mitannian expansion was probably reached under King Saushshattar (fl.1500 B.C.). The disintegration of the Mitannian kingdom began toward the end of the reign of Tushratta (c.1360 B.C.), when the great Hittite King Suppiluliumas (reigned c.1375–1335 B.C.) initiated his drive to conquer North Syria, and it ended with the rule of Mattiwaza, son of Tushratta, the last king of Mitanni. This is the period during which Assyria regained its independence from the Mitannian yoke.

Ashur-uballit and His Successors. The renaissance of Assyria as the leading political power in Mesopotamia, initiated by the Assyrian King Ashur-uballit I (reigned c.1362–1327 B.C.), who collaborated with the Hittites and other allies in destroying Mitanni, was achieved mainly by three Assyrian rulers, Adad-nirari I (reigned c.1304–1273 B.C.), his son Shalmaneser I (reigned c.1272–1243 B.C.), and his grandson Tukulti-Ninurta I (reigned c.1242–1206 B.C.). While Adad-nirari I and his son devoted their energies mainly to the consolidation of their conquests in Upper Mesopotamia in wars against the kingdom of Hanigbalbat, which arose there as the successor state to Mitanni, Tukulti-Ninurta I was able to direct his conquests to areas beyond Upper Mesopotamia. From Syria he deported 28,800 captives to Assyria. In the region of Babylonia he conquered Babylon, destroyed its walls, took

much booty from the temples, and brought the Kassite king captive in chains to Ashur.

Tiglath-pileser I. For a short period after the death of Tukulti-Ninurta I Assyria lost its leading position in Mesopotamia to the Kassite rulers in Babylonia. It was not until the reign of Tiglath-pileser I (c.1114–1076 B.C.) that Assyria regained its supremacy. Throughout his long reign Tiglath-pileser was engaged in repelling the invasions of the Aramaeans. He was the first Assyrian ruler after Shamshi-Adad I to reach the Mediterranean Sea in his campaigns against Syria.

The Aramaeans. The next 150 years represent a period of weakness in Assyrian history, caused most probably by incessant inroads of nomadic Bedouins. Starting in the desert and semidesert regions south of the Euphrates, they crossed the Euphrates, threatening the settled populations of Upper Mesopotamia. These were the Aramaeans, who, even though subjugated by the Assyrians, were able in the course of the following centuries to impose their language upon the whole Fertile Crescent, including Babylonia, Assyria, Syria, and Palestine, relegating the native languages to the status of dead languages.

Growth of Assyria. A spectacular period of political renaissance took place during the reigns of four kings, Adad-nirari II (911–891 B.C.), Tukulti-Ninurta II (890–884 B.C.), Ashur-nasir-pal II (883–859 B.C.), and Shalmaneser III (858–824 B.C.), whose activities represent a story of continuous political expansion. While Adad-nirari II and Tukulti-Ninurta II devoted most of their energies to the reconquest of all the lands in Upper Mesopotamia north of Babylonia, Ashur-nasir-pal II consolidated the reconquered areas in Upper Mesopotamia by organizing them as provinces. He went even farther, beyond the Euphrates, conquering Carchemish and reaching the Mediterranean Sea. The conquest of North Syria was continued by Shalmaneser III as a result of his campaigns against Damascus, Tyre, Sidon, and Israel. During all that period Assyria lived in relative peace with Babylonia, its neighbor to the south.

Assyria as a Dominant Power in the Near East. Assyria's greatest political expansion and cultural influence were reached during a period of about 100 years, from the middle of the 8th to the middle of the 7th century B.C., in the reigns of Tiglath-pileser III (744–727 B.C.), Shalmaneser V (726–722 B.C.), Sargon II (721–705 B.C.), Sennacherib (704–681 B.C.), Esarhaddon (680–669 B.C.), and Ashurbanipal (668–?630 B.C.). This is the period during which Assyria was the leading military power in the whole Near East.

In campaigns against Media and Syria Tiglath-pileser III solidified Assyrian rule in those areas. His greatest military achievement was the conquest of Babylonia. In contrast to other conquered areas, which were placed under Assyrian governors and incorporated as provinces of the Assyrian kingdom, Babylonia preserved a semblance of independence. This was exemplified by Tiglath-pileser III who seated himself on the throne of Babylon under an assumed Babylonian name, Pul. Shalmaneser V ruled in Babylonia under the name Ululaya and continued his father's conquests in Syria, by moving southward against Phoenicia and Palestine. He began the long siege of Tyre in Phoenicia and of Samaria in Israel, but did not live to see their capture, both cities falling to his successor, Sargon

II. The latter concentrated his military operations mainly in the areas situated to the north of Assyria, in Iran, Armenia, and Anatolia. Sennacherib's main preoccupation during his reign was the quelling of revolts in Babylonia. After prolonged campaigns, lasting many years, Sennacherib recaptured Babylonia and destroyed the city of Babylon (689 B.C.). His other campaigns took him to Cilicia, Syria, Phoenicia, and Palestine. The murder of Sennacherib by one of his sons resulted in a civil war, which was resolved in favor of one of Sennacherib's younger sons, Esarhaddon, who put down the rebellion and established himself on the throne of Assyria. In order to prevent fratricidal wars Esarhaddon regulated the succession to the throne by naming two of his sons, Ashurbanipal and Shamash-shum-ukin (reigned 668–648 B.C.), as his successors on the thrones of Assyria and Babylonia, respectively. Esarhaddon's greatest political achievement was his conquest of Egypt, which, however, was not incorporated as part of Assyria, but was organized under local princes, supervised by Assyrian advisers whose main duty was the regular collection of tribute.

Ashurbanipal and the Fall of Assyria. Ashurbanipal's reign, while still marked by successful campaigns in Iran, Asia Minor, Syria, Palestine, and Arabia, contained the germs of decay which ultimately caused the fall of the Assyrian Empire. Early in his reign Egypt was lost, and long-fought rebellions had to be quashed in Babylonia and neighboring Elam. The available sources on Ashurbanipal break abruptly after the year 639 B.C., doubtless because of foreign interference in the affairs of Assyria. Very little is known about the rule of the last three or four kings of Assyria. In 626 B.C. a Chaldaean by the name of Nabopolassar rebelled against Assyrian rule and in the following year established himself on the throne of Babylon. From then on, Assyria suffered a series of defeats, inflicted by Nabopolassar and his ally, Cyaxares, King of Media. The conquest of Nineveh by the Babylonians and Medes took place in 612 B.C., and the last remnants of the Assyrian army under Ashur-uballit II (reigned 611–609 B.C.), the last king of Assyria, were scattered in 609 B.C. The end of Assyria and the destruction of its cities were final and complete. Only 200 years later Xenophon found Assyria proper completely desolated and mistook the ruins of the once proud Nineveh for those of a city of the Medes.

Cultural Contributions

Sharing with Babylonia a common language and writing and the many cultural traits inherited from the Sumerians, the civilization of Assyria cannot be adequately described apart from that of Babylonia. Assyrians have often been called the Romans of the ancient Near East, in contrast to the Babylonians, who have been compared with the Greeks. While the Babylonians were largely peaceful and politically self-contained within their area, the Assyrians were warlike, expanding militarily and politically in all directions. While the Babylonians' great cultural contributions lay mainly in the sciences and literature, Assyrians could justifiably take pride in their great achievements in the field of administration and organization of the state and society, based on their deeper appreciation of law and order.

Social Organization. With the growing expansion of Assyria from a small city-state to an empire encompassing almost the entire Near East, two main classes of population could be distinguished: the Assyrians proper and the peoples of the conquered areas. The growth of the state necessitated an ever-increasing number of Assyrians to take care of the military and administrative affairs of the far-flung empire, resulting at home in a shortage of labor for agriculture and production. This brought about a policy, very highly developed by the Assyrians, of deporting large populations from conquered areas and of settling them in Assyria. The new policy served the double purpose of providing much needed labor in Assyria, thus releasing Assyrians for state duties, and of preventing rebellions in the conquered and largely devastated areas.

At the head of the state stood the king, with all the despotic powers of an oriental monarch. The king was not deified, however, as he was in Egypt. Directly under him were the priests and the warrior class. The state was organized in provinces under governors, whose tasks were the meting out of justice, the raising of levies for war and public construction, and the exaction of taxes and tribute.

Agriculture and Commerce. The principal means of subsistence were agriculture and animal husbandry. Supplementary subsistence was afforded by hunting and fishing. Hunting was the main sport of the king and nobles. Hunting of wild animals such as lions, elephants, and wild bulls was often done by men sitting in horse-drawn chariots. Occasionally, hunting dogs were used. Commerce was highly developed, both internally and internationally. Caravan routes were widely established, and protected caravansaries were built to house traveling merchants.

Sciences and Literature. The Babylonian sciences of mathematics, astronomy, chemistry, and medicine were fully pursued by the Assyrians, although the latter were more interested in copying learned works and organizing them in series than in making original contributions. Literary works included myths, epics and legends, religious texts (prayers, incantations, liturgies, and rituals), and divination series (oracles and astrological omens). There were also innumerable lexical and grammatical texts, private and public letters, and economic and legal texts. Historiographic writing was much more highly developed by the Assyrians than by the Babylonians. The Assyrians' highest achievement in that field was their great annalistic literature. Books were housed in libraries usually attached to temples, although the largest and most famous Assyrian library was assembled by Ashurbanipal. Schools were located on temple grounds and schooling was in the hands of specially trained priests.

The Assyrians developed to an unprecedented degree the art of war and the technique of military engineering. Their standing army consisted of infantry, chariotry, and from the 9th century B.C. on, of cavalry. The soldier, protected by a pointed helmet, shield, and coat of mail, was armed with a sword, spear, and bow and arrows. In besieging towns assault and siege engines such as battering rams moved on wheeled carriages, and catapults, ramps, and scaling ladders were used. Pioneer units were used to mine under besieged fortresses and to build roads and bridges made of boats.

Art and Architecture. In contrast to the Babylonians, who lived in an alluvial area devoid of stone, which had to be imported from distant countries, the Assyrians found stone plentiful in their surroundings and made full use of it, both in art and architecture. Their great cities, often planned in a rectangular shape, such as Sargon's residence, Dur Sharrukin, were full of magnificent palaces and temples. Cities often contained animal parks and botanical gardens for the pleasure of the citizens, and canals and aqueducts brought fresh water from the mountains to the cities. Stone sculpture, both in the round and in relief, abounded, winged lions and bulls providing a particularly favorite subject for the sculptor. Besides stone, bronze, ivory, and clay were used for artistic purposes.

Law. The rules of conduct were controlled by law and contract. While it seems that the Assyrians never compiled a law code on the scale of the Babylonian Code of Hammurabi, they did put together, in the Middle Assyrian period, a collection of laws, mainly governing family life. A most important source for Assyrian law is found in the thousands of contracts pertaining to family life, transfer of property, finances, and so forth. They were written traditionally in the Assyrian dialect, not in Babylonian, which had become the written language of Assyrian literature. Contracts, as well as historical texts, were dated by the names of eponymous officials, in contrast to the Babylonian habit of dating by year names or regnal years.

Religion. Most of the divinities worshiped in Babylonia were also worshiped in Assyria. However, certain divinities received much greater recognition than they did in Babylonia. The chief god of the Assyrians was Ashur. Originally the god of the city of Ashur, he became the supreme god of the pantheon and national god of the Assyrians, just as Marduk became the national god of the Babylonians. Other important Assyrian divinities were Ishtar, goddess of love and war, worshiped at Nineveh, Ashur, and Arbela; Sin, the moon-god, at Haran; Adad, the storm-god, at Ashur; and Ninurta, the god of war and the chase, at Calah.

Cosmopolitan Aspect. The growth of the Assyrian empire brought together under one rule the peoples of Assyria and Babylonia, of Syria and Palestine, and of vast regions in Iran, Armenia, Anatolia, Arabia, and Egypt. These were peoples who spoke different languages and represented different cultural backgrounds. Organized in provinces, most of the conquered countries must have experienced a strong cultural influence emanating from Mesopotamia. The Assyrian policy of founding new cities and settling them with new inhabitants and of transporting by force large bodies of conquered populations from their homes to Mesopotamia brought large masses of foreigners to the country. The custom of Assyrian warriors' bringing home captive women as slaves and of Assyrian kings' taking as wives daughters of foreign rulers, brought in further foreign influence to Mesopotamia. All these factors led gradually to the first appearance of a cosmopolitan society in the Near East, offering fertile ground for the creation of the more or less uniform level of civilization achieved later, in the Hellenistic period, under Alexander the Great and his successors.

PEOPLE, PLACES, AND TERMS

ASHUR [ăsh'ər], **ASSUR, or ASSHUR,** ancient capital of Assyria, on the right bank of the Tigris River, 65 mi. south of Nineveh, on a major trade route. Its site, Qala Sharqat,

was discovered by Claudius J. Rich in 1821, and later explored by British and French antiquaries. It was scientifically excavated between 1903 and 1914 by the Deutsche Orientgesellschaft (German Oriental Society) under Walter Andrae, yielding a large collection of cuneiform tablets of great historical and religious importance. Continuous ancient occupation of the site has been traced from early in the 3d millennium B.C. to the 3d century A.D.

ASHURBANIPAL [ä-shōōr-bä'nĭ-päl] (Assyrian name, Ashshur-bani-apli or Ashshur-ban-apli), Assyrian King, son of Esarhaddon, reigned 668–630 B.C. He was one of the greatest of Assyrian rulers, and his long reign was filled with wars on all the frontiers of his widespread empire— in Iran, Babylonia, Armenia, Asia Minor, Arabia, Syria, Palestine, and Egypt. Only in Egypt did Ashurbanipal suffer a setback, losing the country (654 B.C.) to the victorious Egyptians, who were led by Psamtik I of Saïs and supported by Greek and Carian soldiers. After a period of co-operation, Babylonia under Shamash-shum-ukin, brother of Ashurbanipal, rebelled against Assyria, but was subdued in 648 B.C. by Ashurbanipal, who himself occupied the throne of Babylonia, probably under the name Kandalanu. The ever-rebellious Elam was finally defeated in 639 B.C., losing forever its leading position in Iran to the growing power of the Medes.

His greatest achievement at home was the creation of a giant library in his palace in Nineveh. It contained literary works in Akkadian and Sumerian, which were either collected or copied under the King's orders in the scattered temple libraries of Babylonia and then brought to Nineveh. The available sources on Ashurbanipal break off abruptly after the year 639 B.C., and nothing is known about the last years of his reign. He is sometimes identified with Sardanapalus of Greek history.

ASHUR-NASIR-PAL [ä-shōōr-nä'zĭr-päl] II (883–859 B.C.), Assyrian King, son of Tukulti-Ninurta II, under whom began the expansion of Assyria westward to the Mediterranean coast. He was known for his terroristic tactics and cruel treatment of captured enemies. During his reign cavalry was first used extensively in warfare and Assyrian governors were first placed in conquered lands.

ASSYRIOLOGY [ə-sĭr-ē-ŏl'ə-jē], an area of study dealing primarily with records of Assyria and Babylonia written in cuneiform script and the Akkadian language. The Akkadian language, or Assyro-Babylonian, as it is sometimes called, includes two main dialects, Assyrian and Babylonian. Of these, the Assyrian dialect was limited to Assyria proper, while the Babylonian dialect, originally used only in Babylonia, became in the course of time the written language of Assyrian religious and historical literature. Early in the Old Babylonian period, the Babylonian dialect began to be used extensively outside Babylonia and Assyria in recording business transactions and writing letters in Elam and in Syria. In the Middle Babylonian period the Babylonian dialect became the international language of diplomatic correspondence and was used practically throughout the Near East, including Egypt and Asia Minor. The use of the term "Assyriology," rather than "Babyloniology," was established in the first half of the

19th century, and is due to the fact that the earliest explorations and discoveries in Mesopotamia had taken place in Assyria rather than in Babylonia.

The wide field of Assyriology includes many subbranches: (a) the central core, consisting of the study of Assyrian and Babylonian, both within and outside Mesopotamia; (b) Sumerology, or the study of Sumerian in its two main periods, the 3d millennium B.C., when the Sumerians represented the dominant political and cultural element in Mesopotamia, and the 2d and 1st millennia B.C., when, after the extinction of Sumerian as a living language and its replacement by Akkadian, it became limited in its use to historiographic, legal, and religious writings; (c) the study of Elamite in Iran, of Hurrian in parts of Upper Mesopotamia, Syria, and Asia Minor, and of Urartian in Armenia, all native languages written in different varieties of the Mesopotamian cuneiform script; (d) the study of Hittite and other languages of Asia Minor, originally pursued mainly by Assyriologists, but now an independent discipline, called Hittitology; and (e) the study of Ugaritic in Syria and of the Achaemenid Persian language of Iran, all written in varieties of cuneiform script which cannot be derived directly from the cuneiform script of Mesopotamia.

CALAH [kā'lə] **or KALAKH** [kä'läκH], ancient city of Assyria, called Kalkhu in Assyrian sources, represented by the mound of Nimrud, 20 mi. southeast of Mosul, Iraq. Kalkhu, an ancient settlement, was made a city by Shalmaneser I (1272–1243 B.C.) and rebuilt as capital by Ashur-nasir-pal II in 879 B.C., with an initial population of about 70,000. It remained the Assyrian capital until about 710 B.C. Nimrud was excavated in 1845–47 and 1849–50 by Austen Henry Layard, and from 1949 by M. E. L. Mallowan. Several palaces and administrative buildings were traced, with important finds of state archives, business documents, sculptures, carved ivories, and a quay wall 30 ft. deep of dressed limestone blocks a cubic yard or more in size.

DUR SHARRUKIN [door shä-roo'kĭn] ("Sargon's Fort"), ancient Assyrian city, represented by modern Khorsabad, 12 mi. northeast of Mosul, Iraq. The city was founded c.710 B.C. by Sargon II as a fortified capital to protect Assyria from invasion from the north. Khorsabad was excavated in 1843 by Paul Emile Botta and in 1851–55 by Victor Place; but most of their finds were lost when the boats carrying them sank in the Tigris. The city was again excavated between 1929 and 1935 by an expedition from the Oriental Institute of Chicago.

ESARHADDON [ē-sär-hăd'ən], Assyrian King (reigned 680–669 B.C.), son of Sennacherib. Throughout his reign he was busy fighting and enlarging the frontiers of the Assyrian Empire. He first crushed a rebellion of the Chaldaeans, then reconstructed the city and temples of Babylon, destroyed by his father. He conquered Media, broke Elam's power, and subdued Palestine and Syria. He also repelled the Cimmerians in the northwest. His greatest military achievement, however, was the conquest of Egypt, begun in 674 B.C. and completed in 671 with the taking of the Egyptian capital Memphis. Esarhaddon reorganized Egypt into 22 administrative units placed under

local princes who were supervised by Assyrian officials, whose main duty was the regular collection of tribute. Esarhaddon named two of his sons to succeed him— Ashurbanipal in Assyria, and Shamash-shum-ukin in Babylonia.

NINEVEH [nĭn'ə-və], ancient Assyrian city on the east bank of the Tigris opposite the modern city of Mosul in Iraq. Nineveh began as a Neolithic settlement more than 5,000 years ago. Its earliest settlers, with primitive stone tools and crude pottery, were culturally related to the contemporary peoples of northern Mesopotamia, whose racial identity is uncertain.

It was King Sennacherib (705–681 B.C.) who expanded the city and made it the capital; and it is from his records that we have our best picture of the city. Sennacherib more than doubled its size, so that the inner walls, 8 mi. in circumference, enclosed about 1,800 acres. The walls, chiefly of limestone, were approximately 45 ft. thick and 75 ft. high, and were protected by many towers. A water moat extended more than 100 ft. before these walls. An outer double wall with a moat in between offered further protection. Fifteen gates, each with its own name, led into the city. An elaborate canal and aqueduct brought fresh water from the hills. A broad royal street was built. A large part of the city was occupied by official buildings, temples, and a great governmental armory. Another feature of the city was a park with strange flora and fauna, gathered from distant parts of the world by the ruler. Ashurbanipal, last great ruler of Assyria (668–?630 B.C.), built himself a palace in Nineveh.

The fall of Nineveh and of the Assyrian Empire occurred in the summer of 612 B.C. through the united efforts of the Medes and Babylonians under the leadership

An Assyrian relief from Nineveh depicting the sack of the city of Hamanu. The limestone carvings date from 650 B.C. (BRITISH MUSEUM)

of their respective Kings, Cyaxares and Nabopolassar. The profound impression which the fall of Nineveh made on contemporary peoples is reflected in several Old Testament references to it.

SARGON [sär'gón] **I,** ancient Mesopotamian King. Formerly vizier of the King of Kish, he founded (c.2350 B.C.) the Semitic dynasty of Akkad, with its capital at Agade. He exercised centralized control over the cities of Babylonia by installing citizens of Agade as senior administrators, backed by garrisons. Gaining suzerainty over much of the Near East, Sargon facilitated trade from the Persian Gulf to the Mediterranean and, according to tradition, deep into Asia Minor.

SARGON II, Assyrian King (721–705 B.C.), the son of Tiglath-pileser III. Though once considered a usurper, he was actually a legitimate King, according to information on an ancient plaque in the İstanbul Museum made known in 1933. Sargon II extended the boundaries of his kingdom in all directions, toward Iran, Armenia, Anatolia, and Palestine. In his vast empire he claimed tribute from faraway countries, from Tilmun (Bahrain) in the east to Cyprus in the west. At home, his great achievement was the building of the royal residence Dur Sharrukin (modern Khorsabad), situated about 10 mi. north of Nineveh, the capital of Assyria. "Sargon" is the Biblical form (Isa. 20:1) of his Assyrian name Sharru-kin.

SENNACHERIB [sə-nāk'ər-ĭb], Assyrian King (704–681 B.C.), son of Sargon II. He was involved throughout most of his reign in solving the Babylonian problem. Babylonia, united with Assyria under Tiglath-pileser III, rebelled against Assyrian rule under Sargon II and again soon after Sennacherib's accession to the throne. There was a long period of strife, during which Babylonia was alternately under Assyrian rule and that of local dynasts. Then the defeat of the Babylonians in the battle of Halule (691 B.C.) set the stage for the destruction of the city of Babylon (689 B.C.) and the final subjugation of Babylonia. During this campaign Sennacherib successfully used a river flotilla of ships for battle and transport purposes.

Sennacherib's campaign in Palestine in 701, reported in Assyrian sources as well as in the Old Testament and Herodotus, must have ended inconclusively, since he retired to Assyria without taking Jerusalem. His retreat was the result of losses inflicted probably by pestilence. Sennacherib gave up the royal residence at Dur Sharrukin,

built by his predecessor Sargon II, and moved the capital back to Ashur, and then to Nineveh. He devoted much effort to enlarging, strengthening, and beautifying Nineveh. To secure an abundant water supply for the city he built a canal 31 mi. long. Its waters were carried over part of its course by a real aqueduct. "Sennacherib" is the Biblical form (II Kings 19:16, 20, 36) of the Assyrian name Sin-ahhe-eriba. He was murdered by his sons.

TIGLATH-PILESER [tĭg'lăth pī-lē'zər], Biblical form of the Assyrian name Tukulti-apil-esharra, borne by at least three kings, of whom two have historical import. TIGLATH-PILESER I, King of Assyria (reigned c.1114-c.1076 B.C.), fought successfully during his reign of some 39 years on all frontiers of his kingdom, especially against Armenia, Syria, and Babylonia. A great hunter of wild animals, such as lions, wild bulls, and elephants, he set up the first zoological garden in Ashur, his capital. TIGLATH-PILESER III, (reigned 744–727 B.C.), son of Adad-nirari III, was the first in the series of Assyrian kings who succeeded in establishing political hegemony over the whole Near East. Conquering Babylonia and ruling there under the Babylonian name Pul, he succeeded in uniting the two sister countries under one rule. Tiglath-pileser organized conquered Syria into 13 provinces and exacted tribute from the Israelites. He also carried out an extensive policy of transporting captured people and settling them in faraway lands.

ZIGGURAT [zĭg'ŏŏ-răt], a great rectangular, stepped tower, up to 150 ft (45 m) high, rising from a base whose sides were as much as 300 ft (90 m) long, and dominating the temple area of Sumerian, Babylonian, and Assyrian cities. Noted surviving examples are at Ur, Aqarquf, and Birs Nimrud (ancient Borsippa). One is mentioned in the Bible as the Tower of Babel. Known examples consisted of from two or three to seven stages, each approximately square, with corners orientated to the points of the compass. A small temple stood on the summit of the ziggurat. It is uncertain in some cases whether approach to this temple was by an external spiral staircase or by a ramp.

Despite some external similarities, ziggurats, which were solid, were not parallel in function to pyramids. Earlier theories considered ziggurats symbolic tombs of dying and resurgent gods, as thrones of deities, or as giant altars. But according to the prevailing modern view, the ziggurat supported a "high temple" for the god on his way down to the "low temple" at ground level.

Drawing of the ziggurat of Urnammu, a temple in the form of a stepped tower, built of brick c.2060 B.C.

(UNIVERSITY MUSEUM, PHILADELPHIA)

Babylonia (Southern Mesopotamia)

BACKGROUND

BABYLON, celebrated ancient city of Babylonia on the Euphrates River, about 55 mi. south of Baghdad, and just north of Hillah. The best contemporary description of the city of Babylon comes from the Greek historian Herodotus (fl. 5th century B.C.).

Babylon first assumed great importance under Hammurabi (c.1728–1686 B.C.), the greatest King of the First Dynasty of Babylon, who made it the capital of his empire. It remained the religious and economic center of the Mesopotamian valley, barring one short period, until the building of Seleucia in the Hellenistic age. In 689 B.C. the Assyrian King Sennacherib completely destroyed the city. His son Esarhaddon, in a gesture of friendship to the Babylonians, restored it.

Excavations between 1899 and 1917 were carried on there by the Germans under Robert Koldewey. Owing to ground water conditions, however, the little that remained of the city of Hammurabi's time could not be adequately recovered.

The new city that Esarhaddon built was greatly expanded and beautified by the two Chaldaean kings, Nabopolassar and Nebuchadnezzar II. The latter was particularly instrumental in its reconstruction. A deep moat surrounded the high, thick walls. The main artery through the city, the well-known Procession Street, was paved and led to the temple of Marduk, which was really a grand enclosure containing not only the ziggurat, but also numerous other smaller shrines. Procession Street ended at the Ishtar Gate, a double gateway with towers, which was faced with brilliantly enameled brick. The ruins of Nebuchadnezzar's palace have been recognized, and attempts have even been made to identify the famous Hanging Gardens. Captured by Cyrus the great in 539 B.C., Babylon remained a great city under Persian rule. Alexander the Great died there. Its decline was rapid in the Seleucid period, and soon it became only a series of ruins never to be rebuilt.

BABYLONIA [băb-ə-lō′nē-ə], ancient Near Eastern kingdom prominent in the 2d and 1st millennia B.C., located in an area corresponding approximately to modern Iraq south of Baghdad; the name is also applied anachronistically to this region before the 2d millennium B.C. The land comprised two parts: the northern, called Akkad, and the southern, Sumer, the boundary between them approximately at the city of Nippur. This alluvial plain created by the silt deposits of the Euphrates and Tigris rivers was, under irrigation, of high fertility. The older view that a southward extension of Babylonia resulted during historical times from the silting up of the Persian Gulf is challenged by recent geological research.

Prehistoric Cultures. The earliest settlement occurred around the head of the Persian Gulf. The first culture, designated Eridu (c.4000 B.C.), is regarded by some authorities as the basis of the succeeding Al-Ubaid culture. Ubaid (c.3900–3500 B.C.) represented an efficient peasant economy based on drainage of the swamps and irrigation, with houses of unburnt brick, and a distinctive painted pottery. Temples developed into buttressed buildings on platforms. Spreading into northern Mesopotamia and Syria, the Ubaid became the only prehistoric culture which encompassed the whole area. Within the Ubaid period falls the "Flood stratum" at Ur, now recognized as purely local, and no evidence for the historical authenticity of the Biblical Flood story.

History

Early Dynastic Period (c.2700–c.2350 B.C.). In the succeeding Early Dynastic period, which is divisible into three phases, the Sumerians—probably the people associated with the Uruk culture—come into prominence. Their characteristic social unit was the city-state centered about the temple and lands of the local god. The early Sumerian society of this period is reflected in later myths and epics. Prominent was the En, a cult functionary originally appointed by the citizens, living in the temple in intimate relationship with the city deity. The En could acquire considerable secular authority, as the example of the legendary hero Gilgamesh illustrates. By the middle of the 3d millennium, in response to pressures on the city-state, the official called Ensi, probably originally an organizer of the community's agricultural operations and steward of the god's estates, became city ruler. In some cities this office became hereditary and dynasties arose—a notable case being that of Lagash, where seven rulers reigned for nearly a century and a half.

Conflicts between cities are recorded, and in some cases a ruler who obtained a wider hegemony received the title of King (Sumerian *lugal*, literally "great man"), through his recognition by the god Enlil of Nippur. The most notable was Lugalzaggesi of Umma (c.2375–2351 B.C.), who, after overthrowing the neighboring city of La-

"Dragon of Marduk," from the glazed tile frieze of the Ishtar Gate, built by Nebuchadnezzar II (r.605–562 B.C.)

gash, established control over Sumer, and claimed hegemony from the Persian Gulf to the Mediterranean.

From the Early Dynastic period onward, waves of Semites entered Babylonia from the west, exerting particularly strong influence on the Diyala region and the cities of Mari and Kish, the last being, according to the *Sumerian King List*, the seat of the first postdiluvian dynasty in north Babylonia. Semitic influences continued to increase in the northern cities, and the last King of Kish had a Semitic vizier, Sharrum-kin (Sargon I), who founded the city of Agade, and subsequently overthrew Lugalzaggesi, his master's conqueror (c.2350 B.C.).

Akkadian Dynasty (c.2350–c.2150 B.C.). The Semitic dynasty founded by Sargon of Agade lasted less than two centuries, but had far-reaching consequences, for Sargon's attempt at centralization weakened the old city-state system. International trade flourished by sea and land. Under Sargon's grandson, Naram-sin, his third and greatest successor, pressure began to be felt from the Hurrians, centered on Armenia, and from the Guti in the northeastern highlands. The tensions led to a major rebellion of the cities of Sumer and Akkad toward the end of Naram-sin's reign. The central authority finally collapsed under Naram-sin's son, Shar-kali-sharri.

The Gutian Period (c.2150–c.2100 B.C.). In the succeeding anarchy, the land fell to the barbarian Guti, who were later remembered with abhorrence. Southern Babylonia suffered less than the north, and with Agade eliminated, Lagash regained its old importance as a river port, its Ensis forming a new dynasty. The inscriptions of Gudea,

the best-known ruler, though primarily concerned with temple restorations, mention trading activities with Iran, Asia Minor, Lebanon, and lands beyond the Persian Gulf.

Third Dynasty of Ur (c.2100–1950 B.C.). The last Gutian ruler was defeated by Utu-hengal of Erech, who imposed suzerainty over other city-states, ruling them through governors. One governor, Ur-nammu, secured independence and founded (c.2060 B.C.) the Third Dynasty of Ur. This dynasty, lasting over a century, represents the final flowering of Sumerian civilization—a time of much temple building and canal construction. Politically it was a bureaucracy, as the tens of thousands of extant economic and administrative documents attest. Cities of the empire were ruled through governors shorn of military authority and liable to transfer as a precaution against insurrection. Ur-nammu's son Shulgi (reigned c.2046–1998 B.C.) extended the empire by military expeditions to Elam and Assyria. For the reigns of Shulgi's sons, Amar-sin (c.1998–1989 B.C.) and Shu-sin (c.1989–1980 B.C.), there is evidence of renewed Semitic infiltration by the Amorites, in response to which Shu-sin built a defensive wall. Under Shu-sin's successor, Ibbi-sin (1979–1955 B.C.), these invaders brought about the collapse of the empire city by city. Since Ur relied upon imported corn, severe inflation and famine ensued; and with the collapse of central authority, raids by the eastern mountain-dwellers could no longer be controlled. In Ibbi-sin's 24th year (1955 B.C.) Ur itself was captured and devastated by raiders from Elam.

Isin-Larsa Period (c.1960–1700 B.C.). Meanwhile the

governors of certain cities had been consolidating their position, one being Ishbi-erra of Isin, who, eight years after the destruction of Ur, expelled the invaders. Under Ishbi-erra (1955–1927 B.C.) and his successors, the kingdom of Isin temporarily included most of Babylonia. Farther north, Assyria was emerging, and its ruler Ilushuma made a raid into Babylonia, weakening Isin. Advantage was taken of this by the city-state of Larsa to thrust northward and capture Erech and Nippur.

First Dynasty of Babylon (c.1830–1530 B.C.). During this period infiltrating western Semites, known as Amorites, were consolidating their hold on northern Babylonia, so that small Amorite dynasties arose, among them Mari and Babylon. Archives found at Mari illustrate the keen diplomatic activity in which these small kingdoms engaged. Ultimately, under Hammurabi (1728–1686 B.C.), Babylon, for the first time, became paramount in north Babylonia. In the south, the old dynasty in Larsa had been replaced by a family with Elamite and Amorite affinities, whose second King, Rim-sin, defeated Isin shortly before Hammurabi's succession. In his 30th year, Hammurabi decisively defeated Rim-sin, who was allied with Elam and Eshnunna. Hammurabi thus became supreme ruler of Babylonia; some outlying city-states such as Mari were captured in the following years. With his capital at Babylon, Hammurabi administered his empire with conspicuous success, his correspondence showing meticulous attention to details. Considerable works of canal building were executed during his reign, and his laws show concern for social justice and reform.

The Kassite Domination (c.1530–1150 B.C.). In the 28th year of the reign of Hammurabi's successor, Samsu-iluna (1685–1648 B.C.), the south of Babylonia broke away, forming an independent Dynasty of the Sealands (1658 B.C.). Pressure from the Kassites to the northeast was now felt, and the political history of Samsu-iluna's successors largely concerns defensive measures on the Babylonian borders. In 1531 B.C. Babylon was sacked when the Hittite King Mursilis made a raid from Asia Minor down the Euphrates. Babylonian defenses and administration were thrown into chaos, and on the withdrawal of Mursilis, Babylonia fell a victim to the Kassites, who swept down under their King Agumkakrime (Agum II).

The Kassites, a non-Semitic people from the Zagros Mountains, rapidly adopted Babylonian language and culture. They appear to have constituted only a ruling aristocracy. To judge by the absence of native risings and the ease with which they subsequently regained control of the Sealands, their rule was unoppressive, and not destructive of Babylonian institutions. During this period Babylonian scholars gave canonical form to the principal works of literature. At this time the horse-drawn chariot was introduced as an instrument of warfare.

Four of the Kassite rulers are named in diplomatic correspondence discovered at Tell el-Amarna in Egypt, among them the most important Kassite King, Kurigalzu I (c.1400 B.C.), who maintained good relations with Amenhotep III of Egypt. This ruler restored temples in south Babylonia, and built a new fortified capital, whose remains, at Aqarquf near Baghdad, still form a prominent landmark.

In the 14th century Assyria again came into prominence with the collapse of Mitanni, the Aryan-dominated Hurrian kingdom in the northwest. Rivalry and border disputes between Assyria and Babylonia were temporarily prevented by a marriage alliance, but war ultimately broke out after 1319 B.C., weakening both kingdoms.

Aramaean Infiltration (1300–1000 B.C.). Increasingly in the 13th century Mesopotamia was subject to fresh pressure from the west, this time from the Akhlamu and Sutu—tribes closely connected with the Aramaeans. Their effect was felt chiefly in Assyria, and it was possibly their pressure on Assyria's western borders that prompted an Assyrian attempt to gain control of Babylonia. The Assyrian King Tukulti-Ninurta I (1243–1207 B.C.) conquered the Kassite Kashtiliash IV (1241–1234 B.C.), bringing Babylonia for the first time under Assyrian rule, and transporting the statue of Marduk to his capital, Ashur. This greatly extended Babylonian religious influence in Assyria. Babylonia recovered independence after Tukulti-Ninurta's murder. Subsequent war weakened both countries, and the Kassite dynasty was finally overthrown from within and replaced by the native Second Dynasty of Isin (c.1150–1050 B.C.). Of this dynasty the strongest King was Nebuchadnezzar I (c.1128–1107 B.C.), who inflicted defeats upon the mountain peoples to the east and northeast. He initially exercised suzerainty over Assyria, which ultimately threw off his yoke.

Aramaean pressure increased from 1100 B.C., threatening both Assyria and Babylonia, and in the latter an Aramaean usurper, Adad-apal-iddina, seized the kingship (c.1050 B.C.). For a century there was widespread administrative dislocation in both countries, until the Aramaean tribes began to settle as small kingdoms in Syria and along the Upper and Middle Euphrates. In Babylonia, Aramaeans reached the eastern banks of the Tigris, while the related Kaldu (Chaldaeans) settled in the Sealands in south Sumer.

Assyrian Supremacy (900–626 B.C.). By the end of the 10th century, Assyria, under Adad-nirari II (911–889 B.C.), had begun to expand. For the next three centuries Babylonia was, though nominally independent, usually politically subordinate to Assyria. Ashurnasirpal II of Assyria (884–859 B.C.) wrested from Nabu-apal-iddin of Babylonia suzerainty over the Aramaean tribes along the Middle Euphrates. Nabu-apal-iddin's son, Marduk-zakir-shum, acknowledged the suzerainty of Shalmaneser III (859–824 B.C.), to whose support he owed his throne.

With Assyria too weak between 782 and 746 B.C. to protect the great trade routes, Babylonia also suffered, the Chaldaeans and Aramaeans becoming independent of the central authority and subverting civil order. The strong Assyrian ruler Tiglath-pileser III (745–727 B.C.) restored order to Babylonia, defeating the Aramaeans and strengthening the native Babylonian King, Nabonassar (747–734 B.C.). The Chaldaeans in the southern marshes were less accessible, and at Nabonassar's death in 734 B.C. a Chaldaean chieftain, Ukin-zer, reigned as usurper for three years. By diplomacy Tiglath-pileser divided the Chaldaean tribes, finally making a devastating attack upon those which remained recalcitrant. He personally took the throne of Babylonia (729 B.C.), under the name Pul, a policy continued by his successor Shalmaneser V (727–722 B.C.).

Upon the accession of Sargon II (722–705 B.C.) in Assyria, another Chaldaean chieftain, Marduk-apal-iddin

(Merodach-baladan II, 721–710 B.C.) claimed the kingship of Babylonia. With Elamite support he held the throne for ten years, during which Chaldaean interference severely damaged Babylonia's economy. By 710 B.C. Sargon was able to defeat Marduk-apal-iddin, whom he magnanimously confirmed as tribal chieftain, himself taking the title of Prefect (not King) of Babylon. After the accession of Sennacherib (705–681 B.C.), a native Babylonian was appointed to the throne of Babylonia in 703 B.C. Marduk-apal-iddin rebelled, and with Elamite and Arab assistance seized the throne. Following Assyrian attack, Marduk-apal-iddin fled to Elam. Sennacherib reduced the Chaldaean tribal areas, appointing as King of Babylonia first a native Babylonian and, subsequently, his own younger son. Constant interference by Chaldaean tribesmen, with Elamite support, provoked further Assyrian campaigns. A pro-Chaldaean Babylonian seized the throne, and in 689 B.C. Sennacherib besieged and sacked Babylon, himself assuming the kingship.

Sennacherib's successor, Esarhaddon (680–669 B.C.), Assyrian governor of Babylonia since 689 B.C., likewise assumed the kingship of Babylonia but, reversing his father's policy, rebuilt Babylon. Esarhaddon arranged a succession whereby at his death one son, Ashurbanipal (669–626 B.C.), received Assyria, and another, Shamash-shum-ukin (668–648 B.C.), Babylonia. This worked for several years until Shamash-shum-ukin, under Chaldaean and Elamite influence, engaged in hostilities against his brother. Babylon was besieged and, after three years, starved into submission (648 B.C.), Shamash-shum-ukin himself committing suicide in a fire. For the remainder of the reign of Ashurbanipal, Babylonia was governed through a puppet King, Kandalanu.

The New Babylonian Empire (626–539 B.C.). At Ashurbanipal's death (626 B.C.) the central administration apparently broke down in both kingdoms. Nabopolassar, a Chaldaean governor of the Sealands, assumed the kingship of Babylonia in 626 B.C., though Assyria still exercised intermittent control in some areas. By 617 B.C. Nabopolassar had finally cleared out the Assyrian garrisons. In alliance with the Medes and Scythians, Nabopolassar, in 612 B.C., attacked and captured the Assyrian capital Nineveh. An Egyptian army coming to Assyria's aid was defeated by Nabopolassar's son Nebuchadnezzar II at Carchemish in 605 B.C. Assyria, Cilicia, Syria, and Palestine thereby fell to the New Babylonian Empire. Nebuchadnezzar II, succeeding in 605 B.C., took measures to strengthen his empire in the west, twice (597 and 586 B.C.) besieging and conquering Jerusalem, and taking the wealthy mercantile port of Tyre after a long siege. Both areas became Babylonian provinces. It is Nebuchadnezzar who deported the Jews to their Babylonian captivity. No details are known of an attack he made against Egypt. Inside Babylonia there was great building activity; the famed Hanging Gardens of Babylon date from this time. It is Nebuchadnezzar's Babylon that is known from excavations.

Nebuchadnezzar's successor, Amel-Marduk (561–560 B.C.), the Evil-merodach mentioned in the Bible, was assassinated after two years, Neriglissar (559–556 B.C.) coming to the throne. This ruler undertook a campaign to extend Babylonian authority in Cilicia. After initial success, he suffered a serious setback, dying shortly after. His son was removed in 556 B.C. by a rebellion, and Nabonidus (556–539 B.C.) was installed in his place. This able statesman sought to strengthen the empire by controlling the western trade routes and by favoring the cult of the moon-

University Museum, Philadelphia

Bull's head of gold foil and lapis lazuli adorns a harp found at Ur, dating from 3000–2700 B.C.

BABYLONIAN EMPIRE

Babylonian Empire in 1686 B.C., at end of Hammurabi's reign

Impression from a Sumerian cylinder seal dating from c.2750 B.C.

British Museum

Black diorite figure is one of many stone portraits of King Gudea of Lagash, c. 2100 B.C.

The Metropolitan Museum of Art, Dick Fund, 1955

Sumerian cast-copper statuette, c.2700 B.C., is 15 in high.

The Metropolitan Museum of Art, Excavations of the University of Pennsylvania Museum and the British Museum, 1927-1928; Dodge Fund, 1933

Chaplet found at Ur dates from 3500-2800 B.C. Gold leaves are attached to beads of carnelian and lapis lazuli.

The Metropolitan Museum of Art, Dick Fund, 1959

god (widely worshiped among Semites generally) above the national Babylonian cult of Marduk. To promote the former objective, he spent a decade in northwest Arabia, finally reaching Yathrib (Medina) on the Red Sea. In Babylon his son Belshazzar was left as regent. The religious objective of Nabonidus aroused violent antagonism in Babylonia, while his own and his predecessors' military and building activities began to produce inflation and economic hardship. Thus when the Persian Cyrus began his attack upon the Babylonian Empire in 547 B.C., he received considerable support within Babylonia. In 539 B.C. Babylon fell with only token resistance, Cyrus being hailed as a deliverer from the impious Nabonidus. Cyrus allowed no disturbance of the city's religious institutions, and his son Cambyses officiated at the New Year Festival. Administratively Babylonia became a province under a Persian governor. Later it came, successively, under the rule of Alexander, the Seleucids, Parthians, Sassanians, and Arabs.

Society and Culture

Social Organization. The earliest form of Sumerian society was what the Assyriologist Thorkild Jacobsen calls "primitive democracy," in which community decisions were taken by the assembly of all free citizens. Slaves, though known as war captives, formed no substantial part

of society till late in the 3d millennium. By the time of Hammurabi a tripartite society existed—there being the freeman, the dependent (a class which subsequently disappeared), and the slave. In the 1st millennium, temple-slaves constituted a distinct class. The position of women, as judged by the Code of Hammurabi, was relatively advanced in the 2d millennium.

Economy and Trade. Babylonia lacked metals, stone, and large timber, and from at least the Protoliterate (earliest literate) period these were imported. Mesopotamian influence in Egypt in the late Protoliterate period implies encounters between Egyptian and Sumerian traders, probably in south Arabia or Somaliland. From the Early Dynastic period there are indications in art motifs of contacts with India; and from the middle of the 3d millennium, maritime trade with Tilmun (Bahrain), Magan (Oman) and Meluhha (Somaliland, south Arabia, or northwest India) is attested in texts. At the end of the 3d millennium sea trade flourished between Ur and Magan or Tilmun, with Mesopotamian textiles, oil, and leather goods being bartered for copper, precious stones, and ivory. Overland trading with Iran, Lebanon, and Asia Minor is attested from the Early Dynastic period onward.

In the Sumerian period the whole economy of the city-state was originally controlled by the temples, but toward the end of the 3d millennium the system began to crumble under Semitic influence. Thus, while under the Third Ur Dynasty the sea trade of Ur was organized by the temple of the moon-god, in the Larsa period it was capitalistic. By the time of Hammurabi trade was largely organized by capitalists who were in part bankers, brokers, merchants, and government officials. In the 1st millennium trade was largely controlled by the temple corporations.

Law. The maintenance of justice, not necessarily implying the promulgation of written laws, was a claim of many 3d-millennium rulers. Collections of laws are now known from about 2100 B.C. onward, the principal lawgivers being Ur-nammu, who published the earliest law code yet recovered from Babylonia; Lipit-ishtar of Isin, an unidentified king of Eshnunna; and Hammurabi (*see* HAMMURABI, CODE OF). In earliest Sumerian society judicial decisions were made in the assembly, and the assembly still often administered justice till the New Babylonian period, although, from at least Hammurabi's time, royal judges sat with it. The object of legal procedure was to reach a decision acceptable to all parties.

Religion. The religion of Babylonia was so strongly influenced by Sumerian antecedents that some authorities have denied that it was Semitic. While this extreme view is not generally accepted, there are, certainly, substantial Sumerian features present, even in the latest stages of Babylonian religion. In the Sumerian conception, the city-state was the demesne of the local god, with the ruler as his steward, and throughout Babylonian history this idea remained. Besides local gods, there were high gods and gods personifying aspects of nature and society. Archaic tablets list 4,000 deities, a number later reduced by assimilation.

In 3d-millennium Sumerian religion chthonic, or earth, deities were strongly represented, and goddesses were prominent. The growth of Semitic influence was accompanied by emphasis upon the astral aspect of religion and by the virtual elimination of almost all goddesses except Ishtar and the shadowy consorts of the great gods. The principal Sumerian chthonic deity, Dumuzi (Tammuz), remained prominent in popular Babylonian religion till the 1st millennium, his cult even spreading abroad, as into Jerusalem (Ezek. 8:14).

At the head of the Sumerian pantheon stood the two great gods, An, lord of heaven, and Enlil, lord of the earth, the latter the national god of Sumer and specifically associated with Nippur. These two bestowed kingship and presided over the divine assembly. Both had an ambivalent attitude toward humans, and it was the third great god, Enki (or Ea in Akkadian texts), who was mankind's unfailing friend. Enki, god of sweet waters, magic, and wisdom, was associated with Eridu, which, in Sumerian tradition, was the original center of civilization. A myth relates how the goddess Innin gained for her city, Erech, the gifts of civilization originally held by Enki at Eridu. In later Babylonian theology, Anu (the Semitized spelling of An), Enlil, and Ea constituted virtually a triad. Another group of deities was comprised of the moon-god Sin (Sumerian Nannar); the sun-god Shamash (Sumerian Utu), god of justice; and Ishtar (Sumerian Innin or Inanna), goddess of war and love, who manifested herself as the planet Venus. Associated with these was the storm-god Adad (Sumerian Ishkur). After Babylon gained political

supremacy, its city-god Marduk absorbed the characteristics of Enlil, thus becoming the national god of Babylonia. As such, he played the leading part in the *Epic of Creation*, which recounts the creation of the world order by the destruction of the primeval monster Tiamat. Under the name Asalluhi, Marduk was also a potent god of magic.

Notable in Babylonian religion was its polydaemonism. Illness and misfortune of all kinds were attributed to the attacks of lurking demons. Witchcraft was widespread. Cures were effected by exorcisms or countermagic performed by special priests, and protection was secured by wearing amulets and observing taboos. There was no developed conception of sin. Ritual faults or accidents such as contact with a person under a curse could rouse the divine wrath equally with ethical offenses. A man had a personal god who could supplicate the great gods on his behalf. The divine order was not essentially moral, and mankind existed only to free the gods from toil. The Babylonian was imbued with a sense of man's transitoriness and his powerlessness before the willful forces of nature and gods. Any order could be found only by integrating his will with that of the gods. The divine will could be discovered by divination, notably by the examination of the entrails of a sacrificial beast. Neither the Sumerians nor the Semitic Babylonians had any conception of retribution after death. The lot of the shades depended not upon a good life, but upon due performance of funeral and memorial rites.

The temple was the house of the god, splendidly finished in semiprecious stones and fine timber. Basically all temples were built around an oblong chamber, in one short side of which stood the statue of the god. The gods received daily offerings of food and drink, with special sacrifices on particular monthly and annual feasts, of which the principal was the New Year Festival. By the 1st millennium the latter embraced several elements (notably the sacred marriage and the agricultural *akitu* festival) which were originally distinct. In the temple cults the director was the *Sheshgallu*, sacrifices being performed by *Shangu*-priests. Other classes of priests dealt with special rituals. There were priestesses of various kinds, from the *Entu*, the consort of the god, often of royal blood, who lived in chastity, down to temple harlots.

Mathematics. Babylonian mathematical texts, comprising about 200 table texts and 100 problem texts, are known from two periods—the Old Babylonian and the Seleucid. The problem texts are algebraic or geometric, while the others contain tables for multiplication, division, and the calculation of reciprocals, powers, and roots of numbers. The practical substance, though not the proof, of the Pythagorean theorem was known, a method for solving quadratic equations was found, and the value of π was known to within 0.6%.

Astronomy. The earliest Babylonian astronomical records are observations of the planet Venus from the reign of the Old Babylonian King Ammisaduqa. The text *Mul Apin* of 700 B.C., based on earlier material, gives a basic account of astronomical knowledge, and refers to the zodiacal belt and its constellations. From before 700 B.C. systematic astronomical reports were made to the Assyrian court, giving by 400 B.C. a series long enough for

Babylonian Collection—Yale University

Mathematical problems, each requiring calculation of the area of a rectangle, are listed on a tablet inscribed c.1900 B.C.

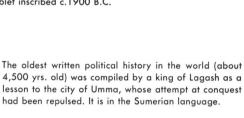

The oldest written political history in the world (about 4,500 yrs. old) was compiled by a king of Lagash as a lesson to the city of Umma, whose attempt at conquest had been repulsed. It is in the Sumerian language.

Babylonian Collection—Yale University

the average apparent movements of celestial bodies to be calculated. With this as a basis, Babylonian astronomers were able by 250 B.C. to apply corrections to predict positions of celestial bodies.

Medicine. Physicians are frequently mentioned in Babylonian texts. As illness was generally attributed either to the "hand" of a deity or possession by a devil, treatment might take the form either of exorcising the malevolent influence or of reducing the symptoms, and physicians employed a blend of magic and practical medicine. Many diagnostic and prognostic texts and prescriptions are extant from the Third Ur Dynasty period onward. The Babylonians had little knowledge of anatomy or physiology and did not understand the functions of most internal organs. Surgery, restricted to setting broken limbs and lancing abscesses, was a risky business inasmuch as, if the operation failed, the surgeon was punishable by law.

Writing on Clay. Writing was invented to assist in keeping temple accounts. In the earliest writing, an outline picture of the object concerned was drawn on a lump of clay, with marks denoting numbers. The writing subsequently took the shape called cuneiform. The utility of the system was extended by the invention of syllograms, signs being divorced from the ideas of the original pictograms and used for the sounds alone.

Language and Literature. Sumerian, an agglutinative language with no known cognates, was spoken and written from the Protoliterate period. Akkadian, the general term for a number of Semitic dialects introduced into Mesopotamia by waves of immigrants from the west, began to be written in cuneiform by 2500 B.C., was widely used in the Sargonic period (2350 B.C.), and became predominant after 1900 B.C., Sumerian no longer being used, except for scholarly and liturgical purposes.

Ninety-five per cent of all extant cuneiform tablets are economic in content. The most important noneconomic documents from the 3d millennium are royal building inscriptions and hymns. The principal Sumerian myths and epics date in their extant form only from 1900 B.C., but incorporate traditions from the Early Dynastic period. All the great Sumerian epics, concerning such heroes as Gilgamesh and Enmerkar, are centered on Erech, suggesting that a school of poets arose there. Sumerian literature strongly influenced the less civilized Semitic immigrants into Babylonia, and many myths and epics extant in Akkadian are borrowed from Sumerian. The influence of Sumerian and Akkadian literature on Biblical literature has sometimes been exaggerated. The story of Noah could be a direct borrowing, but the two creation stories in Genesis (1,2) show only isolated points of contact with Babylonian myths, while no Babylonian analogue of the Garden of Eden has yet been established.

Art and Architecture. Very few fragments of the palaces and temples of Babylonia remain today, due to the perishable nature of the bricks employed in building. However, Babylonian art is represented by pottery, mosaics, cylinder seals, wall-paintings, sculpture in the round, reliefs, metalwork, and carving on ivory. These can be seen in the Louvre, the British Museum, the Boston Fine Arts Museum, the University Museum in Philadelphia, at the Oriental Institute in Chicago, the Berlin Museum, and the Iraq Museum in Baghdad.

PEOPLE, PLACES, AND TERMS

AKKAD or ACCAD [ăk′ăd], name applied originally to a city sometimes called Agade, in southern Mesopotamia, mentioned in Gen. 10:10. Later it denoted that part of Babylonia north of Nippur and the Semitic empire and dynasty founded by Sargon I (fl. 2600 B.C.). The principal cities of the land of Akkad were Akshak, Babylon, Borsippa, Cuthah, Dilbat, Hursagkalama, Kish, and Sippar. From the 3d dynasty of Ur onwards rulers claiming kingship of all Babylonia used the title "King of Sumer and Akkad." The adjective "Akkadian" is applied to institutions of the empire founded by Sargon I, and to the Semitic dialects written in cuneiform after 2500 B.C.

AMORITES [ăm'ə-rīts], one of the ancient peoples inhabiting Palestine before the Hebrew settlement. In this connection they are known principally through references to them in the Old Testament (Gen. 48:22; Josh. 24:15; Judg. 6:10). Some passages (Deut. 20:17; Josh. 3:10; I Kings 21:26) speak of them as being eradicated; but more probably they were largely assimilated, and Ezekiel 16:3 regards them as one of the formative elements of the Hebrew nation. There are references to Amorite communities down to the reign of David (I Sam. 7:14; II Sam. 21:2).

The Amorites represent the originally nomadic people found in cuneiform sources as Amurru, also referred to by modern authorities as West Semites or East Canaanites. Widespread Amorite invasion from the west into the middle Euphrates area and northern Babylonia occurred during the period of the 3d Dynasty of Ur, and brought about its downfall (c.2000 B.C.). Of the numerous Amorite kingdoms established, Babylon, under its 1st Dynasty, ultimately rose to supremacy. The Amorite kingdom of Mari on the middle Euphrates has become well known from the archives excavated by the French at Tell Hariri between 1933 and 1939.

ARAMAEANS [ăr-ə-mē'ənz], ancient Semitic people of Syria and Mesopotamia. Originally nomadic, they were closely associated in the Old Testament (Gen. 25:20; Deut. 26:5) with the family of Abraham, and were possibly mentioned in cuneiform sources before 2000 B.C. From 1100 B.C. on, Aramaean tribes began to settle along the Euphrates and on the borders of Assyria, forming small kingdoms which Assyria sought to control. In the north of Babylonia they had a considerable effect on Babylonian language and institutions. The Chaldaean (Kaldu) tribes, who occupied southernmost Babylonia from 1000 B.C., were closely related to the Aramaeans.

ARAMAIC [ăr-ə-mā'ĭk], a Semitic language once used widely throughout the Near and Middle East. Originally it was spoken by the Aramaean tribes who, beginning with the 14th century B.C., conquered and settled various parts of Mesopotamia and Syria (or Aram). By the 8th century B.C., Aramaic had replaced Akkadian as the international language of the Mesopotamian region. After the 6th century B.C., it became an official language of the Achaemenid or Early Persian Empire; the Persian language itself was frequently written in Aramaic characters. Inscriptions written in this universal, or "common," Aramaic during this period of florescence have been found from Egypt to India. Portions of the Old Testament were recorded in Aramaic (for example, Ezra 4:8–6:18, 7:12–26; Dan. 2:4–7:28). Christ spoke Aramaic, but most of His words in the New Testament were translated into Greek. After the 3d century B.C., Common Aramaic tended to divide into two main dialects, Eastern and Western. Western Aramaic

dialects included Jewish Palestinian, Christian Palestinian, Samaritan, Nabatean, Palmyrene, and Neo-Aramaic. Neo-Aramaic is still spoken in some Lebanese mountain villages, although the other languages are defunct. Eastern Aramaic dialects included Jewish Babylonian, Syriac, Mandaic, and Neo-Syriac. Neo-Syriac survives in parts of northern Iraq and Iran, eastern Turkey, and the Georgian S.S.R. An extensive literature exists in some of these dialects, largely of a religious or philosophical nature. Aramaic lost its importance as a common language when it was supplanted by Arabic, the language of the Muslims who conquered most of the area where Aramaic was spoken.

BABEL [bā'bəl], **TOWER OF,** according to Gen. 11:1–9, a tower built of brick in the land of Shinar (Sumer) to reach to heaven. The plan was frustrated by the Lord giving to mankind, previously of one speech, many different languages to prevent co-operation. The Hebrew name Babel, although related in Gen. 11:9 to the verb balal ("to confuse"), actually represents Akkadian *Babili* (Babylon), "gate of the gods." It is generally accepted that the Biblical tradition incorporates a memory of the great stepped towers, or ziggurats, of Babylonia, of which Abraham would have seen many examples on his migration from Ur to Haran (Gen. 11:31). Benjamin of Tudela (12th century A.D.) proposed to recognize the Tower of Babel in the majestic remains at Birs Nimrud (ancient Borsippa), near Hillah, while Niccolò de' Conti (15th century) identified it with the ziggurat of Aqarquf near Baghdad. Other identifications have included the ziggurats of Babylon itself and of Ur. The theme of the Tower of Babel has been frequently represented in Christian art from the 11th century onward, most notably by Pieter Brueghel.

CHALDAEA or CHALDEA [kăl-dē'ə], properly the marsh region of southern Babylonia extending eastward from Ur and occupied by the Kaldu tribes from about 1000 B.C. As the New Babylonian dynasty to which Nebuchadnezzar belonged was of Kaldu origin, Chaldaea was used by Nebuchadnezzar's contemporaries Jeremiah and Ezekiel as a synonym for Babylonia. Other Biblical writers used the term "Chaldaean" variously to mean "pertaining to the Kaldu" or "Babylonian." As astrology (with astronomy) was the aspect of Babylonian learning which remained in greatest prominence after the political collapse of Babylonia, Daniel and some classical writers used the term "Chaldaean" to denote "astrologer."

The supposed anachronism of qualifying Ur in southern Mesopotamia as "of the Chaldees" at the time of Abraham has occasioned the theory (not generally accepted) that Chaldaea in some Biblical and classical contexts denoted part of Armenia, where a city Ura is attested in cuneiform sources.

CUNEIFORM [kū-nē'ə-fôrm] ("having the form of a wedge," from Lat. *cuneus*, wedge), denotes the writing characteristic of the Sumerians and their neighbors and successors in Mesopotamia and surrounding areas. It was written from left to right. The earliest writing (c.3000 B.C.) consisted of outline pictures drawn on lumps (or "tablets") of damp clay. Each picture represented a word whose meaning was identical with, or close to, the object pictured. The curves of these original pictograms were, in the course of time, replaced by straight lines and the signs came to be drawn 90° counterclockwise relative to their original position; by 2500 B.C. there were few signs whose original pictorial origin remained recognizable. By impressing the edge of a reed (later a metal stylus) of triangular cross section, straight lines were made without the blurred edges which drawing produced; this technique gave the characteristic wedge shape designated "cuneiform." Though cuneiform was also carved on stone and impressed on wax-coated boards, clay tablets (usually square to oblong, 2 to 18 in. long, with one or both sides slightly convex) remained the dominant material. Both sides of a tablet were normally inscribed, the scribe turning it so that the writing on the reverse appeared upside-down relative to the obverse. Each face might contain several columns. Clay cones, prisms, and cylinders were also used.

Hundreds of thousands of cuneiform tablets have been found, the most notable groups coming from Erech, Fara, Nippur, Lagash, Mari, Nineveh, and Ashur. Cuneiform inscriptions on stone are also known.

The language represented by the earliest pictographs, found at Erech, is not known, though that of the succeeding period (Jemdet Nasr) was certainly Sumerian. Sumerian was an agglutinative tonal language with roots largely monosyllabic, with large numbers of homophones, or words with like sounds but diverse meanings. The Sumerians devised a system wherein a sign could be divorced from its ideographic meaning and employed to denote either a homophone of the original ideogram or simply a syllable with a phonetic value. Thus the sign originally representing an arrow (Sumerian TI) could be used for the verb "to live" (Sumerian TI(L)) or for the syllable -ti-.

By 2500 B.C. cuneiform was adapted to the Semitic language called Akkadian. Sumerian ideograms were employed to denote corresponding Akkadian words, and the use of syllabic values was extended. After 300 B.C. cuneiform was written only for astrological or astronomical purposes, the last datable example coming from 75 A.D.

Syllabic cuneiform was also used to represent other languages, such as Elamite (from 2350 B.C.), Hurrian (from 2200 B.C.), Hittite (after 1800 B.C.), and Urartian (after 1000 B.C.). A simplified syllabary was used by the Achaemenids to write Old Persian (c.500 B.C.). A script written by the same technique as syllabic cuneiform but with only 29 signs, representing consonants and not syllables, was employed at Ugarit (c.1400 B.C.); this cuneiform alphabet probably had no influence on the Phoenician alphabet.

Cuneiform inscriptions in Achaemenid ruins were described by travelers in the 17th century. Carsten Niebuhr in 1778 recognized that inscriptions at Persepolis contained three distinct languages. One, Old Persian, was recognized by G. F. Grotefend as alphabetic and partially deciphered in 1802, the task being completed by him, and independently, by H. C. Rawlinson, by 1837. The decipherment of Babylonian cuneiform was begun by Edward Hincks in 1846; by 1851 Rawlinson, using a long trilingual (Old Persian, Elamite, and Babylonian) inscription, had substantially deciphered Babylonian and laid the basis for subsequent research. The recognition of Sumerian as a distinct language occurring on bilingual tablets followed.

Cuneiform texts have carried our detailed knowledge of ancient history back to about 2700 B.C., and have shed much light upon the historical and religious background of the Old Testament.

ELAM [ē'ləm], ancient country of southwest Asia, lying at the head of the Persian Gulf east of the Tigris, now in southwestern Iran. In the 3d millennium B.C., Elam developed a state, a dynasty, and a local language written in cuneiform. Culturally related to neighboring Akkadians and Guti, the Elamites were frequently subjugated by these people during their early history. In the 2d millennium B.C., Elam was under the Kings of Anshan and Susa. Elam reached its cultural and political apogee under a new dynasty in the early 12th century B.C. The Elamite Empire then included the Tigris valley, much of the Persian Gulf shore, and the Zagros Mountains. Elam re-

The wedge-shaped marks of cuneiform writing can be seen on a clay tablet that contains the inventory records of a Babylonian merchant. The marks were stamped in clay with a piece of reed or metal that was pointed at one end and broad at the other. When pressed into wet clay, this tool left the wedge-shaped mark from which cuneiform derives its name.

Wilson and MacPherson Hole

mained strong, successfully resisting Iranian and Assyrian encroachments until it fell c.642 B.C. to Ashurbanipal. In the 6th century it was dominated by Babylonia and thereafter by the Achaemenid Persians. Susa, the Elamite capital, was made a royal residence by Cyrus the Great whose ancestors had come from northern Elam. Elam was called Susiana by classical geographers.

ERECH [ē′rĕk] **or URUK** [o͞o′ro͞ok], ancient city of south Mesopotamia, on the Euphrates. It flourished from before 3000 B.C. to the Parthian period. It is mentioned in Genesis 10:10. It was the center of Sumerian civilization in the Protoliterate period (c.3000 B.C.), when the earliest writing (in its later stages called cuneiform) was invented there. From earliest times Erech was a center of the cults of Anu, god of the heavens, and of Ishtar, goddess of love and war. Eanna, the temple of Ishtar, owned vast estates, and in consequence Erech became in the 1st millennium B.C. virtually the administrative capital of south Babylonia. Impressive ruins at the site (modern Warka) were briefly explored by W. K. Loftus in 1854, and have been scientifically excavated by German expeditions (1912–13, 1928–39, and since 1954).

ERIDU [ā′rĭ-do͞o], southernmost city of ancient Babylonia and, in Sumerian tradition, its first center of civilization. The city, which in antiquity lay on a lagoon of the Persian Gulf, was sacred to the god Enki (Ea). Its ruins (in modern Iraq), excavated in 1946–49 by Fuad Safar, antedate those of Al-Ubaid (c.3900–3500 B.C.).

GILGAMESH [gĭl-gə-mĕsh], hero of the ancient Babylonian epic which bears his name. In 1872 George Smith, a young British scholar, discovered several Assyrian tablets in the British Museum with an account of a flood reminiscent of the Biblicial story of Noah. Although these tablets date from the reign of King Ashurbanipal in 7th century B.C., later scholars demonstrated the story's existence in the 2d millennium B.C. It was part of a larger epic, or cycle of poems, in which Gilgamesh is the tyrannical ruler of Erech.

His people pray to the goddess Araru who creates a wild creature Enkidu as a match for Gilgamesh. Enkidu is tamed by the love of a woman, then fights Gilgamesh, but their battle is indecisive. They become friends and join together to fight a monster. The goddess Ishtar falls in love with Gilgamesh but he spurns her. She goes to the chief god Anu and asks him to create the Bull of Heaven to destroy Gilgamesh, but the bull is killed by Gilgamesh and Enkidu.

Later Enkidu dies and Gilgamesh undertakes a quest to the underworld to learn the secret of eternal life. He meets Utnapishtim who says the gods once decided to destroy mankind by flood but Ea, the god of wisdom, warned Utnapishtim who built a ship and escaped. His ship finally came to rest on Mount Nisir and, because he sacrificed to the gods, he was rewarded with immortality. Utnapishtim puts Gilgamesh to a test which he fails, but Utnapishtim's wife tells Gilgamesh the secret of a rejuvenating agent, a thorny plant at the bottom of the sea. He gets the plant but a serpent steals it, and, finally,

Gilgamesh returns to Erech with the knowledge that the gods created men to die.

Some of these stories remind us of the Bible, but other elements are similar to Homer's *Odyssey*. A good translation with commentary is: Heidel, Alexander, *The Gilgamesh Epic and Old Testament Parallels* (1949).

HAMMURABI [häm-o͞o-rä′bē], King of Babylonia (reigned 1728–1686 B.C. or 1792–1750 B.C.), son and successor of Sin-muballit of the Amorite Dynasty. The events of his reign are known chiefly from date-formulae and letters. During the first 30 years of his reign he was leader of one of several coalitions struggling for domination. In his 31st year he overcame his chief rival, Rim-sin of Larsa, thereby gaining control of the whole region from Babylon to the Persian Gulf. In subsequent years he undertook military action against neighboring states to the north, sacking Mari in his 35th year as King. His empire was consolidated by the 40th year of his rule. Hammurabi owed his success not only to military ability but also to attention to administration and economic justice, reflected in his correspondence and his laws (*see* HAMMURABI, CODE OF).

HAMMURABI, CODE OF, collection of laws promulgated in the early 2d millennium B.C. by Hammurabi, King of Babylonia. Most of the code is extant on a diorite monument, 8.2 ft. high, discovered at Susa (now Shush, Iran) in 1902 and now in the Louvre, Paris. At the top of the stele a relief shows Hammurabi paying homage to the sun-god Shamash, also the god of justice; below is engraved the cuneiform text, in finely executed writing reading vertically from top to bottom in a series of horizontal bands. Portions of the text are also extant on clay tablets from Babylonia and Assyria from periods down to the middle of the 1st millennium B.C.

The text comprises (1) a prologue telling of Hammurabi's divine call and his piety, (2) the corpus of laws, and (3) an epilogue extolling Hammurabi's establishment of justice in the land. The laws, arranged largely according to subject matter, deal with such topics as offenses against the administration of justice and property, land tenure, trade and commerce, marriage, family, and inheritance, assault, regulations governing surgeons and builders, agriculture, wages, and slavery. Penalties included death by drowning and impalement, mutilation, scourging, banishment, enslavement, and the payment of reparations.

Similarities between certain laws in the Pentateuch and those of Hammurabi formerly led to the suggestion of direct borrowing by Moses. This theory has been discountenanced by the discovery of other collections of Mesopotamian laws, which show that Hammurabi was neither the only nor the first lawgiver in the ancient Near East.

Though commonly referred to as a code, Hammurabi's laws have been shown by F. R. Kraus and others to be not a codification of statute law, but a collection of specimen decisions given by Hammurabi as judge, arranged in the literary form, "if so-and-so happened, so-and-so will follow," known as "omen-form." The epilogue recommends the judgments and decisions recorded on the stele to future rulers and people.

Monument on which is engraved most of Hammurabi's code discovered in 1902 at the site of the ancient city of Susa.

The contents of the "code" show that its authors were familiar not only with the specific decisions incorporated, but also with earlier related documents such as the "codes" of Ur-Nammu and Lipit-ishtar.

HANGING GARDENS OF BABYLON, one of the seven wonders of the ancient world. Berossus narrates that Nebuchadnezzar, in the course of his restoration of Babylon, built an artificial hill-like structure to gratify his Queen from mountainous Media. It consisted of a series of terraces, supported by stone platforms and laid out with groves and flower beds irrigated by the Euphrates.

ISHTAR [ĭsh′tär], principal Babylonian and Assyrian goddess, equivalent to the Sumerian Innin and the Phoenician Astarte. Manifesting herself as the planet Venus she assumed the functions of the Great Mother of primitive Near Eastern religions, and, being intimately concerned with the giving or spilling of life, was goddess both of sexual activities and of war. Her cult was widespread, being especially important at Erech, Nineveh, and Arbela. Ishtar was prominent in the Epic of Gilgamesh and in the myth "The Descent of Ishtar to the Underworld."

KISH [kĭsh], ancient Sumerian city of Mesopotamia, south of Baghdad, Iraq. Investigated by early travelers, it was excavated in 1912 by Henri de Genouillac and in 1923–33 by Ernest Mackay (later replaced by L. C. Watelin) and Stephen Langdon. Kish flourished from the early 3d to the late 1st millennium B.C. In Sumerian tradition it was the site of the first dynasty in north Babylonia after the Flood, a claim consistent with archeological evidence, which proves occupation from the Jemdet Nasr period. Literary evidence suggests a hegemony by the king of Kish over all Babylonia before 2600 B.C.

LARSA [lär′sə], ancient city of south Babylonia, just southeast of Erech, referred to as Ellasar in the Bible. The site, excavated by W. K. Loftus in 1854 and by André Par-

rot in 1933, reveals occupation from the Jemdet Nasr period, or earlier, to Seleucid times. Larsa was important among Sumerian cities of the 3d millennium. It attained its greatest prominence between 1867 and 1698 B.C., when its dynasty, partly contemporary with that of Isin, governed much of Babylonia, its last king being overthrown by Hammurabi.

MAPS. Maps are among the oldest forms of imparting knowledge. Even today primitive peoples, unable to read or write, are often excellent map makers, possessing a natural instinct or skill at presenting graphically the land on which they live. Among these, the best known are the charts of the Marshall Islanders made by attaching shells to palm-leaf ribs representing islands and wave fronts. Eskimos and Australian aborigines have also proved adept at natural map making. Early settlers in North America frequently carved maps of their regions on their bone powder horns.

The oldest cartographic records surviving in any number are those of the Babylonians and Egyptians. The earliest extant map is believed to be an Assyrian clay tablet of c.3800 B.C., representing part of northern Mesopotamia. Babylonian clay tablets dating from 2500–600 B.C. and showing surveys of lands, plans of cities, and representations of the world can be seen in some of the great museums. The Babylonians were also successful astronomers and left us a legacy of mathematical concepts such as the 360° circle and the division of the day into hours, minutes, and seconds. The measurement of land for taxation purposes prompted much of the Egyptian mapping. Rameses II (d.1225 B.C.) is known to have begun a land survey of the empire of the Nile. The oldest known papyrus map, in the Turin Museum, is a sketch of a Nubian gold mine dating from about 1320 B.C.

MERODACH-BALADAN [mǐ-rō′dăk-băl′ə-dăn] II (8th century B.C.), King of Babylonia. A Chaldaean chieftain, he usurped the Babylonian throne c.721. Supported by Elamites and certain allies in Syria and Palestine, Merodach-baladan resisted the Assyrians for 11 years. But Sargon of Assyria defeated his western allies, and in 710, after attacking Babylon, assumed the throne. After Sargon's death (705) Merodach-baladan regained the throne.

NEBUCHADNEZZAR [nĕb-yŏŏ-kəd-nĕz′ər] II or **NEBUCHADREZZAR** [nĕb-yŏŏ-kəd-rĕz′ər] II, Babylonian King (605–562 B.C.), son and successor of Nabopolassar. As crown prince, he defeated the Egyptian army at Carchemish shortly before his father's death and annexed Syria. He captured Jerusalem in 597 B.C. and again in 586 B.C., carrying off many Jews into the Babylonian captivity. His military achievements, which included a prolonged siege of Tyre and an attack upon Egypt, brought temporary glory to Babylonia but seriously damaged its economy. Nebuchadnezzar is noted for his restoration of Babylon, including the creation of the hanging gardens and the construction of the city's great walls.

SELEUCIA-ON-TIGRIS [sǐ-lŏŏ′shə; tī′grǐs], ancient Mesopotamian city west of the Tigris, opposite Ctesiphon, 20 mi.

southeast of Baghdad. It was founded about 300 B.C. by Seleucus I to replace Babylon as capital and chief city of Babylonia and continued to be commercially important during the Parthian period. According to Pliny, it was a city of 600,000, with a mixed population of Greeks, Asiatics, and Jews. The Romans destroyed it in 164 A.D. Its site, modern Tell Umair, was excavated (1927–32; 1936–37) by American expeditions, which discovered pottery, coins, palaces, temples, and theaters extending from Seleucid times to the late Parthian period (early 3d century A.D.). From the older period there are the remains of a ziggurat, showing that Seleucia was founded upon the site of an earlier city. Some objects with cuneiform inscriptions suggest an identification with the Sumerian city Akshak.

SIPPAR [sĭ-pär'], ancient Babylonian city, 20 mi. southwest of Baghdad. The most northerly city of Akkad, it was important for the defense of Babylonia against the north. In Sumerian tradition the site of an antediluvian dynasty, Sippar remained important down to the Achaemenid Persian period. The site was excavated in 1880–82 by Hormuzd Rassam (who looted perhaps 50,000 tablets) and in 1894 more scientifically by Vincent Scheil. Buildings traced included a ziggurat, a temple of the sun-god (the tutelary deity of ancient Sippar), private houses, and a supposed school building. The commonly accepted identification with Biblical Sepharvaim is without proof.

SUMER [soo'mər], Biblical Shinar, a land of ancient Mesopotamia, occupying what is now the southernmost third of Iraq. With Akkad to the north, it constituted Babylonia (q.v.).

Sumerian statuette of a male figure dating from c.3000 B.C.

The Metropolitan Museum of Art, Fletcher Fund, 1940

Following several prehistoric cultures, there settled there before 3000 B.C. a new group, the Sumerians, of unknown antecedents, who invented the system of writing called cuneiform and developed urban civilization. Conditions of the period down to about 2600 B.C. are reflected in Sumerian myths and epics, committed to writing in the early 2d millennium B.C.

The organization of early Sumer was based on independent city-states, each centered on a temple estate. Noteworthy among Sumerian cities were Adab, Erech, Eridu, Lagash, Larsa, Nippur, and Ur. Sumerian civilization, also predominant in Akkad, particularly Mari and Kish, influenced the regions further north.

Before the middle of the 3d millennium, individual cities achieved temporary control over greater areas. Semitic immigration gradually altered the social structure of northern Babylonia, and about 2350 B.C. a Semitic empire, based on Agade, but embracing Sumer, arose. When this collapsed, it was Sumer which recovered first, a bureaucratic Sumerian empire, ruled from Ur, being dominant for the final century of the 3d millennium. This collapsed under Amorite pressure, and Sumerian civilization, already heavily admixed with Semitic influence, had no further separate existence.

UR [ûr], ancient Sumerian and Babylonian city in southern Mesopotamia. Formerly on the Euphrates and now 10 mi. southwest of it, the site is marked by the mound Tell al-Muqayyar. It is the site of the best preserved ziggurat (temple tower), first created in the Early Dynastic period (c.2700–2350 B.C.) and last restored by Cyrus the Great. Occupied from the Ubaidian period (c.3900–3500), Ur was known in Sumerian tradition as the seat of an ancient dynasty, datable to the Early Dynastic period. Its tutelary deity was the moon-god Nannar, or Sin. Fortified with a great wall, it was the capital of the Third Dynasty of Ur (c.2100–c.1950), which governed all Mesopotamia. The dynasty finally collapsed when the city was destroyed by the Elamites.

Shortly afterward, about 1850, Ur regained importance as the main port of entry into Mesopotamia for the Tilmun (Bahrain) copper trade. It remained important as an administrative, commercial, and religious center under the First Dynasty of Babylon and the Kassites and down to the Persian period. With the entry of the Chaldaean (Kaldu) tribes onto the marshlands of south Babylonia after c.1200, and their extension northward, Ur was the principal city in their area and might well be called "Ur of the Chaldees." In the Bible (Gen. 11:28,31) it is mentioned, probably anachronistically, under this designation as the place from which Abraham's family migrated northward in the early 2d millennium B.C. Some scholars, however, deny this identification.

Explored by various British archeologists since 1850, Tell al-Muqayyar was excavated in 1919 by H. R. Hall and between 1922 and 1934 by C. Leonard Woolley. Their two most noted finds were the royal tombs and the supposed evidence of the Biblical Flood. The royal tombs comprised 16 subterranean structures of stone or brick, containing one to four chambers, the oldest datable to about 2500 B.C. Besides the principal burial in each tomb, a number of persons—74 in one instance— had been sacrificed. According to one theory, the tombs were those of actual kings of the First Dynasty of Ur, the subsidiary burials being courtiers accompanying their ruler in death. According to another theory, the tombs were those of the priests and priestesses representing the divinities and their attendants in the "sacred marriage" upon which fertility was thought to depend.

Woolley's supposed evidence for the Biblical Flood was a deposit of silt up to 11 ft. thick between two strata of the Ubaidian period. Though this could represent the sand deposited by a severe flood, it could not have been caused by a deluge of the extent of that mentioned in the Bible, as a silt stratum at the corresponding level is lacking at other Sumerian cities not far from Ur. Inscribed cuneiform tablets of periods from the archaic (Early Dynastic I) to the Persian (6th century B.C.) have been found, including about 100 Sumerian literary texts, still unpublished, of the early 2d millennium B.C.

PERSIAN CIVILIZATION

BACKGROUND

PERSIA [pûr′zhə, pûr′shə], a name long current in the western world for Iran, a country in southwest Asia. The word is derived from the Greek *Persis*, which in ancient times was the seat of the Persian Empire founded by the Achaemenid Dynasty.

Prehistory. The prehistoric people of the high Iranian plateau were of a different ethnic stock from the Semites of the Mesopotamian plains to the west. The earliest skeletal remains of these people come from the excavations of some of the caves in which they lived in the Paleolithic Age. Certain of the skulls are of the Nordic type, while others are more similar to the Mediterranean type. The tentative label of "the Caspians" has been applied from the view that they may have moved to the plateau from a region west and north of the Caspian Sea.

The cave excavations brought to light artifacts of the Paleolithic, Mesolithic, and Neolithic ages which indicate that prior to 6000 B.C. these people hunted gazelle and wild sheep and goats. Later they domesticated the sheep and goats and then, about 4000 B.C., moved from their caves to settlements of mud brick houses, to become agriculturists, to weave, and to make pottery. As a result of centuries of rebuilding, these settlements rose higher and higher above the plains and now appear as conspicuous mounds. Many such mounds have been excavated, while countless others remain unexplored. Of the objects found, the most artistically important are the quantities of decorated pottery. The finds from many occupational levels establish comparative dates (stratigraphy) and indicate stylistic affinities.

Prehistory ends when writing begins. The records of Mesopotamian civilizations reveal that groups called Guti, Lullubi, Kassites, and Elamites lived in the mountains along the west of the plateau, while other groups not in touch with Mesopotamia were in other areas. The inhabitants of Luristan, in the western mountains, were horse breeders, as is shown by the kind of bronzes found in this region. The probability that all these groups led a semi-nomadic life may help to explain why the inhabitants of the plateau emerged so slowly from the prehistoric stage to that of urban civilization. However, the Elamites were the exception. Moving south to the hot plains at the head of the Persian Gulf, they established a powerful state, centered at Susa, which maintained close contacts with the adjacent Mesopotamian civilizations.

The Coming of the Iranians. In the 2d millennium B.C. waves of Aryan peoples—nomadic horsemen—began moving west from the heartland of Asia. Some of these tribes turned south toward the Indian subcontinent, while about 1500 B.C. others traveled across the northern limits of the plateau. About the year 1000 B.C. larger groups arrived to settle in the western mountains of the Zagros range. Later this region was to be called Iran, or "the home of the Aryans." These groups included the Medes (Mada), Persians (Parsa), Parthians, Bactrians, Sogdians, Sacae, and Scythians. Although they soon began to acquire new concepts and habits from the established population, they had traditions and distinctive features of their own. For example, excavations at a site to the west of Teheran in a 9th-century-B.C. necropolis have brought to light pottery in the form of animals quite unlike types from earlier sites.

The Medes and the Persians. Initially, the Medes were the most powerful of these tribes and established a kingdom at Ecbatana (modern Hamadan) before the opening of the 6th century. Under Cyaxares (reigned c.625–585 B.C.) they also conquered Assyria. The Persians had moved south into the Elamite lands, giving them the names of Anshan and Parsa. Prominent in this group was the Achaemenid clan, and c.550 Cyrus, its head, overthrew the Median King, Astyages, and brought into being a powerful kingdom of the united Medes and Persians. He led its armies in successful campaigns to the Mediterranean, as well as to the eastern edge of the plateau, and established his capital at Pasargadae. Under his successors the kingdom became an empire, and in their inscriptions its rulers refer to their family (Vishtaspa), their clan (Achaemenid), their tribe (Parsa), and their nation (Aryan). From Parsa came the Greek word *Persis*, the European word "Persia," and the later designation of southwestern Iran as "Fars," together with the description of its language as "Farsi."

Cambyses II (reigned 529–521), son of Cyrus, conquered Egypt and was succeeded by Darius I (reigned 522–486), who came from another branch of the family. A builder and capable administrator who organized the empire on a centralized basis, Darius conquered in the east as far as northwest India, fought the Scythians on the

Danube, and in 494 put down the revolt of the Ionian Greeks in Asia Minor, thus starting the Persian Wars. In 490 he crossed the Bosporus to campaign on the Greek mainland, where he met defeat at Marathon. His son, Xerxes I (reigned 486–465), captured and burned Athens, but the destruction of his fleet by the Greeks at Salamis ended efforts to attach the mainland of Greece to the Achaemenid empire. Under his son, Artaxerxes I (reigned 465–424), revolts broke out in distant areas, and it was not until the reign of Artaxerxes III (358–338) that the earlier limits were briefly restored.

Greek Control. Suddenly Alexander of Macedon appeared in Asia Minor to confront the massed armies of Darius III (reigned 336–330), the ninth Achaemenid ruler. Engagements at Issus and Gaugamela proved disastrous to the Persians, and the Achaemenid empire collapsed. Alexander pressed on to take Babylon, Susa, Persepolis (the spiritual capital of the empire), and Ecbatana (the site of its treasury). In 330, by accident or by design, Persepolis was burned to the ground. Alexander the Great led his forces as far east as the Indus River, founding colonies of Greek settlers along the way, and then returned to Susa to formulate plans for a world state in which Macedonians and Persians would have equal status.

Still a young man, in 323 Alexander was smitten with a mortal fever. Immediately his conquests were parceled out among his generals: from one of them, Seleucus, sprang the Seleucid Dynasty which ruled Iran as part of a vast, loosely affiliated, heterogeneous Asian empire from its capital at Seleucia in Syria. For almost two centuries the Seleucids continued the Hellenization of Iran begun by Alexander, but they could not exert firm control over the native Iranians, who remained relatively independent.

Parthian Domination. A nomadic Scythian tribe, the Arsacid, successfully revolted against the Seleucid Governor of the satrapy of Parthava in the middle of the 3d century B.C. Later historians were to refer to these people as the Parthians. Arsaces I, the first ruler of the line, came to the throne c.249. Between 160 and 140 Mithridates I took over former Achaemenid territory as far west as the Tigris River, while his son Phraates II (137–c.127) forever ended Seleucid pretensions. Mithridates II (reigned c.123–88) repulsed attacks on both flanks of the kingdom and, assuming the title "King of Kings," extended Parthian control from India to the western fringes of Mesopotamia. Then the reign of Phraates III (70–57 B.C.) saw the beginning of nearly three centuries of struggle against the Roman Empire, whose legions pushed eastward from the Mediterranean coastal areas. Notable Parthian vic-

Right, a relief carving from the palace of Xerxes at Persepolis depicts the King attended by two servants.

Below, at Persepolis two remaining columns of the hypostyle hall of Xerxes I (reigned 486–465 B.C.) frame the ruins of the palace of Darius I (reigned 522–486).

Covello—Black Star

Philcarol—FPG

tories were the defeats of Crassus at Carrhae in 53 and of Mark Antony near Lake Rezzieh in northwestern Iran in 36.

Sasanian Dynasty. With the Parthian forces heavily concentrated in the areas threatened by Rome, the situation became favorable for revolt within Iran. In Fars, Ardashir I (reigned 224–41 A.D.) overthrew the Parthian King, Artabanus V, and proclaimed the independence of the region. He then went on to take Ctesiphon on the Tigris, the Parthian capital. A grandson of Sasan, a high priest of Istakhr near Persepolis, and a member of an important family descended from the Achaemenids, Ardashir founded the Sasanian Dynasty, which reigned over a new Iranian empire for some 400 years.

His son Shapur I (reigned 241–72) campaigned as far to the east as the Indus River and then returned to confront the armies of Rome, capturing the Emperor Valerian in battle and taking many thousands of prisoners. Shapur established his capital, Shapur, the chief Sasanian center, in the home province of Fars, and Gundeshapur, near Susa, later a medical center under Khosrau I.

Shapur II (reigned 309–79) waged three wars against Rome during his very long reign. There followed nearly two centuries of war and internal dissolution, during which Bahram Gur (reigned 421–38) scored notable successes against the invading Ephthalites (White Huns). Finally, Khosrau I (reigned 531–79), famed in Persian history as "the Just," ended the Ephthalite threat, temporarily halted Roman encroachments, and asserted the monarchy above all contending factions. In this relatively stable political and social climate, Iranian civilization reached its apogee.

By the opening of the 7th century A.D. the Byzantine Empire had succeeded that of Rome as the major challenge to Sasanian power in Asia. In 611 the Sasanians captured and burned the famed city of Antioch, and Khosrau II (reigned 589–628) was successful in several campaigns, in Egypt and in Constantinople itself. But a major defeat inflicted on his forces in 627 suddenly disclosed that the long years of war had undermined the power of the Sasanian empire.

After his death a series of 12 short-lived rulers strove to establish their authority. In 632 Yazdegird III did achieve a measure of success, but by this time the Arab followers of the Prophet Mohammed were bursting out of the Arabian Peninsula. Victorious at the battle of Kadisiya in 636, the Arabs moved on to capture Ctesiphon and inflicted a final, crushing defeat on the Sasanian forces at Nihawand in 641. Yazdegird III was relentlessly pursued until his assassination in 651 marked the end of the last of the empires of ancient Persia and of nearly 2,000 years of control of the plateau by Iranian stock.

Imperial Organization

The Achaemenid empire consisted of 20 satrapies, or provinces, each governed by a satrap who was a nobly born Persian or Median. These posts tended to become hereditary. These semi-independent governors reported to the absolute monarch, who sought advice from the members of a royal council. The satrap's authority was limited by the presence of civil and military officials who were directly responsible to the king, as well as by itinerant inspectors known as the "eye of the king." The armed forces numbered 360,000 soldiers in six corps, while some 10,000 men from leading families formed the personal bodyguard of the ruler, the so-called Immortals.

A well-developed system of roads facilitated the movement of troops, the conduct of trade, the collection of taxes, and the rapid passage of relays of horsemen carrying the mails. For example, the so-called royal road ran some 1,500 mi. from Susa to the Mediterranean. Gold coinage was in use throughout the empire, administration was based upon carefully kept records, and justice was uniform and fair. The subject peoples of the empire were permitted to practice their own religions and to enjoy semiautonomy. The tolerance and clemency shown toward them was a feature without earlier precedent and one which was to be conspicuous throughout later periods of the country's history.

Nearly all the information about the organzation and operations of the Achaemenid empire comes from the historians of Greece, who were not without bias against the invaders of their homeland. Rock-cut inscriptions, carved in parallel columns of Old Persian, Elamite, and Babylonian, such as at Behistun, and inscribed metal plaques have survived and furnish edicts and statements of a number of the rulers. But no storehouses of official records, comparable to those of the earlier Mesopotamian civilizations, have come to light. However, limited finds of clay tablets reveal that these records were kept in Old Persian, in Aramaic, and in Elamite.

The Parthian rulers, initially under the influence of the language and customs of the Greek colonies of the Seleucid kingdom, later considered themselves to be the heirs of the Achaemenids. Adopting the earlier system of satrapies governed by the families of feudal lords, the Parthians were successful in stemming the pressure of barbarian tribes from Asia on the Iranian plateau. The royal succession was not always to an immediate relative of the ruler, since the feudal lords had a voice in determining succession. This factor led to frequent and serious internal warfare between the supporters of rival contenders for the throne. Parthian organization and culture were eclectic in character, distinctive only in the military field, where the major striking forces were groups of mounted archers. While Greek was the lingua franca of trade throughout most of the period, the Parthians spoke so-called Middle Persian and wrote it in a script called Pahlavi by modern scholars.

The Sasanians outdid the Achaemenids in building up a highly centralized and efficient administration for the kingdom which they called Iranshahr. Each province was governed by a *shahrdar* who was a member of the family of Sasan. The majestically remote and aloof King of Kings was also the supreme judge. He was served by a prime minister who supervised the officials and the skilled secretariat of several ministries. As in Parthian times royal succession was influenced by the wishes of the religious hierarchy and the feudal lords. According to very ancient Aryan practice, society was composed of the classes of priests, warriors, farmers, and traders. In the Sasanian period this social structure was modified on the basis of the Mazdean clergy, warriors, scribes, and commoners—

the latter class incorporating the farmers, shepherds, and traders.

Internal prosperity was fostered by highly developed systems of irrigation. At a number of points in Iran are the remains of dams and aqueducts of the Sasanian period, while the vast, spreading plains of Elam—the modern province of Khuzistan—were irrigated by a complex network of canals fed by rivers flowing out of the high ranges. In later times these canals and their control works fell into ruin, but present-day efforts to restore the ancient fertility of this region have brought back into service many of these canals. Communications were also well developed, as is shown by the surviving stretches of stone-paved highways and the remains of brick and stone bridges spanning many stream beds. The Sasanians spoke Middle Persian, writing it in a developed form of the Pahlavi script, while the sacred books of the period were written in distinctive scripts which could be read only by the trained Mazdean clergy.

Religion

As elsewhere in the prehistoric world, the earliest inhabitants of the plateau held in awe and veneration the forces of nature and the processes of reproduction. By representing these elements symbolically or realistically, they hoped to win protection and avert disaster. Thus, on the earliest pottery are stylized designs of water, trees, and the sun. Later the sun and the earth were personified by a goddess whose consort represented the moon and all growing things. In addition, a mother goddess of reproduction and fertility was worshipped from remote times.

Her image, with enormous breasts and a wide pelvic structure, was reproduced in countless figurines of terra cotta, bone, and bronze well down into Sasanian times. Clans, tribes, and towns had their own local deities to protect them from outsiders, while the great divinities of the Mesopotamian civilizations were also known on the plateau. Finally, the Aryans brought with them such Indo-European deities as Mithra, the sun-god, and Anahita, goddess of fertility.

The Middle East was to give rise to the monotheistic religions of Judaism, Christianity, and Islam. In Iran the movement away from polytheism took place in Achaemenid times through the efforts of the prophet and reformer Zoroaster, or Zarathushtra. Probably born in Balkh, east of the Caspian Sea, some time before 600 B.C., Zoroaster emphasized the eternal opposition of good and evil. Ahura Mazda, symbol of truth and light, was the spirit of good, whereas his opponent, Ahriman, was the spirit of evil. Inscriptions of the Achaemenid rulers include the name of Ahura Mazda, and carved reliefs show them worshiping the divinity at fire altars. The fire temples and the rites of the faith were in the charge of the Magi, a Median clan whose members became the hereditary clergy. The conduct of the believers was based upon good deeds, good thoughts, and good words. An inscription of Darius I states that he followed the truth and hated the lie.

In time some of the principles and instructions expounded by Zoroaster were incorporated into the ancient ritualistic faith called Mazdaism. The cults of Mithra and Anahita had survived throughout the Achaemenid period

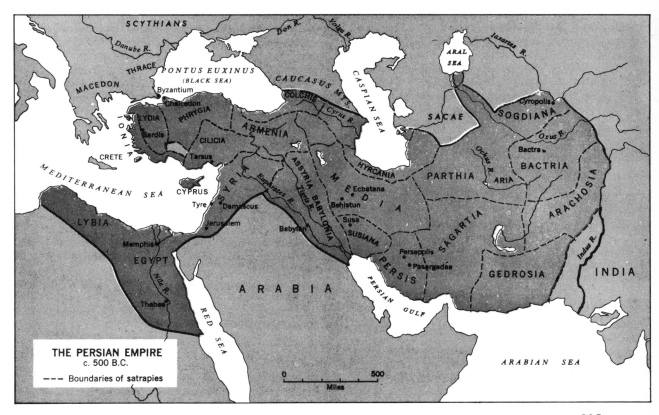

THE PERSIAN EMPIRE
c. 500 B.C.

- - - Boundaries of satrapies

into that of the Parthians, with Mithraism achieving enormous popularity within the Roman Empire. Growing communities of Christians were tolerated by the Parthian rulers. The Sasanians clung to Mazdaism, their state religion, and in this period the old oral traditions were collected and written in the sacred books known collectively as the Avesta. The Magian clergy continued to care for three national fires as well as for those in hundreds of local fire temples. In the 3d century A.D. another prophet, Mani, appeared. He preached a doctrine containing elements from Mazdaism, Christianity, and Buddhism, which emphasized spirituality over materialism and renounced sacrifices and the worship of images. Shapur I seems to have been a convert and considered making Manicheanism the state religion.

The Magians were alarmed by this heresy and by the fact that Mani had set up a celibate clergy of his own, and in 272 A.D. they succeeded in having him put to death. However, Manicheanism survived for many centuries in Asia and as far to the west as Egypt. Near the end of the 5th century Mazdak advocated a doctrine which stemmed from Mazdaism, but included such new features as vegetarianism, abstinence from violence, and communal life. Again, this new faith attracted one of the Sasanian rulers, and again the clergy was too powerful, so that in 528 A.D. Mazdak was put to death and his followers massacred. During the Sasanian period Christians were often persecuted because of their alleged association with Rome and Byzantium, but near the end of this dynasty the Nestorian sect made considerable headway in Iran.

Continuity of Cultural Tradition

Evolving much later from the stages of prehistory than the dwellers of the river valleys of Mesopotamia, the inhabitants of the plateau came slowly to such subjects as astronomy, law, medicine, and the recording of legend, history, and religious and speculative thinking. Only in the Sasanian period were important studies made in some of these fields. The writings survive in Middle Persian and in translations made into Arabic in later times. In this period scholars studied primary works in Greek, Latin, and the languages of India, using them as models and sources for their own writings. However, the strong continuity of tradition and the ability to adopt, change, and assimilate patterns of society and artistic expression from other cultures which typified ancient Persia continued throughout the succeeding Islamic centuries in Iran. As one result, the legends and tales of the kings were told and retold in prose and verse. As another, the Iranians of all later generations felt very close to their distant ancestors.

PEOPLE, PLACES, AND TERMS

ACHAEMENIDS [ăk-ĭ-mĕn'ĭds], ancient Persian dynasty ruling from c.550–330 B.C. Descended from Achaemenes, the dynasty spread westward from southwestern Iran after the decline of Elam. Cyrus the Great established Achaemenid rule by his defeat of Astyages of Media, and brought all western Asia under Persian control by the con-

quest of Babylonia in 539 B.C. Subsequent rulers included Cambyses, Smerdis, Darius I, Xerxes I, Artaxerxes I, Darius II, Artaxerxes II, and Darius III. Alexander the Great ended the dynasty by his victory at Gaugamela.

ALEXANDER THE GREAT (356–323 B.C.), Macedonian King, conqueror of the Persian empire, and one of the greatest leaders in history. Son of Philip II and Olympias, who traced her ancestry back to Achilles, Alexander derived outstanding traits from both parents—diplomatic astuteness and military ability from his father, and a fiery and imaginative temperament from his mother. He received the best education obtainable, including instruction in riding, hunting, and fighting from his father, and in natural science, literature, and moral philosophy from the great Aristotle. He became expert in every skill befitting an aristocrat. Boldly handsome, courageous to the point of rashness, personally magnetic, and intensely loyal, Alexander was at the same time imperious and subject to sudden fierce anger and resentment. His favorite author was Homer, and he imagined himself a second Achilles.

Alexander led the impetuous attack at the battle of Chaeronea, which ended the era of the independent Greek city-state. Two years later his father was murdered (336 B.C.), leaving to him his throne and his almost-completed plans for an expedition to free the Greeks of Asia Minor from Persian control. At Philip's death rebellions broke out in the south, north, east, and west. Although only 20, Alexander handled the trouble with characteristic energy. A prompt show of force intimidated Thebes and checkmated the plans of Demosthenes and others at Athens. At a meeting of the so-called Corinthian League, Alexander, like his father, was named commander in chief of the allied Greek army for service against Persia. The next year (335 B.C.), while he campaigned in the north against Thracian and Illyrian tribes, a rumor of his death prompted a second rebellion by Thebes. Alexander returned suddenly, took the city, destroyed every building except the temples and the house where Pindar had lived, and killed or enslaved the entire population. This fearful lesson kept the Greeks in line for years afterward when he was far off in the East.

The following spring Alexander crossed into Asia Minor with an army of about 40,000, of whom perhaps half were Macedonians. He first visited the site of Troy and there paid tribute to the heroes of Homer. He may at first have intended no more than the capture of the eastern coastal area of the Aegean, or perhaps also the Persian naval bases in Phoenicia and Egypt, but his rapid and relatively easy success must have encouraged him to raise his sights continually. As he overcame hardships and risks, his egotism grew. His interest in geography and scientific exploration also drove him on, and he was genuinely convinced (as were all Greeks) that he was conferring a benefit on Asiatics by introducing them to Greek culture.

His first major victory, at the Granicus River, exposed Asia Minor. Alexander's use of cavalry under his personal command was the deciding factor in this and other engagements. Passing through the Cilician Gates, he defeated the Persians at the battle of Issus (333 B.C.) in northern Syria, and this opened the way to the heart of the empire. After the capture of his family, King Darius offered to negotiate, but Alexander refused. He turned south to secure the eastern Mediterranean coast, but was delayed seven months by the siege and capture of Tyre (332 B.C.), his greatest military feat, and by the resistance of Gaza. Egypt surrendered without a struggle, as did most Persian subjects. At the mouth of the Nile Alexander founded the greatest of the many new cities to be named after himself; this Alexandria soon became the main link between the Western and Eastern worlds. In Egypt he also journeyed into the western desert to the shrine of Zeus Ammon, and was there supposedly greeted as the god's own son. As divine kings were common in the East, such a claim strengthened Alexander's position with his new subjects. But he seems also, either from policy or conviction, to have insisted on being treated as superhuman by his Greek soldiers. This they deeply resented.

Turning eastward (331 B.C.), Alexander met and defeated Darius' greatest army at Gaugamela, in the northern Tigris plain. He then occupied the principal Persian cities, Babylon, Susa, Persepolis, and Ecbatana, with their vast royal treasures. The burning of the palace at Persepolis, whether intentional or not, marked the end of the Persian monarchy. Alexander was now the conqueror of all southwestern Asia; yet he pushed on. In pursuit of Darius, he reached the Caspian Sea, and crossing the Hindu Kush, invaded Bactria and Sogdiana (330–327). After fierce resistance, this area acknowledged his sovereignty, which was perhaps lightened somewhat by his marriage to their beautiful princess Roxana. In the next three years he broke into northwestern India, defeated the gallant King Porus on the Hydaspes River, founded Buchephala to honor his horse, who had died in the battle, overran the Punjab, and was only prevented from pressing

further, perhaps to find the fabled "eastern ocean," by a determined mutiny. He returned west along the Indus River and from its mouth sent a fleet under Nearchus to explore the sea route to the head of the Persian Gulf, while the army proceeded through the desert to Babylon. Both army and fleet reached their destination (324 B.C.), after great danger and privation. The military results were negligible, but from then on trade flowed in increasing volume between the Mediterranean and India.

Back in Babylon, which he apparently intended to make his capital, Alexander devoted himself with the same concentration to the organization of the conquered territories. He wished to make Greeks and Asiatics partners in civil administration, and even in the army. This policy caused resentment among the conquerors, espe-

Coin portrait of Alexander the Great. (AMERICAN NUMISMATIC SOCIETY)

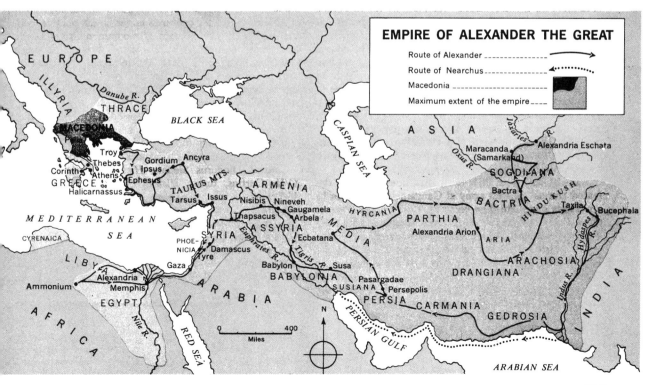

EMPIRE OF ALEXANDER THE GREAT

Route of Alexander
Route of Nearchus
Macedonia
Maximum extent of the empire

cially when Alexander insisted that his officers follow his own example and marry Persian women.

But Alexander's interests and abilities lay more in conquest and exploration than in administration. Preparations were made for an Arabian expedition. Representatives at his court included envoys from the western Mediterranean, and there was speculation that he might turn his restless energies in that direction. But in May or June, 323 B.C., Alexander was stricken with a fever and in 11 days was dead. Only 32, he had reigned less than 13 years. His resistance had been weakened by continuous overexertion, wounds, fierce fits of anger, and heavy drinking. He had not provided for a successor, although it is said that at the last he handed his ring to his second-in-command, Perdiccas. Probably not even Alexander himself could have long held together the vast territory he had conquered. Certainly it rapidly disintegrated without him, to be fought over by his generals. Yet large areas of Asia remained for centuries under Greek political control, and Alexander's dream of a common Greco-Asiatic culture was at least partially realized. Perhaps no single individual in ancient times had so great an impact on world events as did Alexander. It is only natural that time should have magnified and distorted his fame into a legend which history can hardly match. Already legendary during his lifetime, Alexander passed into the literature of many nations after his death, adopted by Arabic-Persian tradition under the name Iskander, and becoming especially popular in the romances of the Middle Ages.

ARSES [är′sēz], youngest son of the Persian King Artaxerxes III. He was enthroned in 336 B.C. by the eunuch Bagoas, his father's confidential minister, who had previously murdered Artaxerxes III. In 336 Arses attempted to assert his authority and consequently he and all his children were killed by Bagoas.

ART AND ARCHITECTURE

The art of Persia, which covers a period of about 7,000 years, expressed itself in many mediums. These include architecture, some of the world's best; pottery, rivaled only by that of China; tiles; metalwork in gold, silver, and bronze, combining power and magnificence; miniature painting and book-binding, nowhere surpassed; and textiles and carpets that are the world's standard.

Other arts—calligraphy, jewelry, arms and armor, glass and lacquer, implements such as surgeons' and craftsmen's tools—were executed with imagination and taste. The long development of Persian art meant maturity, authority, and a close identification with the life and spirit of the people.

The peoples living on and around the Persian plateau were of varied character, speech, and race, but common conditions of life imposed common values and ultimately gave to their arts a specific recognizable character. Their artistic tradition was enriched and perpetuated by the lively cultural interchange continuously promoted by war, trade, and population movements.

Persian arts, marked by a vigorous sense of form, are always lucid and definite, possibly a reflection of the brilliantly clear atmosphere of the region. The vague and obscure were always avoided. Even fantastic animals—

Philcarol—FF
Joseph Kosta

Above, detail of sculptured frieze from the palace of Darius I in Persepolis portrays Phoenicians bringing gifts to the Persian ruler.

Left, thin-walled goblet of painted pottery, found at Susa. This prehistoric piece is an early example of Persian mastery of design.

Buffalo Museum of Science

griffins and winged lions and bulls (products of early religious symbolism in which each element stands for some aspect of a cult)—were always specific, clearly articulated, and must have been quite convincing to the ancient viewer.

The simple forms provided opportunity for decorative designs, rich colors, and elaborately worked surface textures. By 4500 B.C. the walls of the Temple at Tepe Gawra (in northeast Mesopotamia, settled by people from the Persian plateau), were colored soft red both inside and out. By 4000 B.C. painted pottery had appeared (for the first time anywhere), forceful in shapes, colored dark brown on chamois-colored paste, ornamented with abstract patterns and lively animal figures. Tall goblets from Susa (labeled Susa I, meaning the deepest archeological level at that site) are almost paper-thin and decorated with superlative patterns arranged in separate zones. Their symbols represent much-needed water. Thus, at the very start Persian art was concerned with a symbolic appeal to the heavens for life and power. Quite superior to those of adjoining regions, the finest of these goblets (Louvre, Paris) are clearly entitled to be called works of art. Others are in the Hermitage in Leningrad and the Buffalo Museum of Science.

A sculpture in the round (Collection Mohsen Foroughi, Teheran), realistically representing a forceful human figure, dates from the 3d millennium B.C. It shows that at this early date the characteristics of Persian art already existed. Its compact form is elaborately ornamented; the sturdy body is composed of black and red disks, encrusted with gold; the eyes are coated with mica; the limbs are treated to look as if they are covered with scales. It is an impressive work of art.

The following centuries saw the development of bronze implements (especially in Luristan, in the west of Iran). Assyrian carvings depict fortified Iranian cities with lofty, crenelated towers and gabled temples, while archeological research has disclosed walled cities and palaces (for example, at Damghan, Syalck, and Susa), dating from the 2d millennium B.C.

From the 9th century B.C. on, vessels, flagons, weapons, and ritual objects were made in gold, silver, and stone. These were ornamented with animals and human figures (sometimes of great beauty), incised or carved either in relief or the full round. The animals were rendered with vivid realism and sympathetic insight into their character and feelings, qualities lasting through the whole history of Persian art.

The Achaemenid empire, founded by Cyrus (reigned 550–530 B.C.) and consolidated by Darius the Great (reigned 522–486 B.C.), included all western Asia to the Nile and the Aegean. Prodigious wealth poured into Persia from the well-governed dependent states, making possible the creation of an imperial religious architecture, particularly at Persepolis (begun 518 B.C.). This city was distinguished by a series of temples and royal residences of great size and magnificence. They featured widely spaced, fluted columns 65 ft. high, representing trees, symbols of cosmic vitality. The base courses were enriched by long sculptured friezes of tribute bearers—dignified, lucid, graceful, tranquil, infused with a reverential spirit appropriate to the religious monotheism of Darius, who planned the city.

Political and religious revival under the powerful Sasanian empire (222–640 A.D.) inspired impressive architecture with notable dome and vault construction. The main vault of the gigantic barrel-vaulted hall of Taq-i-Kisra, the ruins of which still stand in Ctesiphon, was 86 ft. wide and 96 ft. high. Such halls were richly ornamented with mother-of-pearl, polychrome stucco, and heroic murals. The floor was decorated with a vast silk million-jeweled carpet. Sasanian textiles, bronze vessels, and silver plates with vigorously drawn ritualistic animals and hunting scenes are in the heroic mood, expressing confidence and power.

In the 9th century A.D. eastern Persia (Nishapur and Samarkand) produced pottery ornamented largely with lustrous black designs on milk-white, of such decorative energy that these wares are now ranked among the noblest examples of ceramic art. Luxury wares in pottery reached a climax of elegance and poetic feeling in the early 13th century, especially at Rayy and Kashan. Rich and sophisticated in color, these were sometimes coated in flashing golden luster and decorated with abstract traditional patterns or lively miniature paintings. Bronze vessels of expressive shape inlaid with silver and gold, sometimes brilliantly pictorial, competed for favor among the royalty.

The dignified and austere architecture of the Seljuk period (1037–1190) includes some of the noblest buildings in Persia or anywhere else. Unexcelled masters of brickwork, Seljuk builders constructed single-shell domes approaching mathematical perfection, which have stood intact for nearly 900 years. Their Gothic-looking vaults may have influenced medieval architecture in Europe. The finest of these structures is the Great Mosque at Isfahan.

The Mongol period (1220–1404) saw a succession of buildings of colossal size. These include the Tomb of Ghazan Khan (c.1293), 200 ft. high; the Mosque of Ali Shah, with a vault 100 ft. wide and almost 150 ft. high; the beautiful domed Mausoleum of Uljaitu at Sultaniyeh (c.1305); and similar, even larger buildings in Samarkand. All were lavishly polychromed by painting, colored stucco paneling, and in the later part of the period by faïence mosaic. These major structures expressed the power and the glory of the Mongol rulers, although throughout Persia there were many more modest mosques and tombs of beautiful design and exquisite color (for example, at Varamin, Natanz, Yezd, and Formurad).

In the 15th, 16th, and 17th centuries Persian love of color combined with brilliant and sophisticated patterns came to a dazzling fulfillment not only in sumptuous and subtle fabrics, often gold enriched, but also in miniature paintings of intense jewel-colors and in exquisite drawings —revelations that have "the glory and freshness of a dream." Great carpets, unique in splendor, and vessels of gold and enamel, completed ensembles of furnishings that dazzled European travelers.

Architecture, by this time refined and matured, was everywhere incrusted with dazzling tile—turquoise, cobalt, yellow, white, emerald, black—in harmony and intensity not equaled in any other land. The finest examples are in Meshed (especially in a mosque dedicated in 1418) and in Isfahan (15th to 17th century). These styles continued into the 18th century, gradually losing quality as the economic and political power of Persia steadily declined.

Gardens, symbols of Paradise, were from earliest days (perhaps 4000 B.C.) one of the essential arts of Persia. No home, palace, or mosque ever lacked its pool. These gardens, such as Ferahabad in Isfahan, might be miles in extent, with canals, fountains, and exquisite pavilions in abundance. This art spread to India, where the great gardens were of Persian inspiration, as were many structures, such as the Taj Mahal.

ARTABAZUS [är-tə-bā′zəs] (c.387–325 B.C.), Persian general during the reigns of Artaxerxes II, Artaxerxes III, and Darius III. He was hereditary satrap of Phrygia. Ariobarzanes, administrator of the province during Artabazus' minority, refused to relinquish it in 367, and thereby started the Satraps' Revolt (367–353).

ARTAPHERNES [är-tə-fûr′nēz] (fl. late 6th century B.C.), Persian general, son of Hystaspes, and brother of Darius I (the Great). He was one of "The Seven" who helped Darius seize the Achaemenid throne. As satrap of Sardis he supervised the Ionian Greek cities, surveyed Ionia, fixed city taxes, and was instrumental in suppressing the Ionian revolt of 499–498 B.C. His son, Artaphernes (fl.5th century B.C.), was satrap of Lydia. Darius appointed him and the Mede, Datis, generals to take Athens and Eretria in the Persian invasion of Greece which was defeated at Marathon (490 B.C.). In 481 he led the Lydians in the expedition of Xerxes I against Greece.

ARTAXERXES [är-tə-zûrk′sēz] I, called Longimanus, Persian King of the Achaemenid dynasty (reigned 465–424 B.C.), second son of Xerxes I. Enthroned by Artabanus, his father's murderer, he was persuaded to kill his elder brother. In 464 Artaxerxes turned on Artabanus and killed him. During his reign an Egypto-Athenian revolt and a Bactrian rebellion were suppressed by peaceful diplomacy. He sanctioned the return of the Jews to Palestine and supported the missions of Ezra and Nehemiah for the rebuilding of Jerusalem.

ARTAXERXES II, called Mnemon (reigned 404–358 B.C.), son of Darius II and his successor on the Persian throne. In 401 B.C. he put down a rebellion by his brother Cyrus, satrap of Asia Minor, whose defeat and death at Cunaxa occasioned the famous retreat of his 10,000 Greek mercenaries, recorded by Xenophon in the *Anabasis*. A series of rebellions marked the reign of Artaxerxes II, but he maintained Persian supremacy by fostering dissension among the rival city states in Greece.

ARTAXERXES III, originally Ochus (reigned 358–338 B.C.), son of Artaxerxes II. Seizing the throne after murdering his family, he proceeded to strengthen the declining Persian Empire by compelling the satraps to dismiss their Greek mercenaries. His reconquest of Egypt and Phoenicia led Philip of Macedon to negotiate a Greco-Persian alliance. His death at the hands of his minister Bagoas ended the greatness of the Achaemenids.

CAMBYSES [kăm-bī′sēz] **II,** King of Persia (reigned 529–521 B.C.), son of Cyrus the Great. Soon after his accession he had his brother Bardiya (Smerdis) murdered, though he kept this secret. In 526 he invaded Egypt, where popular unrest prevailed, and by 525 had taken the capital Saïs, defeated and killed King Psamtik III, and made Egypt a satrapy. He also received the submission of Libyans and Greeks at Cyrene and Barca. But further expeditions against Carthage, Siwa, and Ethiopia failed. He died by suicide in Syria while returning to suppress a revolt raised by the Magian priest Gaumata (the false Smerdis) who, claiming to be the real Bardiya, had seized the throne. His reputation for cruelty is considered by modern scholars to be exaggerated.

CYAXARES [sī-ăk′sə-rēz] (reigned c.625–585 B.C.), King of Media, founder of the Median Empire. The son of Phraortes, he established Median independence by reducing the Achaemenids (Persians) to vassalage, and by defeating the Scythians, to whom the Medes had paid tribute for 28 years. With Nabopolassar of Babylonia he destroyed the Assyrian capital Nineveh in 612, and thereafter subjected northern Assyria, northern Mesopotamia, Armenia, and Cappadocia. His decisive battle against Lydia was stalemated by a solar eclipse (May 28, 585), resulting in the establishment of the Halys River as the boundary between the two kingdoms.

CYRUS [sī′rəs] **THE GREAT** (reigned 550–530 B.C.), King of Persia, founder of the Persian Empire. He was the son of Cambyses I and Mandane, daughter of the Median King Astyages. Ascending the throne of Anshan at Pasargadae in Parsa in 559 as vassal of Astyages, Cyrus in 550 overthrew the Median King in battle, assumed the throne of Media, and established a capital at Ecbatana. Median control gave Cyrus authority over Assyria, northern Mesopotamia, Syria, Armenia, and Cappadocia. In 547 he conquered Lydia from Croesus, and thereafter subdued the Greek cities of the Asia Minor coast.

In 546 Gobryas, Governor of Elam, which was then subject to Nabonidus of Babylonia, revolted, and Elam was incorporated into the Medo-Persian Empire. Then, turning eastward, Cyrus rapidly built an empire that extended from the southeast Caspian to the Jaxartes River in Sogdiana and beyond the Indus River in India. In 539 Cyrus's army captured Babylon. The Kings of Syria paid him homage, and Syria, Phoenicia, Palestine, and Babylonia became one great satrapy.

As King of the Universe, Cyrus proclaimed peace for all. In 537 he permitted 40,000 captive Jews to return to Palestine to rebuild the Temple of Solomon and was called by them "the Lord's Anointed." Virtually everywhere he appeared as a liberator, a tolerant, just, and efficient administrator. Restoring temples, honoring local divinities and customs, supporting native pride, he created an organic complex of cultures, joined for mutual advantage. Cyrus was killed while subduing nomad revolts on the eastern border, and was buried at Pasargadae.

CYRUS THE YOUNGER (424–401 B.C.), son of Darius II of Persia. Appointed commander of Asia Minor in 408, he helped finance Sparta in the Peloponnesian War. On the accession of his brother Artaxerxes II in 404, Cyrus plotted for the throne. Tissaphernes, satrap of Lower Asia, denounced him to Artaxerxes, but he was saved from death by his mother, Parysatis. However, he again plotted rebellion. With an army totalling perhaps 30,000, including 13,000 Greek mercenaries, Cyrus in 401 advanced from Sardis to Babylonia, demonstrating masterful skill throughout these difficult preparations. He met Artaxerxes at Cunaxa. Though his army was at first victorious, Cyrus was himself slain. In his *Anabasis*, Xenophon characterizes Cyrus in glowing terms.

DARIUS [də-rī′əs] **I**, also known as Darius the Great (c.550–486 B.C.), King of Persia (reigned 522–486 B.C.), son of Hystaspes. As one of the seven noble Persians who killed the usurper Gaumata, he was chosen to succeed Cambyses. At his accession, the empire was in chaos; his first two years were devoted to suppressing revolts in Persia, Media, Babylonia, and the eastern provinces. Darius then reorganized the empire into 20 satrapies, each governed by a satrap, who was checked by a general and secretary of state; all three received their orders separately and were directly responsible to the Great King. Special traveling agents (secret police) also reported to the court. Although Darius centralized authority to prevent anarchy, he allowed each province a certain autonomy in its form of government and institutions, and encouraged regional cultures and religions. His successful system of government outlasted the Achaemenid period and was adopted by Alexander the Great.

Darius was the first Persian monarch to coin money and to base the economy on a yearly fixed tax. To facilitate commerce and aid centralization he extended the Royal Road connecting his capital, Susa, with Sardis, in Asia Minor, 1,500 mi. distant. He also completed a canal from the Nile to the Red Sea. In 513 he invaded India, annexing the Punjab Sind, and in 512 he temporarily subdued Thrace and Macedonia, though his punitive attack on the Scythians was inconclusive. He put down the rebellious Greek cities of Ionia in 497, but his punitive expeditions against Athens and the rest of Greece met disaster in 492, when his fleet was wrecked off Mount Athos, and again in 490 when his troops were defeated at Marathon. Before he could lead another campaign against Greece, Egypt revolted (486) and Darius died, after ruling ably for 36 years.

DARIUS II, original name Ochus, Persian King, reigned 424–404 B.C., illegitimate son of Artaxerxes I. He gained the throne by killing his half brother Sogdianus, who had murdered the legitimate heir, Xerxes II. By his half sister and wife, Parysatis, he fathered Artaxerxes II and Cyrus the Younger. His misgovernment led to successive insurrections and the loss of Egypt in 410. However, his satraps Tissaphernes and Pharnabazus successfully interfered in Greek politics to effect the defeat of Athens in the Peloponnesian War.

DARIUS III, original name Codomannus (c.380–330 B.C.), last King of Persia, reigned 336–330 B.C. He was enthroned by the clever eunuch Bagoas, who had murdered Artaxerxes III and his son Arses, and who intended to make him a puppet; but Darius executed Bagoas. Darius was routed by Alexander the Great on the plain of Issus in 333, and again at the battle of Gaugamela in 331. He himself escaped to Ecbatana, but his disorganized army could thereafter sustain only guerrilla resistance. Darius was

Museo Nazionale, Naples

Detail from a mosaic discovered in Pompeii depicts Darius III in battle with Alexander the Great on the plain of Issus.

eventually murdered by Bessus, satrap of Bactria, on the approach of Alexander.

FIRDAWSI [fĭr-dou'sē] **or FIRDUSI** [fĭr-dōō'sē], pseudonym of Abu'l-Qasim (c.940–c.1020), renowned Persian epic poet. Author of Iran's greatest epic, the *Shahnama* (Book of Kings), he is reputed to have spent 30 years (980–1010) on its 60,000 rhyming couplets. Virtually nothing certain is known of his life, but Firdawsi was an impoverished country gentleman of northeastern Iran, the area most resistant to Islam and to Arab influences generally. Doubtless a good Muslim, he yet embodied in his poem all his countrymen's pride in their ancient, pre-Islamic civilization. He drew on oral traditions and earlier writings to present, in the purest Persian, all Iranian legend and history from the beginning of time to the fall of the Sassanian Dynasty (c.652). Iranians of all classes have always loved to sing from their great national song. Western critics who complain of its monotony and stereotyped style often overlook passages of wit, urbanity, beauty, and narrative power. *The Shahnama of Firdausi* (9 vols., 1905–25; trans. by A. G. and E. Warner) is the latest annotated translation.

MANI [mä'nē] (c.216–76), founder of Manichaeism (q.v.). A noble Iranian of Ecbatana, born in Ctesiphon, he was brought up in an eclectic Babylonian Christian cult. About 242 he proclaimed his own "revealed" religion, adding to Babylonian and Christian factors dogmas adapted from Buddhism and Iranian mythology. It focused on the opposition between Light and Darkness. He proselytized in northern India, Tibet, Chinese Turkestan, and Khurasan. Returning (c.270) to Shapur's court, he had to flee to avoid arrest. Hormizd (reigned 272–73) apparently was friendly, but Bahram I (reigned 273–76) did not protect him. The Zoroastrian Magi flayed (c.276) him alive; his stuffed skin was publicly hung, and his followers were relentlessly persecuted.

MANICHAEISM [măn-ə-kē'ĭz-əm], a religion founded by the fanatic Persian mystic Mani (c.242 A.D.). Manichaeism was dualistic, holding that there are two major conflicting forces in the world. There is the good, spiritual power of Light and the evil, material power of Darkness. Man, a creation of Evil, but compounded in part of Light, was to strive to release the Light within himself in order to bring about the ultimate triumph of Light over Darkness. Members of this secretive sect who rejected the material in favor of austerity became "elect" or perfect, assured that death would mean immediate entry into eternal bliss. Adherents of lesser purity, known as auditors—St. Augustine was an auditor for a decade prior to his conversion to Christianity—could be reborn to try to perfect themselves and become "elect." Those who rejected the Manichaean revelation were doomed to eternal darkness.

Manichaeism was a blending of Zoroastrianism, with notions borrowed from Buddhism, Gnosticism, and orthodox Christianity. The Manichaeans were thought of by some people, including some of their own followers, as heretic Christians. Mani had in fact declared that his message superseded that of Jesus. Despite persecution, Manichaeism spread widely in the East and the West, and traces of it were still found in Asia in the 17th century.

MARDONIUS [mär-dō'nē-əs] (d.479 B.C.), Persian general, son of Gobryas and nephew of Darius I. In 492 B.C. he was sent by Darius to punish Athens and Eretria for aiding the Ionians; he subdued Macedonia, but half his supply fleet was destroyed in a storm off Mount Athos, thus preventing extension of the campaign. Mardonius later persuaded Xerxes to renew the effort against Greece. The Persian attempt of 480 was at first successful but collapsed with the failure at Salamis. Mardonius and his army remained in Greece, where he was killed in the defeat at Plataea in 479.

MITHRA [mĭth'rə] **or MITHRAS** [mĭth'rəs], ancient Indo-Iranian god. The worship of this deity was brought by migrating Indo-European people into India, northern Mesopotamia, and Iran. In India the god was called Mitra and was associated with Varuna in the highest heaven. A treaty, concluded by the Indo-European rulers of the Hittite and Mitannian empires in the 14th century B.C., reflects the early spread of Mithra to northern Mesopotamia. In Iran the cult achieved considerable importance. Mithra was first worshiped as a god of light, whose chief functions were the protection of contract, the fostering of justice, and the dispelling of darkness and evil. The early Achaemenid kings of Persia (6th-5th century B.C.) viewed him as the heroic helper of the great god Ahura Mazda. In the reign of Artaxerxes II (404–358 B.C.), Mithra joined Ahura Mazda and Anahita in the official Achaemenid pantheon. With the collapse of that dynasty, the cult declined. It was briefly revived by the Parthians in the 1st century A.D., and declined once again in the East under the Sassanid dynasty (3d-7th centuries A.D.).

Mithraism enjoyed its greatest growth and influence in the West. Spreading to Anatolia in the 5th century B.C., it was influenced by Chaldean astrology and Greek mystery religions. It was adopted in Cappadocia and by the pirates of Cilicia. Mithra was gradually transformed into a sacrificial sun-god and had great appeal for the lower

An antique statue of Mithra killing the sacred bull. In Mithraic belief, the bull gave birth to all living things by its death.
(ALINARI—ART REFERENCE BUREAU)

classes in particular. The cult was very popular among the Roman legions in Asia Minor, who saw Mithra, the god of justice, as the soldier's comrade. The legionaries spread the cult along the Danube and Rhine rivers, and as far west as Britain. The central event of Mithraism during the Roman Empire was Mithra's sacrificial slaying of the sacred bull. This was alien to the god's earlier Zoroastrian associations. In Mithraic reliefs, the hero, wearing the Phrygian cap, is depicted plunging his dagger into the bull. Because the death of the bull was thought to give birth to all living things, Mithra, its slayer, was considered a creative force.

Mithraism was a mystery religion into which any male of any social class might be inducted. This initiation involved a seven-stage process, which reflected the belief in seven planetary levels through which the devout ascended to Heaven. All initiates were of equal standing since there was no priestly hierarchy. Mithraism included rites, such as baptism and a sacred meal. Mithra promised immortality to the faithful at the end of time and thus took on the aspect of a savior, or intercessor. Believers were expected to adhere to a rigorous moral code. Mithraic emphasis on the triumph of good over evil, its promise of immortality, and its moral content enabled it to compete with Christianity for the hearts of men for three centuries. Mithra even exerted some influence on Christianity through a 3d-century cult called Manichaeism, an offshoot of Zoroastrianism.

PASARGADAE [pə-sär′gə-dē], earliest capital of ancient Persia, 54 mi. northeast of Persepolis, the later capital, and 60 mi. northeast of modern Shiraz, Iran. Cyrus the Great (reigned 550–530 B.C.) established his capital here, presumably on the site of his decisive victory (550 B.C.) over the Median King Astyages. A vast platform of cyclopean stones laid without mortar, the antecedent of the better-known Persepolis terrace, was built. On this platform was an imposing complex of palaces and temples surrounded by parks and gardens, of which only a few standing columns and masses of fragments remain. A square temple-tower built by Cyrus encloses a stairway to the single room where the sacred fire burned perpetually. The impressive tomb of Cyrus also stands here. Darius I (reigned 522–486 B.C.), who belonged to another branch of the family, abandoned Pasargadae, but the coronation ceremony of all Persian kings was held here until the fall of the Achaemenid Empire.

PERSEPOLIS [pər-sĕp′ə-lis], residential and ceremonial capital of the Achaemenid dynasty of ancient Persia, located 30 mi. northeast of Shiraz, Iran. Darius the Great, who reigned 522–486 B.C., was anxious to avoid associations with Pasargadae, the former capital. He began construction of a new palace complex called, like the country, Parsa. The Greeks mistakenly used the name Persepolis, "the city of the Persians." Susa, Babylon, and Ecbatana remained the administrative centers of the Persian Empire.

The impressive ruins of Persepolis date chiefly to the period c.518–460 B.C. The palace complex was erected upon a 32-acre terrace built partly from natural rock and partly from large stone blocks. Access to the terrace was provided on the west by means of a magnificent double staircase, wide enough to accommodate 10 men abreast and gradual enough to permit horses to mount the stairs. Dominating the ruins atop the terrace is the Apadana (Pers. "Hall of Pillars"), the royal audience hall of Darius and Xerxes. This structure consisted of 72 columns, each about 65 ft. high, surmounted by capitals of back-to-back forequarters of bulls and lions. South of the Apadana is the palace of Darius and the larger *hadish* (palace) of Xerxes. The latter consists of a pillared hall flanked by various rooms. A throne room with 100 columns was completed by Artaxerxes I. Other important remains are those of the Treasuries, the gate of Xerxes, flanked by human-headed bulls, the Harem, and the palace of Artaxerxes III.

The styles employed at Persepolis were largely borrowed from earlier Achaemenid structures at Susa and Parsargadae. They also show some influences from various parts of the Persian Empire. Persepolis was partly burned by Alexander the Great in 330 B.C.

PERSIAN WAR (499–479 B.C.). The struggle between the Persian Empire and mainland Greece can be said to have begun with the revolt of the Ionian Greek cities of Asia Minor against Persia and ended only with the conquest of Persia by Alexander the Great 170 years later. But the end of the first phase (known as the Persian War) is marked by the repulse of the most serious direct Persian attack on European Greece in 480–479 B.C.

The flourishing Greek states on the Asia Minor coast resented even indirect Persian interference with their political autonomy. Under the leadership of Aristagoras of Miletus they revolted and called on their mainland kin for help. While there was considerable sympathy for the insurgents, only Athens and Eretria sent tangible aid. This was provocation enough, however, to harden King Darius' intention to subjugate Greece.

When the Ionian revolt had been suppressed (494 B.C.), the Persian general Mardonius conquered Thrace and Macedonia (492 B.C.). Then a powerful fleet under Datis

and Artaphernes crossed the Aegean in 490 B.C., captured Eretria, and proceeded to attack Athens. Probably on the advice of the exiled tryant Hippias, who accompanied them, the Persians landed at Marathon on the east coast of Attica, intending to march on the city overland. Spartan aid did not arrive in spite of Pheidippides' 150-mi. run to notify them of the threat, and the Athenian army faced the Persians with no allies except 1,000 soldiers from Plataea. The battle of Marathon was won through the bold strategy of the Athenian general Miltiades. The victory resulted in a great surge of self-confidence in Athens. Themistocles began building a powerful fleet. Efforts at Panhellenic co-operation were now more seriously undertaken, for there was no doubt that Persia would try again.

Xerxes, the new King, launched a diplomatic offensive which neutralized much of northern and central Greece. Then in 480 B.C. he mounted a huge attack by land and sea. Units of the Greek army under King Leonidas of Sparta attempted to hold the pass of Thermopylae, while the fleet engaged the Persians at the nearby straits of Artemisium. The Greeks were defeated in both engagements; the Greek army retreated to the Isthmus of Corinth, while their fleet evacuated the whole population of Athens and took up its position in the straits of Salamis. There Themistocles, the Athenian admiral, forced a decisive sea battle, perhaps by falsely warning the Persians that the Greeks intended to slip away. In a confined area the superior maneuverability of the Greek ships and discipline of their crews overwhelmed the Persians.

Xerxes' surviving ships fled and the King retreated by land with most of his troops, leaving Mardonius in command of a still formidable force. The next year a large Greek army commanded by the Spartan King Pausanias invaded central Greece and routed the Persians at Plataea in Boeotia. Concurrently the Greek fleet invaded east Aegean waters and (by tradition on the same day as Plataea) defeated the Persians off Cape Mycale. This action initiated a series of Greek counterattacks on Asia Minor which continued until the mid-5th century and which secured independence for the Asiatic Greeks. Greek success in exploding the myth of Persian invincibility had a profound psychological effect. Henceforth Persian prestige gradually deteriorated and a balance of power was barely maintained through Persian exploitation of rivalries among the Greeks themselves.

SASANIDAE [să-săn'ĭ-dē], Persian dynasty which ruled Iran from 224 to 641 A.D., founded by Sasan, a Mazdean priest at Persepolis. Some 555 years after the fall of the Achaemenid empire, the Sasanians, claiming descent from the Achaemenids, re-established Iranian traditions undiluted by Greek influence. This period marks the apogee of Zoroastrianism (q.v.).

ARDASHIR I, grandson of Sasan, in 224 seized power from the Parthian King, Artabanus V, and claimed the title "King of Kings." Ardashir's son, SHAPUR I (241–72), established the international prestige of the dynasty by capturing Roman Emperor Valerian at Edessa in 260.

Wars with Rome were recurrent in the 4th and 5th centuries, the balance of power at first tipping in Iran's favor, especially under SHAPUR II, in whose reign (309–79) the

Romans temporarily abandoned Armenia. But during the 5th century conditions throughout the Sasanian empire deteriorated in almost every respect. Confusion was deliberately increased by separatist trends in the feudal aristocracy and by the revolutionary Mazdakite movement, which opposed Zoroastrianism and the Sasanian social order. Added danger came from Roman encroachments in Persian Armenia.

However, under KHOSRAU I (531–79), who defeated the Ephthalites (White Huns) and the Byzantines, restored political coherence and prosperity brought about a brilliant cultural renaissance. But stability was short-lived. KHOSRAU II (590–628), after conquering Asia Minor and threatening Constantinople itself, was defeated by the Emperor Heraclius and then assassinated by his own people. The last Sasanian King, YAZDEGIRD III (632–51), after being driven from Mesopotamia in 636, was finally defeated by the Arabs at Nihawand in 641. Iran then became a Muslim country.

SATRAP [să'trăp], governor of a satrapy, or province, of the ancient Persian Empire. His responsibilities included collecting taxes, controlling local administration, and insuring road safety. To check the ambition of the satraps, Darius I (reigned 522–486 B.C.) reorganized the provincial system by centralizing control of imperial troops and installing royal secretaries and advisers known as the "eye of the king." As the Empire decayed, however, the satrapies obtained greater autonomy.

SHAPUR [shă-pōōr'] I, Sasanian Persian King (241–72), son of Ardashir I. In 244 he terminated the war with Rome begun by his father, gaining control of Armenia. He then subdued various areas in Azerbaijan, the Caspian region, and Khurasan. In a second war with Rome he took the Emperor Valerian prisoner in 260—a triumph illustrated in a rock relief at Naksh-i-Rustam. After ravaging Syria c.262, he was defeated by a Palmyra-Roman alliance but retained his power and prestige. He authorized construction of large-scale public works, including the extant Karun dam.

SHAPUR II, Sasanian Persian King (309–79). He succeeded to the Iranian throne as a minor under his mother's regency. In the second half of his reign he appears as a vigorous monarch, annexing Kushan territory in the east and confronting the Romans in the west. Internal dissensions in Armenia provoked a new Perso-Roman war in 359, in which the Emperor Julian was killed (363). A 30-year peace negotiated shortly thereafter was soon broken by recurrent Roman-Armenian plotting, which Shapur eliminated only shortly before his death.

TISSAPHERNES [tĭs-ə-fûr'nēz] (d.395 B.C.), Persian satrap of Lydia from 413 B.C. and of all western Asia after 401. By intrigue he acquired great power in Greek politics, using a Spartan alliance against Athens to weaken both states. He warned Darius II (reigned 424–404 B.C.), just before his death, of the perfidy of Cyrus the Younger, the King's second son. But when Artaxerxes II (reigned 404–358 B.C.) succeeded to the throne, he forgave Cyrus, who assembled Greek troops and attacked Artaxerxes' army in the battle of Cunaxa (401 B.C.). Cyrus was killed, and Tissaphernes negotiated a truce, permitting the Greeks to undertake the famous retreat of the 10,000, but treacherously seized their generals. Tissaphernes and the satrap Pharnabazus sustained elaborate but inconclusive intrigues in Asia Minor. After being defeated by the Spartans, Tissaphernes was assassinated by order of Artaxerxes.

XERXES [zûrk'sēz] **I,** King of Persia (486–465 B.C.), son of Darius I and Atossa. By 483 he had crushed rebellions in Egypt and Babylonia, and had begun to assemble a vast imperial army and navy to invade Greece in retaliation for the Greek victory over Darius at Marathon in 490. In the spring of 480 Xerxes set forth from Sardis at the head of the greatest force ever assembled in antiquity. Crossing the Hellespont by a bridge of boats, he marched through Thrace, Macedonia, and Thessaly, and after overcoming the Spartans at Thermopylae, quickly overran central Greece and Attica.

Meanwhile, though a storm had seriously damaged the Persian fleet, the Greek navy withdrew from Artemisium. The Persian fleet arrived at Phalerum as Xerxes captured Athens. From Mount Aigaleos Xerxes witnessed the naval battle of Salamis, in which the Greeks under Themistocles routed the Persians. Cut off from his supplies, Xerxes withdrew to Asia, leaving his general Mardonius to complete operations in Greece. The Persians, however, met defeat in 479 at both Plataea and Mycale. After 12 more years of fighting, Xerxes' forces were driven out of Asia Minor. Xerxes was later assassinated by a Guard captain, Artabanus. Xerxes is the Ahasuerus of Esther 1:1 in the Old Testament.

XERXES II, King of Persia (424 B.C.), son of Artaxerxes I. He was murdered, shortly after succeeding to the throne, by his brother Sogdianus.

ZOROASTRIANISM [zō-rō-ăs'trē-ən-ĭz-əm], Persian religion founded by the reformer Zoroaster (q.v.) in the late 7th or early 6th century B.C. The official religion of the Achaemenid dynasty, it was revived by the Sassanid rulers. As a state religion, Zoroastrianism was abolished after the Islamic conquest in the 7th century A.D. It is still practised by the Ghebers of Iran and Parsis of India, in somewhat modified form. The sacred books of Zoroastrianism, known collectively as the Zend Avesta, were not written down until the early Christian era. The Avesta represents a confused and sometimes contradictory compilation of the teachings of Zoroaster and the doctrinal accretions of subsequent centuries.

Zoroastrianism was a monotheistic faith with a strong ethical emphasis centering about the dualistic concept of the conflict between Good and Evil. Good was manifest in the creator-god of light and truth, Ahura Mazda, the great, beneficent Wise Lord. His evil opponent was Angra, Mainyu, or Ahriman, the spirit of darkness. The ultimate triumph of Ahura Mazda was assured. But during the struggle, men could aid the cause of Ahura Mazda by making free ethical choices and judgments in their daily lives. These were made with reference to the Amesha Spentas, moral entities created by Ahura Mazda. They were Justice, or Truth, Good Thought, Dominion, Piety, Prosperity, Immortality, and Obedience. It was believed by some that Zoroaster would return to prepare the coming of the final judgment.

The belief in a future life and in immortality is revealed in the concept of the Last Judgment. On that day, Ahura Mazda was to assign the upright to Heaven (immortality) and consign the followers of Ahriman to the regions of eternal darkness. Pride, sloth, and gluttony were among the sins, while representative virtues were tilling the soil, obedience to authority, fulfilling contracts, and showing mercy. Traditional Zoroastrianism was opposed to excessive fasting or grief, animal sacrifice, idol worship, or asceticism. Zoroastrianism influenced Christianity indirectly through other religions to which it gave birth, such as Mithraism and Manichaeism.

ROMAN CIVILIZATION

ANCIENT CITY

The ancient city was never completely buried or forgotten. Many buildings remained visible and in use throughout the centuries. But with the renewed interest in the antique which characterized the Renaissance, a new impetus was given to study and investigation of the ancient remains. Since the 19th century, excavations in the modern sense, especially of the second quarter of the 20th century, have revealed the history of the monuments of ancient Rome, from the foundation of the city through the period of the kings, the Republic, and the Empire.

Rome in the Regal Period. Traditionally, the earliest settlement was made on the Palatine hill in 753 B.C., and post holes for simple oval houses of this period have been found there. Gradually habitation extended to other nearby hills. The valleys between (notably the area later to become the Roman Forum) were first used as cemeteries for the inhabitants of these villages on the hills, but were later occupied by houses. The incorporation of these originally separate settlements into one community is attested by the cemeteries showing more than one set of burial customs. By the early 6th century the valley between the Palatine and the Capitoline was drained and paved with pebbles to serve as the civic center for the now united settlements on the surrounding hills (Palatine, Quirinal, Viminial, Esquiline, Caelian).

In this earliest period of the Forum the essential monuments of the kingdom were established. These included the shrines of Vesta and Janus, and the Regia, seat of the king as both chief priest and head of government, at one end, with an early inscription marking a sacred area at the other. The Capitoline hill, rising west of the Forum, served as the center of the state religion, as it was to remain throughout antiquity. By the late 6th century B.C. a monumental temple to Jupiter Optimus Maximus, in the Etruscan style, decorated with terra-cotta sculpture, was erected by the last of those Etruscan kings who made 6th-century Rome an Etruscan town. For entertainment they provided the Circus Maximus, between the Palatine and Aventine hills, for races and games, the taste for which they had brought to Rome and which were to remain a principal interest of Romans throughout antiquity.

The Face of Republican Rome. With the expulsion of the last King and the establishment of the Republic in 510 B.C. provision had to be made for meetings of the senate and the assembly of the people. At the northwest end of the Forum, the Curia, an enclosed rectangular room for the senate, was erected above the center of the open, roughly semicircular area for the people, facing the rostra, the speaker's platform. From the 5th to the 1st century many temples were built in the Forum Romanum, in the Forum Boarium and Forum Holitorium, the cattle and vegetable markets along the Tiber, and in the Campus Martius, the open space between the Capitoline and the river. All deities of the old Roman religion were housed within the official religious limits of the early unified city (pomerium). But the many foreign gods, those imported by other Latin peoples or the Greek deities imported by official priestly command or the Oriental cults imported by popular demand, had to be settled outside the pomerium on the Aventine, or farther still in the Campus Martius.

Some of the few temples which survive today can be identified. These are the temples of Saturn, Castor and Pollux, and Concordia in the Forum Romanum; of Janus, Juno Sospita, and Spes and Pietas in the Forum Holitorium; of Magna Mater on the Palatine, Apollo in the Campus Martius, and Aesculapius on the island in the Tiber (scantily preserved). The identity of others is in dispute: for example, the rectangular and round temples in the Forum Boarium (traditionally ascribed to Fortuna Virilis and Vesta), the pair in the neighborhoring Sant'-Omobona area, and the four in the modern Largo Argentina. All these were built originally in the Etruscan style, which continued to be the artistic tradition in Rome until the 2d century B.C., when the conquest of Greece brought Greek artists and ideas to Rome. Then the terra-cotta revetted timber and mud brick structures gave way to all stone or stone and concrete buildings in the Greek orders, still retaining the native Italic plan and podium. Most Republican temples were rebuilt more than once, often both in late Republican times and again later, in marble.

Utilitarian Building. Business of the Republic was conducted, when not in the open forums, in wooden shops along the sides. These tabernae in the Forum Romanum gave way in the 2d and 1st centuries to basilicas. They offered larger covered space for business establishments and law courts, such as the Basilicas Porcia, Aemilia, Sempronia, and Opimia, of which the Aemilia and the Sempronia, rebuilt by Caesar, remain in part. The basement of the Temple of Saturn served as the treasury. An archives building was added to the Senate House. A large circular former cistern at the foot of the Capitoline (known today as the Mamertine Prison) served as state prison and housed many prisoners famous in history, including St. Peter according to tradition. Remains of warehouses along the river for the storage of grain still exist.

By the late Republic the majority of Romans were living in the many-storied apartment houses, constructed of wood and unbaked brick, which were the prototype for the typical urban dwelling in Italy thereafter. Material and construction improved in the Empire and later, but there has been little change in the general design of multiple stories of groups of rooms facing onto an open court, with the ground floor occupied by shops. These *insulae* along narrow streets crowded the Caelian and Aventine hills and the lower slopes of the Quirinal, Viminal, and Esquiline hills. The wealthier classes lived on the Palatine and the upper parts of the Esquiline and Quirinal hills, in fine private houses, with rooms decorated with wall paintings, surrounding open courts and gardens. Many of these houses have been found in excavating for modern construction.

To provide water for the rapidly expanding population, the city built the Appian aqueduct, an underground channel, in 312 B.C. to bring water to Rome from about 10 mi. away in the Campagna. By 144 B.C., this and the later Anio Vetus (272 B.C.) were inadequate, so the Marcian aqueduct, first of the great aqueducts of the Republic and Empire, was built on stone arches to bring spring water from 56 mi. away in the Sabine hills. The same springs serve Rome today. Claudius' aqueduct in the early Empire surpassed all these in length.

In the 2d century stone arch construction was also applied to the bridges across the Tiber which carried the main roads leading out of Rome to all parts of Italy. First built was the Pons Aemilius (142 B.C.), which replaced the earliest wooden bridge (from regal times) across to the Janiculum. Then the Milvian Bridge (109 B.C.) which carried the Via Flaminia northeastward (the original piers still standing) was constructed. In 62 B.C. the Fabricius, whose arches have carried traffic to the island ever since it was built, was erected. A few years later the Pons Cestius completed the passage from the island to the Transtiberim (modern Trastevere) section of the city. These two bridges still form one of the principal routes to the Janiculum. The first of those freestanding monumental arches so favored in the Empire was built by Fabius Maximus across the Sacred Way at the entrance to the Forum in 121 B.C.

The increasing population also demanded further entertainment facilities. An additional circus was built in the Campus Martius by the censor Flaminius in 221 B.C. and given his name. Interest in theatrical performances came later. The earliest permanent stone theater was built in 55 B.C. on a vaulted substructure near the Circus Flaminius by Pompey, who provided it with works of art and with a great portico surrounding a garden. In its halls Julius Caesar was murdered in 44 B.C.

Tradition ascribes to King Servius Tullius a wall surrounding the city of the 6th century, the Four Regions. But the so-called Servian Wall of squared stone blocks, existing in considerable stretches around that area, dates rather from the early 4th century, after the Gallic invasion of 390. Some earlier bits of walls may represent the defenses of the early settlements thrown into one by Servius. Not until the 3d century A.D. was another wall built—the brick-faced concrete wall with towers, with which Aurelian surrounded the extended imperial city. This stands almost complete, having enclosed the whole modern city until recent times.

A City of Marble. The famous remark that Augustus found Rome a city of brick and left it a city of marble epitomizes the change that came over Rome during the Empire. The victorious generals of the late 2d century B.C., returning from Greece and the East, had donated the first marble buildings. Increasingly in the last century of the Republic more marble had been used for temples. Above all, Greek orders and architectural style were copied and adapted more than before. Beginning with Augustus (27 B.C.–14 A.D.), however, Greek orders with new Roman variations were regularly employed and adapted to all kinds of buildings. The building material was the brick-faced concrete, faced with white or colored marble, which made possible the engineering achievements in vaulted space.

Julius Caesar had recognized the need to open up more space in the heart of the city for public use and to facilitate movement of traffic from the Forum to the Campus Martius. Besides rebuilding much of the old Forum, he built his own forum which filled those needs and set the pattern for the subsequent forums added by Augustus, Vespasian, Nerva, and Trajan. It consisted of a temple set against the back wall of an open area, surrounded by colonnades with shops behind.

Augustus substituted *exedrae* (semicircular areas) for shops and decorated them with statues glorifying great Romans of the past. Throughout the city he set about rebuilding old temples, repairing altars and aqueducts, and erecting new temples and civic buildings, baths, monuments, utilities, and fire and police stations. His theater of Marcellus by the Tiber later housed a medieval fortress and Renaissance palace and modern apartments in the three-storied arcades and supporting vaults of its auditorium. His Altar of Peace, with sculptured reliefs depicting its actual dedication in 13 B.C., as well as symbolic figures, stands again in the Campus Martius, although not on its original site. Nearby is the circular mass of concrete which was the core of his mausoleum, originally topped with a mound of earth planted with cypresses.

Greatest was the change instituted on the Palatine. Here Augustus, still on a modest scale, initiated the imperial residence. Subsequent emperors, particularly Tiberius, Caligula, Nero, Domitian, Hadrian, and Septimius Severus, extended it over the entire hill, building up great vaulted substructures to increase the area available for the gradually evolving elaborate network of luxurious vaulted rooms and courts. This vast complex set a pattern for, and also gave the name "palace" (*palatium*) to, later European royal residences. Much of this palace, with its private and public rooms, temples, libraries, and gardens, still exists, now uncovered from the Renaissance villa built atop it.

For Nero (54–68 A.D.) even the spacious Palatine did not suffice. His Golden House extended across the valley and on to the Oppian hill, where huge underground painted and stuccoed vaulted chambers, models for the Renaissance style known as grotesque, remain. Nero was also concerned with the dangerously flammable slums of the city and after the fire (64 A.D.) enforced safer concrete construction and height limits on the *insulae*. The Circus Vaticanus, on the site of St. Peter's Square, and the first of the great imperial bathing establishments were completed in his reign.

Vespasian (69–79 A.D.) added another forum (of Peace), and built an amphitheater for gladiatorial games, the Colosseum, over what had been a lake in Nero's garden. His son Titus (79–81 A.D.) erected baths over part of Nero's Golden House and to the Forum Romanum added, at one end, a temple to Vespasian, and at the other, the richly sculptured arch commemorating his victories in Jerusalem. The major part of the great public rooms of the palace on the Palatine are due to Domitian's gifted architect, Rabirius, and are usually called the palace of the Flavians. Domitian's stadium in the Campus Martius remains today as the Piazza Navona.

Architect-Emperors. Before the next great building period in Rome, under Trajan, Nerva (96–98) filled the narrow space between the forums of Augustus and of Vespasian with his own forum, the walls surmounted by a sculptured frieze and housing a Temple of Minerva. To Trajan (98–117) and the genius of his architect, Apollodorus, fell the task of completing the imperial forums. This they did by opening a vast area in the valley and up the slopes of the Viminal. The arched gateway, the colonnaded court, the many-columned Basilica Ulpia, and the Greek and Latin libraries on either side of the column of Trajan (sculptured in relief in a continuous spiral frieze recording his military campaigns) are symmetrical on axis, the essence of Roman design. However, the *exedra* on one side of the court leads into a semicircular market of several stories of arcaded and vaulted passages and streets of shops, a masterpiece of engineering ingenuity as they climb the hill. Trajan, too, built large baths over Nero's Golden House.

To Hadrian (117–38), himself a daring architect, Rome owed the enormous double-cella temple to Venus and Rome facing the Colosseum; the enlargement of the Palatine palace; and his mausoleum (following Augustus' form). Under the name Castel Sant'Angelo, the mausoleum served medieval and Renaissance Popes as a fortress and is now a museum. Above all, Hadrian contributed the Pantheon, the circular-domed temple, a triumph of engineering and architectural design, preserved complete through the ages as a church. Marcus Aurelius (161–80) completed the temple to divine Antoninus and Faustina (now the Church of San Lorenzo in Miranda) in the Forum, and erected a column like Trajan's (in Piazza Colonna). His bronze equestrian statue, on the Capitoline since the 16th century, has stood in various places.

The Late Empire. Septimius Severus (193–211) added a monumental triple arch to the Forum Romanum and a smaller elegant one (Arch of the Money Changers) in the Forum Boarium, both covered with sculpture. He also extended the Palatine complex toward the Caelian to include Domitian's hippodrome and a seven-storied entrance (the latter destroyed in the 16th century). The colossal Baths of Caracalla (completed 216) out beyond the Caelian remain in great part, one small section being now used for summer opera. Enormous size and sym-

metrical vaulted rooms also characterize the Temple to the Sun built by Aurelian (270–75) on the Quirinal, and the Baths of Diocletian (built 298–305), into portions of which were later built the church of Santa Maria degli Angeli, the National Museum, and the Piazza dell'Esedra. The last great buildings of ancient Rome, from the time of the first Christian Emperor, Constantine (306–37), include the celebrated triple Arch of Constantine, the Baths of Constantine on the Quirinal, yielding much sculpture, and the crowning glory of Roman architectural achievement, the Basilica of Constantine (or of Maxentius) in the Forum. The central third of this is now used for the summer symphony concerts.

Destruction of the ancient city began in the 5th century A.D., when pagan temples were dismantled to furnish material for Christian churches. As government authority weakened in the wake of barbarian invasions in succeeding centuries, neglect planted seeds of destruction, followed by plundering for new building as late as the late 16th century.

ARCHITECTURE

ROMAN ARCHITECTURE, building style that flourished in Italy between 100 B.C. and the mid-4th century A.D. It was by far the most important style of ancient building, not only in grandeur of effect but also in its influence on later times. It utilized the post and lintel employed by all early peoples and combined this with the arch and tunnel vault derived from Mesopotamia. The Romans so perfected monumental construction in masonry that several of their finest buildings—for example, the Pantheon in Rome (2d century A.D.)—stand intact today, still in use after more than 18 centuries. Others, now ruined, served as models for famous Christian churches and also, surprisingly, for great modern structures such as railway terminals.

These attainments of Roman architecture were sparked by brilliant advances on two fronts. The first was in structural engineering, particularly in developing concrete reinforced by embedded brick arches and in using this powerful material for creating new vault forms. These were the flexible groined cross vault and the domical vault, each supported on a framework of arches and capable of expansion over vast areas. The Romans also perfected the hemispherical dome, which they first used on buildings of cylindrical shape (as the Pantheon), then on polygonal structures, and at last, through the use of rudimentary pendentives, on rectangular buildings.

The second pioneering advance was in design, notably in planning cities in orderly blocks determined by two straight avenues crossing at right angles, and in creating the balanced layout of the great civic centers called forums. In the Forum of Trajan (2d century A.D.) in Rome, a triumphal arch led to a broad plaza flanked by two-story semicircles of shops and offices. Beyond were a sumptuous basilica or courthouse, two libraries, a famous military memorial enshrining the tomb of the Emperor Trajan, and a great temple.

Equally significant progress was made in designing spacious interiors such as those of the huge public baths.

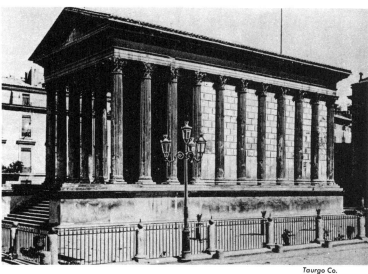

Right, the Maison Carrée (1st century B.C.) in Nîmes, France. The temple with a high base, deep columnar portico, and front steps reveals Etruscan influence.

Below, the Colosseum, framed by the Arch of Titus (both 1st century A.D.), in Rome. A marvel of engineering genius, the amphitheater seated about 45,000 people.
Italian State Tourist Office

Taurgo Co.

Below, Rome's Pantheon (2d century A.D.), a great circular temple with a rotunda.
Brown Brothers

These sumptuous structures—with their lofty central halls, their swimming pools, gymnasiums, steam baths, dressing rooms, and complex service facilities—were beautifully organized for the comfort and convenience of their patrons. They were also magnificently decorated with sculptures, frescoes, mosaic floors, and walls sheathed with slabs of richly colored marbles. The Baths of Caracalla (3d century A.D.) in Rome, raised on substructures 20 ft. high and measuring more than one-fifth of a mile on each side, provided accommodation for 1,600 bathers. It served as model for New York City's Pennsylvania Station.

Sources

The two chief sources of Roman architecture are easily distinguished: Etruscan and Greek. Etruscan architecture, in addition to contributing its use of broad flat bricks and colorful terra-cotta ornament, influenced the Roman in several important types of buildings: (1) The rectangular temple, raised on a high base and fronted by a deep columnar portico, with steps on the entrance end. This is best seen in the Maison Carrée at Nîmes, France (1st century B.C.). (2) The circular tomb. An example is that of Hadrian (2d century A.D.), in Rome, now also known as the Castel Sant'Angelo. Its burial chamber was covered originally by a high conical mound of earth. (3) The early Roman house-type, with its central atrium, or courtyard, open to the sky and surrounded by small bedrooms.

From the Greeks came the three "classic" orders of column and entablature—Doric, Ionic, and Corinthian—to which the Romans added two new ones. The Tuscan is a simplified version of the Doric. The Composite is a more ornate form of the Corinthian, its leafy capital enriched by spiral volutes taken from the Ionic. For utilitarian structures the Doric was soon displaced by the simpler Tuscan.

229

ROMAN ARCHITECTURE

The Ionic, though modified, never became popular. Thus the great majority of Roman columnar buildings employed the more showy Composite and Corinthian orders. Greek architectural ornament, including the use of figure sculpture in frieze and gable, was also adopted and enriched by the Romans. They likewise surrounded the exteriors of their largest temples with single or double rows of columns in the old Greek manner. It is particularly noteworthy that all five of the so-called Roman orders, with their carved ornament and principles of design, were revived and copied by Renaissance architects, who in turn bequeathed them to modern times. Hence they still may be seen in many great public buildings, such as the Capitol and Supreme Court at Washington, D.C., and governmental capitols and courthouses throughout the world.

Development

From early republican Rome (began, 527 B.C.), the chief architectural remains are fortification walls, great arched aqueducts outside the city, and a few atrium-type houses. Although the first Emperor, Augustus (reigned 27 B.C.–14 A.D.), boasted that he "found Rome of brick and left it of marble," few traces of his buildings remain. During the Flavian Dynasty (69–96 A.D.), however, was built the world-famous Colosseum, where thousands of early Christians were martyred and which has since served as model for the largest sports arenas, such as bull rings and football bowls.

The excavations at Pompeii, which was overwhelmed by the eruption of Vesuvius in 79 A.D., show that in typical dwellings the early atrium unit had been extended by the addition of a Greek peristyle (a range of columns surrounding a court). Thus garden space and a focus for social and family life were provided. The flowing continuity in this attractive arrangement of living quarters has strongly influenced the most progressive designs in modern domestic architecture. Yet in Roman lands from the 2nd century onward, the great majority of city dwellers lived in large brick apartment houses. These comprised three to eight identical floors behind continuous façades, with large windows and balconies at each level. Many were provided with plumbing systems for running water and the finest were of spacious duplex-type.

Because of their influence on Christian architecture, two classes of Roman buildings must again be mentioned —those of circular plan and the oblong rectangular basilica. The first was used for tombs and temples and was adopted for shrines of martyrs and also for baptisteries. For the Christian Church the civil basilica served as model. Its typical form was ideally suited to the early ritual: the interior was divided into central nave and flanking aisles by long ranges of columns, and, at the far end, a raised tribunal within a semicircular apse was adapted for the Christian sanctuary.

ART

Roman art is a style of artistic expression that flourished in Italy from about 200 B.C. into the 4th century A.D. Although considered inferior to Greek art in ideal beauty, it was more varied, progressive, and in many ways closer to the modern spirit. It exerted a decisive influence on the arts of the Middle Ages and Renaissance. Roman architecture was particularly important because of its brilliant contributions to structural engineering and design. Other art forms reveal the Roman genius for assimilating earlier styles and developing them along new lines. Artists combined many elements to produce effects of sumptuous magnificence and imposing grandeur, thus expressing Roman ideals of military might and world empire.

The clearest influences came from Greece. Thousands of plundered statues and paintings were shipped to Italy after the conquest of Greece (146 B.C.). Their beauty and perfection inspired generations of Roman artists. As the ancient Etruscan civilization was absorbed into Rome by conquest, it also made distinctive contributions. These appear in the realistic aspects of Roman art, its blatant luxury, and its love for pompous display.

The general development of Roman art, inspired by Greek idealism and Etruscan realism, was irregular and inconsistent, as first one trend and then the other assumed control. The more creative stream, leading to a realistic and then to an impressionistic rendering of nature, was occasionally checked by Greek idealism. Strongly Greek-dominated interludes, inspired by the taste of individual

"The Aldobrandini Marriage," now in the Vatican Library, is an ancient Roman fresco depicting a nuptial scene.

Alinari—Art Reference Bureau

emperors, occurred during the reigns of Augustus (31 B.C.–14 A.D.) and Hadrian (117–38 A.D.). Because Roman official art was designed to glorify the emperor by chronicling his exploits, it concentrated on historical relief sculptures. Here it perfected a novel method of pictorial narration, similar to that of modern comic strips, that was later adopted by Christian artists.

Sculpture. Roman artists excelled in three types of sculpture—portraits, historical reliefs, and naturalistic ornament. Portraiture reveals clear Etruscan influence because it grew out of Etruscan and Roman ancestor worship. It is the most typical Roman art, graphically reflecting the realism, materialism, and ostentation of the ancient Latins. Earlier portraits were unsparingly realistic ("Roman Carrying Ancestral Busts," 1st century B.C., Palazzo Barberini, Rome). Those of the emperors were, however, often ennobled by Greek idealism ("Augustus of Prima Porta," c.16 B.C., Vatican Museum, Rome; "Equestrian Marcus Aurelius," c.180 A.D., Campidoglio, Rome).

Historical reliefs preserve a vivid record of Roman imperialism. Some show the pomp of official ceremonies (the procession relief on the Ara Pacis, or Altar of Peace, 13 B.C., Rome). Others illustrate the glittering march of military triumph (reliefs on the Arch of Titus, 81 A.D., Rome). Most impressive is the continuous spiral band encircling the huge Column of Trajan (113 A.D.) in Rome. In hundreds of scenes and thousands of figures appears the relentless drive of conquering legions, with a pictorial history of their marches, skirmishes, and battles in an important and bloody campaign. The famous "Rose Column" (Lateran Museum, Rome) presents a beautifully naturalistic rendering in marble of delicate blossoms, fruits, and twining vines.

Painting. Thousands of fine frescoes and mosaics were discovered in the excavating of Pompeii and Herculaneum, cities buried by lava in the famous eruption of Vesuvius in 79 A.D. Many more were uncovered in Rome itself. They reveal two different modes of representation.

One style, which emphasizes ideal mythological figures carefully outlined and solidly modeled in clear brilliant tones, obviously derived from Greece. Its compositions, gracefully arranged in spaces of limited depth, continue the classic tradition of ideal formal beauty. Outstanding masterpieces from Pompeii are "Three Graces" and "Hercules Discovering His Son" (National Museum, Naples); and, from Rome, "The Aldobrandini Marriage" (Vatican Library).

The other style, amazingly novel and progressive, anticipated the triumphs of 19th-century impressionist painting by creating, in atmospheric perspective, effects of vast depth and distance. Its famous frescoes produce, by a skillful blending of low color tones, the illusion of distant landscape vistas. Among its masterpieces are "The Odyssey Landscapes," about 50 B.C. (Vatican Library), and "A Naval Battle," 1st century A.D., from Pompeii (National Museum, Naples).

Minor Arts. Silversmiths, gemcutters, and metalworkers attained pre-eminence in fashioning luxurious products. Magnificent treasures of silver plate (bowls, platters, drinking cups, and other objects), exquisitely worked with figures and scenes in relief, come from Pompeii and other parts of the ancient world. Beautifully engraved gems, cameos, and deluxe bronze furnishings are preserved in many museums and private collections.

DEMOCRACY

Ancient Rome. The Romans, perhaps because they were more interested in political practice than in theory, were able to develop institutions capable of solving many of the problems of democracy that had baffled the Greeks. Thus it may be argued that the contribution of Roman lawyers and magistrates has been both more significant and more enduring than that of Greek philosophers so far as the actual operation of democratic institutions is concerned. By viewing citizenship as a matter of legal rights and duties, rather than a matter of active participation in public affairs, the Romans found the key to the orderly expansion of the body politic. Evidence of this achievement is to be found in the New Testament, for St. Paul, a Christianized Jew from Cilicia in Asia Minor, was released from prison in Greece when he reminded the magistrates that he was a Roman citizen.

Order and unity over large areas were for the first time achieved in ways that were compatible with the ideals of democracy. In the complex and pragmatically evolving constitution of republican Rome, a substantial degree of political democracy was combined with monarchical and aristocratic elements in such a way as to ensure a continuing popular voice in the conduct of Roman affairs. The rudiments of the system of checks and balances, including the concept of the separation of powers, are to be found in this constitution. These, together with the characteristically Roman notion of a system of law guaranteeing uniform rights and equal treatment, constitute the fundamental bases of democratic government even down to the present day.

GAMES

Traditionally, Rome held its first games (Ludi) in the reign of Romulus, but its athletic program was restricted to one event: horse racing. Later, Ludi assumed a greater importance when they were held regularly in the Circus Maximus at a fixed annual date, and after chariot races, farces, gladiatorial contests, beast hunts, and other novelties calculated to amuse were introduced from Etruria. From beginning to end these Ludi Magni or Ludi Romani were always spectacles, Romans seldom competing except in equestrian events or occasionally in foot races. In 186 B.C. Greek actors and athletes were introduced. In time the number of Ludi increased, often serving to celebrate military triumphs. Though the Romans as individuals appreciated the value of exercise like running, swimming, riding, hunting, wrestling, and boxing, they never seem to have cared to train themselves professionally for competition. The general impact of the excesses and bestiality of the Ludi under the Roman Empire upon the Roman character was the reverse of the noble, unifying influence of Greek festivals on Greece during the days of its independence.

GAMES, SECULAR Roman centennial celebration comprising games, dramatizations, and sacrifices. The purifying rites were intended to sweep away the accumulated evils of the last hundred years. They were introduced in 249 B.C. during the First Punic War to calm the frightened populace. The revival of the games by Augustus in 17 B.C., celebrated in Horace's *Carmen saeculare,* symbolized the beginning of the Imperial era.

LITERATURE

LATIN LITERATURE, CLASSICAL. Except for certain rituals, crude ballads, and nursery rhymes, Latin literature began with a translation of Homer's *Odyssey* into native Latin verse by Livius Andronicus, sometime after 272 B.C. The Romans were centuries behind the Greeks in civilization, and the history of their literature is for many years a story of translation and adaptation of Greek models. Gnaeus Naevius (c.240 B.C.) wrote the first original epic, the story of the First Punic War, in native Saturnian verse. It was soon eclipsed by the *Annals* of Quintus Ennius (239–169), in hexameters, which covered the whole history of Rome. Cato (234–149), the patron of Ennius, was author of the first surviving prose work, *On Agriculture,* a manual for gentlemen farmers, as well as of the *Origins,* which included the early history of Rome and the foundation traditions of many Italian towns. At the end of the 3d century B.C., Plautus produced a series of comedies for the Roman festival games, based on Greek models, but highly original, full of boisterous fun, and of great vitality and variety, of which 20 have survived. Caecilius succeeded him as Rome's most popular comic dramatist. Tragedy was never as popular with the holiday crowd as comedy, but the names of Pacuvius and Accius, 2d-century writers of tragedy, were always honored by the Romans. A generation after Plautus, Terence (195–159), an enfranchised slave from North Africa, wrote six comedies which have all survived, more polished than those of Plautus, but also less boisterously funny, less realistic, and far less popular. He was the protégé of a literary group headed by Scipio the Younger which consciously tried to promote a Latin literature to rival the Greek. The interest of the group was largely confined to prose and was responsible for the deliberate development of oratory, and of prose style in general. They were also devoted to Stoic philosophy.

Prose style had a practical value for the Roman; poetry developed more slowly. Toward the end of the 2d century B.C., Gaius Lucilius wrote what came later to be called satire, short verse essays with little or no claim to poetic quality on a wide variety of subjects, expressing the writer's personal views on contemporary manners and morals, events and characters. Lucilius' originality lay in abandoning the traditional poetry of epic and drama and expressing directly personal ideas and emotions. Within a generation there appeared a group of poets priding themselves on just such revolutionary ideas. They did not wholly abandon Greek influence, but they turned to the more nearly contemporary Greek poetry which flourished at Alexandria in Hellenistic times. This was of two sorts, personal poems of emotion or wit, and academic productions of complex form, loaded with learned allusions. The greatest representative of this group of modernists was Catullus, who came, c.62 B.C., as a young man from Verona to Rome. There he experienced all the excitements of a wealthy and uninhibited society, and whatever he experienced he revealed in verse which was equally uninhibited. His great contributions to poetry were his passionate short poems, never surpassed in the expression of love, disillusion, and hate. His longer, more elaborate narrative poems have had less universal acclaim, but in the perfection of their complex construction they profoundly influenced the poetry of the following generation.

A contemporary of Catullus, Lucretius, exhibited the independence of the new poets in a totally different direction. Disgusted with the puritanical dogmas of Stoicism and the superstitions of official religion, Lucretius undertook in his only work, *On the Nature of Things,* to expound the materialistic philosophy of Epicurus. Writing in hexameter verse and often rising to magnificent poetic heights, he developed his theory of the atomic nature of matter which made unnecessary both creation and the gods, and freed man from the fear of death.

Latin Prose in the Age of Cicero. Meanwhile, prose literature had been developing from the rugged, practical style of Cato to something far more studied and sophisticated. Greek rhetoricians had inspired the development of two types of style, one elaborately ornate (Asianic), the other starkly simple (Attic). Hortensius and Calvus represented these schools in oratory, but their speeches are lost. Julius Caesar, in his *Commentaries on the Gallic War* and his *Civil War,* is a model of the plain style. Sallust (86–c.34) was an individualist of the more elaborate school. He was the first to write the history of a restricted period, in a varied, concise, epigrammatic style. His *Catiline* and his *Jugurthine War* have deservedly survived. His longer history of the ten years following the death of Sulla has largely disappeared.

The great writer who so far dominated the period of Catullus and Caesar as to give his name to the age was Cicero (106–43 B.C.). Whatever his political significance, as an orator and writer he dominated the age. His style, a compromise between the plain and ornate, with its rotund periods, was to be the standard of formal Latin for the indefinite future. His published writings, for the most part extant, fall into four groups: first, speeches, private and official; second, essays on rhetoric and orators; third, essays on philosophy, ethics, and politics; and fourth, his correspondence, collected and published by his secretary Tiro. Cicero was not an investigating scholar: his rhetorical and philosophical essays are eloquent presentations of the theories of others, past and contemporary. In sympathetic essays such as *On Friendship* and *On Old Age,* the warmth and enthusiasm of originality seems to glow. But Cicero's published work has always been valued chiefly for its historical content and for the pleasure given by artistic perfection of expression. Equaling Cicero in volume of production only, his contemporary Varro (116–27) was the most distinguished encyclopedist of the Roman Republic, best known for his *On the Latin Language* and *On Agriculture.*

The Augustan Age. The Ciceronian Age was followed by the Augustan. After the battle of Actium (31 B.C.) the new master of Rome, pursuing a policy of peace and

Aeneas, carrying his aged father and leading his son, flees from Troy. The ancient relief is in the National Museum of Budapest.
Alinari—Art Reference Bureau

reconciliation, and with the active support of his minister Maecenas, constructively encouraged literary production, especially poetry. The great names of this golden age are the evidence of his success. Vergil (70–19), after the early publication of his pastoral poems, the *Eclogues*, wrote the *Georgics*, exalting Italian agriculture in perhaps the most perfect of all Latin hexameters. Finally, his great epic masterpiece, the *Aeneid*, glorified Rome's foundation by the Trojan Aeneas. Meanwhile, Horace (65–8) established not only the satire which Lucilius had originated but the lyric in stanzaic form as used by Sappho, Alcaeus, and other Greek lyricists of the best periods. He wrote "public" poems, enthusiastically supporting the policies of Augustus, and personal poems whose human appeal still withstands the passage of time. Aside from these two preeminent figures, the Augustan Age produced three outstanding writers of elegiac verse. Tibullus had too much respect for the old Roman tradition to be thoroughly successful in erotic poetry, but Propertius, with no inhibitions, was the supreme exponent of the subjective erotic elegy. Ovid (43 B.C.–c.17 A.D.) was the expert master of the art of love. His *Amores*, *Heroides*, and *Ars Amoris* are sophisticated to the highest degree. Without the passion and sentimentality of Propertius, he easily surpassed him in polish, versatility, and wit. His elegies were followed by the *Metamorphoses*, 15 books of fluent hexameters, telling the tales of transformation culled from the whole range of mythology. Finally, the *Fasti*, unfinished when

he died, was a calendar of Roman religious festivals in elegiac verse. One great prose writer adorned the Augustan Age, the historian Livy (59 B.C.–17 A.D.), who wrote the history of Rome from the earliest myths of its foundation down to 9 B.C. with the ardor of a Republican enthusiast and the simplicity and charm of a true literary artist.

The Age of Rhetoric and Artificiality. The creative greatness of the Augustan Age passed rapidly into a period of imitation and artificiality. The gradually decreasing general participation in government and the encroachment of absolutism on freedom of speech had some influence in this direction by tending to make literature an end in itself. Largely, however, the change was brought about by the increasing artificiality of the rhetoric which had absorbed Roman education, and the growing popularity of the socially sponsored recitation. This custom originated with the idea of obtaining literary criticism, but rapidly developed into a competition for popularity. One writer of Tiberius' reign still showed the Augustan urge to make a new contribution to the body of Latin literature: Phaedrus, a freedman of Augustus, was most successful in his humble ambition to present in Latin verse the fables of Aesop. Another contemporary aspirant to similar recognition was Manilius, who tried to do for Stoic philosophy what Lucretius had done for Epicurean. But his five books on astrology, in creditable hexameters, are already infected with the rhetorical influences of the day.

The first true production of the new age is a general history by Velleius Paterculus which is in reality a rhetorical eulogy of Tiberius, introduced by a summary of preceding history. Encyclopedic works were popular, furnishing material for ambitious writers. Valerius Maximus published nine books of *Memorable Deeds and Sayings*. Seneca the Elder, a learned scholar and rhetorician, produced a collection of real and imaginary law cases, with notable quotations from great lawyers, past and contemporary. A minor historian of the Claudian period was Curtius Rufus, who wrote a history of Alexander the Great in 10 books.

By the time of Nero the new influences had been somewhat assimilated and a group of important writers appeared. Persius wrote six hexameter satires, earnestly preaching Stoic ethics. He drew one vivid picture of a fashionable recitation, which he ridicules bitterly, though he himself was a victim of the custom. Lucan (39–65 A.D.) came nearer than anyone else ever has to making rhetoric into great poetry. His *Pharsalia*, an epic in 10 books on the civil war between Pompey and Caesar, scintillates with quotable phrases. It contains magnificent character sketches and a few great action pictures, but lacks unity of construction and is overburdened with learned digressions. Lucan's uncle, Seneca the Younger, spent his life largely in Nero's service, first as tutor, then as minister. He was a prolific writer of ethical essays of a fairly popular type, written in a colloquial style, which repudiated both the periodic Latin of Cicero and the flagrant rhetoric of the day. Seneca also wrote 10 tragedies adapted from the Greek, and still extant, which were destined to become a popular source of melodrama for the predecessors of Shakespeare, and for Shakespeare himself. Petronius Arbiter was the author of a work unique in Latin literature, the *Satyricon*, a satiric, picaresque novel picturing, with astonishing vividness and ironic understanding, the contemporary middle class. Calpurnius Siculus composed feeble pastorals in imitation of Vergil; and Columella wrote *On Agriculture* in 12 books, the tenth, in hexameter verse, as a continuation of Vergil's *Georgics*.

During the revolution of 68–69, or shortly thereafter, a scholar from Spain, Quintilian, was made professor of rhetoric at Rome, with a salary from the Emperor. For over 20 years he was the most influential Latin rhetorician. His book on education, the *Institutio Oratoria*, was not published until the 90's, but his teaching influenced all writers from Nero's day to Trajan's. He attempted to revive the style of Cicero, but succeeded in only partially discrediting the popular rhetoric. Somewhat older than Quintilian was Pliny the Elder (c.24–79), scientist and historian. His encyclopedia of natural history in 37 books presents some 20,000 facts without any pretense to literary distinction. He also wrote two historical works, highly praised by Tacitus, one a general history, the other a history of Rome's wars with Germany. His nephew, Pliny the Younger, a leading lawyer of Rome at the end of the 1st century, left behind him a carefully revised and edited collection of personal letters and correspondence with Trajan, full of interesting material about the social, political, and literary personalities of the day. Tacitus (c.54–c.117) was the outstanding figure of the period in prose literature. His earliest work was a dramatic dialogue on the decline of oratory, written in Ciceronian form and style. Two essays followed, a eulogistic *Life of Agricola* and the *Germania*, disclosing an individual style which reached perfection in his great historical works, the *Histories* and the *Annals*. These covered respectively the years 69–96 and 14–68. In a total of 30 books, of which 13 are lost, these two works give a powerfully vivid picture of the early Empire, biased because of Tacitus' hatred of imperialism, but accurate as far as facts are concerned. The style is unique, reminiscent of Sallust, but more powerful in its brevity and variety of expression, its dramatic form, and its command of irony and innuendo. A friend of Tacitus and Pliny, Suetonius (c.69–c.140), imperial secretary and librarian, wrote *The Lives of the Caesars*, covering the same ground as Tacitus, without literary distinction but with a wealth of incident and scandal.

In poetry the second half of the 1st century was slower in ridding itself of the popular rhetoric. Valerius Flaccus wrote an epic, with too many long digressions, the *Argonautica*, based on the Greek poem of Apollonius of Rhodes, but in many ways original. Statius, himself a rhetorician and inveterate reciter, wrote a *Thebaid* and an *Achilleid*, in fluent and smooth hexameters. More important were his *Silvae*, or Improvisations, something between satires and lyrics, which at times reach real distinction. Silius Italicus rebelled against the rhetorical epic and reverted to the early Ennian style, in the longest of all Roman epics, the story of the war with Hannibal. Contemporary with Pliny and Tacitus were two great poets, Juvenal, the satirist, and Martial, the epigrammatist. Juvenal (c.50–after 127), while deriving from Horace, was largely moved in his 16 satires by indignation at the discomforts of city life and at the manners and morals of the immigrant and the newly rich. He is powerful in attack

and often brilliant in phrase and word picture. Martial (c.40–c.104) looked to Catullus as his model, but his 15 books of epigrams are less passionate than Catullus', more urbane and witty, and consist mainly of shrewd comment on the people and doings of the Rome of his day.

The Decline of Latin Literature. After Tacitus and Martial, there is no distinguished literature which can, strictly speaking, be called Latin. Several writers made brave attempts. Aulus Gellius, in the 2d century, wrote 20 books of *Attic Nights*, a miscellany rich in quotations from earlier writers. Macrobius' *Saturnalia* (c.400) was a similar miscellany. In the late 4th century, Ammianus Marcellinus wrote a continuation of Tacitus' history, with reasonable accuracy but clumsy style. In poetry, Ausonius, in the 4th century, wrote lyrics, of which the best known is a description of the Moselle River; and a little later Claudian wrote epics on recent history. None of this is of great importance. Fronto, tutor of Marcus Aurelius, in the 2d century, published letters of little interest, but he wrote in a new style, which blended the simple archaic Latin of pre-Ciceronian days with current colloquialism, producing a new Latin, which his prestige made popular. Apuleius (c.123–after 161), a far greater writer than Fronto, but without his professional influence, also used this style. Latin was showing signs of a transformation into the Romance languages. Apuleius wrote a romantic novel called *The Golden Ass* because it describes the adventures of Lucius, who was changed by magic into an ass. The finest piece of poetry in the new style is the *Pervigilium Veneris*, a romantic spring song with a haunting refrain and new suggestions of assonance and even rhyme.

For the rest, Christianity had taken over literature, along with the government. While the polemics of the Church fathers, the magnificent Church hymns, and the great essays of St. Augustine are in a Latin which is often classical, and while they are deeply in debt to Latin literature, they still represent a departure into a new culture. When, in the 6th century, Justinian produced the great Code of Civil Law, he was preserving the Roman past for the benefit of a distant future.

RELIGION

In the development of Roman religion we can distinguish several stages: (1) the primitive religion of the farmer, (2) the religion of the community, (3) the systematized religion of the pontifices, (4) the period of Etruscan and Italian influence, and (5) the final stage in which the old gods were identified with the more personal gods of the Greeks.

In the earliest period the gods were conceived as impersonal shapeless powers, called numina, which effected everything inexplicable and mysterious: the growth of crops, rain and lightning, diseases, birth and death. The household was the starting point of Roman religion. In the household were worshiped the Lares, the numina of the field who had special charge of the house; the Penates, protective spirits of the store-cupboard; Vesta, goddess of the blazing hearth; and the genius, or spirit of developed manhood, of the paterfamilias.

All manifestations of divine power were isolated divinities. The power which made the crops grow was different from that which protected the seeds. The number of numina was ever increasing. Religious activities were mainly confined to magical acts. For example, foxes with burning tails were chased to protect the crops against fire or pregnant cows were sacrificed to the earth to strengthen the fertility of the soil. The dead played no important role. They had lost all individual shape and existed only as Manes, a gray, uniform mass. Ancestors were worshiped as "divine parents," but not even the most distinguished had personal cults.

The religion of the community was focused essentially on warfare. In spring, warriors, horses, weapons, and horns had to be ritually cleansed and strengthened for the expedition. In fall, when they returned, similar rites were performed to prevent hostile magic from entering the town. Prisoners had to pass under a yoke to deprive them of magic power. War was declared by a special priesthood, the Fetiales, by flinging a lance into enemy territory.

Other rites of the community were derived from old farm rites, although they lost their original meaning in the city. For instance, on every estate the boundary stone was worshiped. The boundary stone of Rome was fixed 6 mi. from the town, however, without reference to the actual state boundaries. Here priests of the community performed the old ceremonies. Another example involved the Arvalians, who executed rites for the protection of crops in a grove near Rome far from any fields. Festivals, through all stages of Roman culture, were directly related to the agricultural year.

At burial ceremonies the parade of dead ancestors with their official emblems was probably Etruscan. Divination from the entrails of victims was permanently left to Etruscan priests known as Haruspices. The most important Etruscan contribution to Roman religion, however, was the introduction of images of the gods. On the Capitoline hill the last king of the Etruscan dynasty built the temple of Jupiter, Juno, and Minerva and erected statues of them. For the first time divinities were no longer shapeless powers, but assumed visible features. The old Indo-European sky-god, worshiped "since a Latin language existed," became the principal god of the community. The worship of these deities was highly organized by the state, under the leadership of the pontifical college and lesser sacred priesthoods.

Changing economic conditions encouraged the emphasis of certain aspects of old gods and also brought new gods to Rome. Craftsmen worshiped Minerva, merchants Mercury. Greek influence was implicit in the acceptance of the Sibylline Books. Greek anthropomorphism infiltrated the Roman concept of the gods: Ceres acquired features from Demeter, Diana from Artemis. A pestilence in 433 B.C. brought Apollo, and another plague in 393 B.C. brought Aesculapius, as healing gods to Rome. In 206 B.C. the worship of Magna Mater was introduced from Phrygia. Later the cults of Bacchus, of the Anatolian Ma, and the Egyptian Isis were established.

During the 3d century B.C. the Roman aristocracy, skeptical of popular religion and influenced by Stoicism (q.v.), worshiped ideal values, such as Honor, Reliability, Bravery, and the Welfare of the State, and built temples to them. However, the general trend led away from these late offsprings of shapeless gods. Though the old formalistic religion experienced a revival under Augustus, it eventually was replaced by emperor worship. As it lost its hold on the people, the Oriental cults filled the vacuum. Until the final period, however, Roman religion was characterized by an absence of dogmatism and by a responsiveness to foreign ideas, with its emphasis primarily on discipline and patriotism.

REPUBLIC AND EMPIRE

Rome, which started as a village on the Tiber, eventually expanded to include all of the civilized peoples in Europe, western Asia, and northern Africa. Its governmental institutions, its cultural and social practices, its ideals of patriotic duty and national aspirations have had a lasting influence on the civilization of Europe.

The Legendary Period

According to legends recorded in Vergil and Livy, Rome was settled by a mixture of native Latins with the survivors of the Trojan War brought to Italy by Aeneas in the 12th century B.C. Under the leadership of Aeneas' son a joint kingdom was established at Alba Longa. On a date corresponding to Apr. 21, 753 B.C., the city of Rome was founded on the spot where it still stands. It is likely that the site of the forum, the oldest part of Rome, had become a common center for the villages on the surrounding hills.

Romulus and Remus. Legend has it that the thirteenth King of Alba Longa, Proca, had two sons. The younger, Amulius, dispossessed his elder brother, Numitor, and seized his throne. Numitor's daughter, Rhea Silvia, although a Vestal Virgin, gave birth to twin sons whose father, she claimed, was the god Mars. Amulius, pretending to be outraged by his niece's treachery to her vow of perpetual chastity, seized this opportunity to destroy his brother's descendants, imprisoned Rhea Silvia, and set the twins adrift in a basket on the Tiber, expecting them to be drowned. The basket drifted ashore, however, and the infants were found and nursed by a she-wolf. Later they were reared by a shepherd, Faustulus, and his wife.

When the brothers, Romulus and Remus, reached manhood, they discovered that they were Numitor's grandsons. Gathering a band of fellow shepherds, they went to Alba Longa, killed Amulius, and restored the throne to Numitor. The twins then decided that with their band of followers they would found a city. But they quarreled over which should give his name to the city and be its ruler. One story has it that Romulus was proclaimed ruler; when the walls were under construction but still very low, Remus derisively jumped over them, whereupon Romulus killed him in anger. Romulus, in any case, became sole leader, gave the new city his name, and was its first King.

The new city had one serious lack: most of its men had no wives. Romulus therefore invited the neighboring Sabine tribe to a religious festival celebrated by games. When the show was at its height, the young Romans each seized a Sabine girl and carried her off. The Sabine men, having come unarmed to the festival, were forced to flee, but returned later to fight for the return of their women.

When a battle was about to take place, the Sabine women, now all married to Romans, intervened and begged their husbands and fathers to make peace and not war. And so it was decided not only to make peace but to combine the two states into one.

After many years, in which Romulus enlarged the city, established many customs, and chose 100 citizens to be called Fathers or Senators, Romulus disappeared in a cloud while reviewing the army on the Campus Martius. It was believed that he, the son of a god, had been translated to heaven.

The Monarchy. Romulus was the first of seven Kings, the following six being Numa Pompilius, Tullus Hostilius, Ancus Marcius, Tarquinius Priscus, Servius Tullius, and Tarquin the Proud. The reigns of these seven comprise the Regal Period (753–510 B.C.). Numa traditionally established Rome's most ancient religious institutions. Under Tullus Hostilius, Alba Longa was destroyed and its citizens absorbed by Rome. Servius Tullius is said to have reorganized the political basis of the state for the purpose of creating a larger and more efficient fighting force. The last three reigns of the Regal Period are marked by considerable expansion to the north, and it is possible that the story of these Kings masked domination of Rome by the Etruscans. This little-known people probably came from the east, and had a higher and richer civilization than Rome. Certain Roman usages, such as the curule chair for the chief magistrates, the fasces, and the Roman style of temple, with its high podium and frontal arrangement of columns, were almost certainly influenced by Etruscan patterns.

Many Roman legends clustered about the figures of the Etruscan Kings. The most celebrated is that of the rape of Lucretia. According to this story, Sextus Tarquinius, son of Tarquin the Proud, violated Lucretia, the wife of the noble Collatinus. Lucretia thereupon summoned her husband and father to tell them what had taken place, and then took her own life. It was this violent deed that spurred the Romans to remove the last Tarquin from the throne, exile the Tarquin family, and establish a republic.

Collatinus and Lucius Junius Brutus became the first two consuls.

The Republic

The Republican Institutions. The institutions of the Republic were actually a continuation of the institutions of the Regal Period, but with precautions against a revival of monarchy. The powers of the king were transferred to the magistrates: quaestors, aediles, praetors, and consuls. Quaestors administered public finances. Aediles were in charge of public works and buildings. Praetors acted as judges. The consuls, of whom two were elected each year, were the chief executives. These four offices comprised the *cursus honorum*, election to each office, beginning with the quaestorship, being prerequisite to the next higher. The fact that there were always two consuls prevented supreme power from being vested in one individual. Such terms as *"interregnum"* (used for the period of time between the election of consuls in times of stress), "abdication" (consuls were said to *abdicate*, like kings, when they retired from office), and *"rex sacrorum"* (the Republican official who performed the priestly duties of the king) clearly indicate that practices from the earlier period persisted with necessary adaptation. So we shall find, at the change of Republic to Empire, that certain Republican institutions survived under a monarchy.

After the expulsion of the Tarquins, the Etruscan ruler Lars Porsena, of the city of Clusium, allied himself with Tarquin. It seems likely that the heroic tales of the war which followed are a cover for at least a temporary defeat of the Romans.

Roman Expansion in Italy. The external history of Rome for the next few centuries is one of gradual and then of more rapid expansion toward the rule of all Italy. It is not known exactly when Etruscan domination over Rome ended, but at the beginning of the 4th century the Romans were waging a considerable war against the Etruscan city of Veii. Rome had also to meet the pressure of encroaching hill tribes to the east, such as the Sabines, the Aequi, and the Volscians. In 396 B.C. Veii was conquered and de-

The Colosseum is one of Rome's best-known landmarks. It was begun in 72 A.D. during the reign of Vespasian and completed by his sons, Titus and Domitian. The great amphitheater, scene of many gladiatorial contests, seated about 45,000 spectators. It was originally faced with stone.

Stockpile

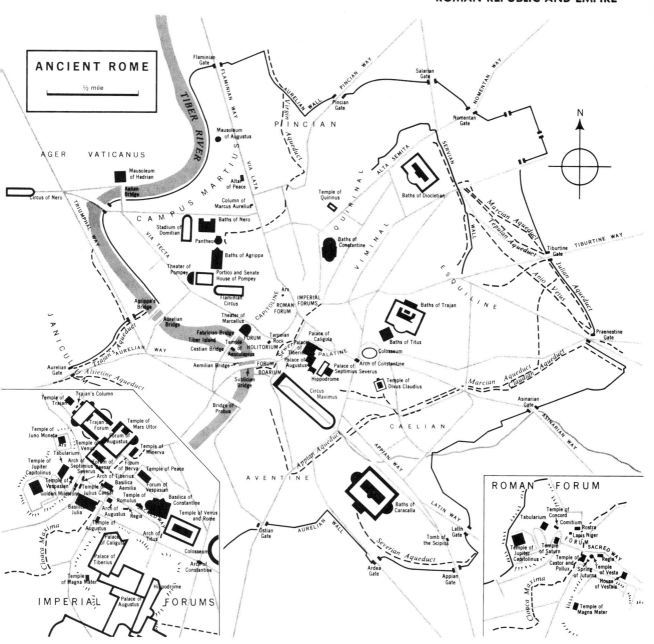

ANCIENT ROME
½ mile

ROMAN FORUM

stroyed, but an enemy from outside Italy, the Gauls, sacked Rome in 390 B.C. Although the Gallic invasion was a setback for Rome, it doubtless served to weaken the power of the Etruscans, who do not seem to have threatened the expansion of Rome after this period.

Rome now began to expand southward along the western shore of Italy. The Greek cities in that area called for Rome's help against the Samnites, a mountain people from the interior of Italy, and in three Samnite Wars (343–290 B.C.) Rome came to dominate a large part of lower Italy. Tarentum, in the far south, called in the assistance of Pyrrhus, King of Epirus, against Rome, but despite his trained troops and war elephants, by means of which he

won a number of victories, Pyrrhus made no permanent dent on Roman power. When he withdrew to Greece in 275 B.C., Rome was undisputed mistress of Italy south of the Po. During the 4th century she had either absorbed or allied herself with the Latin cities north of Rome. The attitude of Greek writers at this time makes it clear that Rome was now to be reckoned with as a world power.

Civil Dissension. While this expansion went on, there was continual friction within the city between the patrician and plebeian orders. In the period immediately after the expulsion of the kings, all power lay with the patricians. The story of the secession of the plebeians in 494 B.C. is evidence that the lower class was fighting for its rights. This secession was ended by the creation of tribunes, plebeian magistrates who could not themselves initiate legislation but could halt legislation unfavorable to the common people by calling "*veto*," or " I forbid." As time went on, more rights were granted. In 445 B.C. marriage between plebeians and patricians was legalized. By 367 B.C. the principle was set forth that at least one consul had to be a plebeian; eventually all political offices were opened to plebeians. Finally, in 287 B.C., laws (plebiscita) enacted by the separate plebeian assembly were made binding upon all. From the mid-4th century on, the political distinction between plebeians and patricians gradually lost its importance, although social distinctions still existed. Henceforth lines were drawn between the wealthier officeholding class, usually called *nobiles*, and the lower class, or *populares*.

Conquests Abroad. Expansion to the extreme south of Italy brought Rome into direct conflict with Carthaginian interests in Sicily. Carthage was the other growing power in the western Mediterranean, but as long as Rome's interests lay within Italy, there was no reason for open conflict. When Carthage occupied the city of Messana in Sicily, and a faction in the city called in Roman aid, the First Punic War (264–241 B.C.) began. This ended in victory for the Romans, the development of Rome as a naval power, and the Carthaginian evacuation of Sicily.

The Second Punic War (218–201 B.C.) was the most decisive in the history of Rome. Despite the military genius of Hannibal. the chief Carthaginian general, who invaded Italy and crushed the Romans repeatedly, Roman superiority in manpower and on the sea, Hannibal's difficulties in conducting a war at so great a distance from his base, and the military skill of Scipio Africanus and others ultimately defeated Carthage. Hannibal had expected that the Italian peoples subject to Rome would join him to effect their own liberation. That they did not suggests that Rome was creating an Italian patriotism. In this war Rome took Spain from Carthage, destroyed Carthage as a world power, and made herself by far the dominant power in the Mediterranean. The Third Punic War (149–146 B.C.) saw the complete destruction of Carthage, her territory becoming the Roman province of Africa.

Responsibility for the protection of Greek interests in southern Italy eventually led to involvement in Greece itself. There the Greek republics looked to Rome for aid in their struggle with Macedon. In 197 B.C., after driving the Macedonians from the Greek cities, Rome proclaimed the freedom of Greece. The appearance in Greece of the dynamic Seleucid King of Syria, Antiochus III, in whose court Hannibal had taken refuge after his defeat in 202 B.C., threatened Rome and forced her to fight again in Greece. Carrying the war to Asia, the Romans defeated Antiochus at the battle of Magnesia in 190 B.C. Their object at this time was not to annex territory, but to prevent any single power from growing strong enough to threaten Roman positions. However, in 168 B.C. Rome dismembered Macedon, making it a province in 148, and in 146 B.C., after the defeat of the Achaean League all Greece was subjugated. In 133 B.C., when Attalus III of Pergamum in Asia Minor died and bequeathed his kingdom to Rome,

the Romans gained an actual foothold in the east. Attalus' kingdom became the rich province of Asia.

A Century of Revolution

Reforms of the Gracchi. In Rome, meanwhile, the conflict between *nobiles* and *populares* was becoming acute. When Rome began to receive tribute in the form of grain from abroad, it became unprofitable to grow it in Italy, and instead, large landowners turned to grazing, which naturally occupied fewer workers than farming. Much of the land thus employed was public domain which the nobles had pre-empted. The reforms of Tiberius Gracchus, who was elected tribune in 133 B.C., were initially motivated by a desire to restore the hardy peasant class which had been the mainstay of Rome's strength. He wished to divide the public lands into small allotments for distribution among landless citizens; the capital necessary to start them in farming would be provided by the legacy which King Attalus had bequeathed to Rome.

But though the land was legally public, noble "squatters" had held it so long that they had come to regard it as their own, and were indignant at being expropriated. To block his reforms a mob of these nobles murdered Tiberius. Gaius Gracchus, elected tribune 10 years later, carried his brother's program forward with greater circumspection; among his other measures he provided grain at a low rate and proposed the establishment of new colonies to favor the landless element, and passed economic measures favorable to the *equites* (middle class) as a means of weakening the *nobiles*. But in 121 B.C. Gaius too was killed.

The Struggle Between Marius and Sulla. The Senate now controlled affairs unchecked. The corrupt state of the government became clear during the Jugurthine War in North Africa, when Senate leaders were openly bribed by Jugurtha, who was convinced that everything at Rome was for sale. This war offered Gaius Marius his chance at power. Marius was a general of genius but not a reformer of the Gracchus type. Rather he was an opportunist who used the grievances of the *populares* to climb to power. He defeated Jugurtha in 105 B.C., and later (102–101 B.C.) the Cimbri and Teutones, Germanic tribes that had invaded Gaul and whose approach was causing panic in Rome. During his period of leadership, Marius reorganized the Roman army, making it a professional body enlisted for long periods rather than a citizen army. The effect of this change was to make the army loyal to its general rather than to the state, thus enabling the general to use the army as a tool in his rise to power. No Republican levy would follow its leader against Rome, but professional armies did. Sulla, Pompey, and Caesar all took advantage of this change; indeed, it was what enabled Caesar to subvert the Republic.

The Social War (90–88 B.C.), fought between Rome and her Latin and Italian allies, who wanted and eventually gained Roman citizenship, brought into prominence Sulla, formerly Marius' second-in-command. When Mithridates, King of Pontus on the Black Sea, began a serious revolt against Rome in 88 B.C., Sulla was given the command against him. Sulla, however, was of the party of the *nobiles*, and in his absence from Rome followers of Marius passed a law giving Marius the command against Mithridates. Sulla then led his army into the city and had laws passed strengthening the power of the Senate. Marius fled, but when Sulla marched to the war against Mithridates, Marius returned with his army, and a blood bath ensued. Marius died in 86 B.C., but the *populares* retained power until Sulla's victorious return from the east in 83. He defeated the Marians, took over the city, and ruled with more systematic bloodshed than Marius, making himself dictator with a reactionary program and "proscribing" all his opponents. Sulla retired in 79 and died the next year.

The Rise of Pompey. Sulla's chief lieutenant, Pompey, held a series of military commands which brought him deserved acclaim—against the rebel Sertorius in Spain, then against Spartacus and his army of gladiators and slaves whom Pompey and Crassus defeated in 71 B.C. Pompey and Crassus were consuls in 70; Pompey's most important military command came in 67 B.C., when he was given unlimited power for three years over the Mediterranean and the shores around it. He quickly accomplished his primary task—to clear the sea of pirates—then went on to defeat Mithridates, who was again being troublesome in the east, and also Tigranes, King of Armenia. He also settled quarrels concerning the succession in Judaea, and visited the Temple in Jerusalem. In 62 B.C. he returned at the head of his victorious army to Rome, where the Senate expected him to act as Sulla had done earlier under similar circumstances—make himself dictator.

In Rome itself, at the same time, the unsettled conditions and discontent are illustrated by the conspiracy of 63 B.C. Catiline, a dissolute noble, placed himself at the head of reckless malcontents in a plot to assassinate the consuls and seize the government. By frustrating this attempt, Cicero, who was consul in 63 B.C. and already a prominent orator, whose policy was to reconcile opposing parties, reached the apex of his career. Caesar was moving into prominence at this time as a leader of the old party of Marius, whose nephew he was. Pompey did not seize power upon his return, but asked the Senate to ratify what he had done in the east and provide land for his veterans. When the Senate did not respond, Pompey, Caesar, and Crassus, Pompey's former colleague and the richest man in Rome, combined to protect their joint interests; this group is usually but inaccurately called the First Triumvirate. Caesar was consul in 59 B.C., together with an ineffectual colleague, and procured the legislation that each of the three wanted, including a five-year command in Gaul for himself.

The Career of Julius Caesar. Caesar at once proceeded to the conquest of Gaul, where he proved his military genius. In 56 B.C. the three leaders met at Luca and renewed their arrangement, but the interests of Pompey and Caesar were inevitably to clash. In 54 Julia, Caesar's daughter and Pompey's wife, who had been a bond between the two men, died, and in 53 B.C. Crassus was killed at the battle of Carrhae in Parthia. When the Senate decreed at the beginning of 49 B.C. that Caesar should lay down his command, which had been renewed for a second five years, he crossed the Rubicon, the boundary of his province, under arms, which was tantamount to rebellion against the state.

At this time Pompey held a magistracy in Spain, but this he administered through legates, while he himself remained at Rome to counter the movements of Caesar. When Caesar, marching southward, had taken Corfinium and was approaching Rome, Pompey and the Senatorial party quickly retired to Greece. His plan evidently was to suppress Caesar by a pincer movement between his troops in Spain and those in Greece. Instead of following Pompey to Greece, Caesar first went to Spain, where he defeated Pompey's lieutenants in a hard campaign; then, after returning to Rome and regulating affairs there, he proceeded to Greece. His brilliant campaign against Pompey's superior forces ended in his victory at Pharsalus (48 B.C.). Pompey fled to Egypt, where he was murdered.

Caesar then fought a successful war against the Alexandrians, subsequently proceeding to Asia Minor. There he defeated Pharnaces of Pontus at Zela, from which he sent the Senate his famous message, *"Veni, vidi, vici"* ("I came, I saw, I conquered"). Next turning to North Africa, he defeated the remnants of the Senatorial party under Cato at Thapsus in 46 B.C. After Thapsus he returned to Rome where he celebrated triumphs, but was soon called to Spain, where Pompey's eldest son was fomenting resistance. Here he defeated Gnaeus Pompey at the battle of Munda in 45 B.C. Then returning to Rome, he set about reorganizing the state and preparing a campaign against the Parthians to recover the standards lost by Crassus at Carrhae. However, he was assassinated on the Ides of March, 44 B.C., at the hands of Brutus and Cassius, who thought that the removal of Caesar would automatically restore the Republic.

In his impatience with the ineffectiveness and venality of the Senatorial leaders, Caesar had in fact concentrated power in his own hands, though he had refused the title of Rex ("King"). Although he had been ruthless in his rise to power, once attained, he made beneficial use of it for the common welfare. He had put an end to a century of civil war, but behaved magnanimously toward his former opponents. He extended citizenship to the people of Cisalpine Gaul (northern Italy), and admitted Gauls to the Senate. He showed consideration for the lower classes. As part of other administrative reforms he regularized the calendar.

Continuing Civil War. But Caesar's death could not restore the Republic. Antony, who had been his colleague in the consulship, proceeded to rule the state on the basis of papers allegedly left by Caesar. Then Octavian, Caesar's 19-year-old great-nephew and adopted son, against the advice of his family, came forward to claim his legacy. The Senatorial party thought it could use him against Antony, but instead Octavian combined with Antony and forced the Senate to name Antony, Octavian, and Lepidus as a triumvirate to rule the state with unlimited power for five years. The first business of the triumvirate was to avenge the death of Caesar. Brutus and Cassius had collected an army in Greece, and there at Philippi they were defeated (42 B.C.) and died in battle against Antony and Octavian.

Now the triumvirs divided their rule, Antony taking the luxurious and attractive eastern provinces, Octavian the more difficult but politically advantageous administration in Italy. Lepidus, who was assigned Africa, was soon eliminated, and conflict between Octavian and Antony was inevitable. Though Antony was the more popular, Octavian discredited him by alleging that he proposed to bestow the eastern parts of the Empire upon Cleopatra, whereas Octavian himself was a patriotic Roman. Octavian was also opposed by remnants of the Pompeian party under the leadership of Pompey's younger son, Sextus, who controlled a private fleet. The defeat of Sextus in 36 B.C. left Octavian free for the conflict with Antony. At the sea battle of Actium in 31 B.C. Cleopatra's flotilla fled, and Antony proved Octavian's charges by following her from the scene of the battle. Both Antony and Cleopatra, by committing suicide in Alexandria, foiled Octavian's plan to take them alive. The battle of Actium is the closing scene in the long civil wars, and established Octavian's sole power beyond question.

The Empire

The Augustan Age. In 27 B.C. Octavian returned to Rome and restored the state to the Senate and the Roman people. He himself professed to be content with the designation of Princeps ("leading citizen"). To suggest the reverence due his person he took the title of Augustus (meaning "the revered one"). This title, like Caesar, became the official designation of all succeeding emperors. The one office which Augustus retained permanently was the tribunate, which enabled him to veto any measure which did not please him. Furthermore, no candidate ran for higher office without his approval. Hence, though the forms of the Republic were observed, real power rested in the hands of Augustus alone.

Augustus' long tenure of office (27 B.C.–14 A.D.) enabled him to institute social and administrative reforms. Attempting to restore the ancient simple virtues of the Republic, he encouraged morality, family life, and a return to the land. He patronized the arts, especially literature, which reached its golden age in his reign. He regularized the administration of the provinces and the civil service, divided the city into "regions," and provided the first public fire department. He cared for the religious institutions of the city, building or renewing 82 temples, and made loyalty to himself and the Empire part of a cult. He added a new and magnificent Forum. So lavish was his building program that it was said of him that he found Rome a city of brick and left it a city of marble.

The weakness of the Augustan system was that in its pretense to being Republican it did not provide for a recognized succession. Until the system of imperial adoptions instituted in the 2d century provided an heir apparent, and even afterward, the absence of a regular succession frequently caused violent rivalries. Augustus himself chose one successor after another, all of whom died before him. His last choice was his stepson Tiberius, who ruled from 14 to 37 A.D.

The Julio-Claudian Emperors. Tiberius and the other Julio-Claudian Emperors were painted in the blackest colors by Roman historians. More recent scholarship indicates that, except for Caligula, who was an insane and cruel autocrat, they were much better rulers than they have been represented to be. Tiberius, though far from popular, was efficient and faithful to the precedents laid down by Augustus. He was succeeded by his nephew Gaius, called Caligula (37–41). Upon Caligula's assassina-

tion the Praetorian Guard, a military elite permanently garrisoned in Rome, put his uncle Claudius on the throne. Claudius (41–54), although represented by ancient authors as little better than an idiot, is now known, from evidence in inscriptions and papyri, to have been an excellent administrator. During his reign Britain first became a Roman province.

Nero (54–68), Claudius' stepson, succeeded him as Emperor. In his early years, under the guidance of Seneca and other advisers, Nero ruled well. But as he matured he became autocratic and vain, extravagant and cruel. When there was a great fire in Rome during his reign he blamed it on the Christians and persecuted them, an act which has made his reputation in other respects perhaps worse than he deserved. After the fire Nero did excellent work in restoring the city. There were revolts against him in Gaul, Spain, and Africa in 68, and to avoid a worse fate Nero committed suicide.

The following year is called "the year of the four emperors." Galba succeeded Nero, was killed in a few months, and followed successively by Otho and Vitellius. The fourth Emperor of this year was Vespasian (69–79), who at the time of his accession was besieging Jerusalem.

The Flavian Emperors. After the effete Julio-Claudians, Vespasian introduced the peasant virtues of his Sabine ancestors into the public life of Rome. The enormous and elaborate gardens which Nero had laid out for his private enjoyment Vespasian transformed to public uses. He began the enormous Colosseum on the site of Nero's private lake. He introduced thrift into the administration of the state, but also endowed the first public professorship in rhetoric and extended the frontiers of the Empire in Britain and Germany. During his reign the revolt of the Jews, begun in 66, was put down by his son Titus, and the Temple in Jerusalem was burned.

Vespasian was succeeded by his sons Titus (79–81) and Domitian (81–96). Titus, known as "the darling of the human race," inherited his father's virtues and enjoyed great popularity. Domitian, on the other hand, was arrogant, cruel, and openly tyrannical. After a number of unsuccessful plots, punished by many executions, Domitian was finally assassinated.

The Five Good Emperors. The election of Nerva (96–98) as Emperor by the Senate ushered in the era of "the five good emperors." Already an old man when elected, he lived less than two years more, but turned the direction of the government away from autocracy and back to constitutionalism. He adopted Trajan as his son, thus avoiding uncertainty over the choice of his successor.

Trajan (98–117), of Spanish birth and little known before his accession, was looked back upon in later years as the greatest Emperor since Augustus. His achievements clearly justify this belief. He continued to rule constitutionally and to increase social benefits begun by Nerva. He also inaugurated much public building, notably the Forum which bears his name, with its splendid Column of Trajan at its center, commemorating his fighting in Dacia. Both conscientious and efficient, Trajan completely controlled the enormous provincial administration.

During Trajan's reign the Roman Empire reached its greatest extent. Sicily had been acquired first in 241 B.C., Sardinia and Corsica in 238, and Spain in 197—all from

ROMAN EMPERORS

AUGUSTUS (OCTAVIAN)	27 B.C.[1]–14 A.D.	AEMILIANUS	253
TIBERIUS	14–37	VALERIAN	253–60
CALIGULA (GAIUS CAESAR)	37–41	GALLIENUS[5]	253–68
CLAUDIUS I	41–54	CLADIUS II, SURNAMED GOTHICUS	268–70
NERO	54–68	AURELIAN	270–75
GALBA	68–69	TACITUS	275–76
OTHO	69	FLORIAN	276
VITELLIUS	69	PROBUS	276–82
VESPASIAN	69–79	CARUS	282–83
TITUS	79–81	NUMERIANUS[6]	283–84
DOMITIAN	81–96	CARINUS[6]	283–85
NERVA	96–98	DIOCLETIAN[7]	284–305
TRAJAN	98–117	MAXIMIAN[7]	286–305
HADRIAN	117–38	CONSTANTIUS I[8]	305–6
ANTONINUS PIUS	138–61	GALERIUS[8]	305–11
MARCUS AURELIUS, SURNAMED ANTONINUS	161–80	CONSTANTINE I (CALLED THE GREAT)[9]	306–37
LUCIUS AURELIUS VERUS[2]	161–69	MAXIMIAN[10]	306–8
COMMODUS	180–92	FLAVIUS VALERIUS SEVERUS[10]	306–7
PERTINAX	193	MAXENTIUS[10]	306–12
DIDIUS JULIANUS	193	LICINIUS[11]	308–24
SEPTIMIUS SEVERUS	193–211	MAXIMINUS, SURNAMED DAZA OR DAIA[11]	308–14
CARACALLA (MARCUS AURELIUS ANTONINUS)	211–17	CONSTANTINE II[12]	337–40
GETA[3]	211–12	CONSTANS I[12]	337–50
MACRINUS	217–18	CONSTANTIUS II[12]	337–61
HELIOGABALUS (ELAGABALUS)	218–22	MAGNENTIUS[13]	350–53
ALEXANDER SEVERUS	222–35	JULIAN (KNOWN AS THE APOSTATE)	361–63
MAXIMINUS, SURNAMED THRAX	235–38	JOVIAN	363–64
GORDIANUS I	238	VALENTINIAN I (EMPEROR IN THE WEST)	364–75
GORDIANUS II	238	VALENS (EMPEROR IN THE EAST)	364–78
PUPIENUS MAXIMUS AND BALBINUS	238	GRATIAN (EMPEROR IN THE WEST)[14]	375–83
GORDIANUS III (GORDIANUS PIUS)[4]	238–44	VALENTINIAN II (EMPEROR IN THE WEST)[15]	375–92
PHILIP (CALLED THE ARABIAN)	244–49	THEODOSIUS I (CALLED THE GREAT)[16]	379–95
DECIUS	249–51	MAXIMUS (EMPEROR IN THE WEST)[17]	383–88
GALLUS	251–53	EUGENIUS (EMPEROR IN THE WEST)[17]	392–94

Western Roman Emperors

HONORIUS	395–423	INTERREGNUM	465–67
CONSTANTIUS III[18]	421	ANTHEMIUS	467–72
VALENTINIAN III	425–55	OLYBRIUS	472
PETRONIUS MAXIMUS	455	GLYCERIUS	473
AVITUS	455–56	JULIUS NEPOS	474–75
MAJORIAN	457–61	ROMULUS AUGUSTULUS[19]	475–76
SEVERUS	461–65		

Eastern Roman Emperors

ARCADIUS	395–408	LEO I	457–74
THEODOSIUS II	408–50	LEO II[20]	473–74
MARCIANUS (MARCIAN)	450–57		

[1] Actual ruler from 31 B.C.

[2] Coemperor, sharing power equally with Marcus Aurelius.

[3] Joint Emperor with his brother, Caracalla.

[4] Joint Emperor with Pupienus Maximus and Balbinus; after their deaths, sole Emperor.

[5] Joint Emperor with his father, Valerian, until the latter's capture by the Persian King Shapur I, near Edessa; thereafter sole Emperor.

[6] Joint Emperors until death of Numerianus, who was succeeded by Diocletian. Diocletian became sole Emperor upon Carinus' death.

[7] Joint Emperors (Augusti); Maximian was adopted by Diocletian as his colleague in 286. Both abdicated in 305, in favor, respectively, of Constantius I and Galerius, but Maximian reassumed imperial power in 306.

[8] Augusti, Constantius I in the West and Galerius in the East.

[9] Sole Augustus in the West after defeat of Maxentius in 312; sole Emperor of Roman world after death of Licinius, in 324.

[10] Rival Augusti in the West.

[11] Augusti in the East. Licinius shared power with Galerius until the latter's death. Maximinus, who commanded in Asia, was overthrown by Licinius in 314.

[12] Sons of Constantine I; joint Emperors.

[13] Usurper in the West.

[14] Ruled jointly with his father, Valentinian I, until the latter's death in 375. Also Emperor in the East after 378, choosing Theodosius I as his colleague in 379.

[15] Ruled jointly with his half brother, Gratian.

[16] Emperor in the East until 394, then sole Emperor of Roman world. On his death, in 395, the Empire was permanently divided into the Western Roman Empire and the Eastern Roman (Byzantine) Empire.

[17] Usurpers.

[18] Coemperor.

[19] The deposition of Romulus Augustulus by the barbarian conqueror Odoacer marks the traditional end of the Western Roman Empire. Actually, Odoacer and his successors continued for a time to acknowledge the overlordship of the Eastern Roman Emperors.

[20] Associated with his grandfather, Leo I. Except for the interlude of the Latin Empire (1204–61), Leo's successors continued to rule over the Eastern Roman (Byzantine) Empire until Constantinople's capture by the Turks under Mohammed II in 1453.

Carthage. Macedonia was annexed in 148, Achaea (all Greece south of Macedonia) in 146, and Africa (the area roughly equivalent to modern Tunisia) in the same year. Asia (western Asia Minor) was bequeathed to Rome by Attalus III in 133. Southern Gaul (later Provence) was annexed in 120 to protect Rome's communications with Spain, and Caesar had conquered the rest of Gaul, up to the Rhine, by 51. Syria was added by Pompey, and Roman rule in Asia Minor and Illyricum (now Yugoslavia) was extended in the 1st century B.C. Egypt was annexed after the defeat of Antony and Cleopatra in 31 B.C.

During the reign of Augustus the boundary of the Empire in central Europe was extended to the Danube, and four new provinces (Rhaetia, Noricum, Pannonia, and Moesia), comprising parts of modern Switzerland, Germany, Austria, Hungary, and Yugoslavia, were added. In Claudius' reign Thrace (Rumania and Bulgaria) was added as a province, and also Britain, which Caesar had invaded earlier but had not conquered. Under Trajan, Dacia (roughly, Transylvania) was added, though this was abandoned in the 3d century. Trajan also advanced far into Mesopotamia, but his conquests there were temporary and did not become a part of the Empire. To complete the circle around the Mediterranean, Numidia, west and south of Carthage, supported Pompey in the Civil War and became a Roman province in 46 B.C. Mauretania, on the coast of Africa west of Carthage, was subdued in the 1st century A.D. and divided into two provinces by Claudius.

Hadrian (117–38), also of Spanish birth, was Trajan's adopted son. He consolidated the boundaries of the Empire as established by Trajan, abandoning Trajan's eastern conquests, and fixed the northern boundary of Britain by means of the Wall named for him there. During his reign Judaea revolted under Bar Kokhba, and the Temple was destroyed. Hadrian was a passionate lover of everything Greek, and during his rule there took place a notable revival of Greek literature and art. He was succeeded by his adopted son Antoninus Pius (138–61).

Antoninus' peaceful reign rested on the strong foundations laid by Trajan and Hadrian. Under him the government continued to be centralized in the Emperor's person. The widespread frontiers were uneasy, but really serious revolts did not take place until the next reign. Antoninus' character was so upright and benevolent that he was called a second Numa.

Marcus Aurelius (161–80) was the adopted son of Antoninus, and was married to Antoninus' daughter. Immediately upon his succession he made his adopted brother Lucius Verus coemperor with him, thus setting a precedent for the division of imperial power. Verus was a weakling and of no help to the Emperor during his difficult reign. A student of Stoic philosophy and a retiring scholar by nature, Marcus Aurelius was compelled by circumstances to spend much of his reign fighting to put down revolts north of the Danube and elsewhere. His *Meditations*, a devotional book reflecting his Stoicism, was largely written during his campaigns.

The Decline of the Empire

The reign of Marcus Aurelius' son Commodus (180–92) may be said to mark the beginning of the decline of the Empire. At this time the principate founded by Augustus ended, and its place was taken by military despotism. Commodus, utterly unlike his father and possibly mad, thought himself to be the reincarnation of Hercules, and liked to take part in gladiatorial games dressed in a lionskin and using a club. He was finally killed at the instigation of his own advisers. Pertinax (193), his successor, chosen by the Praetorian Guard, reigned only three months before being assassinated by those who had chosen him. As the sole permanent armed body in Rome, the Praetorians could overawe any civilian power, and so arrogated to themselves the prerogative of making and unmaking emperors. They now put the office of emperor up for auction to the highest bidder, and awarded it to Didius Julianus, a wealthy Senator.

The Severan Dynasty. But meanwhile the army on the Danube had declared Septimius Severus (193–211) Emperor. Upon reaching Rome he deposed Didius, then put down revolts led by two other would-be emperors. Severus' rule was openly autocratic, and as openly rested upon the power of the army. He changed the personnel of the Praetorian Guard from natives of Italy to troops drawn from the provinces, and improved conditions generally in the army. An "Orientalizing" trend began to show in the reign of Severus. His wife, Julia Domna, was a religious enthusiast who probably encouraged him to set up emperor-worship in the army in place of the former worship of the standards.

Caracalla (211–17) and Geta, Severus' sons, ruled jointly until Caracalla murdered Geta. The reign of Caracalla, a vicious and cruel man, was nonetheless notable for his extension of Roman citizenship to all free inhabitants of the Empire (212). Caracalla was assassinated by order of the Praetorian prefect Macrinus (217–18). The army revolted when Macrinus attempted to reduce its pay, and hailed Heliogabalus, the great-nephew of Julia Domna and a Syrian, as Emperor. Heliogabalus (218–22) ruled as a completely Oriental despot, introducing the sun-god, whose hereditary high priest he was, as the supreme deity at Rome. His mad debauchery, however, brought his downfall, and he was succeeded by his cousin Alexander Severus (222–35). Alexander, very young when he came to power, ruled moderately under his mother's guidance. But the army, now thoroughly insubordinate, mutinied, killed Alexander, and put a Thracian soldier, Maximinus, on the throne.

There followed a half-century of repeated civil war in which the army set up 26 recognized Emperors as well as many unrecognized rivals. Almost all these rulers died violent deaths. The internal confusion was compounded by barbarian invasions from many sides of the Empire. During this period the Empire was often disunited, ruled by several Emperors at once. Even so, there were competent Emperors, such as Claudius II (268–70), Aurelian (270–75), who defeated Zenobia's Palmyrene empire in the East, and Probus (276–82), who went far toward restoring the unity of the Empire and toward limiting the inroads of the Germanic invaders.

Imperial Reorganization. With the accession of Diocletian (284–305), a man of great ability put into power by the army, the Empire was reorganized along new lines. Diocletian's plan provided for two coemperors, called Augusti, and two assistants, called Caesares, to be heirs of the Augusti. This arrangement was designed to regularize the succession and to divide the unwieldy Empire into four parts, each ruled by an Augustus or a Caesar. Diocletian himself took most of the East as his province and made Nicomedia in Bithynia his capital, while in the West Milan and later Ravenna gradually eclipsed Rome itself.

The division of the army under four able commanders made it possible for the government to deal with barbarian invaders and internal revolts, and the Empire was again united. Provincial government was reorganized, civil and military authority sharply divided, and provinces subdivided in order to make revolt more difficult. Diocletian also revised the system of taxation, attempted to regularize the currency, and aimed at fixing prices for all commodities and services in order to stabilize the economy, though this last measure proved impossible to enforce. Diocletian revived persecution of the Christians, who had been left in peace for a long period. Although the persecution was severe and many Christians died, the Church remained strongly organized.

In 305 Diocletian and his co-Augustus, Maximian, abdicated according to plan, leaving the succession to Galerius and Constantius. A period of rivalry for power followed, and by 310 there were five Augusti at once in the Empire and no Caesars. From this struggle Constantine, the son of Constantius, emerged victorious, after defeating Maxentius at the Milvian Bridge in 312, where he is said to have seen a vision of a military standard bearing the sign of the cross with the legend *In hoc signo vinces* ("In this sign thou shalt conquer"). Constantine and Licinius now divided the rule and issued a decree of toleration, the Edict of Milan, which made Christianity legal. Constantine's mother Helena, who is credited with having found the relic of the True Cross and the site of the Holy Sepulcher, was a great patroness of Christianity.

Rivalry between the two Augusti soon arose, and Constantine, after defeating Licinius, ruled alone from 324 to 337. Constantine wished to keep the power in his own family, and appointed sons and nephews as Caesars, apportioning the Empire among them. He founded a new capital, Constantinople, centrally located between the European and Asiatic parts of the Empire. Constantine became a Christian shortly before his death, though he continued to tolerate other religions and to maintain the imperial cult.

Constantine's Empire was divided among his three sons, Constantine II, Constans and Constantius II, who ruled jointly (337–40). When Constantine encroached upon the territory of Constans, he was defeated and killed, and the two remaining brothers ruled for 10 years (340–50). Constans gave way to a usurper, Magnentius, who then ruled in Italy and the West until Constantius deposed him in turn. Constantius, who was childless, made first his cousin Gallus and then Gallus' brother Julian, Caesar. Julian, a scholar and writer, proved an effective general against barbarian invaders in Gaul. He was thereupon proclaimed Augustus in the West, at Paris. Constantius died while marching against Julian to contest this claim, and thus Julian was left sole Emperor.

Julian (361–63), called "the Apostate," the last of the Constantine dynasty, is notable for his attempt to restore paganism to its dominant position. Although he did not persecute the Christians, he tried to suppress them by other means, but without success. With Julian's death while fighting the Persians, all overt opposition to Christianity ended.

The Barbarian Tide and the Disintegration of the Empire. After the brief reign of Jovian (363–64), Valentinian I and Valens, his brother, were co-Augusti. Their reign was a constant struggle to protect the Empire against barbarian invaders from many directions. Valens, who ruled in the East, had to contend with the Goths. Meeting them in force at Adrianople (378), the Romans were completely defeated and Valens killed. The Gothic victory at Adrianople was never fully retrieved. Theodosius succeeded Valens and temporarily subdued the Goths, who settled south of the Danube and remained there as an independent people, allied to the Romans. Meanwhile Maximus had usurped power in Britain. He defeated Gratian, successor to Valentinian I, but was defeated in turn by Theodosius in 388. Theodosius died in 395, after putting down one last revolt by the Franks.

Theodosius was the last Roman Emperor to rule East and West together, and indeed the last to rule the West at all in any real sense. The migrations of the barbarians were now a tide not to be stemmed, and the history of the western part of the Empire became that of the Goths, Vandals, and others vying for power, with certain Roman puppet-emperors supported by barbarian generals. The first of these puppets was Honorius, Theodosius' son, whose regent was the Vandal Stilicho. Arcadius, Honorius' brother, was Emperor in the East, and from this time on the Empire was never united again. Stilicho held off the Goths while he lived, but after his death Alaric and the Goths sacked Rome, in 410. The actual fall of Rome is often dated to 476, when the last Emperor of Roman birth, who bore the significant name Romulus Augustulus, abdicated in favor of the German Odoacer.

In several campaigns, Belisarius, the remarkable general of Justinian (527–65), unsuccessfully attempted to recover the rule of the West. It was Justinian who closed the schools of philosophy in Athens. His reign may properly mark the end of ancient and the beginning of Byzantine history in the eastern half of what had been the Roman Empire.

THEATER

The Romans retained the essential Greek form of theater, but, in adapting it to their own purposes, they proceeded to introduce a number of changes which materially affected its structural principles. At the beginning, except when the Romans put existing Greek buildings to use, only temporary wooden playhouses were erected; but by 55 B.C. Pompey's stone theater was built in Rome itself, followed by a second, for which Cornelius Balbus was responsible, and by a third, the theater of Marcellus, the remains of which may still be seen. These were the ancestors of the vast houses which, during the Empire, were built almost everywhere the legions penetrated.

All exhibit similar features. In the first place, the Romans had a passion for precision and for a grandiose

Roman mask of tragedy.

architectural style, and accordingly the various portions of the Greek playhouse were united in a single framework; the skene, the orchestra, and the auditorium (now called the *cavea*) became one. The virtual disappearance of the old Greek chorus materially contributed toward the securing of this unity. Obviously, when no large choral group existed, an extensive circular orchestra was not only useless but left too wide a gap between audience and stage. Hence the whole of the skene was brought forward, leaving merely a semicircular orchestra, while at the same time the *cavea* was similarly made semicircular by cutting off the sweeping sides of the Greek auditorium. Concurrently, the desire to achieve imposing architectural symmetry led to the elaboration of the scene-building and to the enclosing of the entire structure within massive walls. A comparison of the ruins of the great Roman theater at Orange in southern France with the remaining relics of the Hellenistic theater at Epidaurus immediately demonstrates the basically fresh principle governing the later theatrical form.

The Greek playhouses had been entirely open to the sky, and, since they were often erected on hillsides that offered to spectators' eyes a wide vista of mountain, plain, or seacoast, the impression created by the performances must have gained much from the setting of the plays' actions against a natural landscape. In Roman times this impression was lost. Usually, the sites chosen were on level ground and thus the spectators' view was circumscribed by the theater's structure. Still further, the larger playhouses, apart from having a projecting roof over the stage, were provided with canvas awnings that could be drawn over the entire auditorium; and there were even some smaller houses completely covered over. Scenery was freely displayed and even the front curtain invented. The Roman theater clearly had moved far in the direction of what we conceive of when we speak of theater today.

There was another significant change. In ancient Athens the performances had had a dignified religious-patriotic character; during Roman times this vanished. Certainly, the plays were given during the course of civically sponsored "ludi," or games, but, whereas the Greek festivals were restricted to a few days each year and were blessed by the presence of the priest of Dionysus, the Roman games were freely spread over the entire twelve months and possessed little or no religious significance. Amid such conditions the performances rapidly became professional. A manager gathered a company of actors, purchased new plays, even indulged in advertising through public criers and other means—selling his theatrical wares in the hope of gain. Whereas the Greek productions had been eagerly awaited and significant occasions attended by all the citizens, the Roman productions became merely shows, matters of entertainment. At the beginning the acting profession seems to have been held in fair esteem, so that the fame of Roscius (126?–?62 B.C.) has caused his name to stand as a kind of symbol for supreme histrionic skill, but soon the performers (often slaves) degenerated into becoming a despised section of the community and sank still lower in esteem when the early Church turned to lash the stage.

Decline of Drama. Naturally in these circumstances drama declined. The writing of tragedies continued, but, so far as we can tell, they inclined now to melodrama and rhetorical bombast, and even so, soon ceased to appeal. The well-known dramas of Seneca (c.4 B.C.–65 A.D.) were not intended for theatrical production but only for reading or recitation. Comedy for a time enjoyed greater success, especially in the hands of Terence (185–159 B.C.) and Plautus (254?–184 B.C.); but gradually all forms of literary drama were submerged in popular displays of a debased kind. Gladiatorial shows and chariot races caught the attention of the mob, as did richly mounted sea fights— when the orchestras were actually filled with water. Displays of boxing and rope dancing won plaudits. The *mimi*, or mimes, who had carried on a farcical tradition from Greek times now came into their own and substituted for comedy rough shows, vulgar in tone and largely improvised. For courtly spectators highly indecent dance performances based on classical legend took the place of tragedy. When the Roman Empire fell it left dozens of sumptuous theaters, but hardly anything that was truly dramatic.

When the modern theater came to be established in the 16th century, it was the Roman and not the Greek model that was followed. The relics of the imperial playhouses were examined and much use was made of the *De architectura*, a work discovered in manuscript and printed in 1486, which was written by Vitruvius, Roman architect and engineer of the 1st century B.C. Thus was stimulated a lively attempt to adapt the Roman playhouse to later conditions, an attempt that resulted, on the one hand, in the erection of the academically inspired Teatro Olimpico in Vicenza (completed in 1584), and in the evolution of the "picture-frame" stage where the artists experimented in pictorial settings modeled upon what they had learned about the scenic methods in use in Roman theaters. At the same time the new dramatists, Shakespeare among them, gained inspiration, not from Sophocles and Aristophanes, but from Seneca, Terence, and Plautus. From them the playwrights learned things good and bad; a sense of form, the true Roman heritage, came from this source, but from it also derived Seneca's melodramatic flavor and Plautus' love of farce.

PEOPLE, PLACES, AND TERMS

AGRIPPA [ə-grĭp'ə], **MARCUS VIPSANIUS** (c.63–12 B.C.), Roman general and statesman. One of the chief supporters of Octavian in his struggle to gain control of the empire after Caesar's assassination, he was largely responsible for the naval victories, 36 B.C., over Sextus Pompey at Mylae and Naulochus, and especially for Octavian's victory over Antony at Actium in 31 B.C. After Octavian became Emperor Augustus, Agrippa was one of his most trusted subordinates as both soldier and administrator, and he worked closely with the Emperor in the immense task of organizing the empire, carrying out diplomatic and military missions and assisting in engineering and building enterprises. For a time Augustus apparently considered him his most suitable successor. His third wife was Augustus' daughter Julia.

AGRIPPINA [ăg-rĭ-pī'nə] **THE ELDER** (c.14 B.C.–33 A.D.), daughter of Agrippa and Julia, granddaughter of the Emperor Augustus, and wife of Germanicus Caesar, the heir apparent to Tiberius. After her husband died under suspicious circumstances in 19 A.D., Agrippina accused Tiberius of instigating his murder, and became a caustic critic of his regime. She was exiled to Pandataria Island in 29 A.D. and died there of starvation. Among her nine children were the Emperor Caligula and Agrippina the Younger, wife of Claudius I.

AGRIPPINA THE YOUNGER (15–59 A.D.), daughter of Agrippina the Elder and Germanicus Caesar. Her birthplace was renamed, after her, *Colonia Agrippina* (now Cologne). Her brother, the emperor Caligula, exiled her in 39, but her uncle Claudius, becoming Emperor in 41, recalled her and ultimately married her (49). She persuaded Claudius to choose Nero, her son by her first marriage, over Britannicus, his son by a former marriage, as his heir, and then poisoned him (54). Nero became Emperor and Agrippina was all-powerful, until Nero, resenting her ascendancy, arranged her death.

ALEXANDER SEVERUS [sə-vēr'əs] (208–235 A.D.), Roman Emperor, 222–235. Julia Maesa induced her grandson, the Emperor Heliogabalus, to adopt her other grandson, his cousin, who assumed the name Marcus Aurelius Alexander Severus in 221 and became sole Emperor in 222, on the murder of Heliogabalus by the praetorian guard. His reign was the last bright period before the military anarchy. His mother, Julia Mamaea, and his advisers produced decent government within the empire, but proved unequal to the challenge of war on the eastern and northern frontiers. His own troops murdered him and his mother at their camp near Mainz.

ANCUS MARCIUS [ăng-kəs mär'shē-əs], fourth king of Rome (reigned c.640–616 B.C.). His alleged founding of a colony at Ostia, where the Tiber meets the sea, probably reflects an extension of Roman power to this nearby coastal point. Some exploits attributed to him sound like later inventions, designed to glorify the great family of the Marcii with a heroic ancestor.

ANTONINUS PIUS [ăn-tə-nī'nəs pī'əs] (86–161 A.D.), Roman emperor (138–161). From a senatorial family of southern Gaul, Titus Aurelius Fulvus Boionius Arrius Antoninus, later called Antoninus Pius, had a distinguished career, which included a very successful proconsulship of Asia. In 138 he was adopted by the Emperor Hadrian, after he himself, at Hadrian's wish, had adopted the future Emperors Marcus Aurelius and Lucius Verus. Antoninus Pius became Emperor on Hadrian's death. Unlike Hadrian, he remained in and around Rome. Certain reforms of Hadrian produced their results under Antoninus Pius, in whose beneficent reign the Roman Empire for the last time enjoyed a long period of peace with centralization of authority in the city of Rome.

ANTONY [ăn'tə-nē], **MARK**, Lat. name, Marcus Antonius (c.83–30 B.C.), Roman politician and general, member of the Second Triumvirate, and lover of Cleopatra. Notably handsome and energetic, he gained while still young a reputation for military prowess in Syria and Egypt, and later in Gaul. There he became attached to Julius Caesar, supporting him when Caesar defied the Senate and its general, Pompey, in 49 B.C. Antony was left in charge of Italy when Caesar pursued Pompey to Greece, and later brought the reinforcements which enabled Caesar to defeat the Pompeians at Pharsalus in 48. Returned to Italy, he was Caesar's *magister equitum*, or chief lieutenant, in charge of Italian affairs in Caesar's absence, and he was also Caesar's colleague in the consulship in the last year of Caesar's life. After the assassination of Caesar, in 44, it was Antony who delivered the funeral oration, and aroused the populace against the conspirators—a scene familiar from Shakespeare's *Julius Caesar*.

Antony apparently hoped to become Caesar's successor, but joined Octavian (Augustus), who had similar designs, in forming the Second Triumvirate (43) with the nonentity Lepidus. The two rivals collaborated until after the battle of Philippi (42), at which the army of Brutus and Cassius was defeated. In drawing up lists of enemies to be proscribed and executed Antony and Octavian yielded to each other, Antony insisting upon the execution of Cicero, who had attacked him in the so-called Philippic orations. In the division of responsibilities after Philippi, Octavian retained Italy, which was politically important though difficult and dangerous to administer, and Antony took the rich east, which gave him scope for military successes.

In 41 Antony met Cleopatra, Queen of Egypt, and spent the next winter with her in Egypt. He was forced to return to Italy upon the defeat of his brother by Octavian at Perusia in 40. He then married Octavia, sister of Octavian, as a means of strengthening the bond between Octavian and himself; in 37, the Triumvirate was renewed for another five years. In the same year, however, Antony again met Cleopatra. His subsequent behavior as Cleopatra's lover and as an Oriental despot, his disloyalty to Octavia, and his disregard for the interests of Rome led Octavian ultimately to break with Antony and to declare war against Cleopatra. Octavian's fleet met that of Antony and Cleopatra in 31 off Actium, where the Egyptian fleet was defeated. Cleopatra fled, Antony followed her, and his navy surrendered to Octavian. Although his situation was now hopeless, Antony attempted to hold Egypt against Octavian, but at the latter's arrival, Antony committed suicide, possibly believing that Cleopatra had already done so. She was actually still alive, but did kill herself soon after.

APPIAN [ăp′ē-ən] **WAY,** oldest of Roman roads, built in 312 B.C. by the censor Appius Claudius. It ran from Rome 132 mi. south to Capua. The original gravel surface was gradually replaced by lava-block paving throughout its course across the Campagna to the Alban Hills, and down the coast through the Pontine Marshes and the mountains. After 268 B.C. it was extended 32 mi., over the Apennines to Beneventum, and later continued south through Venosa to Tarentum and the Adriatic coast at Brindisi (202 mi.). Of vital importance for contact with the eastern Mediterranean, it continued in use until late antiquity, and was restored in the 18th century. Prominent landmarks on the Appian Way immediately outside Rome are the church of Domine Quo Vadis, various catacombs, the remains of the Circus Maxentius, and the Casal Rotondo.

APPII [ăp′ē-ī] **FORUM,** forum of Appius, a halting place for rest and provisions on the famous Appian Way, between Brindisi and Rome. Located 40 mi. southeast of Rome, it was there that Paul, as a prisoner, was met by Christians of the imperial capital (Acts 28:15).

APULEIUS [ăp-yə-lē′əs], **LUCIUS** (2d century A.D.), Roman rhetorician and philosopher. Of Greek ancestry, he was born and educated in North Africa. He traveled widely as a lecturer on literature and philosophy, but his fame rests upon an 11-book picaresque novel, which he himself called *Metamorphoses*, but which is better known as *The Golden Ass*. Written in the first person, it narrates the adventures of the hero Lucius, who is turned by magic into an ass, though he retains his human understanding. The bare plot was borrowed from a Greek original. The adventures range through every class of society. Irrelevant stories form a large part of it, one of which is the charming tale of Cupid and Psyche. The book ends with the restoration of Lucius to his own form and his initiation into the cult of Isis, in whose service he becomes a recluse. The style is colloquial, but is marked by almost poetic assonance and rhythm—a new Latin, foreshadowing the Romance languages.

AQUEDUCT [ăk′wə-dŭkt′], an artificial conduit in which a large quantity of water flows from a source to a distribution system. Historically, the term denoted a covered masonry channel in which water flowed by gravity, but it now includes an open or closed gravity conduit or a closed pressure conduit made of masonry, concrete, or other strong material.

Ancient Aqueducts. Ruins of aqueducts found in the Near East and Europe show that they were among the earliest engineering works of mankind. Those built by the Greeks and Romans were surprisingly large, considering the limitations in equipment and material. Their aqueducts were designed to use gravity as a source for water pressure. If the elevations were right, the conduits were laid near the ground and sometimes through a tunnel, like the one in Samos, Greece, which was 0.8 mi. long and 8 by 8 ft. in cross-section. The Romans were noted for the high, arched viaducts they built to support the flow of water across valleys or low areas. The first aqueduct to serve Rome was the 11-mi. Aqua Appia, built about 312 B.C. Of the 13 aqueducts built to serve Rome up to 305 A.D., 50 mi. of the total of 359 mi. were on arches. The conduits had vertical sides and flat or arched roofs and were as much as 5 ft. wide and 9 ft. high. Although lined with cement, they cracked and leaked badly. Some of the many magnificent aqueducts built in the Roman Empire provinces still stand in Segovia, Spain, Metz, Germany, and Nîmes, France. The viaduct at Nîmes, now called the *Pont du Gard*, is 900 ft. long and has three tiers of arches rising to a height of 160 ft.

The Appian Way, oldest and most famous of the Roman roads.
(BERNARD G. SILBERSTEIN—RAPHO GUILLUMETTE)

ARMY, ROMAN The early legion was a citizen militia recruited by a yearly draft based upon property. Basic equipment included throwing-spear, sword, shield, and cuirass (breastplate). A small cavalry force was attached to each legion, and siege engines of great efficiency were developed. But the real success of Roman arms depended upon discipline, practice, and organization. Pay was not introduced until 406 B.C. Originally the legions fought in solid ranks like the Greek phalanx, but during the 4th century B.C. this method was abandoned in favor of smaller, more maneuverable units (maniples).

Because of foreign wars and changing conditions, Gaius Marius between 107 and 100 B.C. reformed the army as a professional body. He threw open the legions to non-landowners, enlisting them on his own initiative for a specific number of years. He gave each legion a symbol of its existence, an eagle that was later worshiped as a sacred object. Each legion was divided into ten cohorts, each cohort into three maniples, and each maniple into two centuries. Paper strength was 6,000 men per legion, with 100 in each of the 60 centuries, but actual strength was usually much less. The cohorts soon replaced the maniples as tactical units, and Caesar commonly employed them in three lines: four in the first and three in the other two. The total number of legions reached 60 by the time of Caesar and Antony. The backbone of each legion was the centurion, one commanding each century. The senior centurion (*primipilus*) was an old soldier of great experience, whose judgment was respected even by the commissioned officers (*tribuni militum* and *legati*).

With the birth of the Empire (27 B.C.) the Emperor Augustus put the army on a permanent basis, fixed the enlistment at 20 years, and gave the legions permanent duty in the subject provinces. Each legion henceforth received a number and a name, such as *Legio XII Fulminata*. Augustus was content with 25 legions. Later emperors required 30 and then 33. Gradually the barrier between soldier and officer ranks was broken down and eventually every soldier could dream of high rank for himself or his sons. With the permanent stationing of troops on the frontiers there arose the practice of recruiting locally from the provinces rather than the homeland. Thus Italians slowly disappeared from the legions and provincial recruits took their place. In the 3d century A.D. the legionaries were provincial in origin and predominantly barbarian.

Only citizens could serve in the legions, but the provincials, before receiving citizenship, were allowed to enter one of two special branches called collectively *auxilia*. One was composed of *alae* (cavalry) and the other of *cohortes* (infantry). Honorable discharge brought with it Roman citizenship. For the security of Italy, Augustus reformed the old Praetorian Guard, an elite corps of men who served for 16 years and received three times the pay of legionaries.

AUGURS (Lat. *augere*, "increase"), official Roman diviners. In the 1st century B.C. the college consisted of 15 members, who observed omens thought to manifest the will of the gods. Their interpretation of the flights of birds, for example, determined the propitious moment for action. When belief in magic decreased, they provided the auspices, or favorable signs, required before major political action could be taken.

AUGUSTAN AGE, in Latin literature, the name given to the brilliant literary period during Augustus' reign (27 B.C.–14 A.D.). Horace, in satire and lyric, Vergil in epic, and Livy in history are the greatest names of the period; but Ovid, with his *Metamorphoses*, and the elegiac poets, Tibullus and Propertius, add to its luster.

AUGUSTUS [ô-gŭs'təs] (63 B.C.–14 A.D.), first Roman Emperor (reigned 27 B.C.–14 A.D.), originally named Gaius Octavius. Born near Rome, he lost his father early, but soon attracted the interest of his great-uncle, Julius Caesar, by whom he was introduced to public life, taken campaigning, and made a pontiff and patrician. At the time of Caesar's murder in 44 B.C., the 19-year-old Octavius was at Apollonia on the east Adriatic coast. In his will Caesar named him his heir and adopted son, whence he was known, until 27 B.C., as Octavian (Caesar Octavianus).

Returning to Italy, Octavian first had to curb Mark Antony's pretensions. He raised a private army and, urged on by Cicero, helped senatorial forces defeat Antony near Modena. Antony, imbued now with respect for Octavian, withdrew to Gaul. After both consuls commanding the senatorial forces had died, Octavian felt strong enough to demand, and obtain, the consulship for himself (43 B.C.). He then struck a bargain with Antony and Lepidus, Caesar's Masters of Horse. They obliged the Senate to sanction their appointment as Triumvirs for Regulating the State, for five years (to Dec. 31, 38 B.C.), and promptly slaughtered their opponents in Italy, including Cicero. Then Antony and Octavian went to Macedonia and suppressed Caesar's murderers, Brutus and Cassius, and their army, at Philippi in 42 B.C. After Philippi, Antony went to Asia Minor, and Octavian to Italy.

Dissension arose when Octavian defeated Antony's wife and brother in civil war at Perugia. The Treaty of Brundisium, giving Antony the East, Octavian the West, and Lepidus Africa, with Italy as joint recruiting ground, restored harmony, and Antony married Octavian's sister in 40 B.C. In 39 B.C. the Triumvirs signed the Treaty of Misenum with Sextus Pompey, who had a powerful navy, and whose kinswoman, Scribonia, Octavian had married. After Antony's departure for his eastern provinces, however, Octavian quickly divorced Scribonia and married Livia, mother of Tiberius and Drusus Germanicus by a previous union. He then made war on Sextus, reassuring Antony with the Treaty of Tarentum (37 B.C.), which prolonged the Triumvirate for another five years (to Dec. 31, 33 B.C.).

More or less successful campaigns near the Dalmatian coast (35–33 B.C.) increased Octavian's confidence against Antony, and soon his propaganda was exploiting Antony's failure against Parthia (36 B.C.), his alleged un-Roman behavior, and especially his love affair with Cleopatra. In 32 B.C., though no longer Triumvir, Octavian retained his army and induced Italy and the western provinces to swear personal allegiance to himself. At his insistence a partisan Senate deprived Antony of all authority and declared war on Cleopatra, and in 31 B.C. Antony and Cleopatra were defeated at Actium. Their flight to Alexandria and subsequent suicides left Egypt and its treasures to Octavian (30 B.C.).

Now master of the Roman world, Octavian reorganized

Roman coin with inscription "Augustus the God."

conducted by various generals, including Agrippa and Augustus' stepsons, Tiberius and Drusus, pacified the empire and consolidated its boundaries. An attempt, however, to advance the northern frontier from the Rhine to the Elbe failed when Varus' army was destroyed in the Teutoburg Forest by Arminius in 9 A.D. In the provinces Augustus established a standing army of 25 legions and correspondingly numerous auxiliaries, and in Italy a garrison of Praetorian Guards, Urban Cohorts, and Vigiles (a combined police and fire brigade). Fleets patrolled the sea lanes. Service in the forces was for a fixed number of years, and retirement bonuses were paid from a special military treasury.

As the Principate did not provide for its own automatic continuation, Augustus sought to assure a smooth transfer of power by procuring before his own death Proconsular Imperium and Tribunician Power for the intended next *princeps*. His first clearly indicated successor was Agrippa, who married Augustus' daughter Julia in 21 B.C. When Agrippa died in 12 B.C., his sons by Julia, Gaius and Lucius, became heirs apparent. Their early deaths, however, obliged Augustus to choose his stepson Tiberius, and it was he who succeeded when Augustus died in 14 A.D.

Ruthless and unscrupulous in acquiring power, Augustus was able and sagacious in using it. He ultimately brought peace, law, and order to a weary Roman world. His system of government worked tolerably well, requiring comparatively few modifications for over two centuries. Autocracy was implicit in it, but antiquity knew no other method for administering large areas.

it as an unavowed monarchy, adroitly avoiding any appearance of dictatorship. In January of 27 B.C. he was proclaimed "Augustus," after he had "restored the Republic" by reactivating, to outward appearances, the consular elections in traditional republican form. Actually, he completely controlled the elections, and was himself consul every year until 23 B.C In addition he enjoyed enormous moral authority. Moreover, a Proconsular Imperium, giving him command of Spain, Gaul, and Syria for the next 10 years, placed practically all the armed forces under his orders.

In 23 B.C. Augustus resigned his consulship, but simultaneously his Proconsular Imperium was pronounced valid and absolute—not only in the provinces specifically entrusted to him—but in all other provinces, too, should he need to intervene in them. The 10-year limit to this Imperium was illusory, since on expiration it was invariably renewed. Similarly, in 23 B.C. he acquired for life the so-called Tribunician Power. This enabled him to veto any official's acts, and regularized his dealings with Senate and People. He numbered the years of his reign from the day this Tribunician Power was conferred.

After 23 B.C. his formal powers remained essentially unchanged, and his system of rule is styled the Principate, from the Latin *princeps* ("the first"), his popular, unofficial title. Officially, he held no unrepublican title. Although he was called Imperator Caesar Augustus, Caesar was actually his name, and Imperator and Augustus designations of republican origin conferred by the Senate.

Augustus carefully supervised all aspects of state life. Religion was cultivated—old temples were repaired, new ones built, and emperor-worship inaugurated. Marriage and family life were fostered and divorce discouraged. Magnificent buildings transformed Rome from a city of brick into one of marble. Grain supply, grain dole, and flood control in Rome; highways in Italy; and a balanced budget received special attention. Military operations

AURELIAN [ô-rē′lē-ən] (c.213–275 A.D.), Roman Emperor (reigned 270–275 A.D.) who reunified the empire. Of humble Illyrian stock but a fine soldier, Lucius Domitius Aurelianus, while commanding troops fighting the Goths, was elevated to the throne by the army about three months after the death of Claudius Gothicus. He first defeated and drove out the Juthungi, who had invaded Italy. He then marched to the east and attacked the Palmyrenes, who, under Queen Zenobia, were attempting to establish an empire of their own in Egypt, Syria, and Asia Minor. By great effort he restored the empire in the east, placing a garrison in Palmyra and capturing Zenobia. Next he attacked the Gallic Empire in the west and brought Gaul, Britain, and Spain back to Rome. He then reformed Rome's inflated currency, and tried to establish the cult of the Sun as the divine sponsor of the empire. He particularly distinguished himself as a disciplinarian, telling the arrogant soldiery that it was not they, but the god, who had made him Emperor. He was murdered in 275, but in his brief reign he performed a miracle of defense and reunification. The city of Rome still preserves the wall, 40 ft. high and 12 mi. in circumference, with which Aurelian fortified it.

BASILICA [bə-sĭl′ĭ-kə], Roman public building used for courts of law, public administration, and business; also, a building of the same type used as an Early Christian church. The Roman basilica was almost always rectangular in plan and divided into three aisles. At the end of the central aisle, the widest of the three, was located a semicircular area that projected from the rectangular shape of

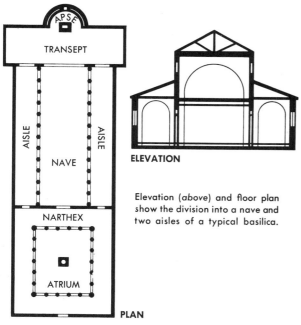

ELEVATION

Elevation (*above*) and floor plan show the division into a nave and two aisles of a typical basilica.

PLAN

Photo Alinari

Bust of Marcus Junius Brutus by Michelangelo.

the building and provided the tribunal for the judges and government officials. An important feature of the developed basilica was that the roof over the central aisle was raised above the side aisles to form a clerestory with windows that lighted the interior.

The plan of the Roman basilica is related to that of the Greek temple, both being rectangular and divided into three aisles. The early basilicas were also like Greek temples in that they were of post-and-lintel construction, that is, based on uprights that support horizontal beams. The main entrance to the Roman basilica was not in a fixed location, in some examples being located on a long side and in others on a short side. Some basilicas had double side aisles flanking the central aisle. Many constructed during the imperial period were built of concrete and had vaulted roofs.

Important basilicas in Rome, the ruins of which still exist, are the Basilica Ulpia (c.113 A.D.) and the Basilica of Constantine (c.312 A.D.), also known as the Basilica of Maxentius. The former was integrated into the design of the forum built by Emperor Trajan. The interior was divided into five aisles separated by marble columns. Its roof was of timber and tile. The Basilica of Constantine, adjoining the Roman Forum, was of concrete construction. The central aisle was roofed by a clerestory with groined or intersecting vaults in each bay.

BIBULUS [bĭb′yə-ləs], **MARCUS CALPURNIUS** (d.48 B.C.), co-consul with Julius Caesar in 59 B.C. After unsuccessfully opposing Caesar's agrarian reforms, he ceased to take any active part in affairs, inspiring the witticism that 59 was the year of the co-consulship of Julius and Caesar. Bibulus died while supporting Pompey in the Civil War.

BRUTUS [brōō′təs], **DECIMUS JUNIUS** (d.43 B.C.), conspirator against Julius Caesar, although he had served under

Caesar in Gaul and had been favored by him. He took part in the war between the forces of Marcus Junius Brutus and Cassius and those of Antony and Octavian, and for a while held chief command of the senatorial forces. While fighting in Cisalpine Gaul he was captured and killed by order of Antony.

BRUTUS, LUCIUS JUNIUS, first of the old Romans, instrumental in the expulsion of King Tarquinius from Rome in 509 B.C. and one of the two praetors, or joint annual magistrates, chosen to preside over the first year of the new Republic. Finding his sons involved in a plot to return the Tarquins to the throne, he tried them and put them to death. He somehow managed to have his colleague removed from the consulship on the ground that he was related to the Tarquins, and had a law passed exiling all the Tarquins. His name is traditionally connected with many conservative ceremonies, such as taking the auspices before entrance on an office. Brutus was killed by Tarquin's son in single combat.

BRUTUS, MARCUS JUNIUS (c.85–42 B.C.), chief conspirator, with Cassius, in the assassination of Julius Caesar. Serving Pompey in the Civil War, he was pardoned by Caesar after the battle of Pharsalus. Although close to Caesar, Brutus may have been influenced by the ideal of the ancient founder of his family, Lucius Junius Brutus, who, according to tradition, established the Roman Republic. Brutus' mother, Servilia, was at one time Caesar's mistress, and some have thought that Brutus may have been the dictator's illegitimate son. Plutarch wrote that, after being stabbed by Brutus, Caesar exclaimed, "*Kai su, technon!*" ("You too, my son!"), rather than the traditional

249

"Et tu, Brute!" ("You too, Brutus!"). After Caesar's death Brutus took a chief part in the war against Antony and Octavian, commanding the senatorial forces in the Balkans. He committed suicide after his defeat at Philippi.

CAELIUS RUFUS [sē'lē-əs roō'fəs], **MARCUS** (82–48 B.C.), Roman politician. A protégé of Cicero as a youth, he became an associate of Catiline and the lover of Clodia. After his affair with Clodia ended in a quarrel, he was accused, in 56 B.C., of plotting against her life, but was defended by Cicero in his oration *Pro Caelio* and acquitted. In the civil war between Caesar and Pompey, Caelius sided with Caesar, and tried unsuccessfully to influence Cicero to do the same. Becoming disillusioned with Caesar in 48, he tried to head a revolt against him, but was captured and executed. Much of our knowledge of Caelius comes from letters exchanged between him and Cicero.

CAESAR [sē'zər], **GAIUS JULIUS** (102–44 B.C.), Roman statesman and general, one of the greatest figures of antiquity. Born of an ancient patrician family, he nevertheless became a champion of the popular party, influenced probably by his aunt's husband Marius, the great popular leader. In 82 B.C. Caesar was proscribed by the reactionary Sulla for refusing to divorce his wife Cornelia. Though he spared Caesar, Sulla recognized that "in young Caesar there are many Mariuses." Following military service in Asia, Caesar returned to Rome after the death of Sulla (78 B.C.) to begin his political career. His prosecution of Dolabella for extortion as governor of Macedonia earned him popularity as well as a reputation as an orator. From 76 to 74 B.C. Caesar sojourned in the eastern Mediterranean, studying oratory in Rhodes, and campaigning against a Cappadocian army in Asia. En route he had been captured by pirates. Setting an even higher price on his ransom than the pirates had named, he vowed to return and punish his captors after his release. Caesar soon kept his word by crucifying this same pirate band. This anecdote in Plutarch testifies to the steadfastness and ruthlessness which were to serve Caesar well in his subsequent rise to power.

Rise to Power. His first step in his official career was as quaestor in 68 B.C. During his term as aedile in 65 he went heavily into debt in an effort to win the support of the masses by impressive public works and entertainment. Caesar was helped by enormous loans from the millionaire Crassus, who expected Caesar's political support in return. While pontifex maximus in 63 B.C., at the trial of the men involved in the Catilinarian conspiracy, Caesar favored leniency, thereby stiffening the opposition of the senatorial party. In 62 B.C. he initiated proceedings against his second wife, Pompeia, for her involvement with Clodius Pulcher in the profanation of the rites of Bona Dea which had been held in Caesar's home.

In 62 he was praetor and in the next year was propraetor, or governor, of Further Spain. Here he discovered his talent for generalship. Upon his return to Rome in 60 B.C. he entered into a political coalition, usually called the First Triumvirate, with Pompey, who was reputed to be the greatest general of his day, and Crassus, who was willing to spend his fortune to obtain a political career. His alliance with Pompey was cemented by the marriage of his daughter Julia to Pompey, who was six years Caesar's senior.

By agreement with his fellow triumvirs Caesar was consul for 59 B.C.; at this time he ingratiated himself with two important economic groups by passing an agrarian law which provided land for poor citizens and veterans and by reducing the equestrians' tax contracts in Asia. Caesar obtained a five-year command in Cisalpine and Transalpine Gaul and Illyricum which was renewed before the end of this period (58–54 B.C.) and extended to 49 B.C. Here his vigorous campaigns resulted in the subjugation of all Gaul, the invasion of Britain, and, even more important for his career, the winning of the personal loyalty of the legions.

The death of Julia in 54 B.C., and of Crassus in 53, brought the rivalry and hostility between Pompey and Caesar into the open. In 49 Caesar asked permission to stand for the consulship *in absentia* on the grounds that if he first laid down his command, as he was legally required to do, he would not be safe from threatened prosecution. By crossing the Rubicon, which was the boundary of his province, under arms, Caesar became technically a rebel, and Pompey was made commander in chief to resist his advance on Rome. Pompey withdrew the senatorial forces to Greece; he had a strong army in Spain, controlled the seas, and evidently expected to crush Caesar in Italy by a pincer movement from east and west. Caesar first disposed of the Pompeian forces in Spain by a brilliant campaign; stormed Marseilles, which had elected to stand neutral; and then crossed to Greece, where, after a retreat at Dyrrachium, he won a complete victory over the Pompeian forces at the battle of Pharsalus in Aug., 48. Pompey fled to Egypt, where he was killed.

In Egypt Caesar encountered Cleopatra, who became his mistress for her own political ends, and bore him a son. After establishing her firmly on the throne, he departed for Pontus, in Asia Minor, where he defeated Pompey's ally Pharnaces II at the battle of Zela. He reported the victory to the Senate in his terse message: *"Veni, vidi, vici"* ("I came, I saw, I conquered"). In 46 B.C. he defeated the Pompeian forces under Scipio at the battle of Thapsus in Africa, and the next year destroyed the remnants of the senatorial forces under Pompey's sons at the battle of Munda in Spain. He returned to Rome in Sept., 45, and spent the months remaining before his death in reorganizing the state and preparing for an expedition against the Parthians, who had defeated Crassus. His assumption of dictatorial powers, however, occasioned increasing fear and distaste. On the Ides (15th) of March, 44, he was assassinated by a senatorial group who believed that with the removal of Caesar the state would revert to the old republican order.

Accomplishments. Although Caesar appears to have been unscrupulous in his rise to power, there can be no question that once at the top, he used his power for the welfare of Rome and of mankind. In the short time given him he did much in the direction of reorganizing the Roman economy and administration, raising the political position of the provincials, and safeguarding the frontiers. The great weakness of Roman political theory was that it persisted in thinking in terms of the old city-state long

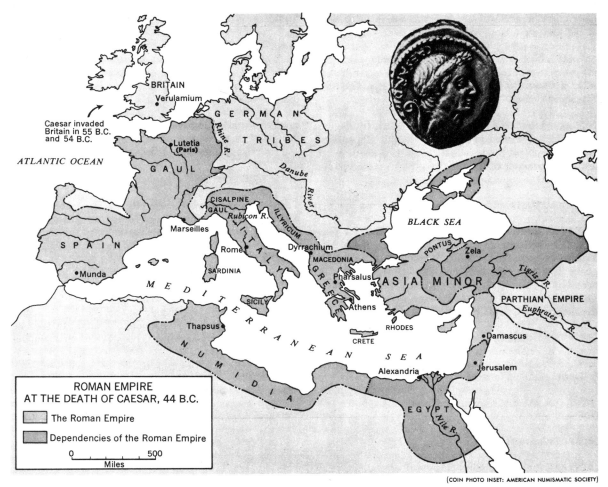

ROMAN EMPIRE
AT THE DEATH OF CAESAR, 44 B.C.

The Roman Empire

Dependencies of the Roman Empire

0   500

Miles

Caesar invaded Britain in 55 B.C. and 54 B.C.

(COIN PHOTO INSET: AMERICAN NUMISMATIC SOCIETY)

after Rome had outgrown that form of government. Had he lived, Caesar might well have attempted to weld the empire into an organic whole with a strong central authority. His successor Augustus had autocratic control over the state, but disguised the fact somewhat by preserving republican forms. Because Caesar was impatient with the old forms, and did not disguise his impatience, the aristocratic party feared the curtailment of its privileges, and, suspecting Caesar of aspiring to kingship, assassinated him. Sincere as they may have been in their desire to restore an older way of life, they did not accomplish it. Their impracticality and Caesar's realism are proven by the bloody interval that elapsed before Augustus finally established a permanent autocracy.

Caesar's name survives in another connection. In 46 B.C. he reformed the Roman calendar by adding a month to make the lunar year correspond to the solar. The result, known as the Julian calendar, continued in use until the 16th century.

Not only do Caesar's accomplishments mark him as the most competent of the Romans; he appears also to have been endowed with extraordinary personal magnetism. He had the power to inspire extreme loyalty in his subordinates; and even Cicero, who was his political opponent, grudgingly admitted Caesar's charm. His intellect was keen, and his mind original and imaginative. He

would have an important place in Roman literature even if he had not been outstanding in other fields. The *Commentaries on the Gallic War*, comprising seven books, each covering the campaigns of a single year, written ostensibly to give a history of the Gallic campaigns, actually attempted to justify Caesar's actions in the eyes of his contemporaries. Cicero characterized its style as "sinewy, forthright, and charming, stripped of all finery as of a garment."

The *Commentaries on the Civil War* (between Caesar and Pompey), a more personal book, is his other major extant work. He also wrote poetry and works of literary criticism, and was much admired as an orator by such competent judges of oratory as Cicero and Quintilian.

There are more complete sources for the life and career of Caesar than for any other major political and military figure of antiquity. In addition to his own writings, Caesar figures in many of Cicero's letters and speeches, and is the subject of biographies by Suetonius and Plutarch.

CAESAR, title used by Roman emperors. First used by Augustus who had inherited the name from Julius Caesar, it was subsequently handed down to all his male descendants by adoption. Though the Julian family died out with Nero, Claudius and later emperors assumed the name as a title, and after Hadrian the title Caesar was also be-

251

stowed on the heir presumptive. Under Diocletian's system of four emperors (tetrarchy), the two junior emperors, who were to succeed as senior emperors (Augusti), were called the two Caesars. From this term derive the titles "tsar" and "kaiser."

CALIGULA [kə-lĭg'yə-lə] (12–41 A.D.), Roman Emperor, reigned 37–41. Son of Germanicus and Agrippina the Elder, he was named Gaius Caesar. He passed his infancy in a military camp on the Rhine and there was dubbed Caligula ("Bootikins") by the soldiers because of the military boots he wore. After Germanicus' death in 19 A.D. he lived successively with his mother, great-grandmother (Livia), and grandmother (Antonia) until 32 A.D., when he joined his great-uncle, the Emperor Tiberius, on the island of Capri. On Tiberius' death in 37 Caligula succeeded him. For some months he ruled well and popularly, but then, after a serious illness, began committing murders and other enormities. In 39 he went to Gaul to prepare an invasion of Britain, which, however, never materialized, and while at Mainz he became the object of a conspiracy. The plot was discovered, however, and ruthlessly suppressed. Returning to Rome, Caligula behaved even more despotically until another conspiracy led to his assassination.

Certainly a more autocratic Emperor than either of his predecessors, Caligula may have been aiming at a monarchy of Near Eastern type; his insistence on extravagant homage and his alleged incest with his sisters, especially Drusilla, might suggest as much. Perhaps, however, he was merely unbalanced; his caprices, extortions, profligacies, and follies, if correctly recorded, appear to be the actions of an eccentric or worse.

CAMILLUS [kə-mĭl'əs], **MARCUS FURIUS** (died c.365 B.C.), Roman hero, elected dictator of the Roman Republic five times. His greatest victory was the capture of the Etruscan city of Veii (396 B.C.), the acquisition of whose territory increased Rome's size, importance, and military strength. In 394 he reduced Falerii, and in 390, emerging from voluntary exile, defeated the invading Gauls, who had already conquered most of the city of Rome. He later gained victories over the Volsci and Aequi, took Praeneste, and once again dispersed the Gauls in 367. The account of his splendid career was continuously embellished in later times.

CANNAE [kăn'ē], site on the River Ofanto (anc. *Aufidus*) in southern Italy, where the Carthaginian general Hannibal annihilated a large Roman army under Aemilius Paulus and Terentius Varro in 216 B.C. Weakening his center and strengthening his wings, Hannibal enveloped the Romans after sucking in their center. His cavalry completed their destruction. Paulus was slain, but Varro managed to escape. The exact site of the battle is disputed, though finds of bones and weapons point to the south bank. A museum houses mementos of the battle.

CARACALLA [kăr-ə-kăl'ə] (188–217 A.D.), Roman Emperor (reigned 211–217), elder son of Septimius Severus and Julia Domna. His original name was Septimius Bassianus, but he was renamed Marcus Aurelius Antoninus

by his father in 196. His nickname "Caracalla" derived from the long Gallic tunic he wore. Caracalla in 198, and his younger brother Geta in 209, were associated with Septimius Severus on the throne. The two brothers quarreled constantly, and a year after their father's death in 211 Caracalla murdered Geta in his mother's presence, and then massacred his adherents, including the eminent jurist Papinian. Claiming to have forestalled Geta's murder of himself, he gave public thanks to the gods, particularly by issuing the famous Constitution Antoniniana of 212, which granted Roman citizenship to all free inhabitants of the Empire, and which thus increased the number who could worship the gods of Rome. In 213 Caracalla pacified the German frontier, defeating the Alamanni and completing defensive walls. Tyrannical by nature, Caracalla's extravagance (including the splendid Baths of Caracalla) and inflationary policies contributed to Rome's financial decline. During a war against the Parthians he was murdered near Carrhae. This was done at the order of the praetorian prefect Macrinus, who succeeded him as Emperor.

CARAUSIUS [kə-rô'shē-əs], **MARCUS AURELIUS** (c.245–293 A.D.), Roman officer of Belgic ancestry, usurper in Britain, 286–293. An able and energetic officer of Maximian I at the beginning of Diocletian's reign, Carausius helped subdue the Franks in Gaul, then took advantage of unsettled conditions to establish himself as emperor in Britain. Diocletian and Maximian recognized him as coemperor (c.289) and he extended his rule to northeast Gaul. He controlled the fleet in the English channel and was able to maintain himself until Constantius I attacked him at Boulogne. He was then murdered by his principal minister, Allectus.

CARINUS [kə-rī'nəs], **MARCUS AURELIUS** (d.285 A.D.), Roman Emperor (283–85). The elder son of the Emperor Carus, he was left behind to govern the West when Carus and Numerianus went east to fight the Persians. After the deaths of Carus and Numerianus, Diocletian was proclaimed Emperor by the army of the East. Carinus would not recognize him and proved himself a formidable adversary, but was murdered by one of his own officers in Moesia in the very hour of victory.

CARUS [kâr'əs], **MARCUS AURELIUS**, Roman Emperor (282–83 A.D.). Discontented with the severe discipline of the Emperor Probus, the army of Rhaetia proclaimed the praetorian prefect Carus emperor. On the murder of Probus, Carus associated his sons Carinus and Numerianus with him on the throne, and then turned his attention to frontier problems. He defeated the Quadi and Sarmatians on the Danube, and then resumed Aurelian's plan for a war against the Persians. Before his death, by accident or murder, he had penetrated deeply into Persian territory and captured the capital, Ctesiphon.

CASSIUS LONGINUS [kăsh'əs lŏn-jī'nəs], **GAIUS** (d.42 B.C.), chief conspirator, with Brutus, against Julius Caesar. He distinguished himself as a soldier under Crassus; later he joined the Pompeian party, but after the defeat of Pompey's army at Pharsalus surrendered to Caesar. Caesar treated him generously, making him praetor in 44 B.C., but he evidently felt Caesar to be his enemy still, and formed the plot against him. He and Brutus together led their army against Octavian and Antony at Philippi (42 B.C.), but when the battle began to go against them, Cassius committed suicide.

CASSIUS VECELLINUS [vĕs-ə-lĭ′nəs], **SPURIUS,** Roman statesman. He negotiated a treaty in 493 B.C. between Rome and her neighbors of the Latin League. In his 3d consulship (486) he was accused by the patricians of plotting for royal power by courting the people, and was put to death.

CATILINE [kăt′ə-lĭn], Latin name Lucius Sergius Catilina (c.108–62 B.C.), Roman politician, leader of a plot against the state which was foiled by Cicero. Catiline began his career as a lieutenant of Sulla, and was propraetor (governor) in Africa for two years. He wished to be a candidate for consul in 66 B.C. but was prevented by his impending prosecution for misgovernment. With others he plotted to murder the new consuls at the beginning of 65 B.C, but the plot was discovered. He was tried but acquitted, and was a candidate for the consulship of 63 B.C. He was defeated by Cicero, but ran again the next year, advocating the abolition of debts. Defeated again, he abandoned legal methods of attaining leadership and organized a conspiracy, with the intention of killing Cicero and then seizing power. It was this plot which Cicero described in the First Oration against Catiline. Exposed in this speech, Catiline fled from Rome and joined the forces collected by his confederates in Etruria. The other leading conspirators were apprehended and executed, at the urging of Cicero and Cato, although Caesar pleaded for leniency. Catiline himself was killed in battle against Roman forces.

It is difficult to obtain an accurate picture of Catiline from ancient sources, since both Cicero and the historian Sallust paint him in the blackest possible colors. He seems to have been unscrupulous, but to have had personal courage and the ability to attract loyal followers. His plot doubtless drew to him many who had legitimate grievances against the ruling class.

CATO [kā′tō], **MARCUS PORCIUS** (234–149 B.C.), Roman statesman, known as "the Censor" or "the Elder." An able member of the municipal aristocracy, which was composed of the leading men of the Italian towns of the Roman federation, he gained influence by his vigor, uncompromising uprightness, and oratorical and literary ability. He fought with distinction in the Second Punic War, was elected consul in 195 B.C., and next served in Spain. In 184 he was elected censor, and earned his surname by his sternness and devotion to the old Roman ideals. He advocated laws to control luxury, and with unusual severity expelled men from the Senate for unbecoming conduct. In later years, while on an embassy to Carthage, he was alarmed by the prosperity of Rome's old rival, then devoting itself to peaceful commerce. Relentlessly proclaiming "Carthage must be destroyed" in every speech, he helped instigate the Third Punic War. Often considered an enemy of things Greek, Cato was rather opposed to the invasion of Greek luxuries and vices in Rome. He appropriated Greek techniques in his oratory, in his handbook on farming, and in the buildings he built as censor.

CATO, MARCUS PORCIUS (95–46 B.C.), Roman statesman, also called Cato Uticensis and Cato the Younger, to distinguish him from his great-grandfather, Cato the Censor, or Cato the Elder. Cato was known in life and after his death as a man of stern morality, an adherent of Stoic philosophy, and an impassioned upholder of republican principles. Together with Cicero he opposed Catiline, and it was his speech which finally influenced the Senate to vote Catiline's execution. He consistently opposed Caesar, and, after 52 B.C. supported Pompey. After Pompey's defeat at Pharsalus (48 B.C.) Cato led the remnants of the senatorial forces across North Africa to Utica, where, when resistance to the Caesarian forces proved hopeless, he took his own life.

CATULLUS [kə-tŭl′əs], **GAIUS VALERIUS** (84?–?54 B.C.), Latin poet of the personal lyric. Born in Verona, he lived in Rome and was one of a group of young poets there who, following the lead of their teacher, Valerius Cato, rebelled against the contemporary trend of endlessly imitating classical Greek drama and epic. These "new poets" expressed their own thoughts and emotions, as had the later Greek poets of Alexandria, to whom they turned for inspiration. The result was, as at Alexandria, a combination of vivid realism (involving personal experiences and reactions) with pedantic scholarship (involving recondite learning and intricate form).

Catullus' tragic love affair with the woman he calls Lesbia produced poems of concentrated love and hatred, scorn and devotion, which have never been surpassed. Equally affecting in a quieter vein are the short lyrics on his beloved villa at Sirmio, and on his brother's grave in the distant Troad. He also wrote violent personal attacks on Caesar and his political associates and incidental poems of the greatest variety, all of which became models for the later Roman epigram. The longer, more elaborate poems include wedding hymns, erotic elegies, an epyllion, or short epic (*Marriage of Peleus and Thetis*), brilliantly complex in structure and full of unforgettable pictures and phrases, and *Attis*, a unique picture of the dedication, frenzy, and remorse of a young devotee of the savage goddess Cybele. Catullus is not only the first but the greatest Roman poet of lyric passion.

CATULUS [kăt′ū-ləs], **GAIUS LUTATIUS,** Roman statesman. As commander of the Roman fleet in the First Punic War, he crushed the Carthaginian fleet off the Aegates Islands in 241 B.C., cut off Carthage's communication with her troops in Sicily, and thus ended the war.

CATULUS, QUINTUS LUTATIUS (c.152–87 B.C.), Roman statesman and general. He shared with Gaius Marius credit for defeating the invading Germanic Cimbri, near Vercellae in northern Italy, in 101 B.C. An aristocrat, Catulus later supported Sulla, and after his proscription by Marius, committed suicide.

CENSOR [sĕn′sər], (Lat., *censere*, "to estimate") the title

253

of an ancient Roman magistrate. Two censors were elected by the Centuriate Assembly every five years for a term of 18 months. Usually chosen from the ranks of ex-consuls, the censors were without *imperium*, the power to command. Their main function was to take the census (Lat. *censere*, "to estimate"), assessing the property qualifications of citizens and assigning them to the appropriate military and voting classes. Acquiring the right to review the membership of the Senate gave the censors power to oversee the public and private morals of the senators. The censors were also in charge of letting out public contracts for building and tax collection. Established in 443 B.C., the office was opened to plebeians, or common people, in 351 B.C. In 81 B.C., Sulla stripped the censors of the right to control membership in the Senate, but this was restored by Pompey in 70 B.C. The censorship declined in importance and use under the principate and ceased to be a distinct office under Domitian (81–96 A.D.). Two famous censors were Appius Claudius (312 B.C.) and Cato the Elder (184 B.C.), the latter noted for severity.

CICERO [sĭs′ər-ō], **MARCUS TULLIUS** (106–43 B.C.), Roman orator, author, and statesman. Born in Arpinum, he was well educated in Rome and in Athens and Rhodes. He was a *novus homo*, or new man, that is, the first of his family to go through the steps of a political career in Rome, from aedile to consul. His prosecution of the corrupt governor Verres in 70 B.C. established his reputation and gained him recognition as the leading lawyer and orator of Rome. Cicero's election to the consulship for 63 was due to the fact that as a member of the equestrian order, and therefore a defender of the banking interests, he was a safe man, whereas his opponent, the noble Catiline (q.v.), openly advocated cancellation of debts. His suppression of the Catilinarian conspiracy was regarded by Cicero himself as the high point of his career, but the execution without the sanction of the people of certain conspirators who were Roman citizens antagonized the popular party.

Cicero's middle-of-the-road policy led him to reject an invitation to co-operate with the triumvirs Caesar, Pompey, and Crassus, and he was consequently left without their or the senate's protection. Clodius Pulcher (q.v.), as tribune, effected Cicero's exile in 58, but he was recalled in 57 and resumed his legal practice. When Caesar and Pompey were estranged after the deaths of Julia (Caesar's daughter and Pompey's wife) and Crassus, Pompey, who was Cicero's patron, cultivated the senate. In 51–50 Cicero was proconsul of Cilicia, but returned as civil war was breaking out between Caesar and Pompey. He joined Pompey, but Caesar, after his victory, permitted him to return to Rome in 47. He remained in political retirement and had no part in the assassination of Caesar in Mar., 44, but he applauded the deed and returned to the forum to attack Antony, who had inherited Caesar's policies, in the series of violent speeches called Philippics. The virulence of his attack made his proscription and murder in the following year inevitable.

Cicero's continuing importance stems not from his political career, but from his pre-eminence as an orator and from the great service he performed in putting the ideas of Greek philosophy into Latin, thus making them available to the Western world at a time when Greek was

Bust of Marcus Tullius Cicero by sculptor of the period.

Culver Pictures, Inc.

lost to Europe. His contribution to the shaping of European thought through his philosophical writings is incalculable. Not an original thinker, he freely admitted that his essays were adapted from the Greek. Among his works, *On the Republic* and *On the Laws* deal with political philosophy; *On Ends* discusses views of the highest good; *On the Nature of the Gods* presents the views of Epicurean, Stoic, and Academic schools of philosophy on this question; and *On Old Age* and *On Friendship* are charming ethical essays.

Cicero also wrote a number of works on the art of rhetoric or oratory, an art of which he was considered by the Romans of his own time and later the acknowledged master. His own speeches are the best examples of his theory and practice. Fifty-eight speeches are extant, while 48 others are known to be lost. The best known of the speeches deal with four subjects: the impeachment of Verres, the corrupt governor of Sicily; the Catilinarian conspiracy; the recovery of property confiscated at the time of his exile; and the 14 Philippics, attacking Antony. Other speeches deservedly well-known are *For Archias*, which defends the Roman citizenship of a Greek poet and expounds the practical uses of poetry; *For Cluentius*, which defends Cluentius on a charge of poisoning and reads like a mystery thriller; and *For Murena*, which defends Murena on a charge of bribery and shows Cicero's masterful urbanity at its best. His oratorical style is characterized by richness of vocabulary, beauty of phrasing, and great attention to cadence or sound.

Cicero's letters, of which we have over 900, serve as a commentary on the political events, social climate, and leading personalities of his day. A very large number were addressed to Cicero's intimate friend Atticus, the rest to his family and various friends. Some of the longer and more important letters may have been revised, but the great bulk are untouched, and give a remarkably vivid and intimate picture of Cicero and his world.

CINCINNATUS [sĭn-sĭ-nā′təs], **LUCIUS QUINCTIUS,** Roman hero. He left his plow in 458 B.C. when a deputation of fellow senators appointed him dictator (a temporary office for emergencies) to rescue a trapped Roman army. Within 16 days he had defeated the enemy, celebrated a triumph, relinquished his dictatorship, and returned to his plowing.

CINNA [sĭn′ə], **LUCIUS CORNELIUS** (d. 84 B.C.), Roman politician and leader of the popular party, though himself a patrician. He was elected consul in 87 B.C. Although until then a supporter of Sulla, in the latter's absence he promulgated proposals for changes in the voting methods that would have caused the overthrow of Sulla and the conservatives. His colleague Octavius and the conservatives defeated his proposed measures, and he left Rome. Recalling Marius from Africa, he returned to Rome to slaughter large numbers of Sulla's followers. He was re-elected consul for the next three years (86–84 B.C.), with various democratic colleagues. On Sulla's return to Rome after his defeat of Mithridates, Cinna raised an army against him, but was killed in a mutiny before his army could meet Sulla's. Cinna's daughter Cornelia was Julius Caesar's first wife.

CIRCUS, ROMAN, name applied to both the building and the chariot races and other contests held in it. The circus was brought to Rome by the Etruscans and quickly became one of the most popular activities of Roman life. The original, largest (seating some 250,000), and most important circus, the Maximus, was founded traditionally by Tarquinius Priscus, the first Etruscan King of Rome, in the 6th century B.C. in the valley between the Palatine and Aventine hills. The long narrow flat race course (1969 × 492 ft.) ran along the valley with seats for spectators along the slopes of the hills on both sides and in a semicircle around one end. At the open end was the starting line. An embankment (*spina*) down the center of the track divided it in half. Gradually there were built and rebuilt through Republican and especially Imperial times the spectators' seats, the Emperor's box, and 12 openings of the starting line with the judges' boxes above. On the *spina* were goal posts (*metae*) at each end, seven eggs and seven bronze dolphins (reversed to mark each of the seven laps of the race), two obelisks brought from Egypt by Augustus and Constantine, as well as many statues and shrines, including the very ancient altar of Consus around which the earliest races had been held. For the games were always religious, held at the numerous festivals of the gods. During the Empire their luxurious magnificence (at the Emperor's expense) was a means of keeping the populace happy and gave rise to the saying "the Roman longs for two things, bread and circuses." The Romans reveled in these races and in their partisanship of the rival parties (*factiones*) of charioteers (the Whites and Greens versus the Blues and Reds). The victorious charioteers were public heroes and amassed large fortunes as well as honor. Other circuses included the Circus Flaminius in the Campus Martius, built in 221 B.C., and the Circus Gai et Neronis, built by the Emperor Caligula on the Vatican hill; the obelisk from its *spina* now stands in front of St. Peter's.

CLAUDIUS [klô′dē-əs] **I** (10 B.C.–54 A.D.), Roman Emperor (reigned 41–54 A.D.). The son of Drusus Germanicus, he was named Tiberius Claudius Drusus Nero Germanicus. Childhood illness left him physically impaired. Consequently despised, he held few public offices before 41, instead devoting himself to history and literature. When the Emperor Caligula, Claudius' nephew, was assassinated, the Praetorian Guard proclaimed Claudius Emperor and the Senate perforce concurred. Claudius immediately gave large donations to the Guard and styled himself Caesar (this not being his legal name), thereby setting precedents for future Emperors. He also crushed a rebellion led by Scribonianus.

Ancient writers depict his reign as vicious, his wives and freedmen, especially Narcissus and Pallas, being allowed excessive power. However, recent findings indicate otherwise. The provinces and empire generally were efficiently governed; Augustus' rudimentary civil service was developed; judicial procedures were closely supervised, and useful engineering projects undertaken. Britain, Mauretania, and Thrace were annexed.

In 50 Claudius' niece and fourth wife, Agrippina the Younger, persuaded him to pass over Britannicus, his own son by Messalina, and name her son Nero to succeed him. Four years later Claudius died suddenly, poisoned, according to report, by Agrippina. Claudius was the second Emperor to be posthumously deified, Augustus being the first.

CLAUDIUS II (d. 270 A.D.), Roman Emperor (reigned 268–70). The men who murdered the Emperor Gallienus chose an able Illyrian officer, Marcus Aurelius Claudius, to succeed him in the crisis. Claudius concentrated on the Alamanni, who had invaded Rhaetia and threatened Italy, defeating them in 268. He then turned his attention to the Goths, who were plundering the Balkans. Brilliant strategy brought victory to the Romans and the epithet Gothicus to the Emperor, who died shortly afterward in a plague.

CLAUDIUS CAECUS [sē′kəs], **APPIUS,** aristocratic Roman statesman. In his censorship (312–308 B.C.) he commenced the Appian Way and constructed Rome's first aqueduct. He is said to have made the forms of action used in the courts available to all instead of only to the aristocracy and to have given the rights of citizenship to the unpropertied free men of the city of Rome. In 280, old and blind, he persuaded the Senate not to make peace with the invading Greek King Pyrrhus.

CLAUDIUS CRASSUS [krăs′əs], **APPIUS,** Roman patrician. Consul in 471 and 451 B.C., he served as decemvir, 451–450. He supported the plebeian insistence on a written code of laws, and courted the people in the hope of abolishing the tribunate in exchange for plebeian admission to higher offices. Legend has it that his arrogant and tyrannical attempt to gain possession of Virginia, the daughter of the plebeian centurion Virginius, led to the secession of the people to the Sacred Mount and the resignation of the decemvirs. He died in prison.

CLODIUS PULCHER [klō′dē-əs pŭl′kər], **PUBLIUS** (c. 93–52 B.C.), Roman politician. Although, as a Claudian, he belonged to one of the most ancient patrician families, Clodius throughout his life played the role of demagogue and leader of mobs. The most scandalous incident of his life occurred in 62 B.C. when he appeared in female dress at the woman's festival of Bona Dea, which was being celebrated at the house of Caesar, then Pontifex Maximus. As a result of this episode Caesar divorced his wife Pompeia, because, although she was apparently not to blame, he felt that "Caesar's wife should be above suspicion." Cicero prosecuted Clodius for sacrilege, and though he was acquitted by a bribed jury, he hated his prosecutor and was later responsible for sending Cicero into exile after the Catilinarian conspiracy, by passing a law against anyone who put Roman citizens to death without trial. Clodius was finally killed by Milo, the leader of a rival mob.

COLOSSEUM [kŏl-ə-sē'əm], Flavian amphitheater built in Rome by the Emperor Vespasian, 72 A.D., and completed by his sons Titus and Domitian. Erected on the site of the lake on the grounds of Nero's Golden House, it represented a powerful political move to replace the hated Emperor's private luxury with a building for the entertainment of the Roman people. Fifty thousand spectators (5,000 standing) could view the gladiatorial and wild beast combats provided by the Emperors. An architectural masterpiece, the Colosseum (so named for its huge size or because it stood beside the colossal statue of the Sun god, originally Nero) was the supreme expression of Roman engineering skill in supporting an auditorium on a framework of vaulted corridors. The oval plan measured 620 by 513 ft.; total height of the outer wall was 157 ft. Around the oval arena, 287 by 180 ft., radiating walls of concrete and three stories of concentric arcades of travertine stone supported vaults which carried the rows of seats and stairways. From the concentric corridors surrounding the building access was gained to the seats. The two lower zones of seats, of marble, were supported by the radiating vaults; the upper zones over the concentric corridors were of wood. The exterior wall of three superimposed arcades was decorated on the ground floor with Tuscan columns, on the second with Ionic, on the third with Corinthian; above the third floor of arcades rose a solid wall with Corinthian pilasters and with corbels for the masts of the awning habitually stretched over the spectators during the games. Under the arena were vaulted corridors and cells for wild animals used in gladiatorial combats, with a mechanism to lift them up to the arena. Although the seats and parts of the supporting walls were dismantled during the Renaissance and their component materials taken for other buildings, most of this monument still remains and constitutes one of the most imposing and celebrated of all Roman landmarks.

COMITIA [kō-mĭsh'ē-ə], in ancient Rome, the assembly of all the Roman people convoked in groups by the highest magistrates. The vote of each group was determined by the majority. Though comitia antedate the foundation of the Republic, their development and importance belong largely to republican times.

The oldest comitia were the comitia curiata in which the people voted by curiae, 30 religio-military units into which the population had been organized in Regal times. At the beginning of the Republic their legislative functions were largely absorbed by the comitia centuriata, and their duties limited to investing magistrates with imperium, or

power of command, to recognizing adoptions and wills, and to officiating at certain religious functions.

The comitia centuriata were assemblies of patricians and plebeians divided into military units (centuries) on the basis of property holding. The comitia centuriata elected consuls, praetors, and censors, legislated when so requested by the consuls, declared war and peace, and inflicted the death penalty in criminal matters. As the voting groups were unequal, the wealthy dominated. In spite of reorganization in the 3d century B.C., the comitia centuriata remained essentially timocratic.

A third assembly, the comitia plebis tributa, was established in 471 B.C.; here the voting was by tribes into which the city was divided, and within a tribe each man's vote, regardless of his wealth, counted equally. Originally, they elected only lower magistrates and judged minor criminal offenses. This became a second legislative body, whose position, however, was largely inherited after 287 B.C. by the concilium plebis, in which plebeians alone voted, when the Hortensian law recognized their resolutions or plebiscites as binding on the entire community. The important plebeian tribunes and plebeian aediles were elected here. During the Principate the centuriate and tribal assemblies became almost as vestigial as the curiate assembly, the real decisions being made elsewhere, and the people serving merely to shout approval of the Emperor's will. Formalities of election were observed until the early 3d century A.D., though no choice was given; the candidate was previously designated by the Senate.

COMMODUS [kŏm'ə-dəs] (161–92 A.D.), Roman Emperor (reigned 180–92), son of Marcus Aurelius. In 177 Lucius Aelius Aurelius Commodus was made Co-Emperor with his father, assuming sole authority on the latter's death. He is famous as the inferior son of a brilliant father who broke the remarkable series of good emperors, each chosen by a predecessor without a son. Commodus acquired a reputation for vice, partly through his own cruelty, weakness, and extravagance, and partly through the hostility of the Senate from which he openly turned away, choosing his advisors from nonsenators instead. He frequently participated in gladiatorial combats and demanded worship as a god. He was strangled by a wrestler, Dec. 31, 192.

CONSUL [kŏn'səl], chief magistrate of the Roman Republic. Two consuls of equal rank, with power to block each other, were elected by the centuriate assembly for one year. From the beginning of the Republic to 534 A.D. the year was officially named the consulship of so and so. They held the *imperium* (right of command) and were at first the only real magistrates. Throughout most of the Republic the command of the army was their most important duty; they also presided over the senate and the assemblies, elicited the expression of senatorial opinion, conducted elections and votes on legislative matters, and carried the decrees of senate and people into effect. At the end of their terms, consuls usually served as governors of provinces. Under the Principate their duties became chiefly ceremonial. However, the rank of ex-consul remained essential for the highest commands.

CONSTANS I [kŏn'stănz], **FLAVIUS JULIUS** (c.323–50),

Roman Emperor (reigned 337–50), youngest son of Constantine the Great. After his father's death he became ruler of Illyricum, Italy, and Africa, and after the defeat of his brother Constantine II, of the whole West. A sincere Christian, Constans made many gifts to the Church, and in the Arian controversy protected Athanasius. He was killed by an agent of the usurper Magnentius.

CONSTANTINE [kŏn′stan-tīn, kŏn′stan-tan] **I**, called the Great (died 337), Roman Emperor. Flavius Valerius Constantinus was the son of Constantius I, Emperor (Augustus) in the West (305–06), and Helena a woman of obscure origins whose later fervent conversion to Christianity won her sainthood. Born in Naissus in Moesia (modern Serbia), Constantine was educated in the retinue of Emperor Diocletian (reigned 285–305) where he had been sent, probably as a hostage, in 293. When his father died at York in 306, Constantine was proclaimed Augustus (emperor) by his army in Britain. However, Galerius, emperor in the East (reigned 305–11), insisted that Severus, the legal successor, become Augustus in the West, and Constantine had to be content with the title of Caesar (vice-emperor) for the moment. In the power struggle that ensued in the West, Constantine gradually eliminated all his rivals. His victory over Maxentius, son of Maximian (emperor of the West, 286–305), at the Milvian Bridge near Rome (312) established him as Augustus in the West. The night before this battle, Constantine is supposed to have seen a vision in the sky of the cross and the words "By this sign shall you conquer." His soldiers went into the battle with shields bearing the Christian monogram formed from the Greek letters *chi rho*, the first two letters of Christ's name. This marks Constantine's spiritual, if not formal, conversion to Christianity.

In the East, the death of the Emperor Galerius (311) produced two rivals—Licinius, who allied himself with Constantine, and Maximinus Daia, who supported the ill-fated Maxentius. Licinius emerged victorious and his relations with Constantine were peaceful at first. In 313, the emperors met at Milan and agreed to grant freedom of worship to Christians and to restore their confiscated property. This agreement is called the Edict of Milan, although no formal law seems to have been promulgated.

War broke out between them the following year and Constantine gained control of all Europe, except Thrace. Constantine's incursion into that territory in 323 brought him into conflict with Licinius. His brilliant victories in 324 at Adrianople, the Hellespont, and Chrysopolis forced Licinius to surrender. His life was spared at first, but he was soon after executed for new intrigues, leaving Constantine sole master of the Roman Empire.

Constantine next turned to the task of trying to strengthen the shaky economic, political, social, and military structure of the empire. In government, he continued and developed the autocratic policies of Diocletian, expanding the bureaucracy, dividing the empire into four administrative prefectures, and creating new ministers of state called *comes* (counts). The need to protect the frontiers against barbarian attacks was made clear to Constantine during his successful campaigns against the Goths on the Danube in 332 and 334. He organized his frontier forces into highly mobile units stationed back from the borders, which could be quickly moved to deal with emergencies along a wider segment of the border. Barbarians were enrolled in the army. The tax burden necessary to support these forces was considerable. To strengthen the economic situation, Constantine adopted measures binding peasants to the land and craftsmen and tradesmen to their occupations. Thus a hereditary manpower supply was produced in key economic sectors, establishing a precedent for later feudal practices.

In 324 construction was begun on a new city at the site of ancient Byzantium. Named Constantinople, it was dedicated in 330. Intended not to replace Rome, but rather to provide a major imperial city near the Danubian and Persian frontiers, it had the effect of shifting the center of gravity of the Roman Empire to the more prosperous East. This not only hastened the decline of Rome but laid the foundation for the Byzantine Empire.

Constantine's greatest accomplishment, however, was the initiation and furthering of the transformation of pagan Rome into a Christian state. Prior to his conversion, the vaguely monotheistic Constantine had begun to develop some sympathy for Christianity. His victories under the symbol of Christ confirmed him in his faith, although he was not actually baptized until he lay on his deathbed. From 313 Constantine concerned himself with the affairs of the church. He summoned the Synod of Arles (314) in an unsuccessful attempt to settle the Donatist controversy. In 325 he presided at the Council of Nicaea, hoping to settle the doctrinal dispute between the adherents of Arius and Athanasius. This first ecumenical council produced the Nicene creed, but while Arianism was declared heretical, it remained influential and divisive for some time. Constantine's attempts to unify the church were probably motivated as much by political considerations as by personal conviction. A united church would support a united empire. Thus Constantine, the first Christian emperor, protected and advanced Christianity, though of necessity paganism was still tolerated.

Constantine died in 337 on the eve of a Persian war. His acts had a profound influence on both Western Christendom and the Byzantine Empire.

CONSTANTINE II, full name Flavius Claudius Constantinus (317–340), Roman Emperor (reigned 337–340). On the death of his father, Constantine I, Constantine II received Britain, Gaul, and Spain as his share of the empire, and acted as supervisor of his younger brother Constans, to whom Italy, Africa, and Illyricum had been assigned. However, Constans refused to acknowledge the primacy of Constantine and appealed for help to Constantius, another brother. Constantine invaded Italy, but was slain near Aquileia.

CONSTANTINE III (d.411), Roman soldier who usurped the imperial power in Gaul (407–11). The Roman legions which garrisoned Britain, discontented with the rule of Stilicho, set up a series of revolutionary Emperors, of whom Constantine was third. Evacuating Britain, Constantine crossed into Gaul with his army, and won over the legions there. He defeated the German tribes which were about to invade Britain; then, having secured control of Gaul, occupied Spain. Emperor Honorius was compelled to recognize him as a colleague in 408. After the death of Alaric, however, Honorius defeated Constantine at his capital, Arles, and executed him.

CONSTANTIUS I [kən-stăn′shē-əs] (c.250–306 A.D.), Roman Emperor (reigned 305–306), whose full name was Flavius Valerius Constantius (called Chlorus). An army officer of Dardanian descent, he served under Diocletian and was made Caesar (subemperor) in the West in 293. He recovered Britain from the usurper Allectus in 296, and defeated the Alamanni in Gaul in 298. When Diocletian abdicated (305), Constantius became Augustus in the West, senior to Galerius, the Augustus in the East. Constantius' son, who became Constantine I, was educated at the court of Galerius, almost as a hostage. When Constantius died at York, Constantine succeeded him.

CONSTANTIUS II (317–61), Roman Emperor (reigned 337–61), son of Constantine the Great and Fausta. At the death of his father, Constantius became ruler of the eastern provinces, where he had already been active as a military commander against the Persians. After the deaths of his brothers, he defeated the usurper Magnentius in the West, and became sole ruler of the Empire (353). An energetic general and administrator, he completed the organization of the authoritarian state which had been begun by his father, and in particular he expanded the bureaucracy. In his last years he had to deal with the usurpation of Julian the Apostate in the West.

CONSTANTIUS III, Western Roman Emperor (reigned 421). He began his career as a general and adviser to the Emperor Honorius. He broke the power of the usurper Constantine, whom he captured at Arles in 411, and was thereafter virtual ruler of the West. He was consul in 414, and in 417 married Galla Placidia, sister of Honorius. Honorius reluctantly made him his colleague (421), but Constantius died soon after his elevation.

CRASSUS [krăs′əs], **MARCUS LICINIUS** (c.115–53 B.C.), Roman politician and general, a member of the First Triumvirate. He began his career as a military leader under Sulla, and continued it by defeating the rebel Spartacus in 71 B.C. He became the richest man in Rome by clever speculation in land, and used his money to buy political influence. Pompey was always his great rival, but Caesar managed to reconcile the two to his own advantage, and in 60 B.C. Caesar, Pompey, and Crassus formed the First Triumvirate, an arrangement for sharing power which had no official standing. Crassus had long wished for an important military command, and in 55 he was made proconsul of Syria for a five-year period. He and his army met a crushing defeat at the hands of the Parthians in 53 B.C. at Carrhae where he was killed by treachery.

DECIUS [dē′shē-əs] (201–251 A.D.), Roman Emperor (reigned 249–251). Gaius Messius Quintus Decius was raised to the throne, apparently against his will, by the army of Moesia, which he commanded and which overthrew the reigning Emperor Philip at the Battle of Verona. He tried to co-operate with the senate and to restore army discipline and the state religion. In this he came into conflict with the Christians whom he persecuted for

nonconformity. He died in Moesia in a disastrous battle against the invading Goths.

DIDIUS JULIANUS [dĭd′ē-əs jōō-lē-ā′nəs], **MARCUS**, Roman Emperor (reigned 193 A.D.). Upon the murder of the Emperor Pertinax he is said to have bribed the Praetorian Guard to proclaim him Emperor, though he was a Senator of no particular distinction. His reign lasted only a few weeks. He was deposed and murdered on the approach of Septimius Severus with the army of the Danube.

DIO CASSIUS [dī′ō kăsh′ē-əs] (c.155–after 230 A.D.), Roman historian. Engaged under the emperors Commodus and Alexander Severus in the administration of Roman provincial government, Dio undertook the composition of a history of Rome from its beginnings. Originally numbering 80 books, the work survives in somewhat less than one third its original size. Treating history not only in the manner of the chronicler, but also, like Thucydides, underlining important events by the insertion of dramatic speeches, Dio divided his work into three large epochs: the first covers the history of the Republic; the second, ending with the reign of Marcus Aurelius, gives an account of the Roman Empire at its height; the last relates the story of Rome during Dio's own lifetime.

DIOCLETIAN [dī-ə-klē′shən] (c.243–313), Roman emperor (reigned 284–305), born in Salonae in Dalmatia. He was responsible for the recovery of the Roman Empire from the near collapse of the mid-3d century and was the author of the military and administrative system of the later Roman Empire, which developed into the Byzantine state. Rising in a military career by his ability, Diocletian was chosen by the army to succeed Numerian. He took Maximian I as his colleague, and the two in a series of wars with the barbarians rescued the Empire from the external dangers through which it had been passing. To assure the defense of the Empire and make the government more efficient, Diocletian instituted (293) the system of the Tetrarchy (rule of four), by which the Empire was divided into two parts, east and west, each half being ruled by a senior Emperor, the "Augustus," assisted by a junior ruler, the "Caesar," who was his heir-designate.

The administration was completely overhauled. The provinces were reduced in size and increased in number, and were grouped into 12 dioceses, each administered by a *vicarius*, who was responsible to the praetorian prefect. Military and civil commands were separated, as they had not been previously. The army, which had become demoralized, was strengthened and reorganized. The currency, which had been inflated and unstable, was completely reformed, though an edict of price control (301) proved unsuccessful. A new system of taxation, based on units of agricultural land, was introduced, and payments were collected in kind as well as in money. To increase the dignity of the Emperor's position, Diocletian introduced the costume and ceremonial of the Persian royal court and made the Emperor a remote figure. His political principles led him to initiate a severe persecution of the Christians (303). After a serious illness (304) Diocletian abdicated and retired, being succeeded by Galerius. His policies were continued and developed by Constantine I.

DOLABELLA [dŏl-ə-běl′ə], **PUBLIUS CORNELIUS** (c.70–43 B.C.), Roman politician. His career exemplified that of many unscrupulous and ambitious Romans of his day. He began as a follower of Pompey, but changed over to Caesar's side. He divorced his first wife and married Cicero's daughter, Tullia, in order to win Cicero's support. After Caesar's assassination he first joined the conspirators, then switched to Antony's side because it was to his advantage. After dubious activities in Syria, he was declared a public enemy by the senate, and committed suicide to escape capture.

DOMITIAN [dō-mǐsh′ən], in full Titus Flavius Domitianus Augustus (51–96 A.D.), Roman Emperor (81–96). He narrowly escaped death during the troubles of the year 69, and enjoyed little real power during the reigns of his father Vespasian and his brother Titus. His own reign was autocratic and, after Saturninus' rebellion (88), positively despotic, with arbitrary arrests, treason trials, and judicial murders. Yet administration was efficient: provinces were well governed (notably Britain under Agricola), morality was enforced, and literature encouraged. Ancient calumnies notwithstanding, the Rhine frontier was strengthened. Along the Danube there were some defeats (85–92), but peace was nevertheless signed with Decebalus, King of Dacia. A conspiracy, one of many, procured Domitian's assassination in 96. Ancient writers probably exaggerate the Domitianic terror, but their version contains much truth. By cowing the senate Domitian accelerated its decline into complete impotence, and by claiming quasi-divine honors he helped promote the absolutism of the late Empire.

ENNIUS [ĕn′ē-əs], **QUINTUS** (c.239–169 B.C.), early Latin poet of Greek birth, considered the father of Roman poetry. He served in the Roman army and attracted the attention of Cato. After miscellaneous productions, he wrote *The Annals*, until Vergil's day the accepted epic of Rome. In dignified, if somewhat crude, hexameters it told the story of Rome from its foundation to 171 B.C. Only fragments of Ennius' writings survive.

EQUESTRIANS [ĭ-kwĕs′trē-ənz] (from Lat. *equestris*, of or pertaining to *equites*, "cavalry"), Roman order for which some reputation for decency, and usually free birth, were general prerequisites, and for which a minimum of 400,000 sesterces was the main requirement. An equestrian census rating goes back to the 6th century B.C. for those with sufficient wealth to afford service in the cavalry, but the history of the equestrian order as a group distinct from the senatorial order, on the one hand, and from the people, on the other, begins in 123 B.C. Then, Gaius Gracchus, who needed a counterweight to the senatorial oligarchy, proposed the bill which transferred from senators to equestrians the court where governors were tried for extortion, and excluded senators from serving as equites. Equestrian capitalists, who invested in state contracts, often resented senatorial policy in the last century of the Republic; but rivalry ended with the principate when careers were progressively opened to equestrians.

ETRURIA [ĭ-trŏor′ē-ə], in antiquity, the region of central Italy corresponding roughly to modern Tuscany, northern

Lazio, and western Umbria. It was bounded on the north by the Macra River and the Apennines, on the south and east by the Tiber River, and on the west by the Tyrrhenian Sea. In ancient times it was famous for copper, iron, and apparently tin.

Apart from Falerii in the southeast corner near Mount Soracte (which contained a Latin-type population), Etruria was inhabited from 800 B.C. or later by the Etruscans, a materially advanced but mysterious people, whose origins are still uncertain. Included in the population of Etruria were numerous serfs who may have been the descendants of its pre-Etruscan inhabitants. Etruria was divided among a large number of city-states, all quite separate from, and politically independent of, one another. Mention is made of a league of 12 Etruscan cities, but these 12 cannot be certainly identified, and the league was anything but cohesive; its primary purpose may have been religious. Etruscan cities were celebrated for their architectural impressiveness, wealth, and even luxury.

From north to south the great Etruscan cities were Faesulae (modern Fiesole), traditionally the forerunner of Florence, with its Etruscan wall and Etrusco-Roman temple; Arretium (modern Arezzo), city of Maecenas and site of the bronze Chimaera, now in the Archeological Museum of Florence; Cortona, on a well-nigh impregnable site, noted for its bronzes; Volaterrae (modern Volterra), famed for its alabaster industries and its imposing Etruscan walls, gateway, and sepulchral urns; Perusia (modern Perugia), with town wall and gate built on Etruscan foundations; Clusium (modern Chiusi), in the heart of Etruria, on whose territory painted tombs have been found, including the celebrated Tomb of the Monkey; Populonia, which smelted iron ore from nearby Elba, the only Etruscan town of consequence to lie on the coast containing tombs of the archaic period; Vetulonia, which has large archaic tombs and has yielded the earliest example of the Roman emblem, the fasces; Orvieto, with temples and tombs; Volsinii, on Lake Bolsena; Vulci, which has yielded 4th-century B.C. fresco battle scenes from the François tomb, in addition to many Greek vases and bronzes; Tarquinii (modern Tarquinia), rich in tomb paintings; Caere (modern Cerveteri), with its extensive necropolis, including huge tumuli and subterranean tombs shaped like Etruscan homes, which has yielded a wealth of bronze and gold artifacts; and Veii, a near neighbor of Rome, notable for its terra-cotta statuary, particularly the Apollo of Veii. Other lesser cities of Etruria were Rusellae (unexcavated), Telamon, Cosa, Pyrgi, and Graviscae on the coast, and Suana, Blera, and Sutrium inland. Outside of Etruria proper lay the Etruscan cities of Marzabotto, Felsina (modern Bologna), Spina at the mouth of the Po, and in the south of Italy, Capua.

ETRUSCAN ART AND ARCHITECTURE. The art of the Etruscans, who created the highest civilization in Italy be-

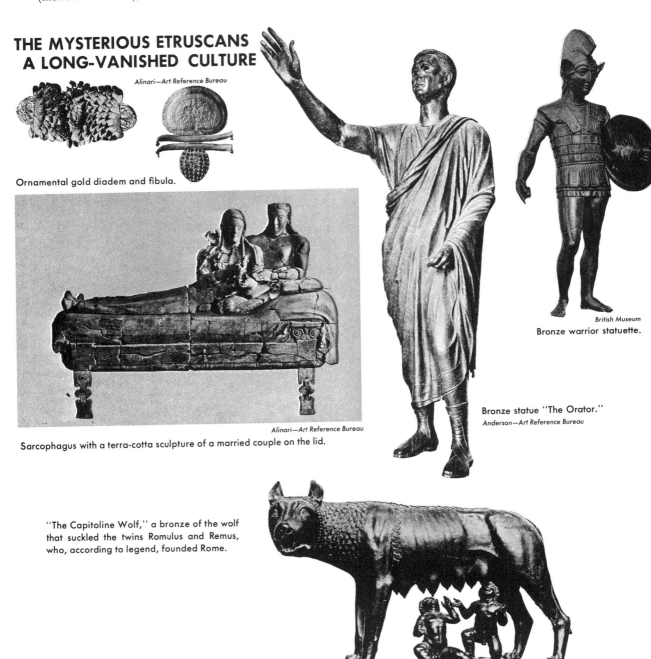

THE MYSTERIOUS ETRUSCANS
A LONG-VANISHED CULTURE

Alinari—Art Reference Bureau

Ornamental gold diadem and fibula.

Sarcophagus with a terra-cotta sculpture of a married couple on the lid.

Alinari—Art Reference Bureau

British Museum
Bronze warrior statuette.

Bronze statue "The Orator."
Anderson—Art Reference Bureau

"The Capitoline Wolf," a bronze of the wolf that suckled the twins Romulus and Remus, who, according to legend, founded Rome.

Alinari—Art Reference Bureau

Alinari—Art Reference Bureau

The Metropolitan Museum of Art, Gift of J. Pierpont Morgan, 1917
Covered vase (*left*), bronze pail (*center*), and
funerary urn (*right*).

Anderson—Art Reference Bureau
Two views of the "Apollo" from
Veii, a painted terra-cotta figure.

Alinari—Art Reference Bureau
"The Chimaera from Arezzo," a bronze.

Alinari—Art Reference Bureau

Alinari—Art Reference Bureau
Pieces of early Etruscan pottery.

wo mural details of a dancer and musicians from the Tomb of the Triclinium at Tar-
uinia. Such paintings reveal the people's love of music, dance, and colorful dress.

Anderson—Art Reference Bureau

A marble tablet showing
the still undeciphered
Etruscan writing.

Art Reference Bureau

fore the rise of Rome, was strongly influenced by Greece, especially after the 6th century B.C. It is nevertheless a vigorous and original creation that went through several centuries of independent development and produced works that have a distinctive character.

Architecture. Since the Etruscans commonly employed wood and terra cotta in their buildings, very scant remains of their architecture, other than foundations, exist. The Etruscan temple, described by the Roman architect Vitruvius, was based on Greek prototypes. In some ways, however, it was unlike the Greek temple: the cella, or interior space, was often divided by interior walls into three rooms; it was set on a high platform, or podium, approached by a broad flight of steps on one end; and it had a deep porch with one or more rows of wooden columns

that supported an entablature of the same material. The columns did not extend around the other three sides of the building to form a peristyle, as in Greek temples.

The few remaining examples of Etruscan architecture are works of masonry, such as city walls (notably a city gate in Perugia), fortifications, and tombs. The last were also cut into bedrock and then covered with an artificial mound of earth.

Sculpture. It was in sculpture, despite obvious Greek influence, that the Etruscans best demonstrated their originality. From earliest times there was a strong vogue for realistic portraiture, especially in figures on sarcophagus lids. This taste for the portrait carried over into Roman art. The Etruscans employed terra cotta, stone, and bronze. Survivals include portrait statues; antefixes, or

261

works for the eaves or roofs of temples in terra cotta; sculpture for temples; and sarcophagus figures, which often were depicted reclining on a couch while propped up on an elbow. The "Apollo" from Veii (now Veio), now in Rome, a large, painted, terra-cotta work, is probably the finest surviving piece. A number of well-known bronzes have also escaped destruction: "The Mars from Todi," "The Capitoline Wolf" (both Rome), "The Orator," and "The Chimaera from Arezzo" (both Florence).

Painting. The originality and creativity of the Etruscans are also revealed in their mural paintings, which have survived in tombs, particularly those at Tarquinii (now Tarquinia) and Caere (now Cerveteri). These vital works, in a flatly painted, decorative style, supply us with information on both the religious beliefs and daily life of the Etruscans. Most of the painted tombs date from the 5th century B.C. and reflect contemporary Greek painting.

Other Works. A horde of artifacts—bronze containers, urns, mirrors, tripods, candelabra, and chariots (the finest of which is in the Metropolitan Museum of Art in New York); ivories; statuettes; funerary urns; vases; and gold jewelry—have also survived. The greatest collections of Etruscan art are in Florence, Rome, and Tarquinia.

ETRUSCANS, a people of ancient Italy who dominated Etruria, the region corresponding to modern Tuscany, from the 8th to the 1st centuries B.C. and, for a portion of that time, Campania and the eastern plain of the Po River. The Etruscans identified themselves as Rasenna, but they were called Tusci or Etrusci by their Roman neighbors. The question of their origins, disputed in ancient and modern times, remains unsolved; their "mysterious" origins are suggested by three distinct theories. The first and most generally accepted, the "migration," or Oriental, theory, follows Herodotus, who relates that the Etruscans emigrated from Lydia in Asia Minor because of a severe famine. Led by Tyrrhenus, son of the Lydian King, they eventually settled on the west coast of Italy, probably in the 8th century B.C., where they became known to the Greeks as Tyrrhenoi (hence the name Tyrrhenian Sea). In general, the second, the autochthonous, or indigenous, theory, claims that they were native to Italy, that they evolved from a mixture of the Iron-Age peoples of Italy (*see* VILLANOVAN), and that any eastern elements cited by supporters of the Oriental theory can be explained by strong influences, primarily due to commerce, from the eastern Mediterranean. The third, the northern theory, proposes an Alpine origin for the Etruscans, a hypothesis no longer upheld because early evidence for a movement from north to south has been found to be quite misleading. On the basis of chronology, Etruscan traces in the Alpine regions can be attributed to Etruscan fugitives from the Po Valley during the Gaulish invasions of the 5th century B.C.

Interest in the Etruscans has not been confined to modern times, for many of their major works of art, such as the famous bronzes—the Capitoline She-wolf, the Arezzo Chimaera, and the Trasimene Orator—were already known in the Middle Ages and the Renaissance. With increasing frequency from the 17th to the 19th centuries—at first accidentally, and later by planned exploration—numerous richly appointed tombs and monumental wall paintings were discovered. During this time it was common practice for landowners to claim as their own any antiquities discovered on their property. This practice encouraged unscientific "excavations," which led to the establishment of great private collections that, happily, later became public. Scientific archeological investigations, such as that by Zannoni at Bologna in the late 19th century, set the stage for similar campaigns throughout Etruscan territory. Recent activity, primarily under the supervision of Italian authorities, has unearthed much new data which may shed light on the true relationship between Iron-Age Italy and the Etruscans.

Government. Their political structure, as deduced from existing archeological and literary evidence, was based on a loose federation of 12 independent cities, the number of which remained constant, although the particular cities varied. Among these can be cited Caere (Cerveteri), Tarquinii (Tarquinia), Vulci, Rusellae (Roselle), Vetulonia, Populonia, Volsinii (Bolsena), Clusium (Chiusi), Arretium (Arezzo), Perusia (Perugia), Volaterrae (Volterra), Veii, Faesulae (Fiesole), and Cortona. Unity was based on religious rather than political ties, a feature which proved a serious weakness when the Etruscans were confronted with the rise of Rome. Most likely a King, or Lucumon, ruled each city, which was composed of the nobility, common people, and slaves. A supreme head, or rex, whose kingly attributes—the crown, scepter, and throne—were later appropriated by Rome, was elected annually for the federation, or "league," during the general assembly held at the still unidentified sanctuary of Voltumna.

Economy. Recognition of Etruscans as mariners is often encountered in the writings of early classical authors, who often regarded them as pirates. During the 6th century B.C., together with the Carthaginians and the Greeks, the Etruscans were numbered among the three leading maritime powers. Their fame as metalworkers has also been recorded by Greek writers of the 5th century B.C. and supported by archeological finds, not only in Italy, but also in France and Greece. It is very probable that the actual presence of the Etruscans in certain areas of Etruria was prompted by rich mineral deposits (iron ores, tin, among others). Even today, Populonia and the nearby island of Elba are active mining centers. Some insight into the Etruscan economy of the 3d century B.C., particularly agriculture, can be gleaned from the Roman historian Livy, who reports the contributions of wheat, corn, and wood made by various Etruscan cities for the outfitting of a Roman military expedition to Africa.

Rise and Fall. At the end of the 6th century B.C. the Etruscans moved north across the Apennines with comparative ease to establish such cities as Marzabotto, Felsina (modern Bologna), and others in the Po River plain. However, they were hindered in the east by rugged mountain tribes, and to the south they met with considerable opposition from the Greek colonists who had been firmly established in southern Italy and Sicily since the beginning of the 7th century B.C. Etruscan ambition clashed also with that of Carthage, which desired complete control of the western Mediterranean and possession of the islands of Corsica, Sardinia, and Sicily. An Etruscan alliance with Carthage against the threat of westward and northward expansion by the Greeks resulted in the great naval battle of 535 B.C. off the city of Alalia on the eastern coast of Corsica. Although the Greeks claimed a victory, archeological evidence indicates their defeat, for they were forced to withdraw from Corsica and to give up further thoughts of expansion. The Carthaginians, rather than the Etruscans, however, gained most from the combined victory, for the Carthaginians effectively secured their trade routes, chiefly for tin and silver, in the western Mediterranean, and at the same time limited Etruscan sea control to the Tyrrhenian Sea, a restriction which signaled the decline of Etruscan maritime power.

On land, however, the Etruscans occupied the whole of Etruria, and their presence in Latium, particularly in Rome, is supported by tradition. Livy gives a detailed account of the Etruscan dynasty of the Tarquins, who ruled Latium during the greater part of the 6th century B.C., until their expulsion c.510. The loss of dominion in Latium cut off Etruria from Campania, where the Etruscans had the prosperous city of Capua. It was through this city and through the rival Greek coastal city of Cumae that the Etruscans maintained their commercial and cultural contacts. Attacks against Cumae failed, and from the beginning of the 5th century B.C. Etruscan sway over Campania was gradually weakened, with Campania falling eventually to the wild Italic mountain tribes who descended into the plains.

The Gauls put an end to Etruscan power in the Po River plain about the beginning of the 4th century B.C. But it was the Romans, who, after the "Expulsion of the Kings," brought about the complete and final collapse of the Etruscans by dealing them a series of drastic military defeats and by ruthlessly destroying many of their cities (Veii in 396, Volsinii in 280, Falerii in 241). Only a few cities which had displayed good will in the past were spared and subsequently absorbed peaceably into the growing Roman state (for example, Caere in 351 B.C.). By the 3d century B.C. Rome had traded roles with the Etruscans, to become the major power in Italy. Toward the beginning of the 1st century B.C. Etruria had officially become a part of Rome. The consistent decline of Etruscan power and prestige is reflected in the known switch from a knowledge of Etruscan letters, for the educated Roman of the 4th century B.C., to Greek letters during the Empire period.

Language. A final decipherment and understanding of the Etruscan language are yet to be accomplished. Although the script is known to be derived from a very old Greek alphabet, the language, which stands quite apart from any known language, remains unintelligible. The only true parallel to the Etruscan script has been discovered on the island of Lemnos, near Turkey, and presents to those who favor the Oriental theory of Etruscan origin a forceful argument. At least 10,000 Etruscan inscriptions are known and recorded. Of these, unfortunately, only a handful are of any "serviceable" length, as the rest, engraved or painted on various works of art, consist of very few words. About 90% of these are funerary in character, merely brief epitaphs giving name, age, and lineage. From an era conscious of public decrees, it is curious that no bilingual inscription (Etruscan with a translation into another language) has yet come to light, particularly in areas where Etruscan contact with Latin- or Greek-speaking peoples existed.

Religion. Like many peoples, Etruscans believed in some aspects of life after death, to judge by the contents of their burials and the nature of their funeral urns and tomb interiors, which imitated the dwellings of the living, evidently in an attempt to recreate eternal homes for the dead. What is known of Etruscan religion suggests that they were a strongly superstitious people, surrounded by an intricate system of taboos and regulations. Unlike the Greeks, the Etruscans believed themselves to be completely dominated by the will of their deities, who were often rather vague in conception. The primitive character usually attributed to Etruscan religion, when compared with Greek religion, is very probably due to the survival of certain beliefs long relinquished by the latter. Basically, Etruscan religion can be classified as revealed. It was thought that certain occurrences could be predicted or interpreted through the art of divination, which was the practice of searching for specific signs in the livers or entrails of sacrificial animals. Well known and respected by the Romans and frequently mentioned by ancient historians (Livy and Pliny) were the haruspices, or Etruscan priests, who performed divination, a ritual whch had antecedents in ancient Babylonia. In general, the Etruscans and Greeks displayed substantially similar elements of worship: an organized priesthood, temples and sacred enclosures, and large accumulations of votive offerings. A strong Greek influence may be surmised from Etruscan equivalents for many of the major Greek divinities: Zeus, Hera, and Athena had their Etruscan counterparts in the triad of Tinia, Uni, and Menerva, later called by the Romans Jupiter, Juno, and Minerva. However, a number of Etruscan deities may have been of purely local origin, as no foreign parallels are known for them.

Legacy. The spontaneity and originality that characterize Etruscan art are perhaps most readily seen in their bronze and terra-cotta sculptures and vivid tomb paintings. The impressive tumuli surrounding numerous Etruscan cities, the multichambered tombs, sepulchral sculpture, and monumental city walls and gateways attest the material wealth and power attained by Etruscan civilization. Remains of this culture are represented in museum collections throughout the world, notably at the Louvre, the British Museum, the Metropolitan Museum of Art in New York, and the Hermitage in Leningrad. However, they can be seen in greatest quantity and to best advantage at the Archeological Museum of Florence and the Villa Giulia Museum of Rome, as well as in smaller local collections at Tarquinia, Volterra, Chiusi, and other sites of ancient Etruria.

That the Etruscan legacy to Roman civilization was large is becoming increasingly evident. The Romans early adopted the Etruscan emblems of magisterial power, including the fasces, or symbol of authority, and the triumphs permitted victorious Roman generals can be traced to the Etruscans, as can also gladiatorial combats, which are known to have originated at Capua. Early Roman military tactics and weapons were influenced by the Etruscans, and many features of Roman law, religious ritual, art, and architecture were directly derived from them. So numerous were the contributions made by the

Etruscans, in fact, that it can be said that the material culture of Rome was dependent on the earlier Etruscan civilization until the 4th century B.C.

FABIUS MAXIMUS RULLIANUS [fā′bē-əs măk′sĭ-məs rŭl-ē-ā′nəs], **QUINTUS** (fl. about 300 B.C.), Roman leader prominent in Rome's struggle to control Italy. He is best known for his defeat of the Samnites, Gauls, and Etruscans at Sentinum in 295. He was consul five times between 322 and 295, and also served as dictator, master of horse, proconsul, censor, and chief of the Senate.

FABIUS MAXIMUS VERRUCOSUS [vĕr-ōō-kō′səs], **QUINTUS** (died 203 B.C.), Roman politician and general. As leader of the conservative faction, he was appointed dictator in 217 B.C. after Hannibal's victory at Lake Trasimene. Recognizing Hannibal's military genius, Fabius avoided a set battle and adopted harassing tactics, hoping to force the Carthaginians to leave Italy for lack of supplies. This policy ("Fabian tactics") earned him both the epithet *cunctator*, the Delayer, and the suspicion of more impatient and aggressive Romans who forced the unusual appointment of a second dictator, Minucius Rufus.

In 216 B.C. the consuls decided to engage Hannibal in formal battle at Cannae and suffered a catastrophic defeat. For the next ten years Fabius' strategy was followed, leading to a stalemate. However, over Fabius' strenuous opposition, the Romans allowed P. Cornelius Scipio (later called Africanus) to lead an invasion of Africa in 204 B.C., designed to draw Hannibal home to defend Carthage. His death in 203 B.C. prevented Fabius from witnessing Hannibal's defeat at Zama in 202 B.C.

FABRICIUS LUSCINUS [lōō-sī′nəs], **GAIUS**, Roman statesman and soldier. While consul in 282 and 278 B.C. he won important battles over the Bruttians, Lucanians, Samnites, and Tarentines. In negotiating with Pyrrhus of Epirus during the war with Tarentum he refused a bribe, and likewise reported to Pyrrhus the offer of a traitor to kill him. He was distinguished for his stern simplicity and moral probity and served as an exemplar of old Roman virtue.

FELIX [fē′lĭks], **ANTONIUS**, a freedman of the Claudian House in Rome. Brother of Pallas, a favorite of the Emperor Claudius, Felix became governor or procurator of Palestine in 52–53 A.D. He was governor at the time of St. Paul's arrest (Acts 23:24–24:26). Tacitus (*Historiae*, Vol. IX) says that Felix "revelled in cruelty and lust, and wielded the power of a king with the mind of a slave."

FIRE FIGHTING. The ancient Romans were the first to organize a resistance to the menace of fire. Rome was the first city to organize a regular fire-fighting force—numbering over 7,000. The homes of the poorer Romans, in the most populous area of the City, were usually built of wood and straw. Each family maintained a fire on a small altar in honor of the domestic gods. Fires frequently broke out.

In those days, long before the discovery of electricity,

there were human alarm boxes, officially called nocturns. These nocturns were strategically stationed throughout the city. The alarm was relayed from one nocturn to another until it reached the nearest castra, which we know as a firehouse. The duty of the nocturn was then to rush to the scene of the fire, driving back crowds and establishing fire lines. Then would come a centurion leading a company of firemen, complete with leather trousers, jackets, and helmets. They were equipped with wooden hand pumps that worked like bellows or syringes (siphons), axes, hammers, saws, iron bars, and short ladders, so made that the ends could be clamped together to reach the roofs of buildings.

Following these came hundreds of aquarii, carrying light earthenware jars or vases. The aquarii formed chains from the nearest cistern, supplied from the great aqueducts leading into the city, and presently the jars would begin emptying a stream of water in the siphons for application to the fire. The prefectus vigilum, equivalent to the fire chief of today, would take command of the fire on his arrival. Surgeons, too, would be in attendance. Usually three were attached to each castra (firehouse). Also, pillow bearers in groups of four, carrying huge leather pillows, about 4 ft. square and stuffed with feathers, would respond. Their purpose was to rescue people trapped at upper windows of buildings. As the forerunner of today's fire marshall, the questionarius was also on the scene. His job was to question the people and try to ascertain the cause of the fire. Roman law at that time demanded that responsibility be fixed for every fire. The questionarius established a board of inquiry before the flames had died.

FLAMINIAN [flə-mĭn′ē-ən] **WAY**, principal northern Roman road, built by the censor Gaius Flaminius (220 B.C.). Augustus restored it and rebuilt almost all its bridges. Beginning at the foot of the Capitoline Hill, it ran due north to cross the Tiber at the Milvian Bridge, followed the Tiber, traversed difficult country in Umbria and across the Apennines to the Adriatic, then followed the coast to Rimini (209 mi. originally, later 215). The line of the road is still followed in large part; and the arch of Augustus, which marked its end at Rimini, and part of his high bridge at Narni still stand.

FLAMININUS [flăm-ĭ-nī′nəs], **TITUS QUINCTIUS** (c.230–c.174 B.C.), Roman general and statesman. He became consul in 198, and in 197 defeated Philip V of Macedon at Cynoscephalae. The Senate kept him in Greece as proconsul to arrange the peace. In 196 he proclaimed to the Greeks assembled at Corinth for the Isthmian Games that henceforth all Greek city-states were to be free. The implementation of this proclamation gave the Romans much trouble.

FLAMINIUS [flə-mĭn′ē-əs], **GAIUS** (d.217 B.C.), Roman general and statesman. In 232 B.C. he secured passage of a law to distribute public land in small lots to landless citizens. This law offended senators who wanted to lease the lands profitably. As censor in 220, he built the Circus Flaminius and the Via Flaminia. In 218 he supported a measure designed to keep senators out of trade, since landowning seemed less likely to conflict with the interests of government. In 217 B.C. popular favor brought him to command against Hannibal, but at Lake Trasimeno he lost his army and his life.

FORUM [fo'rəm], the center of business and public life in ancient Roman cities. The term is derived from the Lat. *foras, foris,* words denoting any open space in front of a tomb, temple, or public building. In Rome the term came to be applied specifically to the flat, roughly rectangular area between the Palatine and Capitoline hills. This Forum Romanum served originally as both a marketplace and an area for the conduct of public business. Later it was devoted more to civic business and to religious observances. In early Republican times, gladiatorial contests were held in the Forum, with galleries for spectators atop the surrounding buildings. The various structures comprising the Forum Romanum were erected at different periods over the course of about 1,000 years. Naturally, several were replaced, repaired, or rebuilt. Buildings attributed to the Regal period (753–509 B.C.) include the Regia, originally the royal palace, later used by the Pontifex Maximus, head of the Roman state religion; the sanctuary of Vesta, goddess who guarded the public hearth, and the adjacent House of the Vestals; the Curia, or Senate house; the fountain of the goddess Juturna; a number of small shops and booths called *tabernae;* and a public altar, associated by some with the tomb of Romulus. The Forum, like the Greek *agora,* was a place where people met to discuss the affairs of the commonwealth.

Republic. During the Republic (509–27 B.C.), the Forum was enhanced by the construction of magnificent temples, public buildings, and basilicas. The venerable temple of Saturn, built c.497 B.C., served for some time as a public treasury. The temple of Castor and Pollux, built c.484 B.C., of which only three columns remain standing, was a favorite meeting place for Romans and also housed the standard weights and measures. Part of the open space of the Forum was called the *Comitium,* the place where the assembly (*comitia*) met to consider legislation or other proposals. Speakers addressed the people from a raised platform, called the Rostra. As Rome became more commercially oriented after 200 B.C., the older stalls and shops were replaced by new ones, built under colonnades and next to basilicas, such as the Basilica Porcia (184 B.C.), the Basilica Aemilia (179 B.C.), the Sempronia (170 B.C.), Opimia (121 B.C.) and the Julia, erected by Julius Caesar in 46 B.C. Passing through the Forum was the Via Sacra, the Sacred Way, along which victorious generals marched in their triumphs up to the Capitoline hill. The first triumphal arch over this road was built by Fabius Maximus in 121 B.C. In 29 B.C. a temple to Divus Julius (the deified Julius Caesar) was constructed.

Imperial Rome. More additions were made in the imperial period. Augustus in 19 B.C. and Tiberius in 16 A.D. built arches, which marked off the eastern and western entrances to the Forum. The temple of Vespasian dates to 79–81, and the Arch of Titus (81 A.D.) still bears witness to that emperor's capture of Jerusalem. Later imperial monuments were a temple dedicated jointly to Venus and Roma (135 A.D.); the arch of Septimius Severus (203), which is still preserved; the temple of Romulus (307); and a basilica, begun by Maxentius, but completed by Constantine (306) and still used for outdoor concerts. The last monument was that of the Byzantine Emperor Phocis (608 A.D.).

As early as 46 B.C. the increase in the size of the city's population made the need for another forum apparent. In that year Julius Caesar built a new forum. Its chief building was a temple to Venus Genetrix, the goddess from whom Caesar claimed descent. The continuing expansion of Rome's population and the complexity of public affairs led to the construction of still other fora during the imperial period. Some were little more than monuments to the reign of an emperor. These fora continued to be built on a rectangular plan. In the imperial period, there were two classes of fora. One was the *fora veniala,* market and commercial centers. Examples are the *forum boaricium* (cattle) and the *forum olitorium* (vegetables).

THE FORUM IN ROMAN TIMES AND TODAY

(1) The Colosseum, inaugurated by the Emperor Titus in 80 A.D.
(2) The temple of Antoninus and Faustina, built in 141 A.D.
(3) Honorary columns set up at the beginning of the 4th century A.D.
(FOTOTECA UNIONE)

The *fora civilia* were devoted to civic and religious affairs. As a rule the imperial fora were not thoroughfares, but the Forum of Nerva (97 A.D.) had a vehicular street running through it. The extremely large Forum of Trajan (111–14) consisted of a triumphal arch, the Basilica Ulpia, libraries, and a tall column, still standing, whose carved surface depicts important events in Trajan's conquest of Dacia (modern Rumania). A temple in honor of Trajan was added to his forum by his successor, Hadrian.

Decline. From the beginning of the 4th century A.D., Rome began to lose her position as the hub of the Empire. With the selection of a succession of new capitals, first at Milan and then at Constantinople and Ravenna (4th century), large-scale building operations ceased. The sack of the city by Vandals and Goths in the 5th century accelerated the decay of the fora. Later they became quarries for builders of fortresses and for Renaissance architects. By the 18th century the Forum Romanum was 40 ft. below ground level. In 1870 Rodolfo Lanciani and Giacomo Boni began the systematic excavations which have brought to light the pitiful but impressive remains of the fora that were the glory of ancient Rome.

GALBA [găl′bə], **SERVIUS SULPICIUS** (3 B.C.–69 A.D.), Roman Emperor (68–69). While governor of Spanish Tarraconensis, Galba joined Vindex's revolt against the Emperor Nero, and after the deaths of both Vindex and Nero was proclaimed Emperor by the Praetorian Guard. His reign was marked by avarice, severity, and favoritism. His choice of Piso Licanianus as his successor proved fatal: Otho, eager himself for the succession, bribed the Praetorian Guard to assassinate Galba.

GALERIUS VALERIUS MAXIMIANUS [gə-lēr′-əs və-lēr′ē-əs măk-sĭm-ē-ā′nəs], **GAIUS**, Roman Emperor (reigned 305–11). After serving in the army under Diocletian, Galerius was made Caesar in the East (293). As such he was chiefly concerned with the defense of the Danube and Persian frontiers. He instigated Diocletian's persecution of the Christians (303). When Diocletian abdicated (305), Galerius became Augustus in the East, nominally second to Constantius I in the West, but actually superior to him. Galerius refused to accept Maxentius as successor to Constantius in the West (306) and succeeded in having Severus appointed. An illness prompted Galerius to issue an edict of partial toleration to the Christians in 309.

GALLA PLACIDIA [găl′ə plə-sĭd′ē-ə] (388–450), Western Roman Empress, daughter of Theodosius I. Taken prisoner by the Visigoths, she married Ataulphus in 414, but after his death returned to the imperial court. In 417 she married Constantius who in 421 became co-Emperor with her brother Honorius. After the death of Constantius she quarreled with Honorius, and retired to Constantinople, where she ruled for 25 years as Regent for her son, Valentinian III. Her tomb at Ravenna, adorned with famous mosaics and sculptured sarcophagi, is preserved.

GALLIC WARS, famous campaigns in Gaul waged by Julius Caesar against Gallic and Germanic tribes from 58 to 51 B.C. As proconsul (governor) of Transalpine Gaul, Caesar undertook the conquest of the region in order to

SCENE OF THE GALLIC WARS

The Roman Republic about 57 B.C.

Caesar's conquests

end the threat from the restive tribes north of the Roman-held territory (Provence). In 58 B.C. he defeated the Helvetii at Bibracte, halting their attempt to penetrate southern Gaul. In the same year, Caesar defeated the German chief and drove him and his people back across the Rhine. With the defeat of the Belgae (57 B.C.) and the Aquitanians and Veneti (56 B.C.), Caesar had placed practically all Gaul under Roman control. In 55 B.C. Caesar crossed over to Britain, returning there the following year with a larger force. After another German campaign, the Romans were faced by a general revolt of the Gallic tribes. Caesar defeated the leader of this revolt, the Arvernian Vercingetorix, at Alesia in 52 B.C. By 51 B.C. all Gaul was pacified.

Caesar's campaigns extended Roman rule from the Pyrenees to the Rhine and from the Atlantic to the Mediterranean. They also provided Caesar with an opportunity to train an army personally loyal to its commander, thus ensuring his political future. The campaigns are described by Caesar in his *Commentaries on the Gallic War.*

GALLIENUS [găl-ē-ē′nəs], **PUBLIUS LICINIUS VALERIANUS EGNATIUS** (218–68), Roman Emperor (253–68). Born into a distinguished family, and well educated, he was co-Emperor with his father Valerian until the Persians captured the latter in 260. Gallienus seems to have displayed energy, loyalty, and intelligence in the struggle to preserve a rapidly disintegrating empire. However, the miseries of inflation, indiscipline, plague, the growth of powerful states in the East, and barbarian pressure from the north, produced devastating effects in his reign, for which he unfairly received the blame and was assassinated. His wife Salonina was the patroness of the philosopher Plotinus.

GALLUS [găl′əs], **GAIUS VIBIUS TREBONIANUS** (c.207–253), Roman Emperor (251–53). As a successful governor of Lower Moesia (249–51) during the Gothic invasion, Gallus appeared to the soldiers a suitable replacement when the Emperor Decius died in battle. But Gallus made a shameful treaty with the Goths which brought no peace, and after more than a year of disaster his soldiers murdered him.

GAUL [gôl] (Lat. **GALLIA**), ancient Roman name designating two areas: Cisalpine Gaul, the area in northern Italy between the Apennines and the Alps; and Transalpine Gaul, the area between the Alps, Pyrenees, Atlantic, and Rhine, corresponding roughly to modern France.

Cisalpine Gaul was inhabited by Ligurians, Veneti, and others in prehistoric times, but in the 5th century B.C. Celts crossed the Alps, seized the fertile Po Valley, and inflicted severe defeats even upon Rome. Rome, however, began conquering these Celts before 222 B.C. and by 191 B.C. had subjugated them. Acquiring many south Italian settlers, Cisalpine Gaul became very populous, productive, and prosperous. In 42 B.C. it was incorporated into Italy.

Transalpine Gaul was Gallia par excellence. Its unidentified prehistoric peoples have left impressive memorials—Paleolithic cave art and Neolithic dolmens and menhirs. Iron-using Celts appeared c.900 B.C., and by 500 B.C. controlled virtually all Transalpine Gaul except Greek Massilia (Marseille). Tombs at Vix and elsewhere confirm Julius Caesar's picture of a wealthy ruling caste in the quarreling Gallic tribes.

To safeguard communications with its Spanish provinces, Rome annexed southern Gaul and made it a province (whence Provence) c.121 B.C. Julius Caesar's campaigns (58–51 B.C.) won central and northern Gaul for Rome. Under Augustus, Gaul was divided into six provinces: Narbonensis (the heavily urbanized south, whose cities today exhibit numerous Roman monuments and still bear their ancient names); Lugdunensis, Aquitania, and Belgica (the relatively unurbanized "Three Gauls," where today's cities bear the names of Gallic tribes, not Gallic towns); and Upper and Lower Germany (military zones along the Rhine). In the 1st and 2d centuries A.D. Romanization, despite occasional revolts, was rapid, and Gaul achieved great prosperity. Because of its magnificent rivers and fertile soil, agriculture and stock raising flourished, and its industries—especially pottery—burgeoned. In the 3d century, Gaul, already partly Christianized, suffered severely from invasion, separatism, and the brigandage of the Bagaudae. Order, however, was reestablished, and in the Late Empire, Latin literature, moribund elsewhere, still flourished in Gaul—for example, Ausonius, Paulinus of Nola, and Apollinaris Sidonius. In the 5th century Roman garrisons withdrew, and although Gaul retained its Latin character, Germanic invaders, notably the Franks under Clovis (c.486), consolidated independent kingdoms there. Thereafter Gaul became France.

GENS [jĕnz], in ancient Rome, a clan or group of families supposedly descended from a common ancestor, particularly old landowning families who from early days shared cult ceremonies (*sacra gentilicia*). Members of the same gens had a common burial place, and, under the Republic, in the absence of direct male relatives, they inherited on intestacy. In Roman nomenclature the *nomen gentilicium*, or the common name borne by all members of the gens, came in second place in a man's name, for example, Julius in the name of Gaius Julius Caesar. Freedmen received the family's *nomen gentilicium* and perhaps the right to participate in certain religious rites, but they did not become part of the gens.

GERMANICUS CAESAR [jər-măn'ĭ-kəs sē'zər] (15 B.C.–19 A.D.), Roman general, son of Drusus Germanicus (Augustus' stepson) and maternal grandson of Mark Antony. In 4 A.D., when Augustus adopted his stepson Tiberius, the latter was compelled to adopt his nephew Germanicus, whose father had died in 9 B.C. Germanicus married Augustus' granddaughter, Agrippina the Elder, who bore him nine children, including the future Emperor Caligula. Germanicus was also the brother of the Emperor Claudius and the grandfather of Nero. At Tiberius' accession in 14 A.D., Germanicus, now heir apparent, ended a mutiny among the legions on the Rhine and led them on two inconclusive campaigns into Germany. Recalled by Tiberius, he celebrated a spectacular triumph in 17 A.D. The emperor sent Germanicus on a diplomatic mission to the East (18 A.D.). He went to Egypt without the necessary imperial permission and accomplished his mission, but quarreled bitterly with Piso, whom Tiberius had assigned to give aid and advice to Germanicus. When Germanicus died in 19 A.D., many thought that Piso had poisoned him, perhaps at the Emperor's instigation. Piso committed suicide before his trial.

GLADIATOR, Roman armed fighter who performed in public shows. Originally combats to the death were part of funeral observances in Etruria. The first gladiatorial show in Rome (264 B.C.) was given by Marcus and Decimus Brutus in the Forum Boarium for their father's funeral. As the taste for these performances grew, they were included in many public festivals, and candidates for office provided lavish shows in the forum or the circus. The first state games were held in 105 B.C. by the consuls, and perhaps were intended to instruct soldiers, but they continued rather as public entertainment staged in amphitheaters, reaching their greatest extent (117 days of shows with 4,941 pairs of gladiators) during the Empire, especially in the 3d century A.D. Although some Emperors tried to limit shows to mimic combats, they ceased only with Constantine (326 A.D.) in the east and in 404 A.D. in the west.

Gladiators, trained in schools and hired out by contractors, were mostly prisoners of war or slaves, but sometimes criminals who were condemned to fight as gladiators; occasionally Roman citizens hired themselves out voluntarily. They were classed according to their equipment: Thracians with round shield and curved dagger; Samnites with long shield and sword; Mirmillones as Gallic warriors, their helmets crowned with fish; and Retiarii with net and trident. Shows began with a procession round the amphitheater, testing of weapons, and exhibition combats with wooden swords; then came the deadly duels in which each pair fought until the wounded man signaled his defeat. If he had fought well the audience shouted approval and he was saved; otherwise their thumbs down meant immediate death. The victor received gold, costly prizes, and a hero's fame. After a number of victories he could win the wooden sword of liberation and honor.

GORDIAN [gôr'dē-ən], name of three Roman Emperors. GORDIAN I, proconsul of Africa, in 238 was raised to the purple at the age of 80 in a movement of landowners outraged by the confiscatory taxation of Maximinus, but he soon committed suicide when his son and co-Emperor GORDIAN II was defeated and slain in battle. GORDIAN III (reigned 238–44), son of a daughter of Gordian I, became Caesar to two senatorial co-emperors, succeeding as Emperor upon their deaths. His father-in-law, Timesitheus, supplied efficient government and military success against the Persians, but after he died, Gordian III was killed, in battle probably.

GRATIAN [grā'shən], also known as Flavius Gratianus (359–83 A.D.), Roman Emperor (reigned 375–83). The eldest son of Valentinian I, Gratian became Emperor of the West on his father's death, the army appointing his infant half-brother, Valentinian II, co-Emperor. After the death of Valens, Gratian appointed Theodosius I Emperor of the East in 379. He managed to repel barbarian attacks, but the army was dissatisfied with his rule and proclaimed Maximus Emperor in 383. Gratian, defeated by Maximus, was then deserted and murdered by his own troops.

HADRIAN, full name Publius Aelius Hadrianus (76–138), Roman Emperor, reigned 117–138. When nine years old he became the ward of his fellow Spaniard and kinsman Trajan (later Emperor), and on reaching manhood held the various posts expected of a Roman senator. On Aug. 9, 117, Trajan reportedly adopted Hadrian, then Governor of Syria, as his successor; on Aug. 11, Trajan's death was announced (he had possibly died before Aug. 9), and thus Hadrian became Emperor. He immediately renounced Trajan's eastern conquests by withdrawing to the Euphrates, thereby preventing the overextension of the Empire. This evidently alienated Trajan's generals, four of whom were promptly executed. Hadrian then gave thought to imperial defense. Frontier fortifications were built in Britain (Hadrian's Wall) and in Germany (the limes joining the Rhine and Danube). He spent years visiting many parts of the Empire in order to promote its unification, and Rome saw comparatively little of him.

Aiming at efficiency, he fostered centralization and developed the imperial civil service, which he staffed largely with equites; he gave particular attention to legal procedures and codes. His reign was generally peaceful except in Palestine, where his Romanizing policies touched off the furious revolt of Bar Cocheba (132–135). Hadrian's last years were unhappy: in 135 he became incurably ill; in 136 he executed his brother-in-law Servianus and Servianus' grandson Fuscus; and in 138 his chosen successor, L. Aelius, died. In 138 Hadrian himself died "hated by all" (for many notables were under sentence of death). Only the insistence of Antoninus Pius, Hadrian's adopted successor, induced the Senate to proclaim Hadrian's deification.

Hadrian was an efficient, if autocratic, monarch. A versatile intellectual, he successfully pursued literature, the fine arts, and especially Greek culture. His memorials include his celebrated villa near Tivoli, the Olympieum and Arch of Hadrian at Athens, and the Pantheon and Castel Sant'Angelo (Hadrian's mausoleum) at Rome.

HADRIAN'S VILLA, favorite residence of the Emperor Hadrian, 18 mi. from Rome near Tivoli. Designed by Hadrian himself, this huge complex of buildings (built 125–135 A.D.) attempted to reproduce the places which had most impressed him on his travels abroad. The villa included a Greek theater, the Poikile (rectangular peristyle surrounding a swimming pool), the Philosophers' Hall, the Canopus (imitating the temple to Serapis in Egypt), and the Imperial Palace. The buildings, embellished with colored marble, gilded stucco, mosaics, paintings, and sculpture, embody some of the most significant innovations in Roman architecture.

HADRIAN'S WALL, ancient Roman battlemented stone rampart between the Tyne and Solway estuaries in

Hadrian's Wall, in northern England, was built (122–128 A.D.) by Emperor Hadrian as a boundary and protection for Roman Britain.

Britain. It was built (122–128 A.D.) under Emperor Hadrian to mark the northern limit of the Roman province. The wall was 20 ft. high, 8 ft. thick, and 73½ mi. long, with 16 forts, fortlets (mile castles) a mile apart, and two turrets between fortlets. It had a large ditch in front and another behind. The whole complex forms the best surviving example of Roman frontier fortifications. It remained the border barrier until Antonine's Wall was built farther north (after 139); but c.212, after the Romans had withdrawn from Antonine's Wall, Hadrian's again became the barrier. It remained the barrier despite massive assaults in 296 and 367 until the Romans abandoned it after 383.

HELIOGABALUS [hē-lē-ō-găb′ə-ləs] **or ELAGABALUS** [ĕl-ə-găb′ə-ləs] (c.205–222 A.D.), Roman Emperor (218–22). He was a cousin of Caracalla and was from the Syrian city of Emesa, where as hereditary priest he had served the local sun-god, who was worshiped in the form of a black stone. His maternal grandmother, Julia Maesa, was sister of Julia Domna, hence sister-in-law of Septimius Severus. The army was induced to murder the usurper Macrinus and proclaim this 14-year-old would-be scion of the Severi, whose real name was Varius Avitus Bassianus, as another M. Aurelius Antoninus. The effective government remained in the hands of Julia Maesa, while Heliogabalus, as he was called after his black stone, outraged Roman sentiment by flaunting his oriental religious practices and foreign ways, so that all sorts of perversions were attributed to him. He obviously had no education or feeling for the public duties and decorum of an emperor. He and his mother were murdered by the Praetorian Guard. His cousin Alexander Severus succeeded him.

HONORIUS (384–423), Roman Emperor (395–423). Son of Theodosius I, Honorius on his father's death became Emperor of the West under the protection of the general Stilicho, his brother Arcadius receiving the East. His reign was troubled by the second invasion of Italy by Alaric and the three sieges of Rome (408–10), by the German invasions of Gaul and Spain, and by the usurpations of Constantine and Jovinus. He witnessed the settlement of the Visigoths in Gaul and of the Vandals and Suevi in Spain, events which affected the whole future of the Roman Empire and of Europe. His sister Galla Placidia was taken captive and married a Visigothic chief. Honorius himself did little to defend the empire against the barbarians.

HORACE [hôr′ĭs], full name Quintus Horatius Flaccus (65–8 B.C.), Rome's greatest lyric poet and satirist. Horace was born in Venusia, a poor mountain town in Apulia. His father was a former slave, ambitious to give his son the privileges which he himself had lacked, and equally anxious to shield him from the vices which, he felt, frequently accompanied those privileges. He took Horace to Rome for his elementary schooling and enabled him to continue his studies at Athens. There Horace was lured by Brutus into the revolutionary army of Caesar's assassins. On his return to Rome, a defeated rebel, Horace supported himself by means of a clerkship and began writing. His work attracted the attention of the recognized poets, Varius and Vergil. Through them he met Maecenas, the cultural ad-

The Roman poet Horace, from a contemporary marble relief.
(MUSEUM OF FINE ARTS, BOSTON)

viser of Augustus, and received an official stipend, and later a small villa in the Sabine hills.

Horace's early poems (called *Epodes*, because they were written in alternating longer and shorter lines) were largely vituperative attacks on persons whom he scorned or disliked, or were satires in rather bad taste, including personal attacks, with no little indecency, all calculated to draw attention to the unknown clerk. But they also contained much evidence of real genius, and their crudity was not, as time proved, typical of the real Horace.

When he had received recognition, he put his heart into the creation of a body of poetry which was to make him, with Vergil, one of the foremost poets in Latin literature. This consisted of a small collection of less violent *Epodes*, in better taste and with evidence of more poetic imagination and skill; two books of *Satires*, verse essays on miscellaneous subjects treated from the personal point of view of the writer and presented in more and more dramatic form with lively dialogue; and four books of *Odes*. These last are lyric poems in stanzaic forms used by the Greek poets Sappho and Alcaeus. They are not the passionate type of emotional lyric that Catullus wrote, but spring from the head rather than from the heart. However, they are not coldly intellectual. They touch human experience at almost every point and from every angle, and have a sincerity and sympathetic appeal of truth.

Horace also wrote two books of *Epistles*. These are really satires cast in the form of letters, still in hexameter verse, with increasing emphasis on literary criticism. The best-known has usually been called the *Art of Poetry*. Finally, Horace wrote a national hymn, to be sung by a chorus of boys and girls at the celebration of the Secular Games in 17 B.C. Among the odes there had been a considerable number of patriotic poems of strong feeling and effective power. To Horace, the commission to write the *Carmen Saeculare* was the peak of his achievement, but he remains one of the best-loved and most quoted of Latin poets because of the appeal of his satires and odes.

HORATII [hə-rā′shē-ī], in Roman legend, three brothers, born triplets, who defended Rome against Alba. The battle was fought between the Horatii and three brothers from Alba, the Curiatii, also triplets. Two of the Horatii were killed at once. The third fled to separate his enemies. His tactic was successful and the Curiatii were slain, singly. The hero, returning to Rome, was cursed by his sister who had had a Curiatii for a lover. Horatius stabbed her. He was condemned, but spared when he appealed to the populace.

HORATIUS COCLES [hə-rā′shəs kŏk′lēz], "Horatius at the Bridge" of Macaulay's *Lays of Ancient Rome*. In Roman legend, he singlehandedly held the Tiber bridge against attacking Etruscans (508 B.C.) for the last few minutes before it was destroyed and then swam to safety. Livy's account of Horatius' stand against Lars Porsenna is an admirable example of his technique of glorifying old Rome and the old Roman.

JOVIAN [jō′vē-ən], Roman Emperor (reigned 363–64). Jovian was a Christian officer who was proclaimed Emperor by the army when Julian was killed in Persia. He concluded a peace with the Persians in which too great concessions were made to the enemy. Jovian's election represented a reaction against the anti-Christian policies of the pagan Julian; but at the same time Jovian was tolerant toward the pagans. He chose his advisers from among the men who had served under Constantius II. Jovian died suddenly of suffocation.

JULIA (c.83–54 B.C.), daughter of Julius Caesar and Cornelia. In 59 she was married to Pompey as a means of cementing the friendship between Pompey and Caesar, but she died in childbirth.

JULIA DOMNA (170–217 A.D.), Roman Empress and influential patron of learning in the reigns (193–217) of her husband and son. She came from Emesa in Syria, married the future Emperor Septimius Severus, and, after his accession, greatly promoted religious syncretism. She attracted a circle of brilliant physicians (Galen, Sammonicus Serenus) and literary men (Athenaeus, Philostratus, Diogenes Laertius, Aelian, Oppian). After the assassination of her son Caracalla she presumably committed suicide.

JULIAN THE APOSTATE, born Flavius Claudius Julianus (332–63), Roman Emperor (reigned 361–63), last member of the dynasty of Constantine the Great and last pagan Roman Emperor. Brought up a Christian, Julian as a youth was secretly converted to paganism. Kept apart from the imperial court in Constantinople, he developed bookish interests, and was allowed to complete his studies of Greek literature and philosophy at Athens. When a Caesar of the Constantinian house was needed, Constantius II put Julian in charge of defending Gaul against the Germans (355). Julian, fearing that Constantius was jealous of his success, accepted when his troops proclaimed him Emperor (360).

On the death of Constantius, Julian was recognized as sole Emperor. He proceeded to Antioch, which he made the headquarters of his preparations for war with Persia. In 363 he successfully invaded Persia as far as Ctesiphon, but then was killed in a skirmish. In his campaign for the revival of paganism, Julian had underestimated the strength of Christianity, and had counted too heavily on the enthusiasm of the pagans for the revival of their religion. His program was a failure, and no other large-scale attempt to revive paganism was made.

JULIA THE ELDER (39 B.C.–14 A.D.), daughter and only child of Augustus. She was married first (25 B.C.) to her cousin Marcellus, Augustus' nephew and heir apparent, and after his death to Agrippa, then Augustus' supposed successor. After Agrippa's death she became, in 11 B.C., the wife of Tiberius, who did succeed Augustus as Emperor; but in 2 B.C. Augustus banished her for licentious behavior to Pandateria Island.

JUVENAL [jōō′və-nəl], full name Decimus Junius Juvenalis (c.50–130 A.D.), Roman satiric poet. His 16 satires follow Horace in the choice of literary genre, but lack Horace's distinguished use of dramatic dialogue. Also, Juvenal lacked Horace's moderation and urbanity. With forthright, even brutal, directness and with burning indignation, he attacked the social and political abuses of the Empire, as well as every human vice, but for safety's sake used the figures of the preceding generation as his ostensible targets. He was the rhetorical satirist rather than the philosophical—the ideal of Samuel Johnson who, in his *London* and *The Vanity of Human Wishes*, closely imitated two of Juvenal's most successful satires. For brilliant characterization and epigrammatic phrases Juvenal was never surpassed: witness his word pictures of old age, of the newly rich, of the horrors and discomforts of life in a crowded metropolis, and his ever-quoted ideal—"a sound mind in a sound body."

LATIFUNDIA [lăt-ə-fŭn′dē-ə] (Lat. *latus*, "wide"; *fundus*, "estate" or "field"), large, capitalistically operated estates which took over much of Italy in the 2d century B.C. as a result of the increase of slaves from foreign wars and slave raids. The latifundium, worked by gangs of slave herdsmen managed for the owner by a slave steward (*vilicus*), was given over partly to pasturage and stock rearing, partly to the cultivation of olives and vines. Methods of management can be studied in Cato's book, *On Agriculture*.

LATINS, ancient peoples of west-central Italy, who settled in Latium about 1000 B.C. and absorbed the indigenous Neolithic population. Early settlements have been found at Alba Longa and on the Palatine Hill in Rome.

By the 6th century B.C., the Latin-speaking peoples, including the Romans, were confined to Latium. Contact with the Etruscans to the north quickened the cultural growth of the Latin cities. Feelings of common ancestry, and competition, led to the formation of various religious and political federations.

Rome's defeat of Alba Longa (c.600 B.C.) resulted in her dominance of the Latin League. By 338 the League was dissolved and Rome, by arms and treaties, had reduced the Latins to the status of dependent allies. The Romans granted the Latins less than full Roman citizenship, but a status superior to that of most Italians after c.265 B.C. As a result of the Italic wars of 90–88 B.C., in which the Latins remained faithful, the Latins and many Italians were accorded full Roman citizenship.

LAW, ROMAN. Aside from Greek art and philosophy and the Judaeo-Christian tradition, no cultural force has exercised so much influence on the development of Western civilization as the Roman ideas of law and state. These evolved as Rome expanded from a small city-state to a great Empire embracing the Mediterranean world and extending beyond. In the West that Empire lasted until the 5th century A.D., and in the East until the 15th. Roman law, the law of the Roman people and state, did not die with the Empire. It became the "common" law of continental Europe during the Middle Ages and continued in modern times until partially codified and replaced by the codes of the 19th and 20th centuries. Today its influence is felt around the globe, even in areas never touched by Roman rule. Most civilized non-English-speaking nations, including those of the Far East and the Soviet bloc, use Roman law in modernized forms.

In the English-speaking part of the world the influence of Roman law was less pronounced, but it made itself felt through many channels. Germanic-Frankish-Norman law, which forms the foundation of the law of England, reflected some Roman law influence, and was again affected, during the 13th and 14th centuries, by Henry de Bracton and other clerics who had studied Roman law in Italy. Furthermore the English common law absorbed some of the Roman law practiced in English ecclesiastical courts, which long retained jurisdiction over large areas of law, including decedents' estates, family law, and parts of criminal law. Roman law also guided much of the law administered by the courts of equity and admiralty and the mercantile courts. Finally, there were important continuing contacts during various periods of English and American history through scholars and lawyers who were refugees from the Continent. But some sections of the English-speaking world, such as Scotland, Louisiana, the Republic of South Africa (Roman-Dutch law), Ceylon, and Quebec, adopted Roman law itself and continue its use in modernized form.

The differences between the Roman-based civil law and the Anglo-Saxon common law of England and the United States are many. They cannot be summarized, though it has often been tried, as the formal distinction between written, or codified (Roman), law and unwritten, or uncodified (common), law. At the risk of vast overgeneralization, one could characterize the chief differences as follows: Roman law in its mature form (Justinian) is an all-inclusive, systematized law, with a minimum of conflict of rules, directed toward the inclusion of even unforeseen fact controversies. It is the product and tool of the legal academician. Common law, even in its present form, consists of the rules formed in the resolution of past human controversies. Hence it is a relatively unsystematized body of decisional law (though some of it may be in statutory form), with a fair amount of irreconcilable legal propositions. Common law is not necessarily directed toward the solution of future fact controversies, though it is capable of being extended to them. It is the product and tool of the legal practitioner.

In the search for the differences, historians frequently have overlooked the similarities. These point to a parallel development of all legal systems from decisional law via rigid primitive codes, through unsystematized decisional law with ever-broadening equitable modifications, to a systematized all-inclusive codification. The common law is only now beginning to reach the last stage.

The Republic

Twelve Tables. When Roman law made its first imprint on history, it appeared in the form of a primitive code, the Twelve Tables (451–449 B.C.). These were written by members of the dominant patrician class under political pressure of the suppressed masses, the plebeians. The Twelve Tables put into writing legal rules of long standing and formed the core of *the* Roman law, often referred to as civil law, or quiritarian law. For many centuries it constituted a bill of rights for Roman citizens. Anglo-Saxon law reached this stage in its development a millennium later.

During the period of the legendary Roman monarchy (753–510 B.C.) and the government of the patrician aristocracy (510–367 B.C.), this rigid and inflexible law, administered by the priesthood (pontifices and flamines), was largely sufficient for the predominantly rural Roman people. Occasional legislation, enacted by the popular assemblies, kept it current with the needs of the time. These legislative bodies also exercised some trial and appeal jurisdiction for several centuries, though proxies (*lictores*) later took the place of the original assemblies.

The Praetor. As Rome grew militarily, politically, and economically, the formalistic, ritualistic civil law and the method of amending it through popular legislation proved inadequate. In 367 B.C., which marked the beginning of the Republic, the high office of the praetor was created. Praetors were magistrates, next to the consuls in rank, and had chiefly judicial duties. They had jurisdiction in all civil cases among Roman citizens. Thus the basis was laid for expansion of the law through interpretation, analogy, and adaptation in the process of adjudicating actual controversies. The praetors and other officers with judicial power were members of the high civil service, an "honorary career" sought by wealthy and ambitious Romans. Hence the law created by those in the "honorary career" came to be known as the honorary law (*jus honorarium*), or edictal law. The latter name arose because the law rested on the edicts of the judicial officers, before whom the legal issues were joined and the pleadings framed prior to trial of the facts before a trial judge (*judex*).

The *jus honorarium* rapidly expanded through the precedents of the *praetor peregrinus*, a parallel office established in 242 B.C. to deal with cases involving non-Romans, who were not entitled to the benefits of Roman law. In an endeavor to render substantial justice to litigants from many different nations, this officer created a separate body of law. It was composed af those rules of law which were deemed "natural" (*jus naturale*), or common to all nations (*jus gentium*), or merely commonly equitable (*aequitas*), with strong components of Roman law. It was considerably influenced by Greek philosophy, especially that of the Stoics. This new law and the relatively informal method of its application ultimately proved so superior that it gained force for purely Roman legal problems as well, and it ultimately absorbed the original civil law. When the priesthood lost all control over the law, a class of professional lawyers consisting of solicitors (*jurisconsulti*) and barristers (*oratores*) came into being.

The Empire

The Classic Period. During the first half (27 B.C.–284 A.D.) of the Empire, Roman law reached its classic stage, with illustrious jurists in imperial service. Lawyers had to be licensed to practice. The freedom of judges to create law was terminated in 131 A.D. by an edict of Emperor Hadrian. It was drafted by the imperial jurisconsult Julianus. His compilation of edicts of the past, supplemented by the Emperor's laws (*constitutiones*) and occasional senate legislation (*senatus consulta*), thenceforth constituted the positive law of Rome, practiced now in regular imperial courts. During the reign (98–117) of Trajan and the reign (117–38) of Hadrian, Roman law and Roman power were at their mightiest, although the morals of the people were already on the decline.

Decline. During the following period of Roman history, called the Dominate (284 to the middle of the 6th century), Roman law, as well as statesmanship, declined rapidly and severely. Various Emperors (after 326 A.D. residing in Constantinople) felt compelled to publish comprehensive, yet technically mediocre, codes, or compilations of laws. They thus tried to simplify, adapt, and render available the principles of classic law, which for the then ill-trained jurists had become too sophisticated. The "law of citations" (426) arbitrarily decreed that the writings of only certain jurists should have the force of law to the exclusion of all other secondary sources. To some extent, newly created law schools (Beirut and Constantinople) checked the decline of legal craftsmanship by training competent practitioners. When, during the 5th century, Germanic tribes conquered and ruled Italy, classic Roman law, for the most part, disappeared there, being replaced by vulgate codes of mixed Roman-Germanic content.

Codex of Justinian. The last and greatest rally of Roman law, as of Roman military power, occurred under Emperor Justinian (reigned 527–65) of the Byzantine (Eastern Roman) Empire. His commission of law professors, under the chairmanship of Tribonian, codified all Roman law from its classic sources, a gigantic task completed in six years. This code comprised the Digest, or Pandects (530–33), a 50-volume treatise of Roman law;

the Institutes (533), a superb student text; the Codex (534), containing all imperial laws then in force; and the Novels (534–65), holding all Justinian's subsequent laws.

This greatest codification of all time came too late to be of practical benefit to the Empire. Although sent to the reconquered Western part of the Empire, it remained without effect there. Even in the East it proved intellectually too demanding for the then ill-equipped judges and practitioners. Popular brief summaries and abridgments served them. In this manner, and through partial integration into the canon law of the Roman Catholic Church, it survived during the Middle Ages, but the magnificent Digest, in all its copies, seemed lost.

Influence on Modern Law

Rediscovery of the Digest. In the middle of the 11th century the study, understanding, and knowledge of Roman law experienced an astounding upswing. The impetus for this change was the startling discovery of one of the few original copies of the Digest, handwritten under Justinian himself. The find was made in Italy's then most important port city, Pisa, which traditionally had carried on trade with Constantinople. It is disputed whether this copy of the Digest (called *littera Pisana* or *Florentina*) is a copy sent by Justinian himself, for official use in Rome, and lost in transit, or whether the copy was brought by ship to Pisa in the 11th century. In any event, the discovery inaugurated a period of renewed study and practice of Roman law for all Europe.

In the 12th and 13th centuries a group of scholars (Irnerius, Azo, and Accursius), called glossators because of their custom of writing marginal comments, or glosses, on their copies of the Digest, rediscovered the true meaning of the great Roman law of Justinian. Their successors, the so-called postglossators (Bartolus and Baldus), adapted this ancient law for contemporary use in the 14th century. From then on Roman law replaced the vulgate systems of the Continent. Systematically taught at all Continental universities, it became a truly "common" law of all Europe. This reception of the Roman law was aided particularly by the labors of the refugee scholars from Constantinople, which in 1453 A.D. had been conquered by the Turks.

Contribution to Modern Law. Roman law has been the great teacher for all modern systems of law. It has taught that law, to be most effective, must be systematized and codified. Thus the infinite number of possible controversies among men can be reduced to a relatively few types which can be solved by the application of a few relatively clear principles. Simplicity is one of the basic lessons of the Roman judicial experience. Roman law avoided hypertechnical abstractions, to which modern Continental law inclines.

Yet codification need not destroy the valuable continuity of development, for Roman law, despite its dynamic changes, remained conservative and bound by tradition. Rarely were legal institutions abolished. They simply vanished with the creation of better institutions. Moreover the Romans demonstrated that the positive law of codes is fully capable of utilizing and supporting ethical values and humanitarian principles. The famous introductory passage to Justinian's Digest is descriptive of Roman jurisprudence: "Jurisprudence is the knowledge of things divine and human; the science of the just and the unjust." It is for this reason that Roman law continues to be taught at English and major American law schools, not only as a necessary introduction to a study of foreign, comparative, and international law, but also as the very foundation of legal philosophy and juridical statesmanship.

LEPIDUS [lĕp'ĭ-dəs], **MARCUS AEMILIUS** (d.13 B.C.), Roman statesman, general, and triumvir. Son of the consul of the same name, Lepidus was a supporter of Caesar in the Civil War and after Caesar's death supported Antony. He soon left Rome to rule Gallia Narbonensis and Hither Spain. In Oct., 43, Lepidus joined the so-called Second Triumvirate, an alliance with Octavian and Antony, to govern the Roman world. In the division of provinces after the battle of Philippi (42), Lepidus received Africa. In 36 he fought in the war against Sextus Pompey but, attempting to gain Sicily for himself, was defeated by Augustus, who compelled him to withdraw from the triumvirate and retire to private life. He had been made Pontifex Maximus in 44, after the death of Caesar, and retained this office until his death.

LICINIUS [lĭ-sĭn'ē-əs], **VALERIUS LICINIANUS**, Roman Emperor (reigned 308–24). After a military career as comrade of the Emperor Galerius, Licinius was made Augustus. Following Galerius' death he formed an alliance with Constantine I, whose sister he married. While Constantine destroyed his rival Maxentius in the West, Licinius defeated Maximinus II, thus becoming sole Emperor in the East (313). In that year Constantine and Licinius jointly issued the Edict of Milan, granting toleration to Christianity. But Licinius broke with Constantine in 315 and was defeated in a brief war. After 320 rivalry between the two Emperors intensified with Licinius' renewal of the persecution of the Christians. He was defeated by Constantine in 323 and later executed.

LIVIA DRUSILLA [lĭv'ē-ə drōō-sĭl'ə] (c.58 B.C.–29 A.D.), first Roman Empress, wife of Augustus from 38 B.C., and mother, by a previous marriage, of Tiberius (the future Emperor) and Drusus Germanicus. Although childless by Augustus, Livia influenced him greatly. The story that she murdered Augustus' grandsons and even Augustus himself to ensure the succession of her own son Tiberius is probably malicious. By Augustus' will she became Julia Augusta; Claudius I subsequently deified her.

LIVY [lĭv'ē] (**TITUS LIVIUS**) (59 B.C.–17 A.D.), Roman historian. He wrote the history of Rome from its supposed foundation in 753 B.C. to 9 B.C. Of the original 142 books of the work, only 35 survive, though there are later epitomes of the rest. The extant books narrate the mythical tales of early Rome and the historical story of Roman conquest from 219 to 167 B.C. Livy came from Patavium, noted for its provincial conservatism, and was an ardent believer in the greatness of the Roman Republic, of which his history is a sincere encomium. In spite of this republican bias he was a protégé of the Emperor Augustus. His history, written in a clear and straightforward style, without undue concern for investigative scholarship, is an enthralling narrative of the life of a nation. Only the short rhetorical introduction, assailing the degeneracy of contemporary Rome, is a concession to the growing artificiality of his own day. The history itself has the charm of a story told with direct simplicity and wholehearted enthusiasm, the characters made vivid by their actions and by the speeches which Livy conceived and ascribed to them. These speeches give dramatic effect to the great events which he narrates. From his own day onward Livy has been the accepted historian of republican Rome. For the modern world, Romulus and Remus, Horatius at the bridge, as well as Hannibal and Scipio, are creations of Livy's pen.

LUCAN [loō'kən] (**MARCUS ANNAEUS LUCANUS**) (39–65), Roman poet. A nephew of Seneca, the philosopher, he was author of the *Pharsalia*, an epic in 10 books on the civil war between Caesar and Pompey. Some scholars have rated Lucan with or even above Vergil. His epic is, however, a wholly rhetorical production, brilliant in parts, teeming with quotable lines, but wholly lacking in over-all construction and overburdened with learned digressions. It also lacks a hero to give it unity. Lucan had an idealistic passion for the old republic which made him eloquent but warped his poetic judgment. While still young, he found himself the object of Nero's jealousy, and brought about his own end by entering into a conspiracy against the Emperor.

LUCILIUS [loō-sĭl'ē-əs], **GAIUS** (148–103 B.C.), father of Roman verse satire. Satire in Roman usage was a short hexameter poem expressing the author's views on almost any subject—philosophy, politics, people, incidents— usually with a moral tone of criticism and always with humor and caustic irony. Lucilius' work survives only in fragments; but Roman critics always noted his courageous independence and effective power of invective and criticism. It was he who fixed on hexameter as the meter best suited to satire.

LUCRETIA [loō-krē'shə] **or LUCRECE** [loō-krēs], in Roman legend, the wife of Lucius Tarquinius Collatinus, famous for her beauty and virtue. Raped by Sextus, son of King Tarquinius Superbus, she killed herself in shame after exacting an oath of vengeance from her husband and father. The family, under the direction of Lucius Junius Brutus, then organized a civil uprising which drove the Tarquins from Rome and led to the establishment of the Republic. The legend was used in Shakespeare's *Rape of Lucrece*.

LUCULLUS [loō-kŭl'əs], **LUCIUS LICINIUS** (c. 110–56 B.C.), Roman general. A partisan of Sulla in the civil war with Marius, in 74 B.C. he was placed in command of the war against Mithridates VI of Pontus. He conducted the war with considerable success, but was relieved of his office when Pompey was given the command, by the Manilian Law. Lucullus retired to private life in Rome, where he gained the reputation of living in magnificent luxury; this has given "Lucullan" its meaning.

LUPERCALIA [lōō-pər-kā'lē-ə], Roman festival held on February 15, possibly in honor of Faunus. Originally, young shepherds ran around the earliest settlement to frighten away wolves. Later, the noisy ceremony lost its propitiatory character; and the beating of the people with the skins of sacrificial victims, at first supposed to combat all evil influences, was thence believed to insure fertility in women. The feast became a popular amusement, until Augustus restored its former dignity.

MACRINUS [mə-krī'nəs], **MARCUS OPELIUS** (164–218 A.D.), Roman Emperor (217–18). A native of Mauretania he became imperial procurator, and in 212 rose to the prefecture of the Praetorian Guard, the highest equestrian office. On a campaign in the East he had the Emperor Caracalla assassinated and was himself raised to the purple by the army, the first of nonsenatorial rank ever to be proclaimed. But the soldiers soon tired of him, and he succumbed to a new pretender, Elagabalus, whose generals killed him.

MAGNENTIUS [măg-nĕn'shē-əs], **FLAVIUS POPILIUS,** Roman usurper, in power 350–53 A.D. An officer of barbarian origin, Magnentius was proclaimed Emperor by his troops in Gaul and was acknowledged ruler of the West after he assassinated the Emperor Constans. He appealed for the support of the pagans, who were then being persecuted, and obtained the backing of some of the Roman aristocracy. But Constantius II, Constans' brother, defeated Magnentius (351), ultimately causing him to flee to Gaul, where he committed suicide.

MANLIUS CAPITOLINUS [măn'lē-əs kăp-ĭ-tō-lī'nəs], **MARCUS** (d.384 B.C.), Roman consul in 392 B.C. According to tradition, he held the Capitol against the attacking Gauls in 387, being aroused by the cackling of the sacred geese; from this episode he supposedly received his surname. After the departure of the Gauls he espoused the cause of the plebeians. Because he seemed to be aiming at kingship, he was accused of treason, prosecuted by the tribunes of the people, and thrown from the Tarpeian Rock.

MARCELLUS [mär-sĕl'əs], **MARCUS CLAUDIUS** (c.269–208 B.C.), Roman statesman and general, five times consul. He first distinguished himself by defeating the Gallic Insubres in 222, killing their chieftain in single combat. In 211 B.C. he captured Syracuse after a two-year siege in spite of Archimedes' ingenious defense machines. In the following years he commanded forces in southern Italy against Hannibal and scored some slight successes. He died in 208 in one of Hannibal's ambushes.

MARCELLUS, MARCUS CLAUDIUS (d.45 B.C.), Roman politician, consul in 51, and an enemy of Caesar. After the battle of Pharsalus he was pardoned by Caesar and permitted to return to Rome. In his speech, *Pro Marcello,* Cicero took occasion to thank Caesar for his leniency. While returning to Rome, however, Marcellus was murdered at Piraeus in Greece.

MARCELLUS, MARCUS CLAUDIUS (42–23 B.C.), nephew and heir of Augustus. He was the son of Augustus' sister

Octavia, was adopted by Augustus, and married Augustus' daughter Julia. It is thought that Augustus intended Marcellus to be his successor, but Marcellus died in 23. He is mentioned by Vergil in the *Aeneid,* Book VI, as one of the illustrious descendants of Aeneas.

MARCUS AURELIUS ANTONINUS [mär'kəs ô-rē'lē-əs ăn-tō-nī'nŭs], original name Marcus Annius Verus (121–180 A.D.), Roman Emperor (161-180) and Stoic pilosopher. He was born in Rome to an Italian family from Spain and was raised in the circle of the Emperor Hadrian. In 138 Aurelius Antoninus (Pius) adopted Marcus and Lucius Verus, complying with the wishes of Hadrian, who had adopted Antoninus. Marcus Aurelius Caesar, as he was now called, married Faustina, daughter of Antoninus Pius, in 145, and became Emperor in 161 on the death of the Emperor Antoninus Pius. Marcus at once made Lucius Verus co-Emperor.

Though he had received an excellent education (among his teachers were M. Cornelius Fronto and Herodes Atticus) and had developed a taste for philosophy and meditation, the conscientious, almost saintly Emperor Marcus had to spend his time in wars, which broke out after a long peace. Both the Parthians in the East, and German and other barbarians in the North, invaded the Empire. The Parthians were defeated by troops under Avidius Cassius (nominally commanded by Lucius Verus). Roman troops actually captured Ctesiphon, but on their return from the East in 166 they brought with them a plague. In 168 Marcus defeated the German barbarians, who had reached Aquileia in Italy.

On the death of Lucius Verus in 169 Marcus became

Bust of Marcus Aurelius Antoninus, Roman Emperor (161–180 A.D.).
(BETTMANN ARCHIVE)

sole Emperor. From 170 to 175 he had to fight against the Marcomanni and Quadi along the Danube; raids occurred also in the Aegean and on the Spanish and African coasts. In 175, having secured unsteady peace along the Danube, he went to the East because of an abortive revolt by Avidius Cassius. On this trip he was initiated into the Eleusinian mysteries, endowed professorships at Athens, and met distinguished representatives of Greek culture. A cruel persecution of the Christians occurred in Gaul as a result of an interpretation placed upon the Emperor's order, but in general his administration was just. In fact, he improved the administration of justice, and despite expensive wars he gave some relief from burdensome taxation. His *Meditations*, composed mainly during campaigns along the Danube, combines religious feeling and philosophy. He died of illness on yet another campaign in Pannonia, leaving a name greatly revered. He was succeeded by his son Commodus, who had been co-Emperor since 177.

MARTIAL [mär'shəl] **(MARCUS VALERIUS MARTIALIS)** (c. 40–104), Rome's greatest epigrammatist. Though born in Bilbilis, Spain, Martial spent most of his life in Rome. His genius was essentially urban and cosmopolitan. In type of verse, he recognized Catullus as his source and master, but his epigrams, at times matching in virulence and indecency those of Catullus, had a much wider range and more polished wit. He wrote about the opening of Vespasian's Colosseum, satirized the follies of the social set and the intrigues of the politicians, and flattered the Emperor and his entourage. But he also had true friends among both great and humble, and occasionally wrote verse of real emotion. Had there been daily newssheets at Rome, Martial would have been a successful columnist, for the comments in his 14 books of epigrams cover brilliantly the whole range of contemporary Roman life.

MAXENTIUS [măk-sĕn'shē-əs], **MARCUS AURELIUS VALERIUS,** Roman Emperor (306–12). Son of Emperor Maximian, Maxentius failed to win promotion in 305 and retired to Rome. When Constantine I became Augustus, the Romans proclaimed Maxentius Emperor and summoned Maximian from retirement to be his colleague. Himself a pagan, Maxentius sought to win Christian support by an edict of toleration. After Constantine and Licinius joined forces, Maxentius allied himself with Maximinus. Constantine then invaded Italy and defeated Maxentius outside Rome at the battle of the Milvian Bridge, in which Maxentius lost his life.

MAXIMIAN [măk-sĭm'ē-ən], full name Marcus Aurelius Valerius Maximianus, Roman Emperor (286–305, 306–8). After serving with Diocletian, Maximian was made his assistant as Caesar (285) and promoted to Augustus (286). He was put in charge of the defense of the West, but was unable to overcome the usurper Carausius in Britain. He took part in Diocletian's persecution of the Christians (303) and abdicated (305) along with Diocletian. When his son Maxentius was proclaimed Emperor after the death of Constantius in 306, Maximian came out of retirement to help him. The following year, however, he tried to depose Maxentius, and when he failed he fled

to Gaul to Constantine with whom he had made an alliance. Finally, after an unsuccessful revolt against Constantine, he committed suicide (310).

MAXIMINUS [măk-sə-mī'nəs], **GAIUS GALERIUS VALERIUS,** surnamed Daza or Daia, Roman Emperor (308–14). A nephew of the Emperor Galerius, on becoming Augustus in the East, Maximinus attempted to revive paganism in Asia Minor, but after Constantine's victories in the West abandoned the effort. He quarreled with his co-Emperor in the East, Licinius, but was defeated. Then, seeking the support of the Christians, he issued an edict of toleration (313). He died after a mysterious illness, interpreted by Christians as divine punishment.

MAXIMINUS, GAIUS JULIUS VERUS, surnamed Thrax, Roman Emperor (235–38), the first barbarian to ascend the throne. Born in Thrace, he served as a common soldier, then as centurion, before entering the equestrian rank of Roman officers. Though not a senator, Maximinus was a man of great strength and military ability; on the assassination of the unwarlike Alexander Severus, he was proclaimed Emperor by the troops. He successfully completed the German war, then defended the Danube frontier, but by confiscation and taxation he sacrificed the cities to the demands of the soldiery. The senate proclaimed him a public enemy. Invading Italy, he found himself without food supplies during a siege of Aquileia, and was murdered by his starving men.

MAXIMUS, MAGNUS CLEMENS, Roman Emperor (383–88). A Spanish officer in command in Britain, Maximus was proclaimed Emperor by his troops. He then crossed to Gaul and defeated Gratian, the Emperor of the West. By agreement with Theodosius I, Emperor of the East, Maximus was recognized as Augustus in Gaul, Spain, and Britain, while Valentinian II retained Italy and Illyricum. In 387 Maximus took Italy from Valentinian, whereupon Theodosius marched against Maximus, captured, and executed him.

MAXIMUS, PETRONIUS, Roman Emperor of the West (455). After serving as senator and minister under Honorius, Maximus rose to the imperial power by causing the deaths of Aetius and Valentinian III. His accession brought about the intervention of Genseric and the Vandals, and he was killed by a mob when the Vandals landed in Italy. Thus Maximus was responsible for the Vandals' sack of Rome.

MUMMIUS [mŭm'ē-əs], **LUCIUS,** Roman general. Consul in 146 B.C., he crushed the Achaean League and presided over the destruction of Corinth. Most of central and southern Greece was then incorporated into the new Roman province of Achaea.

NERO [nē'rō], in full Nero Claudius Caesar Drusus Germanicus (37–68 A.D.), Roman Emperor (54–68). He was the son of Agrippina the Younger, and, through her, great-great-grandson of Augustus, and stepson of Claudius I. Nero became Emperor when Agrippina persuaded Claudius to name him as his successor (50) and then had

Claudius murdered (54). Agrippina's influence soon waned. For a few years Seneca, the philosopher, and Burrus, the Praetorian Prefect, advised Nero, and government was good. Nero, however, resented advice, and after Agrippina's murder (59), Burrus' death (62), and Seneca's retirement (62), he followed his own willful bent. Poppaea (the wife he stole from Otho), Tigellinus (the new Praetorian Prefect), and other favorites egged him on.

A suspicious tyrant who executed all potential rivals, and a wasteful poseur who appeared publicly as singer, actor, and charioteer, Nero was one of the worst emperors. A great fire at Rome (64) afforded him opportunity to construct a grandiose "Golden House" and to accuse and massacre Christians as arsonists, Saints Peter and Paul being traditionally among his victims. In his reign Boudicca revolted in Britain (c.60) and the Jews in Palestine (66).

In 67 Nero traveled in Greece, winning prizes at all the games. But retribution now overtook him. Vindex revolted in Gaul and Galba in Spain; when the Praetorian Guard acclaimed Galba, Nero committed suicide (68), thus ending the Julio-Claudian dynasty. Nero's interest in the arts seems to have been genuine, but his fecklessness, cruelty, and cowardice make him contemptible. His memory was officially damned, an unenviable distinction that had befallen no previous emperor.

NERVA [nûr'və], **MARCUS COCCEIUS** (c.30–98 A.D.), Roman Emperor (96–98). After helping Nero suppress the conspiracy of Piso (65), Nerva was consul with Vespasian (71) and Domitian (90). On Domitian's assassination the senate elected Nerva Emperor (96). Some unrest ensued; defying him, the troops lynched Domitian's murderers. Nerva thereupon publicly adopted an outstanding soldier, the Spaniard Trajan, as his successor, thereby setting the pattern for imperial successions in the ensuing century.

ODOACER [ō-dō-ā'sər] or **ODOVACAR** (c.434–493), the first barbarian ruler of the Roman Empire. Little is known of his origin except that his father's name was Edicon (Edecon), and he lived in the eastern part of the Empire. Odoacer entered Italy in 472 with the general Ricimer and a vast horde of Goths and other eastern tribes. The regent Orestes, after driving the Roman Emperor Julius Nepos into exile, had set his own son, Romulus Augustulus, on the throne. Odoacer pursued Orestes and killed him in 476 (the traditional date of the fall of the Roman Empire). Romulus was sent into exile near Naples. Odoacer then proclaimed himself King of Italy, but his status was never acknowledged by the Byzantine Emperor Zeno. He maintained the traditional imperial organization and redistributed one-third of the land to his soldiers. His attempt to unite Gothic and Roman society was fruitless. An Arian heretic, he was in constant conflict with Pope Gelasius and decided upon Ravenna rather than Rome as his capital. In 489 the Eastern Emperor Zeno sent the Ostrogothic King Theodoric into Italy, and Odoacer's forces were disastrously defeated at Isonzo and the Adda River. He withdrew to his stronghold in Ravenna, but his capital was besieged, and he was captured and executed.

OTHO [ō'thō], **MARCUS SALVIUS** (32–69 A.D.), Roman Emperor (69). In 58 Otho acquiesced when the Emperor Nero, coveting Otho's wife, Poppaea Sabina, sent him to govern Lusitania; but in 68 Otho joined Galba's revolt against Nero. Galba became Emperor but failed to choose Otho as his successor; whereupon Otho had him murdered and himself proclaimed Emperor (Jan., 69). The Rhine armies, however, had already proclaimed Vitellius. Marching south, they defeated Otho's forces at Bedriacum in northern Italy, and Otho committed suicide (Apr., 69).

OVID [ŏv'ĭd] (43 B.C.–18 A.D.), most versatile and facile of the poets of ancient Rome. Ovid was a well-to-do member of a moderately distinguished family, born in Sulmo, highly educated and widely traveled, very decidedly a man of the world. His earliest publication was a collection of erotic elegies, which he called *Amores*. In the same category as the poems of Tibullus and Propertius, they show greater sophistication, a lighter touch, and more graceful wit. These qualities, characteristic of Ovid, appear more conspicuously in the poems which followed. *Ars amoris* (The Art of Love) and *Remedia amoris* (The Cure of Love) are manuals for lovers, in scintillating elegiac verse, presenting their author as a cynical and brilliant connoisseur in the field of erotic adventure. They were popular at Rome with all but the Emperor, whose moral legislation was directly challenged by them. After ten years' delay Augustus found grounds on which to punish Ovid, and he was exiled to Tomis on the Black Sea in 8 A.D.

"Combat of Perseus and Phineus over Andromeda" (1930), an etching by Pablo Picasso for Ovid's *Metamorphoses*.
(MUSEUM OF MODERN ART, NEW YORK)

In the meantime he had written the *Heroides*, imaginary letters from wronged heroines of mythology to their faithless lovers, a series less flippant than the *Amores*, more reminiscent of scenes in Euripidean tragedy, but even more marked by rhetorical brilliance. Ovid next turned to narrative poetry in hexameter verse and produced the 15 books of *Metamorphoses*. These treated in simple and delightful style all the stories of miraculous transformation which mythology provided, weaving them into a continuous narrative by means of transitions both ingenious and masterly. At the same time Ovid composed six books of *Fasti*, a calendar in elegiac verse of Roman religious festivals. This work was unfinished when the decree of exile came. Thereafter Ovid, completely shattered, wrote fluently but monotonously his complaints and pleadings which are embodied in five books of *Tristia* and four of *Epistulae ex Ponto* (Epistles from Pontus). For a sophisticated man of the world like Ovid banishment to barbarian Pontus was worse than death.

PANTHEON [păn'thē-ŏn], the largest and most magnificent of Roman circular temples and the oldest domed building in the world still used today. It was built (c.120 A.D.) by Emperor Hadrian on an earlier structure in Rome. Entered through a portico supported by huge, monolithic columns, the cylindrical interior has massive walls that once were sheathed with costly marbles. The great dome, originally roofed by gilded bronze tiles, is relieved internally by sunken coffers, each at one time decorated by a gilded bronze star. At the crown of the dome a circular opening, 27 ft. in diameter and the sole source of light, illuminates the whole interior. In 609 the Pantheon was made a Christian church.

PAPINIAN [pə-pĭn'ē-ən], in full Aemilius Papinianus (d.212), Roman jurist who occupied the highest legal and governmental magistracy of his time, the *praefectus praetorio* (head of the imperial bodyguard). He was killed by order of Emperor Caracalla, for having publicly disapproved of the Emperor's murder of the latter's brother Gaeta. The deep respect in which Papinian's legal scholarship was held by his contemporaries as well as by his later followers is evidenced by the Law of Citations (426) issued by Emperor Theodosius II. This established his opinions as authoritative rules in controversial cases. Emperor Justinian's great codificatory work (530) included many of Papinian's opinions on contracts, servitudes, and civil and criminal responsibility. In their emphasis on equity, Papinian's opinions transcended mere legal technicalities. His legal philosophy offers some guiding principles even for the present time. His works include: *Quaestiones* (37 books), *Responsa* (19 books), and *Definitiones* (2 books).

PATRICIANS [pə-trĭsh'ənz] (from Lat. *patres*, "heads of great houses"), Roman caste, or order, of privileged citizens. At the beginning of the Republic the patricians constituted an aristocracy of leading families who formed the senate and held the magistracies and chief priesthoods. They claimed that plebeians were religiously unable to take the auspices, hence to hold the magistracies: so they cut themselves off from the plebeians and practiced spe-

cial rites. A struggle of the orders continued from the early 5th century down to 287 B.C., when *plebiscita* were recognized as legislation binding on the whole community. Magistracies and priesthoods with political importance were opened to the plebeians, and the leading patrician and plebeian families around 300 B.C. merged in a new aristocracy called the *nobiles*. The *interrex*, appointed if both consuls were killed, and the *princeps senatus* (ranking senator), as well as certain priests, still had to be patricians. The emperors, when patrician families died out, raised new families to the patrician order so that priesthoods might be properly filled. Constantine changed the patriciate to a personal distinction no longer hereditary.

PETRONIUS [pĭ-trō'nē-əs] (d.66 A.D.), Roman novelist, author of the *Satyricon*. Petronius was a member of Nero's court who, in spite of one successful governorship, did not aspire to public office. He was known rather as the arbiter of fashion, concealing under a pose of luxurious idleness a very considerable energy and ability. He committed suicide while under suspicion of conspiring against the Emperor. There have survived under his name large fragments of a satiric novel in the form of a Greek romance but entirely Roman in spirit, boldly realistic, and depicting the life of the lower middle class and the newly rich of Nero's day. The best-known portion is an extravagant description of a dinner given by one Trimalchio, a vulgar upstart millionaire in a small suburban town.

PHILIP THE ARABIAN, Latin name Marcus Julius Philippus (198–249 A.D.), Roman Emperor (244–49). Son of an Arab chief, Philip entered the imperial service and in 243 A.D. became praetorian prefect and foster-parent of the young Emperor Gordian III. When the latter was killed in the Persian War, the troops proclaimed Philip, who in 248 celebrated splendidly the thousandth birthday of Rome. Though he had good relations with the senate and strove hard to establish orderly conditions, his reign was troubled by revolts and invasions. He died in battle against a rival, Decius.

PLAUTUS [plô'təs], **TITUS MACCIUS** (c.254–184 B.C.), Roman comic poet. Of the plays he wrote for presentation at the festival games, 20 have survived. They are comedies of manners with topical songs interspersed throughout the dialogue. The plots are for the most part taken from the Greek New Comedy, especially from Menander, Philemon, and Diphilus, and are drawn from everyday life with about the same degree of realism as that of American musical comedy. The spirit is wholly Roman, the humor is rugged and boisterous, and there is no little melodrama and sentimentality. Types of character recur (the discouraged lover, the miserly old man, the spendthrift son, the noble harlot), but they are never frozen into stock characters. The plays show a remarkable variety. All are built around intrigue and exciting situations, but these situations are sometimes serious, sometimes hilarious, occasionally highly romantic. The slaves are usually more clever than their masters and control the intrigues.

The success of Plautus in his own day was immense, for he had great appeal for the holiday crowd. His range of vocabulary is vast, his dialogue easy and natural—well adapted to his characters—and his command of his metrical vehicle complete. That his plays have universal appeal is evidenced by their successful adaptation and actual reproduction in many lands and languages from medieval times on. The most familiar are the *Menaechmi* (*The Twin Menaechmuses*), the source of Shakespeare's *Comedy of Errors*, the *Mostellaria* (*The Haunted House*), and the *Miles gloriosus* (*The Braggart Soldier*).

PLEBEIANS [plĭ-bē'ənz], (Lat. *plebei*), Roman citizens who were not patricians but belonged to the plebeians (possibly a word borrowed from Greek which meant the totality of the citizens and carried a protest against patrician pretensions). They were divided into the landowning (*assidui*) and the landless (*proletarii*). As the patricians cut themselves off from the plebeians, the word "plebeians" more clearly meant nonpatricians, the many. To gain political and civil rights, the plebeians resorted to a kind of sit-down strike. The First Secession (494 B.C.) and the Second Secession (449 B.C.) probably have a core of truth encased in legends, while the Third Secession (287 B.C.) is undoubtedly historical.

From 494 they chose sacrosanct tribunes to watch the patrician consuls and to protect plebeians. From 470 the plebeians met in a council by themselves for elections of tribunes and their assistants, and to pass *plebiscita*, expressions of opinion which were not automatically binding on the patriciate until 287. By the second half of the 5th century B.C. plebeians had gained the right of intermarriage with patricians and were admitted to a board of consular tribunes, who replaced the consuls. From 367 B.C. they were admitted to the restored consulate and soon to the other magistracies and political priesthoods. Later, descendants of plebeian consuls joined with the patricians in a new aristocracy called the *nobiles*. In the late Republic "plebeian" lost the precision of its earlier political connotations and was often used simply as a designation of all in the lower social ranks.

POMPEY [pŏm'pē] **THE GREAT,** Latin name Gnaeus Pompeius Magnus (106–48 B.C.), Roman soldier and statesman, Julius Caesar's principal rival. He started his brilliant military career as a partisan of Sulla in 83; he defeated several leaders of the popular party and eventually the formidable rebel Sertorius in Spain, and on his return march to Italy in 71 cut off 5,000 of Spartacus' rebellious slaves. He held the consulship with Crassus in 70, though he was not of legal age and had previously held no lower magistracies. In 67 the Lex Gabinia commissioned him to clear the Mediterranean of pirates, a feat he accomplished in three months. And from 66 to 62, by virtue of the absolute power over army and fleet and proconsular authority over Asia vested in him by the Manilian Law, he campaigned in the East. He defeated Mithridates of Pontus and Tigranes of Armenia, annexed Syria, and organized various states, including Judaea, in the Roman interest.

Upon his return the senatorial party, which had grown suspicious of his power, refused to ratify his Eastern arrangements or to reward his veterans. In 60 he entered into an informal coalition, called the First Triumvirate, with Crassus and Caesar (whose daughter Julia he mar-

Roman bust of Pompey the Great, in the Capitoline Museum, Rome.

Alinari—Art Reference Bureau

ried) to control Roman politics for the years 59–54. The arrangement was renewed in 56, but the deaths of Crassus and Julia left Pompey and Caesar in open rivalry. In 52 Pompey was made sole consul by the senate, with which he was reconciled. In 49, after his conquest of Gaul, Caesar desired to stand for the consulship *in absentia;* but Pompey, now representing the senatorial interests, opposed him. In the civil war which followed Caesar defeated Pompey at Pharsalus in 48 B.C., and Pompey fled to Egypt, where he was assassinated. Great as a general (though his opponents said he merely finished wars others had almost won), Pompey was less effective as a statesman. His ambition was not, like Caesar's, to revolutionize the state, but to be its indispensable leader.

POMPEY THE YOUNGER, Latin name Sextus Pompeius (75–35 B.C.), Roman soldier, younger son of Pompey the Great. Sextus Pompeius accompanied his father to Egypt after the defeat at Pharsalus and, after his father's murder, joined the senatorial forces in North Africa. After the battle of Thapsus he went with his elder brother to Spain. Following the defeat of the Pompeian forces by Caesar at Munda and the death of his brother Gnaeus in 45, Sextus was left to carry on his father's tradition alone. He gathered a considerable army of anti-Caesar refugees and waged successful warfare against the garrison which Caesar had left in Spain. After collecting a large fleet, he made himself master of the sea.

Gaining control of Sicily, Pompey so harried his enemies (the Second Triumvirate, since Caesar was now dead), especially by cutting off the crucial grain supply from Egypt to Rome, that they were forced to make peace with him in 39 at Misenum. There he was made Governor of Sicily, Sardinia, and Achaea. This peace was short-lived, however. Sextus soon clashed with the forces of Octavian and, after early success, was defeated by Octavian's fleet under Agrippa's command at Naulochus, in 36. He then fled to Asia Minor, where he was taken prisoner and put to death in 35.

PRAETOR [prē′tər] (from Lat. *prae-itor*, "leader," "general"), a higher Roman magistrate. At the beginning of the Republic even the consuls were called praetors, but from 367 B.C. the name (at Rome) was reserved for a magistrate with a lesser right of command (*imperium*) than a consul. The *praetor urbanus*, created in 367 B.C., relieved the consuls of civil jurisdiction in Rome. The *praetor peregrinus*, created in 242 B.C., took over jurisdiction at Rome in cases between foreigners or between Romans and foreigners. Other praetors were created to command, administer, and to hear cases in provinces as governors until 81 B.C., when proconsuls and propraetors regularly became governors. Praetors, like consuls, were elected in the *comitia centuriata* and received their right of command from the *comitia curiata*. Upon taking office a praetor published an edict with the rules under which he would judge cases during his term. The normal development of Roman law was by gradual changes in these edicts, until Hadrian forbade change.

PRAETORIAN [prĭ-tôr′ē-ən] **GUARD,** elite troops who garrisoned Rome under the early Roman emperors. Special corps of guards are sometimes recorded for the Republic's generals (*praetores*), but under Augustus a permanent garrison of nine praetorian cohorts of Italians was established at Rome. Theoretically, these troops obeyed the emperor chosen by the senate, but being on the scene, they often acted for the whole army in acclaiming a new emperor and forcing the senate to recognize him. After reorganization under Septimius Severus, the guard was recruited from the legions (provincials). The praetorians were suppressed by Constantine in 312.

PREFECT [prē′fĕkt], Roman official to whom certain duties of another officer were assigned, originally a deputy, but later the normal head of an office or branch of administration. The most important were the prefects of the Praetorian Guard (*praefecti praetorio*), one to four in number. Under the early Empire they were members of the emperor's own family or else equites, trusted advisers who, under the Severi, relieved the emperor of much jurisdiction and were sometimes great jurists. They were the heads of the four prefectures into which Constantine divided the Empire. The Prefect of Egypt was the *eques* whom the emperor appointed as his deputy in Egypt. The Urban Prefect (*praefectus urbi*) was the deputy whom the early consuls left at Rome when they were absent and the senator whom Augustus left as his deputy when absent from Italy, and who became permanent under later emperors when he was chosen from the most distinguished senators. The *praefectus vigilium* commanded the Roman fire brigade, and the *praefectus annonae* was in charge of the grain supply.

PRINCIPATE [prĭn′sĭ-pāt] (from Lat. *princeps*, "leading man"), the period or institution of the theoretically elected emperor in the early Roman Empire, as distinct from the "Dominate." Augustus, who, despite his enormous economic and military power, avoided the appearance of monarchy and posed as an elder statesman of the restored Republic, left a tradition to which most emperors more or less conformed until 285 A.D. The principate was institutionalized with its transmission to Tiberius and particularly with the *lex de imperio Vespasiani*, by which Vespasian received at once, for life, the powers of Augustus, namely the tribunitian power, the higher command (*imperium maius*) of a proconsul, and so forth. He became the supreme judge in either first or appellate instance.

PROBUS [prō′bəs], **MARCUS AURELIUS,** Roman Emperor (276–82 A.D.). Born at Sirmium in 232, Probus rose to high army commands during the reigns of Valerian, Claudius Gothicus, and Aurelian. In 276 the Army of the East proclaimed him Emperor. Probus drove the Germans out of Gaul and the Vandals from Illyria and carried on the work of Aurelian in restoring the unity and defenses of the empire, but he fell victim to the insubordination of his troops.

PROCONSUL [prō-kŏn′səl], Roman general operating instead of a consul (*pro consule*) under his own auspices; or from 81 to 27 B.C. a former consul serving as governor of a province; or in the time of the emperors the governor of a senatorial province (whether former consul or merely former praetor). In time of war the Republican consul in command of an army might be kept on as proconsul after his term, or even a nonmagistrate might serve *pro consule*.

PROPERTIUS [prə-pûr′shəs], **SEXTUS** (c.50–after 16 B.C.), most eminent of the Roman writers of subjective erotic elegies. The first two of Propertius' four books of elegies are concerned primarily with the fluctuations of his love affair with Cynthia and with its intrigues, joys, and torture. He was master of the elegiac verse, and in his earlier poems expressed with vivid realism the effects of passion. The brilliance of these poems has never been surpassed. The last two books are more concerned with the assertion of his own achievement and contain many poems which belong to other categories: the epistle, the epyllion, and the extended epigram. He makes a habit of obscure literary allusion in his effort to produce distinction. It is not for these poems that he is remembered but for the brilliant elegiacs depicting the agonies, despair, and triumphs of the hapless lover.

PULCHERIA [pŭl-kēr′ē-ə], **ST.,** original name Aelia Pulcheria Augusta (399–453), Roman Empress of the East, daughter of Arcadius and Eudoxia. When 16 she became Augusta and regent for her brother Theodosius II, but after his marriage, in 421, she retired. In 450, at Theodosius' death, she became Empress and the nominal wife of the aged general Marcian. Her life was spent in pious works, and she founded a number of churches in Constantinople and elsewhere. Her feast day is Sept. 10.

PUNIC [pū′nĭk], **WARS,** three wars between Rome and Carthage in the 3d and 2d centuries B.C. Founded in Africa by the Phoenicians, Carthage had become the dominant commercial and maritime state in the western Mediterranean by the 3d century B.C. By 265 B.C. Rome had gained control of all peninsular Italy and could not ignore the growth of Carthaginian power in nearby Sicily.

The First Punic War (264–261 B.C.) was touched off by an appeal to both Carthage and Rome from the Sicilian city of Messana, requesting aid against Syracuse. Both responded, but Messana's decision to accept Roman help brought Rome into conflict with both Carthage and Syracuse. The Romans soon occupied much of eastern and southern Sicily. In 261 they built the first major fleet in their history and showed their great adaptability by winning major naval victories over the more experienced Carthaginians off Mylae (260) and Encomus (256). The latter battle made possible a Roman invasion of Africa under Regulus which failed (255). In Sicily, the Romans captured Panormus in 254 and seized Mt. Eryx in 248. Hamilcar Barca retook Mt. Eryx in 244 and used it as a base for guerrilla raids. Defeat at Drepana (250) and a storm in 249 weakened the Roman fleet. But by 242, it had recovered sufficiently to inflict such a serious defeat on the Carthaginians at the Aegates Islands, that Carthage sued for peace.

The peace treaty resulted in Carthaginian surrender of Sicily and the payment of a large indemnity. In 238 the Romans took advantage of Carthage's weakness to arbitrarily take Sardinia and Corsica. Under the leadership of the Barcas, Carthage set out, unopposed by Rome, to find new sources of wealth and mercenaries in Spain. A treaty (226) between Rome and Carthage established the Ebro River as the line separating their areas of influence.

The Second Punic War (218–201 B.C.) began when Hannibal, the son of Hamilcar, besieged Saguntum, a Spanish city south of the Ebro, but a Roman ally. Leaving his brother Hasdrubal in Spain, Hannibal marched across the Alps and into Italy. He scored his first major victory at the Trebia (218) in northern Italy, then brilliantly defeated the Romans at Lake Trasimene (June, 217). When the Romans abandoned the sensible delaying tactics of Fabius Maximus in the spring of 216, Hannibal inflicted upon them the bloodiest defeat in their history, at Cannae, in Apulia. Despite these successes, Hannibal's plans to destroy Rome's power depended on his ability to exploit imagined dissatisfactions among Rome's Italian allies. In this he was unsuccessful. Rome's generous treatment of her allies paid off, and comparatively few defected.

Syracuse, Capua, and Tarentum were retaken by the Romans, and the Scipios were able to block Hasdrubal's reinforcements at the Metaurus (207). Roman resumption of the Fabian strategy deprived Hannibal of further victory. P. Cornelius Scipio, having cleared the Carthaginians from Spain, returned to Rome and, over much opposition from the Fabian faction, succeeded in getting permission to invade Africa and thus draw Hannibal out of Italy. At Zama (202), aided by the defection of the Numidian king Masinissa, Scipio defeated Hannibal. By the peace treaty of 201, Carthage surrendered her fleet, Spain, and the right to wage war without Roman consent. A large indemnity was also exacted. Restricted to the area around Carthage, the city ceased to be an important commercial power.

For the next 50 years, peace reigned between the two states. Revived Carthaginian prosperity, although limited, nevertheless excited the fears of such visiting Romans as Cato the Censor, who for years solemnly urged in the Senate that "Carthage ought to be destroyed." Carthage complained to Rome of Masinissa's encroachments on Carthaginian territory but received no relief from Rome.

Goaded by this situation into violating the 201 treaty, Carthage attacked Numidia but was defeated. Carthage sought to appease Rome by surrendering her weapons, but the Romans demanded that the Carthaginians abandon their city and resettle at least 10 mi. from the sea.

The Third Punic War (149–146 B.C.) began when Carthage, unwilling to yield to this virtual death warrant, resolved to fight. In 146 Scipio Aemilianus, grandson of Hannibal's conqueror, captured the city, razed it, and cursed the site. The surviving inhabitants were sold into slavery and Carthaginian territory became the Roman province of Asia. Rome had ruthlessly achieved unchallenged mastery of the western Mediterranean.

The Punic Wars are described in the surviving works of the later Roman historian, Livy, and in the reliable account of the Greek writer Polybius, who was present at the destruction of Carthage in 146.

QUAESTOR [kwĕs'tər], a Roman magistrate who usually handled finances, either those of the state (under consular supervision) or those of an army or of a senatorial province. By Sulla's law a man had to be an ex-quaestor before he could be praetor (a magistrate), and an ex-praetor before he could be consul. This rule still applied under the principate, though an emperor could arrange exemptions. The quaestors began as two assistants freely chosen by consuls, but, perhaps from 449 B.C., they were elected in the *comitia tributa* (assembly). Their number reached 20 in the time of Sulla, 40 a generation later.

REMUS [rē'məs], in Roman legend, twin brother of Romulus (q.v.), cofounder of Rome. Romulus killed Remus in a quarrel and buried him on the Aventine hill.

ROMAN ROADS, one of the greatest achievements of the Romans, a feat of engineering unequaled by earlier peoples and unsurpassed in durability since. Not only did they last without repair for 70 to 100 years while in steady use, but many stretches remain today or have served as foundations for modern roads, which frequently follow the ancient line. Although local conditions and materials required some variation, the standard construction consisted of stone slab curbs sunk in deep ditches, the area between cleared to bedrock or solid ground to receive four layers. These were (1) two or more layers of thin slabs laid in mortar; (2) rubble stones in mortar; (3) smaller stone or gravel concrete; and (4) paving of slabs of lava or other hard stone, rammed gravel, or fine concrete.

The whole was about 3 ft. deep, crowned to provide drainage. The width varied even in the same road, according to conditions, but was usually about 8 to 12 ft. for two-way traffic, and wider over bridges. Near towns were 2-ft. sidewalks on each side about a foot above the roadbed. Roads were laid in a direct course, over mountains at grades up to 20%, on bridges over valleys, on palisades through marshes.

Numerous early local roads to towns near Rome were followed in the 4th century B.C. by the long-distance highway system spreading out from Rome. Beginning with the Appian Way to Capua (312 B.C.), the system grew rapidly throughout Italy in the 3d and 2d centuries with such roads as the Flaminian, Aemilian, Aurelian, Cassian, and

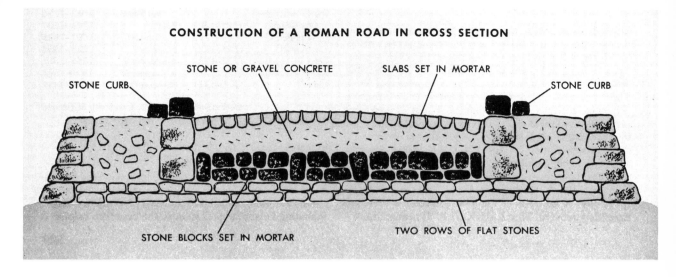

CONSTRUCTION OF A ROMAN ROAD IN CROSS SECTION

STONE OR GRAVEL CONCRETE   SLABS SET IN MORTAR

STONE CURB   STONE CURB

STONE BLOCKS SET IN MORTAR   TWO ROWS OF FLAT STONES

Valerian Ways. The system spread to Greece and Asia Minor in the 2d century and to Gaul and Spain in the 1st century B.C. Roads were a great concern to the Emperors. Augustus repaired them everywhere and built new ones in the east, over the Alps, and along the Rhine. Claudius built in England. Trajan renewed and extended to the limits of the Empire some 56,000 mi. of main roads. Hadrian built the latest. Actual construction was done mostly by the army, but also by captives and slaves. Not only military control but also political administration and the trade and business of the Empire depended on the extensive system of main and secondary highways for mail and transportation.

ROMULUS [rŏm′yə-ləs], in Roman legend, founder and first King of Rome, son of Mars and Rhea Silvia, a Vestal Virgin. Rhea's uncle, King Amulius of Alba Longa, imprisoned her and threw her infant sons, the twins Romulus and Remus, into the Tiber. They were washed ashore at the Palatine Hill, where a she-wolf suckled them. The shepherd Faustulus found and reared them. In a fight with Amulius' herdsmen Remus was captured and taken to Alba. Romulus and his companions then seized Alba, killed Amulius, and freed both Remus and his mother. Restoring their grandfather Numitor to the throne of Alba, they decided to build a new city on the Tiber. However, after quarreling about the site Romulus killed Remus for scornfully leaping over the wall. According to tradition, this happened on Apr. 21, 753 B.C.

Needing wives, Romulus and his men seized Sabine women. When the Sabines attacked Rome, the women, running between their husbands and kinsmen, persuaded them to make peace and become one people. After reigning nearly 40 years, Romulus vanished in a storm on the Campus Martius. According to later legend, the gods took him to heaven to become the god Quirinus.

ROMULUS AUGUSTULUS [rŏm′yĕ-lĕs ô-gŭs′tyŏŏ-ləs], last Western Roman Emperor (reigned 475–76). Romulus was placed on the throne by his father, Orestes, Master of the Soldiers, who drove Emperor Julius Nepos out of Italy. He was not recognized by the Eastern Emperor, Leo I, and so his position was not constitutional. Orestes lost his power when his troops mutinied, and Romulus was deposed by the Herulian chief Odoacer, who became King. Some historians regard the reign of Romulus as the end of the ancient Roman Empire.

SATURNALIA [săt-ər-nā′lē-ə], Roman festival in honor of the god Saturn, held December 17, upon completion of the sowing. During the festival farmhands enjoyed equal rights with their masters. Under the Empire the Saturnalia lost its agricultural character and developed into a general revelry lasting seven days. People exchanged gifts and dined together, and slaves were allowed a certain liberty.

SATURNINUS [săt-ər-nī′nəs], **LUCIUS APPULEIUS** (d.100 B.C.), Roman politician. He was one of the Romans who called themselves *populares* and tried to advance their political fortunes by promoting the interests of the common people through challenging senatorial control of the government. As tribune of the people in 103 and 100 B.C., Saturninus pushed through a law providing allotments of land for Marius' veterans and proposed other bills to establish colonies. Resorting to murder to carry the consular election of Glaucia, he met a violent end.

SCIPIO [sĭp′ē-ō], **PUBLIUS CORNELIUS** (d.211 B.C.), Roman statesman and soldier, father of Scipio Africanus the Elder. Sent to attack Hannibal in Spain at the beginning of the Second Punic War, he learned at Marseille that Hannibal was marching to Italy, and therefore returned to face him in northern Italy. He sustained defeats at the Ticino and Trebbia rivers until other commanders and armies were ready. From 217 on he and his brother Gnaeus fought the Carthaginians in Spain until they were killed in battle in 211. Their Spanish campaigns against Hannibal's brother Hasdrubal did much to keep reinforcements from Hannibal.

SCIPIO AEMILIANUS AFRICANUS NUMANTINUS [sĭp′ē-ō ē-mĭl-ē-ā′nəs ăf-rĭ-kā′nəs nū-mən-tī′nəs], **PUBLIUS CORNE-**

LIUS (185–129 B.C.), Roman statesman and soldier, son of Aemilius Paulus. Having a remarkable faculty for inspiring confidence in his character and abilities, he fought in the Third Punic War as tribune of the soldiers. In 148 he was allowed to return to Rome to stand for the aedileship. The people, dissatisfied with the siege of Carthage, elected him consul, declaring that he should have Africa as his province for the year. Returning to Africa as consul in 147, he conducted the siege so ably that Carthage fell in 146, and Africa was reduced to a Roman province.

SCIPIO AFRICANUS [sĭp′ē-ō ăf-rĭ-kā′nəs], **PUBLIUS CORNELIUS** (235–183 B.C.), Roman general, conqueror of Hannibal. He first saw action against Hannibal in 218 B.C., when he was said to have saved the life of his father, P. Cornelius Scipio. In 210, after his father's death, he was elected proconsul to take command in Spain. There he evolved and taught his troops refinements of Hannibal's best tactics. By 206 he had defeated all the Carthaginian forces and driven them from Spain, though he allowed Hannibal's brother Hasdrubal to slip away to Italy with reinforcements. Returning triumphant to Italy, he secured permission from a reluctant senate, in 205, to carry the war to Africa. Securing a base there, and enlisting the help of the Numidian prince Masinissa with his fine cavalry, he forced the Carthaginians to call Hannibal home from Italy and then defeated him at Zama in 202. The name Africanus was given him for these feats.

His influence with the people became so great as to cause the senate some uneasiness. In 190 B.C. he went as adviser to his brother Lucius, who commanded the army sent against King Antiochus the Great of Asia. Shortly after the successful conclusion of that war, both Scipios were prosecuted for having dealt cavalierly in their accounting for the booty, and Africanus, freed by the intercession of a tribune, retired from Rome in disgust.

SENATE [sĕn′ĭt], **ROMAN** (Lat. *senatus*, from *senes*, "elders"), the council of advisers, first to the King, then to the republican magistrates. Upon the establishment of the Republic, the senate, in which the patrician elders sat for life, dominated the state. It consisted of 300 men throughout most of the Republic. During this time it was difficult for a consul to initiate an important policy without asking the advice of the senate (*senatus consultum*), and having once asked the advice, he was morally bound by it. The composition changed as the senate came to be recruited from ex-magistrates, the majority of whom after 337 B.C. were plebeians.

The consul or praetor, whoever presided, first asked for individual opinions, beginning with the ranking patrician (*princeps senatus*), and then called upon others in order of their rank and seniority, the ex-consuls coming before the ex-praetors. When he had heard enough proposals, he had the senators vote by walking to the man with whom they agreed. From the senate were chosen various committees, consisting of so many ex-consuls, ex-praetors, and others. In like manner embassies and juries were chosen from the senate, though Gaius Gracchus and others temporarily or permanently took courts away from the senate.

As Rome gathered a confederacy and acquired an empire, the conduct of foreign affairs become a concern primarily of the senate, although war could properly be undertaken only after a vote of the people. The senate received foreign ambassadors, and it chose governors by deciding which provinces were to be assigned to elected praetors or ex-magistrates. In the early Empire the senate theoretically elected the emperor and chose even the consuls. Emperors had able men enrolled in the senate before appointing them to high command. Early emperors resorted to the *senatus consulta* when they wished to make new rules for the whole Empire.

SENECA [sĕn′ə-kə], **LUCIUS ANNAEUS** (c.4 B.C.–65 A.D.), Roman statesman, philosopher, essayist, and poet. He was the son of Seneca the rhetorician and uncle of Lucan the poet. Like them, he came from Spain but lived in Rome. Seneca was an avid student of rhetoric and philosophy and was successful in early life as a teacher, lawyer, and courtier. Through Messalina's intrigues he was banished by Claudius in 41 and spent eight miserable years in Corsica. But on the death of Messalina he was recalled, through the influence of Agrippina, who made him tutor to her son Nero. When Nero became Emperor in 54, Seneca was his chief adviser. For five years he tried to check the Emperor's viciousness. His influence vanished, however, after his involvement in the murder of Agrippina and his defense of Nero to the senate. After a few years of semi-retirement Seneca was forced to commit suicide, on the charge of participating in the conspiracy of Piso.

As an author his success was far more memorable. Apart from some early failures in poetry, some undistinguished essays in the field of natural history, and a witty farce (not in the best of taste) on the death of Claudius, his work consisted of essays expounding Stoic ethics, and nine metrical tragedies. His philosophy is not impressive in depth, but the essays are agreeably written in a new and popular style, almost colloquial, and deal with subjects

Antique bust of Lucius Annaeus Seneca, Roman author.

of general interest: *On Anger, On Tranquillity of Mind, On Clemency, On Leisure, On the Happy Life, On Providence.* There are also 124 *Letters to Lucilius,* which are effective short essays in the form of letters on all sorts of ethical questions. The tragedies are highly rhetorical, written for recitation rather than for stage production. They are based on Greek originals but are far from being servile imitations. They had an immense influence, both directly and through English translations, on Shakespeare and his immediate predecessors.

SERVIUS TULLIUS [sûr′vē-əs tŭl′ē-əs] (reigned c.578–534 B.C.), sixth of the seven traditional Kings of Rome. He later enjoyed a great reputation as an organizing genius. He concluded an advantageous treaty with the neighboring Latin peoples. He is believed to have built a famous temple to Diana, but the wall called Servian was built later. He originated a reform of the army, the main purpose of which was to create a basis for enrolling in the army the many people who were being attracted to Rome by its vigorous growth.

SEVEN HILLS OF ROME, a title applied to the original site of Rome, but not always with reference to the same seven hills. Since 390 B.C. they have usually included the Palatine, Capitoline, Quirinal, Viminal, Esquiline, Caelian, and Aventine hills. Another list evidently referring to a very early period names the Palatine, Cermalus, Velia, Fagutal, Oppian, Cispian, and Caelian.

SEVERUS, LUCIUS SEPTIMIUS (146–211 A.D.), Roman Emperor (193–211). Born near Leptis Magna in Libya, he had a good education at Rome and Athens before entering upon a senatorial career and rising to high military commands. On the assassination of Pertinax in 193 the army of the Danube proclaimed Septimius Severus Emperor. He then marched on Italy and received recognition from the senate. However, the Syrian legions had rallied to Pescennius Niger, and the army of Britain, to Clodius Albinus. Severus in three years defeated and executed Niger, and in 197 he defeated Albinus near Lyons. Then he fought successfully against the Parthians and annexed Mesopotamia. In 208 he warred against the Caledonians in Scotland and three years later died at York. In his reign, important for military and jurisdictional changes, the great jurist Papinian served as praetorian prefect, while the jurists Paul and Ulpian belonged to the Emperor's council.

SILIUS ITALICUS [sĭl′ē-əs ĭ-tăl′ĭ-kəs], **TIBERIUS CATIUS ASCONIUS** (c.25–101 A.D.), Roman epic writer. A man of means, culture, and position, Silius wrote the *Punica,* an account of Rome's war with Hannibal in 17 books, the longest and, many believe, the dullest Latin epic. He eschewed the popular rhetoric of his day and often reverted to the manner and vocabulary of Ennius.

SOCIAL WAR (from Lat. *socii,* "allies"), Rome's war against its allies (90–88 B.C.). Rome's Italian allies, although bearing half the sacrifices which created the Roman Empire, found themselves falling constantly into an inferior position compared with the Romans. From the

time of Tiberius Gracchus (d.133 B.C.) they were threatened with the loss of Roman public land which they had been using without ownership. Aspiring to full Roman citizenship, they were yet unwilling to pay the political price of surrendering this public land. When their Roman advocate, Marcus Livius Drusus, tribune in 91 B.C., was repudiated by the oligarchy and assassinated, they conspired against Rome and formed a new state with a common city at Corfinium, renamed Italia.

The open or imminent defection of the Italian half of the Roman confederacy created a mortal peril. The two main groups were the Marsi, commanded by Poppaedius Silo, in the north, and the Samnites, commanded by Papius Mutilus, in the south. With strenuous efforts and heavy Roman losses the Roman generals inflicted defeats on both. In 90 B.C. the consul L. Julius Caesar offered citizenship to communities which had not yet revolted, and in 89 an offer was made to individuals who would lay down their arms. These concessions, approximating what the Italians had asked for before revolting, eventually broke the movement, especially after the victories of Sulla and Gnaeus Pompeius Strabo in 89 B.C.

STILICHO [stĭl′ĭ-kō], **FLAVIUS** (c.359–408 A.D.), Roman general of Vandal origin. By the time of the death of Theodosius I, Stilicho had distinguished himself in his military career, and the dying Emperor entrusted his youthful son Honorius and the Western Empire to his care. Overcoming Rufinus, guardian of Arcadius, the Eastern Emperor, Stilicho was the supreme power in the Roman world from 395 to 408 and became father-in-law of Honorius. He had to combat threats to the Empire on the Rhine frontier and in Greece, Illyricum, Africa, and Italy.

SUETONIUS [swē-tō′nē-əs], full name Gaius Suetonius Tranquillus (c.69–c.140), Roman scholar and biographer. He was a contemporary and friend of Pliny the Younger and one of the secretaries of the Emperor Hadrian. He was the author of *The Lives of the Caesars,* biographies of Julius Caesar and the emperors from Augustus to Domitian. He had access to the state archives, made avid use of published histories, and availed himself to some extent of personal reminiscences. He was primarily a collector of facts, never a historian in the broader sense, and wrote in a plain, sometimes awkward style. He is, however, with Tacitus, one of the two chief sources of our knowledge of the men treated, and his interest in personal details and court gossip and scandal have made him a popular source through the ages. Another book, which survives in part, *On Illustrious Men,* comprises biographies of Roman writers and provided some valuable material for later Roman grammarians.

SULLA [sŭl′ə], **LUCIUS CORNELIUS** (138–78 B.C.), Roman statesman and soldier. He first came into prominence in 107 B.C., when serving under Gaius Marius (q.v.) in Africa, in the Jugurthine War. He distinguished himself in the Social War (90 B.C.), and was elected consul in 88. The chief threat to Rome at this time was the war with Mithridates, King of Pontus. Sulla and Marius, the latter now an elderly man, were both ambitious to command; but Sulla, after marching on Rome, was given the command by the Senate. He conducted the war successfully, both in Greece (where he sacked Athens in 86) and Asia Minor. He returned in 83 with his army to Italy, where Marius and his successors, ruling unconstitutionally, had put to death many of Sulla's followers. There followed an extremely bloody period of civil war in Italy. After defeating Marius' army, Sulla made himself dictator in 81, and then began the systematic extermination of his enemies by "proscription," the posting of public lists of those to be put to death. Thousands died, their property often going to Sulla's supporters. While dictator, Sulla restored the power of the Senate at the expense of the people and passed various measures protecting his form of government. After his retirement in 79, however, Sulla's "reforms" did not last. Sulla died in 78, to be long remembered as the most cruel and autocratic ruler Rome had known up to his time.

TARQUINIUS PRISCUS [tär-kwĭn'ē-əs prĭs'kəs], **LUCIUS,** an Estruscan, fifth of the seven traditional Kings of Rome (reigned 616–579 B.C.). Many details of his reign are uncertain, but it is clear that a great influence was exerted on the Romans by the more civilized Etruscans to the north during this period. And this influence brought to Rome products of Greece and the Near East, such as vases, since the Etruscans were in touch with the world by sea. It also brought artisans who could imitate these sophisticated products. In Tarquin's time Rome became more of a city-state and less of a scattered agricultural community.

TARQUINIUS SUPERBUS [tär-kwĭn'ē-əs soo-pûr'bəs], **LUCIUS,** King of Rome (534–510 B.C.), last of the seven traditional Kings. He was an Etruscan. According to tradition, he murdered his predecessor, Servius Tullius, and ruled despotically. On his expulsion, the Roman Republic was founded. Although Superbus means "haughty" or "cruel," and although there is the striking story of the rape of the noble lady Lucretia by Tarquin's son Sextus, the end of the monarchy is hardly to be explained by the arrogant conduct of the ruling family. There was general resistance to the widespread power of the Etruscan kings both in the region of Rome and, led by the Greeks, farther south in the region of Naples. Circumstances also favored the rise of a noble class hostile to monarchy.

TERENCE [tĕr'əns], in full Publius Terentius Afer (c.195–159 B.C.), Latin comic dramatist. Born in Carthage, Africa, Terence came as a slave to Rome, where he wrote Latin comedies second only to those of Plautus. Unlike his great predecessor, he was not dependent on his earnings, but was the protégé of Scipio the Younger and Laelius, ardent admirers of Greek civilization and patrons of Roman literature. As a result, Terence wrote not for the general public but for a small group of intellectuals. His adaptations of Greek originals are closer to their archetypes than those of Plautus, more polished and less spontaneous and boisterous. Six have survived, probably all that he wrote.

Terence's Latin is astonishingly pure in both style and vocabulary. rivaling even that of Caesar. His plays did not appeal to the holiday crowds but have always had their ardent admirers in the literary circles of every age and nation. Also, because they have less of the robust and often vulgar humor of the Plautine plays, they have been more

generally used as textbooks in the schools. His first play, the *Andria*, was given new fame by Thornton Wilder's adaptation, the novel *The Woman of Andros* (1930). The other plays of Terence are the *Hecyra* (The Mother-in-law), the *Adelphi* (The Brothers), the *Heautontimorumenos* (The Self-tormentor), the *Eunuchus*, and the *Phormio*.

TETRARCH [tĕt'rärk, tē'trärk] (Gr. *tetra,* "four"; *archos,* "ruler"), originally, governor of a fourth part of a province; later, a Roman emperor in Diocletian's system of four rulers. In an attempt to put an end to military uprisings Diocletian and Maximian became Augusti, or senior Emperors, while Constantius and Galerius became Caesars, or junior Emperors. Dividing the work, all four received credit in honorific titles and acclamations for what each did individually. It was planned that the Caesars, already experienced, would succeed the retiring Augusti.

THEODOSIUS [thē-ə-dō'shē-əs] **I,** called Theodosius the Great (c.346–395), Roman Emperor (reigned 379–95). After distinguishing himself in the army, Theodosius was appointed co-Emperor by Gratian and placed in charge of the East. His first achievement was to secure peace with the Goths, who had been plundering the Balkans, by allowing them to settle within the Empire and by employing them in the army. After Gratian's murder in 383 he defeated the usurper Maximus in 388 and recognized Valentinian II as Emperor of the West. Later, after Valentinian's murder in 392, he had to defeat another usurper, Eugenius (394). For the remaining year of his reign Theodosius, with his sons Arcadius and Honorius as colleagues, ruled as sole Emperor. After his death, Arcadius ruled in the East and Honorius in the West, and the Empire remained permanently divided.

By a famous edict Theodosius enforced Christian orthodoxy throughout the Empire and made heresy, particularly Arianism, punishable by the imperial authorities. For a massacre at Thessalonica, St. Ambrose, Bishop of Milan, imposed penance on Theodosius, to which the Emperor submitted. He made a special effort to exterminate paganism, especially in Rome, which had come to be its principal stronghold.

An able administrator, he carried forward the program of Constantine the Great for the creation of a new Christian empire, and by his legislation made plainer the definition of the relations of church and state which had begun to develop in the time of Constantine. Theodosius did not, however, carry this definition of the relationship to its ultimate development, a work which remained for Justinian the Great.

THEODOSIUS II (401–50), Eastern Roman Emperor (reigned 408–50). The son of Emperor Arcadius, Theodosius was a child when he ascended the throne. Not a very strong personality, he was successively dominated by the able prefect Anthemius, by his sister, his wife, and his chamberlain. His strong-willed sister Pulcheria, called the Augusta, picked Eudocia, a cultivated Athenian girl for his wife in 421. After 440, Theodosius was dominated by the corrupt grand chamberlain Chrysaphius. His reign is notable for three reasons. New walls were constructed, which rendered Constantinople almost impregnable. The school of higher learning in Greek and Latin grammar and rhetoric was re-established. Most important was the Theodosian Code, a compendium of the still valid imperial edicts issued since the time of Constantine the Great. This code was the forerunner of the more extensive Code of Justinian. The reign of Theodosius II was marked by successful wars against Persia and unsuccessful attempts to block the advance of the Huns under Attila into the Balkans. Diplomacy and massive bribery were used to induce the Huns to move westward.

TIBERIUS [tĭ-bēr′ē-əs], in full, Tiberius Claudius Nero Caesar (42 B.C.–37 A.D.), Roman Emperor (14–37 A.D.). Tiberius' stepfather was the Emperor Augustus, whom his mother Livia had married in 38 B.C. A brilliant general, Tiberius subjugated Rhaetia-Vindelicia (15 B.C.) with his younger brother Drusus, and Pannonia (12–9 B.C.), campaigned in Germany (9–7 B.C.; 4–6 A.D.), and suppressed revolts in Pannonia-Illyricum (6–9 A.D.). In 12 B.C. Augustus compelled Tiberius to divorce his beloved wife Vipsania and marry Julia, Augustus' profligate daughter. Tiberius thereby became stepfather to Augustus' grandsons Gaius, Lucius, and Agrippa Postumus. Julia's flagrant infidelities and Augustus' patent preference for Gaius and Lucius as his successors caused Tiberius to retire to Rhodes in 6 B.C. He returned to Rome in 2 A.D., however, after Julia's banishment, and to Augustus' service in 4 A.D., after the deaths of Lucius and Gaius. Becoming Augustus' heir apparent, he succeeded him on his death in 14 A.D.

Tiberius' reign seemed bedeviled, starting with mutinies in Germany and Pannonia. Agrippa Postumus was executed in 14; Tiberius' designated successor, the universally popular Germanicus, died in 19; and the ambitious Sejanus, praetorian prefect, acquired and exercised excessive influence from 23 until his execution in 31. Tiberius left Rome permanently for Capri in 26. Germanicus' family was persecuted in 29, and treason trials multiplied. Public misfortunes, such as the disastrous earthquake in Asia Minor in 17, the collapse of an amphitheater near Rome, with great loss of life, in 27, and a serious economic crisis in 33, were events of Tiberius' reign.

The reserved Tiberius was suspected of malevolent hypocrisy and, during his absences from Rome, of extreme vices. Everything contributed to Tiberius' disfavor. Yet he was a conscientious ruler. Military adventures were avoided, public finances carefully managed, and the provinces well administered, governors being given lengthy tenures for that purpose. It is, however, hardly surprising that, although neither Tiberius' memory nor his reign was officially damned, he was not posthumously deified. Christ was crucified during Tiberius' reign (c.30 A.D.), and Gaius (Caligula), the last surviving son of Germanicus, succeeded Tiberius in 37.

TITUS, full name Titus Flavius Sabinus Vespasianus (39–81), Roman Emperor (reigned 79–81). Titus acquired military experience in Britain and Germany. In 67, Nero sent his father, Vespasian, to reconquer rebellious Judaea, and Titus accompanied him. Vespasian returned to Rome to become Emperor in 70, leaving Titus to capture Jerusalem. Titus commemorated his victory there with an arch that is still standing in the Roman Forum. When Vespasian died in 79, Titus easily became emperor.

His two-year reign showed him to be a capable administrator. Despite generous displays for the populace, he generally kept a firm hand on the finances. During his reign, Mt. Vesuvius erupted and buried Pompeii and Herculaneum. A disastrous fire swept Rome for three days in 80. Titus completed the Colosseum which was begun by his father. He was widely mourned at his death and was succeeded by his brother Domitian.

TRAJAN [trā′jən], Latin name Marcus Ulpius Trajanus (53–117), Roman Emperor (reigned 98–117). A Spaniard, Trajan was the first provincial to become Emperor. Like his father, he had a distinguished military career. This led Nerva to adopt him and make him co-Emperor in 97, and Nerva's death in 98 left him sole Emperor. Administrative paternalism and military expansion characterized his reign. Taxation was lowered, philanthropic funds established, public works programs undertaken, important towns such as Timgad founded, sumptuous games and doles provided, and special commissioners appointed to remedy local misgovernment. To enlarge the Empire and consolidate its frontiers, Trajan annexed Dacia, after two wars, in 101–2 and 106, and Arabia Petraea in 105–6. But his conquest of other territories (Armenia, 114; Mesopotamia, 115; Parthia, 116) proved short-lived. Revolt broke out in 116 and soon spread beyond Mesopotamia. Before he could quell it, Trajan died. He was succeeded by his second cousin, Hadrian, who promptly renounced Armenia, Mesopotamia, and Parthia.

Trajan's rule was undoubtedly autocratic, but thanks to his tact and evident determination to provide good government it was also popular. He was styled *Optimus Princeps* (Best of Princes) and deified after death. Impressive memorials of him are his column, forum, and baths in Rome, his arches in Benevento and Ancona, and numerous highways and public buildings throughout the Empire. He is famous for his ruling that, although Christianity was a punishable offense, Christians were not to be deliberately sought out for persecution.

TRIBUNE [trĭb′ūn], an official of the Roman plebs and also an officer in a Roman legion. The tribunes of the plebs were perhaps first chosen in 494 B.C., in the first secession of the plebs, to defend plebeian interests against the patricians, particularly the patrician magistrates. Plebeians swore publicly to kill anyone who harmed a tribune. This is the sacrosanctity, or inviolability, which the tribunes henceforth enjoyed. From 471 B.C. on the tribunes were no longer revolutionary agents but publicly recognized officials elected annually in the plebeian assembly (*concilium plebis*). At first they may have tried to secure a general supervision over the consuls, but from 449 on they seem to have concentrated on the right of assisting individual plebeians who were unfairly treated by patrician magistrates. In the Struggle of the Orders, tribunes were the natural leaders of the plebeians and formulated demands to be backed by a vote of the plebeian assembly. As plebeians became consuls and praetors, the right of assistance (*jus auxilii*) tended to recede in importance, but never disappeared.

With the Lex Hortensia of 287 B.C., by which *plebiscita* (decisions of the plebeian assembly) obtained validity as laws of the Roman people, the position of the tribunes changed. Their proposals now were proposals of laws, whereas the Struggle of the Orders had ceased. Most tribunes from now on saw an opportunity to serve the senate, while some tribunes worked for great nobles like the Scipios against the senatorial majority. Thus the tribunes, whose original function had been to protect the humble, were now, with a change in the social and political environment, much more active as agents of the mighty. And they contributed, despite a few striking cases of opposition, to the entrenchment of senatorial control.

A new period began in the late 2d century B.C. with the Gracchi, who as tribunes introduced revolutionary proposals and tried to break the control of the senatorial oligarchy. Other great tribunes such as Saturninus and Glaucia likewise tried to introduce far-reaching reforms, but they failed.

Sulla destroyed the power of the office, but only temporarily. Opposition groups would get their men elected tribunes and then block each other with tribunician vetoes. But all this ended with the principate, when the tribunate became chiefly a step to higher office.

TRIUMPH, in antiquity, ceremonial entrance of a victorious Roman general into the city of Rome. The honor of a major triumph could be granted by senatorial decree during the republic to a dictator, consul, proconsul, or praetor. Later it could be granted only to an emperor. The triumphator wore the embroidered toga and the laurel crown, rode in a special chariot, and a public slave held a gold crown over his head. The army marched in the procession with prisoners and booty. A lesser triumph (*ovatio*) was often decreed for a general whose victory was less brilliant or less independent. Under the emperors a victorious general might receive *ornamenta triumphalia* but not a triumph, theoretically because he won the victory under the emperor's auspices, not under his own.

TRIUMVIRATE [trī-ŭm′və-rĭt], a Roman commission of three men. The First Triumvirate was established in 60 B.C. by Pompey, Crassus, and Julius Caesar and was renewed in 56 B.C. at the conference of Lucca. It was a secret deal among these three politicians to co-operate and to co-ordinate the efforts of their clients in a single policy. In this way they arranged for the election of each other and their associates and for legislation. The first result was the consulate of Julius Caesar. The Second Triumvirate was a public board consisting of Mark Antony, Marcus Aemilius Lepidus, and Octavian, the young Caesar. This commission for the reorganization of the constitutional structure of the state took office in 43 B.C. on the basis of the Lex Titia. It continued with two members through 32 B.C. after the expulsion of Lepidus in 36. The three dynasts ruthlessly proscribed the enemies of Caesar and the personal enemies of each other and divided the affairs of the Empire among themselves on a geographical basis.

TULLUS HOSTILIUS [tŭl′əs hŏs-tĭl′ē-əs], third of the seven traditional kings of Rome (reigned 673–642 B.C.). According to tradition he was an aggressive warrior who captured the town of Alba, 15 mi. from Rome. This distance suggests the smallness of Roman territory at this time. The warfare between the small cities and towns of the region at this time was generally little more than occasional raids.

TUSCULUM [tŭs′kū-ləm], ancient town of the Latins, over 2,000 ft. above sea level, in the Alban Hills, 15 mi. southeast of Rome. Its extensive but deserted ruins include a charming theater, an amphitheater, a forum, and a primitive corbeled storeroom. Tusculum was the first Latin town whose population obtained Roman citizenship, about 380 B.C. Not a few Tusculans became consuls, notably, Cato the Censor. Wealthy Romans built luxurious villas nearby, Cicero's being especially famous. In medieval times the counts of Tusculum often dominated Rome and controlled the Papacy. In 1191 the town was razed and never rebuilt. Its inhabitants migrated to neighboring but lower lying Frascati.

VALENS [vā′lənz] (c.328–378), Roman Emperor of the East (364–78). He was the younger brother of Valentinian I, Emperor of the West, and coruler with him. Valens suppressed the rebellion of Procopius in 366 and fought the Visigoths from 367 to 369. Then followed campaigns in Armenia and Persia, and against the Huns on the Danube frontier. With the barbarian threat still urgent, Valens, in 376, allowed the Visigoths to escape the Huns by settling in devastated Roman Thrace. Feeling abused, the Visigoths rebelled the following year and the Emperor was killed in the disastrous battle of Adrianople, in 378. Though an Arian Christian, Valens was tolerant toward the orthodox Athanasius.

VALENTINIAN [văl-ən-tĭn′ē-ən] I (321–75), Roman Emperor (364–75). Succeeding Jovian, Valentinian appointed his younger brother Valens as his colleague in the East, while he himself took the West. Valentinian's chief occupation was the defense of the border provinces against the barbarians, in which he was assisted by Theodosius, who later became Emperor. Unlike his brother, who was an Arian, Valentinian supported the Nicene (orthodox) Christians, but tolerated Arians and pagans.

VALENTINIAN II (372–92), Roman Emperor of the West (375–92). On the death of his father, Valentinian I, he was made co-Emperor with his half brother Gratian and given Italy, Illyricum, and Africa, under the regency of his mother Justina. In 387 Valentinian was forced to flee from the usurper Maximus, who had murdered Gratian in 383. Theodosius later defeated Maximus and restored Valentinian in 388. Four years later Valentinian was murdered by order of the Frankish chief Arbogast, governor of Gaul, who was trying to win his independence. In the Christological controversy, Valentinian at first supported the Arians, but was later persuaded to adopt orthodoxy by his protector, Theodosius.

VALENTINIAN III (419–55), Roman Emperor of the West (425–55). The son of Constantius III and Galla Placidia, Valentinian became Emperor as a child, under the regency of his mother. During this period the general

Aetius was a powerful influence, but Aetius and the Empress distrusted each other. Valentinian was spoiled by his mother and his character was weak. He took no interest in imperial business, but devoted himself to astrology and love affairs. His reign witnessed the loss of Africa to the Vandals, civil war between Aetius and Boniface, and Attila's invasion of Italy. Valentinian murdered Aetius in 454, and was in turn slain by Petronius Maximus, who succeeded as Emperor.

VALERIAN [və-lĭr'ē-ən], Latin name Publius Licinius Valerianus (died c.269 A.D.), Roman Emperor (253–60 A.D.). After a distinguished senatorial career Valerian, a good administrator, was proclaimed Emperor by his troops in the turmoil following the uprising of Aemilian. He persuaded the senate to appoint his son Gallienus co-Emperor. The frontiers were under attack both from the northern barbarians and from the new Persian Emperor Shapur I, who conquered much of Syria and Armenia. Valerian, unequal to the military situation, failed to protect the Empire, and was defeated and captured in 260 by Shapur. He died in captivity.

VALERIAN WAY, ancient Roman road extending the old Tiburtine Way (connecting Rome and Tivoli) and running 125 mi. northeastward to the Adriatic coast at Aternum (Pescara). It followed the Anio River, ran past Horace's villa, past Carsioli and Alba Fucens, then over the Apennines to Corfinium, Teate (Chieti), and Hatria (Atri). Built at an unknown date by one of the Valerius family, it was restored by Emperor Claudius.

VALERIUS FLACCUS [və-lĭr'ē-əs flăk'əs], **GAIUS** (died c.90 A.D.), Latin epic writer. He was the author of the *Argonautica*, an unfinished poem in eight extant books, relating the story of the Golden Fleece and the romance of Jason and Medea. Apollonius of Rhodes was Valerius' model, but the Roman poet modified the story extensively.

VERCINGETORIX [vûr-sĭn-jĕt'ə-rĭks] (d.46 B.C.), Gallic leader, chieftain of the Arverni. In 52 B.C., after Caesar had subdued most of Gaul, Vercingetorix organized the Gallic tribes into a confederation and led them in a desperate revolt against the Romans. After some successful battles Vercingetorix retreated to the fortress town of Alesia, where he was forced to surrender after a long siege. He was taken as a prisoner to Rome, made to march in Caesar's triumph, and at last put to death in 46. The French have always regarded Vercingetorix as their first national hero.

VERGIL [vûr'jəl], in full Publius Vergilius Maro (70–19 B.C.), Roman poet and, with Homer, Dante, and Milton, one of the world's great quartet of epic writers. Vergil was born near Mantua, the son of a prosperous farm owner who gave his son the best available education. He studied rhetoric at Rome and philosophy at Naples under Siro the Epicurean. His greatest passion, however, was for poetry and, in particular, the "new poetry" of the school of Catullus. His earliest productions were a privately circulated miscellany of realism, satire, and romantic rhetoric.

In 37 B.C. Vergil published the *Eclogues*, or *Bucolics*, 10

Ancient mosaic portrait of Vergil, found in Sousse, Tunisia.
(ALINARI—ART REFERENCE BUREAU)

pastoral poems closely imitating the Greek poet Theocritus. They were artificial pictures of idealized and highly sophisticated shepherds and their idyllic life of song and love. Seven years later, under the patronage of Maecenas and Augustus Caesar, he produced the *Georgics*, ostensibly a farmer's guide. It consists of four books in matchless hexameters concerning crops and the weather, culture of grape and olive, the breeding of animals, and the raising of bees. The work is a sincere exaltation of Italian agriculture in poetry never surpassed in Latin literature.

The rest of his life Vergil devoted to the creation of the *Aeneid*, an epic in 12 books about the founding of Rome, the story of Aeneas' escape from captured Troy, his long journey to Italy, and his conquest of Latium. The poem was finished, but not finally revised, when Vergil died. With his passion for perfection he directed that it be destroyed, but his patron Augustus disregarded his dying wish. Authorized by the Emperor to remove any blemishes but to add nothing of their own, two of Vergil's poet friends, Varius and Tucca, edited and published the great epic. Vergil died at Brundisium, but was buried in his beloved Naples. The success of his poetry was immediate, and his position as first poet of Rome has never been seriously questioned. Vergil accepted the innovations of the "new poets" who followed the Alexandrian Greeks, but his indelible imprint made his work something far beyond the brilliant productions of the new poets.

The *Aeneid* owes much in its pattern of construction to the short epic of Catullus, but the reader loses sight of this pattern in the dramatic tension of Vergil's narrative. By his insight into human motives and his sympathy with human frailty Vergil created a universal story of heroic achievement out of what might have died as a local ballad. The episode of Dido and Aeneas at Carthage might have grown into a tragic love story with an ending of treacherous desertion. However, the genius of Vergil, with his mighty comprehension of Greek tragedy, was capable of controlling it and making it the final test of Aeneas' consecrated devotion to his god-given mission. It is this development of an ordinary human being into a great but understandable human hero, strengthened by the rites to his dead father and the visit to his immortal father in the lower world, which gives to the *Aeneid* its universal appeal. It is Vergil's loftiness, humanity, and piety that led Dante to choose him as his guide in the *Divine Comedy* and that occasioned the medieval belief that he was a precursor of Christianity.

There are those who remember Vergil for his lighter and more superficially amusing *Eclogues*. Others prefer the polished perfection of the *Georgics*. However, it is the *Aeneid*, with its comprehension of the pity in the world and of the inherent weakness and grandeur of humanity, all embraced in a dramatic tale of high adventure, which makes Vergil the best loved of Roman poets.

VESPASIAN [vĕs-pā′zhən], Latin name Titus Flavius Sabinus Vespasianus (9–79 A.D.), Roman Emperor (69–79). Descended through his mother from the aristocracy of rural Italy, Vespasian had the career typical of a Roman senator. Nero's death in 68 found him commanding in the Jewish War in Palestine. Vespasian cautiously recognized Galba, Otho, and Vitellius in turn as Emperor. In July, 69, the Eastern armies proclaimed him Emperor. The Danubian troops followed suit, marched into Italy, and by December had wrested the Empire from Vitellius for Vespasian.

Although autocratic, Vespasian was a competent ruler. He restored peace throughout the Empire, strengthened the frontiers in Britain, Germany, and the East, rehabilitated finances, and appointed his elder son Titus as virtual co-Emperor. In addition, he suppressed opposition from Stoic and Cynic philosophers, encouraged municipal life and Romanization, recruited provincials into the Roman aristocracy, and continuously held both the consulship and censorship himself. Vespasian was also notable for his pungent wit and for his building program. which included a forum, a Temple of Peace, a new Capitol, and the Coloseum. He founded the Flavian Dynasty, his sons Titus and Domitian succeeding him in turn. After his death he was deified, the third Roman Emperor to be so honored.

VESTAL VIRGINS, priestesses of the Roman hearth goddess Vesta. In early times farmers' daughters had to maintain the fire and prepare the food, while the adult members of the family worked in the fields. Corresponding to old rural customs, the six Vestal Virgins maintained the fire on the state hearth. In case the fire burned out, the guilty Vestal had to rekindle it by the primitive method of rubbing together two pieces of wood. Like the rustic father, the Pontifex Maximus had the right to punish guilty Vestals. Vowed to chastity, they were buried alive if they lost their virginity. Vestals served for 30 years, after which they could marry.

VITELLIUS [vĭ-tĕl′ē-əs], **AULUS** (15–69 A.D.), Roman Emperor (69). He was appointed commander in Lower Germany by the Emperor Galba in 68 . The troops in Germany proclaimed him Emperor in Jan., 69, even before Galba's death. They descended on Italy, and in April defeated the forces of Otho, Galba's murderer, near Cremona. The Eastern armies, however, acclaimed Vespasian in July. The Danubian legions, supporting them, entered Italy, defeated Vitellius' troops near Cremona in October, and advanced on Rome. They arrived there in December. After savage street fighting, they slew Vitellius. Naked militarism, refusal of the title Caesar, general incompetence, and, above all, gluttony characterized Vitellius' short reign.

INDEX